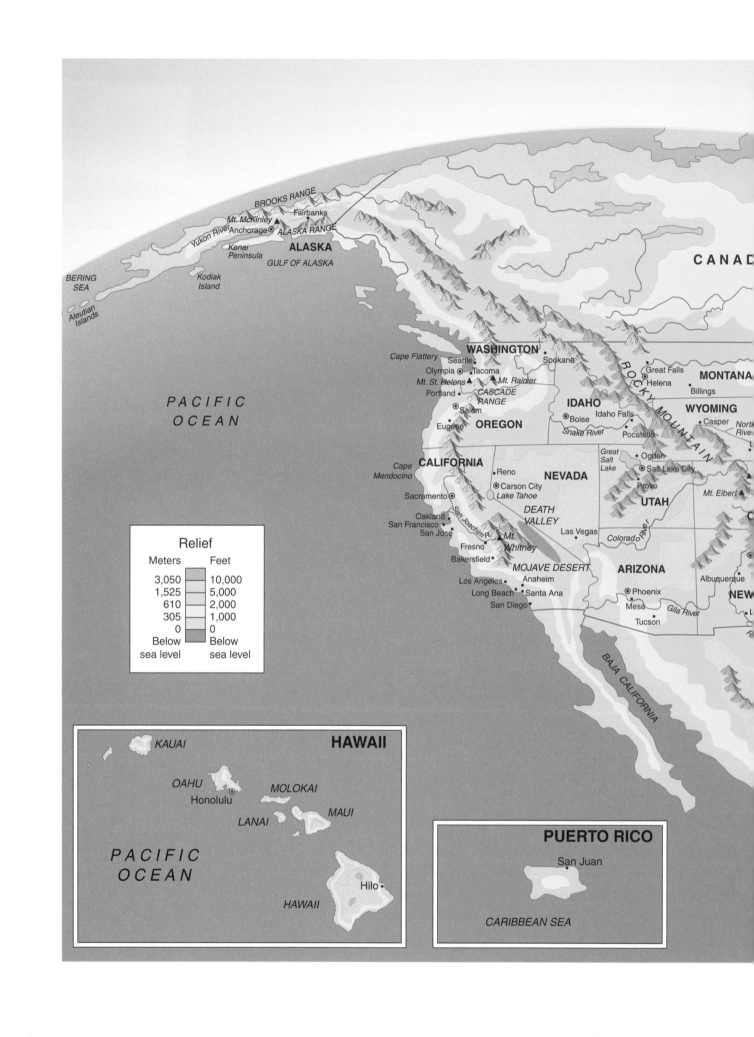

BROOKS RANGE

Fairbanks

Mt. McKinley ▲

Anchorage ⊙  ALASKA RANGE

Yukon River

ALASKA

Kenai
Peninsula

GULF OF ALASKA

BERING
SEA

Kodiak
Island

Aleutian
Islands

CANADA

PACIFIC
OCEAN

WASHINGTON

Cape Flattery

Seattle

Spokane

Olympia ⊙  Tacoma

Great Falls

MONTANA

Mt. St. Helens ▲  Mt. Rainier ▲

Helena

Portland  CASCADE
RANGE

Billings

Salem

IDAHO

WYOMING

Eugene  OREGON

Boise

Idaho Falls

Casper

North
River

Snake River

Pocatello

ROCKY MOUNTAIN

Cape
Mendocino  CALIFORNIA

Reno

NEVADA

Great
Salt
Lake

Ogden

Salt Lake City

Carson City

Lake Tahoe

Provo

Mt. Elbert ▲

Sacramento ⊙

DEATH
VALLEY

UTAH

Oakland

San Joachim R.

San Francisco

Las Vegas

San Jose

Mt.

Colorado River

Fresno  ▲ Whitney

Bakersfield

MOJAVE DESERT

ARIZONA

Los Angeles  Anaheim

Albuquerque

Long Beach  Santa Ana

NEW

San Diego

Phoenix

Mesa  Gila River

BAJA CALIFORNIA

Tucson

### Relief

| Meters | | Feet |
|---|---|---|
| 3,050 | | 10,000 |
| 1,525 | | 5,000 |
| 610 | | 2,000 |
| 305 | | 1,000 |
| 0 | | 0 |
| Below sea level | | Below sea level |

KAUAI

HAWAII

OAHU

MOLOKAI

Honolulu

LANAI

MAUI

PACIFIC
OCEAN

HAWAII

Hilo

**PUERTO RICO**

San Juan

CARIBBEAN SEA

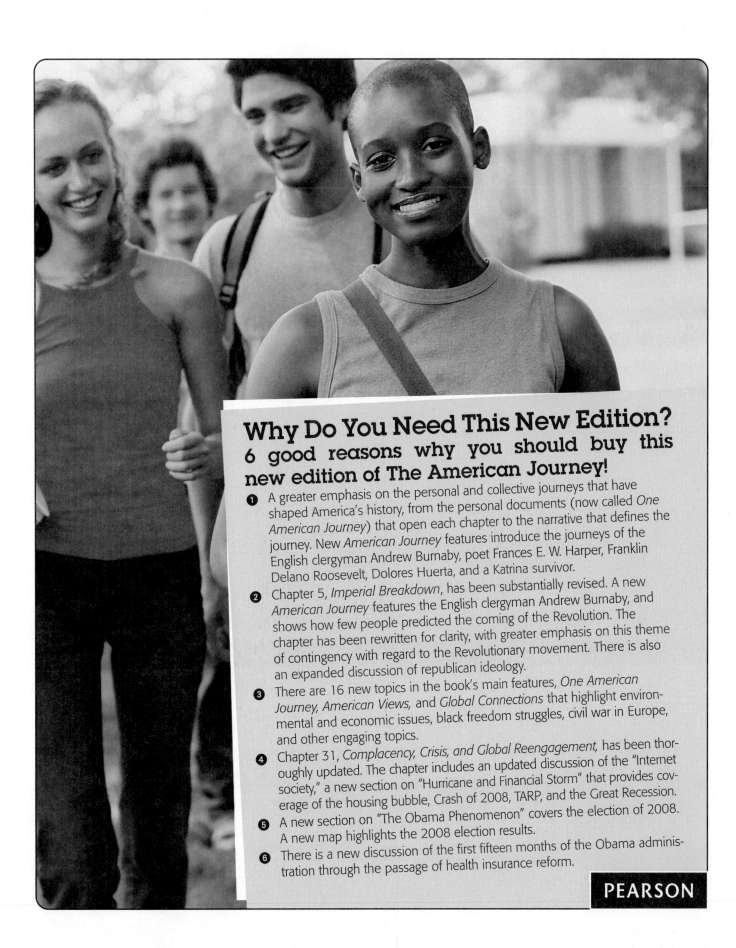

# Why Do You Need This New Edition?
## 6 good reasons why you should buy this new edition of The American Journey!

1. A greater emphasis on the personal and collective journeys that have shaped America's history, from the personal documents (now called *One American Journey*) that open each chapter to the narrative that defines the journey. New *American Journey* features introduce the journeys of the English clergyman Andrew Burnaby, poet Frances E. W. Harper, Franklin Delano Roosevelt, Dolores Huerta, and a Katrina survivor.

2. Chapter 5, *Imperial Breakdown*, has been substantially revised. A new *American Journey* features the English clergyman Andrew Burnaby, and shows how few people predicted the coming of the Revolution. The chapter has been rewritten for clarity, with greater emphasis on this theme of contingency with regard to the Revolutionary movement. There is also an expanded discussion of republican ideology.

3. There are 16 new topics in the book's main features, *One American Journey, American Views,* and *Global Connections* that highlight environmental and economic issues, black freedom struggles, civil war in Europe, and other engaging topics.

4. Chapter 31, *Complacency, Crisis, and Global Reengagement,* has been thoroughly updated. The chapter includes an updated discussion of the "Internet society," a new section on "Hurricane and Financial Storm" that provides coverage of the housing bubble, Crash of 2008, TARP, and the Great Recession.

5. A new section on "The Obama Phenomenon" covers the election of 2008. A new map highlights the 2008 election results.

6. There is a new discussion of the first fifteen months of the Obama administration through the passage of health insurance reform.

# The AMERICAN JOURNEY

# A History of the United States

BRIEF SIXTH EDITION

VOLUME 1

### David Goldfield
UNIVERSITY OF NORTH CAROLINA, CHARLOTTE

### Carl Abbott
PORTLAND STATE UNIVERSITY

### Virginia DeJohn Anderson
UNIVERSITY OF COLORADO, BOULDER

### Jo Ann E. Argersinger
SOUTHERN ILLINOIS UNIVERSITY

### Peter H. Argersinger
SOUTHERN ILLINOIS UNIVERSITY

### William L. Barney
UNIVERSITY OF NORTH CAROLINA, CHAPEL HILL

### Robert M. Weir
UNIVERSITY OF SOUTH CAROLINA

**PEARSON**

Boston   Columbus   Indianapolis   New York   San Francisco   Upper Saddle River
Amsterdam   Cape Town   Dubai   London   Madrid   Milan   Munich   Paris   Montréal   Toronto
Delhi   Mexico City   São Paulo   Sydney   Hong Kong   Seoul   Singapore   Taipei   Tokyo

**Editorial Director:** Craig Campanella
**Publisher:** Charlyce Jones Owen
**Editorial Assistant:** Maureen Diana
**Supplements Editor:** Emsal Hasan
**Senior Manufacturing and Operations Manager
 for Arts & Sciences:** Nick Sklitsis
**Operations Specialist:** Christina Amato
**Director of Marketing:** Brandy Dawson
**Senior Marketing Manager:** Maureen E. Prado Roberts
**Senior Managing Editor:** Ann Marie McCarthy
**Senior Project Manager:** Denise Forlow
**Director of Media and Assessment:** Brian Hyland
**Media Project Manager:** Tina Rudowski
**Digital Media Editor:** Andrea Messineo

**Senior Art Director:** Maria Lange
**Cover Design:** Red Kite Project
**Cover Image:** Painting by American artist George Caleb
Bingham. "Daniel Boone (1734–1820) leading a group of
settlers". GETTY IMAGES INC - HULTON ARCHIVES
**AV Project Manager:** Mirella Signoretto
**Full-Service Production, Interior Design,
 and Composition:** Ashley Schneider/
 S4Carlisle Publishing Services
**Manager, Visual Research:** Beth Brenzel
**Printer/Binder:** Courier/Kendallville
**Cover Printer:** Lehigh-Phoenix Color/Hagerstown
**Text Font:** Adobe Jenson Regular

Credits and acknowledgments for illustrations from other sources reproduced, with permission, in this textbook appear
on appropriate page within text (or on pages C-1–C-2).

**Library of Congress Cataloging-in-Publication Data**

The American journey : a history of the United States / David Goldfield . . . [et al.]. — Brief 6th ed.
   p. cm.
 ISBN-13: 978-0-205-24595-6 (combined volume)
 ISBN-10: 0-205-24595-1 (combined volume)
 ISBN-13: 978-0-205-24596-3 (volume 1)
 ISBN-10: 0-205-24596-X (volume 1)
 ISBN-13: 978-0-205-24597-0 (volume 2)
 ISBN-10: 0-205-24597-8 (volume 2)
 [etc.]
 1.  United States—History—Textbooks.   I. Goldfield, David R., II. Title.

E178.1.A4925 2010
973—dc22

10 9 8 7 6 5 4 3 2 1

Combined Volume:
ISBN 10:     0-205-24595-1
ISBN 13: 978-0-205-24595-6

Examination Copy:
ISBN 10:     0-205-01184-5
ISBN 13: 978-0-205-01184-1

Volume 1:
ISBN 10:     0-205-24596-X
ISBN 13: 978-0-205-24596-3

Books à la carte Volume 1:
ISBN 10:     0-205-24604-4
ISBN 13: 978-0-205-24604-5

Volume 2:
ISBN 10:     0-205-24597-8
ISBN 13: 978-0-205-24597-0

Books à la carte Volume 2:
ISBN 10:     0-205-24606-0
ISBN 13: 978-0-205-24606-9

**PEARSON**

# 1

## WORLDS APART    2

# 2

## TRANSPLANTATION AND ADAPTATION, 1600–1685    30

# 3

## A MEETING OF CULTURES    56

## Interpreting the Past

## ENGLISH COLONIES IN AN AGE OF EMPIRE, 1600s–1763   84

## IMPERIAL BREAKDOWN, 1763–1774   116

# 6

## THE WAR FOR INDEPENDENCE, 1774–1783  140

## Interpreting the Past

**Democratic Roots in New England Soil  166**

# 7

## THE FIRST REPUBLIC, 1776–1789  168

# 8

## A NEW REPUBLIC AND THE RISE OF PARTIES, 1789–1800  194

## Interpreting the Past

**Nullification as a Destructive Force
in U.S. Politics** 218

# 9

## THE TRIUMPH AND COLLAPSE OF JEFFERSONIAN REPUBLICANISM, 1800–1824 220

# 10

## THE JACKSONIAN ERA, 1824–1845 246

## Interpreting the Past

**Jacksonian Democracy and American Politics** 274

# 11

## SLAVERY AND THE OLD SOUTH, 1800–1860 276

# 12

## THE MARKET REVOLUTION AND SOCIAL REFORM, 1815–1850  302

## Interpreting the Past

**The Second Great Awakening and Religious Diversity in America 334**

# 13

## THE WAY WEST, 1815–1850  336

# 14

## THE POLITICS OF SECTIONALISM, 1846–1861  362

## 15

## 16

### Interpreting the Past

# American Views

# Global Connections

# Maps

# Figures and Tables

## Overview Tables

# PREFACE

The path that led us to *The American Journey* began in the classroom with our students. Our primary goal is to make American history accessible to them. The key to that goal—the core of the book—is a strong, clear narrative. We chose our book's title because we believe the theme of *journey* offers an ideal way to give coherence to our narrative and yet fairly represent the complexities of our nation's past.

We employ this theme throughout the book, in its chapters, its pedagogical features, and its selection of primary source documents. The journeys we describe can be geographical, focusing on the movement of people, goods, ideas, or even germs from one place to another. They can also be ideological, political, or social—some eventually codified in our founding documents and institutions, others culminating in patterns of personal behavior and social relationships, still others reaching a dead end because of popular opposition, political or economic changes, or even war.

Not all journeys were straightforward in reaching their destinations. American history contains many examples of thwarted personal hopes and national promises that remained unfulfilled for generations. Americans debated the meaning of the liberty they hailed as their nation's founding principle and the extent of power they were willing to entrust to their government. Did the full measure of liberty apply to all its peoples irrespective of race, gender, or ethnicity? Were American freedoms defined only in the political terms set out in the Bill of Rights of 1791 or were they also to include freedom from economic insecurity and social injustice? Some of the journeys assumed a regional dimension as the environment and inherited cultural patterns imparted a distinctive approach to issues affecting the entire nation.

Most of all, the journeys have been those of individuals. We have tried to include as many of them as possible and to blend their stories into the larger national narrative of which they were and are a part. The voices of contemporaries open each chapter, describing their personal journeys—and detours—toward fulfilling their dreams, hopes, and ambitions as part of the broader American journey. These voices provide a personal window on our nation's history, and the themes they express resonate throughout the narrative. Embedding these individual stories within a broader narrative allows us to address questions of culture, identity, politics, and ideas as they shaped the lives of elites and common people alike.

By including stories from the perspectives of different individuals and groups in the text and Web-based features, we aim to provide students with a balanced overview of the American past. We do not shy away from controversial issues, such as the effects of early contacts between Native Americans and Europeans, why the political crisis of the 1850s ended in a bloody Civil War, how Populists fit into the American political spectrum, or why the United States used nuclear weapons against Japan. If our treatment of these topics provokes debate between students and instructors, we encourage such discussions as an important catalyst to learning.

We invite students and teachers to think about how their own stories and those of their families relate to the theme of our book. Most of all, we hope that *The American Journey* can guide students along their own intellectual paths toward a better understanding of American history and their own place in it.

## APPROACH

In telling our story, we had some definite ideas about what we might include and emphasize that other texts do not—information we felt that the current and next generations of students will need to know about our past to function best in a new society.

**Chronological Organization** A strong chronological backbone supports the book. We have found that jumping back and forth in time confuses students. They abhor dates but need to know the sequence of events in history. A chronological presentation is the best way to help students.

**Geographical Literacy** We also want students to be geographically literate. We expect them not only to know what happened in American history, but where it happened as well. Physical locations and spatial relationships were often important in shaping historical events. The abundant maps in *The American Journey*—all numbered and called out in the text—are an integral part of our story.

**Regional Balance** *The American Journey* presents balanced coverage of all regions of the country. In keeping with this balance, the South and the West receive more coverage in this text than in comparable books.

**Religion** This text stresses the importance of religion in American society as a cultural force and an influence on political action.

**Pedagogical Support** *The American Journey* includes many pedagogical tools to help students understand, analyze, and think critically about the events that unfold in each chapter. The **Student Tool Kit** (see pages xxi–xxxi) provides detailed highlights of these special features, including the MyHistoryLab (www.myhistorylab.com) website that accompanies the text. MyHistoryLab provides many additional resources that expand on the book's themes and content.

## WHAT'S NEW IN THE SIXTH EDITION

In this edition, there is greater emphasis on the personal and collective journeys that have shaped America's history, from the personal documents that open each chapter to the narrative that defines the journey. In addition, every chapter has been thoroughly revised and improved with new special features as well as updated scholarship. Throughout the text, there is an increased emphasis on environmental history in both the chapter narrative and special features. A new **Key Topics** section provides critical thinking questions for each main section of the chapter for study and review. New MyHistoryLab icons are included within the chapters to indicate documents, audio and video clips, interactive maps, and activities available on the MyHistoryLab website that connect to content in the text. There is also a new section, **MyHistoryLab Connections**, listing these and other available resources at the end of each chapter.

## CHANGES BY CHAPTER:

### Chapter 1
A new **Global Connections** feature, "Learning About Chocolate" describes Spanish colonists' fascination with chocolate, a New World food, and their efforts to learn how to make chocolate drinks back in Europe.

### Chapter 2
A new **American Views** document, "A Colonist Marvels at New England's Abundant Wildlife," introduces environmental themes, describing the richness of New England nature at the time of colonization and the colonists' assumptions about exploiting natural resources.

### Chapter 3
There are two new "Where to Learn More" sites that relate to the African American experience in colonial America.

### Chapter 4
A new, expanded section provides discussion on Salem witchcraft.

### Chapter 5
A new **American Journey** features the English clergyman, Andrew Burnaby, and shows how few people predicted the coming of the Revolution. The chapter has been rewritten for clarity, with greater emphasis on this theme of contingency with regard to the Revolutionary movement. There is also an expanded discussion of republican ideology.

### Chapter 7
A new **American Views** focuses on black freedom struggles in the immediate aftermath of the Revolution.

### Chapter 8
A new **American Views** highlights an environmental issue by examining contemporary thinking in the 1790s on water pollution in Philadelphia.

### Chapter 11
A new **Global Connections**, "Cotton Is King," examines the international aspects of the cotton industry.

### Chapter 14
The **American Journey** feature now connects Harriet Beecher Stowe's personal journey to America's journey. The chapter now emphasizes slavery as the primary cause of secession and war, both in the narrative and in the **American Views** feature, "The Cause of the Civil War." A new illustration connects the Revolutions of 1848 (the theme of the Global Connections feature in this chapter) to events in the United States in the 1850s. A second new illustration, the John Brown mural in the Kansas State House, enables students to discuss how art can mix memory and history.

### Chapter 15
There is a new discussion, "The Southern Landscape," on the natural environment and geography of the South and how that affected battles and strategies. A new subhead, "The Real War," includes a quotation from Walt Whitman who lamented that the "real war" would never get into the history books. The narrative now emphasizes the blood, gore, and unnecessary carnage of the war. More information is included on the Native American involvement in the Civil War. The new **Global Connections**, "The Civil War in Europe," covers the reaction to the Civil War in Great Britain, France, and Russia, and their policies. A new **American Views, "The Costs of War,"** is a collection of comments from soldiers and civilians from both sides on the carnage of the war.

### Chapter 16
The major change in this chapter is the emphasis on the theme that Reconstruction did not fail, it was overthrown. The chapter stresses the violence against southern Republican governments, particularly blacks, as the key factor in ending Reconstruction. The new **American Journey** chapter opener is a poem by black poet Frances E. W. Harper, "An Appeal to the American People," that urged northerners not to abandon southern blacks to southern whites. The section "The Democrats' Violent Resurgence" gives more details on the extent and nature of the organized violence. "The Memory of Reconstruction" is expanded, especially on the openness with which future generations of white southerners commended the violence which overthrew Reconstruction.

# SUPPLEMENTARY INSTRUCTIONAL MATERIALS

| FOR INSTRUCTORS | FOR STUDENTS |
|---|---|
| **myhistorylab** www.myhistorylab.com<br>**Save Time. Improve Results.** MyHistoryLab is a dynamic website that provides a wealth of resources geared to meet the diverse teaching and learning needs of today's instructors and students. MyHistoryLab's many accessible tools will encourage students to read their text and help them improve their grade in their course. | **myhistorylab** www.myhistorylab.com<br>**Save Time. Improve Results.** MyHistoryLab is a dynamic website that provides a wealth of resources geared to meet the diverse teaching and learning needs of today's instructors and students. MyHistoryLab's many accessible tools will encourage you to read your text and help you improve your grade in your course. |
| **Instructor's Resource Center** www.pearsonhighered.com/irc This website provides instructors with additional text-specific resources that can be downloaded for classroom use. Resources include the Instructor's Resource Manual, PowerPoint presentations, and the test item file. Register online for access to the resources for The American Journey. | www.coursemart.com<br>CourseSmart eTextbooks offer the same content as the printed text in a convenient online format—with highlighting, online search, and printing capabilities. You **save 60% over the list price** of the traditional book. |
| **Instructor's Resource Manual** Available for download at www.pearsonhighered.com/irc, *the* Instructor's Resource Manual contains chapter outlines, detailed chapter overviews, lecture outlines, topics for discussion, and information about audio-visual resources. | **Books à la Carte** These editions feature the exact same content as the traditional printed text in a convenient, three-hole-punched, loose-leaf version at a discounted price—allowing you to take only what you need to class. You'll **save 35% over the net price** of the traditional book. |
| **Test Item File** Available for download at www.pearsonhighered.com/irc, the Test Item File contains more than 1,500 multiple-choice, identification, matching, true-false, and essay test questions and 10–15 questions per chapter on the maps found in each chapter. | **Library of American Biography Series** www.pearsonhighered.com/educator/series/Library-of-American-Biography/10493.page Pearson's renowned series of biographies spotlighting figures who had a significant impact on American history. Included in the series are Edmund Morgan's *The Puritan Dilemma: The Story of John Winthrop*, B. Davis Edmund's *Tecumseh and the Quest for Indian Leadership*, J. William T. Youngs's *Eleanor Roosevelt: A Personal and Public Life*, and John R. M. Wilson's *Jackie Robinson and the American Dilemma*. |
| **PowerPoint Presentations** Available for download at www.pearsonhighered.com/irc, the PowerPoints contain chapter outlines and full-color images of maps, figures, and images. | *American Stories: Biographies in United States History* This two-volume collection of sixty-two biographies provides insight into the lives and contributions of key figures as well as ordinary citizens to American history. Introductions, pre-reading questions, and suggested resources helps students connect the relevance of these individuals to historical events. Volume 1 **ISBN-10: 0131826549 ISBN-13: 9780131826540**; Volume 2 **ISBN-10: 0131826530 ISBN-13: 9780131826533** |
| **MyTest** www.pearsonmytest.com MyTest is a powerful assessment generation program that helps instructors easily create and print quizzes and exams. Questions and tests can be authored online, allowing instructors ultimate flexibility and the ability to efficiently manage assessments any-time, anywhere! Instructors can easily access existing questions and edit, create, and store using simple drag-and-drop and Word-like controls. | **Penguin Valuepacks** www.pearsonhighered.com/penguin A variety of Penguin-Putnam texts is available at discounted prices when bundled with *The American Journey, Brief 6/e*. Texts include Benjamin Franklin's *Autobiography and Other Writings*, Nathaniel Hawthorne's *The Scarlet Letter*, Thomas Jefferson's *Notes on the State of Virginia*, and George Orwell's *1984*. |

(*continued*)

| FOR INSTRUCTORS | FOR STUDENTS |
|---|---|
| **Retrieving the American Past**  (www.pearsoncustom.com, **keyword search \| rtap**)<br>Available through the Pearson Custom Library, the *Retrieving the American Past* (RTAP) program lets you create a textbook or reader that meets your needs and the needs of your course. RTAP gives you the freedom and flexibility to add chapters from several best-selling Pearson textbooks, in addition to *The American Journey, Brief 6/e*, and/or 100 topical reading units written by the History Department of Ohio State University, all under one cover. Choose the content you want to teach in depth, in the sequence you want, at the price you want your students to pay. | *A Short Guide to Writing About History, 7/e*  Written by Richard Marius, late of Harvard University, and Melvin E. Page, Eastern Tennessee State University, this engaging and practical text helps students get beyond merely compiling dates and facts. Covering brief essays and the documented resource paper, the text explores the writing and researching processes, identifies different modes of historical writing, including argument, and concludes with guidelines for improving style. **ISBN-10: 0205673708; ISBN-13: 9780205673704** |
|  | **Longman American History Atlas**  This full-color historical atlas designed especially for college students is a valuable reference tool and visual guide to American history. This atlas includes maps covering the scope of American history from the lives of the Native Americans to the 1990s. Produced by a renowned cartographic firm and a team of respected historians, the Longman American History Atlas will enhance any American history survey course. **ISBN: 0321004868; ISBN-13: 9780321004864** |

# myhistorylab (www.myhistorylab.com)

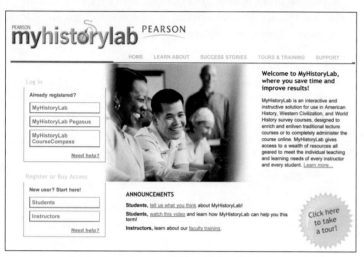

## FOR INSTRUCTORS AND STUDENTS

### Save TIME. Improve Results.

MyHistoryLab is a dynamic website that provides a wealth of resources geared to meet the diverse teaching and learning needs of today's instructors and students. MyHistoryLab's many accessible tools will encourage students to read their text and help them improve their grade in their course.

- **Pearson eText**—An e-book version of *The American Journey* is included in MyHistoryLab. Just as with the printed text, students can highlight and add their own notes as they read the book online.
- **Gradebook**—Students can follow their own progress and instructors can monitor the work of the entire class. Automated grading of quizzes and assignments helps both instructors and students save time and monitor their results throughout the course.
- **History Bookshelf**—Students may read, download, or print 100 of the most commonly assigned history works like Homer's *The Iliad* or Machiavelli's *The Prince*.
- **Audio Files**—Full audio of the entire text is included to suit the varied learning styles of today's students.
- **MySearchLab**—This website provides students access to a number of reliable sources for online research, as well as clear guidance on the research and writing process.

## NEW IN-TEXT REFERENCES TO MYHISTORYLAB RESOURCES

**Read/View/See/Watch/Hear/Study and Review Icons** integrated in the text connect resources on MyHistoryLab to specific topics within the chapters. The icons are not exhaustive; many more resources are available than those highlighted in the book, but the icons draw attention to some of the most high-interest resources available on MyHistoryLab.

### Read the Document

Primary and secondary source documents on compelling topics such as *Brown v. Board of Education of Topeka, Kansas* and Engel, Address by a Haymarket Anarchist enhance topics discussed in each chapter.

### See the Map

Atlas and interactive maps present both a broad overview and a detailed examination of historical developments.

### Watch the Video

Video lectures highlight topics ranging from Columbus to Lincoln to Obama, engaging students on both historical and contemporary topics. Also included are archival videos, such as footage of Ellis Island immigrants in 1903 and the Kennedy-Nixon debate.

### Hear the Audio

For each chapter there are audio files of the text, speeches, readings, and other audio material, such as *Battle Hymn of the Republic* and *The Star Spangled Banner* that will enrich students' experience of social and cultural history.

### Study and Review

MyHistoryLab provides a wealth of practice quizzes, tests, flashcards, and other study resources available to students online.

We would like to thank the reviewers whose thoughtful and often detailed comments helped shape the brief sixth edition and previous editions of *The American Journey*.

## BRIEF SIXTH EDITION:

Troy Bickham, Texas A&M University
Matt Clavin, University of West Florida
Cathy Koken, Pueblo Community College
Susanna Lee, North Carolina State University
Brenda Murray, Arkansas Tech University
Carey Roberts, Arkansas Tech University

## PREVIOUS EDITIONS:

Jacqueline Akins, Community College of Philadelphia
James Barrett, University of Illinois–Urbana-Champaign
Caroline Barton, Holmes Community College
Lawrence Culver, Utah State University
Alan Downs, Georgia Southern University
Kimberly Earhart, Mount San Antonio College
E. J. Fabyan, Vincennes University
Jennifer Fry, Kings College
Michael Gabriel, Kutztown University
Mark Goldman, Tallahassee Community College
Kathleen Gorman, Minnesota State University–Mankato
Don Jacobson, Oakton Community College
Hasan Jeffries, Ohio State University
Thomas Jorsch, Ferris State University
John Klee, Maysville Community and Technical College
Jonathan Mercantini, Canisius College
Loyce Miles, Hinds Community College
James Owens, Oakton Community College
James Page, North Central Texas College
Joshua Schier, Western Michigan University
Larry Wilson, San Jacinto College Central

All of us are grateful to our families, friends, and colleagues for their support and encouragement. Jo Ann and Peter Argersinger would like in particular to thank Anna Champe, Linda Hatmaker, and John Willits; William Barney thanks Pamela Fesmire and Rosalie Radcliffe; Virginia Anderson thanks Fred Anderson, Kim Gruenwald, Ruth Helm, Eric Hinderaker, and Chidiebere Nwaubani; and David Goldfield thanks Frances Glenn and Jason Moscato.

Finally, we would like to acknowledge the members of our Prentice Hall family. They are not only highly competent professionals but also pleasant people. We regard them with affection and appreciation. None of us would hesitate to work with this fine group again. We would especially like to thank our editorial team: Charlyce Jones Owen, Publisher, our marketing team: Maureen Prado Roberts, Senior Marketing Manager, and Brandy Dawson, Director of Marketing; our production team: Ann Marie McCarthy, Denise Forlow, Ashley Schneider, S4Carlisle Publishing Services, Christina Amato, manufacturing manager, Craig Campanella, Editorial Director, and Yolanda deRooy, president of Prentice Hall's Humanities and Social Sciences division.

DG
CA
VDJA
JEA
PHA
WLB
RMW

ACKNOWLEDGMENTS

xix

**David Goldfield** received his Ph.D. in history from the University of Maryland. Since 1982 he has been the Robert Lee Bailey Professor of History at the University of North Carolina in Charlotte. He is the author or editor of fifteen books on various aspects of southern and urban history. Two of his works—*Cotton Fields and Skyscrapers: Southern City and Region, 1607–1980* (1982) and *Black, White, and Southern: Race Relations and Southern Culture, 1940 to the Present* (1990)—received the Mayflower Award for nonfiction and was nominated for the Pulitzer Prize in history. His most recent book is *America Aflame: How the Civil War Created a Nation* (2011). When he is not writing history, Dr. Goldfield applies his historical craft to history museum exhibits, voting rights cases, and local planning and policy issues.

**Carl Abbott** is a professor of Urban Studies and planning at Portland State University. He taught previously in the history departments at the University of Denver and Old Dominion University, and held visiting appointments at Mesa College in Colorado and George Washington University. He holds degrees in history from Swarthmore College and the University of Chicago. He specializes in the history of cities and the American West and serves as coeditor of the Pacific Historical Review. His books include *The New Urban America: Growth and Politics in Sunbelt Cities* (1981, 1987), *The Metropolitan Frontier: Cities in the Modern American West* (1993), *Planning a New West: The Columbia River Gorge National Scenic Area* (1997), and *Political Terrain: Washington, D.C. from Tidewater Town to Global Metropolis* (1999), and *How Cities Won the West: Four Centuries of Urban Change in Western North American (2008).*

**Virginia DeJohn Anderson** is Professor of History at the University of Colorado at Boulder. She received her B.A. from the University of Connecticut. As the recipient of a Marshall Scholarship, she earned an M.A. degree at the University of East Anglia in Norwich, England. Returning to the United States, she received her A.M. and Ph.D. degrees from Harvard University. She is the author of *New England's Generation: The Great Migration and the Formation of Society and Culture in the Seventeenth Century* (1991) and *Creatures of Empire: How Domestic Animals Transformed Early America* (2004). Her current research focuses on the American Revolution.

**Jo Ann E. Argersinger** received her Ph.D. from George Washington University and is Professor of History at Southern Illinois University. A recipient of fellowships from the Rockefeller Foundation and the National Endowment for the Humanities, she is a historian of social, labor, and business policy. Her publications include *Toward a New Deal in Baltimore: People and Government in the Great Depression* (1988), *Making the Amalgamated: Gender, Ethnicity, and Class in the Baltimore Clothing Industry* (1999), and *The Triangle Fire: A Brief History with Documents* (2009). She is currently writing a study of citizenship rights and public housing placing he American experience in the international arena.

**Peter H. Argersinger** received his Ph.D. from the University of Wisconsin and is Professor of History at Southern Illinois University. He has won several fellowships as well as the Binkley-Stephenson Award from the Organization of American Historians, and he is currently president of the Society for Historians of the Gilded Age and Progressive Era. Among his books on political and rural history are *Populism and Politics* (1974), *Structure, Process, and Party* (1992), and *The Limits of Agrarian Radicalism* (1995). His most recent book, integrating legal and political history, is *Courting Chaos: The Politics of Apportionment in the Midwest, 1870–1910* (2011). His current research focuses on the political crisis of the 1890s.

**William L. Barney** is Professor of History at the University of North Carolina at Chapel Hill. A native of Pennsylvania, he received his B.A. from Cornell University and his M.A. and Ph.D. from Columbia University. He has published extensively on nineteenth-century U.S. history and has a particular interest in the Old South and the coming of the Civil War. Among his publications are *The Road to Secession* (1972), *The Secessionist Impulse* (1974), *Flawed Victory* (1975), *The Passage of the Republic* (1987), and *Battleground for the Union* (1989), and *The Civil War and Reconstruction: A Student Companion* (2001). *Most recently, he has finished The Making of a Confederate: Walter Lenoir's Civil War* (2007).

**Robert M. Weir** is Distinguished Professor of History Emeritus at the University of South Carolina. He received his B.A. from Pennsylvania State University and his Ph.D. from Case Western Reserve University. He has taught at the University of Houston and, as a visiting professor, at the University of Southampton in the United Kingdom. His articles have won prizes from the Southeastern Society for the Study of the Eighteenth Century and the *William and Mary* Quarterly. Among his publications are *Colonial South Carolina: A History, "The Last of American Freemen": Studies in the Political Culture of the Colonial and Revolutionary South,* and, more recently, a chapter on the Carolinas in the *new Oxford History of the British Empire* (1998).

# USING *THE AMERICAN JOURNEY*

*When writing history, historians use maps, tables, graphs, and visuals to help their readers understand the past. What follows is an explanation of how to use the historian's tools that are contained in this book.*

## TEXT

Whether it is a biography of George Washington, an article on the Civil War, or a survey of American history such as this one, the text is the historian's basic tool for discussing the past. Historians write about the past using narration and analysis. Narration is the story line of history. It describes what happened in the past, who did it, and where and when it occurred. Narration is also used to describe how people in the past lived, how they spent their days and even, when the historical evidence makes it possible for us to know, what they thought, felt, feared, or desired. Using analysis, historians explain why they think events in the past happened the way they did and try to offer an explanation. In this book, narration and analysis are interwoven in each chapter.

## VISUALS

Visual images embedded thoughout the text can provide as much insight into our nation's history as the written word. Within photographs and pieces of fine art lies emotional and historical meaning. Captions provide valuable information, such as in the example below. When studying the images, consider questions such as: "Who are the people?"; "How were they feeling?"; "What event motivated this photograph or painting?"; and "What can be learned from the backdrop surrounding the focal point?" Such analysis allows for a fuller understanding of the people who lived the American journey.

TRANSPLANTATION AND ADAPTATION **CHAPTER 2** 53

James, Duke of York, received this map of New Amsterdam in 1664, when England seized New Netherland from the Dutch and the Duke became proprietor of the new colony of New York. The top of the map is oriented to the east, with the lower tip of Manhattan Island facing to the right.

labor systems, and worshiped in different churches. In South Carolina, New York, Pennsylvania, and the West Indies, most colonists were not even of English origin. What held these colonies together—besides their establishment under English charters and their enmity toward the Spanish and French—was an overlay of common English institutions of government. By the mid-1680s, all the colonies had legislatures that provided for self-government and laws and judicial institutions based on English models.

The planting of French, Dutch, and English colonies not only ended Spain's monopoly of settlement in North America but also challenged the Indians' hold on the continent. Forced to deal with a rising tide of settlers and often to choose sides between European rivals, native peoples adapted to rapidly changing circumstances. Transplanted Europeans adapted too, not only in their dealings with native peoples but also in finding and controlling the laborers they needed to make their colonies prosper. For English colonists this meant the widespread adoption of slavery, an institution that did not exist in England itself. For millions of Africans, the result was forced migration to the New World.

MAP 5–1 **Colonial Settlement and the Proclamation Line of 1763** This map depicts the regions claimed and settled by the major groups competing for territory in eastern North America. With the Proclamation Line of 1763, positioned along the crest of the Appalachian Mountains, the British government tried to stop the westward migration of settlers under its jurisdiction and thereby limit conflict with the Indians. The result, however, was frustration and anger on the part of land-hungry settlers.

**Why do** you think the Proclamation Line of 1763 was positioned along the crest of the Appalachian Mountains?

# MAPS

Maps are important historical tools. They show how geography has affected history and concisely summarize complex relationships and events. Knowing how to read and interpret a map is important to understanding history. Map 5–1 from Chapter 5 shows the British colonies on the eastern seaboard of North America in 1763, about twelve years before the American Revolution. It has three features to help you read it: a caption, a legend, and a scale. The ❶ **caption** explains the historical significance of the map. Here the caption tells us that in 1763 the British government sought to restrict colonial settlement west of the Appalachian Mountains to prevent conflict between colonists and Indians. Colonial frustration with this policy contributed to the outbreak of the American Revolution.

The legend and the scale appear in the lower right corner of the map. The ❷ **legend** provides a key to what the symbols on the map mean. The solid line stretching along the Appalachian Mountains from Maine to Georgia represents the Proclamation Line of 1763. Cities are marked with a dot, capitals with a dot in a circle and forts by a black square. Spanish territory west of the Mississippi River is represented in gold; territory settled by Europeans is represented in green. The ❸ **scale** tells us that 7/8ths of an inch on the map represents 300 miles (about 480 kilometers) on the ground. With this information, estimates of the distance between points on the map are easily made.

The map also shows the ❹ **topography** of the region—its mountains, rivers, and lakes. This helps us understand how geography influenced history in this case. For example, the Appalachian Mountains divide the eastern seaboard from the rest of the continent. The mountains obstructed colonial migration to the west for a long time. By running the Proclamation Line along the Appalachians, the British hoped to use this natural barrier to separate Indians and colonists.

A ❺ **critical-thinking question** asks for careful consideration of the spatial connections between geography and history.

# STUDY AIDS

Each chapter begins with a collection of historically significant illustrations that provide visual context for the chapter. To help you look ahead at the chapter content, the second page shows the main chapter topics with a question for each to help you carefully consider important themes and developments.

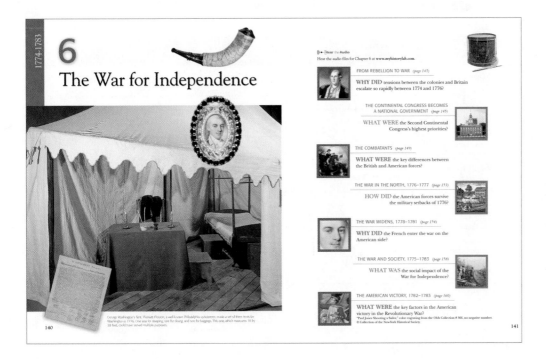

# MARGINAL QUESTIONS

The **Questions** that begin each chapter are repeated at the appropriate place in the margin of the text. You can use these questions to review your understanding of the chapter content.

# MARGINAL KEY TERMS/GLOSSARY

Significant historical terms are called out in bold type throughout the text, defined in the margin, and listed at the end of each chapter with appropriate page numbers. All **key terms** in the text are listed alphabetically and defined in a glossary at the end of the book.

# QUICK REVIEWS

The **Quick Reviews,** placed at key locations in the margins of each chapter, provide pinpoint summaries of important concepts, events, or topics in American history and serve as a mini-review resource.

**WHO WERE** the Regulators, and what were the Regulator movements?

**Pilgrims**   Settlers of Plymouth Colony, who viewed themselves as spiritual wanderers.

### QUICK REVIEW

**Financial Strain on the Empire**

◆ £146-million-pound national debt after French and Indian War

◆ Many Britons believed Americans should bear more of the burden of empire

◆ Economic recession increased pressure for new taxes

# OVERVIEW TABLES

The **Overview tables** in this text are a special feature designed to highlight and summarize important topics within a chapter. The Overview table shown here, for example, shows the predominant colonial labor systems in 1750 by geographic area.

---

52 **CHAPTER 2** TRANSPLANTATION AND ADAPTATION

**OVERVIEW** English Colonies in the Seventeenth Century

| Colony | Date of Founding | Established Religion | Economy | Government |
|---|---|---|---|---|
| Virginia | 1607 | Anglican | Tobacco | Royal (after 1625) |
| Plymouth | 1620 | Puritan | Mixed farming | Corporate |
| St. Christopher | 1624 | Anglican | Sugar | Royal |
| Barbados | 1627 | Anglican | Sugar | Royal |
| Nevis | 1628 | Anglican | Sugar | Royal |
| Massachusetts (including present-day Maine) | 1630 | Puritan | Mixed farming, fishing, shipbuilding | Corporate |
| New Hampshire | 1630 (first settlement, annexed to Massachusetts 1643–1679) | Puritan | Mixed farming | Corporate (royal after 1679) |
| Antigua | 1632 | Anglican | Sugar | Royal |
| Montserrat | 1632 | Anglican | Sugar | Royal |
| Maryland | 1634 | None (Anglican after 1692) | Tobacco | Proprietary |
| Rhode Island | 1636 | None | Mixed farming | Corporate |
| Connecticut | 1636 | Puritan | Mixed farming | Corporate |
| New Haven | 1638 | Puritan | Mixed farming | Corporate |
| Jamaica | 1655 (captured from Spanish) | Anglican | Sugar | Royal |
| Carolina | 1663 | Anglican | Rice | Proprietary |
| New York | 1664 (captured from Dutch) | None | Mixed farming, furs | Proprietary (royal after 1685) |
| New Jersey | 1664 | None | Mixed farming | Proprietary |
| Pennsylvania | 1681 | None | Wheat, mixed farming | Proprietary |

---

## CONCLUSION

Even as England gained a permanent foothold in North America, it faced vigorous competition from France and the Netherlands. A new Atlantic world was beginning to emerge as the migration of people and goods across the ocean linked the Old and New Worlds as never before.

Commerce was the main focus of the short-lived New Netherland colony and a more durable New France. Profits from the fur trade encouraged the French to maintain friendly relations with their Indian allies and ensured that French kings would closely monitor the colony's affairs. English colonization was a more haphazard process. English kings granted charters for new colonies and let them develop more or less on their own. England had no equivalent in the seventeenth century of the imperial bureaucracies Spain and France created to manage their New World holdings.

The result was a highly diverse set of English colonies stretching from the Maine coast to the Caribbean. Settlers adjusted to different environments, developed different economies and

# CHRONOLOGIES

Each chapter includes a **Chronology,** a list of the key events discussed in the chapter arranged in chronological order. The Chronology for Chapter 16 lists the dates of key events during the Reconstruction era from 1861 to 1877. Chronologies provide a review of important events and their relationship to one another.

## CHRONOLOGY

| | | | |
|---|---|---|---|
| **c. 40,000–8000 B.C.E.** | Ancestors of Native Americans cross Bering land bridge. | **1430s** | Beginnings of Portuguese slave trade in West Africa. |
| **c. 10,000–9000 B.C.E.** | Paleo-Indians expand through the Americas. | **1492** | End of *reconquista* in Spain. |
| | | | Columbus's first voyage. |
| **c. 9000 B.C.E.** | Extinction of large land mammals in North America. | **1494** | Treaty of Tordesillas. |
| **c. 8000 B.C.E.** | Beginnings of agriculture in the Peruvian Andes and Mesoamerica. | **1497** | John Cabot visits Nova Scotia and Newfoundland. |
| | | **1497–1499** | Vasco da Gama sails around Africa to reach India. |
| **c. 1500 B.C.E.** | Earliest mound-building culture begins. | **1517** | Protestant Reformation begins in Germany. |
| **c. 500 B.C.E.–400 C.E.** | Adena-Hopewell mound-building culture. | **1519–1521** | Hernán Cortés conquers the Aztec empire. |
| | | **1532–1533** | Francisco Pizarro conquers the Incan empire. |
| **c. 700–1600 C.E.** | Rise of West African empires. | **1534–1542** | Jacques Cartier explores eastern Canada for France. |
| **c. 900** | First mounds built at Cahokia. | **1540–1542** | Coronado explores southwestern North America. |
| | Ancestral Puebloan expansion. | **1542–1543** | Roberval's failed colony in Canada. |
| **c. 1000** | Spread of Islam in West Africa. | **1558** | Elizabeth I becomes queen of England. |
| **c. 1000–1015** | First Viking voyages to North America. | **1565** | Spanish establish outpost at St. Augustine in Florida. |
| **c. 1000–1500** | Last mound-building culture, the Mississippian. | | |
| **c. 1290s** | Ancestral Puebloan dispersal into smaller villages. | **1560s–1580s** | English renew attempts to conquer Ireland. |
| | | **1587** | Founding of "Lost Colony" of Roanoke. |
| **1400–1600** | Renaissance in Europe. | **1598** | Spanish found colony at New Mexico. |

## NATIVE AMERICAN SOCIETIES BEFORE 1492

In 1492 perhaps 70 million people—nearly equal to the population of Europe at that time—lived on the continents of North and South America, most of them south of the present border between the United States and Mexico. They belonged to hundreds of groups, each with its own language or dialect, history, and way of life.

From the start, the original inhabitants of the Americas were peoples in motion. The first migrants may have arrived over forty thousand years ago, traveling from central Siberia and slowly making their way to southern South America. These people, and subsequent migrants from Eurasia, probably traveled across a land bridge that emerged across what is now the Bering Strait. During the last Ice Age, much of the earth's water was frozen in huge glaciers. This process lowered ocean levels, exposing a 600-mile-wide land bridge between Asia and America. Recent research examining genetic and linguistic similarities between Asian and Native American populations suggests that there may also have been later migrations.

**HOW DID** geography shape the development of regional cultures in North America prior to 1492?

**See the Map**
at **www.myhistorylab.com**
*Pre-Columbian Societies of the Americas*

### HUNTERS, HARVESTERS, AND TRADERS

The earliest Americans adapted to an amazing range of environmental conditions, from the frozen Arctic to southwestern deserts to dense eastern woodlands. At first, they mainly subsisted by hunting the mammoths, bison, and other large game that roamed throughout North America.

## NEW! MYHISTORYLAB ICONS

References to relevant primary source documents, audio files, visual sources, interactive maps, and activities available on the MyHistoryLab website have been added throughout each chapter. These references are identified by icons that connect the MyHistoryLab sources to the specific content within the text. Look for these icons as you read the chapter and explore the additional content online at www.myhistorylab.com.

**Read** the **Document**

Primary Source Documents, the History Bookshelf, and Activities.

**See** the **Map**

Interactive and Atlas Maps.

**Hear** the **Audio**

Audio files of the *American Journey* textbook and audio clips of readings, music, and speeches.

**Watch** the **Video**

Video Lectures and archival footage.

## NEW! 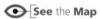 myhistorylab CONNECTIONS

At the end of each chapter, the references in the chapter are listed again along with additional resources that relate directly to the content you will have read in the chapter.

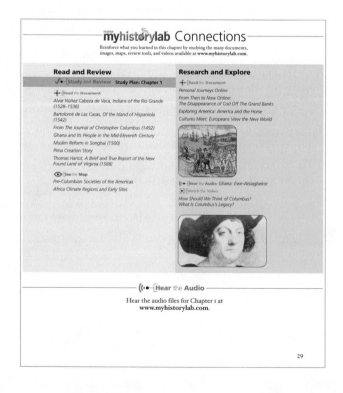

# WHERE TO LEARN MORE, REVIEW QUESTIONS, AND KEY TERMS

At the end of each chapter there are a number of review and enrichment resources. ❶ **Where to Learn More** lists important historical sites and museums around the country and related websites (many of which are also cited at appropriate places in the margins of the text) that provide exposure to historical artifacts and settings. ❷ **Review questions** reconsider the main topics of each chapter. ❸ **Key Terms** reference the page within the chapter where the term is defined. The section called

## WHERE TO LEARN MORE ❶

**Jamestown Settlement, near Williamsburg, Virginia.** Site includes replicas of first English passenger ships to Virginia, a reconstructed Powhatan Village, the re-created James Fort, and galleries with Indian and English artifacts. Visitors can also see archaeological excavations of site of the actual James Fort, as well as sample artifacts recovered from the area. The website http://www.virtualjamestown.org/ offers a wealth of fascinating information about English and Indian settlement in the Jamestown area.

**St. Mary's City, Maryland.** Visitors to this site of the first permanent settlement under the Calvert family may tour the area and view exhibits and living history programs that describe life in early Maryland. The website http://www.stmaryscity.org/ contains information about the historic site of St. Mary's City and has links to a virtual tour of the area.

**Plimoth Plantation, Plymouth, Massachusetts.** A living history museum, Plimoth Plantation re-creates colony life in the year 1627. There are reproductions of the English village and a Wampanoag settlement. Visitors may also see a replica of the *Mayflower*. The website http://www.plimoth.org/ provides information for visitors.

**Pennsbury Manor, Morrisville, Pennsylvania.** A reconstruction of William Penn's seventeenth-century plantation, this site includes furnished buildings and restored gardens. Visitor information about the site and William Penn's life can be found at http://www.pennsburymanor.org/.

## REVIEW QUESTIONS ❷

1. To what extent was Richard Frethorne's experience typical of that of English colonists in the New World? What were the causes of his distress?

2. Comparing French, Dutch, and English colonies, which ones attracted the most settlers, and which the fewest? In what colonies were women scarce? What impact did these differences in emigration have on the various colonies' development?

3. Which English settlements were proprietary colonies? Did they share any common characteristics? What plans did the various proprietors have for their colonies, and to what extent were those plans put into effect?

4. When Virginia's settlers first arrived, they encountered a numerous and powerful confederation of Powhatan Indians. New England's colonists, in contrast, began their settlements after epidemics had drastically reduced the local native population. In what ways did the presence or absence of substantial Indian populations affect each region's early history?

5. In both Massachusetts and Pennsylvania, religion figured prominently as a motive for settlement. What were the religious beliefs of the settlers in each colony, and how did those beliefs help shape each colony's development?

6. Three colonial regions—the Chesapeake, the West Indies, and Carolina—developed economies dependent on staple crops. What were those crops? In what ways did staple-crop agriculture shape society in each region?

7. In what ways did events in Europe affect the founding of colonies in North America?

## KEY TERMS ❸

**Act for Religious Toleration** (p. 41)
**Anglican** (p. 42)
*Coureurs de bois* (p. 34)
**Covenant** (p. 44)
**Frame of Government** (p. 51)
**Fundamental Constitutions of Carolina** (p. 49)
**Headright system** (p. 38)
**House of Burgesses** (p. 38)

**Indentured servants** (p. 34)
**Joint-stock company** (p. 37)
**Pequot War** (p. 44)
**Pilgrims** (p. 43)
**Proprietary colony** (p. 40)
**Puritans** (p. 40)
**Quakers** (p. 50)
**Separatists** (p. 43)
**Slave codes** (p. 48)

54

## SPECIAL FEATURES

*Historians find most of their information in written records and original documents that have survived from the past. These include government publications, letters, diaries, newspapers—whatever people wrote or printed, including many private documents never intended for publication. Several features in the text highlight the written record so important to understanding historical events.*

## ONE AMERICAN JOURNEY

Each chapter begins with **One American Journey,** a brief firsthand account of a time in history. Each of these personal journeys relates to the themes that follow in the chapter. For example, in Chapter 18 is an excerpt from a letter written by Mary Antin, a Russian-Jewish immigrant who came to America at the turn of the last century.

### Personal Journeys Online
At the end of each document is a list of additional firsthand accounts that are included on the *MyHistoryLab* website.

---

4   **CHAPTER 1**   WORLDS APART

ONE AMERICAN JOURNEY

*After a difficult journey of over two hundred miles, the exhausted man arrived at the royal palace in the grand city of Tenochtitlán. He had hurried all the way from the Gulf Coast with important news for the Aztec leader, Moctezuma.*

> *Our lord and king, forgive my boldness. I am from Mictlancuauhtla. When I went to the shores of the great sea, there was a mountain range or small mountain floating in the midst of the water, and moving here and there without touching the shore. My lord, we have never seen the like of this, although we guard the coast and are always on watch.*
>
> *[When Moctezuma sent some officials to check on the messenger's story, they confirmed his report.]*
>
> *Our lord and king, it is true that strange people have come to the shores of the great sea. They were fishing from a small boat, some with rods and others with a net. They fished until late and then they went back to their two great towers and climbed up into them.... They have very light skin, much lighter than ours. They all have long beards, and their hair comes only to their ears.*

Miguel Leon-Portilla, *The Broken Spears: The Aztec Account of the Conquest of Mexico* (Boston, 1962).

 Read the Document at **www.myhistorylab.com**

Personal Journeys Online

- **Christopher Columbus,** *Journal of the First Voyage,* October 12, 1492. Account of his first meeting with Caribbean islanders.
- **Martin Frobisher,** *Account of First Voyage to the New World,* 1576. Description of his arrival in Canada and his encounter with native people.

MOCTEZUMA was filled with foreboding when he received the messenger's initial report. Aztec religion placed great emphasis on omens and prophecies, which were thought to foreshadow coming events. Several unusual omens had recently occurred—blazing lights in the sky, one temple struck by lightning and another that spontaneously burst into flames. Now light-skinned strangers appeared offshore. Aztec spiritual leaders regarded these signs as unfavorable and warned that trouble lay ahead.

The messenger's journey to Tenochtitlán occurred in 1519. The "mountains" he saw were in fact the sails of European ships, and the strange men were Spanish soldiers under the command of Hernán Cortés. Before long, a variety of peoples—Native Americans, Africans, and Europeans—who had previously lived worlds apart would come together to create a world that was new to all of them.

This new world reflected the diverse experiences of the many peoples who built it. Improving economic conditions in the fifteenth and early sixteenth centuries propelled Europeans overseas to seek new opportunities for trade and settlement. Spain, Portugal, France, and England competed for political, economic, and religious domination within Europe, and their conflict carried over into the Americas. Native Americans drew upon their familiarity with the land and its resources, patterns of political and religious authority, and systems of trade and warfare to deal with the European newcomers. Africans did not come voluntarily to the Americas but were brought by the Europeans to work as slaves. They too would draw on their cultural heritage to cope with a new land and a new, harsh condition of life. ✦

# AMERICAN VIEWS

Included in each chapter is a selection from a primary source document. The example shown here is the published account of Mary Rowlandson from Lancaster, Massachusetts, who in 1676 was taken captive with two of her children by Indian warriors. Each American Views feature begins with a brief introduction followed by several questions–for discussion or written response–on what the document reveals about key issues and events.

---

the Indians too far. Officials reduced demands for tribute and ended the *encomienda* system. The Franciscans eased their attacks on Pueblo religion. New Spanish governors, backed by military force, kept the peace as best they could in a place where Indians still outnumbered Europeans.

**Resumption of the Beaver Wars.** The Iroquois experience in the last phase of the Beaver Wars threatened to parallel that of the Indians of New England and Virginia. What began as a struggle between the Iroquois and western native peoples for control of the fur trade blossomed into a larger

## AMERICAN VIEWS

### Mary Rowlandson among the Indians

In February 1676, in the midst of King Philip's War, Indian warriors attacked the town of Lancaster, Massachusetts. They killed many inhabitants and took 23 colonists captive, including Mary Rowlandson and three of her children. Rowlandson spent the next three months traveling with various groups of Nipmucs, Narragansetts, and Wampanoags. She suffered physically and emotionally, watching her youngest daughter die in her arms and worrying about her other two children, from whom she was frequently separated. During her captivity, Rowlandson survived by accepting her fate and adapting to the Indians' way of life. Finally, with an English victory imminent, Rowlandson was ransomed and rejoined her husband (who had been away at the time of the attack) and family. In 1682, she published an account of her captivity in which she explored the meaning of her experience. Rowlandson's narrative proved so popular that three editions were printed in the first year.

- **How** did Rowlandson describe the Indians? How did she characterize her encounter with King Philip?
- **In** what ways did Rowlandson accommodate herself to the Indians' way of life? How did she employ her skills to fit in? Did her gender make a difference in her experience of captivity?
- **How** did Rowlandson's Puritan faith shape her narrative?

We travelled on till night; and in the morning, we must go over the River to Philip's crew. When I was in the Cannoo, I could not but be amazed at the numerous crew of Pagans that were on the Bank on the other side. When I came ashore, they gathered all about me, I sitting alone in the midst: I observed they asked one another questions, and laughed, and rejoyced over their Gains and Victories. Then my heart began to fail: and I fell a weeping which was the first time to my remembrance that I wept before them. Although I had met with so

much Affliction, and my heart was many times ready to break, yet could I not shed one tear in their sight: but rather had been all this while in a maze, and like one astonished: but now I may say as, Psal. 137.1 *By the rivers of Babylon, there we sat down: yea, we wept when we remembered Zion.* There one of them asked me, why I wept, I could hardly tell what to say: yet I answered, they would kill me: No, said he, none will hurt you. Then came one of them and gave me two spoon-fulls of Meal to comfort me.... Then I went to see King Philip, he bade me come in and sit down, and asked me whether I would smoke (a usual Complement now adayes amongst Saints and Sinners) but this no way suited me. For though I had formerly used Tobacco, yet I had left it ever since I was first taken, *It seems to be a bait, the devil lays to make men loose their precious time....*

During my abode in this place, Philip spake to me to make a shirt for his boy, which I did, for which he gave me a shilling: I offered the money to my master, but he bade me keep it: and with it I bought a piece of Horse flesh. Afterwards he asked me to make a Cap for his boy, for which he invited me to Dinner. I went, and he gave me a Pancake, about as big as two fingers; it was made of parched wheat, beaten, and fryed in Bears grease, but I thought I never tasted pleasanter meat in my life. There was a Squaw who spake to me to make a shirt for her *Sannup* [husband], for which she gave me a piece of Bear. Another asked me to knit a pair of Stockins, for which she gave me a quart of Pease.... Hearing that my son was come to this place, I went to see him, and found him lying flat upon the ground: I asked him how he could sleep so? He answered me, *That he was not asleep, but at Prayer;* and lay so, that they might not observe what he was doing. I pray God he may remember these things now he is returned in safety.

*Source:* Neal Salisbury, ed., *The Sovereignty and Goodness of God, Together with the Faithfulness of His Promises Displayed....* (Boston, 1997), pp. 82–83.

# GLOBAL CONNECTIONS

This feature places the American journey within a broader world wide context. That journey not only influenced other countries and peoples, but we in turn have been shaped by global economic, migratory, technological, and political trends. The example shown here is about a mass exodus of German-speaking people from the Rhineland to various parts of the world, including the United States. Critical thinking questions encourage analysis of the global connections.

---

TRANSPLANTATION AND ADAPTATION    **CHAPTER 2**        37

## GLOBAL CONNECTIONS

### NORTH AMERICA'S FIRST JEWISH COMMUNITY

In 1654, twenty-three Jews arrived in New Amsterdam after a long voyage from Brazil. The reasons why they ended up in the Dutch colonial town relate to a much larger story of repeated Jewish migrations, undertaken time and again to escape religious persecution. In New Amsterdam these settlers found a home, establishing the first permanent Jewish community in North America.

Many of them could trace their ancestry back to Spain, where there had been a flourishing Jewish community during the Middle Ages. By the fifteenth century, however, the same Christian militancy that inspired the *reconquista* against the Muslims brought trouble for Spain's Jewish population in the form of the Inquisition. Jews who refused to convert to Christianity risked execution as heretics. In 1492, the same year as Columbus's first voyage, Spanish authorities ordered all Jews to leave Spain. Refugee Spanish Jews relocated all over the Mediterranean world, with perhaps a hundred thousand settling in Portugal, Spain's neighbor on the Iberian Peninsula. Many who did so were forced to accept Christian baptism, but continued to follow their own faith in secret. When the authorities threatened to prevent such practices, many Jews chose to leave Portugal. Some sought refuge in the Netherlands, where they found religious toleration and commercial opportunities.

In the early seventeenth century, the same Dutch West India Company that founded New Netherland tried to dislodge the Portuguese from their prosperous sugar-producing colony of Brazil. The company succeeded in capturing the city of Recife in 1630, and for the next twenty-four years the Dutch ruled over northeastern Brazil. During that time, more than a thousand Jews moved to the colony from the Netherlands. But when the Portuguese regained control of Brazil in 1654, the Jews were forced to move yet again. Most returned to the Netherlands, but a few decided to take their chances in New Amsterdam. At last they found a place where they could stay. When New Netherland became New York in 1664, English authorities continued the Dutch practice of toleration. Even though Jewish colonists were only supposed to worship in private, there was a synagogue in New York City by 1700. Jews eventually settled in other colonies, such as Rhode Island, Pennsylvania, and South Carolina. Wherever they formed their communities, they contributed to the remarkable religious diversity of England's New World empire.

- How did religious persecution in early modern Europe affect the lives of its Jewish inhabitants?

---

Roanoke's dismal fate. But it endured, eventually developing into the prosperous colony of Virginia. The reason for Virginia's success was an American plant—tobacco—that commanded good prices from European consumers. Tobacco also underlay the economy of a neighboring colony, Maryland, and had a profound influence on the development of Chesapeake society.

### THE ORDEAL OF EARLY VIRGINIA

In 1606, several English merchants petitioned King James I for a charter incorporating two companies to attempt New World settlement. One, the London, or Virginia, Company, included merchants from the city of London; the other, the Plymouth Company, included merchants from England's western ports. These **joint-stock companies** sold shares to investors (who expected a profit in return) to raise money for colonization.

**The Jamestown colony.**    Three small ships carried 104 settlers, all men, to the mouth of Chesapeake Bay in May 1607 (see Map 2–2). On a peninsula about 50 miles up a river they named the James in honor of their king, the colonists built a fortified settlement they called Jamestown. Hoping to earn quick profits for Virginia Company investors, they immediately began hunting for gold and searching for the Northwest Passage to Asia. Spending all their time searching for riches, the settlers neglected to plant crops, and their food supplies dwindled. By January 1608, only thirty-eight colonists were still alive.

**joint-stock company**    Business enterprise in which a group of stockholders pooled their money to engage in trade or to fund colonizing expeditions.

**Read the Document**
at **www.myhistorylab.com**
*Exploring America:*
*Jamestown*

# INTERPRETING THE PAST

These two-page features at the end of selected chapters analyze important topics in U.S. history through images and short document excerpts. A focus question and an introductory narrative give a careful examination of the historical implication of each topic in question. In this example, the accounts of an African and a slave trader on their voyages across the Atlantic from Africa are underscored by the stark images of the slave trade to provide an in-depth perspective on this topic.

---

## INTERPRETING the PAST

### The Voyage to Slavery

**WHAT WERE** the dehumanizing experiences faced by Africans as they were kidnapped and transported to the New World as slaves? Under what conditions were Africans taken for slavery, and what was their fate when they arrived in the New World?

Most Africans were captured by other Africans in interior wars between tribes or specifically for sale as slaves. The slaves were moved to the West Coast of Africa where European and American slavers awaited to purchase a human cargo. Slavers inspected their potential cargo for health and strength. Males were preferred because the work on New World plantations would be hard. Human cargo was packed into ships' holds in the most efficient manner and carried under horrible, inhumane conditions to the New World for sale to the highest bidder. It was not unusual for Africans to prefer death to such a fate and individuals would dive overboard or even throw their children into the sea because drowning was considered a better end than that of slavery. For this reason slaves would be kept below decks in leg irons with the exception of an hour or so of exercise each day. During the exercise period slaves would be forced to jump up and down or "dance" to keep their muscles limber and the sale price for each individual at its highest level. Each day dead slaves would be cast overboard and tales abound of schools of sharks trailing slave ships for hundreds of miles.

## *The shrieks of the women, ...*

*Olaudah Equiano, captured in Nigeria at a very early age, later gave this report of the experience crossing the Atlantic in a slave ship in 1789.*

The closeness of the place [ship's hold], and the heat of the climate, added to the number in the ship, which was so crowded that each had scarcely room to turn himself, almost suffocated us. This produced copious perspirations, so that the air soon became unfit for respiration, from a variety of loathsome smells, and brought on a sickness amongst the slaves, of which many died, thus falling victims to the improvident avarice, as I may call it, of their purchasers. This wretched situation was again aggravated by the galling of the chains, now become insupportable; and the filth of the necessary tubs, into which the children often fell, and were almost suffocated. The shrieks of the women, and the groans of the dying, rendered the whole a scene of horror almost inconceivable. Happily perhaps for myself I was soon reduced so low here that it was thought necessary to keep me almost always on deck; and from my extreme youth I was not put in fetters. In this situation I expected every hour to share the fate of my companions, some of whom were almost daily brought upon deck at the point of death, which I began to hope would soon put an end to my miseries. . . . One day, when we had a smooth sea and moderate wind, two of my wearied countrymen who were chained together (I was near them at the time), preferring death to such a life of misery, somehow made through the nettings and jumped into the sea: immediately another quite dejected fellow, who on account of his illness, was suffered to be out of irons, also followed their example; and I believe many more would very soon have done the same if they had not been prevented by the ship's crew who were instantly alarmed. Those of us that were the most active were in a moment put down under the deck, and there was such a noise and confusion amongst the people of the ship as I never heard before, to stop her, and get

*This eighteenth-century engraving of a slave ship shows how tightly Africans were packed below the decks of these vessels, evidence that the thirst for profit overrode concerns for their health or welfare.*

the boat out to go after the slaves. However two of the wretches were drowned, but they got the other, and afterwards flogged him unmercifully for thus attempting to prefer death to slavery.

*Alexander Falconbridge served as a ship's surgeon aboard a slaver in 1788. He was so horrified by what he witnessed during that time that he became involved in the British abolition movement.*

When the Negroes, whom the black traders have to dispose of, are shown to the European purchasers, they first examine them relative to their age. They then minutely inspect their persons, and inquire into the state of their health; if they are afflicted with any infirmity, or are deformed; or have bad eyes or teeth; if they are lame, or weak in their joints, or distorted in the back, or of a slender make, or are narrow in the chest; in short, if they have been, or are afflicted in any manner, so

*African men, women, and children are tied together while walking in chains after being captured by slave traders.*

as to render them incapable of much labour; if any of the foregoing defects are discovered in them, they are rejected. But if approved of, they are generally taken on board the ship the same evening. The purchaser has liberty to return on the following morning, but not afterwards, such as upon re-examination are found exceptionable.

The traders frequently beat those Negroes which are objected to by the captains and use them with great severity. It matters not whether they are refused on account of age, illness, deformity, or for any other reason. At New Calabar, in particular, the traders have frequently been known to put them to death. Instances have happened at that place that the traders, when any of their Negroes have been objected to, have dropped their canoes under the stern of the vessel, and instantly beheaded them, in sight of the captain.

*Two men brand an African woman kneeling helplessly on the ground.*

## *The purchaser has liberty to return...*

82

83

# 1

# Worlds Apart

Mexico: Hernán Cortés is greeted by Moctezuma's messenger in 1519. Mexican Indian painting, sixteenth century.

### ONE AMERICAN JOURNEY

*After a difficult journey of over two hundred miles, the exhausted man arrived at the royal palace in the grand city of Tenochtitlán. He had hurried all the way from the Gulf Coast with important news for the Aztec leader, Moctezuma.*

*Our lord and king, forgive my boldness. I am from Mictlancuauhtla. When I went to the shores of the great sea, there was a mountain range or small mountain floating in the midst of the water, and moving here and there without touching the shore. My lord, we have never seen the like of this, although we guard the coast and are always on watch.*

*[When Moctezuma sent some officials to check on the messenger's story, they confirmed his report.]*

*Our lord and king, it is true that strange people have come to the shores of the great sea. They were fishing from a small boat, some with rods and others with a net. They fished until late and then they went back to their two great towers and climbed up into them.... They have very light skin, much lighter than ours. They all have long beards, and their hair comes only to their ears.*

Miguel Leon–Portilla, *The Broken Spears: The Aztec Account of the Conquest of Mexico* (Boston, 1962).

**•◄• Read the Document** at **www.myhistorylab.com**

### Personal Journeys Online

- Christopher Columbus, *Journal of the First Voyage,* October 12, 1492. **Account of his first meeting with Caribbean islanders.**
- Martin Frobisher, *Account of First Voyage to the New World,* 1576. **Description of his arrival in Canada and his encounter with native people.**

MOCTEZUMA was filled with foreboding when he received the messenger's initial report. Aztec religion placed great emphasis on omens and prophecies, which were thought to foreshadow coming events. Several unusual omens had recently occurred—blazing lights in the sky, one temple struck by lightning and another that spontaneously burst into flames. Now light-skinned strangers appeared offshore. Aztec spiritual leaders regarded these signs as unfavorable and warned that trouble lay ahead.

The messenger's journey to Tenochtitlán occurred in 1519. The "mountains" he saw were in fact the sails of European ships, and the strange men were Spanish soldiers under the command of Hernán Cortés. Before long, a variety of peoples—Native Americans, Africans, and Europeans—who had previously lived worlds apart would come together to create a world that was new to all of them.

This new world reflected the diverse experiences of the many peoples who built it. Improving economic conditions in the fifteenth and early sixteenth centuries propelled Europeans overseas to seek new opportunities for trade and settlement. Spain, Portugal, France, and England competed for political, economic, and religious domination within Europe, and their conflict carried over into the Americas. Native Americans drew upon their familiarity with the land and its resources, patterns of political and religious authority, and systems of trade and warfare to deal with the European newcomers. Africans did not come voluntarily to the Americas but were brought by the Europeans to work as slaves. They too would draw on their cultural heritage to cope with a new land and a new, harsh condition of life. ✦

## CHRONOLOGY

| | | | |
|---|---|---|---|
| c. 40,000–8000 B.C.E. | Ancestors of Native Americans cross Bering land bridge. | 1430s | Beginnings of Portuguese slave trade in West Africa. |
| c. 10,000–9000 B.C.E. | Paleo-Indians expand through the Americas. | 1492 | End of *reconquista* in Spain. |
| | | | Columbus's first voyage. |
| c. 9000 B.C.E. | Extinction of large land mammals in North America. | 1494 | Treaty of Tordesillas. |
| c. 8000 B.C.E. | Beginnings of agriculture in the Peruvian Andes and Mesoamerica. | 1497 | John Cabot visits Nova Scotia and Newfoundland. |
| | | 1497–1499 | Vasco da Gama sails around Africa to reach India. |
| c. 1500 B.C.E. | Earliest mound-building culture begins. | 1517 | Protestant Reformation begins in Germany. |
| c. 500 B.C.E.–400 C.E. | Adena-Hopewell mound-building culture. | 1519–1521 | Hernán Cortés conquers the Aztec empire. |
| | | 1532–1533 | Francisco Pizarro conquers the Incan empire. |
| c. 700–1600 C.E. | Rise of West African empires. | 1534–1542 | Jacques Cartier explores eastern Canada for France. |
| c. 900 | First mounds built at Cahokia. | 1540–1542 | Coronado explores southwestern North America. |
| | Ancestral Puebloan expansion. | 1542–1543 | Roberval's failed colony in Canada. |
| c. 1000 | Spread of Islam in West Africa. | 1558 | Elizabeth I becomes queen of England. |
| c. 1000–1015 | First Viking voyages to North America. | 1565 | Spanish establish outpost at St. Augustine in Florida. |
| c. 1000–1500 | Last mound-building culture, the Mississippian. | | |
| c. 1290s | Ancestral Puebloan dispersal into smaller villages. | 1560s–1580s | English renew attempts to conquer Ireland. |
| | | 1587 | Founding of "Lost Colony" of Roanoke. |
| 1400–1600 | Renaissance in Europe. | 1598 | Spanish found colony at New Mexico. |

# NATIVE AMERICAN SOCIETIES BEFORE 1492

In 1492 perhaps 70 million people—nearly equal to the population of Europe at that time—lived on the continents of North and South America, most of them south of the present border between the United States and Mexico. They belonged to hundreds of groups, each with its own language or dialect, history, and way of life.

From the start, the original inhabitants of the Americas were peoples in motion. The first migrants may have arrived over forty thousand years ago, traveling from central Siberia and slowly making their way to southern South America. These people, and subsequent migrants from Eurasia, probably traveled across a land bridge that emerged across what is now the Bering Strait. During the last Ice Age, much of the earth's water was frozen in huge glaciers. This process lowered ocean levels, exposing a 600-mile-wide land bridge between Asia and America. Recent research examining genetic and linguistic similarities between Asian and Native American populations suggests that there may also have been later migrations.

**HOW DID** geography shape the development of regional cultures in North America prior to 1492?

See the **Map**

at **www.myhistorylab.com**
*Pre-Columbian Societies of the Americas*

## HUNTERS, HARVESTERS, AND TRADERS

The earliest Americans adapted to an amazing range of environmental conditions, from the frozen Arctic to southwestern deserts to dense eastern woodlands. At first, they mainly subsisted by hunting the mammoths, bison, and other large game that roamed throughout North America.

Archaeologists working near present-day Clovis, New Mexico, have found carefully crafted spear points—some of which may be over thirteen thousand years old. Such efficient tools possibly contributed to overhunting, which, along with climate change, led to the extinction of many big-game species. By about 9000 B.C.E. the world's climate began to grow warmer, turning grasslands into deserts and reducing the animals' food supply. Humans too had to find other food sources.

Between roughly 8000 B.C.E. and 1500 B.C.E. the Native American societies changed in important ways. Native populations grew and men and women assumed more specialized roles in their villages. Men did most of the hunting and fishing, activities that required travel. Women remained closer to home, harvesting and preparing wild plant foods and caring for children.

Across the continent, native communities also developed complex networks of trade. They not only exchanged material goods, but also marriage partners, laborers, ideas, and religious practices. Trade networks sometimes extended over great distances. Ideas about death and the afterlife also passed between groups. So too did certain burial practices, such as the placing of valued possessions in the grave along with the deceased person's body. In some areas, the increasing complexity of exchange networks, as well as competition for resources, encouraged concentrations of political power. Chiefs might manage trade relations and conduct diplomacy for groups of villages rather than for a single community.

## THE DEVELOPMENT OF AGRICULTURE

No Native American adaptation was more momentous than the domestication of certain plants and the development of farming. Native Americans may have turned to farming when population growth threatened to outrun the wild food supply. Women, with their knowledge of wild plants, probably discovered how to save seeds and cultivate them, becoming the world's first farmers.

Wherever agriculture took hold, important social changes followed. Populations grew, because farming produced a more secure food supply than did hunting and gathering. Permanent villages appeared as farmers settled near their fields. In central Mexico, agriculture eventually sustained the populations of large cities. Trade in agricultural surpluses flowed through networks of exchange. In many Indian societies, women's status improved because of their role as the principal farmers. Even religious beliefs adapted to the increasing importance of farming.

The adoption of agriculture further enhanced the diversity of Native American societies that developed over centuries within broad regions, or **culture areas** (see Map 1–1). Within each area, inhabitants shared basic patterns of subsistence and social organization, largely reflecting the natural environment to which they had adapted. Most, but not all of them, eventually relied upon farming.

## NONFARMING SOCIETIES

Agriculture was impossible in the challenging environment of the Arctic and Subarctic. There, nomadic bands of Inuits and Aleuts moved seasonally to fish or hunt whales, seals, and other sea animals, and, in the brief summers, gather wild berries.

Along the Northwest Coast and the Columbia River Plateau, one of the most densely populated areas of North America, abundant natural resources permitted native peoples to prosper without farming. Local rivers and forests supplied fish, game, and edible plants.

Farther south, in present-day California, hunter-gatherers once lived in smaller villages, which usually adjoined oak groves where Indians gathered acorns as an important food source. Nomadic hunting bands in the Great Basin, where the climate was warm and dry, learned to survive on the region's limited resources.

**QUICK REVIEW**

**The Earliest Americans**
- The first North Americans were resourceful hunters.
- The earliest Americans adapted to a wide range of regional environments.
- Farming began in central Mexico nine to ten thousand years ago.

**culture areas** Geographical regions inhabited by peoples who share similar basic patterns of subsistence and social organization.

Women were the principal farmers in most Native American societies, growing corn, beans, and other crops in fields cleared by Indian men. Many of these New World foods would be transported across the Atlantic to become important to Old World diets.

## MESOAMERICAN CIVILIZATIONS

Mesoamerica, the birthplace of agriculture in North America, extends from central Mexico into Central America. A series of complex, literate, urban cultures emerged in this region beginning around 1200 B.C.E. The Olmecs, who flourished on Mexico's Gulf Coast from about 1200 to 400 B.C.E., and their successors in the region built cities featuring large pyramids, developed religious practices that included human sacrifice, and devised calendars and writing systems. Two of the most prominent Mesoamerican civilizations that followed the Olmecs were the Mayans in the Yucatán and Guatemala and the Aztecs of Teotihuacán in central Mexico.

**The Mayans.**   Mayan civilization reached its greatest glory between about 150 and 900 C.E. in the southern Yucatán, creating Mesoamerica's most advanced writing and calendrical systems. The Mayans of the southern Yucatán suffered a decline after 900, but there were still many thriving Mayan centers in the northern Yucatán when Europeans arrived in the Americas. The great city of Teotihuacán dominated central Mexico from the first century to the eighth century C.E. and influenced much of Mesoamerica through trade and conquest.

**The Aztecs.**   Some two hundred years after the fall of Teotihuacán, the Toltecs, a warrior people, rose to prominence, dominating central Mexico from about 900 to 1100. In the wake of the Toltec collapse, the **Aztecs** migrated from the north into the Valley of Mexico and built a great empire that soon controlled much of Mesoamerica. The magnificent Aztec capital, Tenochtitlán, was a city of great plazas, magnificent temples and palaces, and busy marketplaces. In 1492, Tenochtitlán was home to some 200,000 people, making it one of the largest cities in the world at the time.

The great pyramid in Tenochtitlán's principal temple complex was the center of Aztec religious life. Here Aztec priests sacrificed human victims. Human sacrifice had been part of Mesoamerican religion since the time of the Olmecs. People believed that such ceremonies pleased the gods and prevented them from destroying the earth. The Aztecs, however, practiced sacrifice on a much larger scale than ever before.

The Aztec empire expanded through military conquest, driven by a quest for sacrificial victims and tribute payments of gold, food, and handcrafted goods from hundreds of subject communities. But as the empire grew, it became increasingly vulnerable to internal division. Neighboring peoples submitted to the Aztecs out of fear rather than loyalty.

**Aztecs**   A warrior people who dominated the Valley of Mexico from 1100–1521.

### QUICK REVIEW

**Mesoamerica**

- Mesoamerica was the birthplace of agriculture in North America.
- Olmecs were the first literate urban culture in the region.
- Mayan civilization reached its height between 150 and 900 C.E.

MAP 1–1　**North American Culture Areas, c. 1500**　Over the course of centuries, Indian peoples in North America developed distinctive cultures suited to the environments in which they lived. Inhabitants of each culture area shared basic patterns of subsistence, craft work, and social organization. Most, but not all, Indian peoples combined farming with hunting and gathering.

**How might** major geographical features (mountains, rivers, deserts, etc.) have shaped the migration patterns and cultural development of the peoples of the Americas?

## NORTH AMERICA'S DIVERSE CULTURES

North of Mexico, the development of a drought-resistant type of maize around 400 B.C.E. enabled a series of cultures sharing certain characteristics with Mesoamerica to emerge. Beginning about 300 B.C.E., the Hohokams settled in villages in southern Arizona and devised elaborate irrigation systems that allowed them to harvest two crops of corn, beans, and squash each year. Trade networks linked the Hohokams to people living as far away as California and Mexico. Their culture endured for over a thousand years but mysteriously disappeared by 1450.

**Ancestral Puebloans.**   Early in the first century C.E., Ancestral Puebloan peoples (sometimes called Anasazis) began to settle in farming communities where the borders of present-day Colorado, Utah, Arizona, and New Mexico meet. Scarce rainfall, routed through dams and hillside terraces, watered the crops. Ancestral Puebloans originally lived in villages, or pueblos (*pueblo* is the Spanish word for "village") built on mesas and canyon floors. In New Mexico's Chaco Canyon, perhaps as many as fifteen thousand people dwelled in a dozen large towns and hundreds of outlying villages. But after about 1200, villagers began carving multistoried stone houses into canyon walls, dwellings that could only be reached by difficult climbs up steep cliffs and along narrow ledges. Warfare and climate change may have worked together to force the Puebloans into these precarious homes.

Around 1200, the climate of the Southwest grew colder, making it more difficult to grow enough to feed the large population. Food scarcity may have set village against village and encouraged attacks by outsiders. Villagers probably resorted to cliff dwellings for protection as violence spread in the region. By 1300, survivors abandoned the cliff dwellings and dispersed into smaller villages along the Rio Grande. Their descendants include the Hopis and Zunis, as well as other Puebloan peoples in the desert Southwest.

**Plains Indians.**   The Great Plains of the continent's interior were much less densely settled than the desert Southwest. Mandans, Pawnees, and other groups settled along river valleys, where women farmed and men hunted bison. Plains Indians moved frequently, seeking more fertile land or better hunting. Wherever they went, they traded skins, food, and obsidian (a volcanic glass used for tools and weapons) with other native peoples.

**Mound-building cultures.**   As agriculture spread to the Eastern Woodlands, a vast territory extending from the Mississippi Valley to the Atlantic seaboard, several "mound-building" societies—named for the large earthworks their members constructed—developed in the Ohio and Mississippi valleys. The oldest flourished in Louisiana between 1500 and 700 B.C.E. The members of the Adena-Hopewell culture, which appeared in the Ohio Valley between 500 B.C.E. and 400 C.E., built hundreds of mounds, often in the shapes of humans, birds, and serpents. Most were grave sites, where people were buried with valuable goods, including objects made from materials obtained through long-distance trade.

The last mound-building culture, the Mississippian, emerged between 1000 and 1500 in the Mississippi Valley. Mississippian farmers raised enough food to support sizable populations and major urban centers. The largest city by far was **Cahokia,** located near present-day St. Louis in a fertile floodplain with access to the major river systems of the continent's interior. Cahokia dominated the Mississippi Valley, linked by trade to dozens of villages in the midwestern region. Mississippian culture began to decline in the thirteenth century, perhaps due to an ecological crisis.

What followed in the Eastern Woodlands region was a century or more of warfare and political instability. In the vacuum left by Cahokia's decline, other groups sought to exert more power. In the Northeast, the Iroquois and Hurons moved from dispersed settlements into fortified villages. Both the Hurons and the Iroquois formed confederacies that were intended to diminish internal conflicts and increase their collective spiritual strength. Among the Iroquois, five separate nations—the Mohawks, Oneidas, Onondagas, Cayugas, and Senecas—joined to create the **Great League of Peace and Power** around the year 1450. Similar developments occurred in the Southeast, where chronic instability led to regional alliances and shifting centers of trade and political power.

**WHERE TO LEARN MORE**

★ Mesa Verde National Park, Colorado
http://www.nps.gov/meve/index.htm

●●◖Read the **Document**

at **www.myhistorylab.com**
*Alvar Núñez Cabeza de Vaca, Indians of the Rio Grande (1528–1536)*

**WHERE TO LEARN MORE**

★ Cahokia Mounds State Historic Site, Collinsville, Illinois
http://cahokiamounds.org/

**Cahokia**   One of the largest urban centers created by Mississippian peoples, containing 30,000 residents in 1250.

**WHERE TO LEARN MORE**

★ Mashantucket Pequot Museum, Mashantucket, Connecticut
http://pequotmuseum.org/

**Great League of Peace and Power**   Spiritual union of five Iroquois nations that aimed to maintain peace among them and unite them to fight against common enemies.

This artist's rendering, based on archaeological evidence, suggests the size and magnificence of the Mississippian city of Cahokia. By the thirteenth century, it was as populous as medieval London and served as a center of trade for the vast interior of North America.

Eastern Woodlands peoples were the first to encounter English explorers, and later, English settlers, at the start of the seventeenth century. By that point these native peoples relied on a mixture of agriculture and hunting, fishing, and gathering for their subsistence. They lived in villages with a few hundred residents, with greater densities of settlement in the South (where a warmer climate and longer growing season prevailed) than in the North.

## THE CARIBBEAN ISLANDERS

The Caribbean islands were peopled by mainland dwellers who began moving to the islands around 5000 B.C.E. Surviving at first by hunting and gathering, island peoples began farming perhaps in the first century C.E. Canoes carried trade goods throughout the Caribbean, as well as to Mesoamerica and coastal South America.

By 1492, as many as 4 million people may have inhabited the Caribbean islands. Powerful chiefs ruled over villages, conducted war and diplomacy, and controlled the distribution of food and other goods obtained as tribute from villagers.

Long before Europeans reached North America, the continent's inhabitants had witnessed centuries of dynamic change. Empires rose and fell, and new ones took their place. Large cities flourished and disappeared. Periods of warfare occasionally disrupted the lives of thousands of individuals. The Europeans' arrival, at the end of the fifteenth century, coincided with a period of particular instability, as various Native American groups competed for dominance in the wake of the collapse of the centralized societies at Cahokia and Chaco Canyon. Yet at the same time, Native American societies experienced important continuities. These included an ability to adapt to widely varying environmental conditions, the preservation of religious and ceremonial traditions, and an eagerness to forge relationships of exchange with neighboring peoples. Both continuities with past experience and more recent circumstances of political change would shape the ways native peoples responded to the European newcomers.

# WEST AFRICAN SOCIETIES

**WHAT WERE** the key characteristics of West African society?

In the three centuries after 1492, six of every seven people who crossed the Atlantic to the Americas were not Europeans but Africans. Like the Americas, Africa had witnessed the rise of many ancient and diverse cultures (see Map 1–2). They ranged from the sophisticated Egyptian

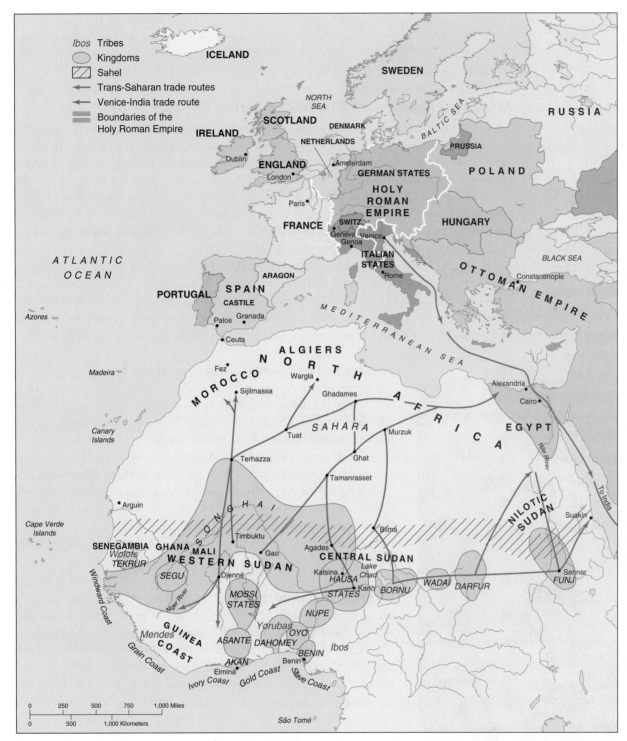

**MAP 1–2** **West Africa and Europe in 1492** Before Columbus's voyage, Europeans knew little about the world beyond the Mediterranean basin and the coast of West Africa. Muslim merchants from North Africa largely controlled European traders' access to African gold and other materials.

**How does** this map help explain the focus of Portuguese exploration in the fifteenth century?

civilization that developed in the Nile Valley over five-thousand years ago, to the powerful twelfth-century chiefdoms of Zimbabwe, to the West African empires that flourished in the time of Columbus and Cortés. The vast majority of Africans who came to the Americas after 1492 arrived as slaves, transported by Europeans eager to exploit their labor.

## GEOGRAPHICAL AND POLITICAL DIFFERENCES

Most African immigrants to the Americas came from the continent's western regions. Extending from the southern edge of the Sahara Desert toward the equator and inland for nearly a thousand miles, West Africa was an area of contrasts. On the whole a sparsely settled region, West Africa nevertheless contained numerous densely inhabited communities. Many of these settlements clung to the coast, but several important cities lay well inland. Perhaps the greatest of these metropolises was Timbuktu, which had as many as seventy-thousand residents in the fifteenth century. At that time, Timbuktu served as the seat of the powerful **Songhai Empire** and was an important center of trade and government.

> Geographical as well as political differences marked the inland and coastal regions. In the vast grasslands of the interior, people raised livestock and cultivated millet and sorghum. Rice also served as an important food crop. In the 1500s, Europeans brought an Asian variety to add to indigenous African rice strains. On the coast—where rain falls nearly every day—people grew yams, bananas, and various kinds of beans and peas in forest clearings. They also kept sheep, goats, and poultry.

**Songhai Empire** A powerful West African state that flourished between 1450 and 1591, when it fell to a Moroccan invasion.

### QUICK REVIEW

**West African Society**

- West Africans were skilled artisans and metalworkers.
- Most West Africans were farmers.
- Most West African clans were patrilineal.

**Artisans and merchants.** West Africans excelled as skilled artisans and metalworkers. Smiths in Benin produced intricate bronze sculptures, and Asante craftsmen designed distinctive miniature gold weights. West African smiths also used their skills to forge weapons, attesting to the frequent warfare between West African states.

Trade networks linked inland and coastal states, and long-distance commercial connections tied West Africa to southern Europe and the Middle East. West African merchants exchanged locally mined gold with traders from North Africa for salt. North African merchants also bought West African pepper, leather, and ivory. The wealth generated by this trans-Saharan trade contributed to the rise of the Songhai and earlier empires.

**Farming and gender roles.** Most West Africans were farmers, whose lives were defined by a daily round of work, family duties, and worship. West African men and women shared agricultural tasks. Men prepared fields for planting, while women cultivated and harvested the crops. Men also hunted and, in the grassland regions, herded cattle. Women in the coastal areas owned and cared for other livestock, including goats and sheep. West African women regularly traded goods, including the crops they grew, in local markets and were thus essential to the vitality of local economies.

## FAMILY STRUCTURE AND RELIGION

Family connections were exceedingly important to West Africans, helping to define each person's place in society. While ties between parents and children were of central importance, West Africans also emphasized their links with aunts, uncles, cousins, and grandparents. Groups of families formed clans that further extended an individual's kin ties within the village.

Craftsmen from the West African kingdom of Benin were renowned for their remarkable bronze sculptures. This intricate bronze plaque depicts four African warriors in full military dress. The two tiny figures in the background may be Portuguese soldiers, who first arrived in Benin in the late fifteenth century.

Benin bronze plaque. National Museum of African Art, Smithsonian Institution, Washington, DC, U.S.A. Aldo Tutino/Art Resource, NY.

Elmina Castle, located on the coast of what is now Ghana, was founded by the Portuguese in 1482 as a trading post. In 1637, the Dutch West India Company seized the castle and converted it for use in the slave trade.

Religious beliefs magnified the powerful influence of family on African life. Ideas and practices focused on themes of fertility, prosperity, health, and social harmony. Because many West Africans believed that their ancestors acted as mediators between the worlds of the living and the dead, they held elaborate funerals for deceased members and performed public rituals at their grave sites.

West Africans believed that spiritual forces suffused the natural world, and they performed ceremonies to ensure the spirits' goodwill. West Africans preserved their faith through oral traditions, not written texts.

Islam began to take root in West Africa as early as the tenth century, introduced by Muslim traders and soldiers from North Africa. Urban dwellers, especially merchants, were more likely to convert to the new religion, as were some rulers. Farmers, however, accustomed to religious rituals that focused on agricultural fertility, tended to resist Islamic influence more strongly or adopt religious practices that mingled Islamic and traditional beliefs.

## EUROPEAN MERCHANTS IN WEST AFRICA AND THE SLAVE TRADE

Before the fifteenth century, Europeans knew little about Africa beyond its Mediterranean coast. But some Christian merchants had traded for centuries with Muslims in the North African ports. When stories of West African gold reached European traders, they tried to move deeper into the continent. But they encountered powerful Muslim merchants intent on monopolizing the gold trade.

The kingdom of Portugal sought to circumvent this Muslim monopoly. Portuguese forces conquered Ceuta in Morocco and gained a foothold on the continent in 1415. Because this outpost did not provide direct access to the sources of gold, Portuguese mariners began exploring the West African coast. They established trading posts along the way.

By the 1430s, the Portuguese had discovered perhaps the greatest source of wealth they could extract from Africa—slaves. A vigorous market in African slaves had existed in southern Europe since the middle of the fourteenth century, and within West Africa itself for centuries. The expansion of this trade required not only eager buyers of slaves, but also willing suppliers. Most slaves within Africa lost their freedom because they were captured in war, but others had been kidnapped or were enslaved as punishment for a crime. First the Portuguese, and later other

**Read** the **Document**
at **www.myhistorylab.com**
*Muslim Reform in Songhai (1500)*

Europeans, exploited rivalries among various West African states to encourage them to take war captives who could be sold into an expanding transatlantic slave trade. Virtually all of the African slaves who ended up in the New World had first been enslaved by fellow Africans.

European visitors who observed African slaves in their homeland often described them as "slaves in name only" because they were subject to so little coercion. African merchants who sold slaves to European purchasers had no reason to suspect that those slaves would be treated any differently by their new owners.

Africans caught in the web of the transatlantic slave trade, however, entered a much harsher world. Separated from the kinfolk who meant so much to them, isolated from a familiar landscape, and hard-pressed to sustain spiritual and cultural traditions in a new environment, Africans faced daunting challenges as they journeyed across the ocean and entered into the history of the New World.

# WESTERN EUROPE ON THE EVE OF EXPLORATION

**HOW DID** events in Europe both shape and inspire exploration of the Americas?

When Columbus sailed from Spain in 1492, he left a continent recovering from the devastating warfare and disease of the fourteenth century and about to embark on the devastating religious conflicts of the sixteenth century. Between 1337 and 1453, England and France had exhausted each other in a series of conflicts known as the Hundred Years' War. And between 1347 and 1351, an epidemic known as the Black Death wreaked havoc on a European population already suffering from persistent malnutrition. Perhaps a third of all Europeans died, with results that were felt for more than a century.

The plague left Europe with far fewer workers, a result that contributed to southern Europeans' interest in the African slave trade. To help the economy recover, the survivors learned to be more efficient and rely on technological improvements. Innovations in banking, accounting, and insurance also fostered economic recovery. Although prosperity was distributed unevenly among social classes, on the whole, Europe had a stronger, more productive economy in 1500 than ever before.

In much of Western Europe, economic improvement encouraged an extraordinary cultural movement known as the Renaissance, a "rebirth" of interest in the classical civilizations of ancient Greece and Rome. The Renaissance originated in the city-states of Italy, where a prosperous and educated urban class promoted learning and artistic expression.

The daily lives of most Europeans, however, remained untouched by intellectual and artistic developments. Most Europeans resided in agricultural communities that often differed in important ways from Native American and West African societies. In European societies, men performed most of the heavy work of farming, while women focused on household production of such goods as butter, cheese, and cloth, as well as on caring for the family. Europeans lived in states organized into more rigid hierarchies than could be found in most parts of North America or West Africa, with the population divided into distinct classes. European society was also patriarchal, with men dominating political and economic life.

## QUICK REVIEW

**European Society**

- European states were hierarchical.
- Most Europeans were peasant farmers.
- European society was patriarchal.

## THE CONSOLIDATION OF POLITICAL AND MILITARY AUTHORITY

By the end of the fifteenth century, a measure of stability returned to the countries about to embark on overseas expansion. The monarchs of Spain, France, and England successfully asserted royal authority over their previously fragmented realms, creating strong state bureaucracies to control political rivals. They gave special trading privileges to merchants to gain their support, creating links that would later prove important in financing overseas expeditions.

The consolidation of military power went hand in hand with the strengthening of political authority. Before overseas expansion began, European monarchs exerted military force to extend their authority closer to home. Louis XI and his successors used warfare and intermarriage with the ruling families of nearby provinces to extend French influence. In the early sixteenth century, England's Henry VIII sent soldiers to conquer Ireland. And the Spain of 1492 was forged from the successful conclusion of the ***reconquista*** ("reconquest") of territory from Muslim control.

Muslim invaders from North Africa first entered Spain in 711 and ruled much of the Iberian Peninsula (which includes Spain and Portugal) for centuries. Beginning in the mid-eleventh century, Christian armies embarked on a long effort to reclaim the region. After the marriage of Ferdinand of Aragon and Isabella of Castile in 1469 united Spain's two principal kingdoms, their combined forces completed the *reconquista*. Granada, the last Muslim stronghold, fell in 1492, shortly before Columbus set out on his first voyage.

**reconquista** The long struggle (ending in 1492) during which Spanish Christians reconquered the Iberian peninsula from Muslim occupiers.

## RELIGIOUS CONFLICT AND THE PROTESTANT REFORMATION

Even as these rulers sought to unify their realms, religious conflicts began to tear Europe apart. For more than a thousand years, Catholic Christianity had united Western Europeans in one faith. By the sixteenth century, the Catholic Church had accumulated enormous wealth and power. In reaction to this growing influence, many Christians, especially in Northern Europe, began to criticize the popes and the church itself for worldliness and abuse of power.

In 1517, a German monk, Martin Luther, invited open debate on a set of propositions critical of church practices and doctrines. Luther believed that the church had become too insistent on the performance of good works, such as charitable donations or other actions intended to please God. He called for a return to what he understood to be the purer beliefs of the early church, emphasizing that salvation came not by good deeds but only by faith in God. With the help of the newly invented printing press, his ideas spread widely, inspiring a challenge to the Catholic Church that came to be known as the **Reformation.**

**Reformation** Martin Luther's challenge to the Catholic Church, initiated in 1517, calling for a return to what he understood to be the purer practices and beliefs of the early church.

Luther urged people to take responsibility for their own spiritual growth by reading the Bible, which he translated for the first time into German. What started as a religious movement, however, quickly acquired an important political dimension.

Sixteenth-century Germany was a fragmented region of small kingdoms and principalities. They were officially part of a larger Catholic political entity known as the Holy Roman Empire, but many German princes were discontented with imperial authority. Many of these princes also supported Luther. When the Holy Roman Empire under Charles V (who was also king of Spain) tried to silence them, the reformist princes protested. From that point on, these princes—and all Europeans who supported religious reform—became known as **Protestants.**

**Protestants** All European supporters of religious reform under Charles V's Holy Roman Empire.

The Protestant movement took a more radical turn under the influence of the French reformer John Calvin, who emphasized the doctrine of **predestination.** Calvin maintained that an all-powerful and all-knowing God chose at the moment of Creation which humans would be saved and which would be damned. Nothing a person could do would alter that spiritual destiny. Once the ideas of Luther and Calvin began to spread in Europe, no one could contain the powerful Protestant impulse. In succeeding years, other groups formed, split, and split again, increasing Europe's religious fragmentation.

**predestination** The belief that God decided at the moment of Creation which humans would achieve salvation.

The Reformation fractured the religious unity of Western Europe and spawned a century of warfare unprecedented in its bloody destructiveness. Protestants fought Catholics in France and the German states. Popes initiated a "Counter-Reformation" to strengthen the Catholic Church—in part by internal reform and in part by persecuting its opponents and reimposing religious conformity. Europe thus fragmented into warring camps just at the moment when Europeans were coming to terms with their discovery of America. Some of the key participants in exploration, such as Spain and Portugal, rejected Protestantism, while others, including England and the Netherlands, embraced religious reform.

**QUICK REVIEW**

**Religious Conflict in Europe**

- 1517: Martin Luther sparks Reformation.
- John Calvin promotes a more radical vision of Protestantism.
- The Catholic Church launches a "Counter-Reformation."

**WHAT WERE** the biological consequences of contact between Europeans and Native Americans?

# CONTACT

Religious fervor, political ambition, and the desire for wealth propelled European nations into overseas expansion as well as conflict at home. Portugal, Spain, France, and England competed to establish footholds on other continents in an intense scramble for riches and dominance.

## THE LURE OF DISCOVERY

The potential rewards of overseas exploration captured the imaginations of a small but powerful segment of European society. Most people, busy making a living, cared little about distant lands. But certain princes and merchants anticipated spiritual and material benefits from voyages of discovery. The spiritual advantages included making new Christian converts and blocking Islam's expansion. On the material side, the voyages would contribute to Europe's prosperity by increasing trade.

Merchants especially sought access to Asian spices. Wealthy Europeans paid handsomely for small quantities of spices, making it worthwhile to transport them great distances. But the overland spice trade—and the trade in other luxury goods such as silk and furs—spanned thousands of miles, involved many middlemen, and was controlled at key points by Muslim merchants. When Constantinople fell to the Ottomans—Muslim rulers of Turkey—in 1453, Europeans feared that caravan routes to Asia would be disrupted. This encouraged merchants to turn westward and seek alternative routes. Mariners ventured farther into ocean waters, seeking direct access to the African gold trade and, eventually, a sea route around Africa to Asia.

**Advances in navigation and shipbuilding.** Ocean voyages required sturdier ships than those that plied the Mediterranean. Because oceangoing mariners traveled beyond sight of coastal features, they also needed reliable navigational tools. In the early fifteenth century, Prince Henry of Portugal sponsored the efforts of shipbuilders, mapmakers, and other workers to solve these practical problems. By 1500, enterprising artisans had made several important advances. Iberian shipbuilders perfected the caravel, a ship whose narrow shape and steering rudder suited it for ocean travel. European mariners adopted two important navigational devices—the magnetic compass (first developed in China) and the astrolabe (introduced to Europe by Muslims from Spain)—that allowed mariners to determine their position in relation to a star's known location in the sky.

## CHRISTOPHER COLUMBUS AND THE WESTWARD ROUTE TO ASIA

Christopher Columbus was but one of many European mariners excited by the prospect of tapping into the wealth of Asia. Born in Genoa in 1451, he later lived in Portugal and Spain, where he read widely in geographical treatises and listened closely to the stories and rumors that circulated among mariners.

Columbus was not the first European to reach the New World. Explorers from Scandinavia, known as Vikings, occupied Iceland by the late ninth century C.E. and later moved on to Greenland. Between 1001 and 1014, Leif Erikson made several voyages to the northern coast of Newfoundland, where he helped to establish a short-lived Viking colony. After the Viking colony disappeared, European fishermen continued to make seasonal voyages to the area, but it would be several centuries before Columbus initiated another attempt at settlement.

Neither was Columbus the first European to believe that he could reach Asia by sailing westward. Most Europeans, however, scoffed at the idea of a westward voyage to Asia in the belief that no ship could carry enough provisions for such a long trip.

Columbus's confidence that he could succeed grew from a mathematical error. He mistakenly calculated the earth's circumference as 18,000 (rather than 24,000) miles and so concluded that Asia

**QUICK REVIEW**

**Discovery and Exploration**

- Europeans sought access to Asian spices.
- Technological innovations made longer sea voyages possible.
- State sponsorship funded voyages of exploration.

**Watch** the **Video**

at **www.myhistorylab.com**
*How should we think of Columbus?*

**Read** the **Document**

at **www.myhistorylab.com**
*From the Journal of Christopher Columbus (1492)*

lay just 3,500 miles west of the Canary Islands. Columbus first sought financial support for a westward voyage from the king of Portugal, whose advisers disputed his calculations and warned him that he would starve at sea before reaching Asia. Undaunted, he turned to Portugal's rival, Spain.

Columbus tried to convince Ferdinand and Isabella that his plan suited Spain's national goals. If he succeeded, Spain could grow rich from Asian trade, send Christian missionaries to Asia (a goal in keeping with the religious ideals of the *reconquista*), and perhaps enlist the Great Khan of China as an ally in the long struggle with Islam. The Spanish monarchs nonetheless kept Columbus waiting nearly seven years—until 1492, when the last Muslim stronghold at Granada fell to Spanish forces—before they gave him their support.

After thirty-three days at sea, Columbus and his men reached the Bahamas. They spent four months exploring the Caribbean and visiting several islands. Although puzzled by his failure to find the fabled cities of China and Japan, Columbus believed that he had reached Asia. Three more voyages between 1493 and 1504, however, failed to yield clear evidence of an Asian landfall or Asian riches.

Frustrated in their search for wealth, Columbus and his men turned violent, sacking native villages and demanding tribute in gold. But Caribbean gold reserves, found mainly on Hispaniola, Puerto Rico, and Cuba, were not extensive. Dissatisfied with the meager results, Columbus sought to transform the Indians themselves into a source of wealth.

In 1494, Columbus suggested to the Spanish monarchs that the Indies could yield a profit if islanders were sold as slaves. In succeeding decades, the Spanish government periodically called for fair treatment of Indians and prohibited their enslavement, but such measures were ignored by colonists on the other side of the Atlantic.

Columbus died in Spain in 1506, still convinced he had found Asia. What he had done was to set in motion a process that would transform both sides of the Atlantic. It would eventually bring wealth to many Europeans and immense suffering to Native Americans and Africans.

A decidedly European view of Columbus's landing appears in this late sixteenth-century print. Columbus and his men, armed with guns and swords, are resplendent in European attire, while nearly naked Indians offer them gifts. To the left, Spaniards erect a cross to claim the land for Christianity. In the upper right, frightened natives flee into the woods.

**QUICK REVIEW**

**Christopher Columbus**

◆ Columbus believed he could sail westward to Asia and find wealth for Spain from Asian trade.

◆ Columbus convinced the Spanish monarchs to support his voyage.

◆ Columbus died in 1506 still believing he had found Asia.

## THE SPANISH CONQUEST AND COLONIZATION

Of all European nations, Spain was best suited to take advantage of Columbus's discovery. Its experience with the *reconquista* gave it a religious justification for conquest (bringing Christianity to nonbelievers) and an army of seasoned soldiers—*conquistadores*—eager to seek their fortunes in America now that the last Muslims had been expelled from Spain. In addition, during the *reconquista*, Spain's rulers developed efficient techniques for controlling newly conquered lands that could be applied to New World colonies.

The Spanish first consolidated their control of the Caribbean, establishing outposts on Cuba, Puerto Rico, and Jamaica (see Map 1–3). The *conquistadores* were more interested in finding gold and slaves than in creating permanent settlements. Leaving a trail of destruction, they attacked native villages and killed or captured the inhabitants.

**The end of the Aztec empire.**    In 1519, Hernán Cortés and six hundred soldiers landed on the coast of Mexico. Their subsequent actions more than fulfilled the Aztec king's belief that the Spaniards' arrival was an evil omen. By 1521, Cortés and his men had conquered the powerful Aztec empire, discovering riches beyond their wildest dreams.

The swift, decisive Spanish victory depended on several factors. In part, the Spanish enjoyed certain technological advantages. Their guns and horses often enabled them to overwhelm larger groups of Aztec foot soldiers armed with spears and wooden swords edged with

To conquer Tenochtitlán, Spanish soldiers had to gain control of the narrow causeways that led to the center of this distinctively designed city.

obsidian. But technology alone cannot account for the conquest of a vastly more numerous enemy, capable of absorbing far higher losses in combat.

Cortés benefited from two other factors. First, he exploited divisions within the Aztec empire. The Spanish acquired indispensable allies among subject Indians who resented Aztec domination, tribute demands, and seizure of captives for religious sacrifice.

A second and more important factor was disease. One of Cortés's men was infected with smallpox, which soon devastated the native population. European diseases had been unknown in the Americas before 1492, and Indians lacked resistance to them. Historians estimate that nearly 40 percent of the inhabitants of central Mexico died of smallpox within a year. Other diseases followed, including typhus, measles, and influenza. By 1600, the population of Mexico may have declined from over 15 million to less than 1 million people.

**The fall of the Inca empire.**    In 1532, Francisco Pizarro and 180 men, following rumors of even greater riches than those of Mexico, discovered the Inca empire high in the Peruvian Andes. It was the largest empire in the Americas, stretching more than 2,000 miles from what is now Ecuador to Chile. An excellent network of roads and bridges linked this extensive territory to the imperial capital of Cuzco. The Spaniards arrived at a moment of weakness for the empire. A few years before, the Incan ruler had died, probably from smallpox, and civil war had broken out between two of his sons. The victor, Atahualpa, was on his way from the empire's northern provinces to claim his throne in Cuzco when Pizarro intercepted him. Pizarro took Atahualpa hostage and despite receiving a colossal ransom—a roomful of gold and silver—had him killed.

**MAP 1–3** **Spanish, English, and French Settlements in North America in the Sixteenth Century** By the end of the sixteenth century, only Spain had established permanent settlements in North America. French outposts in Canada and at Fort Caroline, as well as the English settlement at Roanoke, failed to thrive. European rivalries for North America, however, would intensify after 1600.

**Based on this map,** what factors might help to explain why Spain was more successful in the establishment of permanent settlements before 1600 than either France or England? Do you think geographic location (climate, terrain, etc.) may have played a role?

The Spaniards then captured Cuzco, eventually extended control over the whole empire, and established a new capital at Lima.

By 1550, Spain's New World empire stretched from the Caribbean through Mexico to Peru. It was administered from Spain by the Council of the Indies, which enacted laws for the empire and supervised an elaborate bureaucracy charged with their enforcement. The council aimed to project royal authority into every village in New Spain in order to maintain political control and extract as much wealth as possible from the land and its people.

## GLOBAL CONNECTIONS

 LEARNING ABOUT CHOCOLATE

Long before Europeans arrived in Mesoamerica, native peoples throughout the region—especially elite inhabitants—enjoyed beverages made with cacao. Those who prepared the drinks removed the nibs, or "beans," from cacao fruit, dried and toasted them, then ground them to make chocolate paste. They blended the paste with water, flavored the mixture with chili peppers or dried flowers, and sometimes sweetened it with honey. The aromatic liquid would then be poured at a height from one container to another to produce a foamy, often somewhat bitter, drink. Sufficiently valuable to circulate as currency throughout the region, cacao beans formed an important part of the tribute that subject peoples owed to their Aztec overlords.

After the conquest of Mexico, the Spanish likewise received cacao as tribute. They also developed a taste for chocolate when the Indian women whom they employed as cooks served it to them. To learn how cacao was processed, Spaniards visited Indian villages and markets to watch chocolate being made. By the early seventeenth century, colonial merchants and clergy who returned to Spain introduced their countrymen to what had become a favorite drink.

Spaniards who had learned to drink chocolate in the New World did their best to replicate the familiar taste and appearance of the beverage in their Old World kitchens. But they found it difficult to do so, as the native flowers, peppers, and spices used in Mesoamerica were unavailable in Spain. So they improvised by using products obtained from Asia, such as cinnamon, cloves, and black pepper, to approximate the flavors of New World ingredients. Thus the chocolate consumed in wealthy homes across Spain was a truly global beverage. A mixture of products obtained from all over the world, it testified to the vast expansion of trade networks and served as an important example of the transfer of knowledge and skills from Native Americans to European colonists.

- How did the Indians' knowledge of chocolate affect their relations with the Spanish?

For more than a century, Spanish ships crossed the Atlantic carrying seemingly limitless amounts of treasure from the colonies. To extract this wealth, the colonial rulers subjected the native inhabitants of New Spain to compulsory tribute payments and forced labor. When necessary, Spaniards imported African slaves to supplement a native labor force ravaged by disease and exhaustion.

**Spanish incursions to the north.**   The desire for gold eventually lured Spaniards farther into North America. In 1528, an expedition to Florida ended in disaster when the Spanish intruders provoked an attack by Apalachee Indians. Most of the Spanish survivors eventually perished, but Álvar Núñez Cabeza de Vaca and three other men (including an African slave) escaped from their captors and managed to reach Mexico after a grueling eight-year journey. In a published account of his ordeal, Cabeza de Vaca insisted that the interior of North America contained a fabulously wealthy empire (see "American Views: Cabeza de Vaca among the Indians").

This report inspired other Spaniards to seek such treasures that had eluded its author. In 1539, Hernán de Soto—who tried unsuccessfully to get Cabeza de Vaca to serve as a guide—led an expedition from Florida to the Mississippi River. Along the way, the Spaniards harassed the native peoples, demanding provisions, burning villages, and capturing women to be servants and concubines. In these same years, Francisco Vásquez de Coronado led three hundred troops on an equally destructive expedition through present-day Arizona, New Mexico, and Colorado on a futile search for the mythical Seven Cities of Cíbola, rumored to contain hoards of gold and precious stones.

The failure to find gold and silver halted Spain's attempt to extend its empire to the north. By the end of the sixteenth century, the Spanish maintained just two precarious

WHERE TO LEARN MORE

★ St. Augustine, Florida
http://www.augustine.com/history/

footholds north of Mexico. One was at St. Augustine, on Florida's Atlantic coast. The other settlement was located far to the west in what is now New Mexico.

Almost from the start of the conquest, the bloody tactics used by the Spanish in the New World aroused protest back in Spain. The Indians' most eloquent advocate was Bartolomé de Las Casas, a Dominican priest shamed by his own role (as a layman) in the conquest of Hispaniola. In 1516, the Spanish king appointed him to the newly created office of Protector of the Indians, but his efforts had little effect.

**The seeds of economic decline.** Meanwhile, the vast riches of Central and South America glutted Spain's treasury. Between 1500 and 1650, an estimated 181 tons of gold and 16,000 tons of silver were shipped from the New World to Spain, making it the richest and most powerful state in Europe (see Figure 1–1). But this influx of American treasure had unforeseen consequences that would soon undermine Spanish predominance.

In 1492, the Spanish crown, determined to impose religious conformity after the *reconquista*, expelled from Spain all Jews who refused to become Christians. The refugees included many leading merchants who had contributed significantly to Spain's economy. The remaining Christian merchants, now awash in American riches, saw little reason to invest in new trade or productive enterprises that might have sustained the economy once the flow of New World treasure diminished. As a result, Spain's economy eventually stagnated.

Compounding the problem, the flood of American gold and silver contributed to what historians have called a "price revolution" in Europe. Beginning in the late fifteenth century, as Europe's population recovered from the Black Death, demographic and economic factors led to a rise in prices. This inflationary cycle was made worse by the influx of New World gold and silver.

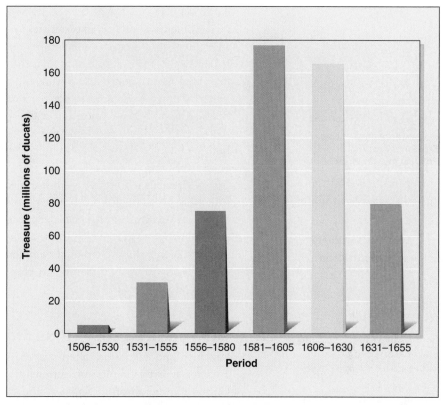

**FIGURE 1–1    Value of New World Treasure Imported into Spain, 1506–1655**  During the sixteenth and early seventeenth centuries, Spain was the only European power to reap great wealth from North America. The influx of New World treasure, however, slowed the development of Spain's economy in the long run. [Note: A ducat was a gold coin.]
*Data Source:* J.H. Elliott, *Imperial Spain, 1469–1716* (1964), p. 175.

●◆●⎤Read the Document
at **www.myhistorylab.com**
*Bartolomé de Las Casas, Of the Island of Hispaniola (1542)*

## THE COLUMBIAN EXCHANGE

Spain's long-term economic decline was just one of many consequences of the conquest of the New World. In the long run, the biological consequences of contact—what one historian has called the **Columbian Exchange**—proved to be the most momentous (see the Overview table, The Columbian Exchange).

The most catastrophic result of the exchange was the exposure of Native Americans to Old World diseases. Europeans and Africans, long exposed to these diseases, had developed some immunity to them. Native Americans, lacking such contact, had not. Epidemics of smallpox, measles, typhus, and influenza struck Native Americans with great force, killing half, and sometimes as many as 90 percent, of the people in communities exposed to them.

Another important aspect of the Columbian Exchange was the introduction of Old World livestock to the New World, which began when Columbus brought horses, sheep,

**Columbian Exchange**  The transatlantic exchange of plants, animals, and diseases that occurred after the first European contact with the Americas.

cattle, pigs, and goats with him on his second voyage in 1493. The large European beasts created problems as well as opportunities for native peoples. With few natural predators to limit their numbers, livestock populations boomed in the New World, competing with native mammals for grazing. At least at first, the Indians' unfamiliarity with the use of horses in warfare often gave mounted European soldiers a decisive military advantage. But some native groups adopted these animals for their own purposes. Yaquis, Pueblos, and other peoples in the Southwest began to raise cattle and sheep. By the eighteenth century, Plains Indians had reoriented their culture around the use of horses, which had become essential for travel and hunting buffalo. Horses also became a primary object for trading and raiding among Plains peoples.

Columbus introduced such European crops as wheat, chickpeas, melons, onions, and fruit trees to the Caribbean. Native Americans, in turn, introduced Europeans to corn, tomatoes, squash, beans, cacao, peppers, and potatoes, as well as nonfood plants such as tobacco and cotton. New World food crops enriched Old World diets and the nutritional benefits eventually contributed to a sharp rise in Europe's population. Over time, many of these more numerous Europeans chose to leave their overcrowded communities for the New World.

## CULTURAL PERCEPTIONS AND MISPERCEPTIONS

Curiosity and confusion often marked early encounters between Europeans and Native Americans. Even simple transactions produced unexpected results. The first Indians whom Cortés allowed aboard a Spanish ship fainted at the sound of a large cannon being fired. French explorers were similarly taken by surprise when they choked while smoking Iroquois tobacco, which they thought tasted like "powdered pepper." These relatively minor mishaps were soon overshadowed by more substantial interactions that highlighted cultural differences between Indians and Europeans.

Most Indians believed that the universe contained friendly and hostile spiritual forces. People interacted with the spirit world through ceremonies that often involved exchanging gifts. North of Mexico, Indians (like West Africans) passed on religious beliefs through oral traditions, not in writing. To Europeans accustomed to worshiping one God in an organized church and preserving their beliefs in a written Bible, Indian spiritual traditions were incomprehensible. Many Europeans assumed that Indians worshiped the Devil. Indians, in turn, often found Christianity confusing and at first rejected European pressure to convert.

Different understandings of gender roles provided another source of confusion. Europeans regarded men as superior to women and thus the natural rulers of society. They disapproved of the less restrictive gender divisions among Native Americans. Europeans, accustomed to societies in which men did most agricultural work, objected to Indian women's dominant role in farming and assumed that men's hunting was more for recreation than subsistence. They concluded that Indian women lived "a most slavish life." Indians, in turn, thought that European men failed to make good use of their wives.

In order for Indians and Europeans to get along peaceably, each side would have to look past these and other cultural differences and adapt to the new circumstances under which both groups now lived. At first, such harmony seemed possible. But it soon became clear that Europeans intended to dominate the lands they discovered. Such claims to dominance sparked vigorous resistance from native peoples everywhere who strove to maintain their autonomy in a changed world.

Read the Document
at www.myhistorylab.com
*Exploring America:
America and the Horse*

Read the Document
at www.myhistorylab.com
*Cultures Meet: Europeans View
the New World*

**QUICK REVIEW**

Sources of Misunderstanding and Mistrust

- Technology.
- Religion.
- Gender.
- Social organization.

Cacao, from which chocolate is made, was one of many New World foods that entered Old World diets as part of the Columbian Exchange. This sixteenth-century illustration shows a native Mexican woman pouring chocolate from a great height to produce a frothy drink.

## AMERICAN VIEWS

### ᧁ Cabeza de Vaca among the Indians (1530) ᧁ

Álvar Núñez Cabeza de Vaca came to the New World in 1527 in search of riches, not suffering. But the Spanish expedition of which he was a member met disaster shortly after it arrived in Florida on a mission to conquer the region north of the Gulf of Mexico. Of an original group of three hundred soldiers, only Cabeza de Vaca and three other men (including one African slave) survived. They did so by walking thousands of miles overland from the Gulf Coast to northern Mexico, an eight-year-long ordeal that tested the men's wits and physical endurance. Instead of entering Indian villages as proud conquistadors, Cabeza de Vaca and his companions encountered native peoples from a position of weakness. In order to survive, they had to adapt to the ways of the peoples across whose land they passed. After Cabeza de Vaca made it back to Mexico City, he described his experiences in an official report to the king of Spain. This remarkable document offers vivid descriptions of the territory extending from northern Florida to northern Mexico and the many peoples who inhabited it. It is equally interesting, as this extract suggests, for what it reveals about Cabeza de Vaca himself and the changes he made in the interest of survival.

- **While** living among the Capoques, what sort of work did Cabeza de Vaca have to do, and why?
- **Why** did Cabeza de Vaca decide to become a merchant? What advantages did this way of life offer him?
- **Why** did the Indians welcome Cabeza de Vaca into their communities even though he was a stranger?

[I remained with the Capoques] for more than a year, and because of the great labors they forced me to perform and the bad treatment they gave me, I resolved to flee from them and go to those who live in the forests and on the mainland, who are called those of Charruco, because I was unable to endure the life that I had with these others; because among many other tasks, I had to dig the roots to eat out from under the water and among the rushes where they grew in the ground. And because of this, my fingers were so worn that when a reed touched them it caused them to bleed, and the reeds cut me in many places. . . . And because of this, I set to the task of going over to the others, and with them things were somewhat better for me. And because I became a merchant, I tried to exercise the vocation as best I knew how. And because of this they gave me food to eat and treated me well, and they importuned me to go from one place to another to obtain the things they needed, because on account of the continual warfare in the land, there is little traffic or communication among them. And with my dealings and wares I entered inland as far as I desired, and I went along the coast for forty or fifty leagues. The mainstay of my trade was pieces of snail shell and the hearts of them; and conch shells with which they cut a fruit that is like frijoles [beans], with which they perform cures and do their dances and make celebrations. . . . And in exchange and as barter for it, I brought forth hides and red ocher with which they smear themselves and dye their faces and hair, flints to make the points of arrows, paste, and stiff canes to make them, and some tassels made from deer hair which they dye red. And this occupation served me well, because practicing it, I had the freedom to go wherever I wanted, and I was not constrained in any way nor enslaved, and wherever I went they treated me well and gave me food out of want for my wares, and most importantly because doing that, I was able to seek out the way by which I would go forward. And among them I was very well known; when they saw me and I brought them the things they needed, they were greatly pleased.

*Source:* Rolena Adorno and Patrick Charles Pautz, eds., *The Narrative of Cabeza de Vaca* (Lincoln: University of Nebraska Press, 2003), pp. 96–97.

## OVERVIEW The Columbian Exchange

| | From Old World to New World | From New World to Old World |
|---|---|---|
| Diseases | Smallpox, measles, plague, typhus, influenza, yellow fever, diphtheria, scarlet fever, whooping cough | Sexually transmitted strain of syphilis |
| Animals | Horses, cattle, pigs, sheep, goats, donkeys, mules, black rats, honeybees, cockroaches | Turkeys |
| Plants | Wheat, sugar, barley, apples, pears, peaches, plums, cherries, coffee, rice, dandelions, and other weeds | Maize, beans, peanuts, potatoes, sweet potatoes, manioc, squash, papayas, guavas, tomatoes, avocadoes, pineapple, chili pepper, cacao |

# COMPETITION FOR A CONTINENT

**WHY DID** early French and English efforts at colonization falter?

**Treaty of Tordesillas** Treaty negotiated in 1494 to resolve the territorial claims of Spain and Portugal.

Spain's New World bonanza attracted the attention of other European states eager to share in the wealth. Portugal soon acquired its own profitable piece of South America. In 1494, the conflicting claims of Portugal and Spain were resolved by the **Treaty of Tordesillas.** The treaty drew a north–south line approximately 1,100 miles west of the Cape Verde Islands. Spain received all lands west of the line, while Portugal held sway to the east. This limited Portugal's New World empire to Brazil, where settlers established sugar plantations worked by slave labor. But the treaty also protected Portugal's claims in Africa and Asia, which lay east of the line.

France and England, of course, rejected this division of the Western Hemisphere between Spain and Portugal. Their initial challenges to Spanish dominance in the New World, however, proved quite feeble. Domestic troubles—largely sparked by the Protestant Reformation—distracted the two countries from the pursuit of empire. By the close of the sixteenth century, both France and England insisted on their rights to New World lands, but neither had created a permanent settlement to support its claim.

## EARLY FRENCH EFFORTS IN NORTH AMERICA

France was a relative latecomer to New World exploration. Preoccupied with European affairs, France's rulers paid little attention to America. But when news of Cortés's exploits in Mexico arrived in the 1520s, King Francis I wanted his own New World empire to enrich France and block further Spanish expansion. In 1524, Francis sponsored a voyage by Giovanni da Verrazano, an Italian navigator, who mapped the North American coast from present-day South Carolina to Maine. During the 1530s and 1540s, the French mariner Jacques Cartier made three voyages in search of rich mines to rival those of Mexico and Peru. He explored the St. Lawrence River up to what is now Montreal, hoping to discover a water route through the continent to Asia (the so-called Northwest Passage).

On his third voyage, in 1541, Cartier was to serve under the command of a nobleman, Jean-François de la Rocque, Sieur de Roberval, who was commissioned by the king to establish a permanent settlement in Canada. This first attempt to found a permanent French colony failed miserably. The Iroquois, suspicious of repeated French intrusions on their lands, saw no reason to help them. A year after they arrived in Canada, Roberval and the surviving colonists were back in France.

Disappointed with their Canadian expeditions, the French made a few forays to the south, establishing outposts in what is now South Carolina in 1562 and Florida in 1564. They soon abandoned the Carolina colony, and Spanish forces captured the Florida fort. Then, back in France, a prolonged civil war broke out between Catholics and Protestants. Renewed interest in colonization would have to await the return of peace at home.

## ENGLISH ATTEMPTS IN THE NEW WORLD

The English were quicker than the French to stake a claim to the New World but no more successful at colonization. In 1497, King Henry VII sent John Cabot, an Italian mariner, to explore eastern Canada on England's behalf. But neither Henry nor any of his wealthy subjects would invest the funds necessary to follow up on Cabot's discoveries.

The lapse in English activity in the New World stemmed from religious troubles at home. Between 1534 and 1558, England changed its official religion several times. King Henry VIII, who had once defended the Catholic Church against its critics, took up the Protestant cause when the pope refused to annul his marriage to Catherine of Aragon. In 1534, Henry declared himself the head of a separate Church of England and seized the Catholic Church's English property. Because many English people sympathized with the Protestant cause, there was relatively little opposition to Henry's actions. But in 1553, Mary—daughter of the spurned Catherine of Aragon—became queen and tried to bring England back to Catholicism. She had nearly three hundred Protestants burned at the stake for their beliefs (earning her the nickname "Bloody Mary"), and many others went into exile in Europe.

Mary's brief but destructive reign ended in 1558, and her half-sister Elizabeth, a committed Protestant, became queen. Elizabeth ruled for forty-five years (1558–1603), restoring Protestantism as the state religion, bringing stability to the nation, and renewing England's interest in the New World. She and her subjects saw colonization not only as a way to gain wealth and political advantage but also as a Protestant crusade against Catholic domination.

**The colonization of Ireland.** England's first target for colonization, however, was not America but Ireland. Henry VIII had tried, with limited success, to bring the island under English control in the 1530s and 1540s. Elizabeth renewed the attempt in the 1560s with a series of brutal expeditions that destroyed Irish villages and slaughtered the inhabitants. Several veterans of these campaigns later took part in New World colonization and drew on their Irish experience for guidance.

Two aspects of that experience were particularly important. First, the English transferred their assumptions about Irish "savages" to Native Americans. Englishmen in America frequently observed similarities between Indians and the Irish. Because the English held the "wild Irish" in contempt, these observations encouraged them to scorn the Indians. When Indians resisted their attempts at conquest, the English recalled the Irish example, claiming that native "savagery" required brutal suppression.

Second, the Irish experience influenced English ideas about colonial settlement. English conquerors set up "plantations" surrounded by palisades on seized Irish lands. These plantations were meant to be civilized outposts in a savage land. Their aristocratic owners imported Protestant tenants from England and Scotland to farm the land. Native Irish people, considered too wild to join proper Christian communities, were excluded. English colonists in America followed this precedent when they established plantations that separated English and native peoples.

**Expeditions to the New World.** Sir Humphrey Gilbert, a notoriously cruel veteran of the Irish campaigns, became fascinated with the idea of New World colonization. He composed a treatise to persuade Queen Elizabeth to support such an endeavor. The queen authorized several exploratory voyages, including Martin Frobisher's three trips in 1576–1578 in search of the Northwest Passage to Asia. Frobisher failed to find the elusive passage and sent back shiploads of glittering ore that proved to be fool's gold. Elizabeth had better luck in allowing privateers, such as John Hawkins and Francis Drake, to raid Spanish ships and New World ports for gold and silver. The plunder taken during these raids enriched both the sailors and their investors— one of whom was the queen herself.

 **Read** the **Document**

at **www.myhistorylab.com**
*From Then to Now Online: The Disappearance of Cod Off The Grand Banks*

John White's picture of the village of Pomeiooc offers a rare glimpse of a sixteenth-century Eastern Woodlands Indian community. The village is surrounded by a palisade with two entrances; evidence suggests that White exaggerated the spacing of the poles in order to depict the houses inside. Eighteen dwellings constructed of poles and mats are clustered around the village circumference; inside some of them raised sleeping platforms can be seen. Many of the villagers are clustered around a central fire, while others are working or conversing.

Algonquian Indian village of Pomeiooc (North Carolina) watercolor, c. 1585 by John White.

**Read the Document**

at www.myhistorylab.com
*Thomas Hariot, A Brief and True Report of the New Found Land of Virginia (1588)*

**QUICK REVIEW**

**Roanoke**

◆ 1578: Gilbert receives permission to set up a colony.

◆ 1585: Raleigh sends men to build a settlement on Roanoke Island.

◆ 1587: Raleigh sends a second expedition led by White.

◆ 1590: White returns to find Roanoke deserted.

Meanwhile, Gilbert continued to promote New World settlement, arguing that it would increase England's trade and provide a place to send unemployed Englishmen. Gilbert suggested offering free land in America to English families willing to emigrate.

In 1578, Gilbert received permission to set up a colony along the North American coast. It took him five years to organize an expedition to Newfoundland, which he claimed for England. After sailing southward seeking a more favorable site for a colony, Gilbert headed home, only to be lost at sea during an Atlantic storm. The impetus for English colonization did not die with him, however, for his half-brother, Sir Walter Raleigh (another veteran of the Irish wars), took up the cause.

**The Roanoke Colony.** In 1584, Raleigh sent an expedition to find a suitable location for a colony. The Carolina coast seemed promising, so Raleigh sent men in 1585 to build a settlement on Roanoke Island. Most of the colonists were soldiers fresh from Ireland who refused to grow their own food, insisting that the Roanoke Indians should feed them. When the local chief, Wingina, organized native resistance, they killed him. Eventually, the colonists, disappointed not to have found any treasure and exhausted by a harsh winter, returned to England in 1586.

Two members of these early expeditions, however, left a more positive legacy. Thomas Hariot studied the Roanoke and Croatoan Indians and identified plants and animals in the area, hoping that some might prove to be profitable commodities. John White drew maps and painted a series of watercolors depicting the natives and the coastal landscape. When Raleigh tried once more, in 1587, to found a colony, he chose White to be its leader. This attempt also failed. The ship captain dumped the settlers—who, for the first time, included women and children—on Roanoke Island so that he could pursue Spanish treasure ships. White waited until his granddaughter, Virginia Dare (the first English child born in America), was born and then sailed to England for supplies. But the outbreak of war with Spain delayed his return for three years. When he finally returned in 1590, White found the colony deserted. The actual fate of the "Lost Colony" at Roanoke will probably never be known.

At this point, Raleigh gave up on North America and turned his attention to his Irish plantations. But England's interest in colonization did not wane. In 1584, Richard Hakluyt had aroused enthusiasm for America by writing the *Discourse on the Western Planting* for the queen and her advisers. He argued that England would prosper from trade and the sale of New World commodities. Once the Indians were civilized, Hakluyt added, they would eagerly purchase English goods. Equally important, England could plant "sincere religion" (that is, Protestant Christianity) in the New World and block Spanish expansion. Hakluyt's arguments fired the imaginations of many people, and the defeat of the Spanish Armada emboldened England to challenge Spain's New World dominance. The experience of Roanoke should have tempered that enthusiasm, illustrating the difficulty of establishing colonies. But the English were slow to learn these lessons; when they resumed colonization efforts in 1607, they repeated Roanoke's mistakes, with disastrous results for the people involved. As it was, the sixteenth century ended with no permanent English settlement in the New World.

# CONCLUSION

Dramatic changes occurred in North America during the century after Moctezuma's messenger spotted the Spanish ships off the Mexican coast. Europeans, eager for wealth and power, set out to claim a continent that just a hundred years earlier they had not dreamed existed. African slaves were brought to the Caribbean, Mexico, and Brazil, and forced to labor under extremely harsh conditions for white masters. The Aztec and Incan empires collapsed in the wake of the Spanish conquest. In the Caribbean and parts of Mexico and Peru, untold numbers of native peoples succumbed to European diseases they had never before encountered.

And yet conditions in 1600 bore clearer witness to the past than to the future. Despite all that had happened, North America was still Indian country. Only Spain had established North American colonies, and even its soldiers struggled to expand north of Mexico. Spain's outposts in Florida and New Mexico staked claims to territory that it did not really control. Except in Mexico and the Caribbean, Europeans had merely touched the continent's shores. In 1600, despite the virulent epidemics, native peoples (even in Mexico) still greatly outnumbered European and African immigrants. The next century, however, brought many powerful challenges both to native control and to the Spanish monopoly of settlement.

# WHERE TO LEARN MORE

**Cahokia Mounds State Historic Site, Collinsville, Illinois.** This site, occupied from 600 to 1500 C.E., was the largest Mississippian community in eastern North America. It now includes numerous exhibits, and archaeological excavations continue in the vicinity. The website http://cahokiamounds.org/ contains a wealth of information and an interactive map.

**Mashantucket Pequot Museum, Mashantucket, Connecticut.** This tribally owned and operated complex offers a view of Eastern Woodlands Indian life, focusing on the Pequots of eastern Connecticut. Exhibits include dioramas, films, interactive programs, and a reconstructed sixteenth-century Pequot village. The homepage for the Mashantucket Pequot Museum and Research Center is http://pequotmuseum.org/.

**Mesa Verde National Park, Colorado.** Occupied by Ancestral Puebloan peoples as early as A.D. 550, the area contains a variety of sites, from early pithouses to spectacular cliff dwellings. The official National Park webpage for Mesa Verde is http://www.nps.gov/meve/index.htm.

**St. Augustine, Florida.** Founded in 1565, St. Augustine is the site of the first permanent Spanish settlement in North America. Today the restored community resembles a Spanish colonial town, with narrow, winding streets and seventeenth- and eighteenth-century buildings. The site also contains the restored Castillo de San Marcos, now a national park. There is an informational website at http://www.augustine.com/history/.

# REVIEW QUESTIONS

1. How did the Aztecs who first glimpsed Spanish ships off the coast of Mexico describe to Moctezuma what they had seen? What details most captured their attention?

2. Compare men's and women's roles in Native American, West African, and European societies. What were the similarities and differences? How did differences between European and Native American gender roles lead to misunderstandings?

3. Many of the first European colonizers in North America were military veterans. What impact did this have on their relations with Indian peoples?

4. Why did Spain so quickly become the dominant colonial power in North America? What advantages did it enjoy over France and England?

5. What role did religion play in early European efforts at overseas colonization? Did religious factors always encourage colonization, or did they occasionally interfere with European expansion?

6. In what ways were trade networks important in linking different groups of people in the Old and New Worlds?

# KEY TERMS

**Aztecs** (p. 7)
**Cahokia** (p. 9)
**Columbian Exchange** (p. 21)
**Culture areas** (p. 6)
**Great League of Peace and Power** (p. 9)

**Predestination** (p. 15)
**Protestants** (p. 15)
*Reconquista* (p. 15)
**Reformation** (p. 15)
**Songhai Empire** (p. 12)
**Treaty of Tordesillas** (p. 24)

# myhistorylab Connections

Reinforce what you learned in this chapter by studying the many documents, images, maps, review tools, and videos available at **www.myhistorylab.com**.

## Read and Review

✓● Study and Review   **Study Plan: Chapter 1**

●●● Read the Document

*Alvar Núñez Cabeza de Vaca, Indians of the Rio Grande (1528–1536)*

*Bartolomè de Las Casas, Of the Island of Hispaniola (1542)*

*From The Journal of Christopher Columbus (1492)*

*Ghana and Its People in the Mid-Eleventh Century*

*Muslim Reform in Songhai (1500)*

*Pima Creation Story*

*Thomas Hariot, A Brief and True Report of the New Found Land of Virginia (1588)*

👁 See the Map

*Pre-Columbian Societies of the Americas*

*Africa Climate Regions and Early Sites*

## Research and Explore

●●● Read the Document

*Personal Journeys Online*

*From Then to Now Online:
The Disappearance of Cod Off The Grand Banks*

*Exploring America: America and the Horse*

*Cultures Meet: Europeans View the New World*

((●● Hear the Audio *Ghana: Ewe-Atsiagbekor*

●● Watch the Video

*How Should We Think of Columbus?
What Is Columbus's Legacy?*

──── ((●● Hear the Audio ────

Hear the audio files for Chapter 1 at
**www.myhistorylab.com**.

# 2

# Transplantation and Adaptation

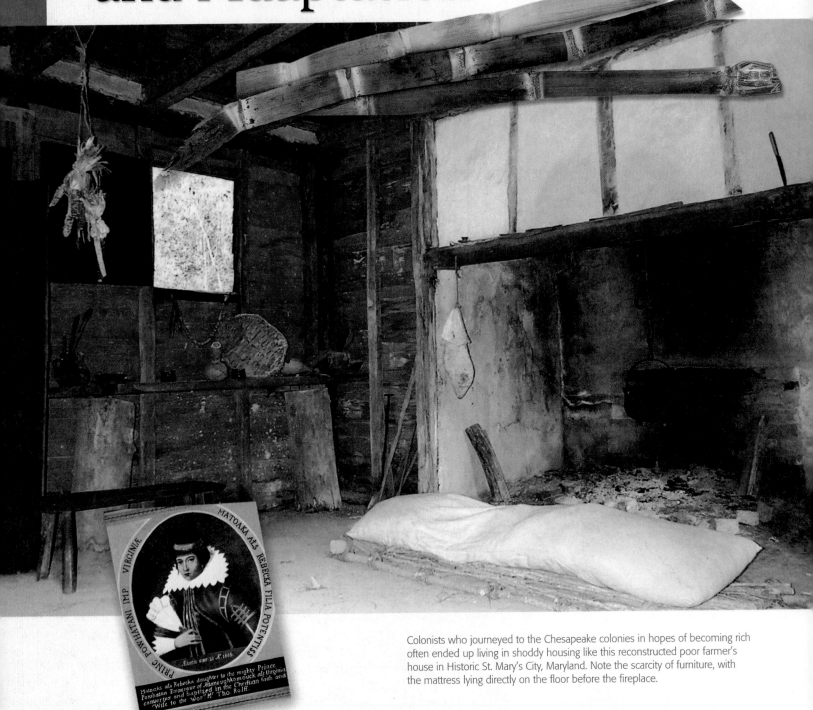

PRINC POWHATANI IMP VIRGINIÆ MATOAKA ALS REBECCA FILIA POTENTISS

Matoaks als Rebecka daughter to the mighty Prince Powhatan Emperour of Attanoughkomouck als Virginia converted and baptized in the Christian faith, and Wife to the Worsh. Mr Tho. Rolff.

Colonists who journeyed to the Chesapeake colonies in hopes of becoming rich often ended up living in shoddy housing like this reconstructed poor farmer's house in Historic St. Mary's City, Maryland. Note the scarcity of furniture, with the mattress lying directly on the floor before the fireplace.

**THE FRENCH IN NORTH AMERICA** *(page 33)*

**WHAT ROLE** did the fur trade and fur traders play in the success of the French colonies?

**THE DUTCH OVERSEAS EMPIRE** *(page 35)*

**HOW DID** conflict between the English and the Dutch affect Dutch colonization in the Americas?

**ENGLISH SETTLEMENT IN THE CHESAPEAKE** *(page 36)*

**HOW DID** tobacco cultivation shape the development of Virginia society?

**THE FOUNDING OF NEW ENGLAND** *(page 42)*

**WHY WERE** the English colonies in New England so different from those in the Chesapeake?

**COMPETITION IN THE CARIBBEAN** *(page 47)*

**WHAT WAS** the connection between sugar cultivation and slavery in the Caribbean?

**THE RESTORATION COLONIES** *(page 49)*

**HOW DID** the proprietors of the Restoration colonies shape their development?

ONE AMERICAN JOURNEY

*Martin's Hundred in Virginia, 1623*

*Loving and kind father and mother:*

*My most humble duty remembered to you, . . . This is to let you understand that I your child am in a most heavy case by reason of the nature of the country, [which] is such that it causeth much sickness, as the scurvy and the bloody flux and diverse other diseases, which maketh the body very poor and weak. . . . [Since] I came out of the ship I never ate anything but peas, and loblollie (that is water gruel). . . . A mouthful of bread for a penny loaf must serve for four men which is most pitiful. . . . [We] live in fear of the enemy every hour . . . for our plantation is very weak by reason of the death and sickness of our company. . . .*

*But I am not half a quarter so strong as I was in England, and all is for want of victuals, for I do protest unto you that I have eaten more in [one] day at home than I have allowed me here for a week. . . .*

*[I] saith that if you love me you will redeem me suddenly, for which I do entreat and beg. . . . Good father, do not forget me, but have mercy and pity my miserable case. I know if you did but see me, you would weep to see me. . . .*

*Richard Frethorne*

Susan M. Kingsbury, ed., *The Records of the Virginia Company of London*, 4 vols. (Washington, D.C., 1935), 4:58–62.

**◆◆◆—[Read the Document** at **www.myhistorylab.com**

Personal Journeys Online

- **Rev. Francis Higginson, July 1629. Letter from Massachusetts to his friends in Leicester, England.**

- **Father Isaac Jogues, *Novum Belgium*, 1646. Description of New Amsterdam.**

- **Hans Sloan, *A Voyage to the Islands*, 1707. Description of early eighteenth-century Jamaica.**

RICHARD FRETHORNE had journeyed across the Atlantic to seek his fortune in the new colony of Virginia. Like many emigrants, he surely hoped that one day he would become a prosperous landowner, a status beyond his reach in England. Instead of health and prosperity, Frethorne found sickness and starvation. Fears of an attack by enemy Indians compounded his misery. Yet the starving young Englishman could not simply board the next ship for England. He was under contract to work for the Virginia Company and could not leave until he had completed his term of service. Hence Frethorne's anguished plea to his father to "redeem" him, or buy out the remainder of his contract so that he could return home sooner.

Frethorne's experience reveals several important aspects of European colonization in the New World. Colonization offered opportunities for advancement, to be sure, but often at the price of sickness, suffering, and danger. Virginia turned out to be England's first permanent colony in the New World, but from Frethorne's perspective in 1623, it was a fragile settlement teetering on the brink of disaster.

Virginia's eventual success, and that of other English colonies, depended upon the willingness of thousands of individuals like Richard Frethorne to face the challenges posed by overseas settlement. Even as their emigration was inspired by hopes of improvement, their quest also reflected England's desire to claim a portion of the New World for itself. In this scramble for American colonies, England's greatest adversaries were France and the Netherlands. If ordinary colonists were often preoccupied with their own tribulations, their leaders could never forget the high stakes involved in the international race for overseas possessions. ◆

## CHRONOLOGY

| | |
|---|---|
| **1581** | Northern Provinces of Holland declare independence from Spain. |
| **1589** | King Henry IV of France signs Edict of Nantes, granting religious toleration to French Protestants and effectively ending civil war over religion. |
| **1602** | Founding of Dutch East India Company. |
| **1603–1625** | James I reigns as king of England. |
| **1607** | Founding of English colonies at Jamestown and Sagadahoc. |
| **1608** | Establishment of French colony at Quebec. |
| **1619** | First Africans arrive in Jamestown. |
| | Virginia's House of Burgesses meets for the first time. |
| **1620** | Founding of Plymouth Colony in New England. |
| | Mayflower Compact signed. |
| **1620s** | Tobacco boom in Virginia. |
| **1624** | Dutch found colony of New Netherland. |
| **1625** | Virginia becomes a royal colony. |
| | Fort Amsterdam founded. |
| **1625–1649** | Charles I reigns as king of England. |
| **1627** | English colony at Barbados founded. |
| **1630** | Massachusetts Bay Colony founded. |
| **1630–1642** | Great Migration to New England. |
| **1634** | Lord Baltimore (Cecilius Calvert) founds proprietary colony of Maryland. |
| **1635–1636** | Roger Williams banished from Massachusetts; founds Providence, Rhode Island. |
| **1637** | Anne Hutchinson banished from Massachusetts. |
| | Pequot War. |
| **1638** | New Haven colony founded. |
| **1640s** | Sugar cultivation and slavery established in West Indies. |
| **1642–1660** | English Civil War and Interregnum. |
| **1649** | Maryland's Act for Religious Toleration. |
| **1654** | Jewish emigrants from Brazil move to New Amsterdam, creating North America's first permanent Jewish community. |
| **1660** | Charles II restored to English throne; reigns until 1685. |
| **1663** | Founding of Carolina colony. |
| **1664** | New Netherland conquered by the English, becomes New York. |
| | New Jersey established. |
| **1673** | French explorers reach the Mississippi River. |
| **1681** | Founding of Pennsylvania. |

# THE FRENCH IN NORTH AMERICA

In the mid-sixteenth century, religious warfare between Catholics and Protestants at home had interrupted France's efforts to establish a foothold in North America. The only French subjects who maintained regular contact with the New World were fishermen making seasonal voyages to the waters off the coast of Newfoundland. But in the early seventeenth century, after King Henry IV restored civil order in France, the situation changed. With the creation of permanent settlements first along the St. Lawrence River and later in the continent's interior, France staked its claim to a New World empire.

**WHAT ROLE** did the fur trade and fur traders play in the success of the French colonies?

## THE QUEST FOR FURS AND CONVERTS

French fishermen who dried their catch along the Newfoundland shore often encountered Indians interested in trading beaver pelts for European goods. There was a ready market for these furs in Europe, where beaver hats had become very fashionable. Thus furs joined fish as a source of wealth, and a reason for French explorers and entrepreneurs to establish the colony of New France.

In 1608, Samuel de Champlain led an expedition up the St. Lawrence River to found a permanent settlement at Quebec. This village was eventually joined by two others located farther up the river (see Map 2–1). For several decades, the colony was managed by the Company of New France, a private corporation working on its own behalf as well as in France's

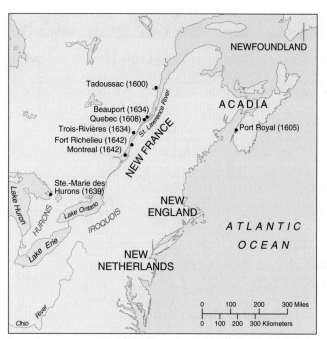

MAP 2–1 **New France, c. 1650** By 1650, New France contained a number of thinly populated settlements along the St. Lawrence River Valley and the eastern shore of Lake Huron. Most colonists lived in Quebec and Montreal; other sites served mainly as fur-trading posts and Jesuit missions to the Huron Indians.

**Why were** so many settlements in New France located along the banks of the St. Lawrence River? How did French settlement patterns reflect the economic goals of the French colonists?

***coureurs de bois*** French for "woods runners," independent fur traders in New France.

### QUICK REVIEW

#### The Fur Trade

- Fur traders were critical to New France's success.
- New France was ruled by royal appointees.
- *Coureurs de bois*: independent fur traders living among the Indians.

**indentured servants** Individuals who contracted to serve a master for a period of four to seven years in return for payment of the servant's passage to America.

### QUICK REVIEW

#### New France under Royal Control

- 1663: King Louis XIV assumes direct control of the colony.
- French officials launch campaign to increase immigration.
- Campaign fails and population is only 15,000 in 1700.

imperial interests. New France grew slowly; by the 1660s, there were only 3,200 colonists clustered in and around the three main villages.

The fur trade supporting the colony's development functioned as a partnership between Indians and Europeans. At first, some colonists anticipated that economic ties between the two peoples would be supplemented by marital ones as French traders took Indian wives. Intermarriage, however, was never widespread, occurring mainly among ***coureurs de bois*** ("woods runners"), independent fur traders who ventured into the forests to live and trade among native peoples.

Indian peoples such as the Montagnais and Hurons welcomed the French not only as trading partners, but also as military allies, making sure that the newcomers understood that the two roles had to be linked. As a result, the fur trade entangled the French in rivalries among Indian groups that long predated European contact.

Some French colonists regarded saving Indian souls as even more important than profiting from furs. Beginning in the 1630s, Jesuit missionaries—members of a Catholic religious order founded during the Counter-Reformation—tried to convince Indians to come to the French settlements to hear Christian preaching and learn European ways. When that tactic failed, Jesuits traveled to native villages and learned native languages, bringing Christianity directly to Indian populations.

## THE DEVELOPMENT OF NEW FRANCE

After 1663, New France underwent several important changes. King Louis XIV disbanded the Company of New France and assumed direct control of the colony. The French government also vastly improved Canada's military defenses, investing money in the construction of forts and sending over professional soldiers.

French officials launched a massive campaign to increase migration to the colony. They sent more than 700 orphaned girls and widows—called *filles du roi*, or "king's daughters"—to provide wives in a colony where there were six men of marriageable age for every unmarried French woman. Many male immigrants were *engagés*, or **indentured servants,** who agreed to work for three years in return for food, lodging, a small salary, and a return passage to France.

Despite these efforts, only about 250 French immigrants arrived each year. Several factors discouraged prospective colonists, not least of which was Canada's reputation as a distant and inhospitable place. Rumors circulated about frigid Canadian winters and surprise Indian attacks. In addition, the government required settlers to be Catholic (although Protestants often resided in Canada temporarily), reducing the pool from which colonists could be recruited. In the end, nearly three out of four immigrants who went to Canada returned home.

By 1700, the population had grown to about 15,000 (less than 7 percent of the English population in the mainland colonies that year; see Figure 2–1). This growth was mostly due to a remarkable level of natural increase.

French officials sought to restrict settlement to the St. Lawrence Valley, fearing that further expansion would render the empire impossible to defend. The impetus to move inland, however, could not be restrained. By the 1670s, French traders and missionaries had reached the Mississippi River. In 1681–1682, Robert, Sieur de La Salle, followed the Mississippi to the Gulf of Mexico, claiming the entire valley (which he named Louisiana in honor of the king) for France. When officials tried to restrict the direct trade between Indians and the *coureurs de bois*, many of these Frenchmen drifted off to settle in what became known as the *pays des Illinois* along the Mississippi. This expansion of French influence alarmed the English, who had founded colonies along the Atlantic seaboard and feared a growing French presence in the west.

Because Indians expected their trading partners also to be military allies, Europeans were often drawn into native conflicts. This illustration, from Samuel de Champlain's 1613 description of the founding of New France, shows him joining his Huron allies in an attack on the Iroquois.

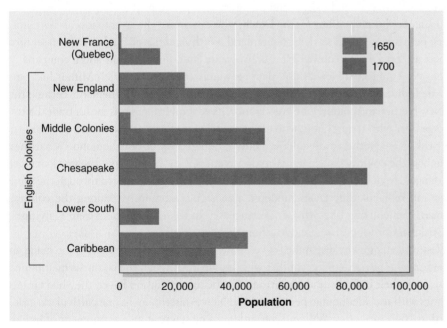

**FIGURE 2–1    European Populations of New France (Quebec) and English Colonies in 1650 and 1700** Although New France's population grew rapidly between 1650 and 1700, it remained only a tiny fraction of the population of England's North American colonies. By 1700, English colonists on the mainland outnumbered New France's inhabitants by a factor of about 16 to 1.

*Data Source:* John J. McCusker and Russell R. Menard, *The Economy of British America, 1607–1789* (1985). University of North Carolina Press.

Prosperous and expansive, Canada provided France with a secure foothold on the North American mainland. Its successful establishment contributed to an escalating European competition for land and trade in the New World. Soon new rivals entered the scene.

# THE DUTCH OVERSEAS EMPIRE

The Dutch Republic joined the scramble for empire in the early seventeenth century. The Northern Provinces, sometimes known as Holland, had in 1581 declared their independence from Spain (whose kings ruled the region as part of the Holy Roman Empire), although sporadic fighting continued for another half-century. The new republic, dominated by Protestants, was intent on challenging Catholic Spain's power in the New World as well as the Old. More than any other factor, however, the desire for profit drove the Dutch quest for colonies.

**HOW DID** conflict between the English and the Dutch affect Dutch colonization in the Americas?

●●●—Read the Document

at **www.myhistorylab.com**

*Exploring America:*
*Exploitation of the Americas*

## THE DUTCH EAST INDIA COMPANY

By 1600, the Dutch emerged as the leading economic power in Europe. The republic earned considerable wealth from manufacturing and Amsterdam soon became Europe's financial capital. The centerpiece of Dutch prosperity, however, was commerce, which expanded dramatically in the early seventeenth century. This commercial vitality provided the context for overseas expansion into both the Atlantic and Pacific.

The instrument of colonial dominance was the Dutch East India Company, founded in 1602 to challenge what had until then been a virtual Portuguese monopoly of Asian trade. Its first success was the capture of the Spice Islands (now Indonesia and East Timor), followed by the takeover of Batavia (Jakarta), Ceylon (Sri Lanka), and Sumatra. The company established slave-trading posts on the Gold Coast of West Africa, where it competed with the Portuguese, and at the Cape of Good Hope on Africa's southern tip. Its far-flung commercial net eventually encompassed parts of India and Formosa (Taiwan).

## THE WEST INDIA COMPANY AND NEW NETHERLAND

The Dutch next set their sights on the Americas, creating the West India Company in 1621. After taking control of West African slave-trading posts and temporarily occupying part of Brazil, the West India Company moved into the Caribbean (acquiring four islands by the 1640s) and North America. Its claim to the Connecticut, Hudson, and Delaware valleys stemmed from the 1609 voyage of Henry Hudson, an Englishman sailing for the Dutch, who discovered the river that bears his name.

The first permanent Dutch settlers on mainland North America arrived in 1624 to set up a fur-trading post at Fort Orange (now Albany). Two years later, Peter Minuit and a company of Protestant refugees established New Amsterdam on Manhattan Island, which Minuit had purchased from the Indians. The Hudson River corridor between these two settlements became the heart of the New Netherland colony. Like New France, its economic focus was the fur trade. Dutch merchants forged ties with the Iroquois, who exchanged furs for European tools and weapons.

At its peak, New Netherland's colonists only numbered about ten thousand. What they lacked in numbers the colonists made up for in divisiveness. New Netherland became a magnet for religious refugees from Europe, as well as a destination for Africans acquired through the slave trade. Ethnic and religious differences hindered a sense of community. Among the colony's Dutch, German, French, English, Swedish, Portuguese, and African settlers were Calvinists, Lutherans, Quakers, Catholics, Jews, and Muslims.

The West India Company dispatched several inept but aggressive governors who made an unstable situation worse by provoking conflict with Indians. Although the colonists maintained good relations with their Iroquois trading partners on the upper Hudson River, they had far less friendly dealings with the Algonquian peoples around New Amsterdam. In one particularly gruesome incident in 1645, Governor Willem Kieft ordered a massacre at an encampment of Indian refugees who had refused to pay him tribute. Ten years later, Governor Peter Stuyvesant antagonized Susquehannock Indians along the Delaware River by seizing a small Swedish colony where the Susquehannocks had traded.

Such actions provoked retaliatory raids by the Indians, further weakening the colony. Though profitable, the fur trade did not generate the riches to be found in other parts of the Dutch empire. By the 1650s, New Netherland increasingly looked like a poor investment to company officials back in Europe.

## ENGLISH SETTLEMENT IN THE CHESAPEAKE

**HOW DID** tobacco cultivation shape the development of Virginia society?

Following the Roanoke Colony's disappearance after 1587 (see Chapter 1), twenty years passed before the English again attempted to settle in America. When they did, in 1607, it was in the lower Chesapeake Bay region. The new settlement, Jamestown, at first seemed likely to share

## NORTH AMERICA'S FIRST JEWISH COMMUNITY

In 1654, twenty-three Jews arrived in New Amsterdam after a long voyage from Brazil. The reasons why they ended up in the Dutch colonial town relate to a much larger story of repeated Jewish migrations, undertaken time and again to escape religious persecution. In New Amsterdam these settlers found a home, establishing the first permanent Jewish community in North America.

Many of them could trace their ancestry back to Spain, where there had been a flourishing Jewish community during the Middle Ages. By the fifteenth century, however, the same Christian militancy that inspired the *reconquista* against the Muslims brought trouble for Spain's Jewish population in the form of the Inquisition. Jews who refused to convert to Christianity risked execution as heretics. In 1492, the same year as Columbus's first voyage, Spanish authorities ordered all Jews to leave Spain. Refugee Spanish Jews relocated all over the Mediterranean world, with perhaps a hundred thousand settling in Portugal, Spain's neighbor on the Iberian Peninsula. Many who did so were forced to accept Christian baptism, but continued to follow their own faith in secret. When the authorities threatened to prevent such practices, many Jews chose to leave Portugal. Some sought refuge in the Netherlands, where they found religious toleration and commercial opportunities.

In the early seventeenth century, the same Dutch West India Company that founded New Netherland tried to dislodge the Portuguese from their prosperous sugar-producing colony of Brazil. The company succeeded in capturing the city of Recife in 1630, and for the next twenty-four years the Dutch ruled over northeastern Brazil. During that time, more than a thousand Jews moved to the colony from the Netherlands. But when the Portuguese regained control of Brazil in 1654, the Jews were forced to move yet again. Most returned to the Netherlands, but a few decided to take their chances in New Amsterdam. At last they found a place where they could stay. When New Netherland became New York in 1664, English authorities continued the Dutch practice of toleration. Even though Jewish colonists were only supposed to worship in private, there was a synagogue in New York City by 1700. Jews eventually settled in other colonies, such as Rhode Island, Pennsylvania, and South Carolina. Wherever they formed their communities, they contributed to the remarkable religious diversity of England's New World empire.

- How did religious persecution in early modern Europe affect the lives of its Jewish inhabitants?

Roanoke's dismal fate. But it endured, eventually developing into the prosperous colony of Virginia. The reason for Virginia's success was an American plant—tobacco—that commanded good prices from European consumers. Tobacco also underlaid the economy of a neighboring colony, Maryland, and had a profound influence on the development of Chesapeake society.

## THE ORDEAL OF EARLY VIRGINIA

In 1606, several English merchants petitioned King James I for a charter incorporating two companies to attempt New World settlement. One, the London, or Virginia, Company, included merchants from the city of London; the other, the Plymouth Company, included merchants from England's western ports. These **joint-stock companies** sold shares to investors (who expected a profit in return) to raise money for colonization.

**The Jamestown colony.**   Three small ships carried 104 settlers, all men, to the mouth of Chesapeake Bay in May 1607 (see Map 2–2). On a peninsula about 50 miles up a river they named the James in honor of their king, the colonists built a fortified settlement they called Jamestown. Hoping to earn quick profits for Virginia Company investors, they immediately began hunting for gold and searching for the Northwest Passage to Asia. Spending all their time searching for riches, the settlers neglected to plant crops, and their food supplies dwindled. By January 1608, only thirty-eight colonists were still alive.

**joint-stock company**   Business enterprise in which a group of stockholders pooled their money to engage in trade or to fund colonizing expeditions.

●●●─Read the **Document**

at **www.myhistorylab.com**
*Exploring America: Jamestown*

**MAP 2–2** **English and Dutch Mainland Colonies in North America, c. 1655** Early English colonies clustered in two areas of the Atlantic seaboard—New England and the Chesapeake Bay. Between them lay Dutch New Netherland, with settlements stretching up the Hudson River. The Dutch also acquired territory at the mouth of the Delaware River in 1655 when they seized a short-lived Swedish colony located there.

**Why might** the Dutch have sought to control the Hudson and Delaware Rivers? What does this map tell us about the differing goals of Dutch and English colonists?

**headright system** Instituted by the Virginia Company in 1616, this system gave fifty acres to anyone who paid his own way to Virginia and an additional fifty for each person (or "head") he brought with him.

**House of Burgesses** The legislature of colonial Virginia. First organized in 1619, it was the first institution of representative government in the English colonies.

**WHERE TO LEARN MORE**

★ Jamestown Settlement, near Williamsburg, Virginia
http://www.virtualjamestown.org/

After the disastrous first year, the colony's governing council turned to Captain John Smith for leadership. He imposed military discipline on Jamestown, organizing settlers into work gangs and decreeing that "he that will not worke shall not eate." When a gunpowder explosion wounded Smith in 1609 and forced him to return to England, his enemies had him replaced as leader.

Once again, the colony nearly disintegrated. More settlers arrived, only to starve or die of disease. Facing financial ruin, company officials back in England tried to conceal the state of the colony. They reorganized the company twice and sent more settlers, including glassmakers, winegrowers, and silkmakers, in a desperate effort to find a marketable colonial product. They experimented with harsh military discipline. When it became clear that such severity discouraged immigration, the company tried more positive inducements.

The first settlers had been expected to work in return for food and other necessities; only company stockholders were to share in the colony's profits. But settlers wanted land, so governors began assigning small plots to those who finished their terms of service to the company. In 1616, the company instituted the **headright system,** giving 50 acres to anyone who paid his own way to Virginia and an additional 50 for each person (or "head") he brought with him.

In 1619, three other important developments occurred. That year, the company began transporting women to become wives for planters and induce them to stay in the colony. It was also the year in which the first Africans arrived in Virginia. In addition, the company created the first legislative body in English America, the **House of Burgesses,** setting a precedent for the establishment of self-government in other English colonies. Landowners elected representatives to the House of Burgesses, which, subject to the approval of the company, made laws for Virginia.

Despite these changes, the settlers were still unable to earn the company a profit. To make matters worse, the headright system expanded English settlement beyond Jamestown. This strained the already tense relations between the English and the Indians onto whose lands they had intruded.

**The Powhatan Confederacy and the colonists.** When the English arrived in 1607, they planted their settlement in the heart of territory ruled by the powerful Indian leader Powhatan. Chief of a confederacy of about thirty tribes with some fourteen thousand people, including 3,200 warriors, Powhatan had little to fear at first from the struggling English outpost. After an initial skirmish with English soldiers, he sent gifts of food, assuming that by accepting the gifts, the colonists acknowledged their dependence on him. Further action against the settlers seemed unnecessary, because they seemed fully capable of destroying themselves.

This conclusion was premature. Armed colonists began seizing corn from Indian villages whenever native people refused to supply it voluntarily. In retaliation, Powhatan besieged Jamestown and tried to starve the colony to extinction. The colony was saved by the arrival of reinforcements from England, but war with the Indians continued until 1614.

The marriage of the colonist John Rolfe to Pocahontas, Powhatan's daughter, helped seal the peace in 1614. Pocahontas had briefly been held captive by the English during the war and had been instructed in English manners and religion by Rolfe. Sent to negotiate with Powhatan in the spring of 1614, Rolfe asked the chief for his daughter's hand. Powhatan gave his consent, and Pocahontas—baptized in the Church of England and renamed Rebecca—became Rolfe's wife.

Powhatan died in 1618, and his brother Opechancanough succeeded him as chief. Still harboring intense resentment against the English, the new chief made plans for retaliation. Early in the morning on March 22, 1622, hundreds of Indian men traveled to the English settlements, as if they meant to visit or trade. Instead, they attacked the unsuspecting colonists, killing 347 by the end of the day—more than one-fourth of the English population.

The surviving colonists almost immediately plotted revenge. English forces struck at native villages, killing the inhabitants and burning cornfields. During the ensuing nine years of war, the English treated the Indians with a ferocity that recalled their earlier subjugation of the Irish.

Although Opechancanough's attack failed to restrain the colonists, it destroyed the Virginia Company. Economic activity ceased as settlers retreated to fortified garrisons. The company went

After years of work, archaeologists have excavated the original site of the English fort at Jamestown. This aerial view of the site shows its close proximity to the James River.

bankrupt, and a royal commission investigating the 1622 attack was shocked to discover that nearly ten times more colonists had died from starvation and disease than at the hands of Indians. King James had little choice but to dissolve the company in 1624, and Virginia became a royal colony the following year. The settlers continued to enjoy self-government through the House of Burgesses, but now the king chose the colony's governor and council, and royal advisers monitored its affairs.

## THE IMPORTANCE OF TOBACCO

Ironically, the demise of the Virginia Company helped the colony succeed. In their search for a marketable product, settlers had begun growing tobacco after 1610. Europeans acquired a taste for tobacco in the late sixteenth century when the Spanish brought samples from the West Indies and Florida. The first cargo of Virginia-grown tobacco arrived in England in 1617 and sold at a profitable 3 shillings per pound.

Between 1627 and 1669, annual tobacco exports climbed from 250,000 pounds to more than 15 million pounds. As the supply grew, the price per pound plunged from 13 pence in 1624 to a mere penny in the late 1660s, where it remained for the next half-century. What had once been a luxury product thus became affordable for Europeans of average means. Now thoroughly dependent on tobacco for their livelihood, the only way colonists could compensate for falling prices was to grow even more, pushing exports to England to more than 20 million pounds per year by the late 1670s (see Figure 2–2).

Tobacco shaped nearly every aspect of Virginia society, from patterns of settlement to the recruitment of colonists. Planters scrambled to claim lands near navigable rivers so that ships could reach their plantations and carry their crops to market. As a result, the colonists dispersed into plantations located along waterways instead of settling in compact communities. Settlers competed to produce the biggest and best crop and get it to market the fastest, hoping to enjoy even a small price advantage over everyone else.

Tobacco kept workers busy nine months of the year. Planters sowed seeds in the early spring, transplanted seedlings a few weeks later, and spent the summer pinching off the tops of the plants (to produce larger leaves) and removing worms. After the harvest, the leaves were "cured"—dried in ventilated sheds—and packed in large barrels. During the winter, planters

Read the **Document**

at **www.myhistorylab.com**
*From Then to Now Online:*
*Tobacco and the American Economy*

C.Smith taketh the King of Pamavnkee prisoner  1608

This illustration shows John Smith seizing the scalplock of Opechancanough, Chief Powhatan's brother, during an English raid on an Indian village. Smith released his prisoner only after Indians ransomed him with corn. Thirteen years later, Opechancanough led a surprise attack against the colonists.

**QUICK REVIEW**

**Tobacco**

- 1617: Virginia-grown tobacco arrives in England.
- 1669: Tobacco exports reach 15 million pounds annually.
- Labor demand of tobacco farming stimulates immigration to the colonies.

**proprietary colony**   A colony created when the English monarch granted a huge tract of land to an individual or group of individuals, who became "lords proprietor."

**Puritans**   Individuals who believed that Queen Elizabeth's reforms of the Church of England had not gone far enough in improving the church. Puritans led the settlement of Massachusetts Bay Colony.

cleared and fenced more land and made barrels for next year's crop. Working on his own, one planter could tend two thousand plants, which yielded about 500 pounds of cured tobacco. When the price was high, this supplied a comfortable income. But as the price plummeted, planters could keep up only by producing more tobacco, and to do that they needed a large labor force.

The planters turned to England, importing thousands of indentured servants, or contract workers, who (like Richard Frethorne) agreed to a fixed term of labor, usually four to seven years, in exchange for free passage to Virginia. The master provided food, shelter, clothing, and, at the end of the term of service, "freedom dues" paid in corn and clothing. Between 1625 and 1640, one thousand or more indentured servants arrived each year. The vast majority, came from the ranks of England's unemployed, who emigrated in hopes of "bettering their condition in a Growing Country."

Most found such hopes quickly dashed. Servants died in alarming numbers from disease, and those who survived faced years of backbreaking labor. Masters squeezed as much work out of them as possible with long hours and harsh discipline. New obstacles faced servants who managed to survive their terms of indenture. For every ex-servant who became a landholder, dozens died in poverty. To prevent freed servants from becoming economic rivals, established planters avoided selling them good land, particularly after tobacco prices hit bottom in the 1660s. Many ex-servants found land only in places less suitable for tobacco cultivation and more vulnerable to Indian attack. As a result, they became a discontented group. In 1675, their discontent would flare into rebellion (discussed in Chapter 3).

## MARYLAND: A REFUGE FOR CATHOLICS

The success of tobacco in Virginia encouraged further English colonization in the Chesapeake region. In 1632, King Charles I granted 10 million acres of land north of the bay to the nobleman George Calvert, Lord Baltimore. Unlike Virginia, which was founded by a joint-stock company, Maryland was a **proprietary colony**—the sole possession of Calvert and his heirs. They owned all the land, which they could divide up as they pleased, and had the right to set up the colony's government.

Calvert, who was Catholic, intended Maryland to be a refuge for others of his faith. When Queen Elizabeth's accession made England a Protestant nation, Catholics became a disadvantaged minority. In Maryland, Calvert wanted Catholic colonists to enjoy economic and political power. He intended to divide the land into manors—large private estates like those of medieval England—and distribute them to wealthy Catholic friends. These manorial lords would live on rents collected from tenant farmers.

Calvert died before settlement began, and it was the sad fate of his son, Cecilius, to see his father's plans unravel. The majority of colonists, who began arriving in 1634, were Protestants who despised Catholics. Refusing to live as tenants on Catholic estates, they claimed land of their own—a process that accelerated after 1640, when Maryland adopted a headright system like Virginia's as a way to recruit settlers.

Maryland's problems intensified when civil war broke out in England in 1642. For years, political and religious disputes had divided the nation. Charles I, who became king in 1625, clashed with the **Puritans,** who called for further reform of the Church of England. He also antagonized many government leaders by dissolving Parliament in 1629 and ruling on his own for

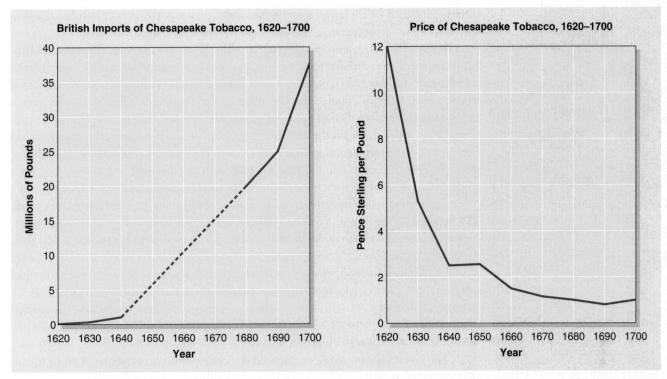

FIGURE 2–2    **The Supply and Price of Chesapeake Tobacco, 1620–1700**    Tobacco cultivation dominated the economy of the Chesapeake region throughout the seventeenth century. As planters brought more and more land under cultivation, the amount of tobacco exported to Britain shot up and the price plummeted. (As the dashed line indicates, no data on tobacco imports are available for the years 1640–1680.)

*Data Source:* Russell R. Menard, "The Tobacco Industry in the Chesapeake Colonies, 1617–1730: An Interpretation," *Research in Economic History,* 5 (1980), app. Jai Press, Inc.

eleven years. Needing funds to suppress a rebellion in Scotland in 1640, however, Charles was forced to recall Parliament. Its leaders, sympathetic to the Puritan cause, quickly turned against him. Both king and Parliament recruited armies and went to war in 1642. Parliamentary forces triumphed, and in 1649, they executed Charles. For the next decade, England was governed as a protectorate, not a monarchy. Oliver Cromwell, a Puritan general, ruled until his death in 1658. His son, Richard, proved an inept successor, however, and in 1660 a group of army officers invited Charles's exiled son to accept the throne.

During the 1640s and 1650s, Maryland Protestants took advantage of the upheaval in England to contest the Calverts' control of the colony. To pacify them, Cecilius Calvert established a legislature, assuming that Protestants would dominate the elective lower house while he could appoint Catholics to the upper house. In 1649, Calvert also approved the **Act for Religious Toleration,** the first law in America to call for freedom of worship for all Christians, but even this brought no peace. The Protestant majority continued to resist Catholic political influence.

Instead of a peaceful Catholic refuge, Maryland soon resembled neighboring Virginia. Its settlers raised tobacco and imported as many indentured servants as possible. Throughout the seventeenth century, Protestants kept up their opposition to the proprietor's control and resisted Catholic efforts to govern the colony that was supposed to have been theirs.

## LIFE IN THE CHESAPEAKE COLONIES

Few people could have predicted how much life in the Chesapeake colonies would differ from England. Many differences stemmed from the region's distinctive population. Because of their labor needs, masters preferred to recruit young men in their teens and twenties as indentured servants, importing three or four times as many of them as women. As a result, the populations of Virginia and Maryland were overwhelmingly young and male. Even as late as 1700, Virginia had

**WHERE TO LEARN MORE**

St. Mary's City, Maryland
http://www.stmaryscity.org/

**Act for Religious Toleration**    The first law in America to call for freedom of worship for all Christians.

three English men for every two women. As a consequence of this gender imbalance, many male ex-servants found that marriage was as remote a possibility as landownership.

Malaria and other diseases inflicted hardship on nearly everyone. Few colonists lived past 50, and women's susceptibility to disease during pregnancy meant that many of them barely made it to 40. Such high mortality, combined with late marriages (because servants could not wed until their terms were up), limited the size of families and slowed population growth. As many as one out of four children died in their first year, and more died before age 20.

Under such conditions, the only way the populations of the Chesapeake colonies could grow during most of the seventeenth century was through immigration. The number of English settlers rose from about 8,000 in 1640 to 24,000 in 1660. Still mostly young and mostly male, the immigrants helped the region's distinctive demographic patterns persist until the end of the century.

These conditions hindered colonists from reproducing customary patterns of family life. The frequency of early death produced unusual households, containing various combinations of stepparents and children from different marriages. There were so many orphans in Maryland that the colony created special courts to protect their property. Many women would be widows at some point in their lives, which gave them temporary control over the family property. Husbands often arranged for their widows to manage their estates until the eldest son reached age 21. Few women received land outright, and if widows remarried, their new spouses usually took control of the estates left by their first husbands. As in England itself, the Chesapeake colonies accorded women little formal authority within society.

The precariousness of life encouraged settlers to invest every penny of profit in land and labor, postponing investment in goods that would bring a more comfortable existence. Poor settlers slept on the floor on straw mattresses and had few other furnishings, often not even a chair or bench to sit on. Rich planters owned more goods, but often of poor quality. Nearly everyone subsisted on a rude diet of pork and corn.

Rough as these conditions were, they far surpassed the circumstances of most native peoples in the Chesapeake. The English population may have been growing slowly, but it still overwhelmed the Indian population, which suffered high mortality from European diseases. By 1685, there were more than ten colonists for every Indian living in eastern Virginia. By that point, many Native Americans in the Chesapeake had retreated to isolated towns, in hopes of preserving control over dwindling lands and maintaining some independence from English domination.

## THE FOUNDING OF NEW ENGLAND

**WHY WERE** the English colonies in New England so different from those in the Chesapeake?

Even before permanent colonists arrived, New England's native population felt the effects of European contact. Between 1616 and 1618, a terrible epidemic swept through coastal New England, killing up to 90 percent of the Indians living there. The devastated survivors were struggling to cope with the consequences of this disaster just as the colonists began to arrive.

### THE PILGRIMS AND PLYMOUTH COLONY

Plymouth Colony, the first of the New England settlements, was founded in 1620. Its origins lay in religious disputes that had plagued England since the late sixteenth century. Most of Queen Elizabeth's subjects approved of her efforts to keep England a Protestant nation, but some reformers believed that she had not rid the Church of England of all Catholic practices. The enemies of these reformers, ridiculing them for wanting to purify the Church of England (or **Anglican** Church) of all corruption, called them Puritans.

English Puritans believed in an all-powerful God who, at the moment of Creation, determined which humans would be saved and which would be damned. They held that salvation came through faith alone, not good works, and urged believers to seek a direct, personal relationship

**Anglican** Of or belonging to the Church of England, a Protestant denomination.

with God. The centerpiece of their spiritual life was conversion: the transforming experience that occurred when individuals felt the stirrings of grace in their souls and began to hope that they were among the saved. Those who experienced conversion were considered saints.

Puritans believed that certain Anglican practices interfered with conversion and the believer's relationship with God. But what they hated most about the Anglican Church was that anyone could be a member. Puritans believed that everyone should attend church services, but they wanted church membership, which conferred the right to partake in the Lord's Supper, or communion, to be limited to saints who had experienced conversion.

Elizabeth and the rulers who followed her—who as monarchs were the "supreme heads" of the Church of England—tried to silence the Puritans. Some Puritans, known as **separatists,** concluded that the Church of England would never change and left it to form their own congregations. One such group, mainly from the village of Scrooby, in Nottinghamshire, became the core of Plymouth Colony.

The Scrooby separatists left England in 1607–1608 for Holland, where they stayed for more than a decade. Although they could worship in peace there, many struggled to make a living and feared that their children were being tempted by the worldly pleasures of Dutch city life. Some Scrooby separatists contemplated moving to America and contacted the Plymouth Company. Called **Pilgrims** because they thought of themselves as spiritual wanderers, they were joined by other separatists and by nonseparatist "strangers" hired to help get the colony started. In all, 102 men, women, and children set sail on the *Mayflower* in September 1620.

After a long and miserable voyage, they landed near Massachusetts Bay. To prevent the colony from disintegrating into factions before their ship had even landed, the leaders drafted the Mayflower Compact, a document that bound all signers to abide by the decisions of the majority.

The Pilgrims settled at Plymouth, the site of a Wampanoag village recently depopulated by disease. Their first winter, the Pilgrims suffered through a terrible "starving time" that left nearly half of them dead.

When two English-speaking natives, Squanto and Samoset, emerged from the woods the next spring, the surviving Pilgrims marveled at them as "special instruments sent of God." Samoset had learned English from traders, and Squanto had learned it in England, where he lived for a time after being kidnapped by a sea captain. The two native men approached the Pilgrims on behalf of Massasoit, the Wampanoag leader. Although suspicious of the newcomers, the Wampanoags thought the Pilgrims might be useful allies against their enemies, the Narragansetts, who had escaped the recent epidemics.

In 1621, the Wampanoags and the Pilgrims signed a treaty of alliance, although each side understood its terms differently. The Pilgrims assumed that Massasoit had submitted to the superior authority of King James, whereas Massasoit assumed that he and the English king were equal partners.

Plymouth remained small, poor, and weak, never exceeding about seven thousand settlers. Although its families achieved a modest prosperity, the colony as a whole never produced more than small shipments of furs, fish, and timber to sell in England. After 1630, the first New England colony was overshadowed by a new and more powerful neighbor, Massachusetts Bay.

## MASSACHUSETTS BAY COLONY AND ITS OFFSHOOTS

The Puritans who founded Massachusetts shared many beliefs with the Pilgrims of Plymouth Colony—with one important exception. Unlike the Pilgrims, most Massachusetts settlers rejected separatism, insisting that the Anglican Church could be reformed. Their goal was to create godly churches to serve as models for the English church.

In 1629, a group of Puritan merchants and gentlemen received a royal charter for a joint-stock enterprise, the Massachusetts Bay Company, to set up a colony north of Plymouth. John Winthrop, a prosperous lawyer, was selected as the colony's governor. In the spring of 1630, a fleet of eleven ships carried Winthrop and about a thousand men, women, and children across the Atlantic.

**covenant** A contract with God, binding settlers to meet their religious obligations in return for God's favor.

**Pequot War** Conflict between English settlers and Pequot Indians over control of land and trade in eastern Connecticut.

John Winthrop (1588–1649) served as the Massachusetts Bay Colony's governor for most of its first two decades. Throughout his life, Winthrop—like many fellow Puritans—struggled to live a godly life in a corrupt world.

**Stability, conformity, and intolerance.** Winthrop described the settlers' mission in New England as a **covenant,** or contract, with God, binding them to meet their religious obligations in return for God's favor. The settlers also created covenants to define their duties to one another. When they founded towns, colonists signed covenants agreeing to live together in peace. Worshipers in each town's church likewise wrote covenants binding themselves to live in harmony.

The desire for peace and purity could breed intolerance. Settlers scrutinized their neighbors for signs of unacceptable behavior. Standards for church membership were strict; only those who could convincingly describe their conversion experiences were admitted. But the insistence on covenants and conformity also created a remarkably stable society.

That stability was enhanced by the development of representative government. By 1634, colony leaders had converted the charter of the Massachusetts Bay Company into a plan of government. The General Court, which initially included only the shareholders of the joint-stock company, was transformed into a two-house legislature. Freemen—adult males who held property and were church members—elected representatives to the lower house, as well as eighteen members (called "assistants") to the upper house. They also chose a governor and deputy governor.

**The Connecticut Valley and the Pequot War.** At least thirteen thousand settlers came to New England and established dozens of towns between 1630 and 1642, when the outbreak of the English Civil War halted emigration. The progress of settlement was generally untroubled in coastal Massachusetts, but when colonists moved into the Connecticut River Valley, tensions with Indians developed. These erupted in 1637 in the brief, tragic conflict called the **Pequot War.**

English settlers from Massachusetts first arrived in the Connecticut Valley in the mid-1630s. When English settlers poured into Connecticut and demanded Pequot submission to English authority, the Pequots turned against them. A struggle for control over the land and trade of eastern Connecticut began.

The colonists allied with the Pequots' enemies, the Narragansetts and Mohegans. Together they overwhelmed the Pequots. After the surviving Pequots had fled or been sold into slavery, more settlers moved to Connecticut, which soon declared itself a separate colony. In 1639, the settlers adopted the Fundamental Orders, creating a government similar to that of Massachusetts, and the English government granted them a charter in 1662.

**Roger Williams and the founding of Rhode Island.** Massachusetts spun off other colonies as its population expanded in the 1630s and dissenters ran afoul of its intolerant government. Roger Williams, who founded Rhode Island, was one of these religious dissenters. Williams was a separatist minister who declared that because Massachusetts churches had not rejected the Church of England, they shared its corruption. He opposed government interference in religious affairs and argued for the separation of church and state. Williams even attacked the Massachusetts charter, insisting that the king had no right to grant Indian lands to English settlers.

When Williams refused to be silenced, the General Court banished him, intending to ship him back to England. But in the winter of 1635, Williams slipped away. He and a few followers found refuge among the Narragansett Indians, from whom he purchased land for the village of Providence, founded in 1636. More towns sprang up nearby when a new religious challenge sent additional refugees to Rhode Island from Massachusetts.

**Anne Hutchinson's challenge to the Bay Colony.**   Anne Hutchinson arrived in Boston from England with her husband and seven children in 1634. Welcomed by the town's women for her talents as a midwife, she began to hold religious meetings in her house. During these meetings, she denounced several ministers, who had taught worshipers that there were spiritual exercises they could perform that might prepare them for sainthood.

Many people, including prominent Boston merchants, flocked to Hutchinson's meetings. But her critics believed her to be a dangerous antinomian (someone who claimed to be free from obedience to moral law), because she seemed to maintain that saints were accountable only to God and not to any worldly authority. Her opponents also objected to her teaching of mixed groups of men and women. Colony magistrates arrested her and tried her for sedition—that is, for advocating the overthrow of the government.

The court found her guilty and banished her. With many of her followers, she moved to Rhode Island, where Roger Williams had proclaimed a policy of religious toleration. Other followers returned to England or moved north to what became in 1679 the colony of New Hampshire.

## Families, Farms, and Communities in Early New England

"This plantation and that of Virginia went not forth upon the same reasons," declared one of Massachusetts's founders. Virginians came "for profit," whereas New Englanders emigrated to bear witness to their Puritan faith. Unlike the unmarried young men who moved in great numbers to Virginia, most New Englanders settled with their families. This had important implications for the development of New England society.

Even though emigration from England slowed to a trickle after 1642, New England's population continued to grow. By 1660, the number of colonists exceeded thirty-three thousand. This demographic expansion stemmed from the initial emigration of families. With a more balanced sex ratio (about three men to two women) than there was in the early Chesapeake, marriage and childbearing were more common.

Settling in a region with a healthier climate, New Englanders were largely spared early deaths from malaria and other diseases that ravaged the Chesapeake settlers. Most children survived to reach adulthood and form families of their own. Many New Englanders enjoyed unusually long lives for the seventeenth century, reaching their seventies and even eighties.

**Women in early New England.**   In New England, as in other colonies and England itself, women were assumed to be legally and economically dependent on the men in their families. Since fewer New England marriages were shortened by the early death of a spouse, fewer New England women experienced widowhood, the one time in their lives when they might enjoy legal independence and exercise control over property.

Women's economic contributions were central to the family's success. In addition to caring for children, cooking, sewing, gardening, and cleaning, most women engaged in household production and traded the fruits of their labor with other families. They sold eggs, made butter and cheese, brewed beer, and wove cloth. Wives of shopkeepers and craftsmen occasionally managed their husbands' businesses when the men had to travel or became ill.

**Community and economic life.**   New Englanders' lives were shaped not only by their families but also by their towns. Unlike Chesapeake colonists, who tended to disperse into separate plantations, New Englanders clustered into communities that might contain fifty or a hundred families. The Massachusetts government strongly encouraged town formation by granting land to groups of families who promised to settle together. Once they found a town they liked, families tended to stay in place. Grown children, inheriting parental estates and finding spouses nearby, often settled in the same community as their parents.

**Read** the **Document**

at **www.myhistorylab.com**
*The Trial of Anne Hutchinson* (1638)

**QUICK REVIEW**

**Anne Hutchinson**

- Arrived in Boston with her family in 1634.
- Began to hold religious meetings in her house.
- Found guilty of sedition and banished from Massachusetts.

## AMERICAN VIEWS

### A Colonist Marvels at New England's Abundant Wildfowl (1634)

William Wood journeyed twice to Massachusetts, arriving first in 1629 for a four-year stay, and then returning from England in 1636 to remain in the colony for the rest of his life. In 1634, he published New England's Prospect, an account of the natural resources of the region, its native inhabitants, and the new towns founded by the colonists. He described an abundance of animal life that would eventually diminish. The millions of pigeons mentioned below, for instance, were almost certainly passenger pigeons, which became extinct in 1914 due to overhunting and the disappearance of the large forests they needed to survive.

- **What** do Wood's descriptions suggest about the colonists' approach to their environment?
- **Why** does Wood assign a monetary value to certain birds?
- **Why** does Wood repeatedly urge his readers to believe him when he describes such large numbers of wildfowl?

The pigeon of that country is something different from our dovehouse pigeons in England . . . They have long tails like a magpie. And they seem not so big, because they carry not so many feathers on their backs as our English doves, yet are they as big in body. These birds come into the country to go to the north parts in the beginning of our spring, at which time (if I may be counted worthy to believed in a thing that is not so strange as true) I have seen them fly as if the airy regiment had been pigeons, seeing neither beginning nor ending, length or breadth of these millions of millions. The shouting of people, the rattling of guns, and pelting of small shot could not drive them out of their course, but so they continued for four or five hours together. . . . Many of them build amongst the pine trees, . . . joining nest to nest and tree to tree by their nests, so that the sun never sees the ground in that place, from whence the Indians fetch whole loads of them. . . .

The turkey is a very large bird, of a black color yet white in flesh, much bigger than our English turkey. . . . Of these sometimes there will be forty, threescore, and an hundred of a flock, sometimes more and sometimes less. . . . Such as love turkey hunting must follow it in winter after a new fallen snow, when he may follow them by their tracks. Some have killed ten or a dozen in half a day. If they can be found towards an evening and watched where they perch, if one come about ten or eleven of the clock, he may shoot as often as he will; they will sit unless they be slenderly wounded. These turkey remain all the year long. The price of a good turkey cock is four shillings, and he is well worth it, for he may be in weight forty pound, a hen two shillings. . . .

The geese of the country be of three sorts: first a brant goose, which is a goose almost like the wild goose in England; the price of one of these is six pence. The second kind is a white goose, almost as big as an English tame goose. These come in great flocks about Michaelmas [September]. Sometimes there will be two or three thousand in a flock . . . The price of one of these is eight pence. The third kind of geese is a great gray goose with a black neck and a black and white head, strong of flight, and these be a great deal bigger than the ordinary geese of England . . . the price of a good gray goose is eighteen pence. . . .

The ducks of the country be very large ones and in great abundance, so is there of teal likewise. The price of a duck is six pence, of a teal three pence. If I should tell you how some have killed a hundred geese in a week, fifty ducks at a shot, forty teals at another, it may be counted impossible though nothing more certain.

*Source:* William Wood, *New England's Prospect,* ed. Alden T. Vaughan (Amherst, MA, 1977), pp. 50–52.

At the center of each town stood the meetinghouse, used as both a place of worship and a town hall. Massachusetts law required towns with at least fifty families to support a school (so children could learn to read the Bible), and men often wrangled at town meetings over the choice and salary of a schoolmaster. Townsmen tried, not always successfully, to reach decisions by consensus. To oversee day-to-day local affairs, they chose five to seven trusted neighbors to serve as selectmen. Each town could also elect two men to represent it in the colony legislature.

New England's stony soil and short growing season offered few ways to get rich, but most people achieved a modest prosperity. Their goal was to achieve a competency—enough property to ensure the family's economic independence. Without the income generated by a staple crop like tobacco, New England farmers could not hire large numbers of indentured servants and so relied on family labor.

New Englanders regularly traded goods and services with their neighbors. A carpenter might erect a house—usually larger and sturdier than the ramshackle Chesapeake dwellings—in return for barrels of salted beef. Men with several teenaged sons sent them to help neighbors whose children were still small. Midwives delivered babies in return for cheese or eggs. Women nursed sick neighbors, whom they might later call on for similar help. These transactions allowed most New Englanders to enjoy a comfortable life, one that many Virginians might have envied.

New England prospered by developing a diversified economy less vulnerable to depression than Virginia's. New Englanders became such skilled shipbuilders and seafaring merchants that by the 1670s, London merchants complained about competition from them. England itself had little use for the dried fish, livestock, salted meat, and wood products that New England vessels carried, but enterprising merchants found exactly the market they needed in the West Indies.

# COMPETITION IN THE CARIBBEAN

The Spanish claimed all Caribbean islands by right of Columbus's discovery, but during the seventeenth century, France, the Netherlands, and England acquired their own island colonies. Europeans competed for these islands at first in the hope that they would yield precious metals and provide bases for privateering expeditions. It eventually became clear that the islands would produce treasure of another sort—sugar, which was in great demand in Europe. In order to reap the enormous profits that sugar could bring, Caribbean planters of all nationalities imported enormous numbers of African people to work as slaves under the harshest conditions to be found in the New World.

**WHAT WAS** the connection between sugar cultivation and slavery in the Caribbean?

## SUGAR AND SLAVES

The Spanish and Portuguese first experimented with sugar production on the Canaries and other Atlantic islands in the fifteenth century. Europeans prized sugar as a sweetener, preservative, decoration—even a medicine—and paid high prices for it. Columbus accordingly brought sugar canes to the New World on his second voyage, in 1493. Soon after the Spanish began growing sugar on Santo Domingo, they began importing African slaves as workers, because Indian slaves were dying in great numbers. The Spanish brought sugar to the South American mainland, as did the Portuguese, who turned Brazil into one of the world's major producers.

At first, English colonists who came to the West Indies in the 1620s and 1630s raised tobacco and imported indentured servants to work their fields. By that time, however, tobacco prices were dropping. Moreover, the disease environment of the West Indies proved even harsher than in the Chesapeake, and settlers died in great numbers.

By the 1640s, a Barbados planter boasted of "a great change on this island of late from the worse to the better, praised be God." That change was a shift from tobacco to sugar cane. Dutch merchants helped finance this transition. Sugar rapidly transformed the West Indies. Planters deforested whole islands to raise sugar cane. They stopped planting food crops and raising livestock—thereby creating a demand for lumber and provisions that boosted New England's economy.

For some years after the transition to sugar, English planters continued to import white indentured servants, including kidnapped English and Irish youths, and supplemented the labor force with African slaves. Due to the islands' unhealthy environment and harsh working conditions, servants died in great numbers. England could barely meet the demand for workers, and English workers, if they survived, often proved rebellious. The English switched to African laborers, whom they considered better suited to agricultural work in a tropical climate. The planters' decision had an enormous impact on English colonial life, first in the islands and then on the mainland, where slavery would develop later in the seventeenth century (see Chapter 3).

African slaves working at a sugar mill in the West Indies, probably on a Dutch-owned island: line engraving, 17th century.

**slave codes** A series of laws passed mainly in the southern colonies in the late seventeenth and early eighteenth centuries to define the status of slaves and codify the denial of basic civil rights to them.

### QUICK REVIEW

#### Slave Codes

- Slavery was a lifelong condition that passed from parents to children.
- Slaves had no legal rights.
- Masters were all but exempt from prosecution for mistreatment of slaves.
- Slaves were subject to punishment at the discretion of masters.

## A BIRACIAL SOCIETY

As happened on virtually all the Caribbean islands, the English West Indies developed a biracial plantation society—the first in the English colonial world. By 1700, more than 250,000 slaves had been brought to the English islands, and they soon constituted a majority of the population.

Laws, sometimes called **slave codes,** declared slavery to be a lifelong condition that passed from slave parents to their children. Slaves had no legal rights and were under the complete control of their masters. Only rarely would masters who killed slaves face prosecution, and those found guilty were subject only to fines. Slaves, in contrast, faced appalling punishments even for minor offenses. They could be whipped, branded, or maimed for stealing food or harboring a runaway compatriot. Serious crimes such as murder or arson brought execution without trial. Slaves who rebelled were burned to death.

Astonishingly, slaves maintained some elements of normal life even under these brutal conditions. When masters began to import African women as well as men—hoping to create a self-reproducing labor force—slaves formed families and preserved at least some African traditions. They gave their children African names. They celebrated and worked to the rhythms of African music. And slaves drew on their West African heritage to perform elaborate funeral rituals, often burying their dead with food and other goods to accompany them on the journey to the afterlife.

White planters, profiting handsomely from their slaves' toil, lived better than many English gentlemen. But sugar made relatively few white colonists wealthy. Its production required a heavy investment in land, slaves, mills, and equipment. As great planters took vast amounts of land for themselves, freed servants and small farmers struggled to survive. After 1650, many of these poor men, looking for other places to live, headed for the mainland. They were joined by planters looking for a place to expand their operations.

# THE RESTORATION COLONIES

The initial burst of English colonization ended in 1640 when England tottered on the brink of civil war. With the restoration of Charles II to the throne in 1660, however, interest in North America revived. During his reign (1660–1685), four new colonies—Carolina, Pennsylvania, New Jersey, and New York—were created (see Map 2–3). All were proprietary colonies, essentially the private property of the people to whom they had been given. (See the Overview table, English Colonies in the Seventeenth Century.)

**HOW DID** the proprietors of the Restoration colonies shape their development?

## EARLY CAROLINA: COLONIAL ARISTOCRACY AND SLAVE LABOR

In 1663, Charles II granted a group of supporters an enormous tract of land stretching from southern Virginia to northern Florida. The proprietors, who included several Barbados planters, called their colony Carolina, after *Carolus*, the Latin form of the king's name.

One of the proprietors, Anthony Ashley Cooper, worked closely with his secretary, John Locke, to devise the **Fundamental Constitutions of Carolina.** This plan to ensure the colony's stability linked property ownership and political rights to a hierarchical social order. It called for the creation of a colonial aristocracy, who would own two-fifths of the land and wield extensive political power. Below them, a large class of freeholders would own small farms and elect representatives to an assembly. At the bottom of the social order would be slaves. This plan never went into effect. People moved in from Virginia and the West Indies and settled where they pleased. They even voted in the assembly to reject the Fundamental Constitutions.

The colonists at first raised livestock to be sold to the West Indies. But the introduction of rice in the 1690s transformed the settlers' economy, making it, as one planter noted, "as much their staple Commodity, as Sugar is to Barbados and Jamaica, or Tobacco to Virginia and Maryland." The English had never grown rice, but West Africans had. Rice cultivation in Carolina coincided with an increase in the number of African slaves there, who probably introduced the crop. Ironically, the profits earned from rice persuaded Carolina planters to invest even more heavily in slave labor.

Carolina society soon resembled the sugar islands from which many of its founders had come. By 1708, there were more black slaves than white settlers; two decades after that, black people outnumbered white people by two to one. Rice farming required a substantial investment in land, labor, and equipment, including dikes and dams for flooding fields. Those who could afford such an investment set themselves up as planters in Carolina's coastal rice district, acquiring large estates and forcing poorer settlers to move elsewhere.

Some of these dislocated settlers went to the northern part of Carolina, where the land and climate were unsuited to rice. There they raised tobacco and livestock, and produced pitch, tar, and timber products from the region's pine forests. So different were the two regions that the colony formally split into two provinces—North and South Carolina—in 1729.

**Fundamental Constitutions of Carolina**   A complex plan for organizing the colony of Carolina, drafted in 1669 by Anthony Ashley Cooper and John Locke.

South Carolina rice planters became some of the wealthiest colonists on the mainland. But their luxurious style of life came at a price. As Carolina's slave population grew, planters dreaded the prospect of slave rebellion. To avert this nightmare, they enacted slave codes as harsh as those of the sugar islands. Carolina evolved into a racially divided society founded on the oppression of a black majority and permeated by fear.

**QUICK REVIEW**

**Rice and Slavery**
- 1690s: Rice introduced in Carolina.
- 1708: Black slaves outnumber white settlers.
- 1730s: Blacks outnumber whites two to one.

## PENNSYLVANIA: THE DREAM OF TOLERATION AND PEACE

Even as early Carolina diverged from the plans of its founders, another Englishman dreamed of creating a colonial utopia. William Penn put his plans into action in 1681, when Charles II

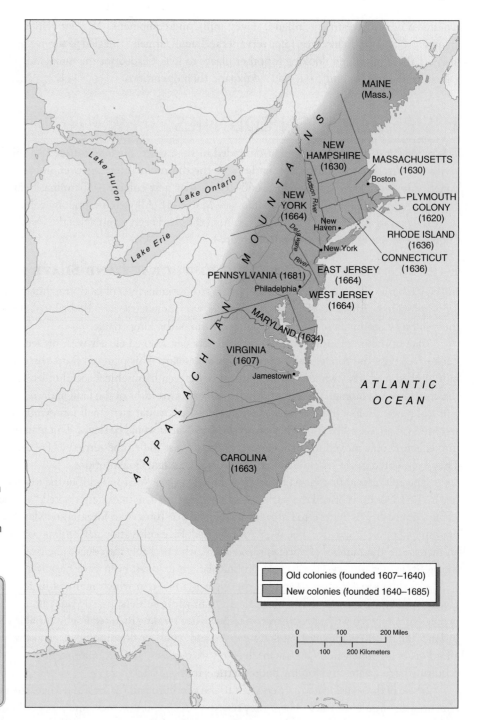

**MAP 2–3 English North American Colonies, c. 1685** After the restoration of Charles II in 1660, several large proprietary colonies joined earlier English settlements in New England and the Chesapeake. By 1685, a growing number of English settlers solidified England's claim to the Atlantic coast from Maine (then part of Massachusetts Bay Colony) to the southern edge of Carolina.

**How might** the establishment of the new colonies (founded 1640–1685) have shaped the development of the old colonies (founded 1607–1640)? What connections were beginning to emerge between the British colonies by the end of the seventeenth century?

**Quakers** Members of the Society of Friends, a radical religious group that arose in the mid-seventeenth century. Quakers rejected formal theology, focusing instead on the Holy Spirit that dwelt within them.

granted him a huge tract of land north of Maryland. Penn intended his colony to be a model of justice and peace, as well as a refuge for members of the Society of Friends, or **Quakers,** a persecuted religious sect to which Penn belonged.

The Society of Friends was one of many radical religious groups that emerged in England during the civil war. Rejecting predestination, they maintained that every soul had a spark of grace and that salvation was possible for all who heeded that "Inner Light." Instead of formal religious services, Quakers held meetings at which silence reigned until someone, inspired by the Inner Light, rose to speak.

Quaker beliefs had disturbing social and political implications. Although they did not advocate complete equality of the sexes, Quakers granted women spiritual equality with men, allowing them to preach, hold separate prayer meetings, and exercise authority over "women's matters." Arguing that social distinctions were not the work of God, Quakers refused to defer to their "betters." Because their faith required them to renounce the use of force, Quakers refused to perform military service, which their enemies considered tantamount to treason.

When English authorities began harassing Quakers, William Penn, who was himself jailed briefly, conceived his plan for a New World refuge. Using his father's connection with the king, he acquired the land that became Pennsylvania ("Penn's Woods") and recruited settlers from among Europe's oppressed peoples and persecuted religious sects. By 1700, about eighteen thousand emigrants had left England, Wales, Scotland, Ireland, and various German provinces for the new colony.

Many came in families and settled in an area occupied by the Delaware Indians, whose numbers, though still substantial, had recently been reduced by disease and warfare. The "holy experiment" required colonists to live "as Neighbours and friends" with the Indians as well as with one another. Penn aimed to accomplish this by paying Indians for land and regulating trade. As long as Penn controlled his colony, relations between the settlers and the Indians were generally peaceful. Relations between Penn and the settlers, however, were less cordial.

In the **Frame of Government** he devised for Pennsylvania, Penn remained true to his Quaker principles with a provision allowing for religious freedom. But true to his aristocratic origins, he designed a legislature with limited powers and reserved considerable authority for himself. When Penn returned to England after a brief stay in the colony (1682–1684), the settlers began squabbling among themselves. The governor and council, both appointed by Penn, fought with elected members of the assembly. Penn's opponents—many of whom were fellow Quakers—objected to his proprietary privileges, including his control of foreign trade and his collection of fees from landholders. Settlers on the lower Delaware River, which the crown had added to Penn's colony to give its port city, Philadelphia, access to the sea, gained autonomy for themselves with their own legislature, in effect creating an unofficial colony that later became Delaware.

By 1720, Pennsylvania's ethnically and religiously diverse colonists numbered more than thirty thousand. The colony, with some of the richest farmland along the Atlantic coast, was widely known as the "best poor man's country in the world." Growing wheat and other crops, the settlers lived mostly on scattered farms rather than in towns. From the busy port of Philadelphia, ships carried much of the harvest to markets in the West Indies and southern Europe.

## NEW NETHERLAND BECOMES NEW YORK

The proprietary colonies of New York and New Jersey were carved out of the Dutch colony of New Netherland. Competition between the English and the Dutch intensified in the mid-seventeenth century as the two peoples struggled for trade supremacy on the high seas. Their antagonism generated two Anglo-Dutch wars in 1652–1654 and 1665–1667. In the New World, tensions were heightened by the presence of English colonists on Long Island, which the Dutch claimed for themselves.

In 1664, Charles II brought matters to a head by claiming that since the site of New Netherland lay within the bounds of the original charter of Virginia, the land belonged to England. He granted the territory to his brother James, duke of York, who sent ships to back up England's claim. Their arrival provoked a rebellion by Long Island's English colonists, leading the Dutch governor, Peter Stuyvesant—who commanded just 150 soldiers—to surrender without firing a shot.

The duke of York became proprietor of this new English possession, which was renamed New York. James immediately created another colony, New Jersey, which he granted to his supporters.

New York, which James retained for himself, was the most valuable part of the former Dutch colony. It included the port of New York City (the former New Amsterdam) and the Hudson Valley with its fur trade. James encouraged Dutch colonists to remain and promoted immigration from England to strengthen the colony and gain income from land sales. By 1700, the settlers numbered twenty thousand.

**WHERE TO LEARN MORE**

Pennsbury Manor, Morrisville, Pennsylvania
http://www.pennsburymanor.org

**Frame of Government** William Penn's constitution for Pennsylvania, which included a provision allowing for religious freedom.

## OVERVIEW English Colonies in the Seventeenth Century

| Colony | Date of Founding | Established Religion | Economy | Government |
|---|---|---|---|---|
| Virginia | 1607 | Anglican | Tobacco | Royal (after 1625) |
| Plymouth | 1620 | Puritan | Mixed farming | Corporate |
| St. Christopher | 1624 | Anglican | Sugar | Royal |
| Barbados | 1627 | Anglican | Sugar | Royal |
| Nevis | 1628 | Anglican | Sugar | Royal |
| Massachusetts (including present-day Maine) | 1630 | Puritan | Mixed farming, fishing, shipbuilding | Corporate |
| New Hampshire | 1630 (first settlement, annexed to Massachusetts 1643–1679) | Puritan | Mixed farming | Corporate (royal after 1679) |
| Antigua | 1632 | Anglican | Sugar | Royal |
| Montserrat | 1632 | Anglican | Sugar | Royal |
| Maryland | 1634 | None (Anglican after 1692) | Tobacco | Proprietary |
| Rhode Island | 1636 | None | Mixed farming | Corporate |
| Connecticut | 1636 | Puritan | Mixed farming | Corporate |
| New Haven | 1638 | Puritan | Mixed farming | Corporate |
| Jamaica | 1655 (captured from Spanish) | Anglican | Sugar | Royal |
| Carolina | 1663 | Anglican | Rice | Proprietary |
| New York | 1664 (captured from Dutch) | None | Mixed farming, furs | Proprietary (royal after 1685) |
| New Jersey | 1664 | None | Mixed farming | Proprietary |
| Pennsylvania | 1681 | None | Wheat, mixed farming | Proprietary |

## CONCLUSION

Even as England gained a permanent foothold in North America, it faced vigorous competition from France and the Netherlands. A new Atlantic world was beginning to emerge as the migration of people and goods across the ocean linked the Old and New Worlds as never before.

Commerce was the main focus of the short-lived New Netherland colony and a more durable New France. Profits from the fur trade encouraged the French to maintain friendly relations with their Indian allies and ensured that French kings would closely monitor the colony's affairs. English colonization was a more haphazard process. English kings granted charters for new colonies and let them develop more or less on their own. England had no equivalent in the seventeenth century of the imperial bureaucracies Spain and France created to manage their New World holdings.

The result was a highly diverse set of English colonies stretching from the Maine coast to the Caribbean. Settlers adjusted to different environments, developed different economies and

James, Duke of York, received this map of New Amsterdam in 1664, when England seized New Netherland from the Dutch and the Duke became proprietor of the new colony of New York. The top of the map is oriented to the east, with the lower tip of Manhattan Island facing to the right.

labor systems, and worshiped in different churches. In South Carolina, New York, Pennsylvania, and the West Indies, most colonists were not even of English origin. What held these colonies together—besides their establishment under English charters and their enmity toward the Spanish and French—was an overlay of common English institutions of government. By the mid-1680s, all the colonies had legislatures that provided for self-government and laws and judicial institutions based on English models.

The planting of French, Dutch, and English colonies not only ended Spain's monopoly of settlement in North America but also challenged the Indians' hold on the continent. Forced to deal with a rising tide of settlers and often to choose sides between European rivals, native peoples adapted to rapidly changing circumstances. Transplanted Europeans adapted too, not only in their dealings with native peoples but also in finding and controlling the laborers they needed to make their colonies prosper. For English colonists this meant the widespread adoption of slavery, an institution that did not exist in England itself. For millions of Africans, the result was forced migration to the New World.

# WHERE TO LEARN MORE

**Jamestown Settlement, near Williamsburg, Virginia.** Site includes replicas of first English passenger ships to Virginia, a reconstructed Powhatan Village, the re-created James Fort, and galleries with Indian and English artifacts. Visitors can also see archaeological excavations of site of the actual James Fort, as well as sample artifacts recovered from the area. The website http://www.virtualjamestown.org/ offers a wealth of fascinating information about English and Indian settlement in the Jamestown area.

**St. Mary's City, Maryland.** Visitors to this site of the first permanent settlement under the Calvert family may tour the area and view exhibits and living history programs that describe life in early Maryland. The website http://www.stmaryscity.org/ contains information about the historic site of St. Mary's City and has links to a virtual tour of the area.

**Plimoth Plantation, Plymouth, Massachusetts.** A living history museum, Plimoth Plantation re-creates colony life in the year 1627. There are reproductions of the English village and a Wampanoag settlement. Visitors may also see a replica of the *Mayflower*. The website http://www.plimoth.org/ provides information for visitors.

**Pennsbury Manor, Morrisville, Pennsylvania.** A reconstruction of William Penn's seventeenth-century plantation, this site includes furnished buildings and restored gardens. Visitor information about the site and William Penn's life can be found at http://www.pennsburymanor.org/.

# REVIEW QUESTIONS

1. To what extent was Richard Frethorne's experience typical of that of English colonists in the New World? What were the causes of his distress?

2. Comparing French, Dutch, and English colonies, which ones attracted the most settlers, and which the fewest? In what colonies were women scarce? What impact did these differences in emigration have on the various colonies' development?

3. Which English settlements were proprietary colonies? Did they share any common characteristics? What plans did the various proprietors have for their colonies, and to what extent were those plans put into effect?

4. When Virginia's settlers first arrived, they encountered a numerous and powerful confederation of Powhatan Indians. New England's colonists, in contrast, began their settlements after epidemics had drastically reduced the local native population. In what ways did the presence or absence of substantial Indian populations affect each region's early history?

5. In both Massachusetts and Pennsylvania, religion figured prominently as a motive for settlement. What were the religious beliefs of the settlers in each colony, and how did those beliefs help shape each colony's development?

6. Three colonial regions—the Chesapeake, the West Indies, and Carolina—developed economies dependent on staple crops. What were those crops? In what ways did staple-crop agriculture shape society in each region?

7. In what ways did events in Europe affect the founding of colonies in North America?

# KEY TERMS

# myhistorylab Connections

PEARSON

Reinforce what you learned in this chapter by studying the many documents, images, maps, review tools, and videos available at **www.myhistorylab.com**.

## Read and Review

✓●─ **Study** and **Review**   **Study Plan: Chapter 2**

●◀●─ **Read** the **Document**

*Richard Frethorne, Letter to His Parents (1623)*

*John Winthrop, "A Model of Christian Charity" (1630)*

*Agreement between the Settlers at New Plymouth (Mayflower Compact) (1620)*

*Captain John Smith to Queen Anne (1617)*

*Father Isaac Jogues, Description of New York (1646)*

*Laws of Virginia (1610–1611)*

*Prenuptial Agreement (1653)*

*The Trial of Anne Hutchinson (1638)*

◉─ **See** the **Map** *The Colonies to 1740*

## Research and Explore

●◀●─ **Read** the **Document**

*Personal Journeys Online*

*From Then to Now Online: Tobacco and the American Economy*

*Exploring America: Exploitation of the Americas*

*Estate Inventories of Early Virginians*

*Exploring America: Jamestown*

((●─ **Hear** the **Audio**

Hear the audio files for Chapter 2 at
**www.myhistorylab.com**.

# 3

# A Meeting of Cultures

This illustration of the African slave trade shows a group of Africans taken from a slave ship that was captured by HMS *Undine*.
Top photo: King Philip's War Club. Published courtesy of Fruitlands Museums, Harvard, Massachusetts. Copyright © North Wind Picture Archives/North Wind Picture Archives – All rights reserved.

((•─Hear the **Audio**
Hear the audio files for Chapter 3 at **www.myhistorylab.com**.

### INDIANS AND EUROPEANS  *(page 59)*

**WHAT WERE** the consequences of trade between Indians and Europeans?

### AFRICANS AND EUROPEANS  *(page 67)*

**HOW AND** why did race-based slavery develop in British North America?

### EUROPEAN LABORERS IN EARLY AMERICA  *(page 76)*

**WHAT METHODS** did Europeans employ to acquire and manage labor in colonial America?

ONE AMERICAN JOURNEY

*One day [in 1756], when all our people were gone out to their work as usual, and only I and my sister were left to mind the house, two men and a woman got over our walls, and in a moment seized us both; and without giving us time to cry out, or to make any resistance, they stopped our mouths and ran off with us into the nearest wood. Here they tied our hands, and continued to carry us as far as they could. . . . Thus I continued to travel, both by land and by water, through different countries and various nations, till at the end of six or seven months after I had been kidnapped, I arrived at the sea coast. . . .*

*The first object that saluted my eyes when I arrived on the coast was the sea, and a slave ship, which was then riding at anchor, and waiting for its cargo. These filled me with astonishment, that was soon converted into terror, which I am yet at a loss to describe. . . . I was immediately handled and tossed up to see if I was sound, by some of the crew; and I was now persuaded that I had got into a world of bad spirits, and that they were going to kill me. Their complexions too, differing so much from ours, their long hair, and the language they spoke, which was very different from any I had ever heard, united to confirm me in this belief. . . . I asked. . . . if we were not to be eaten by those white men with horrible looks, red faces, and long hair. . . .*

*In a little time after, amongst the poor chained men, I found some of my own nation. . . . They gave me to understand we were to be carried to these white people's country to work for them. . . . [Many weeks later] we were landed up a river a good way from the sea, about Virginia county, where we saw few of our native Africans, and not one soul who could talk to me.*

Olaudah Equiano, *The Interesting Narrative of the Life of Olaudah Equiano, or Gustavus Vassa, The African.*

**Read the Document** at **www.myhistorylab.com**

Personal Journeys Online

- Pedro Naranjol, *Indian Account of the Pueblo Revolt,* 1680.
- Job ben Solomon, *Some Memoirs of the Life of Job,* 1734. Description of Job's capture and sale into slavery.
- Gottlieb Mittelberger, *Journey to Pennsylvania,* 1756. Description of the arrival of German redemptioners to Pennsylvania.

OLAUDAH EQUIANO, born in 1745 in the African kingdom of Benin, was only a boy when his terrifying journey to America began. The son of an Igbo chief, he was caught in the web of an expanding transatlantic slave trade that reached from the African interior to nearly every port town in the Americas and the Caribbean. From modest beginnings in the sixteenth century, the slave trade had expanded dramatically, transforming every society it touched. Equiano's Virginia scarcely resembled that of John Smith. Tobacco still reigned supreme, but by the mid-eighteenth century, more workers were black than white.

At the same time, in Virginia and elsewhere in North America, Indian peoples faced new challenges as they endeavored to maintain their independence despite a flood of immigrants from Europe and Africa. Indians employed different tactics—adaptation, coexistence, diplomacy, resistance—to assert their claims to land and their right to participate in the events and deliberations that affected their lives. The America to which Olaudah Equiano had been forcibly transported remained a place where Indian voices had to be heeded.

Equiano's journey did not end in Virginia. Over the next quarter-century, he traveled to other mainland colonies, the West Indies, England, Turkey, Portugal, and Spain. He worked as the servant of a naval officer, a barber, a laborer, an overseer, saving money to purchase his freedom. Such an extraordinary career testified to Equiano's resilience and determination. It also bore witness to the emergence of an international market for laborers, which—like slavery and Indian relations—shaped the development of North America. Thousands of people from England, Scotland, Ireland, and Germany attempted to take advantage of that market and seek their fortunes in America, increasing the white population and expanding onto new lands. The interactions of Indians, Africans, and Europeans created not one but many New Worlds. ✦

## INDIANS AND EUROPEANS

Although, by 1750, European colonists and African slaves together outnumbered Indians north of the Rio Grande, Native Americans still dominated much of the continent. Colonists remained clustered along the coasts, and some native peoples had scarcely seen any Europeans.

**WHAT WERE** the consequences of trade between Indians and Europeans?

The character of the relationship between Indians and Europeans depended on more than relative population size and the length of time they had been in contact. It was also shaped by the intentions of the newcomers—whether they came to extract resources, to trade, to settle, or to gain converts—and by the responses of Native American groups intent on preserving their cultures. The result was a variety of regionally distinctive New World communities.

### INDIAN WORKERS IN THE SPANISH BORDERLANDS

More than any other European colonists, the Spanish sought direct control over Indian laborers. Their success in doing so depended on two factors: the existence of sizable Indian communities and Spanish military force. Native villages provided workers and existing structures of government that the Spanish converted to their own uses. At the same time, Spanish soldiers ensured that the Indians obeyed orders even though they greatly outnumbered the colonists.

## CHRONOLOGY

| | |
|---|---|
| **1440s** | Portuguese enter slave trade in West Africa. |
| **c. 1450** | Iroquois form Great League of Peace and Power. |
| **1610–1614** | First war between English settlers and Powhatan Indians. |
| **1619** | First Africans arrive in Virginia. |
| **1622–1632** | Second war between English settlers and Powhatan Indians. |
| **1637** | Pequot War in New England. |
| **1640s** | Slave labor begins to dominate in the West Indies. |
| | First phase of the Beaver Wars. |
| **1651** | First "praying town" established at Natick, Massachusetts. |
| **1661** | Maryland law defines slavery as lifelong, inheritable status. |
| **1670** | Virginia law defines status of slaves. |
| **1675–1676** | King Philip's War in New England. |
| **1676** | Bacon's Rebellion in Virginia. |
| **1680** | Pueblo Revolt in New Mexico. |
| **1680s** | Second phase of Beaver Wars begins. |

| | |
|---|---|
| **1688–1697** | England and France fight the War of the League of Augsburg (known in America as King William's War). |
| **1690s** | Shift from white indentured servants to black slaves as principal labor force in the Chesapeake. |
| **1701** | Iroquois adopt policy of neutrality toward French and English. |
| **1711–1713** | Tuscarora War in Carolina. |
| **1713** | Beginnings of substantial Scottish, Scots-Irish, and German immigration to colonies. |
| **1715–1716** | Yamasee War in Carolina. |
| **1720s** | Black population begins to increase naturally in English mainland colonies. |
| **1730** | Major slave insurrection in Virginia. |
| **1732** | Georgia established. |
| **1739** | Stono Rebellion in South Carolina. |
| **1741** | Slave conspiracy discovered in New York City. |
| **1750** | Slavery legalized in Georgia. |
| **1760–1775** | Peak of European and African immigration to English colonies. |

**encomienda** In the Spanish colonies, the grant to a Spanish settler of a certain number of Indian subjects, who would pay him tribute in goods and labor.

**repartimiento** In the Spanish colonies, the assignment of Indian workers to labor on public works projects.

One important method of labor control was the **encomienda.** *Encomiendas*, granted to influential Spaniards in New Mexico, gave these colonists the right to collect tribute from the native peoples living on a specific piece of land. The tribute usually took the form of corn, blankets, and animal hides. It was not supposed to include forced labor, but often it did.

The Spanish also relied on the **repartimiento,** a mandatory draft of Indian labor for public projects. Laws stated that native workers should be paid and limited the length of their service, but the Spanish often ignored these provisions and sometimes compelled Indians to work on private estates.

The native peoples strongly resented these Spanish strategies. Spanish demands for labor and tribute remained constant, even when Indian populations declined from disease or crops failed, and workers who resisted were severely punished. Resentments simmered beneath a surface of cooperation until late in the seventeenth century, when long-standing native anger burst forth in rebellion.

## THE WEB OF TRADE

Not all economic exchanges between Indians and Europeans were directly coercive. Indians sometimes used trade relations to exert influence over Europeans. Native Americans thought of trade as one aspect of a broader alliance between peoples. Europeans who wished to trade with Indians had to prove their friendship by offering gifts and military aid as well as manufactured goods.

The French readily adapted to the Native American understanding of trade, realizing that good relations were essential to keeping New France's fur trade operating smoothly. The fur trade benefited Indians too. "The Beaver does everything perfectly well," noted one native leader, "it makes kettles, hatchets, swords, knives, bread; and, in short, it makes everything."

The benefits of trade were immediate and obvious; the problems were slower to appear. The one exception was the problem of disease, which followed almost immediately from Indians' contacts with European traders (see Figure 3–1). The Huron population declined by half in just six years between 1634 and 1640.

This detail from a map illustration depicts an encounter between a French trader and an Indian hunter in the Canadian wilderness. The exchange of European goods for furs was central to the economy of New France.

Although Indian hunters enjoyed considerable autonomy in their work, French merchants began to use economic pressure to control them. By supplying Indians with trade goods in advance, merchants obligated them to bring in furs as payment. Extending credit in this way allowed the French to control native workers without having to subjugate them.

The French could control the Indians through credit because native peoples had grown increasingly dependent on European manufactures. In many communities, Indians abandoned native crafts and instead relied on imported goods. As a result, they had no alternative but to increase their hunting in order to have furs to trade for what they needed. One consequence of this situation was overhunting; as early as the 1640s, beaver could no longer be found in much of New England, New York, and Pennsylvania.

Trade with Europeans eventually encouraged violence and warfare. Indians had fought one another before European colonization, but these wars were generally limited in scope and destructiveness. Warriors conducted raids mainly to seize captives rather than to kill large numbers of their enemies. After Europeans arrived, warriors raided their enemies to replace family members lost to disease and fought to avenge losses resulting from the fierce competition for a diminishing supply of fur-bearing animals. The proliferation of firearms made the conflicts deadlier, and more casualties led to further wars.

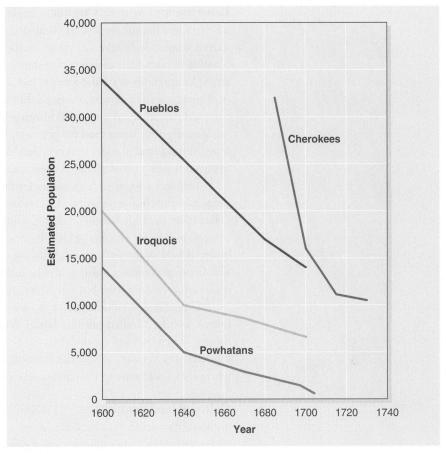

FIGURE 3–1   **Estimated Populations of Selected Indian Peoples, 1600–1730**   Indian populations shrank dramatically due to diseases brought by Europeans from the Old World. By about 1750, native peoples had become a minority of the inhabitants of America north of the Rio Grande.

*Data Sources:* Daniel Richter, *The Ordeal of the Longhouse* (1992); Helen Rountree, *Pocahontas's People* (1990); David Weber, *The Spanish Frontier in North America* (1992); Peter Wood et al., eds., *Powhatan's Mantle* (1989).

The **Beaver Wars,** a long struggle between the Hurons and the Iroquois that began in the 1640s, illustrated the ferocity of such contests. The Hurons were trading partners and allies with the French, and the Iroquois had forged ties with Dutch merchants in the Hudson River Valley. To satisfy the European demand for furs, the Hurons and Iroquois both hunted beaver at an unsustainable rate. By the 1630s, they had killed nearly all the beavers on their own lands and began to look elsewhere. The Hurons raised more corn to trade for furs with Indians living north of the Great Lakes, where beavers were still abundant. The Iroquois, however, began to raid Huron trading parties and attack Huron villages.

The Iroquois triumphed in this struggle largely because the Dutch supplied them with guns, whereas the French were reluctant to arm the Hurons. In the end, thousands of Hurons were killed or captured, and many others fled westward. The cycle of warfare did not end with the Hurons' destruction. The victorious Iroquois went on to challenge Indian nations near the Great Lakes and in the Ohio Valley.

**Beaver Wars**   Series of bloody conflicts, occurring between 1640s and 1680s, during which the Iroquois fought the Hurons and French for control of the fur trade in the east and the Great Lakes region.

**QUICK REVIEW**

**French-Indian Trade: The Costs for Indians**

◆ Disease.

◆ Dependence on European technology.

◆ Increased violence and warfare.

## DISPLACING NATIVE AMERICANS IN THE ENGLISH COLONIES

In New France and New Netherland, where the fur trade took precedence over farming, Indians outnumbered Europeans. This numerical superiority and their key role as suppliers of furs allowed native peoples to negotiate with settlers from a position of strength. The situation was different in the English colonies, whose settlers came to farm and thus competed directly with Indians for land.

**Land use and property rights.**    English settlers at first assumed that there was enough land for everyone. But the settlers misunderstood how Indians used land. Eastern Algonquian peoples moved frequently to take advantage of the land's diversity. They cleared areas for villages and planting fields, which native women farmed until the soil grew less fertile. Then they moved to a new location, allowing the former village site to return to forest. In ten to twenty years, they or their descendants might return to that site to clear and farm it again. In the winter, village communities broke up into small hunting bands. Thus what the colonists considered "vacant" lands were either being used for nonfarming activities such as hunting or regaining fertility in order to be farmed in years to come. Settlers who built towns on abandoned native village sites deprived the Indians of access to these areas.

Disputes also arose from misunderstandings about the definition of land ownership and property rights. Indian villages claimed sovereignty over a certain territory, which their members collectively used for farming, fishing, hunting, and gathering. No Indian claimed individual ownership of a specific tract of land. Europeans, of course, did, and for them ownership conferred on an individual the exclusive right to use or sell a piece of land. The settlers assumed that they had obtained complete rights to the land, whereas the Indians assumed that they had given the settlers not the land itself but only the right to use it.

Colonial agricultural practices also strained relations with the Indians. Cutting down forests destroyed Indian hunting lands. When colonists dammed rivers, they disturbed Indian fishing. When they surrounded their fields with fences, colonists made trespassers of natives who crossed them. Yet the colonists let their cattle and pigs loose to graze in the woods and meadows, where they could wander into unfenced Indian cornfields and damage the crops.

**Colonial land acquisition.**    As their numbers grew, the colonists acquired Indian lands and displaced native inhabitants. Because Indians owned land collectively, only their leaders had the authority to negotiate sales. Settlers, however, sometimes bought land from individual Indians who had no right to sell it. Because land transfers were usually arranged through interpreters and recorded in English, Indians were not always fully informed of the terms of sale. Even Indians who willingly sold land grew resentful as colonists approached them for more. Finally, native peoples could be forced to sell land to settle debts to English creditors.

Settlers occasionally obtained land by fraud. Some colonists simply settled on Indian lands and appealed to colonial governments for help when the Indians objected. Land speculators amplified this kind of unrest as they sought to acquire land as cheaply as possible and sell it for as much as they could.

Finally, colonists often seized Indian lands in the aftermath of war, as befell, among many others, the Pequots in 1637 in Connecticut and, in Carolina, the Tuscaroras in 1713 and the Yamasees in 1715. In each case, settlers moved onto land left vacant after colonial forces killed, captured, and dispersed native peoples. The colonists' hunger for land generated relentless pressure on native peoples. The pattern of mutual suspicion and territorial competition would be difficult to alter.

## BRINGING CHRISTIANITY TO NATIVE PEOPLES

In addition to trade and settlement, religion played a powerful role in shaping relations between Native Americans and Europeans. The three major New World empires of Spain, France, and England competed for Indians' souls as well as their lands and riches.

**Catholic missionaries in Spanish colonies.**    Franciscan priests were the driving force behind Spain's efforts to control New Mexico and Florida (see Map 3–1). Spain valued both regions for strategic reasons. Neither colony attracted many settlers, however, because neither offered much opportunity for wealth. When Franciscan missionaries proposed to move in, Spanish officials, eager to back up their claims with a more visible Spanish presence, provided financial support. Franciscans settled near native villages in New Mexico and Florida in order to

**QUICK REVIEW**

**Native Americans and English Settlers**

◆ Influx of settlers exposed native peoples to disease.

◆ Settlers' desire for land led to violence between settlers and Indians.

◆ By 1650 settlers outnumbered Indians in some areas.

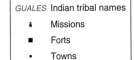

MAP 3–1   **Spanish and French Missions in Seventeenth-Century North America**   Spanish Franciscans in New Mexico (A) and Florida (B) and French Jesuits in New France (C) devoted considerable effort to converting native peoples to Catholic Christianity.

> **What might** explain the geographic distribution of Spanish and French missions? Why were French missions clustered around the Great Lakes? Why did the Spanish missions in Florida form lines of closely connected outposts?

convert their inhabitants to Catholicism. The priests wore their finest vestments and displayed religious paintings and statues, trying to impress the Indians. They gave away bells, knives, cloth, and food. The natives believed that accepting these gifts obliged them to listen to the priests' Christian message and help the Franciscans build houses and churches.

After brief religious instruction, the missionaries convinced many Indians to accept baptism into the Catholic Church. Many of these conversions were doubtless genuine, but they also had practical motivations. Conversions often followed epidemics that devastated native villages but spared the Spanish, leading Indians to wonder if the Christian God might be more powerful than their own gods. In New Mexico, the Spanish promised Pueblo converts protection against

Apache raids and access to Franciscan storehouses in times of famine. Ironically, the corn in the storehouses often came from the Indians' own fields, collected by the Spanish as tribute.

The Franciscans insisted that converts abandon their former ways of life and adopt Spanish food, clothing, gender relations, and work routines along with Catholicism. Their efforts met with mixed success. Many Indians preferred to supplement native beliefs and practices with the new teachings. Because the missionaries reacted to this spiritual mixture with horror, inflicting severe punishments that sometimes led to death, native peoples often practiced their own rituals in secret.

### French Jesuits in Canada.

To a certain extent, French Jesuits in Canada followed a similar strategy, moving to native villages and seeking to awe Indians with European technology and Catholic rituals. By the 1650s, the Jesuits claimed to have produced thousands of converts, some of whom formed separate native Christian communities.

French missionaries combined economic pressure with preaching. They persuaded merchants to sell guns only to converted Indians and to offer them other trade goods at a discount. Such tactics doubtless brought some success, but as in New Mexico, the crises engendered by epidemics more often than not sparked an upsurge in conversions. Converts in New France also preferred to meld Catholic teachings with native beliefs. Missionaries hardly condoned this response but they resigned themselves, at least in the short run, to a gradual approach to conversion. The Jesuits reduced the potential for confrontation with the Indians by accepting small changes in converts at first in hopes of a wholesale transformation to follow.

### Missionaries in English colonies.

The Protestant English were less successful at attracting Native American converts. Protestant practices, including lengthy sermons and Bible study, held little allure for Indians accustomed to a more ritualistic spiritual life. Even so, Protestant missionaries achieved some success, principally in New England. Beginning in the 1650s and 1660s, Puritan ministers such as John Eliot and Thomas Mayhew, Jr., attracted converts. Eliot helped to establish several "praying towns," where Indians received instruction in Protestant Christianity and English ways. By 1674, about 2,300 Indians resided in these towns.

## AFTER THE FIRST HUNDRED YEARS: CONFLICT AND WAR

After nearly a century of European settlement, violence between colonists and Indians erupted in all three North American empires. Each deadly encounter—King Philip's War in New England, Bacon's Rebellion in Virginia, the Pueblo Revolt in New Mexico, and the resumption of the Beaver Wars in New France—reflected distinctive features of English, Spanish, and French patterns of colonization.

### King Philip's War.

The growing frustration of the Wampanoags, who had befriended the Pilgrims more than a half-century earlier, with the land-hungry settlers whose towns now surrounded them, sparked **King Philip's War,** which broke out in 1675. Massasoit's younger son, Metacom—called King Philip by the English—led the Wampanoags in the struggle to preserve their independence. He had little reason to trust English settlers.

In the spring of 1675, a colonial court found three Wampanoags guilty of murdering a Christian Indian who had warned the English of Wampanoag preparations for war. Despite Philip's protest that the evidence against the men was tainted, the court sentenced them to be hanged. This act convinced the Wampanoags that they had to strike back against the English before it was too late. Only "a small part of the dominion of my ancestors remains," declared Philip. "I am determined not to live until I have no country."

Native warriors attacked outlying villages in Plymouth Colony, moved into the Connecticut River Valley, and then turned eastward to strike towns within 20 miles of Boston. As the Narragansetts and other groups joined the uprising, Philip successfully eluded the combined forces of Massachusetts, Connecticut, and Plymouth (see American Views: Mary Rowlandson among the Indians). By the summer of 1676, however, the Indians were exhausted, weakened by disease

**QUICK REVIEW**

Conversion

- Missionaries convinced many Indians to accept baptism.
- Many Indians did not understand the implications of baptism.
- Converts blended Christianity and native religion.

**King Philip's War** Conflict in New England (1675–1676) between Wampanoags, Narragansetts, and other Indian peoples against English settlers; sparked by English encroachments on native lands.

and food shortages. Philip moved into western New England, where his men clashed with the powerful Mohawks, long-standing enemies of the Wampanoags and allies of English fur traders in New York. Philip died in an ambush in August 1676, and the war ended soon after.

At least a thousand colonists and perhaps three thousand Indians died in King Philip's War. The Indians forced back the line of settlement but lost what remained of their independence in New England. The victorious English sold many native survivors, including Philip's wife and young son, into slavery in the West Indies. Philip's head, impaled on a stake, was left for decades just outside Plymouth as a grisly warning of the price to be paid for resisting colonial expansion.

**Bacon's Rebellion.**  As King Philip's War raged in New England, **Bacon's Rebellion** erupted in Virginia and had a similarly devastating effect on that colony's native population. Frustrated by shrinking economic opportunities in eastern Virginia, where established planters controlled the good land, many settlers, including new arrivals and recently freed indentured servants, moved to Virginia's western frontier. There they came into conflict with the region's resident Indians. In the summer of 1675, a group of frontier settlers attacked the Susquehannocks to seize their lands. The Indians struck back, prompting Nathaniel Bacon, a wealthy young planter who had only recently arrived in Virginia, to lead a violent campaign against all Indians, even those at peace with the colonial government. Governor William Berkeley ordered Bacon and his men to stop their attacks. They defied him and marched on Jamestown, turning a war between settlers and Indians into a rebellion of settlers against the colonial authorities.

The rebels believed that Berkeley and the colonial government represented the interests of established tobacco planters who wanted to keep men like themselves from emerging as potential competitors. Desperate because of the low price of tobacco, the rebels demanded voting rights, lower taxes, and easier access to land—meaning, in effect, the right to take land from the Indians. They captured and burned the colonial capital at Jamestown, forcing Berkeley to flee. Directing their aggression against Indians once more, they burned Indian villages and massacred the inhabitants.

By the time troops arrived from England to put down the rebellion, Bacon had died of dysentery and most of his men had drifted home. Berkeley hanged twenty-three rebels, but the real victims of the rebellion were Virginia's Indians. The remnants of the once-powerful Powhatans lost their remaining lands and either moved west or lived in poverty on the edges of English settlement. Hatred of Indians became a permanent feature of frontier life in Virginia, and government officials appeared more eager to spend money "for extirpating all Indians" than for maintaining peaceful relations.

**The Pueblo Revolt.**  In 1680, the **Pueblo Revolt** against the Spanish in New Mexico had a very different outcome than did the rebellion in Virginia or the war in New England. Nearly 20,000 Pueblo Indians had grown restless under the harsh rule of only 2,500 Spaniards. The spark that ignited the revolt was an act of religious persecution. Spanish officials unwisely chose this troubled time to stamp out the Pueblo religion. In 1675, the governor arrested forty-seven native religious leaders on charges of sorcery. The court ordered most of them to be publicly whipped and released but sentenced four to death.

Led by Popé, one of the freed leaders, the outraged Pueblos organized for revenge. A growing network of rebels emerged as Spanish soldiers marched into Pueblo villages and destroyed *kivas*, the chambers that Indians used for religious ceremonies. Working from the village of Taos in northern New Mexico, by the summer of 1680, Popé commanded an enormous force of rebels drawn from twenty Pueblo villages. On August 10, they attacked the Spanish settlements. Popé urged them to destroy "everything pertaining to Christianity." By October, all the surviving Spaniards had fled New Mexico.

They did not return for thirteen years. By then, internal rivalries had split the victorious Pueblo coalition, and Popé had been overthrown as leader. Few Pueblo villages offered much resistance to the new Spanish intrusion. Even so, the Spanish now understood the folly of pushing

**Bacon's Rebellion**  Violent conflict in Virginia (1675–1676), beginning with settler attacks on Indians but culminating in a rebellion led by Nathaniel Bacon against Virginia's government.

**Pueblo Revolt**  Rebellion in 1680 of Pueblo Indians in New Mexico against their Spanish overlords, sparked by religious conflict and excessive Spanish demands for tribute.

**WHERE TO LEARN MORE**

★ Taos Pueblo, Taos, New Mexico
http://www.nps.gov/history/worldheritage/taos.htm

the Indians too far. Officials reduced demands for tribute and ended the *encomienda* system. The Franciscans eased their attacks on Pueblo religion. New Spanish governors, backed by military force, kept the peace as best they could in a place where Indians still outnumbered Europeans.

**Resumption of the Beaver Wars.** The Iroquois experience in the last phase of the Beaver Wars threatened to parallel that of the Indians of New England and Virginia. What began as a struggle between the Iroquois and western native peoples for control of the fur trade blossomed into a larger

## AMERICAN VIEWS

### Mary Rowlandson among the Indians

*In February 1676, in the midst of King Philip's War, Indian warriors attacked the town of Lancaster, Massachusetts. They killed many inhabitants and took 23 colonists captive, including Mary Rowlandson and three of her children. Rowlandson spent the next three months traveling with various groups of Nipmucs, Narragansetts, and Wampanoags. She suffered physically and emotionally, watching her youngest daughter die in her arms and worrying about her other two children, from whom she was frequently separated. During her captivity, Rowlandson survived by accepting her fate and adapting to the Indians' way of life. Finally, with an English victory imminent, Rowlandson was ransomed and rejoined her husband (who had been away at the time of the attack) and family. In 1682, she published an account of her captivity in which she explored the meaning of her experience. Rowlandson's narrative proved so popular that three editions were printed in the first year.*

- **How** did Rowlandson describe the Indians? How did she characterize her encounter with King Philip?
- **In** what ways did Rowlandson accommodate herself to the Indians' way of life? How did she employ her skills to fit in? Did her gender make a difference in her experience of captivity?
- **How** did Rowlandson's Puritan faith shape her narrative?

We travelled on till night; and in the morning, we must go over the River to Philip's crew. When I was in the Cannoo, I could not but be amazed at the numerous crew of Pagans that were on the Bank on the other side. When I came ashore, they gathered all about me, I sitting alone in the midst: I observed they asked one another questions, and laughed, and rejoyced over their Gains and Victories. Then my heart began to fail: and I fell a weeping which was the first time to my remembrance that I wept before them. Although I had met with so much Affliction, and my heart was many times ready to break, yet could I not shed one tear in their sight: but rather had been all this while in a maze, and like one astonished: but now I may say as, Psal. 137.1 *By the rivers of Babylon, there we sat down: yea, we wept when we remembered Zion.* There one of them asked me, why I wept, I could hardly tell what to say: yet I answered, they would kill me: No, said he, none will hurt you. Then came one of them and gave me two spoon-fulls of Meal to comfort me. . . . Then I went to see King Philip, he bade me come in and sit down, and asked me whether I would smoke (a usual Complement now adayes amongst Saints and Sinners) but this no way suited me. For though I had formerly used Tobacco, yet I had left it ever since I was first taken, *It seems to be a bait, the devil lays to make men loose their precious time.* . . .

During my abode in this place, Philip spake to me to make a shirt for his boy, which I did, for which he gave me a shilling: I offered the money to my master, but he bade me keep it: and with it I bought a piece of Horse flesh. Afterwards he asked me to make a Cap for his boy, for which he invited me to Dinner. I went, and he gave me a Pancake, about as big as two fingers; it was made of parched wheat, beaten, and fryed in Bears grease, but I thought I never tasted pleasanter meat in my life. There was a Squaw who spake to me to make a shirt for her *Sannup* [husband], for which she gave me a piece of Bear. Another asked me to knit a pair of Stockins, for which she gave me a quart of Pease. . . . Hearing that my son was come to this place, I went to see him, and found him lying flat upon the ground: I asked him how he could sleep so? He answered me, *That he was not asleep, but at Prayer;* and lay so, that they might not observe what he was doing. I pray God he may remember these things now he is returned in safety.

*Source:* Neal Salisbury, ed., *The Sovereignty and Goodness of God, Together with the Faithfulness of His Promises Displayed.* . . . (Boston, 1997), pp. 82–83.

conflict that was absorbed into the imperial rivalry between England and France. Although the Iroquois suffered devastating losses, they did not lose their independence. The key to Iroquois survival in the war's aftermath was the adoption of a position of neutrality between the European powers.

Looking for new trading partners to replace the Hurons, the French turned in the 1680s to various Indian peoples living near the Great Lakes. But the Iroquois had begun to raid these same peoples for furs and captives, much as they had attacked the Hurons in the first phase of the Beaver Wars in the 1640s. They exchanged the furs for European goods with English traders, who had replaced the Dutch as their partners after the conquest of New Netherland.

The French attacked the Iroquois to prevent them and their English allies from extending their influence in the west. In June 1687, a combined force of French and Christian Indian soldiers invaded the lands of the Senecas, the westernmost of the five nations of the Iroquois League. The Iroquois retaliated by besieging a French garrison at Niagara, where nearly two hundred soldiers starved to death, and killing hundreds of colonists in attacks on French villages along the St. Lawrence River.

The French participated much more directly and suffered greater losses in this renewal of the Beaver Wars than they had in the earlier fighting. In 1688 France and England went to war in Europe, and the struggle between them and their Indian allies for control of the fur trade in North America became part of a larger imperial contest. The European powers made peace in 1697, but calm did not immediately return to the Great Lakes region.

The conflict was even more devastating for the Iroquois. Perhaps a quarter of their population died from disease and warfare by 1689. The devastation encouraged Iroquois diplomats to find a way to extricate themselves from future English–French conflicts. The result, in 1701, was a pair of treaties, negotiated separately with Albany and Montreal, that recognized Iroquois neutrality and, at least for several decades, prevented either the English or the French from dominating the western lands.

# AFRICANS AND EUROPEANS

The movement of Africans to the Americas was one of the largest forced migrations in world history. By the time New World slavery finally ended, with its abolition in Brazil in 1888, over twelve million Africans had arrived on American shores. From a relatively small stream in the sixteenth century, African migration accelerated to a great flood by the 1700s.

**HOW AND** why did race-based slavery develop in British North America?

Virtually all Africans arrived as slaves, making the history of the African experience in the Americas inseparable from the history of slavery and the slave trade. As one eighteenth-century Englishman noted, Africans were "the strength and sinews of this western world," performing much of the labor of colonization. The vast majority of African slaves ended up in Brazil, the West Indies, or New Spain. Only 1 out of 20 Africans came to the British mainland colonies, but this still amounted to nearly 350,000 individuals (see Figure 3–2). Their presence transformed English colonial societies everywhere, but particularly in the South. At the same time, Africans were themselves transformed. Out of their diverse African ethnic backgrounds and the experience of slavery itself they forged new identities as African American peoples.

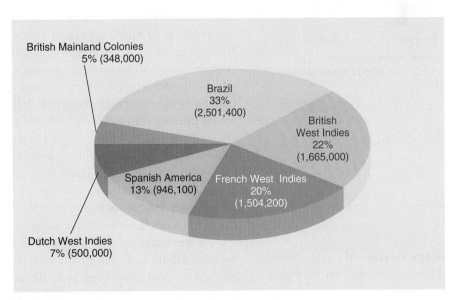

**FIGURE 3–2   Destination of Slaves Imported from Africa to the Americas between 1451 and 1810**   Approximately 7.5 million Africans were brought as slaves to the Americas before 1810. The vast majority went to the Caribbean, Mexico, and South America, where they toiled in mines and on sugar plantations.

*Data Source:* Philip Curtin, *The Atlantic Slave Trade: A Census* (1969), p. 268.

**See the Map**

at **www.myhistorylab.com**
*African Slave Trade, 1500–1870*

**QUICK REVIEW**

**The Demand for Labor**

♦ Indians first forced into slavery in the Americas.

♦ By 1700 Indian slave trade replaced by slaves from Africa.

♦ Over time slaves replaced servants on tobacco plantations.

**Interpreting the Past**
*The Voyage to Slavery* (pp. 82–83)

**Read the Document**

at **www.myhistorylab.com**
*A Slave Tells of His Capture in Africa*
(1798)

**Middle Passage** The voyage between West Africa and the New World slave colonies.

**Read the Document**

at **www.myhistorylab.com**
*Olaudah Equiano, The Middle Passage*
(1788)

## LABOR NEEDS AND THE TURN TO SLAVERY

Europeans in the New World were thrilled to find that land was abundant and quite cheap by European standards. They were perplexed, however, by the unexpectedly high cost of labor. In Europe, the reverse had been true. There land was expensive but labor cheap, because competition for jobs among large numbers of workers pushed wages down. Colonial workers commanded high wages because there were so few of them compared to the supply of land to be developed. In addition, few settlers wanted to work for others when they could get farms of their own. The scarcity and high cost of labor led some colonial employers to turn to enslaved Africans as a solution.

The development of slavery in the colonies was not inevitable. Europeans had owned slaves (both white and black) long before the beginning of American colonization, but slaves formed a small—and shrinking—minority of European laborers. By the fifteenth century, slavery had all but disappeared in northern Europe except as punishment for serious crimes.

Slavery persisted longer in southern Europe and the Middle East. In both regions, religion influenced the choice of who was enslaved. Because neither Christians nor Muslims would hold as slaves members of their own faiths, Arab traders turned to sub-Saharan Africa to find slaves. By the fifteenth century, a durable link between slave status and black skin had been forged in European minds.

Europeans in the New World, beginning with Columbus, first enslaved Indians as a way of addressing the labor shortage. Native American slaves, however, could not fill the colonists' labor needs. Everywhere disease and harsh working conditions reduced their numbers. English colonists also discovered problems with enslaving Indians. When traders incited Indian wars to gain slaves, bloodshed often spread to English settlements. Enslaved Indian men refused to perform agricultural labor, which they considered women's work. And because they knew the land so well, Indians could easily escape. As a result, although the Indian slave trade persisted in the English colonies through the eighteenth century (and into the nineteenth century), by 1700 it had given way to a much larger traffic in Africans.

## THE SHOCK OF ENSLAVEMENT

European traders did not themselves enslave Africans. Instead, they relied on other Africans to capture slaves for them, tapping into and expanding a preexisting internal African slave trade. With the permission of local rulers, Europeans built forts and trading posts on the West African coast and bought slaves from African traders (see Map 3–2). African rulers occasionally enslaved and sold their own people as punishment for crimes, but most slaves were seized in raids on neighboring peoples. Attracted by European cloth, liquor, guns, and other goods, West Africans fought among themselves to secure captives and began kidnapping individuals from the interior.

Once captured, slaves marched in chains to the coast, to be confined in cages until there were enough to fill a ship. Captains examined them to ensure their fitness and branded them like cattle with a hot iron. The slaves then boarded canoes to be ferried to the ships. Desperation overwhelmed some of them, who jumped overboard and drowned rather than be carried off to an unknown destination. Even before the ships left African shores, slaves sometimes mutinied, though such rebellions rarely succeeded.

Slaves who could not escape while still in Africa suffered through a horrendous six- to eight-week-long ocean voyage known as the **Middle Passage.** Captains wedged men below decks into spaces about 6 feet long, 16 inches wide, and 30 inches high. Women and children were packed even more tightly. Except for brief excursions on deck for forced exercise, slaves remained below decks, where the air grew foul from the vomit, blood, and excrement in which the terrified victims lay. Some slaves went insane; others refused to eat. On many voyages, between 5 and 20 percent of the slaves perished from disease and other causes, but captains had usually packed the ships tightly enough to make a profit from selling the rest.

Those who survived the dreadful voyage endured the fear and humiliation of sale. Ship captains sometimes sold slaves at public auctions, where purchasers poked them, looking for signs of disease. Many terrified Africans, like Equiano, thought they were going to be eaten.

## AFRICAN SLAVES IN THE NEW WORLD

The Spanish and Portuguese first brought Africans to the Americas to replace or supplement the dwindling numbers of Indian slaves toiling in silver mines and on sugar plantations. The Dutch, who scrambled for a share of the lucrative slave trade, quickly followed suit. English colonists, less familiar with slavery, adopted it more slowly. West Indian planters were the first English settlers to do so on a large scale in the 1640s. In most other English colonies, however, different economic conditions either postponed or prevented slavery's widespread adoption.

**Slavery in the southern colonies.** Slavery did not fully take hold in Virginia until the end of the seventeenth century, at which point Africans comprised a significant portion of the population (see Figure 3–3). For decades, tobacco planters saw no reason to stop using

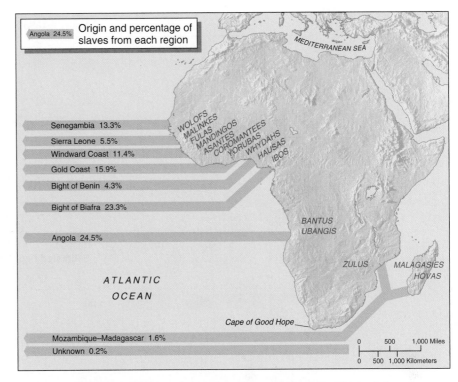

MAP 3–2 **African Origins of North American Slaves, 1690–1807** Nearly all slaves in English North America were West Africans. Most had been captured or purchased by African slave traders, who then sold them to European merchants.

**Why might** the Bight of Biafra and Angola together have made up nearly 50 percent of all slave trading out of West Africa?

white indentured servants. Servants (because they worked for masters only for a period of years rather than for life) cost less than slaves, were readily available, and were familiar. By the 1680s, however, planters in Virginia and Maryland began to shift from servants to slaves.

Two related developments caused this change. First, white indentured servants became harder to find. Fewer English men and women chose to emigrate as servants after 1660 because an improving economy in England provided jobs at home. At the same time, Virginia's white population tripled between 1650 and 1700, increasing the number of planters competing for a shrinking supply of laborers. Planters also faced competition from newer colonies such as Pennsylvania and New Jersey, which had more generous land policies for immigrants.

Second, as white servants grew scarcer, changes in the slave trade made African slaves more available. Before the 1660s, the Dutch and Portuguese merchants who dominated the trade mainly supplied their own colonies and the profitable West Indian market. But beginning in 1674, England's Royal African Company began shipping slaves directly to English buyers. The supply of slaves surged after 1698, when the Royal African Company lost its special trading rights, and many English merchants and New Englanders entered the fiercely competitive trade.

Chesapeake planters eventually found reasons besides availability to prefer slaves to servants. Slaves were a better long-term investment. Because slave status passed from slave mothers to their children, buying both men and women gave planters a self-reproducing labor force. Runaway black slaves were more easily recaptured than escaped servants, who blended into the white population. And unlike indentured servants, slaves were slaves for life.

Chesapeake planters had already come to see white servants as possessions, people whose labor could be bought and sold like any other commodity. This attitude doubtless eased the

◉ See the **Map**
at www.myhistorylab.com
*The Atlantic and Islamic Slave Trades*

•••• Read the **Document**
at www.myhistorylab.com
*Virginia Law on Indentured Servitude* (1705)

•••• Read the **Document**
at www.myhistorylab.com
*Wessell Webling, His Indenture* (1622)

•••• Read the **Document**
at www.myhistorylab.com
*A Virginian Describes the Difference between Servants and Slaves* (1722)

**1650**

| Region | Black | White |
|---|---|---|
| British West Indies | 15,000 | 44,000 |
| Lower South | | |
| Chesapeake | 300 | 12,400 |
| Middle Colonies | 500 | 3,800 |
| New England | 400 | 22,500 |

**1700**

| Region | Black | White |
|---|---|---|
| British West Indies | 115,000 | 33,000 |
| Lower South | 2,900 | 13,600 |
| Chesapeake | 12,900 | 85,200 |
| Middle Colonies | 3,700 | 49,900 |
| New England | 1,700 | 90,700 |

**1750**

| Region | Black | White |
|---|---|---|
| British West Indies | 295,000 | 35,000 |
| Lower South | 59,800 | 82,400 |
| Chesapeake | 150,600 | 227,200 |
| Middle Colonies | 20,700 | 275,700 |
| New England | 11,000 | 349,000 |

FIGURE 3–3　**Estimated Population of Black and White Settlers in British Colonial Regions, 1650–1750**　Settler populations increased rapidly in all colonial regions, but the racial composition varied. By 1750, black people overwhelmingly predominated in the West Indies and were quite numerous in the southern colonies; north of Maryland, however, their numbers remained small.

*Data Source:* John J. McCusker and Russell Menard, *The Economy of British America, 1607–1789* (1985).

transition in the 1680s and 1690s to the much harsher system of slavery. In Carolina, of course, slaves were there from the start, brought in the 1670s by colony founders accustomed to slavery in Barbados. By 1720, slavery was firmly embedded in all the southern colonies except sparsely settled North Carolina. In that year, one-third of Virginia's settler population, and nearly three-quarters of South Carolina's, were black.

Slavery grew rapidly in the southern colonies because it answered the labor needs of planters engaged in the commercial production of tobacco and rice. The demand for slaves became so powerful that it destroyed James Oglethorpe's plan to keep them out of Georgia, the last of England's mainland colonies, founded in 1732. Oglethorpe intended Georgia to be a refuge for English debtors, who normally were jailed until they could repay their creditors. Slaves were initially prohibited not only to prevent them from competing with the debtors, but also to make it difficult for fugitive slaves from South Carolina to escape there. With slavery forbidden, any black person seen in Georgia would be immediately recognizable as a runaway. But when Georgia's colonists began to grow rice, they demanded the right to have slaves. In 1750, the colony's founders reluctantly legalized slavery; by 1770, slaves made up nearly half of the colony's population.

**Slavery in the northern colonies.**   Far fewer slaves lived north of the Chesapeake, although they were present in every British colony. They were too expensive for most northern farmers—who mainly produced food for their families, not staple crops for an international market—to use profitably. This was not true, however, for farmers with larger properties in parts of Long Island, the Hudson Valley, Rhode Island, northern New Jersey, and southeastern Pennsylvania, where commercial wheat farming and livestock raising prevailed. In the eighteenth century, these landowners acquired significant numbers of slaves.

Northern slaves could often be found in cities, especially ports such as Newport, Rhode Island, where newly arrived Africans landed. At the start of the eighteenth century, one out of six Philadelphia residents was a slave; by 1740, slaves made up 15 percent of the city's workingmen. In mid-eighteenth-century New York City, slaves comprised between 12 and 14 percent of the population. Many urban slaves were domestic servants in the homes of rich merchants and professionals. Substantial numbers also labored as artisans.

**Changing race relations in the colonies.**   Race relations in the mainland colonies were less rigid in the seventeenth century than they would later become. Before 1700, slaves did not form a majority of the population in any colony, a situation that may have made them seem less threatening to white people. In some areas, free black people—often slaves who had bought their own freedom—prospered in an atmosphere of racial tolerance that would be unthinkable by the eighteenth century.

The career of an ambitious black Virginian named Anthony Johnson, for example, resembled that of many white settlers. Johnson's master allowed him to marry and start a family while he was still a slave and may even have allowed Anthony to purchase his and his family's liberty. Once free, the Johnsons settled in eastern Virginia, where Anthony and his sons eventually acquired substantial plantations. He and his sons also owned slaves. Anthony Johnson belonged to the first or what one historian has called the "charter" generation of American slaves, and his experience reveals how much slavery changed over time. This generation of slaves mainly came from African port towns, where Europeans and Africans had mingled for generations, or by way of the West Indies or New Netherland. Familiar with European ways, often fluent in European

The freed slave Olaudah Equiano appears in this 1780 portrait by an unknown artist. After purchasing his freedom, Equiano wrote a vivid account of his capture in Africa and his life in slavery. One of the first such accounts to be published (in 1789), this narrative testified to slavery's injustice and Equiano's own fortitude and talents.

Royal Albert Memorial Museum, Exeter, Devon, UK/Bridgeman Art Library.

**Read** the **Document**

at **www.myhistorylab.com**
*Exploring America:*
*Racism in America*

**Read** the **Document**

at **www.myhistorylab.com**
*From Then to Now Online:*
*The Legacy of Slavery*

**WHERE TO LEARN MORE**

Atkinson Site, Colonial Williamsburg, Williamsburg, Virginia
http://research.history.org/Archaeological_Research/MHPage/AAArch.htm

languages, they acquired skills and knowledge that enabled them to bargain with their masters in ways their descendants would not be able to replicate. They came in small groups, cultivated their masters as patrons, negotiated for their own property, and often gained their freedom. They enjoyed such advantages because they came to colonies where slavery had not yet become firmly embedded, where the meaning of bondage was still being worked out.

**Repressive laws and slave codes.** But Johnson's descendants, and the generations of slaves and free black people who came after them, encountered much harsher conditions. Once slavery became the dominant labor system in the Chesapeake, tobacco planters no longer welcomed free black people, fearing that they might encourage slaves to escape. In 1691, Virginia's legislature prohibited individual masters from freeing their slaves. Lawmakers passed another measure in 1699 requiring newly freed black people to leave the colony altogether. Black families like the Johnsons, who were already free, suffered under increasing discrimination.

Bad as the situation of free black people had grown, the condition of slaves was far worse. Slave codes, laws governing slavery, essentially reduced an entire class of human beings to property. In Virginia, from the middle of the seventeenth century on, new laws added to slaves' oppression. A 1662 measure defined slavery as a lifelong and inherited status that passed from slave mothers to their children—even children with white fathers. Masters who might have felt uneasy about holding fellow Christians as slaves were relieved in 1667 when another law stated that baptism would not release slaves from bondage. Two years later, the House of Burgesses gave masters the power of life and death over their slaves, decreeing that masters would not be charged with a felony if their slaves died during punishment. These and other measures were gathered into a comprehensive slave code in Virginia in 1705.

Slave codes appeared virtually everywhere, North and South, but were particularly harsh in the southern colonies. White colonists in the Tidewater Chesapeake and South Carolina feared the consequences of a growing black population. One South Carolina planter predicted in 1720 that slaves would soon rise up against their masters because black people were "too numerous in proportion to the White Men there."

## AFRICAN AMERICAN FAMILIES AND COMMUNITIES

The harshness of the slaves' condition could be relieved somewhat by the formation of close ties with others who shared their circumstances. For such ties to be created, however, several developments had to occur. Slaves had to become sufficiently numerous in specific localities so that black people could have regular contact with one another. Ethnic and language barriers carried over from Africa had to erode so that slaves could communicate. And for families to be formed, there had to be enough slave women as well as men. Because these conditions were slow to develop, occurring at different rates in different colonies, the formation of African American families and communities was delayed until well into the eighteenth century.

**The rise of the creole slave population.** Slaves were most numerous in the southern colonies, and it was there that African American families and communities emerged with greater success. This was especially true in South Carolina and parts of the Tidewater Chesapeake, where in certain localities slaves formed a majority of the population. Even more significant, these regions witnessed the rise of a creole, or American-born, slave population by about the 1750s. This development distinguished slavery in the mainland British colonies from that in the West Indies, where disease and overwork killed so many slaves that the black population grew only because of the constant importation of Africans.

The rise of a creole slave population in the Chesapeake and in Carolina set off a chain of related events that fostered family and community life. Creoles lived longer than African immigrants, and creole women usually bore twice as many children as African-born mothers. This circumstance allowed the slave population to grow by natural increase and more closely resemble a normal population of men and women, children and elders. At the same time, creole slaves grew up without personal memories of Africa, and thus African ethnic differences receded in importance.

**Work and family life.**    Most of a slave's life was structured by work. The vast majority of southern slaves were field hands. On large plantations, masters selected some slave men to be trained as shoemakers, weavers, or tailors and chose others as drivers or leaders of work gangs.

**WHERE TO LEARN MORE**

African Burial Ground, New York, NY
http://www.nps.gov/afbg/index.htm

Although this watercolor of a slave ship bound for Brazil dates from the nineteenth century, it depicts a scene common on slavers in the 1700s. The artist's attention to detail suggests both the misery of the slaves' surroundings and the dignity of the individuals forced to live under such conditions.

The Granger Collection, New York.

This English woodcut, dating from about 1700, served as a label on a tobacco package. In the foreground, planters smoke and take their ease, while in the background, slaves toil under the hot sun.

## QUICK REVIEW

### Slave Society

◆ Traces of African culture remained in slave society.

◆ Labor consumed most of slave's time.

◆ Growth of slave families and communities inhibited escape and rebellion.

With the exception of nurses and cooks, few slave women avoided the drudgery of field labor. If they had families, the end of the day's work in the fields only marked the start of domestic duties back in the slave quarters. But no matter how onerous, work did not absorb every minute of the slaves' lives, and in the intervals around their assigned duties many slaves nurtured ties of family and community that combined African traditions with New World experience.

By the late eighteenth century, more than half of Chesapeake and Carolina slaves lived in family groups. These were fragile units, subject to the whims of masters who did not recognize slave marriages as legal, broke up families by sale, and could take slave women as sexual partners at will. Over time, dense kinship networks formed, reflecting West African influences. Slaves placed great emphasis on kin connections, even using familiar terms such as "aunt" and "uncle" to address friends. Some slave husbands, as was customary in West Africa, took more than one wife. In naming their children, slaves mingled old and new practices, sometimes giving them the African names of distant kin and sometimes using English names.

**Community life and religion.** Community life forged ties between slave families and single slaves on the plantations and offered further opportunities to preserve elements of African heritage. Traces of African religious practices endured in America. Magical charms and amulets have been found buried in slave quarters, indicating that spiritual ceremonies may have been conducted out of sight of white masters. Reflecting their West African background, slaves placed great emphasis on funerals, in the belief that relatives remained members of kin communities even after death. Christianity offered little competition to African religious practices during most of the colonial period. Few masters showed much interest in converting their slaves before the Revolution.

African influences shaped aspects of slaves' recreational activity and material life. Slave musicians used African-style instruments, including drums and banjos, to accompany traditional songs and dances. Where slaves were allowed to build their own houses, they incorporated African elements into the designs—for instance, by using mud walls and roofs thatched with palmetto leaves. Their gardens frequently contained African foods, such as millet, yams, peppers, and sesame seeds, along with European and Native American crops.

## RESISTANCE AND REBELLION

Even as family ties made a life in bondage more tolerable, they made it more difficult for slaves to attempt escape or contemplate rebellion. Slaves who resisted their oppression ran the risk of endangering families and friends as well as themselves. But the powerful desire for freedom was not easily suppressed, and slaves found ways to defy the dehumanization that slavery entailed.

Running away from a master was a desperate act, but thousands of slaves did just that. Deciding where to go posed a problem. Escape out of the South did not bring freedom, because slavery was legal in every colony. After 1733, some runaways went to Florida, where Spanish officials promised them freedom. Others tried to survive on their own in the woods or join the Indians—a choice that carried the risk of capture or death. Perilous as it was, escape proved irresistible to some slaves, especially young males. In a few isolated areas on the South Carolina frontier, runaways formed outlaw "maroon" settlements.

This eighteenth-century painting from South Carolina records the preservation of certain African traditions in American slave communities. The dance may be Yoruba in origin, while the stringed instrument and drum were probably modeled on African instruments.

Abby Aldrich Rockefeller Folk Art Museum, The Colonial Williamsburg Foundation Williamsburg, VA.

Many slaves chose less perilous ways to resist their bondage. Slaves worked slowly, broke tools, and pretended to be ill in order to exert some control over their working lives. When provoked, they also took more direct action, damaging crops, stealing goods, and setting fires. Slaves with knowledge of poisonous plants occasionally tried to kill their owners, although the penalty for being caught was to be burned to death.

The most serious, as well as the rarest, form of resistance was organized rebellion. South Carolinians and coastal Virginians, who lived in regions with slave majorities, had a particular dread of slave revolt. But because rebellions required complete secrecy, careful planning, and access to weapons, they were extremely hard to organize. No slave rebellion succeeded in the British colonies. Rumors usually leaked out before any action had been taken, prompting severe reprisals against the alleged conspirators.

Three major slave revolts did occur and instilled lasting fear in white colonists. In 1712 in New York City, where black people made up 20 percent of the population, about twenty slaves set a building on fire and killed nine white men who came to put it out. The revolt was quickly suppressed, with twenty-four rebels sentenced to death. Another slave insurrection occurred in Virginia in 1730, sparked by a false rumor that local officials had suppressed a royal edict calling for the emancipation of Christian slaves. More than three hundred rebels escaped into the Dismal Swamp along the border with North Carolina, attacking white settlers in the area. Using Indians to hunt down the fugitives, Virginia authorities captured and executed twenty-four of the rebellion's leaders. Another major revolt, the **Stono Rebellion,** struck South Carolina in 1739. About twenty slaves—including several recently arrived Angolans—broke into a store and armed themselves with stolen guns. Marching southward along the Stono River, their ranks grew

**Stono Rebellion**   Uprising in 1739 of South Carolina slaves against whites; inspired in part by Spanish officials' promise of freedom for American slaves who escaped to Florida.

to perhaps a hundred. Heading for freedom in Spanish Florida, they attacked white settlements along the way. White troops (with Indian help) defeated the rebels within a week, but tensions remained high for months. The death toll, in the end, was about two dozen white people and perhaps twice as many black rebels.

In the wake of these rebellions, colonial assemblies passed laws requiring stricter supervision of slave activities. In South Carolina, other measures encouraged more white immigration to offset the colony's black majority. Planters in the southern colonies in particular considered slavery indispensable to their economic survival, even though this labor system generated so much fear and brutality. Their slaves, in turn, obeyed when necessary, resisted when possible, and kept alive the hope that freedom would one day be theirs.

**●◆●—Read the Document**
at **www.myhistorylab.com**
*Slaves Revolt in South Carolina* (1739)

**WHAT METHODS** did Europeans employ to acquire and manage labor in colonial America?

# EUROPEAN LABORERS IN EARLY AMERICA

Slavery was one of several responses to the scarcity of labor in the New World. It took hold mainly in areas where the profits from export crops such as sugar, rice, and tobacco offset the high purchase price of slaves and where a warm climate permitted year-round work. Elsewhere European masters and employers found various ways to acquire and manage European laborers.

## A SPECTRUM OF CONTROL

Slavery was the most oppressive extreme in a spectrum of practices designed to exert control over workers and relieve the problems caused by the easy availability of land and the high cost of labor. Most colonial laborers were, in some measure, unfree (see the Overview table, Predominant Colonial Labor Systems, 1750). One-half to two-thirds of all white immigrants to the English colonies arrived as indentured servants, bound by contract to serve masters for a period of years. But indentured servants, though less costly than slaves, carried too high a price for farmers who raised crops mainly for subsistence. Servants could be found in every colony, but were most common in the Chesapeake and, to a lesser extent, in Pennsylvania, where they worked for farmers producing export crops.

Slaves replaced white indentured servants in Chesapeake tobacco fields during the eighteenth century. Masters continued to import servants for a while to fill skilled jobs but in time trained slaves to fill those positions. Thus, by the middle of the eighteenth century, white servitude, although it still flourished in some places, was in decline as a dominant labor system.

Eighteenth-century Chesapeake planters also availed themselves of another unfree labor source: transported English convicts. Lawmakers in England saw transportation as a way of getting rid of criminals who might otherwise be executed. Between 1718 and 1775, nearly fifty thousand convicts were sent to the colonies, 80 percent of whom ended up in the Chesapeake region. Most were young, lower-class males forced by economic hardship to turn to crime. A few convicts eventually prospered in America, but most faced lives as miserable as those they had known in England.

**redemptioner** Similar to an indentured servant, except that a redemptioner signed a labor contract in America rather than in Europe.

An arrangement similar to indentured servitude—the **redemptioner** system—brought many families, especially from German provinces, to the colonies in the eighteenth century. Instead of negotiating contracts for service before leaving Europe, as indentured servants did, redemptioners promised to redeem, or pay, the costs of passage on arrival in America. They often paid part of the fare before sailing. If they could not raise the rest soon after landing, the ship captain who brought them sold them into servitude. The length of their service depended on how much they still owed.

Purchasing slaves, servants, or convicts did not make sense for everyone. Colonists who owned undeveloped land faced many tasks—cutting trees, clearing fields, building fences and barns—that brought no immediate profit. Rather than buy expensive laborers to accomplish these ends, landowners rented undeveloped tracts to families without property. Both tenants and landlords benefited from this arrangement. Tenants enjoyed greater independence than servants

## OVERVIEW   Predominant Colonial Labor Systems, 1750

| | Colony | Labor System |
|---|---|---|
| New England | Massachusetts | Family farms |
| | Connecticut | Family farms |
| | New Hampshire | Family farms |
| | Rhode Island | Family farms |
| Middle Colonies | New York | Family farms, tenancy |
| | Pennsylvania and Delaware | Indentured servitude, tenancy, family farms |
| | New Jersey | Family farms, tenancy |
| South | Maryland | Slavery |
| | Virginia | Slavery |
| | North Carolina | Family farms, slavery |
| | South Carolina | Slavery |

and could save toward the purchase of their own farms. The landlord secured the labor necessary to transform his property into a working farm, thus increasing the land's value. He also received an annual rent payment and eventually profited from selling the land, often to the tenant family who had rented it.

Merchants eager to develop New England's fisheries devised other means to fill their labor needs. Because it was fairly easy to get a farm, few New Englanders took on the risky job of fishing. Moreover, few could afford the necessary equipment, including boats, provisions, and salt (used for preserving fish). Merchants recruited fishermen by advancing credit to coastal villagers so that they could outfit their own boats. Many fishermen ran up such large debts that they were obliged to continue supplying fish to their creditors, whether they wanted to or not.

In the northern colonies, the same conditions that made men reluctant to become fishermen deterred them from becoming farm laborers, except perhaps for high wages. Paying high wages, however, or the high cost of servants or slaves was difficult for New Englanders with farms that produced no export crops and could not be worked during cold winter months. So northern farmers turned to the cheapest and most dependable workers they could find—their children.

Children as young as 5 or 6 years old began with simple tasks and moved on to more complex work as they grew older. By the time they were in their late teens, girls knew how to run households, and boys knew how to farm. Fathers used their ownership of property to prolong the time their sons worked for them. Young men could not marry until they could set up their own households and relied on their fathers to provide them with land to do so. Fathers often waited until their sons were in their mid-twenties, compelling them until then to invest their labor in the paternal estate.

### NEW EUROPEAN IMMIGRANTS

European immigrants flooded into America in the seventeenth and eighteenth centuries (see Figure 3–4). Nearly 250,000 Scots-Irish people—descendants of Protestant Scots who had settled in northern Ireland in the sixteenth and seventeenth centuries—came to the colonies after

**QUICK REVIEW**

**Child Labor in New England**
- Children began work as young as 5 or 6.
- Teenagers took on adult tasks.
- Fathers used ownership of property to tie sons to the land.

## GLOBAL CONNECTIONS

### EARLY MODERN EUROPE'S BIGGEST MASS MIGRATION

The stream of German immigrants moving to America in the late seventeenth and eighteenth centuries formed only a small part of a much larger flow of emigrants from the Rhineland to many parts of the globe. The Rhineland was not a single political unit, but a region of small states and principalities located along one of Europe's major rivers. Political fragmentation brought religious diversity, with German Reformed or Lutheran churches dominant in some areas and Catholics in others.

Large-scale emigration of Rhineland inhabitants stemmed from many causes, especially warfare. During the Thirty Years' War (1618–1648), much of the Rhineland area was devastated by intense religious conflict and famine. In the 1680s and 1690s, Louis XIV of France invaded the region, sparking more turmoil. Almost continual warfare from the 1730s to the 1760s made the lives of Rhineland inhabitants even worse.

Economic hardship and political repression also spurred emigration. Harsh winters in 1708–1709 and 1709–1710, for instance, destroyed orchards and vineyards, threatening many farmers with impoverishment and even starvation. Harvests failed in many parts of the Rhineland in the 1740s. In addition, religious minorities suffered from persecution, and everyone bore the burden of increasing taxes and arbitrary rule by local princes. For all of these reasons, over the course of the eighteenth century, hundreds of thousands of Rhinelanders decided to flee their homeland.

Many promoters, land speculators, and even governments sought to direct the flow of emigrants to a favored region. Officials from Russia and Prussia offered cheap land and tax exemptions to lure migrants to their countries. As a result of this promotional campaign, by far the largest number of Rhineland refugees relocated to various parts of Eastern Europe, including Prussia, Russia, Hungary, and Poland. A smaller flow of emigrants, mostly Protestants, made their way to North America, settling principally in Pennsylvania, New York, and the Carolinas. Still others moved to Cayenne (French Guiana) in South America. The exodus of these German-speaking emigrants to destinations in the Old and New Worlds constituted the most significant mass migration in early modern Europe.

- Why might more Rhineland migrants have moved within Europe instead of going to the North American colonies?

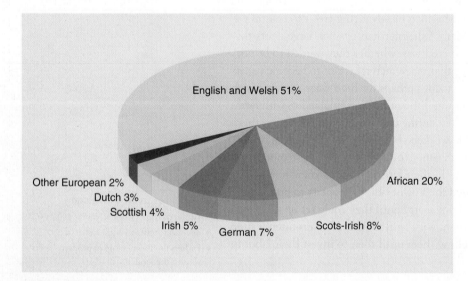

**FIGURE 3–4   Ethnic Distribution of Non-Indian Inhabitants of British Mainland Colonies, c. 1770**   By the third quarter of the eighteenth century, the colonial population was astonishingly diverse. Only two out of three settlers claimed British ancestry (from England, Wales, Scotland, or northern Ireland), while one out of five was African in origin.
*Data Source:* Thomas L. Purvis, "The European Ancestry of the United States Population, 1790," *William and Mary Quarterly*, 3d series, 41 (1984), p. 98.

1718, when their landlords raised rents to intolerable levels. Tens of thousands of immigrants arrived from Scotland during the same period, some seeking economic improvement and some sent as punishment for rebellions against the king in 1715 and 1745. Thousands of Irish Catholics arrived as servants, redemptioners, and convicts.

Continental Europe contributed another stream of emigrants. Perhaps 100,000 German Protestants left the Rhine Valley, where war, economic hardship, and religious persecution had brought misery. French Protestants (known as Huguenots) began emigrating after 1685, when their faith was made illegal in France. Swiss Protestants likewise fled religious persecution. Even a few Poles, Greeks, Italians, and Jews reached the colonies in the eighteenth century.

Many emigrants responded to pamphlets and newspaper articles that exaggerated the bright prospects of life in America. Others studied more realistic accounts from friends and relatives who had already emigrated. Landowners sent agents to port towns to recruit new arrivals to become tenants, often on generous terms.

Streams of emigrants flowed to places where land was cheap and labor most in demand (see Map 3–3). Few went to New England, where descendants of the first settlers occupied the best land. They also avoided areas where slavery predominated—the Chesapeake Tidewater and low-land South Carolina—in favor of the foothills of the Appalachian Mountains, from western Pennsylvania to the Carolinas. There, one emigrant declared, a "poor man that will incline to work may have the value of his labour."

This observation, though partly true, did not tell the whole story. Any person who came as a servant, redemptioner, or tenant learned that his master or landlord received much of "the value of his labour." Not all emigrants realized their dreams of becoming independent landowners. The scarcity of labor in the colonies led as easily to the exploitation of white workers as of slaves and Indians. Even so, for many people facing bleak prospects in Europe, the chance that emigration might bring prosperity was too tempting to ignore.

# CONCLUSION

The ocean voyage that brought Olaudah Equiano across the Atlantic carried him to a land containing a strikingly diverse mosaic of peoples and communities. In communities across North America, peoples from three continents adapted to one another and to American conditions. For some of the people in these communities, emigration and settlement had brought opportunity; for others, including Equiano and his fellow Africans, it brought oppression. For many, though not all, European immigrants, the colonies offered the chance for economic improvement.

Yet at the same time, millions of African slaves suffered under the most repressive colonial labor regime, fighting its grip whenever possible. And even as Europeans and Africans adapted to different New World circumstances, Indians struggled with the consequences of disease, trade, religious conversion, settlement, and warfare resulting from European immigration. Some native peoples managed to preserve their autonomy, others did not.

As the eighteenth century wore on, the North American colonies attracted more attention from their home countries. Spain, France, and England recognized the colonies' growing economic power and strove to harness it to block the expansion of their rivals. Everywhere the effort to strengthen imperial ties created ambivalence among colonists. Because the English settlers were by far the most numerous, their responses were the most pronounced. As they saw more clearly the differences between themselves and England itself, some colonists began to defend their distinctive habits, while others tried more insistently than ever to imitate English ways. The tension between new and old had characterized colonial development from the start. What made the eighteenth century distinctive were the many ways in which the tensions worked themselves out.

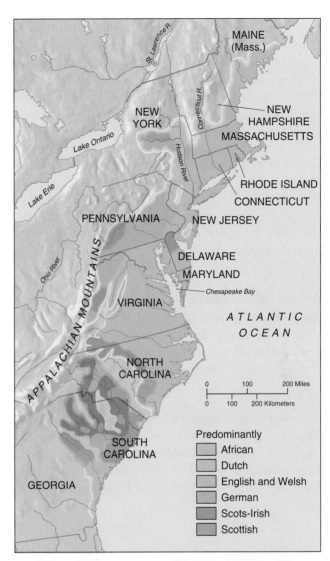

MAP 3–3 **Ethnic Distribution of Settler Population in British Mainland Colonies, c. 1755** Settlers of different ethnic backgrounds tended to concentrate in certain areas. Only New Englanders were predominantly English, while Africans dominated in the Chesapeake Tidewater and South Carolina. German, Scottish, and Scots-Irish immigrants often settled in the backcountry.

**What factors** explain the geographic concentration of colonists of particular ethnic backgrounds?

# WHERE TO LEARN MORE

**Ste. Marie among the Hurons, near Midland, Ontario, Canada.** This site contains a reconstructed Jesuit mission from the seventeenth century. There is a museum with information about seventeenth-century France as well as life among the Huron Indians. Further information may be found at http://www.saintemarieamongthehurons.on.ca.

**Taos Pueblo, Taos, New Mexico.** Still a residence for Pueblo Indians, this multistoried pueblo has portions dating from the fifteenth century. This is the site from which Popé directed the beginnings of the Pueblo Revolt in 1680. Pictures and other information are available at http://www.nps.gov/history/worldheritage/taos.htm.

**African Burial Ground, New York City, NY.** This recently discovered site of an eighteenth-century burial ground for free and enslaved Africans on Manhattan is now a national park and monument. Information about visits and exhibitions can be found at http://www.nps.gov/afbg/index.htm.

**Atkinson Site, Colonial Williamsburg, Williamsburg, Virginia.** Archaeologists are currently excavating this site of an eighteenth-century slave quarter. Information about the site and the artifacts that have been found there is available at http://research.history.org/Archaeological_Research/MHPage/AAArch.htm.

# REVIEW QUESTIONS

1. The first phase of Olaudah Equiano's journey into slavery took him from Africa's interior to the coast. What part of this journey most frightened him? Why? How did the development of a transatlantic labor market shape Equiano's experiences in the New World and the Old?

2. English colonists experienced more frequent, and more violent, conflicts with Indians than the settlers of New France did. Why was this so? What factors affected Indian-European relations in the two colonial regions?

3. Why were Catholic missionaries more successful than Protestants in converting Indians to Christianity in early America?

4. When did Chesapeake planters switch from servants to slaves? What factors contributed to their decision to make this change?

5. By about 1750, more slaves in the mainland British colonies were creoles (American-born) than African-born. What effects did this have on the formation of African American communities in America?

6. Different labor systems predominated in various regions of British America. How did the economy of each region help determine its labor system?

7. Tens of thousands of European immigrants came to America in the eighteenth century, but they tended to settle only in certain colonial regions. What destinations did they favor and why?

# KEY TERMS

**Bacon's Rebellion** (p. 65)  
**Beaver Wars** (p. 61)  
*Encomienda* (p. 60)  
**King Philip's War** (p. 64)  
**Middle Passage** (p. 68)  
**Pueblo Revolt** (p. 65)  
**Redemptioner** (p. 76)  
*Repartimiento* (p. 60)  
**Stono Rebellion** (p. 75)

# PEARSON myhistorylab™ Connections

Reinforce what you learned in this chapter by studying the many documents, images, maps, review tools, and videos available at **www.myhistorylab.com**.

## Read and Review

✓● Study and Review **Study Plan: Chapter 3**

●●●● Read the **Document**

*Olaudah Equiano, The Middle Passage (1788)*

*A Slave Tells of His Capture in Africa (1798)*

*A Virginian Describes the Difference between Servants and Slaves (1722)*

*Runaway Indentured Servants (1640)*

*Runaway Notices from The South Carolina Gazette (1732, 1737)*

*Slaves Revolt in South Carolina (1739)*

*Virginia Law on Indentured Servitude (1705)*

*Wessell Webling, His Indenture (1622)*

👁● See the **Map**

*African Slave Trade, 1500–1870*

*The Atlantic and Islamic Slave Trades*

## Research and Explore

●●●● Read the **Document**

*Personal Journeys Online*

*From Then to Now Online: The Legacy of Slavery*

*Exploring America: Racism in America*

*Watson and the Shark: Reading the Representation of Race*

((•● Hear the **Audio** *I Just Come from the Fountain*

---

((•● Hear the **Audio**

Hear the audio files for Chapter 3 at
**www.myhistorylab.com**.

## The Voyage to Slavery

**WHAT WERE** the dehumanizing experiences faced by Africans as they were kidnapped and transported to the New World as slaves? Under what conditions were Africans taken for slavery, and what was their fate when they arrived in the New World?

Most Africans were captured by other Africans in interior wars between tribes or specifically for sale as slaves. The slaves were moved to the West Coast of Africa where European and American slavers awaited to purchase a human cargo. Slavers inspected their potential cargo for health and strength. Males were preferred because the work on New World plantations would be hard. Human cargo was packed into ships' holds in the most efficient manner and carried under horrible, inhumane conditions to the New World for sale to the highest bidder. It was not unusual for Africans to prefer death to such a fate and individuals would dive overboard or even throw their children into the sea because drowning was considered a better end than that of slavery. For this reason slaves would be kept below decks in leg irons with the exception of an hour or so of exercise each day. During the exercise period slaves would be forced to jump up and down or "dance" to keep their muscles limber and the sale price for each individual at its highest level. Each day dead slaves would be cast overboard and tales abound of schools of sharks trailing slave ships for hundreds of miles.

## The shrieks of the women, ...

*Olaudah Equiano, captured in Nigeria at a very early age, later gave this report of the experience crossing the Atlantic in a slave ship in 1789.*

The closeness of the place [ship's hold], and the heat of the climate, added to the number in the ship, which was so crowded that each had scarcely room to turn himself, almost suffocated us. This produced copious perspirations, so that the air soon became unfit for respiration, from a variety of loathsome smells, and brought on a sickness amongst the slaves, of which many died, thus falling victims to the improvident avarice, as I may call it, of their purchasers. This wretched situation was again aggravated by the galling of the chains, now become insupportable; and the filth of the necessary tubs, into which the children often fell, and were almost suffocated. The shrieks of the women, and the groans of the dying, rendered the whole a scene of horror almost inconceivable. Happily perhaps for myself I was soon reduced so low here that it was thought necessary to keep me almost always on deck; and from my extreme youth I was not put in fetters. In this situation I expected every hour to share the fate of my companions, some of whom were almost daily brought upon deck at the point of death, which I began to hope would soon put an end to my miseries. . . . One day, when we had a smooth sea and moderate wind, two of my wearied countrymen who were chained together (I was near them at the time), preferring death to such a life of misery, somehow made through the nettings and jumped into the sea: immediately another quite dejected fellow, who on account of his illness, was suffered to be out of irons, also followed their example; and I believe many more would very soon have done the same if they had not been prevented by the ship's crew who were instantly alarmed. Those of us that were the most active were in a moment put down under the deck, and there was such a noise and confusion amongst the people of the ship as I never heard before, to stop her, and get

*This eighteenth-century engraving of a slave ship shows how tightly Africans were packed below the decks of these vessels, evidence that the thirst for profit overrode concerns for their health or welfare.*

the boat out to go after the slaves. However two of the wretches were drowned, but they got the other, and afterwards flogged him unmercifully for thus attempting to prefer death to slavery.

*Alexander Falconbridge served as a ship's surgeon aboard a slaver in 1788. He was so horrified by what he witnessed during that time that he became involved in the British abolition movement.*

When the Negroes, whom the black traders have to dispose of, are shown to the European purchasers, they first examine them relative to their age. They then minutely inspect their persons, and inquire into the state of their health; if they are afflicted with any infirmity, or are deformed; or have bad eyes or teeth; if they are lame, or weak in their joints, or distorted in the back, or of a slender make, or are narrow in the chest; in short, if they have been, or are afflicted in any manner, so

African men, women, and children are tied together while walking in chains after being captured by slave traders.

as to render them incapable of much labour; if any of the foregoing defects are discovered in them, they are rejected. But if approved of, they are generally taken on board the ship the same evening. The purchaser has liberty to return on the following morning, but not afterwards, such as upon re-examination are found exceptionable.

The traders frequently beat those Negroes which are objected to by the captains and use them with great severity. It matters not whether they are refused on account of age, illness, deformity, or for any other reason. At New Calabar, in particular, the traders have frequently been known to put them to death. Instances have happened at that place that the traders, when any of their Negroes have been objected to, have dropped their canoes under the stern of the vessel, and instantly beheaded them, in sight of the captain.

Two men brand an African woman kneeling helplessly on the ground.

*The purchaser has liberty to return...*

# 4

# English Colonies in an Age of Empire

New Amsterdam City Hall and Great Dock in the late seventeenth century.

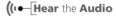 **Hear** the **Audio**

Hear the audio files for Chapter 4 at **www.myhistorylab.com**.

## ECONOMIC DEVELOPMENT AND IMPERIAL TRADE IN THE BRITISH COLONIES *(page 87)*

**WHAT WERE** the goals of British trade policy?

## THE TRANSFORMATION OF CULTURE *(page 93)*

**HOW DID** new intellectual and religious trends reshape colonial culture?

## THE COLONIAL POLITICAL WORLD *(page 98)*

**HOW DID** the "Glorious Revolution" affect colonial politics?

## EXPANDING EMPIRES *(page 102)*

**WHAT WAS** the "backcountry"? Who settled there and why?

North Wind Picture Archives

## A CENTURY OF WARFARE *(page 106)*

**WHAT ROLE** did the colonists play in the French and Indian War?

ONE AMERICAN JOURNEY

*Virginia 26th April 1763*

*Mr. Lawrence*

*Be pleased to send me a genteel sute of Cloaths made of superfine broad Cloth handsomely chosen; I shou[l]d have Inclosed [for] you my measure but in a general way they are so badly taken here that I am convinced it wou[l]d be of very little service; I wou[l]d have you therefore take measure of a Gentleman who wears well made Cloaths of the following size—to wit—Six feet high & proportionably made; if any thing rather Slender than thick for a Person of that highth with pretty long arms & thighs—You will take care to make the Breeches longer than those you sent me last, & I wou[l]d have you keep the measure of the Cloaths you now make by you and if any alteration is required, in my next [letter] it shall be pointed out. Mr Cary will pay your Bill—& I am Sir Yr Very H[um]ble Serv[an]t . . .*
    *George Washington*

W. W. Abbot and Dorothy Twohig, eds., *The Papers of George Washington*, Colonial Series, vol. 7 (Charlottesville, 1990).

●●●─│Read the Document at **www.myhistorylab.com**

**Personal Journeys Online**

- **Eliza Lucas Pinckney,** *Letterbook,* **1742. Description of a South Carolina plantation mistress's day.**

- **Alexander Hamilton,** *Itinerarium,* **1744. Description of sociability in eighteenth-century Philadelphia.**

- **Nathan Cole, "Spiritual Travels," October 23, 1740. A Connecticut farmer hears George Whitefield preach.**

GEORGE WASHINGTON, along with a few dozen other privileged Virginians, had traveled to Williamsburg for a visit that mixed politics, business, and pleasure. Like Washington, these men had come to the capital to represent their respective counties in the House of Burgesses. When not engaged in government business, they attended to private affairs. Washington was surely not the only one to take the opportunity to write to his London tailor and order the fashionable clothing that advertised his status as a gentleman.

April 1763 marked the fourth time Washington had gone to Williamsburg to take his seat in the legislature. Just 31 years old in that year, he had recently married Martha Custis, a wealthy widow, and inherited his older brother's plantation at Mount Vernon. Washington already owned more land than most English gentlemen. With land and wealth to support his ambitions, he wanted to live, look, and behave like an English country gentleman.

Throughout British America, colonists who had achieved wealth and power tried, like Washington, to imitate the habits and manners of the English gentry. Their aspirations testified to important developments in the eighteenth century. Prosperity and the demand of a growing population for English products tied the colonies ever more tightly into a trade network centered on the imperial metropolis, London. The flow of goods and information between Britain and America fueled the desires of Washington and other successful colonists for acceptance as transatlantic members of the British elite.

These developments in Great Britain's American colonies brought them to the attention of European statesmen, who increasingly factored North America into their calculations. Parliament devised legislation to channel colonial products into British ports and away from European competitors. Spain and France viewed the economic growth and geographic expansion of British North America as a threat to their own colonial possessions, and responded by augmenting their own territorial claims. With expansion came conflict, and with conflict, a series of four imperial wars, which themselves became powerful engines of change in the New World. ✦

## CHRONOLOGY

| | |
|---|---|
| **1651–1733** | Parliament passes series of navigation acts to regulate imperial trade. |
| **1660** | Charles II becomes king of England. |
| **1662** | Halfway Covenant adopted by Massachusetts clergy. |
| **1685** | James II becomes king of England. |
| **1686–1689** | Dominion of New England. |
| **1688** | Glorious Revolution in England; James II loses the throne. |
| **1689** | William and Mary become English monarchs; Leisler's Rebellion begins in New York. |
| **1689–1697** | King William's War in America. |
| **1691–1692** | Witchcraft trials in Salem, Massachusetts. |
| **1698** | First French settlements near mouth of Mississippi River. |

| | |
|---|---|
| **1701** | Iroquois adopt policy of neutrality toward France and Britain. |
| **1702–1713** | Queen Anne's War in America. |
| **1707** | Act of Union joins England and Scotland to create Great Britain. |
| **1718** | San Antonio, Texas, and New Orleans founded. |
| **1734–1735** | Jonathan Edwards leads religious revival in Northampton, Massachusetts. |
| **1739** | Great Awakening begins in Middle Colonies with George Whitefield's arrival. |
| **1744–1748** | King George's War in America. |
| **1754–1763** | Seven Years' War in America. |
| **1760s** | Spanish begin establishing missions in California. |

# ECONOMIC DEVELOPMENT AND IMPERIAL TRADE IN THE BRITISH COLONIES

**WHAT WERE** the goals of British trade policy?

England's greatest assets in its competition with other European nations were a dynamic economy and a sophisticated financial system that put commerce at the service of the state. British leaders came to see colonies as indispensable to the nation's economic welfare. Colonies supplied raw materials unavailable in the mother country, and colonists and Indians provided a healthy market for British manufactured goods.

As the eighteenth century progressed, colonial economies grew in tandem with that of Great Britain. Parliament knitted the colonies into an empire with commercial legislation, while British merchants traded with and extended credit to growing numbers of colonial merchants and planters. Over time, these developments integrated the economies of the colonies with that of the mother country in a vast transatlantic system.

## THE REGULATION OF TRADE

To improve its competitive position in transatlantic trade, England adopted a policy of **mercantilism.** The goal was to achieve a favorable balance of trade within the empire as a whole, with exports exceeding imports. Colonies played a crucial role, since they supplied commodities that British consumers would otherwise have to purchase from foreign competitors. Certain colonial products, such as tobacco or rice, could also be exported to foreign markets, further improving the balance of trade. Between 1651 and 1733, Parliament passed four types of mercantilist regulations to put this policy into action (see the Overview table, British Imperial Trade Regulations, 1651–1733).

The first type of regulation aimed at ending Dutch dominance in overseas trade. Beginning with the Navigation Act of 1651, all trade in the empire had to be conducted in English or colonial ships, with crews of which at least half were Englishmen or colonists. The act stimulated rapid growth in England's merchant marine and New England's shipping industry, which soon became the most profitable sector of New England's economy.

**mercantilism**   Economic system whereby the government intervenes in the economy for the purpose of increasing national wealth.

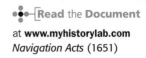

at **www.myhistorylab.com**
*Navigation Acts* (1651)

**enumerated products**   Items produced in the colonies and enumerated in acts of Parliament that could be legally shipped from the colony of origin only to specified locations.

## QUICK REVIEW

### British Trade Policy

- All trade in empire to be conducted on English or colonial ships.
- Colonial trade to be channeled through England or another English colony.
- Subsidization of English goods offered for sale in the colonies.
- Colonists prohibited from large-scale manufacture of certain products.

The second type of legislation stipulated that certain colonial goods, called **enumerated products,** could be shipped only to England or to another English colony. These goods initially included tobacco, sugar, and indigo; other products, such as rice, were added later. These laws also required European goods to pass through England before they could be shipped to the colonies. When these goods entered English ports, they were taxed, making them more expensive and encouraging colonists to buy English-made items.

The third and fourth types of regulations further enhanced the advantage of English manufacturers who produced for the colonial market. Parliament subsidized certain goods, including linen and gunpowder, to allow manufacturers to undersell European competitors in the colonies. Other laws protected English manufacturers from colonial competition by prohibiting colonists from manufacturing wool, felt hats, and iron on a large scale.

England's commercial goals were largely achieved. The Dutch eventually lost their preeminence in the Atlantic trade. Colonial trade helped the English economy to grow and contributed to London's emergence as Western Europe's largest city. Colonists enjoyed protected markets for their staple crops and low prices on English imports. Colonial merchants took full advantage of commercial opportunities within the empire.

Occasionally, merchants evaded these laws by smuggling. Customs officials, sent over from England beginning in the 1670s, were hard-pressed to stop them. Smuggling tended to increase in wartime; the risks may have been higher, but so too were profits. Without the support of colonial authorities (some of whom might be involved in illicit trade themselves), customs officials struggled to enforce parliamentary regulations.

## THE COLONIAL EXPORT TRADE AND THE SPIRIT OF ENTERPRISE

By the mid-eighteenth century, the Atlantic had become a busy thoroughfare of international commerce (see Map 4–1). British and colonial vessels carried goods and people from Great Britain, continental Europe, and West Africa to the colonies and returned raw materials to the Old World. At the heart of Anglo-American trade lay the highly profitable commerce in staple crops, most of which were produced by slave labor.

West Indian sugar far surpassed all other colonial products in importance (see Figure 4–1). By the late 1760s, the value of sugar exports reached almost £4 million per year—nearly 50 percent more than the total value of all other exports from British American colonies.

Tobacco from the Chesapeake colonies was the second most valuable staple crop. Nearly 90 percent of the crop was reexported to continental Europe. Persistent low prices, however, led many tobacco planters to sow some of their land with wheat after about 1750. This change lessened their dependence on tobacco and allowed them to take advantage of the strong demand for flour in southern Europe and the West Indies.

Exports of rice and indigo (a plant that produced a blue dye used in textile manufacture) enriched many South Carolina planters. Parliament encouraged indigo production by granting subsidies to growers and placing stiff taxes on foreign indigo. It also subsidized colonial production of naval stores—such as tar, pitch, and turpentine—to reduce England's dependence on Swedish suppliers.

Wheat exports from the Middle Colonies boomed in the eighteenth century. Since farmers in Great Britain grew enough wheat to supply the domestic market, there was little demand there for colonial flour. But there was a strong market for it in the West Indies and Europe, particularly when a series of poor harvests and warfare disrupted European supplies.

New England had no staple crop and produced little for export. The region's merchants nevertheless prospered by carrying other colonies' goods to market. By 1770, New England's earnings from shipping fees, freight charges, and insurance exceeded the total value of its own exports.

## QUICK REVIEW

### Colonial Exports

- Chesapeake colonies: tobacco.
- South Carolina: rice and indigo.
- Middle Colonies: wheat.

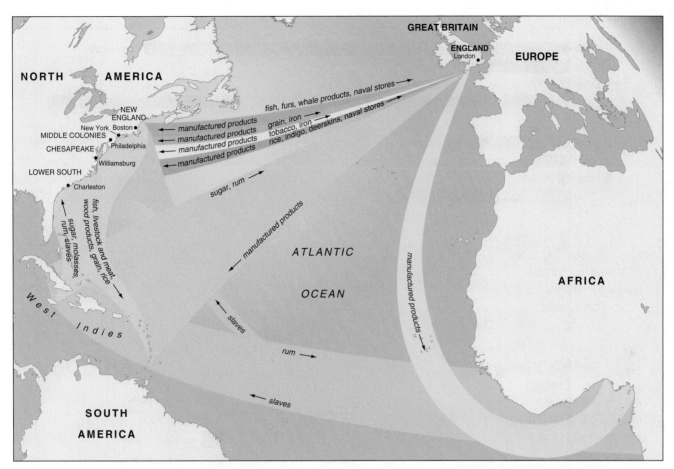

MAP 4–1  **Anglo-American Transatlantic Commerce**  By the eighteenth century, Great Britain and its colonies were enmeshed in a complex web of trade. Britain exchanged manufactured goods for colonial raw materials, while Africa provided the enslaved laborers who produced the most valuable colonial crops.

**The transatlantic** commerce of this era is sometimes referred to as the "triangular trade." Does this map support or complicate this description?

New England merchants also strengthened trade links to the West Indies that had first been forged in the 1650s. By the mid-eighteenth century, more than half of all New England exports went to the islands. Merchants accepted molasses and other sugar by-products in payment, bringing them back to New England to be distilled into cheap rum. Traders then carried rum to Africa to exchange for slaves. Although British merchants dominated the African slave trade, New Englanders also profited. Less than 10 percent of New England's population were slaves, but because New Englanders trafficked in human cargo and provisioned the West Indies, their commercial economy nonetheless depended on slavery.

## THE IMPORT TRADE AND TIES OF CREDIT

By the late 1760s, over £4 million worth of British manufactured goods flowed into the colonies each year. This import trade satisfied a demand for items that could not be produced—at least not cheaply—in North America.

Imported weapons, woolen cloth, knives, and jewelry often made their way into Indian villages. Indians were discerning customers and rejected goods not made to their liking. Native leaders sometimes acquired imported goods for exchange with allies as well as for their own use.

See the **Map**
at **www.myhistorylab.com**
*Colonial Products*

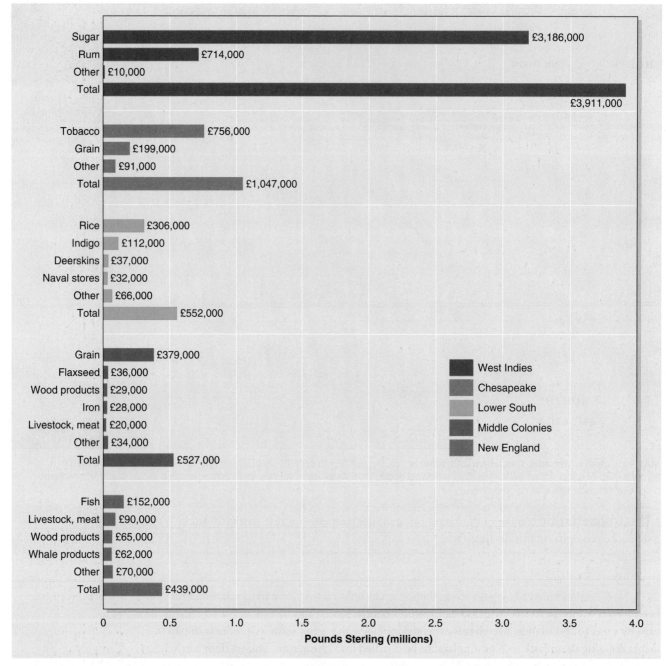

**FIGURE 4–1  Average Annual Value of Colonial Exports by Region, 1768–1772**  Staple crops—especially sugar—produced by slave labor were the most valuable items exported from Britain's North American colonies.

*Data Source:* John J. McCusker and Russell R. Menard, *The Economy of British America, 1607–1789,* rev. ed. (1991). University of North Carolina Press.

The colonists' even heavier consumption of manufactured goods was vital to British overseas commerce. In terms of value, colonists imported more goods than they exported. This imbalance was remedied in good part by colonial earnings from shipping fees and payments from the British government for colonial military expenses.

British merchants extended credit to colonists on generous terms so they could buy British products. Major tobacco planters virtually lived on the easy credit that British merchants provided. These merchants marketed the planters' tobacco and supplied them with English goods, charging the costs of purchase and transportation against the profits they expected the next year's crop to bring.

Scenes like this were common in the dockyards at Deptford and other parts of eighteenth-century London. Boxes and barrels of English goods were loaded aboard sailing ships that returned months later with sugar, tobacco, rice, and other products from every part of England's worldwide empire.

Easy credit let planters indulge themselves with English goods, and many sank into debt. When trade was brisk and tobacco prices high, no one worried. But when tobacco prices dropped or an international crisis made overseas trading risky, creditors called in the debts owed to them. At such times, colonial debtors realized how much they (like the Indians involved in European trade) depended on goods and credit supplied by distant merchants.

## BECOMING MORE LIKE BRITAIN: THE GROWTH OF CITIES AND INEQUALITY

As colonial commerce grew, so did colonial cities—the connecting points in the economic network tying the colonies to London and other British ports. Boston, New York, Philadelphia, and Charleston were as large as many British provincial towns. Only about 5 percent of all mainland colonists lived in cities, but the influence of urban centers far outweighed their size.

## OVERVIEW  British Imperial Trade Regulations, 1651–1733

| Name of Act | Key Features |
| --- | --- |
| Navigation Act of 1651 | Aimed to eliminate Dutch competition in overseas trade<br>Required most goods to be carried in English or colonial ships<br>Required crews to be at least half English |
| Navigation Act of 1660 | Required all colonial trade to be carried in English ships<br>Required master and three-quarters of crew to be English<br>Created list of enumerated goods, such as tobacco and sugar, that could be shipped only to England or another English colony |
| Staple Act of 1663 | Required products from Europe, Asia, and Africa to be landed in England before being shipped to the colonies |
| Plantation Duty Act of 1673 | Attempted to reduce smuggling<br>Required captains of colonial ships to post bond that they would deliver enumerated goods to England or pay the "plantation duty" that would be owed in England |
| Navigation Act of 1696 | Plugged loopholes in earlier laws<br>Created vice-admiralty courts in colonies to enforce trade regulations |
| Woolens Act of 1699 | Forbade export of woolen cloth made in the colonies, to prevent competition with English producers |
| Hat Act of 1732 | Prohibited export of colonial-made hats |
| Molasses Act of 1733 | Placed high tax on French West Indian and other foreign molasses imported into colonies to encourage importation of British West Indian molasses |

All colonial cities (like Britain's major ones) were seaports. With their bustle and cosmopolitan atmosphere, colonial cities resembled British provincial cities more than they did the farming villages of the American countryside. Cities provided such amenities as inns, taverns, coffeehouses, theaters, and social clubs. Their populations were diverse in ethnic origin and religion. In addition, the African American population in the northern colonies tended to live in cities. By 1750, slaves made up 20 percent of New York City's population, about 10 percent of Philadelphia's, and nearly 9 percent of Boston's.

**Artisans in colonial cities.** Colonial cities had higher proportions of artisans than did rural villages. Many of them labored at trades directly related to overseas commerce, such as shipbuilding or ropemaking. Others produced pottery, furniture, paper, glassware, and iron tools.

Colonial manufacturing took place in workshops often attached to artisans' houses. Artisans managed a workforce consisting of their wives and children, along with journeymen or apprentices. Usually teenage boys, apprentices contracted to work for a master for four to seven years. Like indentured servants, they received no wages but worked for food, clothing, shelter, and a small payment at the end of their service. Once an apprentice finished his training, he became a journeyman, working for a master but now earning wages and saving to set up his own shop.

Many artisans flourished in colonial cities, but prosperity was by no means guaranteed. In Philadelphia, skilled artisans typically earned enough for a modest subsistence. Yet workers at less skilled crafts often made only a bare living, and ordinary laborers faced seasonal unemployment.

((•─ Hear the Audio
at www.myhistorylab.com
*The Connecticut Peddler*

This view of the Philadelphia waterfront dates from 1720. It shows how the city had developed into one of British America's principal ports just forty years after its founding.

Peter Cooper, "The Southeast Prospect of the City of Philadelphia," ca. 1720. The Library Company of Philadelphia.

Cities like Philadelphia, New York, and Charleston provided opportunities for some women to support themselves with craft work. Mary Wallace and Clementia Ferguson, for instance, stitched fashionable hats and dresses for New York customers. Nonetheless, even in cities, women's options were limited. Most employed women were widows striving to maintain a family business until sons grew old enough to take over.

**The growing gap between rich and poor.** Wherever colonists engaged heavily in commerce—in cities or on plantations—the gap between rich and poor widened during the eighteenth century. In 1687, the richest 10 percent of Boston's residents owned 46 percent of the taxable property in the town; by 1771, the top tenth held 63 percent of the taxable wealth. Similar changes occurred in Philadelphia. In South Carolina and the Chesapeake, many planters added to the already substantial holdings in land and slaves that they had inherited. It became increasingly difficult for newcomers to enter their ranks. At the same time, the colonies' growing reliance on slave labor—especially in the South—created a sizable class of impoverished people denied the chance to better their condition. By 1770, slaves, for whom America was anything but a land of opportunity, constituted one out of five residents of the British colonies.

To address the growing problem of poverty among white colonists, cities built workhouses, and towns collected funds for poor relief in greater amounts than ever before. Many poor people were aged or ill, without families to help them. Able-bodied workers forced to accept public relief usually owed their misfortune to temporary downturns in the economy.

Even in the worst of times, no more than one out of ten white colonists (mainly city dwellers) depended on public assistance. For free black people who were unemployed and denied public relief, conditions were far worse. A Pennsylvania law went so far as to allow them to be enslaved. And, bad as it was, the problem of poverty among white colonists had not reached anything like the levels seen in Britain. As much as one-third of England's population regularly received relief, and the numbers swelled during hard times. Eighteenth-century white colonists, on average, enjoyed a higher standard of living than most British residents or other Europeans. So long as land was available—even if one had to move to the edges of settlement to get it— colonists could at least eke out a bare subsistence, and many did much better.

# THE TRANSFORMATION OF CULTURE

Despite the convergence of British and colonial society, many influential settlers worried that America remained culturally inferior to Great Britain. During the eighteenth century, some prosperous colonists strove to overcome this provincial sense of inferiority. They built grand houses and filled them with imported goods, cultivated what they took to be the manners of the British gentry, and followed British and European intellectual developments. Some colonial gentlemen

HOW DID new intellectual and religious trends reshape colonial culture?

The Governor's Palace in Williamsburg, Virginia, completed in 1722, was one of the grandest and most expensive dwellings in the colony.

**Read the Document**

at **www.myhistorylab.com**
*Benjamin Wadsworth, from*
*A Well-Ordered Family* (1712)

**W** WHERE TO LEARN MORE

★ Berkeley and Westover Plantations,
Charles City, Virginia
http://www.jamesriverplantations.org

**W** WHERE TO LEARN MORE

★ Mount Vernon, Virginia
http://www.mountvernon.org

even reshaped their religious beliefs to reflect European notions that God played only an indirect role in human affairs.

These elite aspirations, however, were not shared by all settlers. Most colonists, although they might purchase a few imported goods, had little interest in copying the manners of the British elite, and few of them altered their spiritual beliefs to fit European patterns. Indeed, familiar religious practices flourished in eighteenth-century America, and when a tremendous revival swept through the colonies beginning in the 1730s, religion occupied center stage in American life.

## GOODS AND HOUSES

Eighteenth-century Americans imported more manufactured products from England with every passing year. This practice did not simply reflect the growth of the colonial population, for the rate at which Americans bought British goods exceeded the rate of population increase. Colonists owned more goods, often of better quality, than their parents and grandparents had possessed.

In the less secure economic climate of the seventeenth century, colonists had limited their purchases of goods, investing instead in land to pass on to their children. But by the eighteenth century, prosperous colonists felt secure enough to buy goods to make their lives more comfortable. Colonists acquired such goods to advertise their more refined style of life.

Prosperous colonists built grand houses where they lived in greater comfort than ever before. By the 1730s, numerous southern planters had built "great houses" while others transformed older houses into more stylish residences. Washington extensively remodeled Mount Vernon, adding a second story and extra wings to create a home fit for a gentleman. In the northern colonies, merchants built the most impressive houses, often following architectural pattern books imported from England.

These houses were not only larger but also different in design from the homes of less affluent colonists. Most settlers lived in one- or two-room dwellings and thus cooked, ate, and slept in the same chamber. But the owners of great houses could devote rooms to specialized uses, such as kitchens and private bedrooms.

Prosperous colonists did not build such homes merely to advertise their wealth. They wanted to create the proper setting for a refined way of life, emulating the English gentry in their country estates and London townhouses. But they knew that the true measure of their gentility lay not just in where they lived and what they owned but in how they behaved.

## SHAPING MINDS AND MANNERS

Colonists knew that the manners of British gentlefolk set them apart from ordinary people. Many Americans therefore imported "courtesy books" containing the rules of polite behavior. These publications advised would-be gentlemen on how to show regard for social rank, practice personal cleanliness, and respect other people's feelings. Many colonists subscribed to English journals such as the *Tatler* and the *Spectator* that printed articles describing good manners.

Women, too, cultivated genteel manners. In Charleston, South Carolina, and other colonial cities, girls' boarding schools advertised instruction in "Polite Education." Female pupils received only the rudiments of intellectual training in reading, writing, and arithmetic, for it was assumed that women had little need of such accomplishments. The private schools' curricula instead focused on French, music, dancing, and fancy needlework. These were skills that advertised girls' genteel status and prepared them for married lives as elite ladies.

Some people expressed their gentility through more intellectual pursuits, taking advantage of the relatively high literacy rates among white colonists. In New England, where settlers placed great emphasis on Bible study, about 70 percent of men and 45 percent of women could read and write. Only a third of men in the southern colonies, and even fewer women, could read and write, but even these literacy rates were higher than among Britain's general population. Eighteenth-century colonists enjoyed greater access to printed material than ever before. In 1704, the *Boston News-Letter* became the first continuously published newspaper in British America. By the 1760s nearly every colony had a regularly published newspaper, and booksellers opened shops in several cities. Prominent colonists began to participate in a transatlantic world of ideas.

Educated colonists were especially interested in the new ideas that characterized what has been called the **Age of Enlightenment.** The European thinkers of the Enlightenment drew inspiration from recent advances in science that suggested that the universe operated according to natural laws that human reason could discover. The hallmark of Enlightenment thought was a belief in the power of human reason to improve the human condition.

This optimistic worldview marked a profound intellectual shift. Enlightenment thinkers rejected earlier ideas about God's unknowable will and continued intervention in human and natural events. They instead assigned God a less active role as the creator of the universe, who had set the world running according to predictable laws, and then let nature and humans shape events. Such ideas inspired a growing international community of scholars to try to discover the laws of nature and to work toward human progress.

Colonial intellectuals sought membership in this scholarly community. A few of them—the Reverend Cotton Mather of Massachusetts, William Byrd, Benjamin Franklin—gained election to the Royal Society, the most prestigious learned society in England. Most of their scholarly contributions were unimpressive, but Franklin achieved genuine intellectual prominence. His experiments with a kite proved that lightning was electricity (a natural force whose properties were poorly understood at the time) and gained him an international reputation.

If Franklin's career embodied the Enlightenment ideal of the rational exploration of nature's laws, it also revealed the limited impact of Enlightenment thought in colonial America. Only a few prosperous and educated colonists could afford such intellectual pursuits. Franklin came from humble origins—his father was a maker of candles and soap—but his success as a printer allowed him to retire from business at the age of 42. Only then did he purchase the equipment for his electrical discoveries and have the leisure time to begin his scientific work. Franklin's equipment—and leisure—were as much badges of gentlemanly status as George Washington's London-made suit.

Most colonists remained ignorant of scientific advances and Enlightenment ideas, having little leisure to devote to literature and polite conversation. When they found time to read, they picked up not a courtesy book or the *Spectator* but the Bible, which was the best-selling book of the colonial era. Religion principally shaped the way in which they viewed the world and explained human and natural events.

**Age of Enlightenment** Major intellectual movement occurring in Western Europe in the late seventeenth and early eighteenth centuries.

**QUICK REVIEW**

**Enlightenment Thought**

- Inspired by scientific advances.
- Emphasis on the power of reason to improve human life.
- Assigned God a less active role in human affairs.

## COLONIAL RELIGION AND THE GREAT AWAKENING

Church steeples dominated the skylines of colonial cities. By the 1750s, Boston and New York each had eighteen churches, and Philadelphia boasted twenty. Churches and meetinghouses likewise dominated country towns. Often the largest and finest buildings in the community, they bore witness to the diverse and thriving condition of religion in America.

In every New England colony except Rhode Island, the Puritan (or Congregationalist) faith was the established religion. Congregational churches in the region, headed by ministers trained at Harvard College and Yale (founded in 1701), served the majority of colonists, who were required to pay taxes to support them. Though proud of the Puritan tradition that had inspired New England's origins, ministers and believers nonetheless had to adapt to changing social and religious conditions.

By the time he was in his forties, Benjamin Franklin had already achieved considerable fame as an author, scientist, and inventor.

Mason Chamberlain (1727–1787), "Portrait of Benjamin Franklin." 1762. Oil on canvas, 503/8 × 403/4 inches (128 × 103.5 cm). Gift of Mr. and Mrs. Wharton Sinkler, 1956. Location: Philadelphia Museum of Art, Philadelphia, Pennsylvania, U.S.A./Art Resource, NY.

**Halfway Covenant** Plan adopted in 1662 by New England clergy to deal with problem of declining church membership, allowing children of baptized parents to be baptized whether or not their parents had experienced conversion.

**Read the Document**
at **www.myhistorylab.com**
*Exploring America:*
*The Great Awakening*

The principal adaptation consisted of a move away from strict requirements for church membership. In order to keep their churches pure, New England's founders had required prospective members to give convincing evidence that they had experienced a spiritual conversion before they could receive communion and have their children baptized. By the 1660s, however, fewer colonists sought admission under such strict standards, which left them and their unbaptized children outside the church. To address this problem, the clergy in 1662 adopted the **Halfway Covenant.** This allowed adults who had been baptized (because their parents were church members), but who had not themselves experienced conversion, to have their own children baptized.

Congregational churches also had to accept a measure of religious toleration in New England. In 1691, Massachusetts received a royal charter granting "liberty of Conscience" to all Protestants, bringing the colony in line with England's religious policy. At the same time, some Congregationalist preachers began emphasizing personal piety and good works in their sermons, ideas usually associated with Anglicanism. These changes indicated a shift away from the Puritan exclusiveness of New England's early years.

In the South, the established Church of England consolidated its authority in the early eighteenth century but never exerted effective control over spiritual life. Many a parson in England could ride from one side of his parish to the other in an hour, but Anglican clergymen in the southern colonies served parishes that were vast and sparsely settled. One South Carolina parish contained 10,400 square miles and only seven hundred white residents. Ministers also found that influential planters, accustomed to running parishes when preachers were unavailable, resisted their efforts to take control of churches. Aware that the planters' taxes paid their salaries, many ministers found it easiest simply to preach and behave in ways that offered the least offense. Frontier regions often lacked Anglican churches and clergymen altogether. In such places, dissenting religious groups, such as Presbyterians, Quakers, and Baptists, gained followers among people neglected by the Anglican establishment.

No established church dominated in the Middle Colonies of New York, New Jersey, and Pennsylvania. The region's ethnically diverse population and William Penn's policy of religious toleration guaranteed that a multitude of groups would compete for followers. Yet religion flourished in the Middle Colonies. By the middle of the eighteenth century, the region had more congregations per capita than even New England.

Groups such as the Quakers and the Mennonites, who did not have specially trained ministers, easily formed new congregations in response to local demand. Lutheran and German Reformed churches, however, required European-educated clergy, who were always scarce. Pious laymen held worship services in their homes even as they sent urgent letters overseas begging for ordained ministers. When more Lutheran and Reformed clergy arrived in the 1740s and 1750s, they sometimes discovered, as Anglican preachers did in the South, that laymen balked at relinquishing control of the churches.

Bewildering spiritual diversity, relentless religious competition, and a comparatively weak Anglican Church all distinguished the colonies from Britain. Yet in one important way, religious developments during the middle third of the eighteenth century drew the colonies closer to Britain. A great transatlantic religious revival, originating in Scotland and England, first touched the Middle Colonies in the 1730s. In 1740–1745, it struck the northern colonies with the force of a hurricane, and in the 1760s, the last phase of the revival spread through the South.

America had never seen anything like this immense revival, which came to be called the **Great Awakening.**

By 1730, Presbyterians in Pennsylvania had split into factions over such issues as the disciplining of church members and the requirement that licensed ministers have university degrees. What began as a dispute among clergymen eventually blossomed into a broader challenge to religious authority. That challenge gained momentum in late 1739, when one of the most charismatic evangelists of the century, George Whitefield, arrived in the colonies from England.

Whitefield, an Anglican minister, had experienced an intense religious conversion while he was still a university student. Already famous in Britain as a preacher of great emotional fervor, he embarked on a tour of the colonies in the winter of 1739–1740. As soon as Whitefield landed in Delaware, his admirers whipped up local enthusiasm, ensuring that he would preach to huge crowds in Pennsylvania and New Jersey. Whitefield then moved on to New England, where some communities had already experienced local awakenings. In 1734–1735, for instance, the Congregationalist minister Jonathan Edwards had led a revival in Northampton, Massachusetts, urging his parishioners to recognize their sinfulness and describing hell in such a terrifying way that many despaired of salvation.

Whitefield's tour through the colonies knitted these scattered local revivals into the Great Awakening. Crowds gathered in city squares and open fields to listen to his sermons. Whitefield exhorted his audiences to examine their souls for evidence of the "indwelling of Christ" that would indicate that they were saved. He criticized other ministers for emphasizing good works and "head-knowledge" instead of the emotional side of religion.

Whitefield's open-air sermons scarcely resembled the colonists' accustomed form of worship. Settlers normally gathered with family and neighbors in church for formal, structured services. They sat in pews assigned on the basis of social status, reinforcing standards of order and community hierarchy. But Whitefield's sermons were highly dramatic performances. He preached for hours in a booming voice, gesturing wildly and sometimes even dissolving in tears. Thousands of strangers, jostling in crowds that often outnumbered the populations of several villages put together, wept along with him.

In the wake of Whitefield's visits, Benjamin Franklin noted, "it seem'd as if all the World were growing Religious." Revivals and mass conversions often followed his appearances, to the happy astonishment of local clergy. But their approval evaporated when more extreme revivalists appeared. Officials who valued civic order tried to silence such extremists by passing laws that prohibited them from preaching in a town without the local minister's permission.

Disputes between individuals converted in the revivals—called **New Lights**—and those who were not (Old Lights) split churches. New Lights insisted, as the separatist founders of Plymouth once had, that they could not remain in churches with sinful members and unconverted ministers and so left to form new churches.

The Awakening came late to the southern colonies, but it was there, in the 1760s, that it produced perhaps its greatest controversy. Many southern converts became Baptists, combining religious criticism of the Anglicans with condemnation of the wealthy planters' way of life. Plainly dressed Baptists criticized the rich clothes, drinking, gambling, and pride of Virginia's gentry. The planters, in turn, viewed the Baptists as dangerous people who could not "meet a man upon the road, but they must ram a text of Scripture down his throat." Most of all, they hated the Baptists for their willingness to preach to slaves.

Although the revivals themselves gradually waned, the Great Awakening had a lasting impact on colonial society. In addition to introducing colonists to a fervent evangelicalism, it forged new links between Great Britain and the colonies. Evangelical ministers on both sides of the Atlantic exchanged correspondence. Periodicals such as the *Christian History* informed British and American subscribers of advances in true religion throughout the empire.

The revivals also brought newcomers into Christian congregations. Chesapeake slaves responded to the evangelists' message and—often contrary to the intent of the white

**Great Awakening** Tremendous religious revival in colonial America striking first in the Middle Colonies and New England in the 1740s and then spreading to the southern colonies.

⊙⊙⊙─[**Read** the **Document**

at **www.myhistorylab.com**
*Jonathan Edwards, "Some Thoughts"* (1742)

⊙⊙⊙─[**Read** the **Document**

at **www.myhistorylab.com**
*Benjamin Franklin on George Whitefield* (1771)

**New Lights** People who experienced conversion during the revivals of the Great Awakening.

During George Whitefield's tour of the American colonies in 1739–1741, the famous revivalist minister often preached to large crowds gathered outdoors to hear one of his powerful sermons.

preachers—drew lessons about the equality of humankind. A few black preachers circulated in the slave quarters, spreading the message of salvation and freedom. The impact of revivalism on Indians was less dramatic, but still significant. Evangelicals enjoyed their greatest success in small Native American communities, whose inhabitants were attracted to a less formal style of preaching, particularly in New England. Native converts often urged fellow Indians to heed the Christian message of self-discipline, not to emulate English colonists, but to revitalize villages beset by alcoholism and other problems linked to European domination.

The Awakening did not greatly increase women's church membership, since women already constituted majorities in many congregations. But by emphasizing the emotional power of Christianity, revivals accorded greater legitimacy to what was thought to be women's more sensitive temperament.

Everywhere, the New Light challenge to established ministers and churches undermined habits of deference to authority. Revivalists urged colonists to think for themselves in choosing which church to join, and not just to conform to what the rest of the community did. As their churches fractured, colonists faced more choices than ever before in their religious lives.

The exercise of religious choice also influenced political behavior. Voters noticed whether candidates for office were New or Old Lights and cast their ballots for men on their own side. Tactics first used to mobilize religious groups—such as organizing committees and writing petitions and letters—also proved useful for political activities. The Awakening thus fostered greater political awareness and participation among colonists.

## THE COLONIAL POLITICAL WORLD

**HOW DID** the "Glorious Revolution" affect colonial politics?

The political legacy of the Great Awakening—particularly the emphasis on individual choice and resistance to authority—corresponded to developments in the colonial political world. For most of the seventeenth century, ties within the empire developed from trade rather than governance. But as America grew in wealth and population, king and Parliament sought to manage colonial affairs more directly.

## THE DOMINION OF NEW ENGLAND AND THE LIMITS OF BRITISH CONTROL

Before 1650, England made little attempt to exert centralized control in North America. Each colony more or less governed itself, and most political activity occurred at the town or county level. Busy with the routines of daily life, most colonists devoted little time, and even less interest, to politics.

When Charles II became king in 1660, he initially showed little interest in the colonies except as sources of land and government offices with which he could reward his supporters. Charles's brother James, the duke of York, envisioned a more tightly controlled empire. He encouraged Charles to appoint military officers with strong ties of loyalty to him as royal governors. In 1675, James convinced Charles to create the Lords of Trade, a committee of the Privy Council (the group of nobles who served as royal advisers), to oversee colonial affairs.

When James II became king in 1685, the whole character of the empire abruptly changed. Seeking to transform it into something much more susceptible to England's control, James set out to reorganize it along the lines of Spain's empire, combining the colonies into three or four large provinces. He appointed powerful governors to carry out policies that he himself would formulate.

James began in the north, creating the **Dominion of New England** out of eight previously separate colonies stretching from Maine (then part of Massachusetts) to New Jersey. He chose Sir Edmund Andros, a former army officer, to govern the vast region with an appointive council but no elective assembly.

**Dominion of New England** James II's failed plan of 1686 to combine eight northern colonies into a single large province, to be governed by a royal appointee with no elective assembly.

Events in England ultimately sealed the fate of the Dominion. For years, English Protestants had worried about James's absolutist governing style and his conversion to Catholicism. Their fears increased in 1688, when the queen bore a son to carry on a Catholic line of succession. Parliament's leaders invited Mary, James's Protestant daughter from his first marriage, and her husband, William of Orange, the stadtholder of the Netherlands, to take over the throne. In November 1688, William landed in England and gained the support of most of the English army. In December, James fled to France, ending a bloodless coup known as the **Glorious Revolution.**

Bostonians overthrew Andros the following April and shipped him back to England. Massachusetts colonists hoped that their original charter of 1629 would be reinstated, but a new one was issued in 1691. It made several important changes. Massachusetts now included the formerly separate Plymouth Colony as well as Maine. Its colonists no longer elected their governor, who would instead be appointed by the monarch. Voters no longer had to be church members, and religious toleration was extended to all Protestants. The new charter ended exclusive Puritan control in Massachusetts but also restored political stability.

**Glorious Revolution** Bloodless revolt that occurred in England in 1688 when parliamentary leaders invited William of Orange, a Protestant, to assume the English throne.

The impact of the Glorious Revolution in other colonies likewise reflected local conditions. In Maryland, Protestants used the occasion of William and Mary's accession to the throne to lobby for the end of the Catholic proprietorship. They were partly successful. The Calvert family lost its governing powers but retained rights to vast quantities of land. The Anglican Church became the established faith, and Catholics were barred from public office.

## SALEM WITCHCRAFT

In Massachusetts, during the three years between Andros's overthrow and the arrival of a royal governor in 1692, the colony lacked a legally established government. In this atmosphere of uncertainty, an outbreak of accusations of witchcraft in Salem grew to unprecedented proportions. Over the years, New Englanders had executed a dozen or so accused witches, usually older

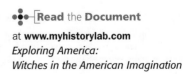

●●●—Read the **Document**
at **www.myhistorylab.com**
*Exploring America:*
*Witches in the American Imagination*

women. But in the winter of 1691–1692, when several young girls of Salem experienced fits and other strange behavior, hundreds of settlers were accused of witchcraft and nineteen were hanged.

Salem's crisis occurred against a backdrop of local economic change, which created friction between agrarian and more commercial parts of the town. Recent conflicts with Indians on the nearby frontier also made many colonists worry that God was punishing them for their sins. Moreover, the town had recently experienced bitter controversy over the appointment of a minister. All of these tensions contributed to the frenzy of witchcraft accusations.

## THE LEGACY OF THE GLORIOUS REVOLUTION

At the time of the Glorious Revolution, colonists rejected James II, not English authority in general. Their motives largely reflected powerful anti-Catholic sentiment. William's firm Protestantism reassured them, and most colonists assumed that life would return to normal. But the Glorious Revolution in England and the demise of the Dominion had long-lasting effects that shaped political life in England and America for years to come.

In England, the Glorious Revolution signaled a return to political stability after years of upheaval. English people celebrated the preservation of their rights from the threat of a tyrannical king. In 1689, Parliament passed the Bill of Rights, which justified James's ouster and bound future monarchs to abide by the rule of law. They could not suspend statutes, collect taxes, or engage in foreign wars without Parliament's consent, or maintain a standing army in peacetime. Parliamentary elections and meetings would follow a regular schedule, without royal interference. In sum, Parliament claimed to be the crown's equal partner in governing England.

Colonists, too, celebrated the vindication of their rights as Englishmen. They believed that their successful resistance to Andros confirmed that their membership in the empire was founded on voluntary allegiance, not forced submission to the mother country. Observing the similarity between Parliament and the colonial assemblies, they concluded that their own legislatures had a critical role in governance and in the protection of their rights and liberties. On both sides of the Atlantic, representative government had triumphed.

In fact, Parliament claimed full authority over the colonies and did not recognize their assemblies as its equal. For more than a half-century, however, it did not vigorously assert that authority. In addition, William and his immediate successors lacked James's compulsion to control the colonies. During the early eighteenth century, Parliament and royal ministers confined their attention to matters of trade and military defense and otherwise left the colonies on their own. This mild imperial rule, later called the era of "salutary neglect," allowed the colonies to grow in wealth, population, and self-government. It also encouraged colonists to assume equality with the English as members of the empire.

## DIVERGING POLITICS IN THE COLONIES AND GREAT BRITAIN

British people on both sides of the Atlantic believed that politics ought to reflect social organization. They often compared the state to a family. Just as fathers naturally headed families, adult men led societies. In particular, adult male property holders, who enjoyed economic independence, claimed the right to vote and hold office. Women (who generally could not own property), propertyless men, and slaves had no political role because they, like children, were subordinate to the authority of others. Their dependence on husbands, fathers, masters, or employers—who could influence their political decisions—rendered them incapable of exercising freedom of choice.

Eighteenth-century people also believed that government should reflect society's hierarchical organization. In Britain, this idea was embodied in the monarchy and Parliament. The crown, of course, represented the interests of the royal family. Parliament represented society's two main divisions: the aristocracy in the House of Lords and the common people in the House

•••┤Read the Document

at www.myhistorylab.com
*Ann Putnam's Confession* (1706)

**QUICK REVIEW**

**Glorious Revolution**

- 1688: James II forced from throne in bloodless coup.
- Massachusetts receives new charter.
- Broad support for Glorious Revolution throughout colonies.

of Commons. Americans shared the view that government should mirror social hierarchies but found it much more difficult to put the idea into practice.

American society grew closer to the British model during the eighteenth century but was never identical to it. Thus, its political structure would never fully mirror that of Britain. One obvious difference was that America lacked an aristocracy. Elite colonists were often just two or three generations removed from humble beginnings. Hence the acute anxiety that inspired George Washington and other colonial gentlemen to seek refinement, to gain the automatic recognition that Britain's elites enjoyed.

In both Britain and America, land ownership was the prerequisite for political participation, because it freed people from dependence on others and gave them a stake in society. In Britain, this requirement sharply limited participation. Landholding in America, however, was much more widespread. A majority of white male farmers eventually owned the land they tilled, and in most colonies, 50 to 75 percent of white men were eligible to vote.

Distinctive social conditions in Britain and America also gave rise to different notions of political representation. Electoral districts for Parliament came in a confusing mixture of shapes, reflecting their status in past centuries. Once-important towns sent representatives on the basis of their former prominence. At the same time, rapidly growing cities, such as Manchester, lacked any representative at all. Most people in Britain, however, accepted the idea of **virtual representation,** which held that representatives served the interests of the nation as a whole, not just the locality from which they came. They maintained that since the colonists held interests in common with British people at home, they were virtually represented in Parliament, just like Manchester's residents.

Since the founding of their colonies, however, Americans had experienced **actual representation** and believed that elected representatives should be directly responsive to local interests. The Americans' experience with actual representation made them extremely skeptical of Parliament's claims to virtual representation. For the first half of the eighteenth century, however, Parliament did not press this claim, and the tensions between the two ideas remained latent.

The most direct political confrontations between Britain and the colonies instead focused on the role of colonial governors. In every colony except Connecticut and Rhode Island (where voters chose the executive), either the king or the proprietor appointed the governor. The governors' interests thus lay with their British patrons and not the colonies. More important, governors exercised great power over the colonial assemblies.

In practice, several conditions hampered governors' efforts to exercise their legal authority. Many arrived with detailed instructions on how to govern, which limited their ability to negotiate with colonists over sensitive issues. Governors controlled few offices or other prizes to use as patronage to buy the allegiance of their opponents. They struggled to dominate assemblies that grew in size as the colonial population expanded. And in several colonies, including Massachusetts and New York, governors relied on the assemblies to appropriate the money for their salaries—a financial dependence that restrained even the most autocratic executive.

Despite concerns about the power of governors, most colonists accepted the loose and sometimes contradictory political ties of empire. They saw their connections to Britain as voluntary, based on common identity and rights. So long as Parliament treated them as partners in empire and refrained from ruling by coercion, colonists could celebrate British government as "the most perfect combination of human powers in society . . . for the preservation of liberty and the production of happiness."

By the middle of the eighteenth century, the blessings of British government extended to more colonists than ever before. The population of British America grew rapidly and spread out over vast amounts of land. The expansion of British settlement, in turn, alarmed other European powers. Both Spain and France launched new settlements as the competition for the continent entered a new and volatile phase.

**virtual representation** The notion that parliamentary members represented the interests of the nation as a whole, not those of the particular district that elected them.

**actual representation** The practice whereby elected representatives normally reside in their districts and are directly responsive to local interests.

# EXPANDING EMPIRES

**WHAT WAS** the "backcountry"? Who settled there and why?

During the first half of the eighteenth century, England, Spain, and France enlarged their North American holdings according to patterns established during the previous century. England's empire expanded in tandem with the unrelenting growth of its colonial population. Spain and France still relied on missionaries, soldiers, and traders to stake their claims to American territory. Over time, these empires came into closer contact with one another, intensifying the competition for land, trade, resources, and Indian allies (see Map 4–2).

## BRITISH COLONISTS IN THE BACKCOUNTRY

Population growth in eighteenth-century British North America was truly astonishing. The non-Indian population in the mainland colonies numbered about 260,000 in 1700; by 1760, it had increased to over 1.5 million (see Figure 4–2). Much of this growth stemmed from natural increase.

**MAP 4–2  Expanding Settlement, c. 1750**  Imperial rivalries drove Spain, France, and England to expand their North American empires in the mid-eighteenth century. Once again, this sparked conflict with native peoples as well as with European competitors.

**How does** this map help pinpoint the role of English backcountry settlement in the escalation of imperial conflict in eighteenth-century North America?

Immigration also boosted the population. Thousands of Scots-Irish and German settlers, in addition to thousands of African slaves, helped the population of the Lower South increase at nearly twice the rate of New England, which attracted few immigrants (and therefore remained the most thoroughly English of all colonial regions). By 1770, Pennsylvania had 240,000 settlers, ten times the number it had in 1710.

Most of the coast from Maine to Georgia was settled by 1760, forcing new immigrants to move inland. The most dramatic expansion occurred in the foothills and valleys of the Appalachian Mountains from Pennsylvania to Georgia, a region known as the backcountry.

Between 1730 and 1770, nearly a quarter of a million German, Scots-Irish, and English colonists entered the backcountry. They mainly raised crops and livestock for subsistence on small, isolated farms. Community life developed slowly, because many backcountry settlers moved frequently and a surplus of men among the first settlers delayed the formation of families.

Contemporary observers, especially eastern elites, derided the crudeness of frontier life. Their disparaging comments reflected emerging tensions between backcountry settlements and older seacoast communities. Many eastern planters acquired vast tracts of western land with the intent of selling it to these "crude" settlers. Their interests collided with those of many backcountry settlers, including squatters who occupied the land without acquiring legal title in the hope that their labor in clearing farms would establish their property rights.

Backcountry settlers often complained that the rich eastern planters who dominated the colonial legislatures ignored western demands for adequate representation. They also argued that the crudeness of frontier life was only temporary. Perhaps the best measure of their desire to resemble eastern planters was the spread of slaveholding in the backcountry.

Tensions grew throughout the backcountry as colonists encroached on Indian lands. Indians moving to avoid friction with whites frequently encroached on lands claimed by other tribes—particularly those of the Iroquois Confederacy—leading to conflict among native peoples.

Even where British settlers had not yet appeared, English and Scottish traders could often be found, aggressively pursuing trade with the Indians. Spanish and French observers feared this commercial expansion even more than the movement of settlers. Knowing that the Indians viewed trade as a counterpart to military alliance, they worried that the British, with cheaper and better trade goods, would lure away their native allies. In response, the Spanish and French expanded their own territorial claims and tried to strengthen relations with Indian peoples.

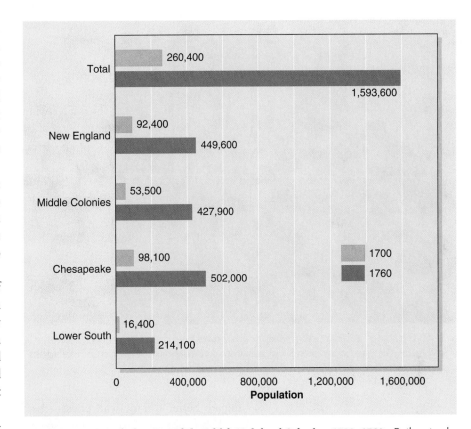

**FIGURE 4–2   Population Growth in British Mainland Colonies, 1700–1760**   Both natural increase and immigration contributed to a staggering rate of population growth in British North America. Some colonists predicted that Americans would soon outnumber Britain's inhabitants—a possibility that greatly concerned British officials.

*Data Source:* John J. McCusker and Russell R. Menard, *The Economy of British America, 1607–1789,* rev. ed. (1991). University of North Carolina Press.

**QUICK REVIEW**

**Population Growth**

- 1700: 265,000 black and white settlers in the mainland colonies.
- 1760: 1.5 million black and white settlers in the mainland colonies.
- Population growth due to natural increase and immigration.

# THE SPANISH IN TEXAS AND CALIFORNIA

To create a buffer zone around their existing colonies, the Spanish moved into Texas and California. Franciscan priests established several missions in east Texas between 1690 and 1720.

An idealized depiction of a California mission, this engraving shows pious Indian converts kneeling before a procession of Spanish clergy. Conditions for native peoples living in the missions were often much harsher than this image suggests.

San Antonio was founded in 1718 as a waystation between the Rio Grande and the east Texas missions; its fortified chapel, San Antonio de Valero, later became famous as the Alamo. The Spanish advance into Texas, however, met with resistance from the French (who also had outposts on the Gulf Coast) and from the Caddos and other Indians armed with French guns. Efforts to fill east Texas with settlers from Spain, Cuba, and the Canary Islands failed when Spanish officials could not guarantee their safety. With only 1,800 settlers there as late as 1742, Spain exerted a weak hold on Texas.

Sixteenth-century Spaniards had considered building outposts in California to supply ships traveling between Mexico and the Philippines but were deterred by the region's remoteness. Spanish interest revived in the 1760s, when it seemed that Russia, which had built fur-trading posts in Alaska, might occupy California. Largely through the efforts of two men—José de Gálvez, a royal official, and Junípero Serra, a Franciscan priest—the Spanish constructed a string of forts and missions from San Diego north to San Francisco between 1769 and 1776.

They initially encountered little opposition from California's Indians, who lived in small, scattered villages. With no European rivals nearby, the Spanish erected an extensive mission system designed to convert and educate Indians and set them to work. Thousands of native laborers farmed irrigated fields and tended livestock. They did so under extremely harsh conditions.

According to one observer, Christian Indians who settled at the missions endured a fate "worse than that of slaves." The Spanish worked them hard and maintained them in overcrowded, unsanitary dwellings. Native women suffered from sexual exploitation by Spanish soldiers. Epidemics of European diseases swept through the Indian population. Signs of native resistance met with quick and cruel punishment.

Spain's empire grew, even as it weakened, during the eighteenth century. Its scattered holdings north of the Rio Grande functioned as colonies of another colony—Mexico—shielding it from foreign incursions. From the beginning, Spain's vision of empire had rested not on extensive settlement but on subjugation of native peoples in order to control their labor. After 1700, the limitations of this coercive approach to empire became apparent.

## THE FRENCH ALONG THE MISSISSIPPI AND IN LOUISIANA

French expansion followed the major waterways of the St. Lawrence River, the Great Lakes, and the Mississippi into the heart of North America. Concerned about defending scattered settlements, French officials forbade colonists to move into the interior. But colonists went anyway, building six villages along the Mississippi in a place they called the *pays des Illinois*.

The first Illinois settlers were independent fur traders (*coureurs de bois*, or "woods runners") unwilling to return to Canada after the French government tried to prohibit their direct trade with Indians. Many found Christian Indian wives and farmed the rich lands along the river. The settlers, using the labor of their families and of black and Indian slaves, produced surpluses of wheat, corn, and livestock to feed the growing population of New Orleans and the lower Mississippi Valley.

See the Map
at www.myhistorylab.com
*French America, 1608–1763*

## AMERICAN VIEWS

### An English Minister Visits the Backcountry

In 1766, Charles Woodmason, a newly ordained Anglican minister, embarked on a six-year-long tour to bring religion to backcountry settlers. Born in England, he came to the colonies around 1752, settling first in Charleston, South Carolina. He lived in the area as a planter and merchant for more than a decade before deciding on a career in the ministry. Assigned to work in the backcountry, he was shocked to find crude living conditions and ethnically diverse settlers with little or no knowledge of religion. As the following excerpt shows, the journal Woodmason kept during these years contains a fascinating mix of his observations and prejudices.

- **How** does Woodmason characterize the behavior of backcountry settlers?
- **What** is Woodmason's opinion of the settlers' religious beliefs?
- **How** accurately do you think Woodmason's account reflects backcountry society? To what extent did his identity as an English-born gentleman shape his impressions of the region?

In this Circuit of a fortnight I've eaten Meat but thrice, and drank nought but Water—Subsisting on my Bisket and Rice Water and Musk Melons, Cucumbers, Green Apples and Peaches and such Trash. By which am reduc'd very thin. It is impossible that any Gentleman not season'd to the Clime, could sustain this. . . . Nor is this a Country, or place where I would wish any Gentleman to travel, or settle. . . . [The settlers'] Ignorance and Impudence is so very high, as to be past bearing—Very few can read—fewer write. . . . They are very Poor—owing to their extreme Indolence for they possess the finest Country in America, and could raise but ev'ry thing. They delight in their present low, lazy, sluttish, heathenish, hellish Life, and seem not desirous of changing it. Both Men and Women will do any thing to come at Liquor, Cloaths, furniture, &c. &c. rather than work for it. . . .

It is very few families whom I can bring to join in Prayer, because most of them are of various Opinions the Husband a Churchman, Wife, a Dissenter, Children nothing at all. . . . Few or no Books are to be found in all this vast Country. . . . Nor do they delight in Historical Books or in having them read to them, as do our Vulgar in England for these People despise Knowledge, and instead of honouring a Learned Person, or any one of Wit or Knowledge be it in the Arts, Sciences, or Languages, they despise and Ill treat them—And this Spirit prevails even among the Principals of this Province. . . . [At Flatt Creek] I found a vast Body of People assembled—Such a Medley! such a mixed Multitude of all Classes and Complexions I never saw. I baptized about 20 Children and Married 4 Couple—Most of these People had never before seen a Minister, or heard the Lords Prayer, Service, or Sermon in their Days. I was a Great Curiosity to them—And they were as great Oddities to me. After Service they went to Revelling Drinking Singing Dancing and Whoring—and most of the Company were drunk before I quitted the Spot—They were as rude in their Manners as the Common Savages, and hardly a degree removed from them.

*Source:* Richard J. Hooker, ed., *The Carolina Backcountry on the Eve of the Revolution: The Journal and Other Writings of Charles Woodmason, Anglican Itinerant* (Chapel Hill, 1953), pp. 52–56.

French Louisiana contained a remarkably diverse population of Indian peoples, French soldiers and settlers, and German immigrants, as well as African slaves, who by the 1730s outnumbered the European colonists. Discouraged by the lack of profits, French officials and merchants neglected Louisiana, and even Catholic missionaries failed to establish a strong presence. Significant European emigration to Louisiana essentially ceased after the 1720s.

But the French approach to empire in Louisiana as in Canada depended more on Indian alliances than on settlement. Louisiana's principal allies were the Choctaws, whom one military official called "the bulwark of the colony." The Choctaws and other native allies offered trade and military assistance in return for guns, trade goods, French help in fighting British raiders seeking Indian slaves, and occasional French mediation of Indian disputes.

French expansion along the Mississippi Valley drove a wedge between Florida and Spain's other mainland colonies; it also blocked the westward movement of English settlers. But France's enlarged empire was only as strong as the Indian alliances on which it rested. Preserving good relations was expensive, however, requiring the constant exchange of diplomatic gifts and trade goods. When France ordered Louisiana officials to limit expenses and reduce Indian gifts in 1745, the officials objected that the Choctaws "would ask for nothing better than to have such pretexts in order to resort to the English."

The fear of losing Indian favor preoccupied officials in 1745 because at that moment France's empire in America consisted of two disconnected pieces: New France, centered in the St. Lawrence Valley and the Great Lakes basin, and Louisiana, stretching from New Orleans to the *pays des Illinois*. Between them lay a thousand miles of wilderness, through which only one thoroughfare passed—the Ohio River. For decades, communication between the two parts of France's North American empire had posed no problem because Indians in the Ohio Valley allowed the French free passage through their lands. If that policy ended, however, France's New World empire would be dangerously divided.

# A CENTURY OF WARFARE

**WHAT ROLE** did the colonists play in the French and Indian War?

The expansion of empires in North America reflected the policies of European states locked in a relentless competition for power and wealth. From the time of the Glorious Revolution, English foreign policy aimed at limiting the expansion of French influence. This, in turn, resulted in a series of four wars. As the eighteenth century wore on, the conflicts between the two countries increasingly involved their American colonies as well as Spain and its colonies. The outcome of each of the wars in America depended no less on the participation of colonists and Indians than on the policies and strategies of the European powers. The conclusion of the final conflict signaled a dramatic shift in North American history (see the Overview table, The Colonial Wars, 1689–1763).

### IMPERIAL CONFLICT AND THE ESTABLISHMENT OF AN AMERICAN BALANCE OF POWER, 1689–1738

When he became king of England in 1688, the Dutch Protestant William of Orange was already fighting the War of the League of Augsburg against France's Catholic king, Louis XIV. Almost immediately, William brought England into the conflict. The war lasted until 1697 and ended, as most European wars of this period did, in a negotiated peace that reestablished the balance of power. Little territory changed hands, either in this war or in the War of the Spanish Succession (1702–1713), which followed it.

In America, these two imperial wars—known to British colonists as **King William's War** and **Queen Anne's War,** after the monarchs on the throne at the time—ended with equal indecisiveness. Neither war caused more than marginal changes for the colonies in North America. Both had profound effects, however, on the English state and the Iroquois League.

All European states of the eighteenth century financed their wars by borrowing. But the English were the first to realize that wartime debts did not necessarily have to be repaid during the following peace. The government instead created a funded debt. Having borrowed heavily from large joint-stock corporations, the government used tax revenues to pay the interest on the loans but not to pay off the loans themselves.

As the debt grew larger, more taxes were necessary to pay interest on it. Taxes also rose to pay for a powerful navy and a standing army. When the treasury created a larger bureaucracy to collect taxes, many Englishmen grew nervous. Their anxiety emerged as a strain of thought known as **Country,** or **"Real Whig," ideology.** Country ideology stressed the threats that a standing army and a powerful state posed to personal liberty. It also emphasized the dangers of taxation to property rights and the need for property holders to retain their right to consent to taxation. Real Whig politicians publicized their fears but could not stop the growth of the state.

**King William's War**   The first Anglo-French conflict in North America (1689–1697), the American phase of Europe's War of the League of Augsburg.

**Queen Anne's War**   American phase (1702–1713) of Europe's War of the Spanish Succession.

**Country (Real Whig) ideology**   Train of thought (focusing on the threat to personal liberty and the taxation of property holders) first appearing in England in the late seventeenth century in response to the growth of governmental power and a national debt.

## OVERVIEW  The Colonial Wars, 1689–1763

| Name in the Colonies | European Name and Dates | Dates in America | Results for Britain |
|---|---|---|---|
| King William's War | War of the League of Augsburg, 1688–1697 | 1689–1697 | Reestablished balance of power between England and France |
| Queen Anne's War | War of the Spanish Succession, 1702–1714 | 1702–1713 | Britain acquired Nova Scotia |
| King George's War | War of the Austrian Succession, 1739–1748 | 1744–1748 | Britain returned Louisbourg to France British settlers began moving westward Weakening of Iroquois neutrality |
| French and Indian War | Seven Years' War, 1756–1763 | 1754–1763 | Britain acquired Canada and all French territory east of Mississippi Britain gained Florida from Spain |

In America, the first two imperial wars transformed the role of the Iroquois League. During King William's War, the Iroquois allied with the English, but received little help from them when the French and their Indian allies attacked Iroquois villages. By 1700, the Iroquois League had suffered such horrendous losses—perhaps a quarter of the population had died from causes related to the war—that its leaders sought an alternative to direct alliance with the English.

With the **Grand Settlement of 1701,** the Iroquois adopted a policy of neutrality with regard to the French and British empires. The Iroquois's strategic location between New France and the English colonies allowed them to serve as a geographical and diplomatic buffer. Neutral Iroquois diplomats could play the English against the French, gaining favors from one side in return for promises not to ally with the other. This neutralist policy ensured that for nearly fifty years neither Britain nor France could gain ascendancy in North America.

Iroquois neutrality offered benefits to the Europeans as well as the Indians. The British began to negotiate with them for land. The Iroquois claimed sovereignty over much of the country west of the Middle and Chesapeake colonies. To smooth relations with the British, the Iroquois sold them land formerly occupied by Delawares and Susquehannocks.

Meanwhile a neutral Iroquois League claiming control over the Ohio Valley and blocking British access across the Appalachian Mountains helped the French protect the strategic corridor that linked Canada and Louisiana. If the British ever established a permanent presence in the Ohio Valley, however, the Iroquois would cease to be of use to the French. The Iroquois remained reasonably effective at keeping the British out of the valley until the late 1740s. The next European war, however, altered these circumstances.

**Grand Settlement of 1701**   Separate peace treaties negotiated by Iroquois diplomats at Montreal and Albany that marked the beginning of Iroquois neutrality in conflicts between the French and the British in North America.

### KING GEORGE'S WAR SHIFTS THE BALANCE, 1739–1754

The third confrontation between Britain and France in Europe, the War of the Austrian Succession—**King George's War** to the British colonists—began as a small war between Britain and Spain in 1739. But in 1744, France joined in the war against Britain and conflict once again erupted in North America.

New Englanders saw yet another chance to attack Canada. This time their target was the great fortress of Louisbourg on Cape Breton Island, a naval base that dominated the Gulf of St. Lawrence. An expedition from Massachusetts and Connecticut, supported by a squadron of Royal Navy warships, captured Louisbourg in 1745. This success cut Canada off from French reinforcement. English forces should now have been able to conquer New France.

**King George's War**   The third Anglo-French war in North America (1744–1748), part of the European conflict known as the War of the Austrian Succession.

WHERE TO LEARN MORE

Fortress of Louisbourg National Historic Site, Cape Breton Island, Canada
http://louisbourg.com/history.html

This contemporary map shows the British seizure of the French fortress at Louisbourg in 1758 during the French and Indian War. In 1745, during King George's War, New Englanders had helped capture the fort, which was returned to France at the war's end in 1748.

Instead, politically influential merchants in Albany, New York, chose to continue their profitable trade with the enemy across Lake Champlain, enabling Canada to hold out until the end of the war. When the peace treaty was signed in 1748, Britain, which had fared badly in the European fighting, returned Louisbourg to France. This diplomatic adjustment, routine by European standards, shocked New Englanders. At the same time, New York's illegal trade with the enemy appalled British administrators. They began thinking of ways to prevent such independent behavior in any future war.

King George's War furnished an equal share of shocks for New France, which had suffered more than in any previous conflict. Even before the war's end, traders from Pennsylvania began moving west to buy furs from Indians who had once traded with the French. The movements of these traders, along with the appearance of Virginians in the Ohio Valley after 1748, gravely concerned the French.

In 1749, the governor general of New France set out to assert direct control over the region by building a series of forts from Lake Erie to the Forks of the Ohio (where the Monongahela and Allegheny rivers meet to form the Ohio River). This decision signaled the end of France's commitment to Iroquois neutrality. The Iroquois now found themselves trapped between empires edging closer to confrontation in the Ohio Valley.

The Iroquois, in fact, had never exerted direct power in the Ohio Country. Their control instead depended on their ability to dominate the peoples who actually lived there. The appearance of English traders in the valley offering goods on better terms than the French or the Iroquois had ever provided undermined Iroquois dominance.

The Ohio Valley Indians increasingly pursued their own independent course. One spur to their disaffection from the Iroquois was the 1744 **Treaty of Lancaster,** by which Iroquois chiefs had sold the rights to trade at the Forks of the Ohio to Virginia land speculators. The Virginians assumed that these trading rights included the right to acquire land for eventual sale to settlers. The Ohio Valley Indians found this situation intolerable, as did the French. When, in 1754, the government of Virginia sent out a small body of soldiers under Lieutenant Colonel George Washington to protect Virginia's claim to the Forks of the Ohio, the French struck back.

## THE FRENCH AND INDIAN WAR, 1754–1763: A DECISIVE VICTORY

In April 1754, French soldiers overwhelmed a group of Virginians who had been building a small fort at the Forks of the Ohio. They erected their own fort, Fort Duquesne, on the spot. The French intended to follow up by similarly ousting Washington's troops, who had encamped farther up the Monongahela River. However, at the end of May, Washington's men killed or captured all but one member of a small French reconnaissance party. The French decided to teach the Virginians a lesson. On July 3, they attacked Washington at Fort Necessity, forcing him to surrender.

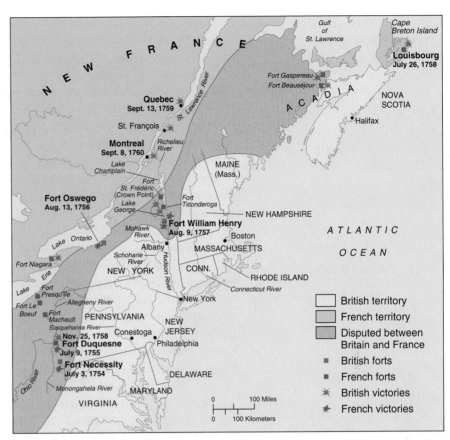

MAP 4–3   **The French and Indian War, 1754–1763**   Most of the battles of the French and Indian War occurred in the frontier regions of northern and western New York and the Ohio Valley. The influx of settlers into these areas created tensions that eventually developed into war.

**Why did** most of the fighting in the French and Indian War take place in the backcountry? How does this map help explain the crucial importance of Louisbourg to the French?

Even before this news reached Britain, imperial officials worried that the Iroquois might ally with the French. Britain ordered New York's governor to convene an intercolonial meeting in Albany—known as the Albany Congress—to discuss matters with the Iroquois. Several prominent colonists, including Governor William Shirley of Massachusetts and Benjamin Franklin, took advantage of the occasion to put forward the **Albany Plan of Union,** which called for an intercolonial union to coordinate defense, levy taxes, and regulate Indian affairs. But the colonies, too suspicious of one another to see their common interests, rejected the Albany Plan, which British officials also disliked. Meanwhile, events in the west took a turn for the worse.

The French expulsion of the Virginians left the Indians of the region, Delawares and Shawnees, with no choice but to ally with the French in what came to be called the French and Indian War (see Map 4–3). The Iroquois tried to remain neutral, but their neutrality no longer mattered. Europeans were at last contending directly for control of the Ohio Country.

The **French and Indian War** blazed in America for two years before it erupted as a fourth Anglo-French war in Europe in 1756. Known in Europe as the Seven Years' War (1756–1763), it involved fighting in the Caribbean, Africa, India, and the Philippine Islands as well as in Europe and North America. It was unlike any other eighteenth-century conflict, not only in its immense scope and expense but also in its decisive outcome.

**Treaty of Lancaster**   Negotiation in 1744 whereby Iroquois chiefs sold Virginia land speculators the right to trade at the Forks of the Ohio.

**Albany Plan of Union**   Plan put forward in 1754 calling for an intercolonial union to manage defense and Indian affairs. The plan was rejected by participants at the Albany Congress.

**French and Indian War**   The last of the Anglo-French colonial wars (1754–1763) and the first in which fighting began in North America. The war ended with France's defeat.

See the **Map**
at **www.myhistorylab.com**
The Seven Years' War

The war had two phases in North America—1754 to 1758 and 1758 through 1760. During the first phase, the French enjoyed a string of successes as they followed their proven strategy—guerrilla war.

The first full campaign of the war, in 1755, saw not only the British colonial frontiers collapsing in terror but also a notable defeat inflicted on the troops Britain had dispatched to attack Fort Duquesne under the command of Major General Edward Braddock. Braddock's defeat set the tone for virtually every military engagement of the next three years and opened a period of demoralization and internal conflict in the British colonies.

Britain responded to Braddock's defeat by sending a new commander in chief with more trained British soldiers. The new commander, Lord Loudoun, insisted on managing every aspect of the war effort, not only directing the campaigns but also dictating the amount of support, in men and money, that each colony would provide. Colonial soldiers, who had volunteered to serve under their own officers, objected to Loudoun's command. By the end of 1757, a year of disastrous military campaigns, colonial assemblies were also refusing to cooperate.

Britain's aim had been to "rationalize" the war by making it conform to European professional military standards. This approach required soldiers to advance in formation in the face of massed musket fire without breaking rank. Few colonial volunteers met professional standards, and few colonists thought them necessary, especially when British soldiers suffered defeat after defeat at the hands of French and Indian guerrillas. British officers assumed that colonial soldiers were simply lazy cowards. But colonial volunteers saw British officers as brutal taskmasters. They resisted all efforts to impose professional discipline on their own units, even to the point of desertion and mutiny.

Despite the astonishing success of their guerrilla tactics, the French, too, began moving toward a more European style of warfare. In the process, they destroyed their strategic and tactical advantages. In 1756, the Marquis de Montcalm assumed command of French forces. In his first battle, the successful siege of Fort Oswego, New York, Montcalm was horrified by the behavior of his Indian allies, who killed wounded prisoners, took personal captives, and collected scalps as trophies. He came to regard the Indians—so essential to the defense of New France—as mere savages.

Following his next victory, the capture of Fort William Henry, New York, Montcalm conformed to European practice by allowing the defeated garrison to go home in return for the promise not to fight again. Montcalm's Indian allies, a thousand or more strong, were not to take prisoners, trophies, or plunder. The tragic result came to be known as the Massacre of Fort William Henry. Feeling betrayed by their French allies, the Indians took captives and trophies anyway. This action not only outraged the New England colonies (most of the victims were New Englanders) but also alienated the Indians on whom the defense of Canada depended.

At the same time that the Europeanization of the war was weakening the French, the British moderated their policies and reached accommodation with the colonists. A remarkable politician came to power in London as England's chief war minister. William Pitt, who as secretary of state directed the British war effort from late 1757 through 1761, realized that friction arose from the colonists' sense that they were bearing all the financial burdens of the war without having any say in how the war was fought. Pitt's ingenious solution was to promise reimbursements to the colonies in proportion to their contribution to the war effort, reduce the power of the commander in chief, and replace the arrogant Loudoun with a less objectionable officer.

Pitt's money and measures restored colonial morale and launched the second phase of the war. He sent thousands of British soldiers to America to fight alongside colonial troops. As the Anglo-American forces grew stronger, they operated more successfully, seizing Louisbourg again in 1758. Once more, Canada experienced crippling shortages of supplies. But this time, the Anglo-Americans were united and able to take advantage of the situation. British emissaries persuaded the Delawares and Shawnees to abandon their French alliance, and late in 1758, an Anglo-American force again marched on Fort Duquesne. In command of its lead battalion was Colonel George Washington. The French defenders, abandoned by their native allies and confronted by overwhelming force, blew up the fort and retreated to the Great Lakes.

**QUICK REVIEW**

**Pitt's Policies**

- Reimbursements to the colonies in proportion to their contribution.
- Deemphasis of the power of the commander in chief.
- More British troops to fight alongside colonial troops.

## GLOBAL CONNECTIONS

### ❧ TEA AND EMPIRE ❧

*We went ashore [near Greenwich, New York] to fill water near a small log cottage on the west side of the river inhabited by one Stanespring and his family. . . . This cottage was very clean and neat but poorly furnished. Yet Mr. Milne observed severall superfluous things which showed an inclination to finery in these poor people, such as a looking glass with a painted frame, half a dozen pewter spoons and as many plates, . . . a set of stone tea dishes, and a tea pot. These, Mr. Milne said, were superfluous and too splendid for such a cottage. . . . As for the tea equipage it was quite unnecessary. . . .*

*Source:* Wendy Martin, ed., *Colonial American Travel Narratives* (New York, 1994), p. 216.

Alexander Hamilton, a Scottish physician, made this observation while traveling from Maryland to New Hampshire in 1744. Few colonists would have agreed that the family's teapot and dishes were "quite unnecessary." By the eighteenth century, many colonists—even residents of Philadelphia's poorhouse—regarded tea as an essential part of their diet. How had a beverage from a native Chinese plant become commonplace in towns and villages located thousands of miles away? The answer lies in the expanding network of British commerce. By the start of the eighteenth century, Britain's

East India Company had established a thriving trade in tea and silks with Chinese merchants in Canton. Large ships, specially designed to withstand the rigors of lengthy voyages around Africa's Cape of Good Hope, carried more tea every year. Imports rose from 50 tons in 1700 to 15,000 tons by 1800. Increased supplies meant that tea became affordable for all classes of British subjects and colonists. Poorer folk relied on the mild stimulant to help them endure hard days at work. For wealthier people, drinking tea became a marker of sociability. This was especially true for women, whose elegant tea parties offered opportunities to display fine porcelain tea pots and cups, silver or pewter spoons, sugar tongs, and other equipment. Until factories began producing porcelain in Britain itself, British and colonial consumers sipped their tea from cups that arrived as ballast aboard the East India Company ships. Only with the onset of the Revolutionary movement, when British taxes on tea discouraged colonial purchases, did American consumers reject the beverage that had previously linked them with Great Britain and, by extension, a commercial empire that virtually circled the globe.

- Why might Alexander Hamilton have thought it unsuitable for a poor family to drink tea?

From this point on, the Anglo-Americans suffered no setbacks, and the French won no victories. The war became a contest in which the larger, better-supplied army would triumph. Montcalm, forced back to Quebec, decided to risk everything in a European-style, open-field battle against a British force led by General James Wolfe. At the Battle of Quebec (September 13, 1759), Montcalm lost the gamble—and his life (as did the victorious General Wolfe).

The French had not yet lost the war. If they could revive their Indian alliances, they still had a chance. What finally decided the outcome of the war in America was two developments: the Battle of Quiberon Bay in France (November 20, 1759) and the Iroquois's decision to join the Anglo-American side in 1760. The sea battle cost the French navy its ability to operate in the Atlantic, preventing it from reinforcing Canada. Montcalm's successor could not rebuild the Indian alliances he so desperately needed. At the same time, the Iroquois decision to enter the war on the Anglo-American side tipped the balance irrevocably against the French. The last defenders of Canada surrendered on September 8, 1760.

## THE TRIUMPH OF THE BRITISH EMPIRE, 1763

The war pitting Britain against France and Spain (which had entered the fighting as a French ally in 1762) concluded with an uninterrupted series of British victories. In the Caribbean, where every valuable sugar island the French owned came under British control, the culminating event was the

**MAP 4–4    European Empires in North America, 1750–1763**    Great Britain's victory in the French and Indian War transformed the map of North America. France lost its mainland colonies, England claimed all lands east of the Mississippi, and Spain gained nominal control over the Trans-Mississippi West.

**Using these** two maps, explain why the position of Native Americans in colonial North America was much more precarious in 1763 than in 1750.

**Treaty of Paris**    The formal end to British hostilities against France and Spain in February 1763.

surrender of Havana on August 13, 1762. Even more spectacular was Britain's capture of the Philippine capital of Manila on October 5—a victory that literally carried British power around the world.

These conquests created the unshakable conviction that British arms were invincible. An immense surge of British patriotism spread throughout the American colonies. When news of the conquest of Havana reached Massachusetts, bells rang, cannons fired salutes, and bonfires blazed.

Hostilities ended formally on February 10, 1763, with the conclusion of the **Treaty of Paris.** France regained its West Indian sugar islands—its most valuable colonial possessions—but lost the rest of its North American empire. France ceded to Britain all its claims to lands east of the Mississippi River (except the city of New Orleans) and compensated Spain for the losses it had sustained as an ally by handing over all claims to the Trans-Mississippi West and the port of New Orleans (see Map 4–4). Britain returned Cuba and the Philippines to Spain and in compensation received Florida. Now Great Britain owned everything east of the Mississippi, from the Gulf of Mexico to Hudson's Bay. With France and Spain both humbled and on the verge of financial collapse, Britain seemed preeminent in Europe and ready to dominate in the New World. Never before had Americans felt more pride in being British, members of the greatest empire on earth.

In his most famous painting, American artist Benjamin West depicted the death of the British general James Wolfe at the Battle of Quebec. He portrays Wolfe as a glorious martyr to the cause of British victory. In the left foreground, West added the figure of an Indian, a "noble savage" who contemplates the meaning of Wolfe's selfless sacrifice of his life.

Benjamin West (1738–1820), "The Death of General Wolfe," 1770, Oil on canvas, 152.6×214.5 cm. Transfer from the Canadian War Memorials, 1921 (Gift of the 2nd Duke of Westminster, Eaton Hall, Cheshire, 1918). National Gallery of Canada, Ottawa, Ontario.

## CONCLUSION

The George Washington who ordered a suit from England in 1763 longed to be part of the elite of the great British Empire. If he feared any threat to his position in that elite, it was not Parliament and the king but the uncomfortably large debts he owed to his London agents or perhaps the unruly Baptists who challenged the superiority of the great planters. But such worries, though real, were merely small, nagging doubts, shared by most of his fellow planters.

What was more real to Washington was the great victory that the British had just gained over France, a victory that he had helped to achieve. For Washington, as for virtually all other colonial leaders and many ordinary colonists, 1763 was a moment of great promise and patriotic devotion to the British Empire. They hoped that the colonies had embarked on a new stage in a political and cultural journey, moving them closer to an equal partnership with England itself in the world's most powerful empire. It was a time for colonists to rejoice in the fundamental British identity and liberty and rights that seemed to ensure that their lives would be better and more prosperous than ever.

# WHERE TO LEARN MORE

**Colonial Williamsburg, Williamsburg, Virginia.** A reconstruction of the capital of eighteenth-century Virginia, this site covers 173 acres and contains many restored and rebuilt structures, including houses, churches, the House of Burgesses, and the Governor's Palace. Many educational and cultural programs are available. Historical interpreters, dressed in period costume, provide information about eighteenth-century Chesapeake life. The website http://www.colonialwilliamsburg.com/history/index.cfm has a variety of links that include biographical information on eighteenth-century residents of Williamsburg, aspects of colonial life, and material culture.

**Mount Vernon, Virginia.** Site of George Washington's much-refurbished home. There is also a reconstructed gristmill and barn, as well as various outbuildings. Exhibits include information on Washington's agricultural experiments. The website http://www.mountvernon.org offers virtual tours of the house and grounds, as well as information on "George Washington, Pioneer Farmer."

**Fortress of Louisbourg National Historic Site, Cape Breton Island, Canada.** This site includes a reconstruction of the fortified French settlement that played a key role in the eighteenth-century wars between Britain and France. More information is available at the website http://louisbourg.com/history.html.

**Berkeley and Westover Plantations, Charles City, Virginia.** These two eighteenth-century James River plantations suggest the elegance of elite planters' lives. The house and grounds at Berkeley are open to the public, the grounds only at Westover, the home of William Byrd. Pictures, descriptions of the sites, and background on their owners can be found at http://www.jamesriverplantations.org/, which has links to each plantation.

# REVIEW QUESTIONS

1. Why did George Washington prefer to order a suit from London rather than trust a Virginia tailor to make him one? How does his decision reflect elite colonists' attitudes about American society and culture in the eighteenth century?

2. In what ways did economic ties between Britain and the colonies grow closer in the century after 1660?

3. What was the Great Awakening, and what impact did it have? How did it affect different groups in colonial society?

4. In what ways were colonial and British political ideas and practices similar? In what ways were they different?

5. Why did England, Spain, and France renew their competition for North America in the eighteenth century?

6. What role did warfare play in North America in the eighteenth century? What role did the Iroquois play?

# KEY TERMS

**Actual representation** (p. 101)
**Age of Enlightenment** (p. 95)
**Albany Plan of Union** (p. 109)
**Country (Real Whig) ideology** (p. 106)
**Dominion of New England** (p. 99)
**Enumerated products** (p. 88)
**French and Indian War** (p. 109)
**Glorious Revolution** (p. 99)
**Grand Settlement of 1701** (p. 107)

**Great Awakening** (p. 97)
**Halfway Covenant** (p. 96)
**King George's War** (p. 107)
**King William's War** (p. 106)
**Mercantilism** (p. 87)
**New Lights** (p. 97)
**Queen Anne's War** (p. 106)
**Treaty of Lancaster** (p. 109)
**Treaty of Paris** (p. 112)
**Virtual representation** (p. 101)

# myhistorylab Connections

PEARSON

Reinforce what you learned in this chapter by studying the many documents, images, maps, review tools, and videos available at www.myhistorylab.com.

## Read and Review

✓ Study and Review **Study Plan: Chapter 4**

Read the Document

*Benjamin Franklin, Observations Concerning the Increase of Mankind, Peopling of Countries (1751)*

*Ann Putnam's Deposition (1692)*

*Ann Putnam's Confession (1706)*

*Benjamin Franklin on George Whitefield (1771)*

*Benjamin Wadsworth, from A Well-Ordered Family (1712)*

*England Asserts Her Dominion through Legislation in 1660*

*Jonathan Edwards, "Some Thoughts" (1742)*

*Navigation Acts (1651)*

See the **Map**

*French America, 1608–1763*

*Colonial Products*

*The Seven Years' War*

*European Claims in North America, 1750 and 1763*

*Regions of Colonial North America, 1683–1763*

## Research and Explore

Read the Document

*Personal Journeys Online*

*From Then to Now Online: The Diversity of American Religious Life*

*Exploring America: The Great Awakening*

*Exploring America: Witches in the American Imagination*

Hear the Audio

*Lookie There!*

*The Connecticut Peddler*

## Hear the Audio

Hear the audio files for Chapter 4 at
**www.myhistorylab.com.**

# 5
# Imperial Breakdown

Having apparently originated in a May Day–like celebration of the repeal of the Stamp Act in the spring of 1766, liberty poles were particularly characteristic of New York City, where citizens of all social classes supported their erection (as in the picture). However, British soldiers repeatedly destroyed them, thereby prompting serious rioting. Elsewhere, liberty trees served similar symbolic functions. John C. McRae of New York published this print in 1875. © North Wind/North Wind Picture Archives

((•●—Hear the **Audio**

Hear the audio files for Chapter 5 at **www.myhistorylab.com**.

### THE CRISIS OF IMPERIAL AUTHORITY *(page 119)*

**WHAT NEW** challenges did the British government face in North America after 1763?

### REPUBLICAN IDEOLOGY AND COLONIAL PROTEST *(page 123)*

**HOW DID** republican ideology inform the colonists' view of their relationship to Britain?

### THE STAMP ACT CRISIS *(page 124)*

**WHY DID** the Stamp Act spark widespread unrest in the colonies?

### THE TOWNSHEND CRISIS *(page 126)*

**HOW DID** the colonists respond to Townshend's colonial policies?

### DOMESTIC DIVISIONS *(page 129)*

**WHAT ISSUES** and interests divided the colonists?

### THE FINAL IMPERIAL CRISIS *(page 131)*

**WHAT PUSHED** the colonists from protest to rebellion?

ONE AMERICAN JOURNEY

*Indeed, it appears to me a very doubtful point, even supposing all the colonies of America to be united under one head, whether it would be possible to keep in due order and government so wide and extended an empire, the difficulties of communication, of intercourse, of correspondence, and all other circumstances considered.*

*A voluntary association or coalition, at least a permanent one, is almost as difficult to be supposed: for fire and water are not more heterogeneous than the different colonies in North America. Nothing can exceed the jealousy and emulation which they possess in regard to each other. . . . Even the limits and boundaries of each colony are a constant source of litigation. In short, such is the difference of character, of manners, of religion, of interest, of the different colonies, that I think, if I am not wholly ignorant of the human mind, were they left to themselves, there would soon be a civil war from one end of the continent to the other; while the Indians and negroes would, with better reason, impatiently watch the opportunity of exterminating them all together.*

Andrew Burnaby, *Travels Through the Middle Settlements in North America in the Years 1759 and 1760* [1775] (3rd edition, 1798; reprinted New York: Augustus M. Kelley, 1970), pp. 152–153.

**Read the Document** at **www.myhistorylab.com**

Personal Journeys Online

- **Mary Ambler, *Diary of M. Ambler,* 1770.** This memoir records Ambler's trip to Baltimore to have her two young children inoculated for smallpox.

- **Reverend John Ettwein, *Notes of Travel from the North Branch of the Susquehanna to the Beaver River, Pennsylvania,* 1772.** This journal recorded the journey of about one hundred Christianized Indians through western Pennsylvania to their new homes at the village of Friedenstadt.

- **Nicholas Cresswell, *The Journal of Nicholas Cresswell,* 1774–1777.** A prospective immigrant sails, having decided to go to America, but the Revolution changes his mind.

ANDREW BURNABY, an English clergyman, made these observations while on a tour of the colonies in 1759 and 1760. Few people on either side of the Atlantic would have disagreed with his assessment. The only union that he or anyone else at the time could imagine was the imperial connection that bound Great Britain to its American possessions. That connection seemed even stronger as Burnaby's journey came to a close in 1760, for by then Britain's victory in the French and Indian War was all but certain.

But the war had changed the British Empire in ways that few people immediately grasped. The first to understand the challenges of victory were British officials, who found themselves with a burdensome debt and vastly increased territory to administer—much of it occupied by erstwhile enemies. Their efforts to meet these challenges resulted in an unprecedented assertion of imperial control over the American colonies in order to secure the fruits of victory. From the vantage point of London, this new model of empire appeared both necessary and, to some officials, long overdue.

To many colonists, however, British reforms represented an unwarranted disruption of a well-functioning imperial relationship. Rather than seeing various reform measures as attempts to deal with practical problems, colonists regarded them as repeated assaults on their property and rights. For more than a decade, Great Britain and its American colonies engaged in an often acrimonious and occasionally violent debate over the proper structure of the postwar empire. Only at the end of that period did it become clear that the survival of the empire itself might be at stake. ✦

## CHRONOLOGY

| | |
|---|---|
| **1759–1761** | Cherokee War takes place. |
| **1760** | George III becomes king. |
| **1761–1769** | British, French, German, Russian, and American astronomers observe transit of Venus across the sun. |
| **1763** | Peace of Paris ends French and Indian War. |
| | Spanish accelerate imperial reforms. |
| | British troops remain in America. |
| | Proclamation Line of 1763 limits western expansion of colonial settlement. |
| | Pontiac's War begins. |
| | Paxton Boys murder peaceful Indians. |
| **1764** | Sugar Act passed. |
| | Currency Act passed. |
| **1765** | Quartering Act passed. |
| | Stamp Act passed. |
| | Stamp Act Congress meets in New York. |
| **1766** | Stamp Act repealed; Declaratory Act passed. |
| | New York Assembly refuses to comply with Quartering Act. |

| | |
|---|---|
| **1767** | Townshend duties imposed. |
| | Regulator movements begin in North and South Carolina. |
| **1769** | James Watt, a British inventor, patents a steam engine. |
| **1769–1770** | Famine kills one-third of the population in Bengal, India. |
| **1770** | Boston Massacre takes place. |
| | Tea duty retained, other Townshend duties repealed. |
| **1771** | North Carolina Regulator movement defeated. |
| **1772** | *Gaspée* burned. |
| | Committees of Correspondence formed. |
| **1773** | Boston Tea Party takes place. |
| **1774** | Coercive Acts passed. |
| | Quebec Act passed. |
| | First Continental Congress meets and agrees to boycott British imports. |

# THE CRISIS OF IMPERIAL AUTHORITY

As the French and Indian War drew to a close, political shifts at the heart of London did not make the task of imperial administration any easier. In 1760, a rather naïve new monarch, George III, ascended the throne at the age of 22. Disputes among his advisers soon led to the resignation of William Pitt, the popular war minister who had helped England achieve its great victory. Political infighting at the highest reaches of government persisted until April 1763, when George Grenville became first lord of the treasury and the man responsible for ushering Britain and her colonies into the postwar era.

**WHAT NEW** challenges did the British government face in North America after 1763?

### CHALLENGES OF CONTROL AND FINANCE

Britain's empire in 1763 was immense, and the problems its rulers faced were correspondingly large. Moreover, it still faced threats, if diminished ones, from its traditional European enemies. French territory on the North American mainland had been reduced to two tiny islands in the Gulf of St. Lawrence. Yet France's spectacular defeat would only whet its appetite for revenge. Spain was a more significant presence on the North American mainland. At the end of the French and Indian War, it surrendered East and West Florida to Britain but got back its possessions in Cuba and the Philippines that the British had captured. Spain acquired Louisiana from its French ally as compensation for the loss of the Floridas.

Protecting Britain's enlarged empire from these familiar European rivals formed just part of the security problems facing British officials. With the Peace of Paris of 1763, Britain acquired

**QUICK REVIEW**

**European Territories, 1763**

- Britain: territories in North America from Hudson's Bay to the Caribbean, from the Atlantic to the Mississippi.
- France: territory on the mainland reduced to two small islands.
- Spain: Cuba, the Philippines, Louisiana, and California.

not only new lands but also new subjects—few of whom had any reason to feel loyal toward George III or the British nation. Thousands of French inhabitants remaining in Canada and the Mississippi Valley would likely side with France in the event of another war with Britain. Even greater numbers of Native Americans, most of whom sided with France during the war, populated these regions.

Concerns about imperial authority extended to the inhabitants of the existing colonies themselves. Worries about the colonists' wartime smuggling and their assemblies' frequent obstruction of military orders fed an ongoing debate in London about the need for a more centralized form of imperial control. The assertiveness of colonial legislatures, many British officials thought, contributed to an unacceptable level of American insubordination. Imperial reform would have to address this problem as well.

But any plan for imperial restructuring, no matter how well designed, faced an enormous obstacle. Wartime expenses had caused England's national debt to balloon. Half of the money collected from hard-pressed British taxpayers went just to pay the interest on this massive debt, and no more revenue could be squeezed from them without risking domestic unrest. Moreover, it seemed unfair to do so. Since the comparatively lightly taxed Americans benefited the most from the war, officials believed they should shoulder more of the financial burden of victory.

## NATIVE AMERICANS AND FRONTIER CONFLICT

As a first response to the new demands of empire, the British government decided to keep a substantial body of troops in America in peacetime—10,000 were initially planned. The soldiers would protect the new territories and existing colonies. More importantly, officials hoped that their presence would help to maintain peace with the Indians.

Even as the war with France had been drawing to a close, conflict with Cherokee Indians on the southern frontier had flared into violence. Longtime allies and trading partners of South Carolina, the Cherokees resented repeated incidents of theft, encroachment on their lands, and violence perpetrated by frontier colonists. By early 1760, their frustration blossomed into the **Cherokee War** when they launched retaliatory attacks on western settlements in all the southern colonies. Three expeditions, manned by British as well as colonial troops, eventually forced the Cherokees to agree, in a 1761 treaty, to surrender land in the Carolinas and Virginia to the colonists.

The end of the Cherokee War did not necessarily ease frontier tensions. France's loss of its North American colonies deprived many Indians of a key ally, trading partner, and counterweight to British pressures for land. Britain's General Jeffrey Amherst confirmed their worst fears when he ordered a reduction in the gifts customarily supplied to the Iroquois and other Native American allies. He saw no reason to continue offering what he regarded as bribes to maintain ties to Indians who could no longer threaten to desert Britain and ally with France. Amherst further infuriated western Indians by reneging on a promise to construct trading posts in the interior and withdraw troops. The persistence of military garrisons and the establishment of farming settlements near them suggested nothing less than a British intent to occupy Indian lands permanently.

The Indian response stunned the British with its fierceness and geographical range. It was also remarkable as an unprecedented example of Indian unity in the face of European expansion. The sources of that unity were as much spiritual as political. In 1761, Neolin,

**Cherokee War**   Conflict (1759–1761) on the southern frontier between the Cherokee Indians and colonists from Virginia southward.

Cunne Shote, one of three Cherokee chiefs who visited London in 1762, had this portrait painted there by Francis Parsons.

sometimes known as the Delaware Prophet, experienced a vision in which God commanded the Indians to reject their dependence on European goods and ways and embrace their own ancestral practices.

By May 1763 the Indians were ready to strike. Led by an Ottawa chief named Pontiac, a loose coalition of at least eight major Native American peoples launched attacks on more than a dozen British forts in the west, beginning at Detroit. Within months, **Pontiac's War** raged along the frontier from the Great Lakes to Virginia. Horrified by the prospect of an Indian victory, General Amherst urged his troops to adopt desperate measures. British tactics included killing Indian prisoners and, most notoriously, distributing smallpox-infected blankets as diplomatic gifts to local chiefs who had come to Fort Pitt during a temporary truce.

It was not smallpox but starvation that ultimately ended Pontiac's War. British forces attacked Indian food supplies as they waited for their adversaries to run out of ammunition. By late summer 1764, the Indian coalition had begun to disintegrate and fighting ceased. Pontiac finally accepted a treaty in 1766. Chastened by the conflict, British officials agreed to follow the practices the French had once used in the Great Lakes area by supplying western Indians with diplomatic gifts, encouraging trade, and mediating disputes.

Yet frontier animosities whipped to a frenzy by the war did not easily dissipate. Few colonists in vulnerable western settlements cared any longer to distinguish between friendly and hostile Indians; as far as they were concerned, all Indians were enemies. This kind of thinking provoked a group of Scots-Irish settlers in Paxton Township, Pennsylvania, upset at the colonial assembly's lack of aggressiveness in dealing with Indians, to take matters into their own hands. Unable to catch the Indians who were attacking their settlements, they slaughtered a defenseless group of Christian Conestogas living nearby. The so-called Paxton Boys went on to murder another group of Christian Indians two weeks later.

## DEALING WITH THE NEW TERRITORIES

Even as Pontiac's War was going on, the king issued the **Proclamation of 1763.** The measure aimed to pacify Indians by prohibiting white settlement west of the ridgeline of the Appalachian Mountains. Colonists who had already moved to the western side of this Proclamation Line were required "forthwith to remove themselves" back to the east (see Map 5–1). The royal proclamation contained two other key features. First, it obligated Britain to establish a regulated Indian trade in the interior in an effort to supply desired

W    WHERE TO LEARN MORE

Fort Michilimackinac National Historic Landmark, Mackinaw City, Michigan http://www.mackinacparks.com/

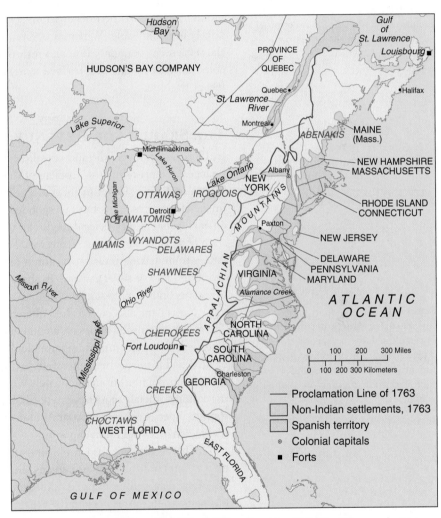

**MAP 5–1    Colonial Settlement and the Proclamation Line of 1763**    This map depicts the regions claimed and settled by the major groups competing for territory in eastern North America. With the Proclamation Line of 1763, positioned along the crest of the Appalachian Mountains, the British government tried to stop the westward migration of settlers under its jurisdiction and thereby limit conflict with the Indians. The result, however, was frustration and anger on the part of land-hungry settlers.

**Why do** you think the Proclamation Line of 1763 was positioned along the crest of the Appalachian Mountains?

See the **Map**
at **www.myhistorylab.com**
*Settlement in North America, c. 1763*

**Pontiac's War**    Indian uprising (1763–1766) led by Pontiac of the Ottawas and Neolin of the Delawares.

**Proclamation of 1763**    Royal proclamation setting the boundary known as the Proclamation Line that limited British settlements to the eastern side of the Appalachian Mountains.

**Quartering Acts**    Acts of Parliament requiring colonial legislatures to provide supplies and quarters for the troops stationed in America.

**Sugar Act**    Law passed in 1764 to raise revenue in the American colonies. It lowered the duty from 6 pence to 3 pence per gallon on foreign molasses imported into the colonies and increased the restrictions on colonial commerce.

goods and curb traders' cheating of their Native American customers. Second, it established civilian governments in East and West Florida. For the time being, Canada—inhabited by more than eighty thousand French Catholics—would remain under military rule.

The 10,000-man force that British officials planned to keep in America was not nearly large enough to ensure that the proclamation would be obeyed. Moreover, both the stationing of troops in peacetime and the establishment of the Proclamation Line aroused considerable resentment among colonists. Americans shared a traditional English distrust of standing armies, and worried that the soldiers could just as easily be used to coerce the colonists as to protect them. Their concerns were heightened when Parliament passed two **Quartering Acts** that required colonial assemblies to provide barracks and supplies for the soldiers.

News of the Proclamation Line was no more welcome. Colonial settlers and land speculators coveted the territories they had fought to win from France and resented the prohibition against their occupation. As it turned out, the prohibition against settlement was largely unenforceable. Within a few years, imperial authorities made several adjustments to the settlement boundary line and returned supervision of the Indian trade to the individual colonies, concessions that revived many of the problems that the Proclamation of 1763 had meant to solve.

## The Search for Revenue: The Sugar Act

In 1764 George Grenville and his fellow ministers turned from territorial control to matters of finance. Compounding the problem of the soaring national debt, a postwar recession had both Britain and the colonies in its grip. Parliament passed two laws that year to address imperial financial concerns. One statute responded to London merchants' protest against Virginia's use of colonial paper money as legal tender for payment of debts, because the money had lost nearly a sixth of its value during the recent war. The Currency Act of 1764 prohibited all colonial legislatures from making their paper money legal tender. It allowed creditors to demand repayment in specie (gold or silver), always in short supply in the colonies, and even more so during the postwar economic recession.

Parliament also passed the American Revenue Act, commonly known as the **Sugar Act.** The Sugar Act placed duties on a number of colonial imports, but its most important provision actually lowered the tax on imported molasses from 6 to 3 pence per gallon. The Molasses Act of 1733 had required the higher duty to discourage colonists from importing molasses (much of it used to make rum) from the French West Indies. But merchants evaded the high tax by bribing customs officials about a penny a gallon to certify French molasses as British. Grenville hoped that the 3 pence per gallon Sugar Act tax was close enough to the going rate for bribes that colonial merchants would simply pay it.

The Sugar Act also took aim at smugglers by requiring that ships carry elaborate new documentation of their cargoes. Customs officials could seize ships for what their owners often regarded as minor technicalities. The act further ordered customs collectors to discharge their duties personally. Previously, these men had often lived in England, leaving the work of collection in the colonies to poorly paid deputies, who were susceptible to bribes. Finally, Parliament gave responsibility for trying violations of the laws to a new vice-admiralty court in Halifax, Nova Scotia. Vice-admiralty courts, with jurisdiction over maritime affairs, normally operated without a jury and were therefore more likely to enforce trade restrictions.

New Englanders predominated among those colonists actively opposed to the Sugar Act. They feared that enforcement of the tax on foreign molasses would damage the northern rum industry. Earnings from rum were crucial to the New England–West Indies trade and also helped to pay for imported British goods. The postwar recession was hardly the time to stir up colonial fears about their economies. The assemblies of eight colonies collaborated on a set of petitions sent to royal authorities to protest the Sugar Act. Officials in London, however, simply ignored the petitions even as they labored to devise new colonial taxes.

# REPUBLICAN IDEOLOGY AND COLONIAL PROTEST

**HOW DID** republican ideology inform the colonists' view of their relationship to Britain?

Colonists stressed economic arguments in their petitions against the Sugar Act, but their unease about the measure also had political dimensions. Parliament had passed similar commercial regulations before, but its new assertiveness and its claim that additional taxes might be necessary stirred colonial fears that more than their pocketbooks were under threat. Colonists treasured their rights as Englishmen, but new imperial reforms threatened to encroach on their enjoyment of those rights as never before. Thus imperial reforms provoked colonists to reflect upon the character of the postwar empire and on the principles that governed their membership in it.

## POWER VERSUS LIBERTY

Many colonists derived their understanding of politics from a set of ideas loosely grouped under the heading of **republicanism.** Influenced by writings from classical Rome, and linked to what was known in England as **Country,** or **"Real Whig," ideology** (see Chapter 4), republican political thinkers acknowledged that governments must exercise power, but simultaneously cautioned that power could easily overwhelm liberty. Too much power in the hands of a ruler meant tyranny. Too much liberty in the hands of the people, however, was no better; it meant anarchy.

Republican ideology thus called upon the people to be ever vigilant against corruption and excessive power. Their main bulwark against tyranny was civil liberty, or maintaining the right of the people to participate in government. The people who did so, however, had to demonstrate virtue. To eighteenth-century republicans, virtuous citizens were those who focused not on their private interests but rather on what was good for the public as a whole. They were necessarily propertyholders, since only these individuals could exercise an independence of judgment impossible for those dependent on employers, landlords, masters, or (in the case of women and children) husbands and fathers.

**republicanism** The idea that governments must exercise power, but simultaneously cautioning that power could easily overwhelm liberty.

**Country (Real Whig) ideology** Train of thought (focusing on the threat to personal liberty and the taxation of property holders) first appearing in England in the late seventeenth century in response to the growth of governmental power and a national debt.

## THE BRITISH CONSTITUTION

The key to good government was preserving a balance between the exercise of power and the protection of liberty. Colonists agreed that no government performed this crucial task better than Great Britain's, based as it was on the **British Constitution.** Then, as now, the British Constitution was not a written document. It consisted instead of the governing institutions, laws, and political customs of the realm as they had evolved over the centuries. It was understood, in short, as the way in which British government and society together *were constituted.*

The genius of Britain's government lay in the fact that its constitution was "mixed and balanced." Society was comprised of three elements—the monarchy, aristocracy, and common people—and they had their governmental counterparts in the Crown, the House of Lords, and the House of Commons. Liberty would be preserved so long as none of the elements acquired the ability to dominate or corrupt the others.

The British Constitution protected that balance in a number of ways. Both Houses of Parliament, for instance, had to consent to laws in order for them to go into effect. Because taxation was such a sensitive subject, the House of Commons—the governmental unit closest to the people—retained the right to initiate tax laws and no tax could pass without the consent of the representatives of both houses. This parliamentary control of taxation operated as a crucial check on the monarch's power.

**QUICK REVIEW**

**Republican Ideology**
- Sought to achieve a balance between power and liberty.
- Saw the British Constitution as the embodiment of political balance.
- Colonists saw in taxation the potential for tyranny.

**British Constitution** The principles, procedures, and precedents that governed the operation of the British government.

## TAXATION AND SOVEREIGNTY

Colonists who had absorbed republican ideas were especially concerned about taxation because anyone who paid taxes in effect surrendered some of his property to do so. As long as the taxpayer consented to those taxes, however, it was unlikely that they would become excessive enough to threaten his independence and liberty. Rumors from England that more taxes might follow passage of the Sugar Act encouraged some colonists to begin thinking about whether they really consented to taxes passed by a Parliament to which they elected no representatives.

The fiscal measures required by imperial reform thus drew attention to differences between British and colonial understandings of representation. British authorities contended that colonists, like all inhabitants of Britain, were virtually represented in Parliament because that body's members served the interests of the British nation and empire as a whole. Colonists, however, thought they could only be represented by men for whom they had actually voted—such as the members of their colonial legislatures (see Chapter 4). And they insisted that the right to be taxed only by their own elected representatives was one of the most basic rights of Englishmen.

Few colonists realized yet that their concerns about taxation connected to the more fundamental issue of political **sovereignty.** Sovereignty was the supreme authority of the state, and it included both the right to take life (as in the case of executions for capital crimes) and to tax. If the state were deprived of its authority, it ceased to be sovereign. Were colonists to reach the point where they denied Parliament's right to tax them, they would in effect be denying that the British government had sovereign power over the colonies.

**Read** the **Document**

at **www.myhistorylab.com**
*James Otis, The Rights of the British Colonies Asserted and Proved (1763)*

**sovereignty**   The supreme authority of the state, including both the right to take life (as in the case of executions for capital crimes) and to tax.

# THE STAMP ACT CRISIS

**WHY DID** the Stamp Act spark widespread unrest in the colonies?

Because revenue from the Sugar Act was hardly enough to solve Britain's debt problems, George Grenville proposed another measure, the **Stamp Act.** This legislation required all valid legal documents, as well as newspapers, playing cards, and various other papers, to bear a government-issued stamp, for which there was a charge. Colonists who opposed the Sugar Act had difficulty justifying their opposition to a measure that appeared to fall within Britain's accepted authority to regulate commerce. The Stamp Act was different. It was the first internal tax (as opposed to an external trade duty) that Parliament had imposed on the colonies.

## COLONIAL ASSEMBLIES REACT TO THE STAMP TAX

Colonial protests arose months before the Stamp Act was due to go into effect on November 1, 1765. Eight legislatures passed resolutions condemning the measure. In Virginia's House of Burgesses, 29-year-old Patrick Henry went so far as to propose a resolution asserting that Virginians could disobey any law to which their own legislature had not agreed. Neither this nor some of Henry's other inflammatory proposals passed, but they testified to colonial outrage at what many regarded as an unconstitutional tax.

In October, nine colonies sent delegates to the **Stamp Act Congress** meeting in New York to coordinate the colonial response. The delegates affirmed their loyalty to the king and their "due subordination" to Parliament, but proceeded to adopt the **Declaration of Rights and Grievances.** This document denied Parliament's right to tax the colonies and petitioned king and Parliament to repeal both the Sugar and Stamp acts. Parliament, shocked at this challenge to its authority, refused to receive this declaration or any other colonial petitions.

While colonial assemblies and the Stamp Act Congress deliberated, a torrent of pamphlets and newspaper essays flowed from colonial presses. Some went beyond opposition to the Stamp

**Read** the **Document**

at **www.myhistorylab.com**
*Exploring America:
The Stamp Act*

**Stamp Act**   Law passed by Parliament in 1765 to raise revenue in America by requiring taxed, stamped paper for legal documents, publications, and playing cards.

**Stamp Act Congress**   October 1765 meeting of delegates sent by nine colonies, which adopted the Declaration of Rights and Grievances and petitioned against the Stamp Act.

**Read** the **Document**

at **www.myhistorylab.com**
*Benjamin Franklin, Testimony against the Stamp Act (1766)*

## GLOBAL CONNECTIONS

### A FRENCHMAN REPORTS ON THE AMERICAN REACTION TO THE STAMP ACT

Britain emerged from the Great War for Empire as the victor, but France had no intention of quietly giving up the struggle. French officials therefore took a keen interest in what was happening in the British North American colonies. The Duc de Choiseul, who was in charge of foreign affairs in the 1760s, was in fact remarkably prescient in believing that the British acquisition of Canada would prompt the thirteen mainland colonies to revolt since they no longer needed protection from the French next door. Choiseul and his successor in office, the Comte de Vergennes, accordingly sent agents to take the temperature of affairs in America and report on items of interest such as fortifications, navigable rivers, and the like.

An anonymous traveler whose journal wound up in the French naval archives may have been such a spy, and his findings doubtless pleased French officials. After landing in North Carolina in early 1765, he went north through Williamsburg, Virginia; Annapolis, Maryland; Philadelphia, Pennsylvania; to New York City. On May 30 he was visiting the Virginia House of Burgesses when Patrick Henry gave an historic speech against the Stamp Act, and the traveler's account remains one of our best sources for what was actually said that day. But at all of his major stops, he found Americans condemning the Stamp Act and claiming that they "would fight to the last Drop of their blood before they would Consent to any such slavery." He was sure that this act "had made a great alteration in the Americans Disposition towards great britain" and turned them toward manufacturing goods for themselves. If the trend continued, he predicted that it would be a "fatal stroke to England, for their Chief Dependance is on their manufactures to which these colonys were a Considerable suport."

British officials, he believed, had encouraged religious and other differences among the colonists to keep them dependent on the mother country. But, he concluded, "great is their mistake in this, for the Inhabitants of north America Can lay aside their religion, when their Interest requires it as well as the English Can, and always have done."

- Do you think the Frenchman was right in his assessment of the American reaction to the Stamp Act and the value of the colonies to Great Britain?

---

Act itself to address broader issues. At the same time, merchants in several colonial cities resorted to economic pressure, pledging to cease importing British goods until the hated taxes were repealed. Important as these various measures were in solidifying colonial opposition, however, defeat of the Stamp Act came largely through actions, not words.

**Declaration of Rights and Grievances** Asserts that the Stamp Act and other taxes imposed on the colonists without their consent were unconstitutional.

### COLONISTS TAKE TO THE STREETS

In Boston, a group composed mainly of artisans and shopkeepers, with a few prominent citizens playing behind-the-scenes roles, organized themselves as the **Sons of Liberty.** As part of their general protest against the Stamp Act, they planned to intimidate Andrew Oliver, who had been appointed to the office of stamp distributor, into resigning. In August 1765, they took to the streets. Violent protests quickly spread to other locations. Up and down the coast, rioters forced nearly every stamp distributor to resign his office before the law went into effect on November 1. After that date, the law was essentially nullified, because there was no one to distribute the hated stamps.

Colonial elites sympathetic to the cause of the rioters were nonetheless appalled at their violent tactics. The Stamp Act Congress convened, in large part, so that elites could try to regain control of the situation. When news of the protests reached London, imperial authorities were astonished by the violence. British merchants, feeling the sting of colonial boycotts of British goods, petitioned Parliament to repeal the Stamp Act and resolve the crisis before matters got further out of hand.

**Sons of Liberty** Secret organizations in the colonies formed to oppose the Stamp Act.

**QUICK REVIEW**

**The Stamp Act Crisis**

- First internal tax imposed on colonists by Britain.
- Protest of the Stamp Act took many forms.
- Repeal of the Stamp Act accompanied by passage of the Declaratory Act.

## REPEAL AND THE DECLARATORY ACT

For reasons that had nothing to do with colonial unrest, George III decided to replace Grenville at the treasury with another man, the Marquis of Rockingham. Rockingham was convinced that repealing the Stamp Act was the only way to calm colonial tempers. He faced a delicate task, however, in getting Parliament and the king to agree to repeal.

Both Crown and Parliament thought it preposterous for the world's mightiest empire simply to give way to unruly American mobs. They did not wish to give the slightest impression that they agreed with the colonists' assertion that the Stamp Act was unconstitutional, for to do so would be to call into question Parliament's right to legislate for the colonies at all. In the end, Rockingham found a three-part solution that linked repeal to an unequivocal assertion of Parliament's sovereignty.

First, the Stamp Act would be repealed only because it had damaged British commercial interests, and not because it allegedly violated the colonists' rights. Second, Parliament passed the **Declaratory Act.** This measure affirmed Parliament's sovereignty, declaring that it had "full power and authority to make laws and statutes of sufficient force and validity to bind the colonies and people of America . . . in all cases whatsoever." Third, Parliament passed the Revenue Act of 1766, which reduced the tax on molasses from 3 pence per gallon to 1 penny, but imposed it on all molasses—British and foreign—that came to the mainland colonies.

In London, Parliament had saved face and calmed the merchant community. In the colonies, people rejoiced. They regarded repeal as a vindication of their claim that the Stamp Act had been unconstitutional, and they saw little threat in the Declaratory Act because it did not explicitly assert Parliament's right to tax the colonies, but only "make laws" for them. The Revenue Act attracted little notice, even though it in fact generated considerable income for the empire. Tacit acceptance of this measure suggested that colonists remained willing to pay "external" taxes that regulated trade.

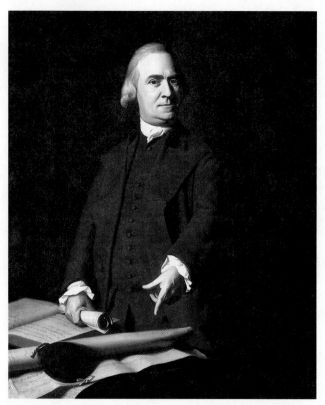

Samuel Adams, the leader of the Boston radicals, as he appeared to John Singleton Copley in the early 1770s. In this famous picture, thought to have been commissioned by another revolutionary leader, John Hancock, Adams points to legal documents guaranteeing American rights.

*Source:* John Singleton Copley (1738–1815), "Samuel Adams," ca. 1772. Oil on canvas 49 1/2 × 39 1/2 in. (125.7 cm × 100.3 cm). Deposited by the City of Boston, 30.76c Courtesy, Museum of Fine Arts, Boston. Reproduced with permission. © 2000 Museum of Fine Arts, Boston. All Right Reserved.

**Declaratory Act**    Law passed in 1766 to accompany repeal of the Stamp Act that stated that Parliament had the authority to legislate for the colonies "in all cases whatsoever."

# THE TOWNSHEND CRISIS

**HOW DID** the colonists respond to Townshend's colonial policies?

Peace between Britain and the colonies did not last long. In 1766 there was another shake-up in the British ministry. The king replaced Rockingham with William Pitt, who had accepted a peerage and was now known as Lord Chatham. Leadership in the House of Commons passed from Pitt to Charles Townshend. Townshend was convinced that the colonists still needed to be taught a lesson in submission to Parliament's authority.

## TOWNSHEND'S PLAN

One focus of Charles Townshend's concern was New York, where the legislature refused to comply with the Quartering Act of 1765 that required colonial assemblies to raise money for housing and supplying British troops. New Yorkers had concluded that this measure amounted to taxation without representation. Townshend's response was to get Parliament to pass an act in 1767 that suspended the New York legislature. Although the New York assembly gave in before the act went into effect, the measure revived concerns about imperial power and showed colonists that Townshend meant business.

A satirical British engraving from 1766 showing English politicians burying the Stamp Act, "born 1765 died 1766." The warehouses in the background symbolize the revival of trade with America.

Much of Britain's postwar debt remained unpaid. Nonetheless, Townshend's fiscal plan was not really designed to reduce that debt. Townshend proposed new duties for the colonies but at the same time lowered certain taxes in Britain itself. He and other British officials were primarily interested in asserting parliamentary sovereignty over the colonies. The result was the **Townshend Duty Act of 1767.** It imposed new duties on imports that colonists got from Britain, including tea, paper, lead, glass, and paint. Revenue from the act would pay the salaries of governors and judges in the colonies, freeing them from dependence on the colonial assemblies that normally paid them.

Colonists suspected that Townshend's plan to pay governors and judges would ensure that these officials would support their parliamentary paymasters rather than the colonial assemblies. Their fears grew when news arrived that there would be a new American Board of Customs Commissioners to see that the Townshend duties were paid. The board would be located in Boston, the presumed home port of many smugglers and the site of the fiercest protests against the Stamp Act.

## RENEWED RESISTANCE

Charles Townshend died suddenly in September 1767 and thus did not live to see the consequences of his actions. Colonial protests were swift, if unorganized. Once again, colonial radicals called for a boycott of British goods. But trade embargoes hurt merchants and consumers alike, making it difficult to guarantee compliance in all port towns. Yet unanimity was critical; a boycott in Boston was meaningless if British goods continued to flow into Philadelphia or New York. Support for nonimportation increased, however, after an incident in Boston in June 1768. When customs commissioners seized John Hancock's ship, *Liberty*, on charges of smuggling, their action sparked a riot. In response to the requests of the terrified commissioners, Britain sent two regiments of troops to Boston.

In the aftermath of the *Liberty* riot and with the impending arrival of British troops, merchants first in Boston and New York, and later Philadelphia, agreed to nonimportation. Enforcement of the trade boycotts energized the populace and drew more people, including artisans and laborers, into political action than ever before. Women, who normally had no

**Townshend Duty Act of 1767** Act of Parliament, passed in 1767, imposing duties on colonial tea, lead, paint, paper, and glass.

**WHERE TO LEARN MORE**

★ Charleston, South Carolina
http://www.nps.gov/nr/travel/charleston/

●●●—Read the **Document**

at **www.myhistorylab.com**
*John Dickinson, from Letters from a Farmer in Pennsylvania (1768)*

((●—Hear the Audio

at **www.myhistorylab.com**
*The Liberty Song*

formal political role because of their dependent status, found that their responsibilities for household production and purchasing gained political meaning. They too could announce their solidarity with fellow colonists by spurning British imports and instead making and wearing homespun clothing. Colonists from all social groups forged a sense of common purpose in their resistance to the Townshend duties (see American Views: Social Status and the Enforcement of the Nonimportation Movement).

The **nonimportation movement** eventually produced a sharp drop in British imports. By early 1770, northern colonies had reduced imports by nearly two-thirds (see Figure 5–1). Once again, colonial economic pressure caught the attention of British merchants and members of Parliament. The troubles in America contributed to the king's decision to appoint a new prime minister, Frederick, Lord North, in January 1770. Lord North was prepared to concede that the Townshend duties had been counterproductive because they interfered with British trade. But even as he worked for their repeal, news arrived of another episode of violence in Boston—this time involving British troops.

**nonimportation movement**    A tactical means of putting economic pressure on Britain by refusing to buy its exports in the colonies.

•••Read the Document
at www.myhistorylab.com
*The Virginia Nonimportation Resolutions (1769)*

## THE BOSTON MASSACRE

Ever since British troops had arrived in Boston in 1768, there had been friction between soldiers and civilians. By the summer of 1769, however, Boston seemed calm enough that British authorities thought it safe to remove half of the 1,000 troops stationed there. This action energized the Sons of Liberty, who saw an opportunity to confront the remaining soldiers more often. Crowds frequently gathered to taunt and throw stones at troops standing at guardposts. Townsmen also targeted off-duty soldiers who sought part-time employment at unskilled jobs. Many Bostonians, unemployed because of the weak economy, resented competition from soldiers who, because they derived some income from the army, could afford to accept lower wages from employers.

In early March 1770, these sporadic incidents culminated in a fatal confrontation. On March 5, a crowd gathered outside the customs house and began pelting the guardsmen with snowballs and rocks. The British officer, Captain Thomas Preston, ordered his men to fix bayonets and push the crowd back. But then one soldier evidently slipped, and his musket discharged as he fell. The remaining soldiers, perhaps believing that in the tumult Preston had ordered them to fire, shot into the crowd, killing five Bostonians and wounding six. Four of the dead men were white artisans or laborers; the fifth was Crispus Attucks, a free black sailor.

Captain Preston and six soldiers were tried for murder. They were defended in court by two prominent Boston lawyers, John Adams and Josiah Quincy Jr. who—despite their radical political leanings—thought the soldiers deserved a proper legal defense.

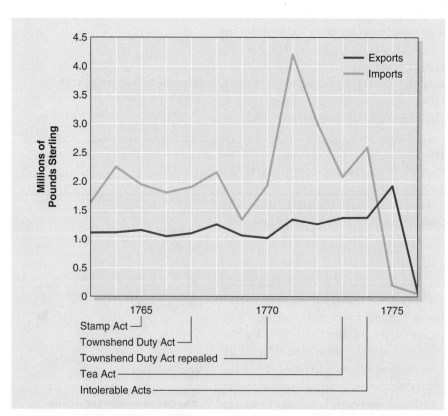

**FIGURE 5–1    Value of American Exports to and Imports from England, 1763–1776**    This figure depicts the value of American exports to and imports from England. The decrease of imports in 1765–1766 and the even sharper drop in 1769 illustrate the effect of American boycotts in response to the Stamp Act and Townshend duties.

*Data Source:* U.S. Bureau of the Census, *Historical Statistics of the United States, Colonial Times to 1970,* Bicentennial Edition, Part 1 (1975).

Preston and four soldiers were acquitted; two others were convicted of the lesser charge of manslaughter.

The **Boston Massacre** seemed to fulfill dire republican prophecies about a tyrannical Britain using military coercion to take away American liberties. Boston's radicals worked to ensure that the memory of the Massacre remained fresh in colonists' minds. Each year, Bostonians commemorated March 5 as "Massacre Day," with public speeches and other events. Orators warned colonists in other cities to be vigilant, since their turn might be next.

## PARTIAL REPEAL AND ITS CONSEQUENCES

Ironically, the Boston Massacre occurred on the same day that Lord North proposed that Parliament repeal all of the Townshend duties except the one on tea. As was the case after the Stamp Act, Parliament feared that complete repeal would make it seem that Britain had given in to the colonists. Retaining the tax on tea served as a statement of parliamentary authority; it also made fiscal sense in that most of the revenue raised by the Townshend duties came from the tax on tea.

The rejoicing that had followed the Stamp Act repeal was not repeated after partial repeal of the Townshend duties. For the colonists, this had been an incomplete victory, and recent events, especially the Boston Massacre, had seriously undermined their trust in British authority. On the surface, the years 1770–1773 looked like a time of relative calm. Underneath, however, colonial animosities against British policies continued to simmer.

Every now and then, some incident brought those animosities to a boil in a dramatic way. Such was the case in 1772, when a British customs vessel, the *Gaspée*, ran aground near Providence, Rhode Island. Because its crew had allegedly harassed local residents, Rhode Islanders got even. Led by John Brown, a local merchant, they boarded and burned the ship. The British government appointed a commission of inquiry with instructions to arrest the culprits and send them to England for trial. Despite its offer of a reward for information, the commission learned nothing.

Such incidents, and in particular the British threat to send Americans to England for trial, led colonial leaders to resolve to keep one another informed about British actions. Twelve colonies established **committees of correspondence** for this purpose. In 1773, Boston radicals established similar committees in towns throughout Massachusetts. The committees aimed not only to keep abreast of events in Britain and in other colonies, but also to try and anticipate what Parliament's next move might be. Radicals were especially concerned that colonists would let down their guard in the relative calm that followed the Townshend duty repeal.

# DOMESTIC DIVISIONS

Even as growing mistrust of Britain encouraged many colonists to see themselves as having common interests, local animosities could still divide them. The same issues that sparked opposition to Britain—property rights and political representation—often pitted colonists against one another.

## REGULATOR MOVEMENTS

The end of the Cherokee War of 1760–1761 had not brought peace to backcountry South Carolina. Gangs of outlaws displaced by that conflict roamed the countryside, plundering the estates of prosperous farmers and challenging anyone to stop them. When the colonial government, based more than a hundred miles away in Charleston, failed to respond, the aggrieved farmers took matters into their own hands. In 1767, they organized what were in effect vigilante

**Read** the **Document**
at **www.myhistorylab.com**
*Boston Gazette, Description of the Boston Massacre (1770)*

**Boston Massacre**   After months of increasing friction between townspeople and the British troops stationed in the city, on March 5, 1770, British troops fired on American civilians in Boston.

**committees of correspondence**
Committees formed in the colonies to keep Americans informed about British measures that would affect them.

**WHAT ISSUES** and interests divided the colonists?

**Regulators** Vigilante groups active in the 1760s and 1770s in the western parts of North and South Carolina. The South Carolina Regulators attempted to rid the area of outlaws; the North Carolina Regulators were more concerned with high taxes and court costs.

companies to fight against the marauders. Calling themselves **"Regulators,"** they aimed to bring law and order to the backcountry. By March 1768, the Regulators succeeding in killing or expelling most of the criminals.

The outlaws' threat to property and order, however, was symptomatic of a larger problem of political representation. By the 1760s, most South Carolina settlers lived in the backcountry, but because the creation of legislative districts in the region had not kept pace with settlement, they elected only 2 of 48 assembly representatives. Moreover, there was no court system in the region for the resolution of disputes. Once the outlaws had been eliminated, the Regulators—many of whom were relatively prosperous farmers and shopkeepers—took it upon themselves to "regulate" the poor settlers in their neighborhoods. The crisis diminished only when the governor agreed to create circuit courts in the backcountry and the assembly established new districts that increased the region's political representation.

At about the same time, a Regulator movement emerged in North Carolina. Once again, political representation was a major grievance, for the western counties elected only 17 of the assembly's 78 members. And while North Carolina's backcountry did have county courts, they were plagued by corruption. Once again, aggrieved westerners resorted to extralegal protests. They refused to pay taxes, closed county courts, and attacked the most detested of tax officials. Governor William Tryon matched force with force, sending a thousand militiamen from eastern counties to subdue the protestors. In May 1771, the militiamen defeated more than 2,000 poorly armed Regulators in a battle at Alamance Creek that left 29 men dead and 150 wounded.

The battle at Alamance Creek was the most serious episode of unrest, but the tensions that produced it simmered throughout the backcountry. Western settlers, often recent immigrants from Scotland, Northern Ireland, and Germany, paid little attention to the threats to liberty and property posed by parliamentary measures. As far as they were concerned, the sources of corruption lay much closer to home, in eastern capitals where officials ignored western demands for good government. Until legislative districts were created in the region, backcountry farmers could legitimately complain about taxation without representation—imposed by their own colonial assemblies.

**QUICK REVIEW**

**Vigilante Justice**

♦ 1766: Regulators form in response to corruption and lawlessness in North Carolina and South Carolina.

♦ Regulators conflict with local elites.

♦ Response to Regulators demonstrated inflexibility of British government.

This depiction of Governor William Tryon's confrontation with the North Carolina Regulators during May 1771 was produced at Philadelphia in 1876 by F.O.C. Darley (1822–1888).

## THE BEGINNINGS OF ANTISLAVERY

In a similar vein, African slaves could have argued that their experience of actual enslavement was far more real than any potential threat to white colonists' liberty posed by imperial reforms. Black colonists, both slave and free, watched white colonists march in parades and riot in the streets, and heard their orators make fervent speeches on behalf of liberty. Although slavery would far outlast these decades, some colonists began to question the legitimacy of the oppressive institution.

Some slaves, particularly in New England, employed the language of liberty when they sued their owners for freedom. In Massachusetts, groups of slaves petitioned both the legislature and the governor for release from bondage. While these legal maneuvers did bring freedom for some individual slaves, taking masters to court was expensive, and slavery as an institution was scarcely undermined.

The slave trade was temporarily interrupted in some colonies during the nonimportation movements. But the first significant attacks on the institution were generated by religious, not economic or political, concerns. Beginning in the 1750s, antislavery movements arose on both sides of the Atlantic. In England, Methodists led the way; in the colonies, Quakers were the first to create an antislavery society and, in 1774, to abolish slaveholding among their membership.

The majority of colonists were nowhere near ready to endorse the end of slavery, and slaveowners regarded calls for abolition as a threat to their property rights. Yet if the antislavery movement could claim few victories in these years, it in fact achieved a major accomplishment. For the first time, colonists who had grown accustomed to taking slavery for granted had to defend an institution that violated the very rights they claimed for themselves.

# THE FINAL IMPERIAL CRISIS

The relative calm that marked the years 1770 to 1773 might have lasted far longer had Parliament not passed another law that reignited colonial protests. Ironically, the despised measure had nothing to do with imperial reform.

**WHAT PUSHED** the colonists from protest to rebellion?

## THE BOSTON TEA PARTY

The measure that outraged colonists was actually designed to help a failing British corporation. The East India Company was tottering on the brink of bankruptcy. Millions of pounds of unsold tea sat in its warehouses, and the imminent failure of Britain's largest corporation alarmed Lord North. If English and colonial consumers, who were purchasing cheaper smuggled Dutch tea, could be induced to buy East India Company tea, the corporation might be saved without needing a major government subsidy.

North's proposed solution was the **Tea Act of 1773.** The measure made East India Company tea cheaper by exempting it from the duty normally collected as the tea was transshipped through Britain. For colonial consumers, the only tax that remained on the tea was the old Townshend duty. North assumed that the lure of cheaper tea would allow the colonists to accept the Townshend duty, and their increased purchases would save the beleaguered East India Company.

As it turned out, North spectacularly misjudged the colonial reaction. Merchants were outraged by a provision in the Tea Act that gave the company and its agents a monopoly on the sale of tea in the colonies. They were joined in protest by Americans in every colony, convinced that North meant to trick them into paying a tax to which they had not consented. Elite colonists and laborers, men and women, united in their opposition.

Colonial leaders realized that their most effective form of resistance was preventing the ships carrying tea from landing. In several ports, the Sons of Liberty threatened ship captains with violence, convincing them to return to England without unloading their cargo. But in Boston, the company agents responsible for the tea happened to be the sons of Governor Thomas Hutchinson. The governor was determined to have the tea unloaded in Boston and the tax paid.

Boston's Sons of Liberty saw no alternative to taking decisive action. On December 16, 1773, a well-organized band of men disguised as Indians raced aboard the *Dartmouth* and two other tea ships, broke open 342 chests of tea, and heaved the contents into the harbor. In a similar action in 1774, residents of Annapolis, Maryland, forced some merchants to burn their own

**WHERE TO LEARN MORE**

★ Boston, Massachusetts, The Freedom Trail http://www.cityofboston.gov/ freedomtrail/

**Tea Act of 1773**    Act of Parliament that permitted the East India Company to sell through agents in America without paying the duty customarily collected in Britain, thus reducing the retail price.

**Read** the **Document**

at www.myhistorylab.com *From Then to Now Online: The Tea Party Movement*

**Read** the **Document**

at www.myhistorylab.com *Hewes, "A Retrospect on the Boston Tea Party" (1834)*

**Boston Tea Party**    Incident that occurred on December 16, 1773, in which Bostonians, disguised as Indians, destroyed £9,000 worth of tea belonging to the British East India Company in order to prevent payment of the duty on it.

**Coercive Acts**    Legislation passed by Parliament in 1774; included the Boston Port Act, the Massachusetts Government Act, the Administration of Justice Act, and the Quartering Act of 1774.

ship when it arrived with dutied tea. But it was the **Boston Tea Party** that captured the attention of Parliament and inspired its angry reaction.

## THE INTOLERABLE ACTS

The destruction of property in the Boston Tea Party shocked many people in Britain and America. Parliament understood that such an affront to its sovereignty demanded a vigorous response. Thus in the spring of 1774, it passed a series of repressive measures known as the **Coercive Acts.**

The first of these, effective June 1, 1774, was the Boston Port Act, which closed the port of Boston until Bostonians paid for the tea and uncollected duties. The Administration of Justice Act allowed any British soldier or official who was charged with a crime while performing his duties to be tried in England (where he would almost certainly receive sympathetic treatment). A new Quartering Act permitted the army to lodge soldiers in any civilian building if necessary. The fourth and most detested measure, the Massachusetts Government Act, drastically modified that colony's charter of 1691. Henceforth, members of the governor's council and sheriffs would be appointed rather than elected. In addition, the act limited the number of town meetings that could be held without the governor's prior approval. As the Coercive Acts made their way through Parliament, the king chose General Thomas Gage, the commander of the British army in North America, as the new governor of Massachusetts.

On the same day that Parliament enacted these measures, it also passed an unrelated law, the **Quebec Act.** This statute extended Quebec's boundaries south to the Ohio River and stipulated that the colony was to be governed by an appointed governor and council but no elected assembly (see Map 5–2). Civil cases would be tried without a jury and the Catholic Church would enjoy the same privileges that it had under the French. The colonists linked the Quebec Act with the Coercive Acts and labeled them the **Intolerable Acts.**

MAP 5–2    **The Quebec Act of 1774**    The Quebec Act enlarged the boundaries of the Canadian province southward to the Ohio River and westward to the Mississippi, thereby depriving several colonies of claims to the area granted them by their original charters.

**Which parts** of Quebec were home to the most British colonists in 1774? Why did they object to the Quebec Act?

## THE AMERICANS' REACTION

The Americans' response to all of these measures was swift, but also revealed divided opinions. The colonists came closest to unanimity in their opposition to the Quebec Act. As one colonist said, the establishment of the Catholic Church in Quebec "gave a General Alarm to all Protestants." Equally disturbing was the fact that the act gave Canada jurisdiction over lands north of the Ohio River claimed by Connecticut, Pennsylvania, and Virginia. Colonial settlers and land speculators in these colonies resented their exclusion from territory they had helped to win for Britain in the French and Indian War. Colonists also suspected that the autocratic government prescribed for Quebec loomed as a model of British plans for their own colonies.

There was little the colonists could do to stop Gage from closing the port of Boston. Many merchants argued that the town should just pay for the tea and thus avoid an economic crisis. They were outnumbered, however, by many more Bostonians who called for another intercolonial boycott of British goods. Yet in New York and Philadelphia, merchants balked at a form of protest that hurt their businesses, and instead wanted an intercolonial congress called to coordinate an American response.

Colonists everywhere expressed real concern about the other Coercive Acts. The Administration of Justice Act—which some with vivid imaginations dubbed the Murder Act—seemed to declare open season on colonists, allowing crown officials to kill them without fear of punishment. The Massachusetts Government Act suggested that no colonial charter was safe. Parliament might decide to abolish the lower houses of all the colonies (see the Overview table, New Restraints and Burdens on Americans, 1763–1774).

If Lord North thought that the Coercive Acts would drive a wedge between radical Boston and the rest of the colonies, he was utterly mistaken. Boston's committee of correspondence produced a steady stream of warnings about this latest and most serious threat to liberty that resonated throughout the colonies. As real economic hardship descended on the city, contributions of food and fuel flowed in from the countryside. The spirit of protest thus spread out from urban areas, where opposition to the Stamp Act and Townshend Acts had mainly occurred, into rural villages. More colonists were politicized than ever before.

When the assemblies in other colonies discussed joining the resistance movement, royal governors shut them down. This led colonists to organize "provincial congresses," or extralegal conventions that acted as proxies for the assemblies in mobilizing the public. Massachusetts's Provincial Congress, meeting in the town of Concord, became the colony's de facto government. It voted to accept the **Suffolk Resolves,** which had been passed at a convention in Suffolk County (where Boston was located). These resolutions called for the payment of taxes to the Provincial Congress, not to Gage in Boston, and demanded creation of an armed force of "minutemen" ready to respond to any emergency. The Provincial Congress also authorized the stockpiling of arms and ammunition in Concord.

Mr. and Mrs. Thomas Mifflin of Philadelphia. Mifflin was a prominent merchant and radical opponent of British policy toward the colonies. He and his wife were visiting Boston in 1773, when John Singleton Copley painted them. Working at a small loom, Sarah Morris Mifflin weaves a decorative fringe. She no doubt did the same during the nonimportation movement against the Townshend duties, thereby helping to make importation of such goods from England unnecessary.

John Singleton Copley, Portrait of Mr. and Mrs. Thomas Mifflin. Philadelphia Museum of Art: Bequest. of Mrs. Esther B. Wistar to the Historical Society of Pennsylvania in 1900 and acquired by the Philadelphia Museum of Art # EW 1999–45–1, Photograph © Museum of Fine Arts, Boston.

**Quebec Act** Law passed by Parliament in 1774 that provided an appointed government for Canada, enlarged the boundaries of Quebec, and confirmed the privileges of the Catholic Church.

**Intolerable Acts** American term for the Coercive Acts and the Quebec Act.

**Suffolk Resolves** Militant resolves adopted in 1774 in response to the Coercive Acts by representatives from the towns in Suffolk County, Massachusetts, including Boston.

**First Continental Congress** Meeting of delegates from most of the colonies held in 1774 in response to the Coercive Acts. The Congress endorsed the Suffolk Resolves, adopted the Declaration of Rights and Grievances, and agreed to establish the Continental Association.

## THE FIRST CONTINENTAL CONGRESS

A consensus emerged in support of an intercolonial congress. In the end, twelve colonies (all except Georgia) sent representatives. The **First Continental Congress** met at Carpenter's Hall in Philadelphia from September 5 to October 26, 1774, with fifty-five delegates present at one time or another. The delegates quickly voted for nonimportation, remembering its utility in previous imperial confrontations. Virtually all of the delegates likewise agreed to a policy of nonexportation, to begin in August 1775 if Britain had not yet addressed colonial grievances. Radical delegates also succeeded in having the Congress endorse the Suffolk Resolves, declaring the Coercive Acts unconstitutional.

Delegates then engaged in an extended debate trying to define colonial rights, in effect specifying the terms by which the colonies would voluntarily retain their membership in the empire. The result was a declaration of rights and set of resolves that responded to a decade of imperial crises. The delegates went beyond declaring the Intolerable Acts unconstitutional to

## AMERICAN VIEWS

### Social Status and the Enforcement of the Nonimportation Movement

**M**any Americans enthusiastically supported the nonimportation movement called in response to the Townshend Duty Act crisis of the late 1760s. A few, however, openly opposed it. Among these was the aristocratic William Henry Drayton of South Carolina, who objected to the composition of the committee chosen to enforce the nonimportation agreement in his region. The committee included artisans and shopkeepers, men who, Drayton claimed, should have no role in public affairs. Their education prepared them only "to cut up a beast in the market to the best advantage, to cobble an old shoe in the neatest manner, or to build a necessary house [privy]," not to make public policy. As the following document makes clear, deference had its limits, and the committeemen emphatically disagreed with him. Drayton was later to reverse himself and actively support the Continental Association's ban on importing British goods in 1775. "The people" wanted it, he would later explain, and "it was our duty, to satisfy our constituents; as we were only servants of the public [at large]."

- **Who** makes policy in the United States today?
- **What** qualifications do you think they should have?
- **How** do your answers to these questions differ from Drayton's? From the "Mechanicks's"?
- **How** would you explain Drayton's later switch?

### The Mechanicks of the General Committee to William Henry Drayton

The gracious Giver of all good things, has been pleased to bestow a certain principle on mankind, which properly may be called common sense: But, though every man hath a natural right to a determined portion of this ineffable ray of the Divinity, yet, to the misfortune of society, many persons fall short of this most necessary gift of God. . . .

The Mechanicks pretend to nothing more, than having a claim from nature, to their share in this inestimable favour, in common with Emperors and Kings, and, were it safe to carry the comparison still higher, they would say with William-Henry Drayton himself; who, in his great condescention, has been pleased to allow us a place amongst human beings: But whether it might have happened from an ill construction of his sensory, or his upper works being damaged by some rough treatment of the person who conducted his birth, we know not; however so it is, that, to us, he seems highly defective in this point, whatever exalted notions he may entertain of his own abilities.

By attending to the dictates of common sense, the Mechanicks have been able to distinguish between RIGHT and WRONG; in doing which indeed no great merit is claimed, because every man's own feelings will direct him thereto, unless he obstinately, or from a pertinacious opinion of his own superior knowledge, shuts his eyes, and stoickally submits to all the illegal encroachments that may be made on his property, by an ill-designing and badly-informed ministry.

Mr. Drayton may value himself as much as he pleases, on his having had a liberal education bestowed on him, tho' the good fruits thereof have not hitherto been conspicuous either in his public or private life: He ought however to know, that this is not so absolutely necessary to these, who move in the low sphere of mechanical employments. But still, though he pretends to view them with so contemptuous and oblique an eye, these men hope, that they are in some degree useful to society, without presuming to make any comparisons between themselves and him, except with regard to love for their country; for he has amply shewn, that an attachment of this sort is not one of his ruling passions. Nor does he appear in the least to have regarded the peace and good order of that community of which he is a member; otherwise he would not wilfully, and without any cause, have knocked his head against ninety-nine out of every hundred of the people, not only in this province, but of all North-America. . . .

Mr. Drayton may be assured, that so far from being ashamed of our trades, we are in the highest degree thankful to our friends, who put us in the way of being instructed in them; and that we bless God for giving us strength and judgment to pursue them, in order to maintain our families, with a decency suitable to their stations in life. Every man is not so lucky as to have a fortune ready provided to his hand, either by his own or his wife's parents, as has been his lot; nor ought it to be so with all men; and Providence accordingly hath wisely ordained otherwise, by appointing the greatest part of mankind, to provide for their support by manual labour; and we will be bold to say, that such are the most useful people in a community. . . .

We are, Yours, &c.

MECHANICKS of the COMMITTEE.

October 3d, 1769.

*Source: South Carolina Gazette, October 5, 1769; reprinted in The Letters of Freeman, etc.: Essays on the Nonimportation Movement in South Carolina by William Henry Drayton, ed. Robert M. Weir (1977), University of South Carolina Press, pp. 111–114.*

## OVERVIEW   New Restraints and Burdens on Americans, 1763–1774

| | Limits on Legislative Action | Curbs on Territorial Expansion | Burdens on Colonial Trade | Imposition of New Taxes |
| --- | --- | --- | --- | --- |
| 1763 | | Proclamation Line keeps white settlement east of the Appalachians. | Peacetime use of navy and new customs officials to enforce Navigation Acts. | |
| 1764 | Currency Act limits the colonial legislatures' ability to issue paper money. | | Vice-admiralty courts strengthened for Sugar Act. | Sugar Act imposes taxes for revenue (modified 1766). |
| 1765 | | | | Quartering Act requires assemblies to provide facilities for royal troops.<br><br>Stamp Act imposes internal taxes on various items (repealed 1766). |
| | Declaratory Act proclaims Parliament's right to legislate for colonies in all cases whatsoever. | | | |
| 1767 | Royal instructions limit size of colonial assemblies. | | Vice-admiralty courts strengthened for Townshend duties.<br><br>American Customs Service established in Boston. | Townshend duties imposed on some imported goods in order to pay colonial officials. (All but tax on tea repealed 1770.) |
| 1773 | | | | Tea Act reduces duty and prompts Boston Tea Party. |
| 1774 (Intolerable Acts) | Massachusetts Government Act limits town meetings, changes legislature, and violates Massachusetts charter. | Quebec Act enlarges Quebec at expense of colonies with claims in the Ohio River Valley. | Boston Port Act closes harbor until East India Company's tea is paid for. | Quartering Act of 1774 declares that troops could be lodged in virtually any uninhabited building in Boston. |

criticize all revenue measures passed since the end of the French and Indian War. They denounced the dissolution of colonial assemblies and the keeping of troops in the colonies during peacetime. Congress defined the colonists' rights to include "life, liberty, and property," and stated that colonial legislatures had exclusive powers to make laws and pass taxes, subject only to the royal veto. About the only concession it made was to pledge that Americans would "cheerfully" consent to trade regulations for the good of the empire.

## THE CONTINENTAL ASSOCIATION

As Congress's proceedings came to an end, some delegates began to tinker with its recommendations to protect their own colonies' interests. Members from the Chesapeake colonies wanted to ensure that, if the nonexportation policy had to go into effect in 1775, it would

**WHERE TO LEARN MORE**

Philadelphia, Pennsylvania
http://www.ushistory.org/tour/index.html

A NEW METHOD OF MACARONY MAKING AS PRACTISED AT BOSTON

This image shows John Malcolm, an unpopular customs commissioner, being tarred and feathered in Boston. By 1774, radicals threatened others who defended British measures with similar punishment.

not begin until that year's tobacco crop had been shipped. Carolina delegates went so far as to threaten to walk out of the meeting if rice was not exempted from the nonexportation agreement. Northern delegates agreed to the Carolinians' demand, but the incident demonstrated how fragile colonial unity was.

Two final tasks remained. First, Congress needed an enforcement mechanism to ensure that its agreed-upon measures were followed. It created the **Continental Association,** a mutual pledge by the delegates to see that their colonies ceased importing any British goods after December 1, 1774, and, if the dispute with Britain was not resolved by September 1775, make sure that their provinces ceased exporting goods to Britain and the West Indies. Voters in every town, city, and county throughout the colonies were to choose committees to enforce the terms of the Association. The approximately 7,000 men who served on these committees during the winter of 1774–1775 in effect formed grassroots radical governments.

Second, Congress concluded its proceedings with an address not to Parliament, but to the king and the British and American people. This gesture confirmed the fact that delegates no longer considered Parliament to be a legitimate legislature over the colonies. Delegates instead asked George III to use his "royal authority and interposition" to protect his loyal subjects in America. So long as the king protected colonial rights, he could count on the Americans' allegiance.

## POLITICAL POLARIZATION

Scarcely anyone called for independence at this point. Even so, many Americans had moved far from the positions they had taken at the start of the imperial crisis. Instead of urging a return to the pre-1763 status quo, they agreed with the Congress's rejection of Parliament's sovereignty and its assumption that only allegiance to the king tied Americans to Britain. But not all colonists accepted such a drastic reinterpretation of the imperial connection. Even if they regarded recent parliamentary measures as threats to American liberty, some colonists continued to recognize parliamentary authority over the colonies. Others had never quarreled with British policies at all. By late 1774, however, it became more dangerous to express such opinions. The local committees created under the Continental Association not only enforced the boycott against British goods but also intimidated their opponents into silence.

A new political order was emerging, requiring colonists to choose one side or the other in an atmosphere of increasing polarization. The advocates of colonial rights began to call themselves **Whigs** and condemned their opponents as **Tories.** These traditional English party labels dated from the late seventeenth century, when the Tories had supported the accession of the Catholic King James II, and the Whigs had opposed it. Colonial Whigs used this label to identify themselves as champions of liberty and called their opponents Tories to represent them as defenders of tyrannical royal government. As imperial ties proceeded to unravel, there appeared to be no third option.

# CONCLUSION

Years of political turmoil inspired colonists to think more systematically about their rights than they had ever done before. As they did so, members of the elite and laborers, men and women, black colonists and white, were all drawn into the politics of resistance. They read (and sometimes wrote) letters and pamphlets, marched in the streets, boycotted tea, and wore homespun clothing. In so doing, they came to recognize their common interests as Americans and their differences from the British. They became aware, as Benjamin Franklin would later write, of the need to break "through the bounds, in which a dependent people had been accustomed to think, and act" so that they might "properly comprehend the character they had assumed."

In the winter of 1774–1775, however, the "character" of the Americans was not yet fully revealed. Although they had achieved an unprecedented level of unity in their opposition to Parliament, they did not all agree on where the path of resistance would lead. Americans had surely rebelled, but had not yet launched a revolution.

**Tories**   A derisive term applied to loyalists in America who supported the king and Parliament just before and during the American Revolution.

# WHERE TO LEARN MORE

**Fort Michilimackinac National Historic Landmark, Mackinaw City, Michigan.** Near the south end of the Mackinac Bridge, the present structure is a modern restoration of the fort as it was when Pontiac's War took a heavy toll on its garrison. The Mackinac State Historic Park's website, http://www.mackinacparks.com/ provides a brief description and photographs of the reconstructed colonial village and fort.

**Charleston, South Carolina.** Many buildings date from the eighteenth century. Officials stored tea in one of them, the Exchange, to prevent a local version of the Boston Tea Party. The website for Historic Charleston, http://www.nps.gov/nr/travel/charleston, provides a map, a list of buildings, and information about them.

**Boston, Massachusetts, The Freedom Trail.** Many important buildings and sites in this area date from the seventeenth and eighteenth centuries. They include Faneuil Hall (Dock Square), where many public meetings took place prior to the Revolution, and the Old State House (Washington and State streets), which overlooks the site of the Boston Massacre. The Freedom Trail, http://www.cityofboston.gov/freedomtrail/, provides a well-illustrated virtual tour of the historic sites.

**Philadelphia, Pennsylvania.** Numerous buildings and sites date from the eighteenth century. Independence National Historical Park contains Carpenter's Hall, where the First Continental Congress met, and the Pennsylvania State House (now known as Independence Hall), where the Declaration of Independence was adopted. Philadelphia's Historic Mile, http://www.ushistory.org/tour/index.html, provides a virtual tour of the great landmarks of the city, including Independence Hall.

# REVIEW QUESTIONS

1. What did Andrew Burnaby see as the main obstacles to colonial union? What did he foresee as the consequences of leaving the colonists "to themselves"?

2. How did the outcome of the French and Indian War affect the relations between Native Americans and white settlers? Between British authorities and Americans?

3. What was the relationship between the French and Indian War and changes in British policy toward America? How did the expectations of Americans and Britons differ in 1763? Why were the new policies offensive to Americans?

4. How was stationing British troops in America related to British taxation of the colonists? Why did the colonists consider taxation by Parliament an especially serious threat to their freedom as well as to their pocketbooks?

5. How did Americans oppose the new measures? Who participated in the various forms of resistance? How effective were the different kinds of resistance? What effect did resistance to British measures have on Americans' internal politics and sense of identity as Americans?

6. What led to the meeting of the First Continental Congress? What steps did the Congress take? What did it expect to achieve?

# KEY TERMS

Boston Massacre (p. 129)
Boston Tea Party (p. 132)
British Constitution (p. 123)
Cherokee War (p. 120)
Coercive Acts (p. 132)
Committees of
    correspondence (p. 129)
Continental Association (p. 136)
Country (Real Whig)
    ideology (p. 123)
Declaration of Rights and
    Grievances (p. 125)
Declaratory Act (p. 126)
First Continental
    Congress (p. 133)
Intolerable Acts (p. 133)
Nonimportation
    movement (p. 128)

Pontiac's War (p. 122)
Proclamation of 1763
    (p. 122)
Quartering Acts (p. 122)
Quebec Act (p. 133)
Regulators (p. 130)
Republicanism (p. 123)
Sons of Liberty (p. 125)
Sovereignty (p. 124)
Stamp Act (p. 124)
Stamp Act Congress (p. 124)
Suffolk Resolves (p. 133)
Sugar Act (p. 122)
Tea Act of 1773 (p. 131)
Tories (p. 137)
Townshend Duty Act of 1767
    (p. 127)
Whigs (p. 136)

# PEARSON
# myhistorylab Connections

Reinforce what you learned in this chapter by studying the many documents, images, maps, review tools, and videos available at **www.myhistorylab.com**.

## Read and Review

✓●─ **Study** and **Review** **Study Plan: Chapter 5**

●●●●─ **Read** the **Document**

*Benjamin Franklin, Testimony against the Stamp Act (1766)*

*John Dickinson, from Letters from a Farmer in Pennsylvania (1768)*

*An Early Abolitionist Speaks Out against Slavery (1757)*

*Boston Gazette, Description of the Boston Massacre (1770)*

*Hewes, "A Retrospect on the Boston Tea Party" (1834)*

*John Andrews to William Barrell, Boston Tea Party (1773)*

*James Otis, The Rights of the British Colonies Asserted and Proved (1763)*

*Slave Petition to the Governor of Massachusetts (1774)*

*The Virginia Nonimportation Resolutions (1769)*

◉─ **See** the **Map** *Settlement in North America, c. 1763*

## Research and Explore

●●●●─ **Read** the **Document**

*Personal Journeys Online*

*From Then to Now Online: The Tea Party Movement*

*Exploring America: The Stamp Act*

((●●─ **Hear** the **Audio** *The Liberty Song*

((●●─ **Hear** the **Audio**

Hear the audio files for Chapter 5 at
**www.myhistorylab.com**.

# 6

# The War for Independence

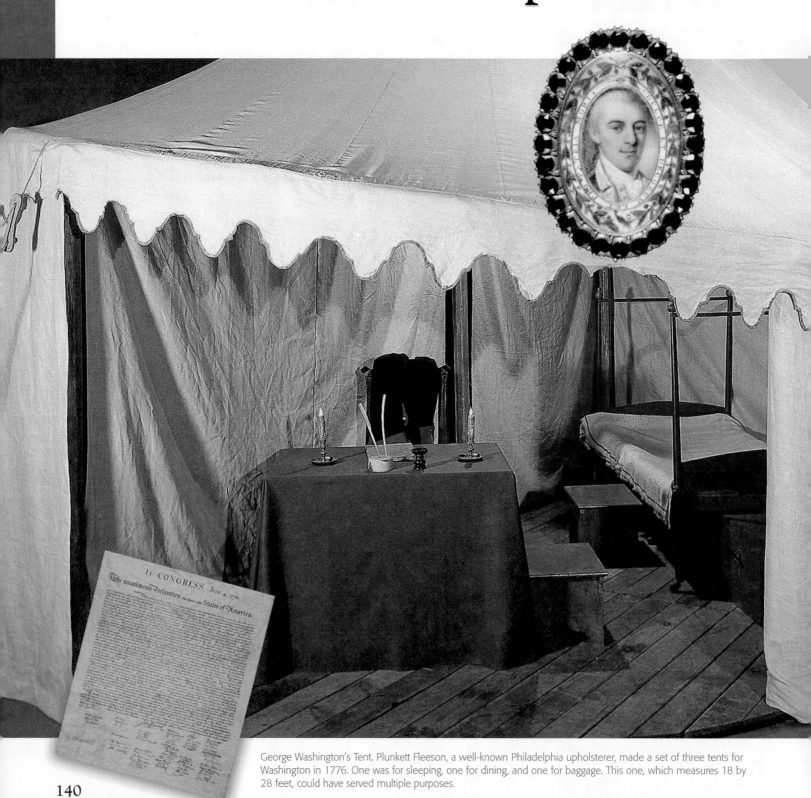

George Washington's Tent. Plunkett Fleeson, a well-known Philadelphia upholsterer, made a set of three tents for Washington in 1776. One was for sleeping, one for dining, and one for baggage. This one, which measures 18 by 28 feet, could have served multiple purposes.

((•─ Hear the Audio

Hear the audio files for Chapter 6 at www.myhistorylab.com.

## FROM REBELLION TO WAR  *(page 143)*

**WHY DID** tensions between the colonies and Britain escalate so rapidly between 1774 and 1776?

## THE CONTINENTAL CONGRESS BECOMES A NATIONAL GOVERNMENT  *(page 145)*

**WHAT WERE** the Second Continental Congress's highest priorities?

## THE COMBATANTS  *(page 149)*

**WHAT WERE** the key differences between the British and American forces?

## THE WAR IN THE NORTH, 1776–1777  *(page 153)*

**HOW DID** the American forces survive the military setbacks of 1776?

## THE WAR WIDENS, 1778–1781  *(page 154)*

**WHY DID** the French enter the war on the American side?

## THE WAR AND SOCIETY, 1775–1783  *(page 158)*

**WHAT WAS** the social impact of the War for Independence?

## THE AMERICAN VICTORY, 1782–1783  *(page 160)*

**WHAT WERE** the key factors in the American victory in the Revolutionary War?

"Paul Jones Shooting a Sailor," color engraving from the Olds Collection # 366, no negative number.
© Collection of the New-York Historical Society.

ONE AMERICAN JOURNEY

*Headquarters, Valley Forge*

*January 14, 1778*

*I barely hinted to you my dearest Father my desire to augment the Continental Forces from an untried Source. . . . I would solicit you to cede me a number of your able bodied men Slaves, instead of leaving me a fortune. I would bring about a twofold good, first I would advance those who are unjustly deprived of the Rights of Mankind to a State which would be a proper Gradation between abject Slavery and perfect Liberty and besides I would reinforce the Defenders of Liberty with a number of gallant Soldiers. . . .*

*Headquarters, Valley Forge*

*February 2, 1778*

*My dear Father,*

*The more I reflect upon the difficulties and delays which are likely to attend the completing our Continental Regiments, the more anxiously is my mind bent upon the Scheme which I lately communicated to you. . . .*

*You seem to think my dear Father, that men reconciled by long habit to the miseries of their Condition would prefer their ignominious bonds to the untasted Sweets of Liberty, especially when offer'd upon the terms which I propose. . . . I am tempted to believe that this trampled people have so much human left in them, as to be capable of aspiring to the rights of men by noble exertions, if some friend to mankind would point the Road, and give them prospect of Success.*

*I have long deplored the wretched State of these men and considered in their history, the bloody wars excited in Africa to furnish America with Slaves. The Groans of despairing multitudes toiling for the Luxuries of Merciless Tyrants. I have had the pleasure of conversing with you sometimes upon the means of restoring them to their rights. When can it be better done than when their enfranchisement may be made conducive to the Public Good.*

*John Laurens*

Henry Laurens Papers, vol. 12, pp. 305, 390–392.

**Read the Document** at **www.myhistorylab.com**

Personal Journeys Online

- **Baikia Harvey, Letter to Thomas Baikie, Snowhill, South Carolina, December 30, 1775.**
  **A new immigrant describes conditions in Georgia in 1775.**

- **Joseph Martin, *The Revolutionary Adventures of Joseph Plumb Martin*, 1776–1783.**
  **A Continental soldier remembers the Revolution.**

**JOHN LAURENS** wrote these letters to his father, Henry, at one of the low points of the American Revolution, when victory seemed most remote. The letters reveal much, not only about the course of the war but also about the aspirations and limitations of the Revolutionary generation. Henry Laurens, a wealthy slaveholder from South Carolina, was president of the Continental Congress; his son John was an aide to General George Washington. The progress of the war had encouraged young John to take an intellectual journey that can only be understood in the context of that conflict.

John, 23 years old in 1778, had been born in South Carolina but educated for the most part in Geneva and London, where he

## CHRONOLOGY

| | |
|---|---|
| **1775** | April 19: Battles of Lexington and Concord. |
| | May 10: Second Continental Congress meets. |
| | June 17: Battle of Bunker Hill. |
| | December 31: American attack on Quebec. |
| **1776** | January 9: Thomas Paine's *Common Sense* published. |
| | July 4: Declaration of Independence. |
| | September 15: British take New York City. |
| | December 26: Battle of Trenton. |
| **1777** | January 3: Battle of Princeton. |
| | September 11: Battle of Brandywine Creek. |
| | October 17: American victory at Saratoga. |
| | Runaway inflation begins. |
| | Continental Army winters at Valley Forge. |
| **1778** | February 6: France and the United States sign an alliance. |
| | June 17: Congress refuses to negotiate with British peace commissioners. |
| | July 4: George Rogers Clark captures British post in the Mississippi Valley. |
| | December 29: British capture Savannah. |
| | Death of the great French Enlightenment writer, François-Marie Arouet Voltaire. |

| | |
|---|---|
| **1779** | June 21: Spain declares war on Britain. |
| | Americans devastate the Iroquois country. |
| | September 23: John Paul Jones captures the British ship *Serapis*. |
| **1780** | May 12: Fall of Charleston, South Carolina. |
| | October 7: Americans win Battle of Kings Mountain. |
| | December 3: Nathanael Greene takes command in the South. |
| **1781** | January 17: Americans defeat British at Battle of Cowpens. |
| | March 15: Battle of Guilford Court House. |
| | October 19: Cornwallis surrenders at Yorktown. |
| **1783** | March 15: Washington quells the Newburgh "Conspiracy." |
| | September 3: Peace of Paris signed. |
| | November 21: British begin evacuating New York. |
| | First manned balloon flight, in France. |
| | Quakers present first antislavery petition to the British parliament. |
| **1784** | United States vessel opens trade with Canton, China. |
| **1788** | Britain transports convicts to Australia. |

had been exposed to some of the most progressive currents of the Enlightenment. Among these were compassion for the oppressed and the conviction that slavery should be abolished.

Laurens saw an opportunity to solve two problems at once when he returned to America in 1777. Enlisting slaves in the army would provide blacks with a stepping stone to freedom and American forces with desperately needed troops. Although his father detested slavery, however, he could never quite accept his son's radical proposition. John was further frustrated when he turned to state legislatures in the Deep South. Convincing them to allow black troops to enlist in return for their freedom proved impossible.

John's idealistic quest for social justice ended on the banks of the Combahee River in South Carolina, where he died in one of the last skirmishes of the war. "Where liberty is," he once wrote, "there is my country." Americans won their independence, but eight long years of warfare strained and in some ways profoundly altered the fabric of American society, though not as much as Laurens had wished. ✦

## FROM REBELLION TO WAR

**WHY DID** tensions between the colonies and Britain escalate so rapidly between 1774 and 1776?

When the First Continental Congress adjourned in October 1774, no one quite knew what the future would hold. Matters indeed seemed to be approaching a crisis. Britain had adopted its harshest policies yet in response to the Boston Tea Party and appeared to be in no mood for reconciliation. At the same time, colonists in New England were stockpiling arms while committees of safety watched their neighbors in the cities and countryside, intimidating defenders of Britain into silence. Yet if tempers ran high, few people wished for bloodshed.

## CONTRADICTORY BRITISH POLICIES

Britain held parliamentary elections in the fall of 1774, but if Americans hoped that the outcome would change the government's policy toward them, they were disappointed. Lord North's supporters won easily. Even so, a few members of Parliament urged their fellow legislators to adopt conciliatory measures before it was too late. However, such efforts failed to gain much support.

Lord North's next actions made matters worse. He ordered Thomas Gage, commander in chief of the British army in America and newly installed governor of Massachusetts, to destroy an arms stockpile in Concord and arrest the radical leaders John Hancock and Samuel Adams. North then introduced a measure that prohibited New Englanders from trading outside the British Empire or sending their ships to the North Atlantic fishing grounds. Both Houses of Parliament followed a similar hard line by declaring the colony of Massachusetts to be in rebellion.

Yet at the same time, Lord North introduced a **Conciliatory Proposition,** whereby Parliament pledged not to tax the colonies if their assemblies would voluntarily contribute to the defense of the empire and the costs of civil government and the judiciary in their own colonies. British officials, however, would decide what was a sufficient contribution—a provision that protected Parliament's claim to sovereignty—and could use force against colonies that did not pay their share. At one time, colonists might have found the Conciliatory Proposition acceptable. By the spring of 1775, it was too late.

## MOUNTING TENSIONS IN AMERICA

Colonists everywhere waited to hear what Britain's next move would be, but those in Massachusetts were most apprehensive. General Gage had begun fortifying Boston and had dissolved the Massachusetts legislature. The delegates assembled anyway, calling themselves the Provincial Congress. In October 1774, this body appointed an emergency executive body, the **Committee of Safety,** headed by John Hancock, to gather arms and ammunition and to organize militia volunteers. Some localities had already formed special companies of **Minute Men,** who were to be ready at "a minute's warning in Case of an alarm." Massachusetts had, in effect, created a revolutionary government.

As tensions grew, colonists everywhere found it increasingly dangerous to express opinions in favor of Britain, or even to avoid taking a position. Moderates who placed their hopes in George III were demoralized when the king declared the New England colonies to be in a state of rebellion. The king's threat that "blows must decide whether they are to be subject to this Country or independent" scarcely reassured those who hoped to avoid spilling blood. The initial clash between British and American forces was not long in coming.

## THE BATTLES OF LEXINGTON AND CONCORD

Gage received his orders to seize the weapons at Concord and arrest Samuel Adams and John Hancock on April 14, 1775. On the night of April 18, hoping to surprise the colonists, he assembled 700 men on the Boston Common for a predawn march toward the towns of Lexington and Concord, some 20 miles away (see Map 6–1). But the army's maneuvers were hardly invisible to vigilant colonists. Adams and Hancock, who were staying in Lexington, escaped. Throughout the night, patriot riders—including the silversmith Paul Revere—spread the alarm through the countryside.

When the British soldiers reached Lexington at dawn, they found about seventy armed militiamen drawn up in formation on the village green. Outnumbered ten to one, the Americans probably did not plan to begin a fight. More likely, they were there in a show of defiance, to demonstrate that Americans would not run at the sight of the king's troops. A British major ordered the militia to disperse. They were starting to obey when a shot from an unknown source shattered the stillness. The British responded with a volley that killed or wounded 18 Americans.

**Conciliatory Proposition**   Plan whereby Parliament would "forbear" taxation of Americans in colonies whose assemblies imposed taxes considered satisfactory by the British government.

**WHERE TO LEARN MORE**

★ Minute Man National Historical Park, Lexington and Concord, Massachusetts
http://www.nps.gov/archive/mima/vcenter.htm

**Committee of Safety**   Any of the extralegal committees that directed the revolutionary movement and carried on the functions of government at the local level in the period between the breakdown of royal authority and the establishment of regular governments.

**Minute Men**   Special companies of militia formed in Massachusetts and elsewhere beginning in late 1774.

•••—Read the Document

at **www.myhistorylab.com**
*Royal Proclamation of Rebellion (1775)*

•••—Read the Document

at **www.myhistorylab.com**
*Joseph Warren, "Account of the Battle of Lexington" (1775)*

The British troops pressed on to Concord and burned what few supplies the Americans had not been able to hide. But when their rear guard came under fire at Concord's North Bridge, the British panicked. As they retreated to Boston, patriot Minute Men and other militia harried them from both sides of the road. By the time the column reached safety, 273 British soldiers were dead, wounded, or missing.

News of the **Battles of Lexington and Concord** spread quickly. The speed with which distant colonies heard about the outbreak of fighting testifies to the extraordinary efforts patriots made to spread word of it.

The shots fired that April morning would, in the words of the nineteenth-century Concord philosopher and poet Ralph Waldo Emerson, be "heard round the world." They signaled the start of the American Revolution, which would help to inspire many revolutions elsewhere.

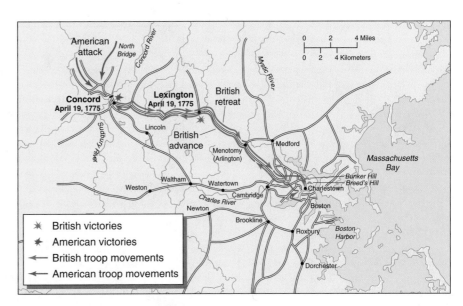

**MAP 6–1  The Battles of Lexington and Concord, April 19, 1775**  This map shows the area around Boston, where in April 1775 British and American forces fought the first military engagements of the Revolution.

**How did** the fighting at Lexington and Concord differ from traditional European military engagements?

# THE CONTINENTAL CONGRESS BECOMES A NATIONAL GOVERNMENT

The First Continental Congress had adjourned in October 1774 with virtually everyone hoping that the imperial crisis could be resolved without war. When the delegates reconvened in Philadelphia on May 10, 1775, however, war had begun. Gage's troops had limped from Concord back into Boston, besieged there by a gathering force of patriot militia from all over New England. With no other intercolonial body available to do the job, the Second Congress by default assumed management of the rebellion as its members also debated what the colonies' ultimate goal should be. Even before America had declared itself a nation, it had acquired a national government.

WHAT WERE the Second Continental Congress's highest priorities?

## THE SECOND CONTINENTAL CONGRESS CONVENES

It would be difficult to overstate the enormity of the task facing the **Second Continental Congress.** On the very day that the Congress convened—May 10, 1775—American forces from Vermont and Massachusetts under, respectively, Ethan Allen and Benedict Arnold captured the British garrison at Fort Ticonderoga at the southern end of Lake Champlain. Just over a month later, General Gage attempted to fortify territory south of Boston, where his cannons could command the harbor. But the Americans seized the high ground first, entrenching themselves on Breed's Hill north of town. On June 17, 1775, Gage sent 2,200 well-trained soldiers to drive the 1,700 patriot forces from their new position. Misnamed for another hill nearby, this encounter has gone down in history as the Battle of Bunker Hill (see Map 6–2).

Taking leadership of the rebellion, the Congress in the succeeding months became, in effect, a national government. Such important tasks as making laws and imposing taxes remained with the colonial assemblies. Congress instead focused on the functions the Crown had formerly performed. It took command of the **Continental Army,** authorized the formation of a navy, established a post office, conducted diplomacy with Indian nations, and printed paper money to meet its expenses.

**Battles of Lexington and Concord**
The first two battles of the American Revolution, which resulted in a total of 273 British soldiers dead, wounded, and missing and nearly one hundred Americans dead, wounded, and missing.

**Second Continental Congress**
Convened in Philadelphia on May 10, 1775, the Second Continental Congress called for the patchwork of local forces to be organized into the Continental Army, authorized the formation of a navy, established a post office, and printed paper continental dollars to meet its expenses.

**Continental Army**  The regular or professional army authorized by the Second Continental Congress and commanded by General George Washington during the Revolutionary War.

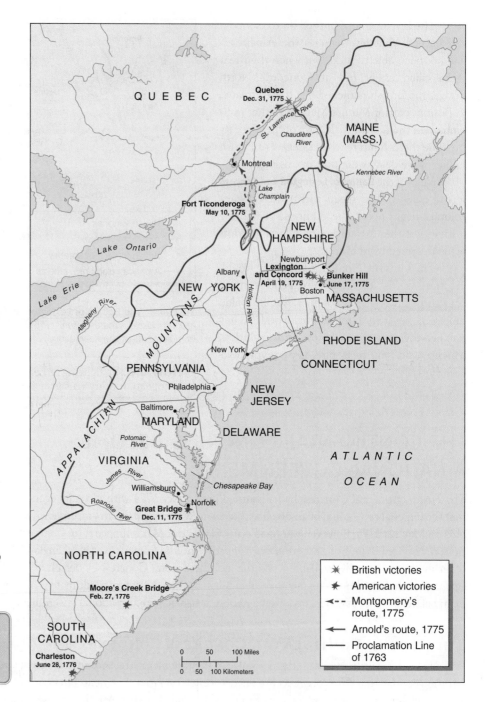

MAP 6–2   **Early Fighting, 1775–1776**   As this map clearly reveals, even the earliest fighting occurred in widely scattered areas, thereby complicating Britain's efforts to subdue the Americans.

**What were** the key components of Britain's strategy in the early years of the war? Why did the British fail to suppress the rebellion?

**Olive Branch Petition**   Petition adopted by the Second Continental Congress as a last effort of peace that avowed America's loyalty to George III and requested that he protect them from further aggressions.

**Declaration of the Causes and Necessity of Taking Up Arms**   Declaration of the Second Continental Congress that Americans were ready to fight for freedom and liberty.

One of Congress's most momentous decisions was choosing a leader for the Continental Army. Although most of the patriot troops around Boston were New Englanders, delegates knew that they had to ensure military support from all colonies. Thus, at John Adams's suggestion, Congress asked a Virginian, George Washington, to take command.

Not yet ready to demand independence, Congress hoped that the fighting would compel Britain to accept a government that acknowledged the sovereignty of colonial assemblies and an imperial tie through allegiance to the Crown. Thus even as delegates managed the war, they approved the **Olive Branch Petition** on July 5, 1775, in which they asked George III to protect his American subjects from the military actions ordered by Parliament. The following day, Congress approved the **Declaration of the Causes and Necessity of Taking Up Arms,** which listed colonial grievances and asserted the resolve of American patriots "to die freemen, rather than to live slaves." And at the end of the month, it formally rejected North's Conciliatory Proposition.

## EARLY FIGHTING: MASSACHUSETTS, VIRGINIA, THE CAROLINAS, AND CANADA

Washington arrived in Boston in early July 1775 to take command of the American forces. Months of military standoff followed, with neither side able to dislodge the other. During the winter of 1775–1776, however, the Americans dragged some sixty cannons 300 miles through snow and over mountains from Fort Ticonderoga to Boston. In March 1776, Washington mounted the newly arrived guns to overlook Boston harbor, putting the British in an indefensible position. The British then evacuated the city and moved their troops to Halifax, Nova Scotia. New England was for the moment secure for the patriots.

Fighting in the South also went well for the Americans. Virginia's last royal governor, Lord Dunmore, fled the capital, Williamsburg, and set up a base in nearby Norfolk. Promising freedom to slaves who joined him, he succeeded in raising a small force of black and white loyalists and British marines. On December 9, 1775, most of these men died when they attacked a much larger force of 900 Virginia and North Carolina troops at Great Bridge, near Norfolk. On February 27, a force of loyalist Scots suffered a similar defeat at Moore's Creek Bridge in North Carolina. And in June 1776, colonial forces successfully repulsed a large British expedition sent to attack Charleston, South Carolina.

## INDEPENDENCE

The American forces' stunning early successes bolstered their confidence. At the same time, Britain continued to lose whatever colonial support remained. In October 1775, the navy attacked and burned the town of Falmouth (now Portland) in Maine, an atrocity that outraged even those moderate colonists who held out hope for reconciliation. Slaveholders, particularly in Virginia, were equally appalled at Governor Dunmore's efforts to lure slaves away with a promise of freedom. When King George III rejected the Congress's Olive Branch Petition in August 1775 and proclaimed the colonies to be in rebellion, he unknowingly pushed more colonists toward independence.

It had taken more than a year of armed conflict to convince many Americans to accept the idea that independence from Britain, not reconciliation, should be the necessary outcome of their efforts. As it turned out, taking that final step required a push from an unexpected direction. It came from Thomas Paine, a ne'er-do-well Englishman, who had recently arrived on American soil. His pamphlet *Common Sense*, published in Philadelphia in January 1776, denounced King George and made a vigorously argued case for independence. *Common Sense*, which sold more than 100,000 copies throughout the colonies, helped propel many Americans toward independence.

Tactical considerations also influenced patriot leaders. Formal separation from Great Britain would make it easier for them to gain desperately needed aid from England's rival France and other foreign countries. France and Spain were already providing a small amount of secret aid, but would do much more for an independent nation. Declaring independence would also provide a better legal basis for American leaders' newly claimed authority. Accordingly, most of the states (as the rebellious colonies now called themselves) either instructed or permitted their delegates in the Congress to vote for independence.

This fine portrait of George Washington appears in multiple versions depicting the victorious general against different backgrounds, including the battles of Princeton and Yorktown. The painter, Charles Willson Peale, served under Washington at Princeton, and the French commander at Yorktown, the Count de Rochambeau, took an appropriate version home with him in 1783.

### QUICK REVIEW

**The Continental Congress Takes Charge**

- Commanded the Continental Army.
- Authorized the formation of a navy.
- Established a post office.
- Conducted diplomacy with Native American nations.
- Printed paper money.

**Read the Document**

at **www.myhistorylab.com**
*Exploring America: Exploring the Geography of the American Revolution*

Thomas Jefferson, author of the Declaration of Independence and future president of the United States. Mather Brown, an American artist living in England, painted this picture of Jefferson for John Adams while the two men were in London on diplomatic missions in 1786. A companion portrait of Adams that Jefferson ordered for himself also survives. Brown's sensitive portrait of a thoughtful Jefferson is the earliest known likeness of him.

**Declaration of Independence**
The document by which the Second Continental Congress announced and justified its decision to renounce the colonies' allegiance to the British government.

**contract theory of government**
The belief that government is established by human beings to protect certain rights—such as life, liberty, and property—that are theirs by natural, divinely sanctioned law and that when government protects these rights, people are obligated to obey it.

**WHERE TO LEARN MORE**

Independence National Historical Park, Philadelphia, Pennsylvania
http://www.nps.gov/inde/index.htm

On June 7, 1776, Virginian Richard Henry Lee introduced in the Congress a resolution stating that the united colonies "are, and of right ought to be, free and independent States." Postponing a vote on the issue, the Congress appointed a committee to draw up a declaration of independence. On June 28, after making revisions in Thomas Jefferson's proposed text, the committee presented the document to Congress. In the debate that followed, a few delegates clung to the hope of remaining loyal to the crown. But when the Congress voted on the resolution for independence on July 2, 1776, all voting delegations approved it. After further tinkering with the wording, the Congress officially adopted the **Declaration of Independence** on July 4, 1776.

Congress intended the declaration to be a justification for America's secession from the British Empire and an invitation to potential allies. But Jefferson's prose transformed a version of the **contract theory of government** into one of history's great statements of human rights. Developed by the late-seventeenth-century English philosopher John Locke and others, the contract theory maintains that legitimate government rests on an agreement between the people and their rulers. The people are bound to obey their rulers only so long as the rulers offer them protection.

The Declaration of Independence consists of a magnificently stated opening assumption, two premises, and a powerful conclusion. The opening assumption is that all men are created equal, that they therefore have equal rights, and that they can neither give up these rights nor allow them to be taken away. The first premise—that people establish governments to protect their fundamental rights to life, liberty, and property—is a restatement of contract theory. The second premise is a long list of charges meant to prove that George III had failed to defend his American subjects' rights. This indictment, the heart of the declaration, justified the Americans' rejection of their hitherto legitimate ruler. Then followed the dramatic conclusion: that Americans could rightfully overthrow King George's rule and replace it with something more satisfactory to them.

Although Jefferson proclaimed "all men" as being equal, in fact many people were excluded from full participation in eighteenth-century American society. Women, Native Americans, slaves, and free black people fell outside the scope of that sweeping phrase. So too did men without property, who had restricted rights in colonial society. But if the words "all men are created equal" had limited practical meaning in 1776, they have ever since confronted Americans with a moral challenge to make good on them.

## THE LOYALISTS

The Declaration of Independence may have clarified matters for American Whigs, but it made the position of Tories—those who professed loyalty to Britain—untenable. With the Declaration of Independence, these loyal subjects of Britain suddenly became enemies of the American people.

An estimated half a million colonists—20 percent of the free population—sided with Britain. Their numbers included rich merchants and farmers as well as poor settlers, and they could be found in every colony. Some were recent immigrants, especially Scots or Scots-Irish newcomers, who trusted the British government more than colonial elites to protect them. In New England, where they were a minority, Anglicans held fast to political as well as religious ties to Britain. Their experiences underscored the important point that the American Revolution was a civil conflict as well as a war for independence. It set neighbor against neighbor and created permanent rifts within families.

These divisions were intensified by the actions of the legislatures of newly independent states. Refusing to swear allegiance to the state and nation brought criminal penalties; taking up arms on behalf of Britain became a capital crime. Even so, about 19,000 colonists fought with the British, often in special units made up solely of loyalists.

Up to 70,000 more loyalists became refugees, fleeing mainly to Nova Scotia and Upper Canada (later the province of Ontario). In addition, some 20,000 escaped slaves who sought freedom with British forces likewise dispersed to other parts of the British Empire. By propelling thousands of people northward, the American Revolution can be said to have created two nations—the United States and, eventually, Canada.

## THE COMBATANTS

Republican theory mistrusted professional armies as the instruments of tyrants. A free people, republicans insisted, relied for defense on their own patriotism. But militiamen, as one American general observed, had trouble coping with "the shocking scenes of war" because they were not "steeled by habit or fortified by military pride." In real battles, they often proved unreliable. Americans therefore faced a hard choice: Develop a professional army or lose the war. In the end, they did what they had to do.

### PROFESSIONAL SOLDIERS

Drawing on their colonial experience and on republican theory, the new state governments first tried to meet their military needs by relying on the militia and by creating new units based on short-term enlistments. Officers, particularly in the North, were often elected, and their positions depended on personal popularity. Discipline became a major problem in both the militia and the new state units, and often volunteers had barely received basic training before their term of duty ended and they returned home.

Washington sought to avoid these problems by professionalizing the new Continental Army. He eventually prevailed on Congress to adopt stricter regulations and to require enlistments for three years or the duration of the war. Although he used militia effectively, his consistent aim was to turn the Continental Army into a disciplined force that could defeat the British in the large engagements of massed troops characteristic of eighteenth-century European warfare, for only such victories could impress the other European powers and establish the legitimacy of the United States.

The enemy British soldiers—and the nearly 30,000 German mercenaries (Americans called them "Hessians") whom the British government employed—offered Americans the clearest model of a professional army. British regulars were not (as Americans assumed) the "dregs of society." Although most of the enlisted men came from the lower classes and from economically depressed areas, many also had skills. British officers usually came from wealthy families and had simply purchased their commissions. Only rarely could a man rise from the enlisted ranks to commissioned-officer status.

The life of a British soldier was tough. They were frequently undernourished, and many more died of disease

**WHAT WERE** the key differences between the British and American forces?

Posters like this one appeared in many cities and towns to recruit soldiers to join the Continental Army. Washington hoped to be able to turn inexperienced young men into a disciplined, professional fighting force.

•••⌐Read the Document

at www.myhistorylab.com
*Letter from a Revolutionary
War Soldier (1776)*

than of injury in battle. Medical care was, by modern standards, primitive. Severe discipline held soldiers in line. Striking an officer or deserting could bring death; lesser offenses usually incurred a beating.

After the winter of 1777–1778, conditions in the Continental Army more closely resembled those in the British army. Like British regulars, American recruits tended to be low on the social scale. They included young men without land, indentured servants, some criminals and vagrants—in short, men who lacked better prospects. The chances for talented enlisted men to win an officer's commission were greater than in the British army. But Continental soldiers frequently had little more than "their ragged shirt flaps to cover their nakedness," and their bare marching feet occasionally left bloody tracks in the snow.

The British and the Americans both had trouble supplying their troops. The British had plenty of sound money, which many American merchants and farmers were happy to take in payment for supplies. But they had to rely mostly on supplies shipped to them from the British Isles. The Continental Army, by contrast, had to pay for supplies in depreciating paper money. After 1780, the burden of provisioning the Continental Army fell on the states, which did little better than Congress had done. Unable to obtain sufficient supplies, the army sometimes threatened to seize them by force. Washington, however, did all he could to prevent his soldiers from foraging through the countryside, stealing much-needed provisions. He knew that such actions would erode public support for the army and the patriot cause and thus had to be stopped.

Often feeling ignored by an uncaring society, the professional soldiers of the Continental Army developed a community of their own. They groused, to be sure—sometimes alarmingly. In May 1780, Connecticut troops at Washington's camp in Morristown, New Jersey, staged a brief mutiny. On January 1, 1781, armed units from Pennsylvania stationed in New Jersey marched to Philadelphia demanding their back pay. The Pennsylvania Executive Council met part of the soldiers' demands, but some of the men left the service. Washington ordered subsequent mutinies by New Jersey and Pennsylvania troops suppressed by force.

**QUICK REVIEW**

**Military Life**

◆ Soldiers suffered from disease and lack of food.

◆ Discipline was severe.

◆ Soldiers of the Continental Army developed a community of their own.

---

## AMERICAN VIEWS

### ∼◎∽ An American Surgeon Reflects on the Winter at Valley Forge, 1777–1778 ∼◎∽

*D*r. Albigence Waldo was a surgeon in the First Connecticut Infantry Regiment of the Continental Army while it was encamped at Valley Forge, Pennsylvania. His diary, from which the following excerpts are taken, reveals much about the attitudes of the soldiers as well as the conditions they faced. Waldo resigned from the service in 1779 because of illness but lived until 1794.

- **How** serious was Waldo in describing the reasons for the location of the soldiers' winter quarters?
- **Did** his griping reflect a serious morale problem?
- **What** do his remarks about the Indian soldier's death reveal about Waldo's values?

[December 13, 1777.—] It cannot be that our Superiors are about to hold consultation with Spirits infinitely beneath their Order, by bringing us into these [remote] regions. . . . No, it is, upon consideration for many good

purposes since we are to Winter here—1st There is plenty of Wood & Water. 2dly There are but few families for the soldiery to Steal from—tho' far be it from a Soldier to Steal. 4ly [sic] There are warm sides of Hills to erect huts on. 5ly They will be heavenly Minded like Jonah when in the Belly of a Great Fish. 6ly They will not become home Sick as is sometimes the case when Men live in the Open World—since the reflections which will naturally arise from their present habitation, will lead them to the more noble thoughts of employing their leisure hours in filling their knapsacks with such materials as may be necessary on the Journey to another Home.

December 14.—Prisoners & Deserters are continually coming in. The Army which has been surprisingly healthy hitherto, now begins to grow sickly from the continued fatigues they have suffered this Campaign. Yet they still show a spirit of Alacrity & Contentment not to be expected from so young Troops. I am Sick—discontented—and out of humour. Poor food—hard lodging—Cold Weather—fatigue—Nasty Cloaths—nasty Cookery—Vomit half my time—smoak'd out of my senses—the Devil's in't—I can't Endure it—Why are we sent here to starve and Freeze—What sweet Felicities have I left at home; A charming Wife—pretty Children—Good Beds—good food—good Cookery—all agreeable—all harmonious. Here all Confusion—smoke & Cold—hunger & filthyness—A pox on my bad luck. There comes a bowl of beef soup—full of burnt leaves and dirt, sickish enough to make a Hector spue—away with it Boys—I'll live like the Chameleon upon Air. Poh! Poh! Crys Patience within me—you talk like a fool. Your being sick Covers your mind with a Melanchollic Gloom, which makes everything about you appear gloomy. See the poor Soldier, when in health—with what cheerfulness he meets his foes and encounters every hardship—if barefoot, he labours thro' the Mud & Cold with a Song in his mouth extolling War & Washington—if his food be bad, he eats it notwithstanding with seeming content—blesses God for a good Stomach and Whistles it into digestion. But harkee Patience, a moment—There comes a Soldier, his bare feet are seen thro' his worn out Shoes, his legs nearly naked from the tatter'd remains of an only pair of stockings, his Breeches not sufficient to cover his nakedness, his Shirt hanging in Strings, his hair dishevell'd, his face meager; his whole appearance pictures a per-son forsaken & discouraged. He comes, and crys with an air of wretchedness & despair, I am Sick, my feet lame, my legs are sore, my body cover'd with this tormenting Itch—my Cloaths are worn out, my Constitution is broken, my former Activity is exhausted by fatigue, hunger & Cold, I fail fast. I shall soon be no more! And all the reward I shall get will be—"Poor Will is dead."

December 21.—[Valley Forge.] Heartily wish myself at home, my Skin & eyes are almost spoil'd with continual smoke. A general cry thro' the Camp this evening among the Soldiers, "No Meat! No Meat!"—the Distant vales Echo'd back the melancholy sound—"No Meat! No Meat!" Immitating the noise of Crows & Owls, also, made a part of the confused Musick.

What have you for your Dinners Boys? "Nothing but Fire Cake & Water, Sir." At night, "Gentlemen the Supper is ready." What is your Supper Lads? "Fire Cake & Water, Sir."

December 30.—Eleven Deserters came in to-day—some Hessians & some English—one of the Hesns took an Ax in his hand & cut away the Ice of the Schuylkill which was 1 1/2 inches thick & 40 Rod wide and waded through to our Camp—he was 1/2 hour in the Water. They had a promise when they engag'd that the war would be ended in one year—they were now tired of the Service.

[January 3, 1778.—] I was call'd to relieve a Soldier tho't to be dying—he expir'd before I Reach'd the Hutt. He was an Indian—an excellent Soldier—and an obedient good natur'd fellow. He engaged for money doubtless as others do;—but he has serv'd his country faithfully—he has fought for those very people who disinherited his forefathers—having finished his pilgrimage, he was discharged from the War of Life & Death. His memory ought to be respected, more than those rich ones who supply the world with nothing better than Money and Vice.

*Source:* "Valley Forge, 1777–1778. Diary of Surgeon Albigence Waldo, of the Connecticut Line," *Pennsylvania Magazine of History and Biography,* 21 (1897): 306–7, 309, 315–16, 319.

What was perhaps the most serious expression of army discontent—one that might have threatened the future of republican institutions and civilian government in the United States—occurred in March 1783, after the fighting was over. Washington's troops were then stationed near Newburgh, New York, waiting for their pay before disbanding. When the Congress failed to grant real assurances that any pay would be forthcoming, hotheaded young officers called a meeting that could have led to an armed coup. General Washington, who had scrupulously deferred to civilian authority throughout the war, asked permission to address the gathering and, in a dramatic speech, subtly warned the men of all that they might lose by insubordination. A military coup would "open the flood Gates of Civil discord" and "deluge" the nation in blood; loyalty now, he said, would be "one more distinguished proof" of their patriotism. With the fate of the Revolution apparently hanging in the balance, the movement collapsed. Washington's quick response set a precedent for the subordination of the military to civilian government.

## WOMEN IN THE CONTENDING ARMIES

Women accompanied many units on both sides, as was common in eighteenth-century warfare. A few were prostitutes. Some were officers' wives or mistresses, but most were the married or common-law consorts of ordinary soldiers." These "camp followers" fulfilled many of the support functions necessary to sustain the army. They cooked and washed for the troops, occasionally helped load artillery, and provided most of the nursing care. A certain number in a company were subject to military orders and were authorized to draw rations and pay.

## AFRICAN AMERICAN PARTICIPATION IN THE WAR

Early in the war, as we have seen, some royal officials like Lord Dunmore recruited slaves with promises of freedom. But these efforts often proved counterproductive, frightening potentially loyalist slaveowners and driving them to the Whig side. Thus it was not until June 30, 1779, that the British commander in chief, Sir Henry Clinton, promised to allow slaves who fled from rebel owners to join the royal troops to "follow . . . any Occupation" they wished. Hedged as this prom- ise of freedom was, news of it spread quickly among the slave communities, and late in the war, African Americans flocked to the British army in South Carolina and Georgia.

Sharing prevailing racial prejudices, the British were often reluctant to arm blacks. Instead, they put most of the ex-slaves to work as agricultural or construction workers (many of the free and enslaved blacks accompanying American troops were similarly employed). However, a few rela- tively well-equipped black British dragoons (mounted troops) did see combat in South Carolina.

On the other hand, approximately 5,000 African Americans fought against the British and for American independence, hundreds of them in the Continental Army. Many were freemen from Massachusetts and Rhode Island.

But farther south, as discussed above, John Laurens, a young Carolina patriot, repeatedly but vainly tried to convince the South Carolina assembly to raise and arm black troops. Instead, the legislature eventually voted to give slaves confiscated from loyalists to white volunteers as a reward for their service. It is therefore scarcely surprising that, as one Whig put it, many African Americans were "a little Toryfied," especially in the South.

## NATIVE AMERICANS AND THE WAR

At first, most of the approximately 200,000 Native Americans east of the Mississippi River would probably have preferred to remain neutral, and both sides initially took them at their word. But Indians' skills and manpower were valuable, and by 1776 both the British and Americans sought their assistance. Forced to choose, many Native Americans favored the British, hoping thereby to safeguard their lands.

Prewar experience convinced Native Americans that British officials would be more apt to protect them against white settlers, and the British could provide more trade goods and arms. Many Indians, including the Cherokees, Creeks, Choctaws, and Chickasaws, therefore decided to back the British, and Cherokee warriors raided the southern frontier starting in 1776. Southern colonists countered with expeditions that repeatedly devastated Cherokee towns. But when older chiefs sought peace, Dragging Canoe (Tsi'yugunsi'ny) and the more militant younger men estab- lished new communities on the Chickamauga River in northern Georgia and continued to fight.

Caught between the British and the Americans, other Indian groups also split. Among these was the powerful Iroquois Confederation in upstate New York. Under the leadership of Thayendanegea—known to whites as Joseph Brant—the Mohawks and Senecas supported the British, while a minority of the Oneidas and Tuscaroras joined the Americans. The Revolution thus created an irreparable divide among the Iroquois, leading many to move to Canada during and after the war.

Frontier racism, which had scarcely dissipated since Pontiac's War (see Chapter 5), flared up again. Few Americans were willing to trust Indian claims of neutrality, and during the war conducted raids against native villages. In 1782, in an event that recalled the earlier Paxton Boys massacre in Pennsylvania (see Chapter 5), a group of Americans slaughtered 100 defenseless Moravian Christian Indians at Gnadenhutten in the Ohio country. Thus American behavior during the war did little to calm native fears for their lives and property in an independent United States.

# THE WAR IN THE NORTH, 1776–1777

The Revolutionary War can be divided into three phases. In the first, from the outbreak of fighting in 1775 through 1777, most of the important battles took place in New England, New York, New Jersey, and Pennsylvania, while the Americans faced the British alone. But in 1778, France entered the war on the American side, opening the second phase of the war in which fighting would rage from 1778 to 1781, mainly in the South, at sea, and on the western frontier. The third phase of the war, from late 1781 to 1783, saw little actual fighting. With American victory assured, attention shifted to the diplomatic maneuvering leading up to the Peace of Paris (1783).

**HOW DID** the American forces survive the military setbacks of 1776?

## Britain Hesitates: Crucial Battles in New York and New Jersey

During the first phase of the war, the British concentrated on subduing New England. Replacing General Gage, the government appointed Sir William Howe as commander in chief of British forces and his brother, Richard Howe, as admiral of the naval forces in North American waters. New York City had been the headquarters of the British army during the late colonial period, and the Howes made it their base of operations. To counter this move, Washington moved his forces to New York in the spring of 1776. In August 1776, the Howes landed troops on Long Island and, in the Battle of Brooklyn Heights, quickly drove the American forces deployed there back to Manhattan Island.

Following instructions to negotiate peace as well as wage war, Richard Howe then met with three envoys from Congress on Staten Island on September 11, 1776. The British commanders were prepared to offer fairly generous terms but could not grant independence. The Americans would accept nothing less. So the meeting produced no substantive negotiations.

In the ensuing weeks, British forces overwhelmed Washington's troops, driving them out of Manhattan and then, moving north, clearing them from the area around the city at the Battle of White Plains. But the Howes were hesitant to deal a crushing blow, and the Americans were able to retreat across New Jersey into Pennsylvania. The American cause seemed lost, however, and the Continental Army almost melted away. Realizing that without a success he would soon be without troops, Washington led his forces back across the icy Delaware and launched a successful surprise attack on a garrison of Hessian mercenaries at Trenton, New Jersey, on the morning of December 26. A week later, Washington overwhelmed a British force at Princeton, New Jersey. By raising morale, the victories at Trenton and Princeton probably saved the American cause.

**QUICK REVIEW**

**Victories at Trenton and Princeton**

- 1776: A series of defeats devastated the Continental Army.
- Christmas night 1776: Washington crosses the Delaware and launches a surprise attack.
- Victories at Trenton and Princeton revive the American cause.

## The Year of the Hangman: Victory at Saratoga and Winter at Valley Forge

Contemporaries called 1777 the Year of the Hangman because the triple sevens suggested a row of gallows. It was in fact a critical year for the American cause. Mounting a major effort to end the rebellion, the British planned to send an army down the Hudson River from Canada. The goal was to have it link up with the Howes in New York City, isolate New England, and defeat the rebellion there. But there was little effort to coordinate strategy between the forces advancing from Canada and those in New York. Thus, the poorly planned and poorly executed campaign ended in disaster for the British.

Some 5,000 Redcoats and 3,000 German mercenaries assembled in Canada during the winter of 1776–1777. Under the command of the high-living and popular "Gentleman Johnny" Burgoyne, the army finally set off in June with 1,500 horses hauling its heavy artillery and ponderous supply

George Washington viewing troops at Valley Forge during the winter of 1777–78. This modern depiction is somewhat romanticized. While making a similar tour on foot, Washington once saw a soldier who was literally clothed in nothing but a blanket.

train. A second, smaller column, supported by an Indian force under Thayendanegea (Joseph Brant) moved to the west to capture an American fort near Oriskany, New York, and then join up with Burgoyne's main force. On July 5, Burgoyne's army recaptured Fort Ticonderoga, but success eluded him after that.

Trouble began as the troops started overland through the woods at the southern end of the lake. Huge trees felled by American axmen blocked their way, and the army crawled along at only two or three miles a day. Early in August, the column sent to capture the American fort near Oriskany turned back to Canada. Burgoyne's Indian allies under Joseph Brant likewise went home. Promised reinforcements never arrived. Ten days later, a Whig militia force wiped out a force of 800 men trying to gather supplies in Vermont.

By October 1777, Burgoyne's army was down to fewer than 6,000 men and faced disaster. Nearly 3,000 Continentals and 9,000 American militia, commanded by General Horatio Gates, exerted relentless pressure on the increasingly dispirited invaders. Unable to break through the American lines, Burgoyne surrendered his entire army to Gates following the Battle of Saratoga on October 17, 1777.

Meanwhile, General William Howe, rather than moving north to support Burgoyne, made plans to destroy Washington's army and capture Philadelphia. In July 1777, Howe's troops sailed from New York to Chesapeake Bay and from there marched on Philadelphia from the south. They met Washington's army on the banks of Brandywine Creek, near the Pennsylvania-Delaware border. The Americans put up a good fight before giving way with a loss of 1,200 killed or captured (twice as many as the British).

**Valley Forge** Area of Pennsylvania approximately 20 miles northwest of Philadelphia where General George Washington's Continental troops were quartered from December 1777 to June 1778 while British forces occupied Philadelphia during the Revolutionary War.

Howe occupied Philadelphia, and his men settled down in comfortable winter quarters. The Congress fled to York, Pennsylvania, and the Continental Army established its own winter camp outside Philadelphia at Valley Forge. The Continental Army's miserable winter at **Valley Forge** has become famous for its hardships. Suffering from cold, disease, and starvation, as many as 2,500 soldiers died. Yet despite the difficulties, the Continental Army completed its transformation into a disciplined professional force. By spring, pleased observers felt that Washington at last had an army capable of meeting the British on equal terms.

# THE WAR WIDENS, 1778–1781

**WHY DID** the French enter the war on the American side?

Since late 1776, Benjamin Franklin and a team of American diplomats had been in Paris negotiating French support for the patriot cause. In the winter of 1777–1778, aware that a Franco-American alliance was close, Parliament belatedly tried to end the rebellion by giving the Americans everything they wanted except independence itself. But France and the United States concluded an alliance on February 6, 1778, and Congress refused to negotiate with the British.

Foreign intervention transformed the American Revolution into a virtual world war, engaging British forces in heavy fighting not only in North America but also in the West Indies and India. In the end, had it not been for French assistance, the American side probably would not have won the clear-cut victory it did.

## THE UNITED STATES GAINS AN ALLY

The American victory at Saratoga in October 1777 had persuaded the French that the United States had a viable future. Eager for revenge against their old British enemy, French officials decided to act quickly lest any military reverses force the Americans to agree to reconciliation with Britain. In a move that astonished the British, France accordingly signed a commercial treaty and a military alliance with the United States. Both sides promised to fight together until Britain recognized the independence of the United States, and France pledged not to seek the return of lands in North America.

French entry into the war was the first step in the consolidation of a formidable alliance of European powers eager to see Britain humbled and to gain trading rights in the former British colonies. France persuaded Spain to declare war on Britain in June 1779. Much of the salt used to preserve American soldiers' provisions came from Spanish territories, and New Orleans became a base for American privateers. More important, the Spanish fleet increased the naval power of the countries arrayed against Great Britain.

Meanwhile, Catherine the Great of Russia suggested that the European powers form a League of Armed Neutrality to protect their trade with the United States and other warring countries against British interference. Denmark and Sweden soon joined; Austria, Portugal, Prussia, and Sicily eventually followed. Britain, which wanted to cut off Dutch trade with the United States, used a pretext to declare war on the Netherlands before it could join. Great Britain thus found itself isolated and even, briefly, threatened with invasion. These threats did not frighten the British leaders into suing for peace, but they forced them to make important changes in strategy.

Accordingly, in the spring of 1778, the British replaced the Howes with a new commander, Sir Henry Clinton, and instructed him to send troops to attack the French West Indies. Knowing that he now faced a serious French threat, Clinton began consolidating his forces by evacuating Philadelphia and pulling his troops slowly back across New Jersey to New York.

On June 28, 1778, Washington caught up with the British at Monmouth Court House. This inconclusive battle proved to be the last major engagement in the North. Clinton withdrew to New York, and Continental troops occupied the hills along the Hudson Valley north of the city. The war shifted to other fronts.

## FIGHTING ON THE FRONTIER AND AT SEA

Known as "a dark and bloody ground" to Native Americans, Kentucky became even bloodier after the British instructed their Indian allies to raid the area in 1777. Because the British post at Detroit coordinated these attacks, the Americans tried to take it in 1778. Three expeditions failed for various reasons, but the last, under a Virginian, George Rogers Clark, did capture three key British settlements in the Mississippi Valley: Kaskaskia, Cahokia, and Vincennes (see Map 6–3). These successes may have strengthened American claims to the West at the end of the war.

In 1778 bloody fighting also occurred on the eastern frontiers. During the summer, a British force of 100 loyalists and 500 Indians struck the Wyoming Valley of Pennsylvania. Four months later, a similar group of attackers burned farmsteads and slaughtered civilians at Cherry Valley, New York. Both raids stimulated equally savage reprisals against the Indians.

The Americans and British also clashed at sea throughout the war. Great Britain was the preeminent sea power of the age, and the United States never came close to matching it. But in 1775 Congress authorized the construction of 13 frigates—medium-sized, relatively fast ships, mounting 32 guns—as well as the purchase of several merchant vessels for conversion to warships. By contrast, the Royal Navy in 1779 had more than a hundred large, heavily armed "ships of the line." The Americans therefore engaged in what was essentially a guerrilla war at sea.

The Congress and the individual states also supplemented America's naval forces by commissioning privateers. In effect legalized pirates, privateers preyed on British shipping. Captured goods were divided among the crew according to rank; captured sailors became prisoners of war. Some 2,000 American privateers took more than 600 British ships and forced the British navy to spread itself thin doing convoy duty.

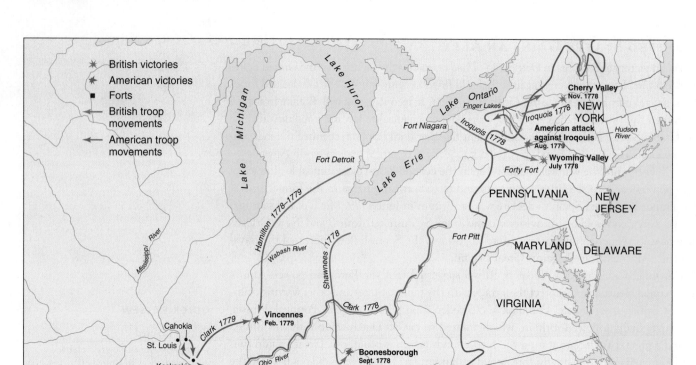

**MAP 6–3    The War on the Frontier, 1778–1779**    Significant battles in the Mississippi Valley and the frontiers of the seaboard states added to the ferocity of the fighting and strengthened some American claims to western lands.

**Why were** the British at more of a disadvantage the farther from the coast they fought?

## THE LAND WAR MOVES SOUTH

During the first three years of the war, the British made little effort to mobilize what they believed to be considerable loyalist strength in the South. But in 1778, the enlarged threat from France prompted a change in strategy: Redcoats would sweep through a large area and then leave behind a Tory militia to reestablish loyalty to the crown and suppress local Whigs. The British hoped thereby to recapture everything from Georgia to Virginia; they would deal with New England later.

The British southern strategy unfolded in November 1778, when General Clinton dispatched 3,500 troops to take control of Georgia. Meeting only light resistance, they quickly seized Savannah and Augusta and restored the old colonial government under civilian control. After their initial success, however, the British suffered some serious setbacks. Spain entered the war and seized British outposts on the Mississippi and Mobile rivers while Whig militia decimated a loyalist militia at Kettle Creek, Georgia.

But the Americans could not beat the British army. In late September and early October 1779, a combined force of 5,500 American and French troops, supported by French warships, laid siege to Savannah. The assault failed, and the French sailed off.

The way was now open for the British to attack Charleston, the military key to the Lower South. In December 1779, Clinton sailed through stormy seas from New York to the Carolina coast with about 9,000 troops. In the Battle of Charleston, he encircled the city, trapping the

**QUICK REVIEW**

**The Southern Strategy**

- Little effort before 1778 by British to mobilize southern loyalists.
- Threat from France forced a new strategy.
- Early successes were followed by setbacks.
- American victory at Yorktown effectively ended the war.

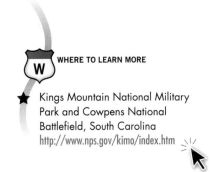

patriot forces inside. On May 12, 1780, more than 5,000 Continentals and militia laid down their arms in the worst American defeat of the war.

The British were now poised to sweep the entire South. Most local Whigs, thinking the Revolution over, at first offered little resistance to the Redcoats striking into the Carolina backcountry. The British success seemed so complete that Clinton tried to force American prisoners to resume their duties as British subjects and join the loyalist militia. Thinking that matters were now well in hand, Clinton sailed back to New York, leaving the southern troops under the command of Lord Cornwallis. Clinton's confidence that the South had returned to British allegiance was premature.

## AMERICAN COUNTERATTACKS

In the summer of 1780, Congress dispatched a substantial Continental force to the South under General Horatio Gates, the hero of Saratoga. Local patriots flocked to join him. But instead of achieving another great victory, Gates and his men blundered into Cornwallis's British army near Camden, South Carolina, on August 16, and suffered a complete rout. More than 1,000 Americans were killed or wounded and many captured. Gates—transformed from the hero of Saratoga into the goat of Camden—fled to Hillsborough, North Carolina.

American morale revived on October 7, 1780, when "overmountain men" (militia) from Virginia, western North Carolina, and South Carolina defeated the British at Kings Mountain, South Carolina. And in December 1780, Nathanael Greene replaced the discredited Gates, bringing competent leadership to the Continentals in the South.

Ever resourceful, Greene divided his small forces, keeping roughly half with him in northeastern South Carolina and sending the other half westward under General Daniel Morgan. Cornwallis ordered Colonel Banastre Tarleton to pursue Morgan, who retreated northward until he reached Cowpens, South Carolina. There, on January 17, 1781, Morgan cleverly posted his least reliable troops, the militia, in the front line and ordered them to retreat after firing two volleys. When they did as told, the British thought the Americans were fleeing and charged after them—straight into devastating fire from Morgan's Continentals.

Cornwallis now badly needed a battlefield victory. Burning his army's excess baggage, he set off in hot pursuit of Greene and Morgan, whose rejoined forces retreated northward ahead of the British. On February 13, 1781, Greene's tired men crossed the Dan River into Virginia, and Cornwallis gave up the chase, marching his equally exhausted Redcoats southward. To his surprise, Cornwallis now found himself pursued—though cautiously—by Greene. On March 15, the opposing forces met at Guilford Court House, North Carolina, in one of the war's bloodiest battles. Although the British held the field at the end of the day, an Englishman accurately observed, "another such victory would destroy the British Army." Cornwallis retreated to the coastal town of Wilmington, North Carolina, to rest and regroup.

By the late summer of 1781, British fortunes were waning in the Lower South. The Redcoats held only the larger towns and the immediately surrounding countryside. With their superior staying power, they won most major engagements, but these victories brought

**W** WHERE TO LEARN MORE

★ Kings Mountain National Military Park and Cowpens National Battlefield, South Carolina
http://www.nps.gov/kimo/index.htm

Watch the Video

at **www.myhistorylab.com**
*The American Revolution as Different Americans Saw It*

**W** WHERE TO LEARN MORE

★ Yorktown Battlefield, Colonial National Historical Park, Yorktown, Virginia
http://www.nps.gov/york/index.htm

The surrender of Lord Cornwallis at Yorktown on October 19, 1781, led to the British decision to withdraw from the war. Cornwallis, who claimed to be ill, absented himself from the ceremony and is not in the picture. Washington, who is astride the horse under the American flag, designated General Benjamin Lincoln (on the white horse in the center) as the one to accept the submission of a subordinate British officer. John Trumbull, who painted *The Battle of Bunker Hill* and some 300 other scenes from the Revolutionary War, finished this painting while he was in London about 15 years after the events depicted. A large copy of the work now hangs in the rotunda of the United States Capitol in Washington, D.C. John Trumbull (American 1756–1843), *Surrender of Lord Cornwallis at Yorktown, October 1781*, oil on canvas, 20 7/8 × 30 5/8 inches. Yale University Art Gallery, Trumbull Collection.

them no lasting gain. When the enemy pressed him too hard, Greene retreated out of reach, advancing again as the British withdrew.

Disappointed and frustrated, Cornwallis decided to conquer Virginia to cut off Greene's supplies and destroy Whig resolve. British forces were already raiding the state. Cornwallis marched north to join them, reaching Yorktown, Virginia, during the summer of 1781.

The final military showdown of the war was at hand. By now, French soldiers were in America ready to fight alongside the Continentals, and a large French fleet in the West Indies had orders to support an attack on the British in North America. Faking preparations for an assault on British-occupied New York, the Continentals (commanded by Washington) and the French headed for the Chesapeake. Cornwallis and his 6,000 Redcoats soon found themselves besieged behind their fortifications at Yorktown by 8,800 Americans and 7,800 French. A French naval victory gave the allies temporary command of the waters around Yorktown. Cornwallis had nowhere to go, and Clinton—still in New York—could not reinforce him quickly enough. On October 19, 1781, the British army surrendered.

# THE WAR AND SOCIETY, 1775–1783

**WHAT WAS** the social impact of the War for Independence?

Regular combatants were not the only ones to suffer during the struggle for independence. Eight years of warfare also produced profound dislocations throughout American society. Military service wrenched families apart, sporadic raids brought the war home to vast numbers of people, and everyone endured economic disruptions. As a forge of nationhood, the Revolution tested all Americans, whatever their standing as citizens.

## THE WOMEN'S WAR

Women everywhere had to see their loved ones go off to fight and die. Such circumstances elevated women's domestic status. Couples began referring to "our"—not "my" or "your"—property. Wives frequently became more knowledgeable about the family's financial condition than their long-absent husbands. Women also assumed new public roles during the conflict. Some nursed the wounded. More wove cloth for uniforms. The Ladies' Association of Philadelphia was established in 1780 to demonstrate women's patriotism and raise money to buy shirts for the army. Similar associations formed in other states.

Despite their increasing private responsibilities and new public activities, it did not occur to most women to encroach on traditional male prerogatives. When John Adams's wife, Abigail, urged him and the Second Continental Congress to "Remember the Ladies," she was not expecting equal political rights. What she wanted, rather, was some legal protections for women and recognition of their value and need for autonomy in the domestic sphere. "Remember," she cautioned, "all Men would be Tyrants if they could."

The Revolution in fact did little to change women's political status. Perhaps the most immediate outcome of the Revolution for American women was the politicization of their maternal responsibilities. As good "republican mothers," they could be trusted to instill patriotism in their sons, helping them to mature into virtuous citizens. Although this idea led to calls for enhancing women's educational opportunities, it was at best a limited improvement in their political role.

## EFFECT OF THE WAR ON AFRICAN AMERICANS

In the northern states, where slavery was already economically marginal and where black men were welcome as volunteers in the Continental Army, the Revolutionary War helped to bring an end to slavery, although it remained legal there for some time (see Chapter 7). In the South, however, slavery was integral to the economy, and white planters viewed it as crucial to their postwar recovery. Thus, although British efforts to recruit black soldiers brought freedom to thousands and temporarily undermined slavery in the South, the war ultimately strengthened the institution, especially in the Carolinas and Georgia. Of the African Americans who left with the British at the end of the war, many, both slave and free, went to the West Indies. Others settled in Canada, and some eventually reached Africa, where Britain established the colony of Sierra Leone for them.

## THE WAR'S IMPACT ON NATIVE AMERICANS

Survivors among the approximately 13,000 Native Americans who fought for the British did not have the option of leaving with them at the end of the war. How many died during the conflict is not known, but certainly many did. Not only the Iroquois but other groups lost much. The Americans repeatedly invaded the Cherokees' homeland in the southern Appalachian Mountains. Americans also attacked the Shawnees of Ohio.

In the peace treaty of 1783, Britain surrendered its territory east of the Mississippi, shocking and infuriating the Native Americans living there. They had not surrendered, and none of them had been at the negotiations in Paris. Because it enabled Americans to claim Indian territory by conquest, the Revolutionary War was a disaster for many Native Americans that opened the floodgates to a torrent of white settlers.

## ECONOMIC DISRUPTION

The British and American armies both needed enormous quantities of supplies. This heavy demand disrupted the normal distribution of goods and drove up real prices seven- or eightfold; in addition, widespread use of depreciating paper money by the American side amplified the rise in prices and triggered severe inflation.

Ki-On-Twog-Ky, also known as Corn Planter (1732/40–1836) was a Seneca Indian chief who raided American settlements for the British, while he observed that "war is war, death is death, a fight is hard business." He later presided over the surrender of much land to the United States.

When the British did not simply seize what they needed, they paid for it in hard currency— gold and silver. American commanders, by contrast, had to rely on paper money because the Congress and the states had almost no hard currency at their disposal. The Continental dollar, however, steadily declined in value, and by March 1780, the Congress was forced to admit officially that it was worthless.

Necessity, not folly, drove Congress and the states to rely on the printing press. Rather than alienate citizens by immediately raising taxes to pay for the war, the states printed paper money supposedly redeemable through future tax revenues. But because the quantity of this paper money rose faster than the supply of goods and services, prices skyrocketed, and the value of the money plunged. Those who had paper money tried to spend it before its value could drop further; whereas those who had salable commodities such as grain tended to hoard them in the hope that the price would go even higher. Prices also climbed faster than wages, leaving many working people impoverished.

The rampant inflation was demoralizing and divisive. Lucky speculators and unscrupulous profiteers could grow rich, while ordinary and patriotic people suffered. As usual, war and its deprivations brought out both the best and the worst in human nature.

Most Americans somehow managed to cope. But during the last years of the conflict, their economic and psychological reserves ran low. The total real wealth of private individuals declined by an average of 0.5 percent annually from 1774 to 1805, even with the returning prosperity of the 1790s. Such statistics suggest the true economic cost of the War for Independence. And the atrocities committed on both sides provide a comparable measure of the conflict's psychological cost.

# THE AMERICAN VICTORY, 1782–1783

**WHAT WERE** the key factors in the American victory in the Revolutionary War?

The British surrender at Yorktown marked the end of major fighting in North America, though skirmishes continued for another year. In April 1782, the Royal Navy defeated the French fleet in the Caribbean, strengthening the British bargaining position. Although George III insisted on continuing the war because he feared that defeat would threaten British rule in Canada and the West Indies, the majority in Parliament now felt that enough men and money had been wasted trying to keep the Americans within the empire. In March 1782, the king accepted Lord North's resignation and appointed a new prime minister, with a mandate to make peace.

## THE PEACE OF PARIS

The peace negotiations, which took place in Paris, were lengthy. The Americans demanded independence, handsome territorial concessions, and access to the rich British-controlled fishing grounds in the North Atlantic. The current British prime minister, Lord Shelburne, was inclined to be conciliatory to help British merchants recover their lost colonial trade. The French had achieved their objective of weakening the British and now wanted out of an increasingly costly worldwide war. Spain had not won its most important goal, the recovery of British-held Gibraltar, and thus gave the Americans no support at all.

The American negotiators, Benjamin Franklin, John Adams, and John Jay, skillfully threaded their way among these conflicting interests. With good reason, they feared that the French and Spanish might strike a bargain with the British at the expense of the United States. As a result, the Americans disregarded Congress's instructions to avoid making peace unilaterally and secretly worked out their own arrangements with the British. On November 30, 1782, the negotiators signed a preliminary Anglo-American treaty of peace whose terms were embodied in the final **Peace of Paris,** signed by all the belligerents on September 3, 1783.

The Peace of Paris gave the United States nearly everything it sought. Great Britain acknowledged that the United States was "free, sovereign and independent." The northern boundary of the new nation extended west from the St. Croix River (which separated Maine from Nova Scotia) past the Great Lakes to what were thought to be the headwaters of the Mississippi River (see Map 6–4). The Mississippi itself—down to just north of New Orleans—formed the western border. Spain acquired the provinces of East and West Florida from Britain. This territory included parts of present-day Louisiana, Mississippi, Alabama, and Georgia.

Several provisions of the treaty addressed important economic issues. Adams, on behalf of New Englanders, insisted on a provision granting American fishermen access to the waters off eastern Canada. The treaty also required that British forces, on quitting American soil, were to leave behind all American-owned property, including slaves. Another provision declared existing debts between citizens of Britain and the United States still valid, giving British merchants hope of collecting on their American accounts. Congress was to "recommend" that the states restore rights and property taken from loyalists during the war. Nothing was said about the slave trade, which Jay had hoped to ban.

## THE COMPONENTS OF SUCCESS

The War for Independence was over. In December 1783, the last British troops left New York. The Continental Army had already disbanded during the summer of 1783. On December 4, Washington said farewell to his officers

---

**QUICK REVIEW**

**Peace of Paris**

◆ Signed September 3, 1783.

◆ United States got virtually everything it sought at peace talks.

◆ Treaty addressed important economic issues, but said nothing about slavery.

**Peace of Paris** Treaties signed in 1783 by Great Britain, the United States, France, Spain, and the Netherlands that ended the Revolutionary War.

*THE HORSE AMERICA, throwing his Master.*

This British political cartoon from 1779 shows the horse "America" throwing its British master. The figure in the distance on the right is a French soldier; his depiction suggests that the cartoonist thought the French alliance would enable America to win the war.

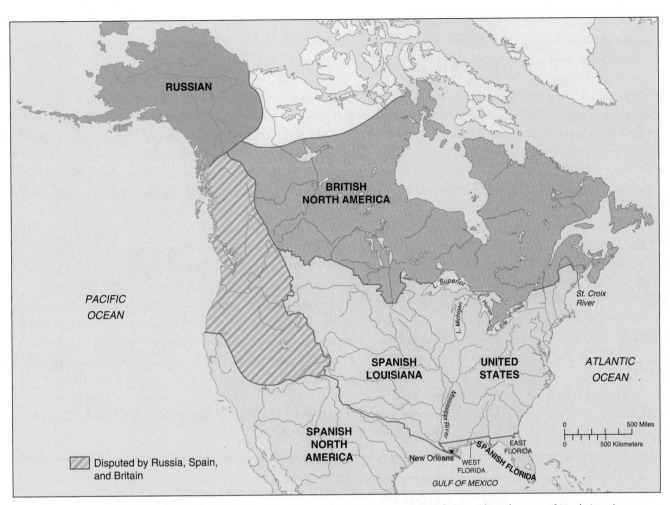

MAP 6-4   **North America after the Peace of Paris, 1783**   The results of the American Revolution redrew the map of North America, confining Britain to Canada and giving the United States most of the area east of the Mississippi River, though Spain controlled its mouth for most of the next 20 years.

**What factors** helped determine the territorial settlement reached in the Peace of Paris?

at New York City's Fraunces Tavern and later that month resigned his commission to the Congress and went home to Mount Vernon. By now he had won the respect of friend and foe alike.

Washington's leadership was just one of the reasons why the Americans won the Revolutionary War. French assistance played a crucial role. Indeed, some historians contend that without the massive infusion of French men and money in 1781, the Revolution would have failed. The British also contributed heavily to their own downfall with mistakes that included bureaucratic inefficiency, hesitant command, and overconfidence. Finally, Great Britain had tried to solve a political problem by military means, but an occupying army is far more likely to alienate people than to secure their goodwill.

Yet it took 175,000 to 200,000 soldiers—Continentals and militia troops—to prevent Great Britain from recovering the colonies. Of these, some 7,000 died in battle. Perhaps 10,000 more succumbed to disease while on active duty, another 8,500 died while prisoners of war, and nearly 1,500 were reported missing in action. More than 8,000 were wounded and survived. Those who served in the Continental Army, probably more than half of all who fought, served the longest and saw the most action. Their casualty rate—30 to 40 percent—may have been the highest of any war in which the United States has been engaged. In proportion to the population, these losses would be the equivalent of more than 2 million people in the United States today.

## GLOBAL CONNECTIONS

### THE BRITISH EMPIRE WITHOUT AMERICA

The American victory in the War for Independence did not deprive Great Britain of its entire New World empire. After 1783, Canada—which now counted thousands of loyalist refugees among its inhabitants—remained British, as did Jamaica, Barbados, and other lucrative sugar-growing Caribbean islands. Over the next few decades, however, the focus of the British Empire moved to the east.

Its centerpiece was India, where Britain expanded its territorial holdings, largely through conquest. Elsewhere, the first boatload of British convicts disembarked in Australia in 1788, and free settlers soon joined them to make good on Britain's claim to the island continent. By 1815, British imperial holdings also included parts of West and South Africa.

At the same time, Britain augmented its global empire by establishing commercial rather than territorial ties to other parts of the world. This was especially true for China, where British trade expanded dramatically, even as merchants' access was restricted to the port of Canton. In 1786, British merchants had also established a foothold at Penang on the Malay Peninsula. As the nineteenth century wore on, the mercantilist regulations that Britain had once imposed on its American colonies gave way to free trade policies.

Although Britain's so-called "second empire" encompassed the globe, it demonstrated some of the same weaknesses that had contributed to the loss of the American colonies. The Revolution had exposed crucial problems with British efforts to strengthen its imperial authority by asserting Parliamentary sovereignty over what had been essentially self-governing colonies. After 1783, imperial officials continued to allow a certain amount of local self-rule for white communities in the remaining British colonies but imposed more authoritarian governments on nonwhite majorities. At the same time, the imperial bureaucracy in London remained as uncoordinated as ever, with colonial responsibilities divided among numerous—and often competing—officials and departments. This new version of the British Empire would last until well into the twentieth century, but it too eventually dissolved.

- How did the British Empire change after the War for Independence?

## CONCLUSION

Despite the devastation and divisiveness of the war, many people in Europe and the United States were convinced that it represented something momentous. The *Annual Register*, a popular and influential British magazine, commented accurately in 1783 that the American Revolution "has already overturned those favourite systems of policy and commerce, both in the old and in the new world, which the wisdom of the ages, and the power of the greatest nations, had in vain endeavored to render permanent; and it seems to have laid the seeds of still greater revolutions in the history and mutual relations of mankind."

Americans, indeed, had fired a shot heard round the world. Thanks in part to its heavy investment in the American Revolution, France suffered a financial crisis in the late 1780s. This, in turn, ushered in the political crisis that culminated in the French Revolution of 1789. The American Revolution helped to inspire among French people (including soldiers returning from service in America) an intense yearning for an end to arbitrary government and undeserved social inequalities. Liberty also proved infectious to thousands of German troops who had come to America as mercenaries but stayed as free citizens after the war was over. Once prosperous but distant provinces of a far-flung empire, the North American states had become an independent confederation, a grand experiment in republicanism whose fate mattered to enlightened men and women throughout the Western world. In his written farewell to the rank and file of his troops at the end of October 1783, Washington maintained that "the enlarged prospects of happiness, opened by the confirmation of our independence and sovereignty, almost exceed the power of description." He urged those who had fought with him to maintain their "strong attachments to the union" and "prove themselves not less virtuous and useful as citizens, than they have been persevering and victorious as soldiers." The work of securing the promise of the American Revolution, Washington knew, would now shift from the battlefield to the political arena.

## OVERVIEW   Important Battles of the Revolutionary War

| | Battle | Date | Outcome |
|---|---|---|---|
| Early Fighting | Lexington and Concord, Massachusetts | April 19, 1775 | Contested |
| | Fort Ticonderoga, New York | May 10, 1775 | American victory |
| | Breed's Hill ("Bunker Hill"), Boston, Massachusetts | June 17, 1775 | Contested |
| | Great Bridge, Virginia | December 9, 1775 | American victory |
| | Quebec, Canada | December 31, 1775 | British repulsed American assault |
| | Moore's Creek Bridge, North Carolina | February 27, 1776 | American victory |
| The War in the North | Brooklyn Heights, New York | August 27, 1776 | British victory |
| | White Plains, New York | October 28, 1776 | British victory |
| | Trenton, New Jersey | December 26, 1776 | American victory |
| | Princeton, New Jersey | January 3, 1777 | American victory |
| | Brandywine Creek, Pennsylvania | September 11, 1777 | British victory (opened way for British to take Philadelphia) |
| | Saratoga, New York | September 19 and October 17, 1777 | American victory (helped persuade France to form an alliance with United States) |
| | Monmouth Court House, New Jersey | June 28, 1778 | Contested |
| The War on the Frontier | Wyoming Valley, Pennsylvania | June and July 1778 | British victory |
| | Kaskaskia and Cahokia, Illinois; Vincennes, Indiana | July 4, 1778–February 23, 1779 | American victories strengthen claims to Mississippi Valley |
| | Cherry Valley, New York | November 11, 1778 | British victory |
| The War in the South | Savannah, Georgia | December 29, 1778 | British victory (took control of Georgia) |
| | Kettle Creek, Georgia | February 14, 1779 | American victory |
| | Savannah, Georgia | September 3–October 28, 1779 | British victory (opened way for British to take Charleston) |
| | Charleston, South Carolina | February 11–May 12, 1780 | British victory |
| | Camden, South Carolina | August 16, 1780 | British victory |
| | Kings Mountain, South Carolina | October 7, 1780 | American victory |
| | Cowpens, South Carolina | January 17, 1781 | American victory |
| | Guilford Court House, North Carolina | March 15, 1781 | Contested |
| | Yorktown, Virginia | August 30–October 19, 1781 | American victory (persuaded Britain to end war) |

# WHERE TO LEARN MORE

**Independence National Historical Park, Philadelphia, Pennsylvania.**   Independence Hall, where Congress adopted the Declaration of Independence, is the most historic building in Philadelphia. The informative website can be accessed through http://www.nps.gov/inde/index.htm.

**Kings Mountain National Military Park and Cowpens National Battlefield, South Carolina.**   Situated approximately 20 miles apart, these were the sites of two battles in October 1780 and January 1781 that turned the tide of the war in the South. Both have museums and exhibits. The official site is accessible through http://www.nps.gov/kimo/index.htm.

**Minute Man National Historical Park, Lexington and Concord, Massachusetts.**   There are visitors' centers at both Lexington and Concord with explanatory displays. Visitors may also follow the self-guided Battle Road Automobile Tour. The official website is accessible through http://www.nps.gov/archive/mima/vcenter.htm.

**Yorktown Battlefield, Colonial National Historical Park, Yorktown, Virginia.**   The park commemorates the great American victory here. Innovative exhibits enable visitors to follow the course of the war from a multicultural perspective. The official website is accessible through http://www.nps.gov/york/index.htm.

# REVIEW QUESTIONS

1. Who were the loyalists, and how many of them were there? What attempts did the British and Americans make in 1775 to avert war? Why did these steps fail?

2. What actions did the Second Continental Congress take in 1775 and 1776? Why did it choose George Washington as the commander of its army? Why was he a good choice?

3. Why did Congress declare independence in July 1776? How did Americans justify their claim to independence?

4. Why were most of the early battles fought in the northern states? What effect did French entry into the war have on British strategy?

5. Why did the initial British victories in the South not win the war for them? Why did the United States ultimately win? What did it obtain by winning?

6. What were the effects of the war on Native Americans, African Americans, women, and American society in general?

7. What were some of the global effects of American independence?

# KEY TERMS

**Battles of Lexington and Concord** (p. 145)
**Committee of Safety** (p. 144)
**Conciliatory Proposition** (p. 144)
**Continental Army** (p. 145)
**Contract theory of government** (p. 148)
**Declaration of Independence** (p. 148)

**Declaration of the Causes and Necessity of Taking Up Arms** (p. 146)
**Minute Men** (p. 144)
**Olive Branch Petition** (p. 146)
**Peace of Paris** (p. 160)
**Second Continental Congress** (p. 145)
**Valley Forge** (p. 154)

# PEARSON myhistorylab™ Connections

Reinforce what you learned in this chapter by studying the many documents, images, maps, review tools, and videos available at **www.myhistorylab.com**.

## Read and Review

✓● Study and Review **Study Plan: Chapter 6**

•••● Read the Document

Joseph Warren, "Account of the Battle of Lexington" (1775)

Thomas Jefferson, "Original Rough Draught" of the Declaration of Independence (1776)

Thomas Paine, A Freelance Writer Urges His Readers to Use Common Sense (1776)

John Adams to Abigail Adams (July 3, 1776)

Letter from a Revolutionary War Soldier (1776)

Peter Oliver, Origin and Progress of the American Rebellion: A Tory View (1781)

Royal Proclamation of Rebellion (1775)

The Declaration of Independence (1776)

👁● See the Map
Revolutionary War: Northern Theater, 1775–1780

Territorial Claims in Eastern America after Treaty of Paris

The American Revolution

## Research and Explore

•••● Read the Document

*Personal Journeys Online*

*From Then to Now Online: Anti-war Churches*

*Exploring America: Exploring the Geography of the American Revolution*

((●● Hear the Audio *The Liberty Song*

COMMON SENSE;

ADDRESSED TO THE

INHABITANTS

OF

AMERICA,

On the following interesting

SUBJECTS.

I. Of the Origin and Design of Government in general, with concise Remarks on the English Constitution.
II. Of Monarchy and Hereditary Succession.
III. Thoughts on the present State of American Affairs.
IV. Of the present Ability of America, with some miscellaneous Reflections.

PHILADELPHIA;
Printed, and Sold, by R. BELL, in Third-Street.
MDCCLXXVI.

(●● Watch the Video *The American Revolution as Different Americans Saw It*

---

((●● **Hear the Audio**

Hear the audio files for Chapter 6 at
**www.myhistorylab.com**.

## Democratic Roots in New England Soil

**WHY COULD** New England society move from a firm condemnation of democracy to embracing the basic ideals that would lead to the Declaration of Independence and the Constitution of 1787?

The Puritans of New England were less than democratic in both beliefs and goals. Contrary to popular myth, Puritans did not migrate to the New World for the purpose of establishing religious freedom. They were seeking to establish a religious utopia to serve as what Governor John Winthrop called a "light upon a hill" for the world to copy. Once they created their utopia, Puritans wanted to keep it pristine, so they forbade the establishment of other religious doctrine, especially the Quaker and Roman Catholic faiths. In Puritan communities, nonconformist behavior was looked upon with deep suspicion, especially if it was religious in nature. The trials of Quaker evangelists and their public whippings and even execution provide evidence of Puritan intolerance.

However, the Puritans unknowingly planted the seeds for the very democracy that they hated as an abomination of the purity of God's social order. In the Mayflower Compact, Puritan separatists agreed to a governmental covenant that allowed for majority rule and later established the idea of the town meeting. In the charter of the Massachusetts Bay Colony, annual election of governors was provided for, as were the election of the colonial legislature and the General Court. Puritan customs forbade church ministers from serving in public office, an early version of separation of church and state although the Puritans would not see it in that way. Most important of all, the Puritans required that all church members be literate enough to read and interpret the Bible. Puritan laws directed all families to educate their children sufficiently to this purpose and towns were encouraged to establish free public schools. This emphasis upon the individual and his right to interpret the Bible, within certain doctrinal limits, without the intercession of a priest or minister would lead to political consequences.

A hundred years after the heyday of the Puritans, the political seeds that they planted would bear democratic fruit.

> We hold these truths to be self-evident, that all men are created equal, that they are endowed by their Creator with certain unalienable Rights, that among these are Life, Liberty and the pursuit of Happiness.—That to secure these rights, Governments are instituted among Men, deriving their just powers from the consent of the governed, . . .
>
> John Adams, *Coauthor of the Declaration of Independence*, *1776*

## Democracy I do not conceyve . . .

*"The Signing of the Mayflower Compact," a painting by E. Percy Moran, shows the historic ceremonial signing on November 21, 1620, below the deck of the Mayflower.*

### Mayflower Compact (1620)

IN THE NAME OF GOD, AMEN. We, whose names are underwritten, the Loyal Subjects of our dread Sovereign Lord King James, by the Grace of God, of Great Britain, France, and Ireland, King, Defender of the Faith, &c. Having undertaken for the Glory of God, and Advancement of the Christian Faith, and the Honour of our King and Country, a Voyage to plant the first Colony in the northern Parts of Virginia; Do by these Presents, solemnly and mutually, in the Presence of God and one another, covenant and combine ourselves together into a civil Body Politick, for our better Ordering and Preservation, and Furtherance of the Ends aforesaid: And by Virtue hereof do enact, constitute, and frame, such just and equal Laws, Ordinances, Acts, Constitutions, and Officers, from time to time, as shall be thought most meet and convenient for the general Good of the Colony; unto which we promise all due Submission and Obedience. IN WITNESS whereof we have hereunto subscribed our names at Cape-Cod the eleventh of November, in the Reign of our Sovereign Lord King James, of England, France, and Ireland, the eighteenth, and of Scotland the fifty-fourth, Anno Domini; 1620.

The wooden Old Ship Meeting House in Hingham, Massachusetts, has served as church and community center for the Puritans of the town since 1681. The village meeting house hosted the annual town meeting where Puritans voted for their town selectmen (town council), voted on laws that would govern them for the next year, and openly debated town policy. All adult male members of the Church were usually allowed to vote.

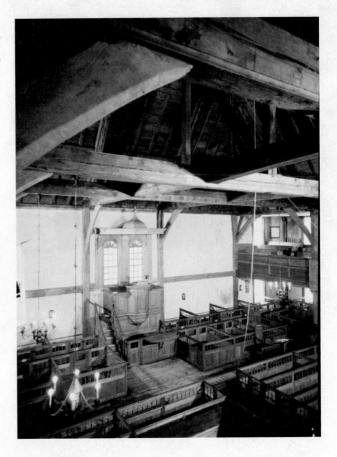

## Fundamental Orders of Connecticut (1639)

It is Ordered, sentenced, and decreed, that there shall be yearly two General Assemblies or Courts, the one the second Thursday in April, the other the second Thursday in September following; the first shall be called the Court of Election, wherein shall be yearly chosen from time to time, so many Magistrates and other public Officers as shall be found requisite: Whereof one to be chosen Governor for the year ensuing and until another be chosen, and no other Magistrate to be chosen for more than one year: provided always there be six chosen besides the Governor, which being chosen and sworn according to an Oath recorded for that purpose, shall have the power to administer justice according to the Laws here established. . . .

It is Ordered, sentenced, and decreed, that the election of the aforesaid Magistrates shall be in this manner: every person present and qualified for choice shall bring in (to the person deputed to receive them) one single paper with the name of him written in it whom he desires to have Governor, and that he that hath the greatest number of papers shall be Governor for that year. And the rest of the Magistrates or public officers to be chosen in this manner: the Secretary for the time being shall first read the names of all that are to be put to choice and then shall severally nominate them distinctly, and every one that would have the person nominated to be chosen shall bring in one single paper written upon, and he that would not have him chosen shall bring in a blank; and every one that hath more written papers than blanks shall be a Magistrate for that year. . . .

It is Ordered, sentenced, and decreed, that the Secretary shall not nominate any person, nor shall any person be chosen newly into the Magistracy which was not propounded in some General Court before, to be nominated the next election; and to that end it shall be lawful for each of the Towns aforesaid by their deputies to nominate any two whom they conceive fit to be put to election. . . .

It is Ordered, sentenced, and decreed, that no person be chosen Governor above once in two years, and that the Governor be always a member of some approved Congregation, and formerly of the Magistracy within this Jurisdiction. . . .

## Fundamental Agreement, or Original Constitution of the Colony of New Haven (June 4, 1639)

. . .

Query II. WHEREAS there was a covenant solemnly made by the whole assembly of free planters of this plantation, the first day of extraordinary humiliation, which we had after we came together, that as in matters that concern the gathering and ordering of a church, so likewise in all public officers which concern civil order, as choice of magistrates and officers, making and repealing laws, dividing allotments of inheritance, and all things of like nature, we would all of us be ordered by those rules which the scripture holds forth to US; this covenant was called a plantation covenant, to distinguish it from a church covenant. which could not at that time be made a church not being then gathered, but was deferred till a church might be gathered, according to GOD. It was demanded whether all the free planters do hold themselves bound by that covenant, in all businesses of that nature which are expressed in the covenant, to submit themselves to be ordered by the rules held forth in the scripture. . . .

Query III. THOSE who have desired to be received as free planters, and are settled in the plantation, with a purpose, resolution and desire, that they may be admitted into church fellowship, according to CHRIST, as soon as GOD shall fit them "hereunto, were desired to express it by holding up hands. According all did express this to be their desire and purpose by holding up their hands twice (viz.) at the proposal of it, and after when these written words were read unto them.

Query IV. All the free planters were called upon to express, whether they held themselves bound to establish such civil order as might best conduce to the securing of the purity and peace of the ordinance to themselves and their posterity according to GOD In answer hereunto they expressed by holding up their hands twice as before, that they held themselves bound to establish such civil order as might best conduce to the ends aforesaid.

*We hold these truths to be self-evident...*

# The First Republic

The illustration on this 1783 map of the United States pairs George Washington on the left with Liberty and Benjamin Franklin on the right with Justice in a symbolic identification of the new republic with the values of equality and individual dignity. The Granger Collection

((•●—Hear the **Audio**

Hear the audio files for Chapter 7 at **www.myhistorylab.com**.

### THE NEW ORDER OF REPUBLICANISM  *(page 171)*

**WHAT WERE** the most significant weaknesses of the Articles of Confederation?

### PROBLEMS AT HOME  *(page 177)*

**HOW DID** economic problems lead to political conflict in the 1780s?

### DIPLOMATIC WEAKNESSES  *(page 182)*

**WHAT STEPS** did Britain and Spain take to block American expansion?

### TOWARD A NEW UNION  *(page 185)*

**WHICH GROUPS** in American society were most likely to support the Constitution? Why?

ONE AMERICAN JOURNEY

*The jurors of the Commonwealth of Massachusetts upon their oath present that Moses Sash of Worthington . . . a negro man & Labourer being a disorderly, riotous & seditious person & minding & contriving as much as in him lay unlawfully by force of arms to stir up promote incite & maintain riots mobs tumults insurrections in this Commonwealth & to disturb impede & prevent the Government of the same & the due administration of justice in the same, & to prevent the Courts of justice from sitting as by Law appointed for that purpose & to promote disquiets, uneasiness, jealousies, animosities & seditions in the minds of the Citizens of this Common-wealth on the twentieth day of January in the year of our Lord Seventeen hundred & eighty seven & on divers other days & times as well before as since that time at Worthington . . . unlawfully & seditiously with force & arms did advise persuade invite incourage & procure divers persons . . . of this Commonwealth by force of arms to oppose this Commonwealth & the Government thereof & riotously to join themselves to a great number of riotous seditious persons with force & arms thus opposing this Commonwealth & the Government thereof . . . and in pursuance of his wicked seditious purposes . . . did procure guns, bayonets, pistols, swords, gunpowder, bullets, blankets & provisions & other warlike instruments offensive & defensive . . . & did cause & procure them to be carried & conveyed to the riotous & seditious persons as aforesaid in evil example to others to offend in like manner against the peace of the Commonwealth aforesaid & dignity of the same.*

*Source:* Indictment of Moses Sash by the Supreme Judicial Court of Massachusetts for Suffolk County, April 9, 1787, cited in Sidney Kaplan and Emma Nogrady Kaplan, *The Black Presence in the Era of the American Revolution* (Amherst: University of Massachusetts Press, 1989), p. 259.

◆●◆┤**Read** the **Document** at **www.myhistorylab.com**

**Personal Journeys Online**

- **William Shepard, Letter to Governor Bowdoin, Jan. 26, 1787.** A militia captain describes the routing of the Shaysites at Springfield Arsenal.

- **Henry Lee, Letter to George Washington, Oct. 1, 1786.** One of Washington's former generals expresses his fears over the outbreak of agrarian insurgencies.

THUS, in the dry, legalistic language of the highest court in Massachusetts was Moses Sash, a twenty-eight-year-old African American veteran of the Revolutionary War, indicted by a grand jury for his role in Shays's Rebellion. Named after its leader, Daniel Shays, another Revolutionary veteran, this armed insurgency pitted debt-ridden farmers in the western half of Massachusetts against conservative interests in the east. Farmers and laborers in western Massachusetts faced hard times in the 1780s. Faced with an unresponsive state legislature controlled by eastern merchants and creditors, angry farmers reacted much as they had during the revolutionary agitation against the British a decade earlier: They organized, protested, and shut down the county courts.

Routed in a battle at Springfield Arsenal in January 1787 by an army raised by Governor Bowdoin, the Shaysites fled into the hills. Nearly all of them, including Sash, were pardoned by the new administration of Governor John Hancock. Sash moved to Connecticut and died in poverty.

More than any other domestic disturbance in the 1780s, Shays's Rebellion dramatized the fragile nature and conflicting values of America's first republic under the Articles of Confederation. White Americans debated the meaning of liberty and whether greater powers should be granted to the very weak national government established by the Articles in 1781. Moses Sash and countless other African Americans—slave or free—insisted that the Revolution bequeathed a promise of greater human rights that extended to all Americans regardless of race. Americans favoring a stronger, more centralized government repeatedly cited Shays's Rebellion as an example of the impending chaos that would destroy the republic unless fundamental changes were made. Those changes came with the writing of the United States Constitution in 1787 and its ratification in 1788. ✦

## CHRONOLOGY

| | | | |
|---|---|---|---|
| **1776** | States begin writing the first constitutions. | **1785** | Land Ordinance of 1785. |
| **1777** | Articles of Confederation proposed. | | States begin to issue more paper money. |
| **1780s** | English textile production begins to surge with new technological advances. | | Treaty of Fort McIntosh. |
| **1781** | Articles ratified. | **1786** | Shays's Rebellion breaks out. |
| **1783** | Americans celebrate independence and the peace treaty with Britain. | | Jay-Gardoqui Treaty defeated. |
| | | | Annapolis Convention. |
| | British West Indies closed to U.S. traders. | **1787** | Constitutional Convention at Philadelphia. |
| **1784** | Onset of the postwar depression. | | Northwest Ordinance. |
| | Opening of China trade by the United States. | **1788** | Constitution ratified and goes into effect. |
| | Spain closes the Mississippi. | | Publication of *The Federalist*. |
| | Separatist plots in the West. | | |
| | Treaty of Fort Stanwix. | | |

# THE NEW ORDER OF REPUBLICANISM

**WHAT WERE** the most significant weaknesses of the Articles of Confederation?

As royal authority collapsed during the Revolution, provincial congresses and committees assumed power in each of the former colonies. The Continental Congress, seeking to build support for the war effort, was concerned that these new institutions should have a firm legal and popular foundation. In May 1776, the Congress called on the colonies to form new state governments "under the authority of the people."

This call reflected the political philosophy of republicanism that animated the Revolution (see Chapter 6). To Americans, republicanism meant, first and foremost, that legitimate political authority derives from the people. Another key aspect of republicanism was the revolutionary idea that the people could define and limit governmental power through written constitutions. These core republican principles held that governmental authority should flow from the people, but it was not always clear just who was included in "the people."

### DEFINING THE PEOPLE

Republicanism rested on the belief that the people were sovereign, but it also taught that political rights should be limited to those who owned private property. Only propertied people were thought to possess the independent will required for informed political judgment. This, in effect, restricted political participation to propertied white men. Virtually everyone else, property-less white men, servants legally bound to others, women, slaves, and most free black people, were denied political rights. As for Native Americans, they were outside the U.S. body politic and exercised political rights within their own nations.

Because the ownership of property was relatively widespread among white men, some 60 to 85 percent of adult white men could participate in politics, a far higher proportion than elsewhere in the world of the eighteenth century. The greatest concentration of the remaining 25 percent or so shut out of the political process were unskilled laborers and mariners living in port cities.

### WOMEN AND THE REVOLUTION

The Revolution did little to change the traditional patriarchal assumption that politics and public life should be the exclusive domain of men. Women, according to republican beliefs, were part of the dependent class and belonged under the control of propertied men, their husbands and fathers.

With the exception of New Jersey, where women meeting the property qualifications were eligible to vote, the state constitutions of the Revolutionary era prohibited women from voting.

**suffrage** The right to vote in a political election.

## QUICK REVIEW

### Property, Race, Gender, and Citizenship

◆ Republicans limited political rights to white male property owners.

◆ 60 to 85 percent of adult white men owned property.

◆ The Revolution did not challenge exclusion of women from politics.

Under common law (the customary, largely unwritten, law that Americans had inherited from Britain), women surrendered their property rights at marriage unless they made special arrangements to the contrary. Legally and economically, husbands had complete control over their wives.

To be sure, some women saw in the political and social enthusiasm of the Revolution an opportunity to protest the most oppressive features of their subordination. Men, Eliza Wilkinson of South Carolina lamented, "won't even allow us liberty of thought and that is all I want." Such protests, however, had little enduring effect. Most women were socialized to accept that their proper place was in the home with their families.

Gender-specific language, including such terms as "men," "Freemen," "white male inhabitants," and "free white men," explicitly barred women from voting in almost all state constitutions of the 1770s. Only the New Jersey constitution of 1776 defined **suffrage,** the right to vote, in gender-free terms, extending it to all adults "worth fifty pounds." As a result, until 1807, when the state legislature changed the constitution, propertied women, including widows and single women, enjoyed the right to vote in New Jersey.

Outside of the political realm, the Revolution did bring women a few limited gains. They benefited from slightly less restrictive divorce laws and gained somewhat greater access to educational and business opportunities, changes that reflected the relative autonomy of many women during the war when their men were off fighting. The perception of women's moral status also rose. As the Philadelphia physician Benjamin Rush argued in his *Thoughts upon Female Education* (1787), educated and morally informed women were needed to instruct "their sons in the principles of liberty and government." Often called republican motherhood, this more positive view of women's influence entrusted mothers with the responsibility of passing on republican virtues from one generation to the next.

**The Revolution and African Americans in the South.** The Revolution had a more immediate impact on the lives of many African Americans, triggering the growth of free black communities and the development of an African American culture. Changes begun by the Revolution were the main factor in the tremendous increase of free blacks from a few thousand at mid-century to more than 100,000 by 1800 (see Figure 7–1). One key to this increase was a shift in the religious and intellectual climate. Revolutionary principles of liberty and equality and evangelical notions of human fellowship convinced many whites for the first time to challenge black slavery. As many whites grew more hostile to slavery, slaves in the North, drawing on republican political theory, submitted petitions for freedom to the new state legislatures and blacks everywhere began to seize opportunities for freedom.

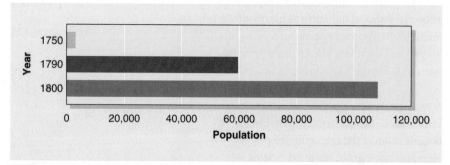

**FIGURE 7–1 Growth of the Free Black Population between 1750 and 1800** Gradual emancipation in the North, the freeing of many slaves by their owners in the South, and the opportunities for freedom offered by the Revolution, all contributed to an explosive growth in the free population of African Americans in the second half of the eighteenth century.

*Data Source: A Century of Population Growth in the United States, 1790–1900* (1909). p. 80. Data for 1750 estimated.

Upwards of 50,000 slaves, or one in ten of those in bondage, gained their freedom as a result of the war. One route was through military service, which generally carried a promise of freedom. When the British began raising black troops, the Americans followed suit. All the states except Georgia and South Carolina recruited black regiments. Some 5,000 blacks served in the Continental Army along with Moses Sash, and they, like their counterparts in British units, were mostly slaves. Most of the slaves who gained freedom during the war, however, had fled their owners and made their way to the port cities of the North.

By making slave property generally less secure, the Revolution encouraged many masters to free their slaves. A manumission act passed by the Virginia assembly in 1782 (but tightened a decade later) allowed individual owners to free their slaves. As the number of free blacks increased, those still enslaved grew bolder in their efforts to gain freedom.

**Northern blacks and the Revolution.**    If the control mechanisms of slavery experienced some strain in the South during the Revolution, in the North, where slaves were only a small percentage of the population, they crumbled. Slaves pressured their owners for freedom by running away, damaging property, and committing arson. Most northern states ended slavery between 1777 and 1784. New York followed in 1799, and New Jersey in 1804. Nonetheless, although a majority of northern whites now agreed that slavery was incompatible a commitment to **natural rights** (the inherent human rights to life and liberty) and human freedom, they refused to sanction a sudden emancipation. The laws ending slavery in most of the northern states called for only the children of slaves to be freed, and only when they reached adulthood.

Once free, northern blacks had to struggle to overcome white prejudice. Facing discrimination in jobs and housing, barred from juries, and denied a fair share of funds for schools, urban blacks had to rely on their own resources. With the help of the small class of property holders among them, they began establishing their own churches and self-help associations.

**The Revolution's impact on Native Americans.**    Most Indian peoples had stayed neutral during the war or fought for the British (see Chapter 6). Just as the Americans sought to shake off British control, so the Indians, especially the western tribes and most of the Iroquois Confederation, sought to free themselves from American dominance. The British defeat was thus a double blow, depriving the Indians of a valuable ally and exposing them to the wrath of the victorious patriots.

The state governments, as well as the Confederation Congress, treated Indian lands as a prize of war to be distributed to white settlers. Territorial demands on the Indians escalated, and even the few tribes that had furnished troops for the American side struggled to maintain control over their homelands. As they did so, it was clear that white Americans did not consider Native Americans to be part of their republican society.

Most Native Americans did not want or expect equal rights within the new American republic. They viewed themselves as belonging to their own nations, composed of distinct villages and settlements, with a common culture and interests. They wanted political rights and control over the land within their nations. Above all, they wanted independence.

In seeking to defend their independence against the growing pressure of white Americans on their lands, Native Americans forged new confederacies in the 1780s that temporarily united them against a common enemy. They were encouraged in these efforts by the imperial powers of England and Spain, both of which sought to curb the westward expansion of the United States. Thus, the immediate impact of the

**natural rights**    Political philosophy that maintains that individuals have an inherent right, found in nature and preceding any government or written law, to life and liberty.

**QUICK REVIEW**

**African Americans and the Revolution**

◆ Revolutionary principles sparked some to challenge slavery.

◆ More than 50,000 slaves gained freedom as results of the war.

◆ By 1800 the free black population reached 100,000.

Phillis Wheatley was an acclaimed African American poet. Kidnapped into slavery as a child in Africa, she was a domestic slave to the Wheatley family of Boston when her first poems were published in 1773.

## AMERICAN VIEWS

### A Quaker Seeks Cooperative Action against Slavery

*Quakers took the lead in pushing for the emancipation of slaves in the northern states. This letter, written in 1784 by James Pemberton, relates the efforts of a Pennsylvania Quaker to enlist the aid of British abolitionists in the cause of black freedom in the United States. It also outlines the struggles within the Society of Friends over admitting African Americans into membership.*

- **What** plan of cooperation does Pemberton propose? What do you believe would be the keys to its success?
- **What** political bodies are cited for the delivery of anti-slavery petitions?
- **Why** were Quakers so reluctant to support the "unrestricted admission" of African Americans into their religious fellowship?
- **How** did some Quakers reason that racial intermarriage would upset a racial order ordained by Providence?

I am much obliged by the kindness in sending me the Essays on Slavery, the case of the oppressed blacks commands our attention to move in endeavors for their relief as opportunities are favorable; altho Congress has done as little in consequence of our address as your Parliament has in favor of your Petition, and I conclude on similar motives; An application is now about to be made by Friends to the Legislature of New Jersey on this Subject, and we have reprinted five hundred copies of the Petition of your yearly meeting and the Representation which followed it from your meeting . . . for general distribution among the people in these States, & the Rulers in particular, a fragment of a letter from T[homas] Day printed in London concise & serious has been reprinted by private procurement in newspapers & otherwise by which it has a general dispersion and will I hope prove useful.

The admission of members into our Religious Society is at all times a matter of weight, a base convincement of the rectitude of our principles and discipline, and a foundation sufficient without satisfactory proof of real conversion, the want of which has been productive of burdens & troubles to meetings in many instances, and in the case of Blacks, considerations of another nature occur which are of great importance, wherein friends here do not agree in sentiment tho religiously affected for the real welfare of those people, the concord of Society therefore requires a mature deliberate consideration of the Subject in a collective capacity, for which no occasion has yet offered and I know of no more than one instance of an application of this sort to any Monthly meeting; while some friends are advocates for an unrestricted admission, others plead if no limitation is proscribed they must become entitled to the privilege of intermarriage, and I believe there are few who would freely consent to such a union in their families which mixture some think would reverse the order of Divine Providence who in his wisdom inscrutable to us has been pleased to form distinction of Colour, for tho[ugh] of one blood he made all nations of men, yet it is also said he has fixed their habitation, which has been changed by avarice & ambition. However when the subject becomes necessary to be religiously discussed, I hope friends will be favored with the true spirit of judgment rightly determined &c.

*Source:* James Pemberton to James Phillips, in London, Nov. 18, 1784, Gilder Lehrman Collection of American History, 04237.

Revolution on Native Americans was a mixed one. On the one hand, the Revolution had created a new expansionist power in the United States that was intent on settling lands already occupied by Indians. On the other hand, American victory in the Revolution had broken the British monopoly of power in the region west of the Appalachian Mountains. Before the United States could consolidate its claim over the region, new imperial rivalries sprang up that allowed Native Americans to stake out a political middle ground between the competing powers. Throughout the 1780s, Native Americans continued to act as independent political agents in playing off outside powers against each other.

# THE STATE CONSTITUTIONS

Ten new state constitutions were in place by the end of 1777. All these constitutions were written documents, a departure from the English practice of treating a constitution as a collection of customary rights and practices that had evolved over time. In the American view, a constitution was a formal expression of the people's sovereignty, a codification of the powers of government and the rights of citizenship that functioned as a fundamental law to which all public authority was held accountable.

Because Americans had come to associate tyranny with the privileges of royal governors, all the new state constitutions cut back sharply on executive power. Most important, for it struck at what patriots felt was the main source of executive domination and corruption, governors lost control over patronage, the power to appoint executive and judicial officials. As the new constitutions curbed the power of governors, they increased that of the legislatures, making them the focal point of government.

To make the legislatures more expressive of the popular will, the new constitutions included provisions that lowered property requirements for voting and officeholding, mandated annual elections, increased the number of seats in the legislatures, and made representation more proportional to the geographical distribution of population. Upper houses were made independent of the executive office and opened to popular election, as opposed to the colonial practice of having their members appointed by the governor.

In a final check on arbitrary power, each state constitution eventually included some form of a bill of rights that set explicit limits on the power of government to interfere in the lives of citizens. By 1784, the constitutions of all thirteen states had provisions guaranteeing religious liberty, freedom of the press, and a citizen's right to such fair legal practices as trial by jury.

**Toward religious pluralism.**   The new constitutions weakened but did not always sever the traditional tie between church and state. Many states, notably in New England, levied taxes for the support of religion. The states of New England also continued to maintain Congregationalism as the established, or state-supported, religion, while allowing dissenting Baptists and Methodists to use funds from the compulsory religious taxes to support their ministers.

The mid-Atlantic states lacked the religious uniformity of New England. This pluralism checked legislative efforts to impose religious taxes or designate any denomination as the established church. In the South, where many Anglican (or Episcopalian) clergymen had been Tories, the Anglican Church lost its former established status.

**Conflicting visions of republicanism.**   Although in general the executive lost power and the legislature gained power under the new state constitutions, the actual structure of each state government reflected the outcome of political struggles between radical and conservative visions of republicanism. The democratically inclined radicals wanted to open government to all male citizens. The conservatives wanted to limit government to an educated elite of substantial property holders. Although they agreed that government had to be derived from the people, most conservatives, like Jeremy Belknap of New Hampshire, thought that the people had to be "taught . . . that they are not able to govern themselves."

In South Carolina, where conservative planters gained the upper hand, the constitution mandated property qualifications that barred 90 percent of the state's white males from holding elective public office. By contrast, Pennsylvania had the most democratic and controversial constitution. Many of Pennsylvania's conservatives had discredited themselves during the Revolution by remaining neutral or loyal to the crown. The Scots-Irish farmers and Philadelphia artisans who stepped into the resulting political vacuum held an egalitarian view of republicanism. The constitution they pushed through in 1776 gave the vote to all free males who paid taxes, regardless of wealth, and eliminated property qualifications for officeholding. In addition, the constitution concentrated power in a unicameral (single-house) legislature, eliminating both the

**QUICK REVIEW**

**New State Constitutions**

♦ New constitutions guaranteed individual rights.

♦ Constitutions weakened tie between church and state.

♦ In general the legislature gained power at the expense of the executive.

office of governor and the more elite upper legislative house. To prevent the formation of an entrenched class of officeholders, the constitution's framers also required legislators to stand for election annually and barred them from serving more than four years out of seven.

Unlike the colonial assemblies, the new state legislatures included substantially more artisans and small farmers and were not controlled by men of wealth. The proportion of legislators who came from a common background—those with property valued under £200—more than tripled to 62 percent in the North and more than doubled in the South from the 1770s to the 1780s.

**Articles of Confederation** Written document setting up the loose confederation of states that comprised the first national government of the United States.

## THE ARTICLES OF CONFEDERATION

Once the Continental Congress decided on independence in 1776, it needed to create a legal basis for a permanent union of the states. According to the key provision of the **Articles of Confederation** that the Congress finally submitted to the states in November 1777, "Each State retains its sovereignty, freedom and independence, and every power, jurisdiction and right, which is not by this confederation expressly delegated to the United States, in Congress assembled." The effect was to create a loose confederation of autonomous states.

The powers the Articles of Confederation delegated to the central government were extremely limited, in effect little more than those already exercised by the Continental Congress. There were no provisions for a national judiciary or a separate executive branch of government. The Articles made Congress the sole instrument of national authority but restricted it with a series of constitutional safeguards that kept it from threatening the interests of the states.

The Congress had authority primarily in the areas of foreign policy and national defense. It could declare war, make peace, conduct foreign affairs, negotiate with Native Americans, and settle disputes between the states. It had no authority, however, to raise troops or impose taxes; it could only ask the states to supply troops and money and hope that they would comply.

Most states quickly ratified the Articles of Confederation, but Maryland stubbornly held out until March 1781. Because they needed the approval of all thirteen states, only then did the Articles officially take effect. The issue in Maryland concerned the unsettled lands in the West between the Appalachian Mountains and the Mississippi River (see Map 7–1). Some states claimed these lands by virtue of their colonial charter rights, and led by Virginia and Massachusetts, they insisted on maintaining control over these territories. The so-called landless

MAP 7–1   **Cession of Western Lands by the States**   Eight states had claims to lands in the West after the Revolution, and their willingness to cede them to the national government was an essential step in the creation of a public domain administered by Congress.

**Why did** the question of control of western lands divide the states both during and after the Revolution? Which states were most in favor of federal control of western lands? Why?

states—those with no claim to the West—insisted that the territories should be set aside as a national domain, a reserve of public land controlled by Congress for the benefit of all the states.

Threatened by the British presence in the Chesapeake area in early 1781, Virginia finally broke the impasse over the Articles. Though it retained control of Kentucky, Virginia gave up its claim in the West to a vast area extending north of the Ohio River. In turn, Maryland, the last holdout among the landless states and now desperate for military aid from the Congress, agreed to ratify the Articles.

# PROBLEMS AT HOME

Neither prosperity nor political stability accompanied the return of peace in 1783. The national government struggled to avoid bankruptcy, and in 1784, an economic depression struck. As fiscal problems deepened, creditor and debtor groups clashed angrily in state legislatures. When legislatures passed measures that provided relief to debtors at the expense of creditors, the creditors decried what they saw as the interference of ignorant majorities with the rights of private property. Raising the cry of "legislative despotism," the abuse of power by tyrannical lawmakers, the creditors joined their voices to those who early on had wanted the power of the states curbed by a stronger central government. The only solid accomplishment of the Confederation Congress during this troubled period was to formulate an orderly and democratic plan for the settlement of the West.

**HOW DID** economic problems lead to political conflict in the 1780s?

## THE FISCAL CRISIS

The Continental Congress and the states had incurred heavy debts to finance the Revolutionary War. Unable to impose and collect sufficient taxes to cover the debts and without reserves of gold or silver, they had little choice but to borrow funds and issue certificates, or bonds, pledging repayment. By the end of the war in 1781, the national debt stood at $11 million. As Congress issued new securities to settle claims by soldiers and civilians, the debt rose to $28 million within just a few years.

The Congress never did put its tottering finances on a sound footing. Its fiscal problems ultimately discredited the Articles of Confederation in the eyes of the **nationalists,** a loose bloc of congressmen, army officers, and public creditors who wanted to strengthen the Confederation at the expense of the states. The nationalists first began to organize in the dark days of 1780 and 1781, when inflation was rampant, the army was going unpaid, the Congress had ceased paying interest on the public debt, and the war effort itself seemed in danger of collapsing. Galvanized by this crisis, the nationalists rallied behind Robert Morris, a Philadelphia merchant appointed as superintendent of finance for the Confederation government.

Morris sought to enhance national authority through a bold program of financial and political reform. He began by securing a charter from Congress in 1781 for the Bank of North America, the nation's first commercial bank. Morris temporarily brought order and economy to the nation's finances. Nonetheless, he was blocked in his efforts to gain the taxing power that was essential for restoring the shattered credit of the Confederation government.

In 1781, Morris proposed a national impost, or tariff, of 5 percent on imported goods. Because this was a national tax, it required an amendment to the Articles of Confederation and the consent of all thirteen states. Twelve of the states quickly ratified the impost amendment, but Rhode Island—critically dependent on its own import duties to finance its war debt—rejected it. When a revised impost plan was considered two years later, New York blocked its passage.

The failure of the impost tax was one of many setbacks that put the nationalists temporarily on the defensive. With the conclusion of peace in 1783, confidence in state government returned, taking the edge off calls to vest the central government with greater authority. The states continued to balk at supplying the money requisitioned by Congress and denied the Congress

**nationalists**   Group of leaders in the 1780s who spearheaded the drive to replace the Articles of Confederation with a stronger central government.

even limited authority to regulate foreign commerce. Most ominously for the nationalist cause, the states began to assume responsibility for part of the national debt. As Morris had warned in 1781, such a policy entailed "a principle of disunion . . . which must be ruinous." Without the power to tax, the Congress was a hostage to the sovereignty of the individual states with no real authority over the nation's economic affairs. When the economy plunged into a severe depression in 1784, Congress could only look on helplessly.

## ECONOMIC DEPRESSION

During the Revolutionary War, Britain closed its markets to American goods. After the war, the British continued this policy, hoping to keep the United States weak and dependent. Meanwhile, British merchants were happy to satisfy America's pent-up demand for consumer goods after the war. Cheap British imports inundated the American market, and coastal merchants made them available to inland traders and shopkeepers by extending easy credit terms. In turn, these local businessmen sold the goods to farmers and artisans in the interior. Ultimately, however, the British merchants required payment in hard currency, gold and silver coins. Without access to its former export markets, America's only source of hard currency was foreign loans obtained by Congress and what money the French army had spent during the war. This was soon exhausted, and America's trade deficit with Britain—the excess of imports over exports—ballooned in the early 1780s (see Figure 7–2).

The result was an immense bubble of credit that finally burst in 1784, triggering a depression that would linger for most of the decade. As merchants began to press debtors for immediate payment, prices collapsed (they fell more than 25 percent between 1784 and 1786), and debtors were unable to pay. The best most could hope for was to avoid bankruptcy.

In the cities, wages fell 25 percent between 1785 and 1789, and workers began to organize. They called for tariffs to protect them from cheap British imports and for legislative measures to promote American manufacturers. In the countryside, farmers faced lawsuits for the collection of debts and the dread possibility of losing their land.

With insufficient money in circulation to raise prices and reverse the downturn, the depression fed on itself. Congress was powerless to raise cash and was unable to pay off its old debts, including what it owed to the Revolutionary soldiers. Many state governments made things worse by imposing heavy taxes payable in the paper money they had issued during the Revolution. The result was to further reduce the amount of money in circulation, thus increasing deflationary pressures and forcing prices still lower.

Britain's trade policies caused particular suffering among New England merchants. No longer protected under the old Navigation Acts as British vessels, American ships were now barred from most ports in the British trading empire. Incoming cargoes from the West Indies to New England fell off sharply, and the market for whale oil and fish, two of New England's major exports, dried up.

In the southern states, British policies compounded the problem of recovering from the physical damage and labor disruptions inflicted by the war. Some 10 percent of the region's slaves had fled during the war, and production levels on plantations fell in the 1780s. Chesapeake planters needed a full decade to restore the prewar output of tobacco, and a

WHERE TO LEARN MORE

South Street Seaport Museum, New York City, New York
http://seany.org

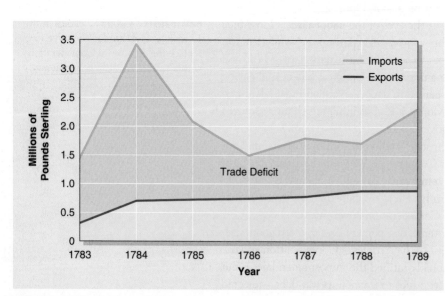

**FIGURE 7–2  American Exports to and Imports from Britain between 1783 and 1789**
During the 1780s, the United States imported far more from Britain than it exported there. The resulting huge trade deficit drained the country of gold and silver and was a major factor in the credit crisis that triggered an economic depression in the middle of the decade.
*Data Source:* U.S. Bureau of the Census, *Historical Statistics of the United States: Colonial Times to 1970,* pt. 2 (1975), p. 1176.

collapse in tobacco prices in 1785 left most of them in the same chronic state of indebtedness that had plagued them on the eve of the Revolution.

Farther south, in the Carolina low country, the plantation economy was crippled. War damage had been extensive, and planters piled up debts to purchase additional slaves and repair their plantations and dikes. Burdened by new British duties on American rice, planters saw their rice exports fall by 50 percent.

By the late 1780s, the worst of the depression was over and an upturn was under way in the mid-Atlantic states. Food exports to continental Europe were on the rise, and American merchants were developing new trading ties with India and China. Commercial treaties with the Dutch, Swedes, and Prussians also opened up markets that had been closed to the colonists. Nonetheless, a full recovery had to await the 1790s.

As the economy stagnated in the 1780s, the population was growing rapidly. There were 50 percent more Americans in 1787 than there had been in 1775. As a result, living standards fell and economic conflict dominated the politics of the states during the Confederation period.

## The Economic Policies of the States

The depression had political repercussions in all the states. Britain was an obvious target of popular anger, and merchants, artisans, and workers, especially in the North, pushed for tariff barriers against cheap British goods. Most northern states imposed anti-British measures, but these varied from state to state, limiting their impact and producing squabbles when goods imported in one state were shipped to another.

State legislatures in the North passed tariffs on foreign goods, but the lack of a uniform national policy doomed their efforts. Shippers evaded high tariffs by bringing their cargoes in through states with no tariffs or less restrictive ones. States without ports, such as New Jersey and North Carolina, complained of economic discrimination. When they purchased foreign goods from a neighboring shipping state, they were forced to pay part of the tariff cost, but all the revenue from the tariff accrued to the importing state.

Tariff policies also fed sectional tensions between northern and southern states that undermined efforts to confer on the Congress the power to regulate commerce. The agrarian states of the South, which had little in the way of mercantile or artisan interests to protect, generally favored free trade policies that encouraged British imports. Southern planters were also happy to take advantage of the low rates charged by British ships for transporting their crops to Europe; by doing so, they put pressure on northern shippers to reduce their rates.

The most bitter divisions exposed by the depression of the 1780s, however, were not between states but between debtors and creditors within states. As the value of debt securities the states had issued to raise money dropped during the Revolutionary War, speculators bought them up for a fraction of their face value from farmers and soldiers desperate for cash. The speculators then pressured the states to raise taxes and repay the debts in full in hard currency. Wealthy landowners and merchants likewise supported higher taxes and the rapid repayment of debts in hard currency.

Arrayed against these creditor groups by the mid-1780s was a broad coalition of debtors: middling farmers, small shopkeepers, artisans, laborers, and people who had overextended themselves speculating in western land. The debtors wanted the states to issue paper money that they could use instead of hard money—gold and silver—to pay their debts. The paper money would have an inflationary effect, raising wages and the prices of farm commodities and reducing the value of debts contracted in hard currency.

**Shays's Rebellion.**    This was the economic context in which **Shays's Rebellion** exploded in the fall of 1786. Farm foreclosures and imprisonments for failure to pay debts had skyrocketed in western Massachusetts. When the creditor and seaboard interests in the legislature refused to pass any relief measures, some 2,000 farmers took up arms against the state government in Shays's Rebellion.

**QUICK REVIEW**

**Debt and the Balance of Trade**

◆ Britain sought to keep America weak and dependent.

◆ Trade imbalance soared in the 1780s.

◆ Collapse of credit bubble in 1784 led to depression.

**Shays's Rebellion**   An armed movement of debt-ridden farmers in western Massachusetts in the winter of 1786–1787. The rebellion created a crisis atmosphere.

●◆●─Read the Document

at www.myhistorylab.com
*Military Reports on Shays's
Rebellion (1787)*

Outside of western Massachusetts, discontented debtors generally stopped short of armed resistance because of their success in changing the monetary policy of their states. In 1785 and 1786, seven states enacted laws for new paper money issues. In most cases, the result was a qualified success. Controls on the supply of the new money kept it from depreciating rapidly, so that its inflationary effect was mild. Combined with laws that prevented or delayed creditors from seizing property from debtors to satisfy debts, the currency issues helped keep a lid on popular discontent.

The most notorious exception to this pattern of fiscal responsibility was in Rhode Island. A rural party that gained control of the Rhode Island legislature in 1786 pushed through a currency law that flooded the state with paper money that could be used to pay all debts. Creditors who balked at accepting the new money at face value were subject to heavy penalties. Shocked, they went into hiding or left the state entirely, and merchants denounced the law as outright fraud.

**Debtors versus conservatives.**    The actions of the debtor party in Rhode Island alarmed conservatives everywhere, confirming their fears that legislative bodies dominated by common farmers and artisans rather than, as before the Revolution, by men of wealth and social distinction, were dangerous. Conservatives, creditors, and nationalists alike now spoke of a democratic tyranny that would have to be checked if the republic were to survive and protect its property holders.

## CONGRESS AND THE WEST

The Peace of Paris and the surrender of charter claims by the states gave the Congress control of a magnificent expanse of land between the Appalachian Mountains and the Mississippi River. This was the first American West. In what would prove the most enduring accomplishment of the Confederation government, the Congress set forth a series of effective provisions for its settlement, governance, and eventual absorption into the Union.

Asserting for the national government the right to formulate Indian policy, the Congress negotiated a series of treaties with the Indians beginning in 1784 for the abandonment of their land claims in the West. By threatening to use military force, congressional commissioners in 1784 coerced the Iroquois Confederation of New York to cede half of its territory to the United States in the Treaty of Fort Stanwix. Similar tactics in 1785 resulted in the Treaty of Fort McIntosh, in which the Wyandots, Chippewas, Delawares, and Ottawas ceded much of their land in Ohio. Against the opposition of states intent on grabbing Indian lands for themselves, Congress resolved in 1787 that its treaties were binding on all the states. And anxious for revenue, Congress insisted on payment from squatters who had filtered into the West before provisions had been made for land sales.

The most pressing political challenge was to secure the loyalty of the West to the new and fragile Union. To satisfy the demands of settlers for self-government, the Congress resolved as early as 1779 that new states would be carved out of the western domain with all the rights of the original states. An early plan for organizing the territories, the Ordinance of 1784, was largely the work of Thomas Jefferson. In it, he proposed to create ten districts, or territories, each of which could apply for admission as a state when its population equaled that of the free inhabitants in the least populous of the existing states. Jefferson also proposed that settlers be permitted to choose their own officials, and he called for the prohibition of slavery in the West after 1800. Shorn of its no-slavery features, the ordinance passed Congress but was never put into practice.

As settlers and speculators began pouring into the West in 1784, however, the Congress was forced to move quickly to formulate a policy for

This clash between Shays's rebels and government troops at the Springfield arsenal marked the violent climax of the agrarian protests of the 1780s.

conveying its public land into private hands. If it could not regulate land sales and pass on clear titles, Congress would, in effect, have surrendered its claim to govern.

The Congress responded with the **Land Ordinance of 1785.** The crucial feature of this seminal legislation was its stipulation that public lands be surveyed in a rectangular grid pattern before being offered for sale (see Figure 7–3). By requiring that land first be platted into townships of 36 uniform sections of 640 acres each, the ordinance adopted the New England system of land settlement, an approach that promoted compact settlements and produced undisputed land titles.

Congress also attempted to attract a certain type of settler to the West by offering the plots of 640 acres at the then-hefty sum of no less than $640, or $1 per acre, payable in hard currency or its equivalent. The goal here was to keep out the shiftless poor and reserve the West for enterprising and presumably law-abiding farm families who could afford the entry cost. Concerned about westerners' reputation for lawlessness and afraid that the primitive living conditions might cause them to lapse into savagery, Congress also set aside the income from the sale of the sixteenth section in each township for the support of public schools.

Before any land sales occurred under the Ordinance of 1785, impatient settlers continued to push north of the Ohio River and claim homesteads as squatters. They clashed both with local Indian tribes and with the troops sent by the Congress to evict them. Impatient with the slow

**QUICK REVIEW**

**Congressional Indian Policy**

◆ Negotiated treaties for the abandonment of Indian land claims in the West.

◆ Made treaties binding on all states.

◆ Used the threat of military force to coerce Indians to cede their lands.

**Land Ordinance of 1785** Act passed by Congress under the Articles of Confederation that created the grid system of surveys by which all subsequent public land was made available for sale.

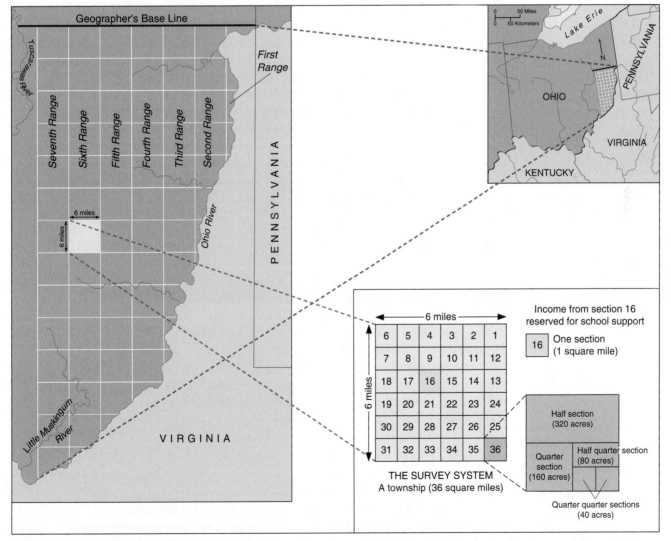

**FIGURE 7–3 Land Ordinance of 1785** The precise uniformity of the surveying system initiated in the Land Ordinance of 1785 created a rectangular grid pattern that was the model for all future land surveyed in the public domain.

process of surveying, the Congress sold off 1.5 million acres to a group of New England speculators organized as the Ohio Company. The speculators bought the land with greatly depreciated loan-office certificates that had been issued to Revolutionary War veterans, and their cost per acre averaged less than 10 cents in hard money. They now pressed their allies in Congress to establish a governmental structure for the West that would protect their investment by bringing the unruly elements in the West under control.

Both the Congress and speculators wanted political stability and economic development in the West and a degree of supervision for settlers. What was needed, wrote James Monroe of Virginia, were temporary controls—made acceptable by the promise of eventual statehood—that "in effect" would place the western territories under "a colonial government similar to that which prevail'd in these States previous to the revolution." The **Northwest Ordinance of 1787,** the most significant legislative act of the Confederation Congress, filled this need, creating a phased process for achieving statehood that neatly blended public and private interests.

According to the ordinance, controls on a new territory were to be strictest in the early stage of settlement, when Congress would appoint a territorial government consisting of a governor, a secretary, and three judges. When a territory reached a population of 5,000 adult males, those with 50 acres of land or more could elect a legislature. The actions of the legislature, however, were subject to an absolute veto by the governor. Once a territory had a population of 60,000, the settlers could draft a constitution and apply for statehood "on an equal footing with the original states in all respects whatsoever."

Most significant, it prohibited slavery. Southern congressmen agreed to the ban, in part because they saw little future for slavery in the region. More important, they expected slavery to be permitted in the region south of the Ohio River that was still under the administrative authority of Virginia, North Carolina, and Georgia in the 1780s. Indeed, slavery was allowed in this region when the **Southwest Ordinance of 1790** brought it under national control, a decision that would have grave consequences in the future sectionalization of the United States.

Although the Northwest Ordinance applied only to the national domain north of the Ohio River, it provided the organizational blueprint by which all future territory was brought into the Union. It went into effect immediately and set the original Union on a course of dynamic expansion through the addition of new states.

## DIPLOMATIC WEAKNESSES

**WHAT STEPS** did Britain and Spain take to block American expansion?

In the international arena of the 1780s, the United States was a weak and often ridiculed nation. Under the Articles of Confederation, the Congress had the authority to negotiate foreign treaties but no economic or military power to enforce their terms. Unable to regulate commerce or set tariffs, Congress had no leverage with which to pry open the restricted trading empires of France, Spain, and most important, Britain.

France and the United States, allies during the Revolutionary War, remained on friendly terms after it. Britain, however, treated its former colonies with contempt, and Spain was also openly antagonistic. Both of these powers sought to block American expansion into the trans-Appalachian West.

### IMPASSE WITH BRITAIN

The Confederation Congress was unable to resolve any of the major issues that poisoned Anglo-American relations in the 1780s. Key among those issues were provisions in the peace treaty of 1783 that concerned prewar American debts to the British and the treatment of Loyalists by the patriots. Britain used what it claimed to be America's failure to satisfy these provisions to justify its own violations of the treaty. The result was a diplomatic deadlock that hurt American interests in the West and in foreign trade.

---

**Northwest Ordinance of 1787**
Legislation that prohibited slavery in the Northwest Territories and provided the model for the incorporation of future territories into the union as coequal states.

**Southwest Ordinance of 1790**
Legislation passed by Congress that set up a government with no prohibition on slavery in U.S. territory south of the Ohio River.

#### QUICK REVIEW

**Slavery and New States**

- Northwest Ordinance of 1787 establishes political structure for new territories.
- Northwest Ordinance prohibited slavery in the Northwest.
- Southwest Ordinance of 1790 allowed slavery in the region south of the Ohio River.

Article 4 of the peace treaty called for the payment of all prewar debts at their "full value in sterling money"—that is, in gold or silver coin. Among the most numerous of those with outstanding debts to British creditors were tobacco planters in the Chesapeake region of Virginia and Maryland. During the Revolution, the British army had carried off and freed many of the region's slaves without compensating the planters. Still angry, the planters were in no mood to repay their debts. Working out a scheme with their respective legislatures, they agreed only to pay the face value of their debts to their state treasuries in state or Continental paper money. Since this money was practically worthless, the planters in effect repudiated their debts.

During the Revolution, all the states had passed anti-Loyalist legislation, and many state governments had seized Loyalists' lands and goods, selling them to raise revenue for the war effort. Articles 5 and 6 of the peace treaty pledged the Congress to "recommend" to the states that they stop persecuting Loyalists and restore confiscated Loyalist property. But wartime animosities remained high, ebbing only gradually during the 1780s. Thus, the states were slow to rescind their punitive legislation or allow the recovery of confiscated property.

Combined with the matter of the unpaid debts, the continued failure of the states to make restitution to the Loyalists gave the British a convenient pretext to hold on to the forts in the West that they had promised to relinquish in the Treaty of Paris. Their refusal to abandon the forts, which extended from Lake Champlain in upstate New York westward along the Great Lakes, was part of an overall strategy to keep the United States weak, divided, and small. The continued British presence in the region effectively shut Americans out of the fur trade with the Indians. Moreover, it insulted the sovereignty of the United States and threatened the security of its northern frontier.

For all of the British provocations in the West, American officials viewed Britain's retaliatory trade policies as the gravest threat to American security and prosperity. John Adams, the American minister to London, concluded that the British would never lift their trading and shipping restrictions until forced to do so by a uniform American system of discriminatory duties on British goods. Retaliatory navigation acts by individual states did little good because they left the British free to play one state against another. Only with a strong, centralized government could Americans fashion a navigation system that would command Britain's respect.

**QUICK REVIEW**

**British Foreign Policy**

- Britain sought to keep the United States small, divided, and weak.
- Maintained forts in the West.
- Exploited divisions among Americans.
- Pursued retaliatory trade policies.

## SPAIN AND THE MISSISSIPPI RIVER

At the close of the Revolutionary War, Spain reimposed barriers on American commerce within its empire. Spain also refused to recognize the southern and western boundaries of the United States as specified in the treaty with Britain in 1783, holding out instead for a more northerly border. And of greatest consequence, it denied the claim of the United States to free navigation of the entire length of the Mississippi River.

The Mississippi question was explosive because on its resolution hinged American settlement and control of the entire western region south of the Ohio River. Only with access to the Mississippi and the commercial right of deposit at New Orleans—that is, the right to transfer cargoes to oceangoing vessels—could the region's farmers, then mostly in what would become Tennessee and Kentucky, profitably reach national and international markets.

In the wake of the Revolution, the settlers of Kentucky, which was still part of Virginia, and Tennessee, which was still part of North Carolina, flirted with the idea of secession. Impatient to secure both political independence and the economic benefits that would come with access to the Mississippi, the separatists were not particular about whom they dealt with. They became entangled in a web of diplomatic intrigue that included the Spanish, the Indians, and American officials east of the mountains.

Spain sought to use the divided loyalties of American speculators and frontier settlers to its advantage, employing some of them as spies and informers. Spain likewise sought to exploit divisions among Indian groups. In a bewildering variety of treaties negotiated by the Congress, individual southern states, and land speculators, white Americans laid claim to much of the

## GLOBAL CONNECTIONS

### ∽ FOREIGN THREATS ∾

"*I think I have done all possible to make it possible for the Government of New Orleans to reap benefit from the present situation of the United States. . . . These people intend to live on friendly terms with Spain and we no longer hear the threats we formerly heard . . . we must not neglect them. I think time will bring them to the King.*"

In this letter of 1788 to the Spanish secretary of state, Don Diego de Gardoqui, the Spanish representative in Philadelphia, outlined Spain's efforts in the 1780s to detach the American settlements in Kentucky from the United States and draw them into an economic alliance with Spanish Louisiana. The goal was to protect Louisiana by both weakening the United States and expanding trading opportunities for the American goods and services desired by the Spanish subjects of Louisiana. Westward expansion by Americans was inevitable, but Spain hoped to control it and turn it to its advantage by offering trading rights on the Mississippi River that would lead to a partnership with the Spanish colony in New Orleans.

The efforts of Spain to draw Kentuckians into its empire, combined with the presence of the British in Canada and the willingness of both of these foreign powers to subsidize Native Americans as they fought to protect their tribal lands against encroachments by white settlers, threatened any effective American control of the trans-Appalachian territory. Meanwhile, British trading restrictions had largely succeeded in reducing the United States to a colonial dependency that furnished British factories with cheap raw materials and purchased British-made goods delivered in British ships. In struggling to establish its sovereign rights in a world of hostile imperial powers, the United States under the Articles of Confederation suffered the crippling disadvantage of lacking any means of formulating or implementing a uniform policy for its defense. More so than any of the other delegates at the Constitutional Convention, Alexander Hamilton drew the obvious conclusion. "You have to protect your rights against Canada in the north, Spain in the south, and your western frontier against the savages. . . . No Government could give us tranquility and happiness at home, which did not possess sufficient strength and stability to make us respectable abroad." Like any new nation confronted with threats to its security, the United States could not afford the luxury or indulge in the utopian hope of dispensing with power politics.

• How could Spain try to control the westward expansion of America and use that expansion to its advantage?

ancestral land of the major Indian nations in the Southeast. Fraud was rampant, and many Native Americans believed, with good reason, that they had never been consulted in the dispossession of their land. The Spanish responded by recruiting disaffected Indians into an alliance system of their own. Their staunchest allies came from a faction of the Creeks led by Alexander McGillivray, the son of a trader father and a half-French, half-Creek mother. Supplied with arms by the Spanish, these Creeks succeeded in forcing white settlers off their tribal land in Georgia.

Spain stepped up pressure on the West in the summer of 1784, when it closed the Mississippi River within Spanish territory to American trade. Hoping now to benefit from American weakness, Spain also opened negotiations for a long-term settlement with the United States. The Spanish negotiator, Don Diego de Gardoqui, offered a deal that cleverly played the interests of the North against those of the South and West. In exchange for an American agreement to surrender claims to navigate the Mississippi for the next thirty years, Gardoqui proposed to grant the United States significant trading concessions in the Spanish Empire that would open new markets and new sources of hard money to the financially pressed merchants of the northeastern states. John Jay, his American negotiating partner, reluctantly accepted the offer.

When Jay released the terms of the proposed treaty with Spain in 1786, southerners who had taken the lead in the settlement of the West, accused Jay of selling out their interests. The treaty threatened the agrarian alliance they hoped to forge with the West, increasing the odds that the West would break from the East and go its own way. Vowing that they would not surrender the West, southern congressmen united to defeat the treaty.

The regional antagonisms exposed by the Jay-Gardoqui talks heightened the alarm over the future of the republic provoked by Shays's Rebellion earlier in 1786. As the sense of crisis deepened in 1786, the nationalists grew in influence and numbers. Led by Alexander Hamilton of New York and James Madison of Virginia, they now argued that only a radical political change could preserve the republic and fulfill the promise of its greatness.

# TOWARD A NEW UNION

In September 1786, delegates from several states met at the **Annapolis Convention,** in Annapolis, Maryland, seeking to devise a uniform system of commercial regulation for the country. While there, a group of nationalist leaders issued a call for a convention at Philadelphia "to devise such further provisions as shall appear to them necessary to render the constitution of the Federal Government adequate to the exigencies of the Union." The leaders who met at the **Constitutional Convention** in Philadelphia forged an entirely new framework of governance, the **Constitution of the United States,** which called for a federal republic with a powerful and effective national government. In 1788, after a close struggle in state ratifying conventions, the Constitution was adopted.

**WHICH GROUPS** in American society were most likely to support the Constitution? Why?

**Annapolis Convention** Conference of state delegates at Annapolis, Maryland, that issued a call in September 1786 for a convention to meet at Philadelphia to consider fundamental changes.

**Constitutional Convention** Convention that met in Philadelphia in 1787 and drafted the Constitution of the United States.

**Constitution of the United States** The written document providing for a new central government of the United States.

## THE ROAD TO PHILADELPHIA

Only nine states sent delegates to the Annapolis Convention, and only those from five states had actually arrived when the nationalists, at the prompting of James Madison and Alexander Hamilton, abruptly adjourned the meeting. They then called on the states and the Congress to approve a full-scale constitutional convention for Philadelphia in May 1787.

The timing of the call for the Philadelphia Convention could not have been better. During the fall and winter of 1786, the agrarian protests unleashed by Shays's Rebellion in Massachusetts spilled over into other states. Coupled with talk of a dismemberment of the Union in the wake of the Jay-Gardoqui negotiations, the agrarian unrest strengthened the case of the nationalists for more centralized authority.

All the states except Rhode Island, which wanted to retain exclusive control over its own trade, sent delegates to Philadelphia. The fifty-five men who attended the convention represented an extraordinary array of talent and experience. Chiefly lawyers by training or profession, most had served in the Confederation Congress, and more than one-third had fought in the Revolution. Extremely well educated by the standards of the day, the delegates were members of the intellectual as well as the political and economic elite. As a group, they were far wealthier than the average American. Most had investments in land and the public securities of the United States. At least nineteen owned slaves. Their greatest asset as a working body was their common commitment to a nationalist solution to the crisis of confidence they saw gripping the republic. Most of the strong supporters of the Articles of Confederation refused to attend.

**WHERE TO LEARN MORE**

Independence National Historical Park, Philadelphia, Pennsylvania
http://www.nps.gov/inde/index.htm

## THE CONVENTION AT WORK

When it agreed to the Philadelphia Convention, the Congress authorized only a revision of the Articles of Confederation. Almost from the start, however, the delegates set about replacing the Articles altogether. The most ardent nationalists immediately seized the initiative by presenting the **Virginia Plan.** Drafted by James Madison, this plan replaced the Confederation Congress with a truly national government, organized like most of the state governments with a bicameral legislature, an executive, and a judiciary.

Two features of the Virginia Plan stood out. First, it granted the national Congress power to legislate "in all cases in which the separate states are incompetent" and to nullify any state laws that in its judgment were contrary to the "articles of Union." Second, it made representation in both houses of the Congress proportional to population. This meant that the most

**Virginia Plan** Proposal calling for a national legislature in which the states would be represented according to population.

This portrait, sketched in about 1790 by John Trumbull, is the only known likeness of Alexander McGillivray, a Creek leader who effectively played off Spanish and American interests in the Southeast to gain a measure of independence for the Creeks in the 1780s.

**New Jersey Plan**    Proposal of the New Jersey delegation for a strengthened national government in which all states would have an equal representation in a unicameral legislature.

●●●—⌐Read the Document
at www.myhistorylab.com
*The New Jersey Plan (1787)*

●●●—⌐Read the Document
at www.myhistorylab.com
*The Virginia Plan (1787)*

**Great Compromise**    Plan proposed at the 1787 Constitutional Convention for creating a national bicameral legislature in which all states would be equally represented in the Senate and proportionally represented in the House.

populous states would have more votes in Congress than the less populous states, giving them effective control of the government.

Delegates from the small states countered with the **New Jersey Plan,** introduced on June 15 by William Paterson. This plan kept intact the basic structure of the Confederation Congress—one state, one vote—but otherwise amended the Articles by giving the national government the explicit power to tax and to regulate domestic and foreign commerce. In addition, it gave acts of Congress precedence over state legislation, making them "the supreme law of the respective states."

**The Great Compromise.**    The New Jersey Plan was quickly voted down, and the convention remained deadlocked for another month over how to apportion state representation in the national government. The issue was finally resolved on July 16 with the so-called **Great Compromise.** Small states were given equal footing with large states in the Senate, or upper house, where each would have two votes. In the lower house, the House of Representatives, the number of seats was made proportional to population, giving larger states the advantage. The Great Compromise also settled a sectional dispute over representation between the free (or about to be free) states and the slave states. The southern states wanted slaves counted for apportioning representation in the House but excluded from direct tax assessments. The northern states wanted slaves counted for tax assessments but excluded for apportioning representation. To settle the issue, the Great Compromise settled on an expedient, if morally troubling, formula: Free residents were to be counted precisely; to that count would be added, "excluding Indians not taxed, three-fifths of all other persons (meaning enslaved blacks)." Thus the slave states gained additional political representation, while the states in the North received assurance that the owners of nonvoting slaves would have to bear part of the cost of any direct taxes levied by the new government.

The Great Compromise ended the first phase of the convention, which had focused on the general framework of a stronger national government. In its next phase, the convention debated the specific powers to be delegated to the new government. It was at this point that the sectional cleavage between North and South over slavery and other issues came most prominently to the fore.

**Regulation of commerce and the issue of slavery.**    The sectional clash first erupted over the power of Congress to regulate commerce. At issue was whether Congress could regulate trade and set tariffs by a simple majority vote. Southerners worried that a northern majority would pass navigation acts favoring northern shippers and drive up the cost of sending southern commodities to Europe. To counter this threat, delegates from the Lower South demanded that a two-thirds majority be required to enact trade legislation.

In the end, the delegates agreed that enacting trade legislation would require only a simple majority. In return, however, southerners exacted concessions on the slavery issue. When planters from South Carolina and Georgia made it clear that they would agree to join a new Union only if they could continue to import slaves, the convention abandoned a proposal to ban the foreign slave trade. Instead, Congress would be barred from acting against the slave trade for twenty years. In addition, bowing to the fears of planters that Congress could use its taxing power to undermine slavery, the convention denied Congress the right to tax exports from any state. And to alleviate southern concerns that slaves might escape to freedom in the North, the new

Constitution included an explicit provision calling on the states to return "persons held to Service or Labour" in any other state.

**The office of the chief executive.**    After settling the slavery question, the convention had one last significant hurdle to clear: the question of the national executive. In large part because of their confidence in George Washington, whom nearly everyone expected to be the first president, the delegates fashioned a chief executive office with broad discretionary powers. The prerogatives of the president included the rank of commander in chief of the armed forces, the authority to conduct foreign affairs and negotiate treaties, the right to appoint diplomatic and judicial officers, and the power to veto congressional legislation. The president's term of office was set at four years, with no limits on how often an individual could be reelected.

Determining how to elect the president proved a thorny problem. The delegates envisioned a forceful, energetic, and independent executive, insulated from the whims of an uninformed public and the intrigues of the legislature. As a result, they rejected both popular election and election by Congress. The solution they hit upon was the convoluted system of an "electoral college." Each state was left free to determine how it would choose presidential electors equal to the number of its representatives and senators. These electors would then vote by ballot for two persons. The person receiving a majority of all the electoral votes would become president and the second highest vote-getter the vice president. If no candidate received a majority of the electoral votes, the election would be turned over to the House of Representatives, where each state would have one vote.

## OVERVIEW OF THE CONSTITUTION

Although not as strong as the most committed nationalists would have liked, the central government outlined in the Constitution was to have far more powers than were entrusted to Congress under the Articles of Confederation (see the Overview table, The Articles of Confederation and the Constitution Compared). The Constitution's provision for a strong, single-person executive had no precedent in the Articles. Nor did the provision for a Supreme Court. The Constitution vested this court, as well as the lower courts that Congress was empowered to establish, with the judicial power of the United States. In addition, the Constitution specifically delegated to Congress the powers to tax, borrow and coin money, regulate commerce, and raise armed forces, all of which the Confederation government had lacked.

Most of the economic powers of Congress came at the expense of the states. Further curbing the sovereignty of the states was a clause stipulating that the Constitution and all national legislation and treaties were to be "the supreme law of the land." This clause has subsequently been interpreted as giving the central government the power to declare state laws unconstitutional.

A no-nonsense realism, as well as a nationalist outlook, infused the Constitution. Its underlying political philosophy was that, in Madison's wonderful phrase, "ambition must be made to counter ambition." Madison and the other members of the national elite who met at Philadelphia were convinced that self-interest, not disinterested virtue, motivated political behavior. Accepting interest-group politics as inevitable and seeking to prevent a tyrannical majority from forming at the national level, the architects of the Constitution designed a central government in which competing blocs of power counterbalanced one another.

The Constitution placed both internal and external restraints on the powers granted to the central government. The functional division of the government into executive, legislative, and judicial branches, each with ways to keep the others from exercising excessive power, created an internal system of checks and balances.

**QUICK REVIEW**

**Checks on Executive Power**

- Senate given the authority to approve or reject presidential appointments.
- Congress, not the president, given the power to declare war.
- Congress given the power to override presidential vetoes.

◆▶ **Read the Document**

at **www.myhistorylab.com**
*The Constitution of the United States of America (1789), page A-5*

◆▶ **Read the Document**

at **www.myhistorylab.com**
*From Then to Now Online: Reshaping the Constitution*

## OVERVIEW    The Articles of Confederation and the Constitution Compared

| | Articles | Constitution |
| --- | --- | --- |
| Sovereign power of central government | No power to tax or raise armies | Power granted on taxes and armed forces |
| Source of power | Individual states | Shared through federalism between states and national government |
| Representation in Congress | Equal representation of states in unicameral Congress | Bicameral legislature with equal representation of states in Senate and proportional representation in House |
| Amendment process | Unanimous consent of states | Consent of three-fourths of states |
| Executive | None provided for | Office of president |
| National judiciary | None provided for | Supreme Court |

**judicial review**    A power implied in the Constitution that gives federal courts the right to review and determine the constitutionality of acts passed by Congress and state legislature.

**federalism**    The sharing of powers between the national government and the states.

**◉ Watch the Video**

at **www.myhistorylab.com**
*Slavery and the Constitution*

**•◦• Read the Document**

at **www.myhistorylab.com**
*Exploring America:*
*Ratification of the Constitution*

**•◦• Read the Document**

at **www.myhistorylab.com**
*Patrick Henry against Ratification of the Constitution (1788)*

**Federalists**    A supporter of the **Constitution** who favored its ratification.

Although the Constitution did not explicitly grant it, the Supreme Court soon claimed the right to invalidate acts of Congress and the president that it found to be unconstitutional. This power of **judicial review** provided another check against legislative and executive authority (see Chapter 9). To guard against an arbitrary federal judiciary, the Constitution empowered Congress to determine the size of the Supreme Court and to impeach and remove federal judges appointed by the president.

The external restraints on the central government were to be found in the nature of its relationship to the state governments. This relationship was based on **federalism,** the division of power between local and central authorities. By listing specific powers for Congress, the Constitution implied that all other powers were to be retained by the states. Thus, while strengthening the national government, the Constitution did not obliterate the sovereign rights of the states, leaving them free to curb the potential power of the national government in the ambiguous areas between national and state sovereignty.

This ambiguity in the federalism of the Constitution was both its greatest strength and its greatest weakness. It allowed both nationalists and advocates of states' rights to support the Constitution. But the issue of slavery, left unresolved in the gray area between state and national sovereignty, would continue to fester, sparking sectional conflict over the extent of national sovereignty that would plunge the republic into civil war three-quarters of a century later.

## THE STRUGGLE OVER RATIFICATION

The last article of the Constitution stipulated that it would go into effect when it had been ratified by at least nine of the states acting through specially elected popular conventions. Congress, influenced by the nationalist sentiments of many of its members, one-third of whom had attended the Philadelphia Convention, and perhaps weary of its own impotence, accepted this drastic and not clearly legal procedure, submitting the Constitution to the states in late September 1787.

The delegates in Philadelphia had excluded the public from their proceedings. The publication of the Constitution lifted the veil of secrecy and touched off a great political debate. Although those who favored the Constitution could most accurately have been defined as nationalists, they referred to themselves as **Federalists,** a term that helped deflect charges that they favored an excessive centralization of political authority. By default, the opponents of the Constitution were known as **Antifederalists,** a negative-sounding label that obscured their support of the state-centered sovereignty that most Americans associated with federalism. Initially outmaneuvered in this way, the Antifederalists never did mount an effective campaign to counter the Federalists' pamphlets, speeches, and newspaper editorials (see the Overview table, Federalists Versus Antifederalists). The Antifederalists did attract some men of wealth and social standing. Most Antifederalists, however, were backcountry farmers, men with mud on their boots who lived far from centers of communication and market outlets for their produce. The Antifederalists clung to the belief that only a small republic, one composed of relatively homogeneous social interests, could secure the voluntary attachment of the people necessary for a free government. They argued that a large republic, such as the one framed by the Constitution, would inevitably become tyrannical because it was too distant and removed from the interests of common citizen-farmers.

However much the Antifederalists attacked the Constitution as a danger to the individual liberties and local independence that they believed the Revolution had been fought to safeguard, they were no political match for the Federalists. They lacked the wealth, social connections, access to newspapers, and self-confidence of the more cosmopolitan and better-educated Federalists. In addition, the Federalists could more easily mobilize their supporters, who were concentrated in the port cities and commercial farming areas along the coast. Conservatives shaken by Shays's Rebellion lined up behind the Constitution. So, too, did groups—creditors, merchants, manufacturers, urban artisans, commercial farmers—whose interests would be promoted by economic development.

In the early stages, the Federalists scored a string of easy victories. Delaware ratified the Constitution on December 7, 1787, and within a month, so, too, had Pennsylvania, New Jersey, Georgia, and Connecticut.

The Federalists faced their toughest challenge in the large states that had generally been more successful in going it alone during the 1780s. One of the most telling arguments of the Antifederalists in these and other states was the absence of a bill of rights in the Constitution. Realizing the importance of the issue, and citing Article 5 of the Constitution, which provided for an amendment process, the Federalists promised to recommend amending the Constitution with a bill of rights once it was ratified. By doing so, they split the ranks of the Antifederalists in Massachusetts. After the Federalists gained the support of two venerable heroes of the Revolution, John Hancock and Sam Adams, the Massachusetts convention approved the Constitution by a close vote in February 1788.

The major hurdles remaining for the Federalists were Virginia, the most populous state, and strategically located New York. To eke out victory in these crucial states, the Federalists drew on their pragmatism and persuasiveness. As in Massachusetts, they were helped by their promise of a bill of rights. And for the New York campaign, Madison, Jay, and Hamilton wrote an eloquent series of eighty-five essays known collectively as *The Federalist* to allay fears that the Constitution would so consolidate national power as to menace individual liberties. In the two most original and brilliant essays in *The Federalist*, essays 10 and 51, Madison turned traditional republican doctrine on its head. A large, diverse republic like the one envisaged by the Constitution, he reasoned,

**Antifederalists**  Opponents of the **Constitution** in the debate over its ratification.

**Read** the **Document**
at **www.myhistorylab.com**
*James Madison, Defends the Constitution (1788)*

**Read** the **Document**
at **www.myhistorylab.com**
*The Federalist No. 51 (1788)*

This c. 1790 folk art depiction of Washington and his wife reveals how quickly Washington's fame became part of the public consciousness and made him the obvious choice to preside over the Constitutional Convention.

## OVERVIEW Federalists versus Antifederalists

| | Federalists | Antifederalists |
|---|---|---|
| Position on Constitution | Favored Constitution | Opposed Constitution |
| Position on Articles of Confederation | Felt Articles had to be abandoned | Felt Articles needed only to be amended |
| Position on power of the states | Sought to curb power of states with new central government | Felt power of states should be paramount |
| Position on need for bill of rights | Initially saw no need for bill of rights in Constitution | Saw absence of bill of rights in proposed Constitution as threat to individual liberties |
| Position on optimum size of republic | Believed large republic could best safeguard personal freedoms | Believed only a small republic formed on common interests could protect individual rights |
| Source of support | Commercial farmers, merchants, shippers, artisans, holders of national debt | State-centered politicians, most backcountry farmers |

not a small and homogeneous one, offered the best hope for safeguarding the rights of all citizens. This was because a large republic would include a multitude of contending interest groups, making it difficult for any combination of them to coalesce into a tyrannical majority that could oppress minority rights. With this argument, Madison had developed a political rationale by which Americans could have both an empire and personal freedom.

North Carolina and Rhode Island did not ratify the Constitution until after the new government was functioning. North Carolina joined the Union in 1789 once Congress submitted the amendments that constituted the Bill of Rights. The obstinate Rhode Islanders stayed out until 1790, when Congress forced them in with a threat of commercial reprisal.

## CONCLUSION

In freeing themselves from British rule, Americans embarked on an unprecedented wave of constitution-making that sought to put into practice abstract principles of republicanism that held that political power should derive from the people. Between 1776 and 1780, Americans developed a unique system of constitutionalism that went far beyond the British model of an unwritten constitution. They proclaimed the supremacy of constitutions over ordinary legislation, detailed the powers of government in a written document, provided protection for individual freedoms in bills of rights, and fashioned a process for framing governments through the election of delegates to a special constitutional convention and the popular ratification of the work of that convention. In all of these areas, Americans were pioneers in demonstrating to the rest of the world how common citizens could create their own governments.

In dealing with the legacy of slavery, however, white Americans were far more cautious, and most denied that their revolutionary experience included African Americans and should embrace black emancipation. Moses Sash and other African Americans, in keeping alive the dream of full black freedom, refused to passively accept the dictates of white authority. The revolution within a revolution they fought for was put off to the indefinite future by the delegates at the Constitutional

Convention in 1787. Instead, they focused on achieving a peaceful, political revolution in securing the ratification of the Constitution. Their victory in creating a new central government with real national powers was built on the foundation of constitutional concepts and mechanisms that Americans had laid down in their state constitutions. The new Constitution rested on the consent of the governed, and it endured because it could be amended to reflect shifts in popular will and to widen the circle of Americans granted the rights of political citizenship and the enjoyment of liberty.

Accepting as a given that self-interest drove political action, the framers of the Constitution designed the new national government to turn ambition against itself. They created rival centers of power that forced selfish factions to compete in a constant struggle to form a workable majority. The struggle occurred both within the national government and between that government and the states in the American system of federalism. The Constitution thus set the stage for an entirely new kind of national politics.

# WHERE TO LEARN MORE

**South Street Seaport Museum, New York City, New York.** Maritime commerce was the lifeblood of the postrevolutionary economy. The artifacts and exhibits here offer a fine introduction to the seafaring world of the port city that became the nation's first capital in the new federal Union. See http://seany.org for more on the impact of trade on the development of New York and information on preservation projects underway in the city.

**Independence National Historical Park, Philadelphia, Pennsylvania.** Walks and guided tours through this historic district enable one to grasp much of the physical setting in which the delegates to the Constitutional Convention met. The website http://www.nps.gov/inde/index.htm includes a virtual tour of many of the collections at the park, a portrait gallery of leading figures in the Revolution, and a look at the archaeological projects underway in the park.

**Northern Indiana Center for History, South Bend, Indiana.** The permanent exhibition on the St. Joseph River valley of northern Indiana and southern Michigan explains the material world of this region and how it changed as first Europeans and then Americans mingled and clashed with the Native American population. At http://www.centerforhistory.org one can learn more about the center and the variety of programs it offers.

# REVIEW QUESTIONS

1. How did the Shaysites justify their taking up arms against the government of Massachusetts? Can you imagine any way in which the crisis could have been resolved short of violence?

2. Why do you think that the U.S. Constitution does not cite God or mention religion in any direct way?

3. What was so unprecedented about the new state constitutions, and what principles of government did they embody? What provisions do you think were made for the newly freed African Americans?

4. What were the problems of the economy in the 1780s, and why did clashes between debtors and creditors become so divisive? Do you think that an economic recovery could have been achieved under the Articles of Confederation?

5. Do you feel that the diplomatic weaknesses of the United States under the Articles were as serious as its internal problems? What were the sources of those weaknesses, and what threat did they pose for national unity?

6. What sorts of men drafted the Constitution in 1787, and how representative were they of all Americans? What explains the differences between the Federalists and the Antifederalists? Do you think they shared the same vision of what they wanted America to become? How widespread was the popular backing for the Constitution, and what accounts for its ratification?

7. Compare and contrast the options open to the United States in the 1780s in developing its economy with those of the new nations that have also emerged out of former colonial empires since World War II.

# KEY TERMS

# PEARSON myhistorylab™ Connections

Reinforce what you learned in this chapter by studying the many documents, images, maps, review tools, and videos available at **www.myhistorylab.com**.

## Read and Review

✓ ● Study and Review **Study Plan: Chapter 7**

●●● Read the Document

*Debates in the Federal Convention (1787)*

*James Madison Defends the Constitution (1788)*

*Patrick Henry against Ratification of the Constitution (1788)*

*A Free African American Petitions the Government for Emancipation of All Slaves (1777)*

*Alexander Hamilton, John Jay, and James Madison, The Federalist Papers (1787–1788)*

*The Federalist No. 51 (1788)*

*James Madison, The Virginia (or Randolph) Plan (1787)*

*Military Reports on Shays's Rebellion (1787)*

*The New Jersey Plan (1787)*

*Thomas Jefferson, Notes on the State of Virginia (1787)*

*Virginia Constitution (1776)*

*The New Jersey Plan (1787)*

*The Virginia Plan (1787)*

## Research and Explore

●●● Read the Document

*Personal Journeys Online*

*From Then to Now Online: Reshaping the Constitution*

*Are you an Anti-Federalist?*

*Exploring America: Ratification of the Constitution*

● Watch the Video *Slavery and the Constitution*

## ((●● Hear the Audio

Hear the audio files for Chapter 7 at
**www.myhistorylab.com**.

# 8

# A New Republic and the Rise of Parties

Washington's Triumphal Entry Into New York. A tapestry, of George Washington and his retinue riding into New York amid cheering crowds standing on a street and balconies.

((●•─ Hear the Audio

Hear the audio files for Chapter 8 at www.myhistorylab.com.

## WASHINGTON'S AMERICA  *(page 197)*

**WHAT EXPLAINS** the differing role of slavery in the country's regional economies?

## FORGING A NEW GOVERNMENT  *(page 202)*

**WHAT CHALLENGES** faced the Congress that assembled in New York between 1789 and 1791?

## THE EMERGENCE OF PARTIES  *(page 206)*

**WHAT FORCES** shaped the development of party politics in America?

## THE LAST FEDERALIST ADMINISTRATION  *(page 212)*

**WHY WAS** Adams defeated in the election of 1800?

ONE AMERICAN JOURNEY

*April 30, 1789*

*New York City*

*This is the great important day. Goddess of Etiquette assist me while I describe it. . . . The President was conducted out of the middle window into the Gallery [of Federal Hall] and the Oath administered by the Chancellor [Robert R. Livingston, Chancellor of New York]. Notice that the Business was done, was communicated to the Croud by Proclamation . . . who gave three Cheers. . . . As the Company returned into the Senate Chamber, the president took the Chair, and the Senate and representatives their Seats. He rose & all arose also and [he] addressed them [in his inaugural address]. This great Man was agitated and embarrassed more than ever he was by the levelled Cannon or pointed Musket. He trembled and several times could scarce make out to read, tho it must be supposed he had often read it before. He put part of the fingers of his left hand, into the side, of what I think the Taylors call the fall, of his Breetches. Changing the paper into his left hand, after some time, he then did the same with some of the fingers of his right hand. When he came to the Words all the World, he made a flourish with his right hand, which left rather an ungainly impression. . . . He was dressed in deep brown, with Metal buttons, with an Eagle on them, White Stockings a Bag and Sword—from the Hall there was a grand Procession to St. Pauls Church where prayers were said by the Bishop. The Procession was well conducted and without accident, as far as I have heard. The Militias were all under Arms. [They] lined the Street near the Church, made a good figure and behaved well. The Senate returned to their Chamber after Service, formed & took up the Address. . . . In the Evening there were grand fire Works . . . and after this the People went to bed.*

[William Maclay]

Kenneth R. Bowling and Helen E. Veit, eds., *The Diary of William Maclay and Other Notes on Senate Debates,* March 4, 1789–March 3, 1791 (Baltimore: Johns Hopkins University Press, 1988), pp. 11–13.

◆━ Read the Document at **www.myhistorylab.com**

Personal Journeys Online

- New York *Daily Advertiser,* April 24, 1789. Newspaper description of Washington's arrival in New York.

- Tobias Lear, Diary, April 30, 1789. Account of presidential procession for Washington's inauguration.

- George Washington, Excerpts from the First Inaugural Address, April 30, 1789.

SENATOR WILLIAM MACLAY of Pennsylvania wrote this account in his personal journal of the inauguration of George Washington as the first president of the United States at Federal Hall in New York City on April 30, 1789. A Presbyterian with a strong sense of rectitude that often made him overly critical of others, he was one of the first of the original Federalists to break with the Washington administration over its fiscal and diplomatic policies.

Washington's shakiness at his inaugural was understandable. He had every reason to dread taking on the burden of the presidency. As head of the new national government, he would put at risk the legendary status he had achieved during the Revolution. Most Americans intensely feared centralized authority, which is why the framers deliberately left the word *national* out of the Constitution. Washington somehow had to establish loyalty to a new government whose main virtue in the eyes of many was the very vagueness of its defined powers.

The Constitution had created the framework for a national government, but pressing problems demanded the fleshing out of that framework. The government urgently needed revenue to begin paying off the immense debt incurred during the Revolution. It also had to address the unstable conditions in the West, where the settlers wavered in their loyalties. Ultimately, the key to solving these and other problems was to inspire popular backing for the government's authority. ✦

## WASHINGTON'S AMERICA

The Americans whom Washington was called on to lead were hardly one unified people. They identified and grouped themselves according to many factors, including race, sex, class, ethnicity, religion, and degree of personal freedom. Geographical factors, including climate and access to markets, further divided them into regions and sections. The resulting hodgepodge sorely tested the assumption—and it was never more than an assumption in 1789—that a single national government could govern Americans as a whole (see Figure 8–1).

**WHAT EXPLAINS** the differing role of slavery in the country's regional economies?

### THE UNIFORMITY OF NEW ENGLAND

The national census of 1790 counted nearly 4 million Americans, one in four of whom lived in New England. Although often viewed as the most typically "American" part of the young nation, New England in fact was rather atypical. It alone of the nation's formative regions had largely shut itself off from outsiders. The Puritan notions of religious liberty that prevailed in the region extended only to those who subscribed to the Calvinist orthodoxy of the dominant Congregationalist Church. Geography conspired with this religious exclusiveness to limit

## CHRONOLOGY

| | |
|---|---|
| **1789** | Inauguration of Washington. |
| | Congress establishes the first federal departments. |
| | French Revolution begins. |
| **1790** | Hamilton submits the first of his financial reports to Congress. |
| **1791** | Bill of Rights ratified. |
| | Congress charters the Bank of the United States. |
| | Slave revolt breaks out in Saint-Domingue (Haiti). |
| **1792** | St. Clair's defeat along the Wabash. |
| | Reelection of Washington. |
| | Austria and Prussia invade France. |
| | Execution of King Louis XVI. |
| **1793** | France goes to war against Britain, Spain, and Holland. |
| | Genêt Mission. |
| | Washington issues Proclamation of Neutrality. |
| **1794** | Ohio is opened with the victory of General Anthony Wayne at the Battle of Fallen Timbers. |

| | |
|---|---|
| | Suppression of the Whiskey Rebellion in western Pennsylvania. |
| **1795** | Jay's Treaty with Britain ratified. |
| | Treaty of Greenville with Ohio Indians. |
| **1796** | Pinckney's Treaty with Spain ratified. |
| | Washington's Farewell Address. |
| | John Adams elected president. |
| **1797** | Beginning of the Quasi-War with France. |
| **1798** | XYZ Affair. |
| | Alien and Sedition Acts. |
| | Provisional army and direct tax. |
| | Virginia and Kentucky Resolutions. |
| **1799** | Fries's Rebellion in Pennsylvania. |
| | Napoleon assumes power in France. |
| **1800** | Franco-American Accord. |
| | Thomas Jefferson elected president. |

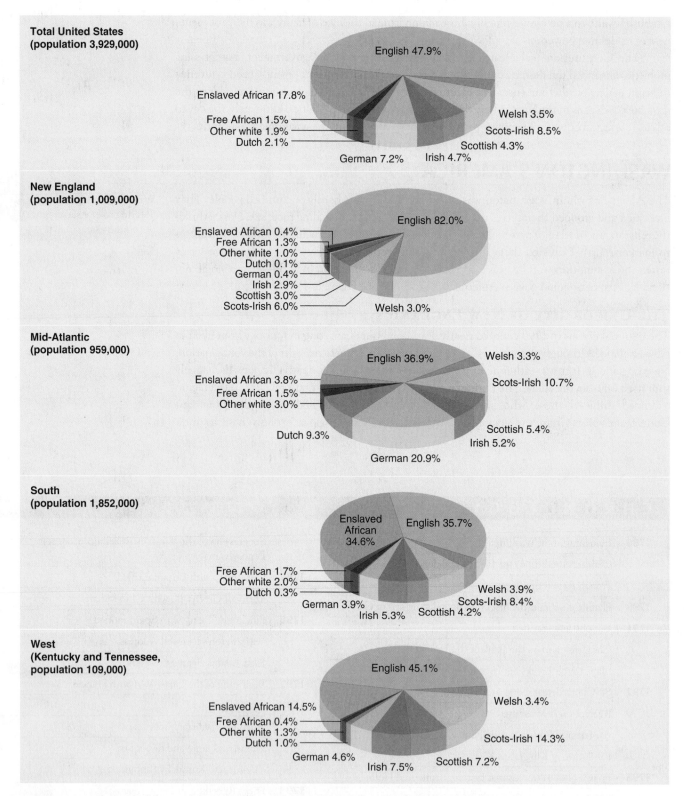

**Total United States**
**(population 3,929,000)**
English 47.9%
Enslaved African 17.8%
Free African 1.5%
Other white 1.9%
Dutch 2.1%
German 7.2%
Irish 4.7%
Scottish 4.3%
Scots-Irish 8.5%
Welsh 3.5%

**New England**
**(population 1,009,000)**
English 82.0%
Enslaved African 0.4%
Free African 1.3%
Other white 1.0%
Dutch 0.1%
German 0.4%
Irish 2.9%
Scottish 3.0%
Scots-Irish 6.0%
Welsh 3.0%

**Mid-Atlantic**
**(population 959,000)**
English 36.9%
Welsh 3.3%
Enslaved African 3.8%
Free African 1.5%
Other white 3.0%
Scots-Irish 10.7%
Scottish 5.4%
Irish 5.2%
Dutch 9.3%
German 20.9%

**South**
**(population 1,852,000)**
Enslaved African 34.6%
English 35.7%
Free African 1.7%
Other white 2.0%
Dutch 0.3%
German 3.9%
Irish 5.3%
Scottish 4.2%
Scots-Irish 8.4%
Welsh 3.9%

**West**
**(Kentucky and Tennessee,**
**population 109,000)**
English 45.1%
Welsh 3.4%
Enslaved African 14.5%
Free African 0.4%
Other white 1.3%
Dutch 1.0%
German 4.6%
Irish 7.5%
Scottish 7.2%
Scots-Irish 14.3%

FIGURE 8–1    **Ethnic Breakdown of the United States in 1790, by Region**    Unique racial and ethnic patterns shaped each of the nation's four major regions in 1790. New England was most atypical in its lack of racial or ethnic diversity.

*Data Source: The Statistics of the Population of the United States,* comp. Francis A. Walker (1872), pp. 3–7; Thomas L. Purvis, "The European Ancestry of the United States Population, 1790," *William and Mary Quarterly,* 41(1984), p. 98.

population diversity. New England's poor soils and long, cold winters made it an impractical place to cultivate cash crops like the tobacco and rice of the South. As a result, New England farmers had little need of imported white indentured servants or black slaves. Puritan values and a harsh environment thus combined to make New England the most religiously and ethnically uniform region in the United States. Most of the people living there were descended from English immigrants who had arrived in the seventeenth century.

New Englanders found slavery incompatible with the natural-rights philosophy that had emerged during the Revolution and gradually began to abolish it in the 1780s (though they remained profitably tied to slavery through shipping plantation crops). Slavery had, in any case, always been marginal in New England's economy. Owning slaves as domestic servants or artisans had been a status symbol for wealthy urban whites in Boston, Portsmouth, and Newport. As a result, about 20 percent of New England's small African American population lived in cities, where jobs were relatively easy to find, in contrast to the white population, only 10 percent of which lived in cities.

Women outnumbered men in parts of New England in 1789. This pattern—not found in other parts of the country—was the result of the pressure of an expanding population and the practice of dividing family farms among male heirs. As farms in the older, more densely settled parts of New England were divided into ever-smaller lots, many young men migrated west in search of cheap, arable land. Thus by 1789, women formed a slight majority in Connecticut, Massachusetts, and Rhode Island.

Despite their superior numbers, women in New England, as elsewhere, remained subordinate to men. Even so, the general testing of traditional authority that accompanied the Revolution led some New England women to question male power. The Massachusetts poet Judith Sargeant Murray, for example, published essays asserting that women were the intellectual equals of men. Republican ideology, emphasizing the need for women to be intellectually prepared to raise virtuous, public-spirited children, led reformers in New England to seek equal access for women to education. In 1789, Massachusetts became the first state to allocate funds specifically for girls' elementary education. Liberalized divorce laws in New England also allowed a woman to seek legal separation from an abusive or unfaithful spouse.

In other respects, political and social life in New England remained rooted in the Puritan past. Age, property, and reputation determined one's standing in a culture that valued a clearly defined social order. The moral code that governed town life promoted curbs on individual behavior for the benefit of the community as a whole. With their notions of collective liberty, New Englanders subscribed to a version of republicanism that favored strong government, setting themselves apart from most other Americans, who embraced a more individualistic idea of liberty and a suspicion of government power. New Englanders perceived government as a divine institution with a moral responsibility to intervene in people's lives. Acting through town meetings, they taxed themselves for public services at rates two to four times higher than in the rest of the country. Their courts were also far more likely than those elsewhere to punish individuals for crimes against public order (like failing to observe the Sabbath properly) and sexual misconduct.

## THE PLURALISM OF THE MID-ATLANTIC REGION

The states of the mid-Atlantic region—New York, New Jersey, and Pennsylvania—were the most ethnically and religiously diverse in the nation. People of English descent constituted somewhat less than 40 percent of the population. Other major ethnic groups included the Dutch and Scots-Irish in New York and Germans and Scots-Irish in New Jersey and Pennsylvania. With ethnic diversity came religious diversity. Transplanted New Englanders made up about 40 percent of New York's ethnic English population. Among others of English descent, Anglicans predominated in New York, and Quakers in New Jersey and Pennsylvania. The Dutch, concentrated in the lower Hudson Valley, had their own Dutch Reformed Church, and most Germans were either Lutherans or **pietists,** such as the Mennonites and the Moravians, who stressed personal piety over theological doctrine. The Presbyterian Scots-Irish settled heavily in the backcountry.

**QUICK REVIEW**

**New Englanders**

◆ Most of population were descendants of seventeenth-century English immigrants.

◆ Congregationalism deemed official religion in Connecticut and Massachusetts.

◆ Women outnumbered men in some parts of the region.

◆ Slavery abolished in 1780s.

**pietists**   Protestants who stress a religion of the heart and the spirit of Christian living.

Idealized classical images of women—white, chaste, and pure—were popular emblems in the early republic to portray national ideals of liberty and republican motherhood.

**QUICK REVIEW**

**The Mid-Atlantic Region**

◆ Most ethnically and religiously diverse area in the nation.

◆ Slavery concentrated in port cities and adjacent rural areas.

◆ Diversity created a complex political environment.

This mosaic-like pattern of ethnic and religious groupings was no accident. In contrast to Puritan New England, the Middle Colonies had offered freedom of worship to attract settlers. In addition, economic opportunities for newcomers were much greater than in New England. The soil was better, the climate was milder, and market outlets for agricultural products were more abundant. These conditions made the mid-Atlantic region the nation's first breadbasket. Commercial agriculture fed urban growth and created a greater demand for labor in both rural and urban areas than in New England. The influx of Germans and Scots-Irish into the region in the eighteenth century occurred in response to this demand.

The demand for labor had also been met by importing African slaves. Blacks, both free and enslaved, made up 5 percent of the mid-Atlantic population in 1790, and, as in New England, they were more likely than whites to live in the maritime cities. New York had more slaveholders in 1790 than any other American city except Charleston, South Carolina.

Despite its considerable strength in the port cities and adjacent rural areas, slavery was never an economically vital institution in most of the mid-Atlantic region. Commercial agriculture did not rest on a slave base, nor did it produce a politically powerful class of planters. As a result, slavery in the mid-Atlantic region gave way to the demands for emancipation inspired by the natural-rights philosophy of the Revolution.

Pennsylvania in 1780, New York in 1799, and New Jersey in 1804 all passed laws of gradual emancipation. These laws did not free adult slaves but provided that children born of a slave mother were to be freed at ages ranging between 18 and 28. Soon after the laws were passed, however, adult slaves began hastening their own freedom. They ran away, set fires, and pressured their owners to accept cash payments in return for a short, fixed term of labor service. But even as they gained their freedom, African Americans had to confront enduring white racism. The comments of one white New Yorker suggest what they were up against. "We may sincerely advocate the freedom of black men," he wrote, "and yet assert their moral and physical inferiority."

The diversity of the mid-Atlantic region created a complex political environment. Competing cultural and economic interests prevented the kind of broad consensus on the meaning of republicanism that had emerged in New England. Those who supported strong government included mercantile and financial leaders in the cities and commercial farmers in the countryside. These people tended to be Anglicans, Quakers, and Congregationalists of English descent. Those opposing them and favoring a more egalitarian republicanism tended to come from the middle and lower classes. They included subsistence farmers in the backcountry and artisans and day laborers in the cities. Fiercely independent and proud of their liberties, they resented the claims of the wealthy to political authority. They resisted government aid to business as a form of political corruption that unfairly enriched those who were already economically powerful.

## THE SLAVE SOUTH AND ITS BACKCOUNTRY

In the South—the region from Maryland and Delaware to Georgia—climate and soil conditions favored the production of cash staples for world markets. Southern planters relied on the coerced labor of African slaves, whose numbers made the South the most populous region in the country.

Just under 40 percent of all southerners were slaves, but their concentration varied within the region. They were a majority in the Chesapeake Tidewater region, where slave ownership was widely distributed among white tobacco planters, including small and middling growers as well as the few great plantation owners. Farther south, in the tidal swamps of the South Carolina and Georgia lowcountry, where draining and clearing the land required huge inputs of labor, blacks outnumbered whites five to one. In the lowcountry, large planters, the richest men in the country, worked hundreds of slaves in the production of rice, indigo, and sea-island cotton.

Slaves were less numerous in the Piedmont, or foothills, region of the South that lies between the coastal plain and the Appalachian highlands. In the southern mountains, sloping to the southwest from the Blue Ridge in Virginia, the general absence of marketable crops diminished the demand for slave labor.

The free black population in the South had grown rapidly during the 1780s. Thousands of slaves fled behind British lines to win their freedom, and patriots freed others as a reward for enlisting in their forces. The Revolutionary values of liberty and equality also led many slave owners to question the morality of slavery. Legislatures in the Upper South passed laws making it financially easier than before for masters to manumit (free) their slaves. In Virginia alone, 10,000 slaves were manumitted in the 1780s. Slavery remained the foundation of the southern economy, however, and whites feared competition from freed blacks. As a result, no southern state embarked on a general program of emancipation, and slavery in the region survived the turbulence of the Revolutionary era.

Many German Lutherans settled in southeastern Pennsylvania. Hung above the gallery in this interior view of a Lutheran church in York are paintings of the 12 apostles and of figures drawn from the Old Testament.

Collection of the New-York Historical Society, Negative number 28824c.

Economic conditions in the South, where the raw poverty of the backcountry offset the great wealth of the low country, stamped the region's politics and culture. Tidewater planters were predominantly Anglican and of English descent. Piedmont farmers were more likely to be Scots-Irish Presbyterians and Baptists. More evangelical in their religion, and with simpler habits and tastes, the backcountry Baptists denounced the lowcountry planters for their luxury and arrogance. The planters retaliated by trying unsuccessfully to suppress the backcountry evangelicals.

The planters were indeed proud, domineering, and given to ostentatious displays of wealth. Planters understood liberty to mean the power of white males, unchecked by any outside authority, to rule over others. The only acknowledged check on this power was the planter's sense of duty, his obligation to adhere to an idealized code of conduct befitting a gentleman and a man of honor.

Backcountry farmers also jealously guarded their liberties. Backcountry farmers shared with the planters a disdain for government and restraints on the individual. But they opposed the planters' belief in a social hierarchy based on wealth and birth that left both poor whites and black slaves in a subordinate position.

## THE GROWING WEST

Between the Appalachian Mountains and the Mississippi River stretched the most rapidly growing region of the new nation, the West. Land-hungry settlers poured across the mountains once

**WHERE TO LEARN MORE**

Cincinnati Historical Society, Cincinnati, Ohio
http://www.cincymuseum.org/

the British recognized the American claim to the region in the Treaty of Paris. During the 1780s, the white population of the West exploded from less than 10,000 to 200,000. The region's Native American population was about 150,000.

Indians strongly resisted white claims on their lands. A confederation of tribes in the Ohio Valley, led by the Miamis and supplied with firearms by the British in exchange for furs, kept whites out of the Old Northwest territory, the area north of the Ohio River. South of the Ohio, white settlements were largely limited to Kentucky and Tennessee. In what is today Alabama and Mississippi, the Creeks and their allies blocked American expansion.

Most white migrants in Kentucky and Tennessee were the young rural poor from the seaboard slave states. The West offered them the opportunity to claim their own farms and gain economic independence, free from the dominance of planters and the economic competition of slave labor. But planters also saw the West as a land of opportunity. The planters of Tidewater Virginia were especially likely to speculate in vast tracts of western land. And many planters' sons migrated to the West with a share of the family's slaves to become planters in their own right. This process laid the foundation for the extension of slavery into new regions.

Isolation and uncertainty haunted frontier life. The Appalachians posed a formidable barrier to social and economic intercourse with the East. Few settlers had the labor resources, which chiefly meant slaves, to produce an agricultural surplus for shipment to market down the Ohio and Mississippi rivers. Most farmers lived at a semisubsistence level. Many of them, mostly Scots-Irish, did not own the land they cultivated. These squatters, as they were called, occupied the land hoping someday to obtain clear title to it.

In Kentucky, squatters, aligned with a small class of middling landowners, spearheaded the movement for political separation from Virginia that gained statehood for the territory in 1792. The settlers wanted to break the control that Tidewater planters had gained over most of the land and lucrative government offices in Kentucky. In their minds, planters, officeholders, land speculators, and gentlemen of leisure were all part of an aristocracy tied to the distant government in Richmond and intent on robbing them of their liberty.

Despite the movement in Kentucky for statehood, the ultimate political allegiance of the West was uncertain. Westerners wanted the freedom to control their own affairs and outlets for their crops. Apparently, they were willing to strike a deal with any outside power offering to meet these needs. Aware of the threat to the region posed by the British and Spanish, Washington had warned in 1784 that the political loyalties of the West wavered "on a pivot." The future of the region loomed as a major test for his administration.

## QUICK REVIEW

**Westerners**

- White population of West 200,000 by end of 1780s.
- Relationship between whites and Indians tense and sometimes violent.
- Most white migrants to Kentucky and Tennessee were young, rural poor from seaboard slave states.

# FORGING A NEW GOVERNMENT

**WHAT CHALLENGES** faced the Congress that assembled in New York between 1789 and 1791?

The Congress that assembled in New York (the temporary capital) from 1789 to 1791 faced a challenge scarcely less daunting than that of the Constitutional Convention of 1787. It had to give form and substance to the framework of the new national government outlined in the Constitution. Executive departments had to be established, a federal judiciary organized, sources of revenue found, terms of international trade and foreign policy worked out, and the commitment to add a bill of rights to the Constitution honored.

## "MR. PRESIDENT" AND THE BILL OF RIGHTS

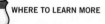

**WHERE TO LEARN MORE**

Federal Hall National Memorial, New York, New York
http://www.nps.gov/feha/index.htm

The first problem for Washington and Congress was to decide just how the chief executive of the new republic should be addressed. In a debate that tied up Congress for a month, agreement was finally reached on "Mr. President." Whatever his title, Washington was intent on surrounding the presidency with an aura of respectability.

Meanwhile, Congress got down to business. James Madison, now a representative from Virginia, early emerged as the most forceful leader in the House. He pushed for speedy action on the bill of rights, which the Federalists had promised to add to the Constitution during the ratification debate. To allay the fears of Antifederalists that the Constitution granted too much power to the national government, the Federalists had promised to consider amendments that protected both individual rights and liberties and the rights of states. But Madison astutely kept the focus of the amendments on personal liberties. He submitted nineteen amendments, and Congress soon settled on twelve. Ten of these, known collectively as the **Bill of Rights,** were ratified by the states and became part of the Constitution as of December 15, 1791.

**Bill of Rights**  A written summary of inalienable rights and liberties.

   The Bill of Rights is one of the most enduring legacies of the first Congress. Most of the first eight amendments are concerned with individual rights. They guarantee religious freedom, freedom of expression, and the safeguarding of individuals and their property against arbitrary legal proceedings. Only three amendments speak of state interests. Citing the necessity of a "well regulated Militia" for "the security of a free State," the Second Amendment guarantees "the right of the people to keep and bear Arms." This assured the states that they could rely on their militias for protection against federal tyranny. The Ninth and Tenth Amendments stipulate that the powers not granted to the national government in the Constitution are retained by the people and the states.

   The Bill of Rights broadened the government's base of popular support. Once Congress submitted the amendments to the states for ratification, North Carolina (1789) and Rhode Island (1790) overcame their lingering objections (see Chapter 7) and joined the Union. The Bill of Rights also assured Americans that the central government would not try to impose a uniform national culture.

## DEPARTMENTS AND COURTS

In the summer of 1789, Congress authorized the first executive departments: the State Department for foreign affairs, the Treasury for finances, and the War Department for the nation's defense. These departments already existed under the Articles of Confederation, and the only debate about them concerned the extent of presidential control over the officials who would head them. The Constitution was silent on whether the president could dismiss an official without the Senate's consent. Congress decided that the president could do so, setting an important precedent that bolstered presidential power. Department heads would now be closely bound to the president. As a group, they would evolve into the cabinet, the president's chief advisory body.

   Greater controversy attended the creation of the federal judiciary. The Constitution called for "one Supreme Court" but left it up to Congress to authorize lower federal courts. The framers were deliberately vague about the federal judiciary, because Antifederalists and proponents of states' rights did not want national courts enforcing a uniform judicial system.

   The **Judiciary Act of 1789** represented an artful compromise that balanced the concerns of the Antifederalists and states' rights advocates with the concerns of nationalists who strongly opposed leaving matters of national law up to state courts. It created a hierarchical national judiciary based on thirteen federal district courts, one for each state. Appeals from these courts were to be heard in one of three circuit courts, and the Supreme Court was to have the final say in contested cases. In a major concession to the Antifederalists, however, the act limited jurisdiction in federal courts to legal issues stemming from the Constitution and the laws and treaties of the national government.

**Judiciary Act of 1789**  Act of Congress that implemented the judiciary clause of the Constitution by establishing the Supreme Court and a system of lower federal courts.

Waterborne commerce was the key in the early emergence of New York City as a trading center. Shown here is the Manhattan end of the Brooklyn Ferry in 1790.

The Metropolitan Museum of Art, The Edward W. C. Arnold Collection of New York Prints. Bequest of Edward W. C. Arnold, 1954. (54.90.491) Photograph © 1986. The Metropolitan Museum of Art. Art Resource, NY.

## REVENUE AND TRADE

The government's most pressing need was for revenue. Aware that Congress under the Articles of Confederation had been crippled by its inability to secure a reliable source of income, Madison acted to put the finances of

**Tariff Act of 1789**  Apart from a few selected industries, this first tariff passed by Congress was intended to raise revenue and not protect American manufacturers from foreign competition.

**WHERE TO LEARN MORE**

Hamilton Grange National Memorial, New York, New York
http://www.nps/gov/hagr/index.htm

**Read** the **Document**

at **www.myhistorylab.com**
*Alexander Hamilton, An Opinion on the Constitutionality of an Act to Establish a Bank (1791)*

**QUICK REVIEW**

**Hamilton's Reports**

◆ Plan to address Revolutionary War debt.

◆ Call for an excise tax on distilled whiskey.

◆ Proposal to charter a national bank.

◆ Recommendation for government to promote industry.

Shown here in 1799, the neoclassical design of the First Bank of the United States in Philadelphia was a fitting expression of the grandeur of Hamilton's vision for a national bank.

the new federal government on a firm footing. Nearly everyone agreed that the government's chief source of income should be a tariff on imported goods and tonnage duties (fees based on cargo capacity) on ships entering American ports.

The **Tariff Act of 1789** was designed primarily to raise revenue, not to protect American manufacturers by keeping out foreign goods with high duties. It levied a duty of 5 percent on most imported goods but imposed tariffs as high as 50 percent on a limited number of items, such as steel, salt, cloth, and tobacco. The debate on the Tariff Act provoked some sectional sparring. Manufacturers, who were concentrated in the North, wanted high tariffs for protection against foreign competition. In contrast, farmers and southern planters wanted low tariffs to keep down the cost of the manufactured goods they purchased.

## HAMILTON AND THE PUBLIC CREDIT

The Treasury was the largest and most important new department. To its head, Alexander Hamilton of New York, fell the task of bringing order to the nation's ramshackle finances. The basic problem was the huge debt left over from the Revolution. With interest going unpaid, the debt was growing, and by 1789, it had reached $52 million. Until the government set up and honored a regular schedule for paying interest, the nation's public credit would be worthless. Unable to borrow, the government would collapse.

At the request of Congress, Hamilton prepared a series of reports on the nation's finances and economic condition. In the first, issued in January 1790, Hamilton proposed a bold plan to address the Revolutionary War debt. The federal government, he maintained, should fund the national debt at full face value. To do this, he proposed exchanging the old debt, including accrued interest, for new government bonds bearing interest at about 4 percent. In addition, Hamilton maintained that the federal government should assume the remaining war debt of the state governments. The intent of this plan was to give the nation's creditors an economic stake in the stability of the new nation and to subordinate state financial interests to those of the central government.

In his second report, issued in December 1790, Hamilton called for an excise tax (a tax on the production, sale, or consumption of a commodity) on distilled whiskey produced within the United States. The purpose of the tax was to raise additional revenue for interest payments on the national debt and establish the government's authority to levy internal taxes on its citizens.

The third report recommended the chartering of a national bank, the Bank of the United States. Hamilton patterned his proposed bank after the Bank of England and intended it to meet a variety of needs. Jointly owned by the federal government and private investors, it would serve as the fiscal (financial) and depository agent of the government and make loans to businesses. Through a provision that permitted up to three-fourths of the value of bank stock to be purchased with government bonds, the bank would create a market for public securities and hence raise their value. Most important, the bank would provide the nation with a stable currency. Hamilton proposed to allow the Bank of the United States to issue money in the form of paper banknotes that would be backed by a small reserve of specie and the security of government bonds. His goal was both to strengthen the economy and to consolidate the power of the national government.

Hamilton's final report, issued in December 1791, recommended government actions to promote industry. Looking, as always, to the British model of economic development, he argued that the United States would never become a great power until it diversified its largely agrarian economy. As long as the nation imported most of its manufactured goods,

Hamilton warned, it would be no more than a second-rate power. Hamilton advocated aid to American manufacturers in the form of protective tariffs (high tariffs meant to make imported goods more expensive than domestic goods) for such industries as iron, steel, and shoemaking—which had already begun to establish themselves—and direct subsidies to assist with start-up costs for other industries. Hamilton believed that such "patronage," as he called it, would ultimately foster interregional economic dependence. Thus, in Hamilton's vision, manufacturing, like a national currency, would be a great national unifier.

## REACTION AND OPPOSITION

The breadth and boldness of Hamilton's program invited opposition. About half the members of Congress owned some of the nation's debt, and nearly all of them agreed with Hamilton that it should be paid off. Some opponents, however, were concerned that Hamilton's plan was unfair. Hard times had forced most of the original holders of the debt—by and large, ordinary citizens—to sell their certificates to speculators at a fraction of their face value. Should the government, asked Madison, reward speculators with a windfall profit when the debt was paid back in full and forget about the true patriots who had sustained the Revolution in its darkest hours?

Others objected, on republican grounds, that Hamilton had no intention of actually eliminating the government's debt. He envisioned instead a permanent debt, with the government making regular interest payments as they came due. The debt, in the form of government securities, would serve as a vital prop for the support of moneyed groups. One congressman saw this as a violation of "that great principle which alone was the cause of the war with Great Britain . . . that taxation and representation should go hand in hand." Future generations, he argued, would be unfairly taxed for a debt incurred by the present generation.

Opposition to Hamilton's proposal to have the federal government assume state debts reflected sectional differences. With the exception of South Carolina, the southern states had already paid back a good share of their war debts. Thus Hamilton's plan stood to benefit the northern states disproportionately. Because Hamilton had linked the funding of the national debt with the assumption of state debts, southern opposition threatened funding as well. Tensions mounted as the deadlock continued into the summer of 1790. Frustrated over southern intransigence, New Englanders muttered about seceding. Southerners responded in kind.

Tempers cooled when a compromise was reached in July. Southerners agreed to accept funding in its original form because, as Hamilton correctly noted, it would be impractical, if not impossible, to distinguish between the original and current holders of the national debt. Assumption passed after Hamilton cut a deal with Virginians James Madison and Thomas Jefferson. In exchange for southern support of assumption, Hamilton agreed to line up northern votes for locating the nation's permanent capital on the banks of the Potomac River, where it would be surrounded by the slave states of Maryland and Virginia. The package was sweetened by extra grants of federal money to states with small debts.

Hamilton's alliance with Madison and Jefferson proved short-lived, dissolving when Madison led the congressional opposition to Hamilton's proposed bank. Madison and most other southerners viewed the bank as evidence of a willingness to sacrifice the interests of the agrarian South in favor of the financial and industrial interests of the North. They feared that the bank, with its power to dispense economic favors, would re-create in the United States the kind of government corruption and privilege they associated with Great Britain. They argued that the Constitution did not explicitly authorize Congress to charter a bank or any other corporation.

The bank bill passed Congress on a vote that divided along sectional lines and Hamilton's bank was chartered for twenty years. Congress also passed a hefty 25 percent excise tax on distilled liquor. Little, however, of Hamilton's plan to promote manufacturing survived the scrutiny of the agrarian opposition. Tariff duties were raised moderately in 1792, but no funds were forthcoming to accelerate industrial development.

# THE EMERGENCE OF PARTIES

**WHAT FORCES** shaped the development of party politics in America?

**Federalists** Supporters of Hamilton's program; they were American's most fully integrated into the market economy—and in control of it.

**Republican** Party headed by Thomas Jefferson that formed in opposition to the financial and diplomatic policies of the Federalist party; favored limiting the powers of the national government and placing the interests of farmers over those of financial and commercial groups.

By the end of Washington's first term, Americans were dividing into two camps. On one side stood those who still called themselves **Federalists.** These were the supporters of Hamilton's program—speculators, creditors, merchants, manufacturers, and commercial farmers. They were the Americans most fully integrated into the market economy and in control of it. Concentrated in the North, they included New England Congregationalists and mid-Atlantic Episcopalians (former Anglicans), members of the more socially prestigious churches. In both economic and cultural terms, the Federalists were drawn from the more privileged segments of society. Jefferson and Madison shrewdly gave the name **Republican** to the party that formed in opposition to the Federalists, thus identifying it with individual liberties and the heritage of the Revolution. The Republicans accused Hamilton and the Federalists of attempting to impose a British system of economic privilege and social exploitation. The initial core of the party consisted of southern planters and backcountry Scots-Irish farmers, Americans outside the market economy or skeptical of its benefits. They feared that the commercial groups favored by Hamilton would corrupt politics in their pursuit of power and foster commerce and manufacturing at the expense of agriculture. The Republicans were committed to an agrarian America in which power remained in the hands of farmers and planters.

In 1792, parties were still in a formative stage. The political divisions that had appeared first in Congress and then spread to Washington's cabinet did not yet extend very deeply into the electorate. Washington remained aloof from the political infighting and was still seen as a great unifier. Unopposed, he was reelected in 1792. However, a series of crises in his second term deepened and broadened the incipient party divisions. By 1796, rival parties were contesting the presidency and vying for the support of an increasingly politically organized electorate.

## THE FRENCH REVOLUTION

The French Revolution began in 1789, and in its early phase, most Americans applauded it. France had been an ally of the United States during the Revolutionary War and now seemed to be following the example of its American friends in shaking off monarchical rule. By 1792, however, as threats against it mounted, the French Revolution turned violent and radical. Its supporters confiscated the property of aristocrats and the church, slaughtered suspected enemies, and executed the king, Louis XVI. In early 1793, republican France was at war against Britain and the European powers.

The excesses of the French Revolution and the European war that erupted in its wake touched off a bitter debate in America. Federalists drew back in horror from France's new regime. They insisted that the terror unleashed by the French was far removed from the reasoned republicanism of the American Revolution. For the Republicans, however, the French remained the standard-bearers of the cause of liberty for common people everywhere.

**Franco-American relations.** When the new French ambassador, Edmond Genêt, arrived in the United States in April 1793—just as the debate in America over the French Revolution was heating up—Franco-American relations reached a turning point. The two countries were still bound to one another by the Franco-American Alliance of 1778. The alliance required the United States to assist France in the defense of its West Indian colonies and to open U.S. ports to French privateers if France were attacked. Genêt, it soon became clear, hoped to embroil the United States in the French war against the British. He commissioned U.S. privateers to attack British shipping and tried to enlist an army of frontiersmen to attack Spanish possessions in Louisiana and Florida.

Genêt's actions, as well as the enthusiastic reception that greeted him as he traveled from Charleston to Philadelphia (chosen in 1790 as the temporary national capital), forced Washington

## OVERVIEW  Federalist Party versus Republican Party

| Federalists | Republicans |
| --- | --- |
| Favored strong central government | Wanted to limit role of national government |
| Supported Hamilton's economic program | Opposed Hamilton's economic program |
| Opposed French Revolution | Generally supported French Revolution |
| Supported Jay's Treaty and closer ties to Britain | Opposed Jay's Treaty and favored closer ties to France |
| In response to threat of war with France, proposed and passed Direct Tax of 1798, Alien and Sedition Acts and legislation to enlarge army | Opposed Alien and Sedition Acts and enlarged army as threats to individual liberties |
| Drew strongest support from New England; lost support in mid-Atlantic region after 1798 | Drew strongest support from South and West |

to call a special cabinet meeting. The president feared that Genêt would stampede Americans into the European war, with disastrous results for the nation's finances. Over Jefferson's objections, Hamilton urged Washington to declare U.S. neutrality in the European war, maintaining that the president could commit the nation to neutrality on his own authority when Congress, as was then the case, was not in session. Washington accepted Hamilton's argument and issued a proclamation on April 22, 1793, stating that the United States would be "friendly and impartial toward the belligerent powers."

**The growth of Democratic-Republican societies.**   Genêt quickly faded from public view, but U.S. politics became more open and aggressive in the wake of his visit. Pro-French enthusiasm lived on in a host of grassroots political organizations known as the Democratic-Republican societies. As their name suggests, these societies reflected a belief that democracy and republicanism were one and the same. This was a new concept in U.S. politics. Democracy had traditionally been equated with anarchy and mob rule. The members of the new societies argued, to the contrary, that only democracy—meaning popular participation in politics and direct appeals by politicians to the people—could maintain the revolutionary spirit of 1776, because the people were the only true guardians of that spirit.

The Democratic-Republican societies attacked the Washington administration for failing to assist France, and they expressed the popular feeling that Hamilton's program favored the rich over the poor. For the first time, Washington himself was personally assailed in the press.

The core members of the societies were urban artisans whose egalitarian views shocked the Federalists, who expected deference, not criticism and political activism, from the people. In their view, the Democratic-Republicans were rabble-rousers trying to dictate policy to the nation's natural leaders. The Federalists harshly condemned the emergence of organized political dissent from below, but in so doing they only enhanced the popular appeal of the growing Republican opposition.

## SECURING THE FRONTIER

Control of the West remained an elusive goal throughout Washington's first term. Indian resistance in the Northwest Territory initially prevented whites from pushing north of the Ohio River. The powerful Miami Confederacy, led by Little Turtle, routed two ill-trained American armies in 1790 and 1791. The southern frontier was quieter, but the Spanish

## GLOBAL CONNECTIONS

### NEUTRALITY IN AN AGE OF REVOLUTION

Whereas it appears that a state of war exists between Austria, Prussia, Sardinia, Great Britain, and the United Netherlands on the one part and France on the other, and the duty and interest of the United States require that they should with sincerity and good faith adopt and pursue a conduct friendly and impartial toward the belligerent powers:

I have therefore thought fit . . . to exhort and warn the citizens of the United States carefully to avoid all acts and proceeding whatsoever which may in any manner tend to contravene such disposition.

In these words President Washington proclaimed the neutrality of the United States in the European war spawned by the French Revolution. He realized, as did most Americans, that the new and still weak nation had far more to lose than gain by embroiling itself in the European war. Still, before the French Revolution turned to regicide and the Reign of Terror in 1793–1794, Americans basked in pride for having first raised the revolutionary banner of liberty and equality that their former ally was now spreading over Europe. But by the mid-1790s exultation had turned into disillusionment and fears of social upheaval. By the time that Napoleon assumed what amounted to dictatorial powers in 1799, most Americans had reverted to their earlier belief in the uniqueness of the American Revolution. As Madison observed when reflecting on the French experience, America remained as "the only Theatre in which true liberty can have a fair trial."

Despite believing that the French had discredited the cause of liberty, Americans clung to the hope that the contagion of liberty they had first unleashed in their Revolution would topple autocratic regimes across the world. And spread it did in a wide arc of revolutionary movements that stretched across the Western world. The French colony of Saint-Domingue (Haiti) exploded in unrest in 1791 once the French Revolution had outlawed slavery. Touissant L'Ouverture, the slave grandson of an African king, led black armies in a ten-year war of liberation that resulted in the independence of Haiti in 1804. Napoleon's invasion of the Iberian Peninsula in 1809 created a power vacuum in Spain's American empire. A host of revolutions broke out to fill the vacuum, and Mexico, Argentina, Bolivia, Chile, Colombia, Ecuador, Peru, and Venezuela all gained their freedom from Spanish rule. None of these revolutions closely followed the American or French model. All, however, were united by a common political language of liberty, popular self-rule, and constitutionalism that the Americans and the French had bequeathed to global politics.

- In what ways did the American Revolution soon serve as a liberating example for revolutionary change elsewhere?

continued to use the Creeks and Cherokees as a buffer against American penetration south of the Tennessee River.

By 1793, many western settlers felt abandoned by the national government. They believed that the government had broken a promise to protect them against Indians and foreigners. Much of the popularity of the Democratic-Republican societies in the West fed off these frustrations. Westerners saw the French, who were at war with Britain and Spain, as allies against the foreign threat on the frontier, and they forwarded resolutions to Congress embracing the French cause. These resolutions also demanded free and open navigation on the Mississippi River. This, in the minds of Westerners, was their natural right. Without it, they would be forever impoverished. "If the interest of Eastern America requires that we should be kept in poverty," argued the Mingo Creek society of western Pennsylvania, "it is unreasonable from such poverty to exact contributions. The first, if we cannot emerge from, we must learn to bear, but the latter, we never can be taught to submit to."

Submission to national authority, however, was precisely what the Federalists wanted from both the Indians and the western settlers. By the summer of 1794, Washington's administration felt prepared to move against the Indians. This time, it sent into the Ohio region not the usual ragtag crew of militia and unemployed city dwellers but a force built around veterans from the professional army. The commander, General Anthony Wayne, was a savvy, battle-hardened war hero.

Wayne's victory on August 4, 1794, at the Battle of Fallen Timbers, near present-day Toledo, broke the back of Indian military resistance in Ohio. In the resulting **Treaty of Greenville,** signed in August 1795, twelve tribes ceded most of the present state of Ohio to the U.S. government in return for an annual payment of $9,500. The Ohio country was now open to white settlement.

**Treaty of Greenville**   Treaty of 1795 in which Native Americans in the Old Northwest were forced to cede most of the present state of Ohio to the United States.

## THE WHISKEY REBELLION

Within a few months of Wayne's victory at Fallen Timbers, another American army was on the move. Its target was the so-called whiskey rebels of western Pennsylvania, who were openly resisting Hamilton's excise tax on whiskey. Hamilton was determined to enforce the tax and assert the supremacy of national laws. Although resistance to the tax was widespread, he singled out the Pennsylvania rebels. It was easier to send an army into the Pittsburgh area than into the Carolina mountains. Washington, moreover, was convinced that the Democratic-Republican societies of western Pennsylvania were behind the defiance of federal authority there. He welcomed the opportunity to chastise these organizations, which he identified with the dangerous doctrines of the French Revolution.

Washington called on the governors of the mid-Atlantic states to supply militia forces to crush the **Whiskey Rebellion.** The army met no resistance and expended considerable effort rounding up 20 prisoners. Two men were found guilty of treason, but Washington pardoned both. Still, at Hamilton's insistence, the Federalists had made their point: When its authority was openly challenged, the national government would use military force to compel obedience.

**Whiskey Rebellion**   Armed uprising in 1794 by farmers in western Pennsylvania who attempted to prevent the collection of the excise tax on whiskey.

The Whiskey Rebellion starkly revealed the conflicting visions of local liberty and national order that divided Americans of the early republic. The non-English majority on the Pennsylvania frontier, Irish, Scots-Irish, German, and Welsh, justified resistance to the whiskey tax with the same republican ideology that had fueled the American Revolution. Mostly poor farmers, artisans, and laborers, they appealed to notions of liberty, equality, and freedom from oppressive taxation that were deeply rooted in backcountry settlements from Maine to Georgia. In putting down the Pennsylvania rebels, Washington and Hamilton acted on behalf of more English and cosmopolitan groups in the East who valued central power as a check on any local resistance movement that might begin unraveling the still fragile republic.

**⊙∙⊡Read the Document**
at **www.myhistorylab.com**
*George Washington, Proclamation Regarding the Whiskey Rebellion (1794)*

## TREATIES WITH BRITAIN AND SPAIN

Much of the unrest in the West stemmed from the menacing presence of the British and Spanish on the nation's borders. Washington's government had the resources to suppress Indians and frontier dissidents but lacked sufficient armed might to push Spain and especially Britain out of the West.

The British, embroiled in what they saw as a life-or-death struggle against revolutionary France, clamped a naval blockade on France and its Caribbean colonies in the fall of 1793. They also supported a slave uprising on the French island of Saint-Domingue (present-day Haiti), enraging southern planters who feared that slave rebellions might spread to the United States. The French countered by opening their colonial trade, which had been closed to outsiders during peacetime, to neutral shippers. American merchants stepped in and reaped profits by supplying France. The British retaliated by seizing American ships involved in the French trade. They further claimed the right to search American ships and impress, or forcibly remove, sailors they suspected of having deserted from the British navy. News of these provocations reached America in early 1794 and touched off a major war scare. Desperate to avert a war, Washington sent John Jay, the chief justice of the United States, to London to negotiate an accord.

From the American point of view, the resulting agreement, known as **Jay's Treaty,** was flawed but acceptable. Jay had to abandon the American insistence on the right of neutrals to ship goods to nations at war without interference. He also had to grant Britain "most favored

**Jay's Treaty**   Treaty with Britain negotiated in 1794 in which the United States made major concessions to avert a war over the British seizure of American ships.

## AMERICAN VIEWS

### An Architect on Water Pollution in Philadelphia

Benjamin Henry Latrobe, the first professional architect in the United States, was living in Philadelphia in 1798. Five years earlier, a major yellow fever epidemic had carried off two thousand of the city's inhabitants. Here, Latrobe offers his views on the sources of water pollution and what the city had to do to obtain a clean water supply and improve public health.

- **What** was the link between mosquitoes and yellow fever missed by Latrobe and his contemporaries?
- **How** then did doctors and others in the eighteenth century account for outbreaks of yellow fever and other diseases?
- **What** led Latrobe to conclude that foul air was not the source of the yellow fever?
- **How** did Philadelphia and other cities dispose of their human wastes and what does this tell us about the spread of waterborne diseases? How widespread in the world today do you suspect are the unsafe conditions that Latrobe described for Philadelphia in 1798?
- **What** solution did Latrobe offer for Philadelphia's water problems?

On inspecting the plan of the city of Philadelphia and observing the numerous wide and straight streets, it will not be easily believed that want of ventilation can be entirely the cause of the yellow fever which has made such dreadful and frequent devastations among the inhabitants. It is true that there are narrow and often very filthy alleys which intersect the interior of the squares bounded by the principal streets and in which the air may stagnate. The back yards of most of the houses are also depositories of filth. [Still,] there must be some cause more powerful and more specific. The cause, I believe, may be found in the following circumstance:

The soil between the Delaware and Schuylkill [rivers] is generally flat [and] consists of a bed of clay of different depth, from ten to thirty feet . . . . Below this bed of clay is universally a stratum of sand. In this sand runs a stratum of water, and as it is impossible to dig into it without finding clear and excellent water in an inexhaustible quantity, let the wells and pumps be ever so near to each other, it appears to me not at all extravagant to suppose that the waters of the two rivers unite through

this sand stratum, which serves as a filtering bed . . . But this very circumstance, the inexhaustible supply of clean water to be found in every possible spot of ground . . . is the great cause, in my opinion, of the contagion which appears now to be an annual disease of Philadelphia, the yellow fever. The houses, being much crowded, and the situation flat, without subterraneous sewers to carry off the filth, every house has its privy and its drains which lodge their supplies in one boghole sunk into the ground at different depths. Many of them are pierced to the sand, and as those which are sunk thus low never fill up, there is a strong temptation to incur the expense of digging them deep at first to save the trouble and noisomeness of emptying them.

In every street, close to the footpath, is a range of pumps at the distance of about sixty or seventy feet from which all the water which is used for drinking or culinary purposes is drawn. The permeability of the stratum in which the water runs, and which the action of the pump draws to itself from all parts round it, must certainly contaminate the water of every pump in the neighborhood of a sink loaded with the filth of the family, and as the number of these sinks is very superior to that of the pumps, each of them is in a manner surrounded by noxious matter.

Thus . . . we have a proof that there does exist in the mode by which the city is supplied with water a very abundant source of disease, independent of the noxious exhalations of the narrow and filthy alleys and lanes [for] the evil lies in the constant fermentation of the stratum of water and production of mephitic [poisonous] air, to which the pumps are so many chimneys to convey it into the streets and open windows at all times, and from which it is regularly pumped up every time the handle is depressed.

The great scheme of bringing the water of the Schuylkill to Philadelphia to supply the city is now become an object of immense importance, though it is at present neglected from a failure of funds. The evil, however, which it is intended collaterally to correct is so serious . . . as to call loudly upon all who are inhabitants of Philadelphia for their utmost exertions to complete it.

*Source:* Benjamin Henry Latrobe, *The Journal of Latrobe: Being the Notes and Sketches of an Architect, Naturalist and Traveler in the United States from 1796 to 1820* (New York: D. Appleton, 1905), pp. 92–98.

nation" status, giving up the American right to discriminate against British shipping and merchandise. And he had to reconfirm the American commitment to repay in full pre-Revolutionary debts owed to the British. In return for these major concessions, Britain pledged to compensate American merchants for the ships and cargoes it had seized in 1793 and 1794, to abandon the six forts it still held in the American Northwest, and to grant the United States limited trading rights in India and the British West Indies.

Signed in November 1794, Jay's Treaty caused an uproar in the United States when its terms became known in March 1795. Southerners saw in it another sellout of their interests. It required them to pay their prewar debts to British merchants but was silent about the slaves Britain had carried off during the Revolution. And the concessions Britain did make seemed to favor the North, especially New England merchants and shippers. Republicans, joined now by urban artisans, were infuriated that Jay had stripped them of their chief weapon, economic retaliation, for breaking free of British commercial dominance. The Senate ratified the treaty in June 1795, but only because Washington backed it.

Jay's Treaty, combined with a string of French victories in Europe in 1795, convinced Spain to adopt a more conciliatory attitude toward the United States. In the **Treaty of San Lorenzo** in 1795 (also known as Pinckney's Treaty), Spain accepted the American position on the 31st parallel as the northern boundary of Spanish Florida and granted American farmers free transit through the port of New Orleans with the right of renewal after three years.

**Treaty of San Lorenzo**   Treaty with Spain in 1795 in which Spain recognized the 31st parallel as the boundary between the United States and Spanish Florida.

## THE FIRST PARTISAN ELECTION

Partisanship, open identification with one of the two parties, steadily rose in the 1790s, fueled in large measure by a new print culture. The first opposition newspaper, the *National Gazette*, appeared in 1791, and the number of newspapers more than doubled within the decade. Circulated and discussed in taverns and coffeehouses, newspapers helped draw ordinary Americans into the political process. Ongoing involvement in the raucous, celebratory political culture that Americans fashioned also politicized them. Through festivals, street parades and demonstrations favoring or opposing such events as the French Revolution or Jay's Treaty, and an endless stream of toasts, speeches, banquets, and broadsides, various groups publicly proclaimed and acted out their version of what it meant to be an American. No single version held sway. National self-identity varied by class, race, sex, and region, but as newspaper reports of local activities were copied and disseminated across the country, Americans could feel that they were joined in a collective effort to define what the nation meant to them. As a national identity was being forged and contested, lines of partisanship were marked and deepened.

Women also participated in this public arena of political activism. Although denied formal political rights, they wrote and attended plays with explicit political messages, joined in patriotic rituals, and organized their own demonstrations. By the late 1790s, both parties were seeking to broaden their popular appeal by including women in their partisan rallies.

As partisanship spread, no symbol of traditional authority, Washington included, was safe from challenge. He devoted most of his Farewell Address of September 1796 to a denunciation of partisanship. He also warned against any permanent foreign alliances and cautioned that the Union itself would be endangered if parties continued to be characterized "by geographical discriminations, *Northern* and *Southern*, *Atlantic* and *Western*."

Confirming Washington's fears, the election of 1796 was the first openly partisan election in American history. John Adams was the Federalist candidate, and Thomas Jefferson, the Republican candidate. Each was selected by a party caucus, a meeting of party leaders. As a result of disunity in the Federalist ranks, the election produced the anomaly of a Federalist president (Adams) and a Republican vice president (Jefferson). Written with no thought of organized partisan competition for the presidency, the Constitution simply stated that the presidential

**Read the Document**
at www.myhistorylab.com
*Exploring America:*
*The Partisan Press*

**Read the Document**
at www.myhistorylab.com
*George Washington, Farewell*
*Address (1796)*

**Read the Document**
at www.myhistorylab.com
*From Then to Now Online:*
*Advice for an Empire*

**QUICK REVIEW**

**The Election of 1796**

◆ First openly partisan presidential election.

◆ Candidates: John Adams (Federalist); Thomas Jefferson (Republican).

◆ Adams won with support in New England and the mid-Atlantic states.

WHY WAS Adams defeated in the election of 1800?

🛡 **WHERE TO LEARN MORE**

★ Adams National Historic Site, Quincy, Massachusetts
http://www.nps.gov/adam/index.htm

**XYZ Affair** Diplomatic incident in 1798 in which Americans were outraged by the demand of the French for a bribe as a condition for negotiating with American diplomats.

**Quasi-War** Undeclared naval war of 1797 to 1800 between the United States and France.

candidate with the second-highest number of electoral votes would become vice president. In this case, that candidate was Jefferson.

Despite the election's confused outcome, the sectional pattern in the voting was unmistakable. Only the solid support of regional elites in New England and the mid-Atlantic states enabled the Federalists to retain the presidency. Adams received all the northern electoral votes, with the exception of Pennsylvania's. Jefferson was the overwhelming favorite in the South.

# THE LAST FEDERALIST ADMINISTRATION

The Adams administration got off to a rocky start from which it never recovered. The vice president was the leader of the opposition party; key members of the cabinet, which Adams had inherited from Washington, owed their primary loyalty to Hamilton; and the French, who saw Adams as a dupe of the British, instigated a major crisis that left the threat of war hanging over the entire Adams presidency.

## THE FRENCH CRISIS AND THE XYZ AFFAIR

An aggressive coalition known as the Directory gained control of revolutionary France in 1795 and denounced the Jay treaty as evidence of an Anglo-American alliance against France. When Jefferson and the pro-French Republicans lost the election of 1796, the Directory turned openly hostile. In short order, the French annulled the commercial treaty of 1778 with the United States, ordered the seizure of American ships carrying goods to the British, and declared that any American sailors found on British ships, including those forcibly pressed into service, would be summarily executed. By the time Adams had been in office three months, the French had confiscated more than 300 American ships.

In the fall of 1797, Adams sent three commissioners to Paris in an effort to avoid war. The French treated the three with contempt. Through three intermediaries, identified by Adams only as X, Y, and Z when he informed Congress of the negotiations, the French foreign minister demanded a large bribe to initiate talks and an American loan of $12 million.

In April 1798, the Senate published a full account of the insulting behavior of the French in what came to be called the **XYZ Affair.** The public was indignant, and war fever swept the country. The Federalists, who had always warned against the French, enjoyed greater popularity than they ever had or ever would again. Congress acted to upgrade the navy, and responsibility for naval affairs, formerly divided between the Treasury and War departments, was consolidated in a new Department of the Navy. By the fall of 1798, American ships were waging an undeclared war against the French in Caribbean waters, a conflict that came to be known as the **Quasi-War.**

The Federalists in Congress, dismissing Republican objections, also voted to create a vastly expanded army. They tripled the size of the regular army to 10,000 men and authorized a special provisional army of 50,000. Congress put the provisional army under Washington's command, but he declined to come out of retirement except for a national emergency. In the meantime, he insisted that Hamilton be appointed second in command and given charge of the provisional army's field operations. To pay for both the expanded army and the naval rearmament, the Federalists pushed through the Direct Tax of 1798, a levy on the value of land, slaves, and dwellings.

## CRISIS AT HOME

The thought of Hamilton in charge of a huge army convinced many Republicans that their worst nightmares were about to materialize. One congressman shuddered that "the monarchy-loving Hamilton is now so fixed, as to be able, with one-step, to fill the place of our present commander in chief." Adams shared such fears. He was furious that Hamilton had been forced on him as commander of the provisional army. As Adams came to realize, Hamilton's supporters, known as the

High Federalists, saw the war scare with France as an opportunity to stamp out dissent, cement an alliance with the British, and strengthen and consolidate the powers of the national government.

The Federalists passed four laws in the summer of 1798, known collectively as the **Alien and Sedition Acts,** that confirmed the Republicans' fears. Three of these acts were aimed at immigrants, especially French and Irish refugees who voted for the Republicans. The president was empowered to deport foreigners who came from countries at war with the United States and to expel any alien resident he suspected of subversive activities. The Naturalization Act extended the residency requirement for U.S. citizenship (and hence the right to vote) from five to fourteen years. Worst of all in the minds of Republicans was the Sedition Act, a measure that made it a federal crime to engage in any conspiracy against the government or to utter or print anything "false, scandalous and malicious" against the government. Federalist judges were blatantly partisan in their enforcement of the Sedition Act. Twenty-five individuals, mostly Republican editors, were indicted under the act, and ten were convicted.

Outraged at this threat to the freedom of speech, Jefferson and Madison turned to the safely Republican legislatures of Kentucky and Virginia for a forum from which to attack the constitutionality of the Alien and Sedition Acts. Taking care to keep their authorship secret, they each drafted a set of resolutions that challenged the entire centralizing program of the Federalists. In doing so, they produced the first significant articulation of the southern stand on **states' rights.**

The resolutions—adopted in the fall of 1798—proposed a compact theory of the Constitution. They asserted that the states had delegated specific powers to the national government for their common benefit. It followed that the states reserved the right to decide whether the national government had unconstitutionally assumed a power not granted to it. If a state decided that the national government had exceeded its powers, it could "interpose" its authority to shield its citizens from a tyrannical law. In a second set of resolutions, the Kentucky legislature introduced the doctrine of **nullification,** the right of a state to render null and void a national law it deemed unconstitutional.

Jefferson and Madison hoped that these resolutions would rally voters to the Republican Party as the defender of threatened U.S. liberties. Yet not a single additional state seconded them. In the end, what aroused popular rage against the Federalists was not legislation directed against aliens and subversives but the high cost of Federalist taxes.

The Direct Tax of 1798 fell on all owners of land, dwellings, or slaves and provoked widespread resentment. Enforcing it required an army of bureaucrats—more than 500 for the state of Pennsylvania alone. In February 1799, in the heavily German southeastern counties of Pennsylvania, a group of men led by an auctioneer named John Fries released tax evaders from prison in Bethlehem. President Adams responded to Fries's Rebellion with a show of force, but the fiercest resistance the soldiers he sent to Pennsylvania encountered was from irate farm wives, who doused them with hot water and the contents of chamber pots. Fries and two other men were arrested, convicted of treason, and sentenced to be executed. (Adams later pardoned them.) But the Federalists had now lost much of their support in Pennsylvania.

## THE END OF THE FEDERALISTS

The events in Pennsylvania reflected the air of menace that gripped the country as the campaign of 1800 approached. The army was chasing private citizens whose only crime was resisting hateful taxes. Federal soldiers also roughed up Republican voters at polling places. Southern Republicans talked in private of the possible need to resist Federalist tyranny by force and, failing in that, to secede from the Union. Hamilton and the High Federalists saw in the Kentucky and Virginia resolutions "a regular conspiracy to overturn the government." Reports that Virginia intended to strengthen its militia heightened their anxieties, and they proposed to meet force with force.

No one did more to defuse the charged atmosphere than President Adams. The Federalists depended for their popular support on the expectation of a war with France, which as late as 1798 had swept them to victory in the congressional elections. Still, Adams refrained from asking for a

**Alien and Sedition Acts**   Collective name given to four acts passed by Congress in 1798 that curtailed freedom of speech and the liberty of foreigners resident in the United States.

**⦁⦁⦁ Read the Document**

**at www.myhistorylab.com**
*The Alien and Sedition Acts (1798)*

**states' rights**   Favoring the rights of individual states over rights claimed by the national government.

**nullification**   A constitutional doctrine holding that a state has a legal right to declare a national law null and void within its borders.

**Interpreting the Past**
*Nullification as a Destructive Force in U.S. Politics* (pp. 218–219).

# REPUBLICANS

## Turn out, turn out and save your Country from ruin !

From an *Emperor*—from a *King*—from the iron grasp of a *British Tory Faction*—an unprincipled banditti of British speculators.  The hireling tools and emissaries of his majesty king George the 3d have thronged our city and diffused the poison of principles among us.

### DOWN WITH THE TORIES, DOWN WITH THE BRITISH FACTION,

Before they have it in their power to enslave you, and reduce your families to distress by heavy taxation. Republicans want no Tribute-liars—they want no ship Ocean-liars—they want no Rufus King's for Lords —they want no Varick to lord it over them—they want no Jones for senator, who fought with the British against the Americans in time of the war.—But they want in their places such men as

### *Jefferson & Clinton,*

who fought their Country's Battles in the year '76

By associating their Federalist opponents with the hated Tories of the American Revolution, the Republicans appealed to the voters as the true defenders of American liberation.

Collection of the New-York Historical Society, Negative # 35609.

**Franco-American Accord of 1800**   Settlement reached with France that brought an end to the Quasi-War and released the United States from its 1778 alliance with France.

**Deism**   Religious orientation that rejects divine revelation and holds that the workings of nature alone reveal God's design for the universe.

## QUICK REVIEW

### Presidential Election of 1800

- Federalists could not overcome party disunity.
- Federalists depicted Republicans as godless revolutionaries.
- Strong party organization won election for Republicans Jefferson and Burr.

declaration of war. The United States had been successful in the Quasi-War and in Europe, the tide of war had turned against the French. As a result, Adams believed that the French would now be more open to conciliation. Of greater importance, Adams recognized that war with France could trigger a civil war at home. Hamilton and the High Federalists, he realized, would use war as an excuse to crush the Republican opposition in Virginia. Fearful of Hamilton's intentions and unwilling to run the risk of militarizing the government and saddling it with a huge war debt, Adams broke with his party and decided to reopen negotiations with France in February 1799.

The **Franco-American Accord of 1800** that resulted from Adams's initiative released the United States from its 1778 alliance with France. It also obligated the United States to surrender all claims against the French for damages done to U.S. shipping during the Quasi-War. Once peace with France seemed likely, the Hamiltonian Federalists lost their trump card in the election of 1800. The Republicans could no longer be branded as the traitorous friends of an enemy state. The enlarged army, with no foe to fight, became a political embarrassment, and the Federalists dismantled it. Although rumors of possible violence continued to circulate, the Republicans grew increasingly confident that they could peacefully gain control of the government.

The Federalists nonetheless ran a competitive race in 1800. Adams's peace policy bolstered his popularity. And because U.S. merchants had profited from supplying both sides in the European war, the country was enjoying a period of prosperity that benefited the president and his party. But the party wounds opened by Adams's decision to broker a peace with France continued to fester. Hamilton wrote a scathing attack on the president in a letter that fell into the hands of Aaron Burr, a crafty politician from New York whom the Republicans had teamed up with Jefferson for the presidential election. Burr published the letter, airing the Federalists' squabbling in public.

The Federalists, hampered by party disunity, could not counter the Republicans' aggressive organizational tactics. They found it distasteful to appeal to common people. Wherever they organized, the Republicans attacked the Federalists as monarchists plotting to undo the gains of the Revolution. The Federalists responded with emotional appeals that depicted Jefferson as a godless revolutionary whose election would usher in a reign of terror. "The effect," intoned the Reverend William Linn, "would be to destroy religion, introduce immorality, and loosen all bonds of society."

Attacks like Linn's reflected the fears of Calvinist preachers that a tide of disbelief was about to submerge Christianity in the United States. Church attendance had declined in the 1790s, particularly among men, and perhaps no more than one in twenty Americans was a member of any church. **Deism,** an Enlightenment religious philosophy popular among the leaders of the Revolutionary era, was now beginning to make inroads among ordinary citizens. Deists viewed God as a kind of master clockmaker who created the laws by which the universe runs but otherwise leaves it alone. They rejected revelation for reason, maintaining that the workings of nature alone reveal God's design.

These developments convinced Calvinist ministers, nearly all of them Federalists, that the atheism of the French Revolution was infecting U.S. republicanism. They lashed out at the Republicans, the friends of the French Revolution, as perverters of religious and social order. Jefferson, a deist known for his freethinking in religion, bore the brunt of their attack in 1800.

The Republicans won the election by mobilizing voters through strong party organizations. Voter turnout in 1800 was twice what it had been in the early 1790s, and most of the new voters were Republicans. The Direct Tax of 1798 cost the Federalists the support of commercial farmers in the mid-Atlantic states. Artisans in port cities had already switched to the Republicans in protest over Jay's Treaty, which they feared left them exposed to a flood of cheap British imports. Adams carried New England and had a smattering of support elsewhere. With New York added to their solid base in the South and the backcountry, the Jeffersonians gained an electoral majority (see Map 8–1).

Party unity among Republican electors was so strong that Jefferson and Burr each received 73 electoral votes. Consequently, the election was thrown into the House of Representatives, which, until the newly elected Congress was seated, was still dominated by Federalists. Hoping to deny Jefferson the presidency, the Federalists in the House backed Burr. The result was a deadlock that persisted into the early months of 1801. On February 16, 1801, the Federalists yielded. Informed through intermediaries that Jefferson would not dismantle Hamilton's fiscal system, enough Federalists cast blank ballots to give Jefferson the majority he needed for election. The Twelfth Amendment to the Constitution, ratified in 1804, prevented a similar impasse from arising again by requiring electors to cast separate ballots for president and vice president.

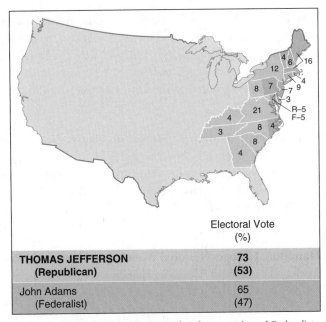

| | Electoral Vote (%) |
|---|---|
| **THOMAS JEFFERSON** (Republican) | **73** **(53)** |
| John Adams (Federalist) | 65 (47) |

MAP 8–1  **The Election of 1800**  The sharp erosion of Federalist strength in New York and Pennsylvania after 1798 swung the election of 1800 to the Republicans.

**Where were** the Federalists strongest? Where were the Republicans strongest? What explains the geographical distribution of political support for the two parties?

# CONCLUSION

In 1789, the U.S. republic was little more than an experiment in self-government. The Federalists provided a firm foundation for that experiment. Hamilton's financial program, neutrality in the wars of the French Revolution, and the diplomatic settlement with Britain in Jay's Treaty bequeathed the young nation a decade of peace and prosperity.

Federalist policies, however, provoked strong opposition rooted in conflicting economic interests and contrasting regional views over the meaning of liberty and government in the new republic. As early as 1789 in the midst of debates in the Senate over a bill to establish a federal judiciary, William Maclay saw the outlines of a plan to subvert Republican liberties. As he put it, "The Constitution is meant to swallow up all the State Constitutions by degrees and this to Swallow by degrees all the State Judiciaries. This at least is the design some Gentlemen seem driving at."

Federalist leadership initially depended on a coalition of regional elites in New England, the mid-Atlantic region, and the slave districts of the South. Fully sharing Maclay's fears over a consolidated government, southern planters were the first of the elites to bolt the Federalist coalition when they joined urban artisans and backcountry Scots-Irish farmers in opposing Jay's Treaty and the commercially oriented program of the Federalists.

During John Adams's administration, Quaker and German farmers in the mid-Atlantic states defected from the Federalists over the tax legislation of 1798, and three of the four regions of the country lined up behind the Republicans. The new Republican majority was united by the belief that the actions of the New England Federalists threatened individual liberty and regional autonomy.

The openly partisan politics of the 1790s surprised the country's founders, who equated parties with the evils of factionalism. They had not foreseen that parties would forge a necessary link between the rulers and the ruled and create a mechanism by which group values and regional interests could be given a political voice. Party formation climaxed in the election of 1800, when the Republicans ended the Federalists' rule.

To the credit of the Federalists, they relinquished control of the national government peacefully. The importance of this precedent can scarcely be exaggerated. It marked the first time in modern political history that a party in power handed over the government to its opposition. It now remained to be seen what the Republicans would do with their newfound power.

# WHERE TO LEARN MORE

**Cincinnati Historical Society, Cincinnati, Ohio.**
Collections include written and visual materials on the history of the Old Northwest Territory. Visit its website, http://www.cincymuseum.org, for information on its programs and the accessibility of its printed and audiovisual collections.

**Federal Hall National Memorial, New York, New York.** This museum and historic site holds artifacts relating to President Washington's inauguration. Its website, http://www.nps.gov/feha/index.htm, includes a printable travel guide to various sites in Manhattan administered by the National Parks Service.

**Hamilton Grange National Memorial, New York, New York.** The home of Alexander Hamilton contains materials on his life. A brief history of the home and Hamilton's life can be found at its website, http://www.nps/gov/hagr/index.htm.

**Adams National Historic Site, Quincy, Massachusetts.**
This site preserves buildings and manuscripts associated with four generations of the Adams family. See its website, http://www.nps.gov/adam/index.htm, for information on guided tours and the various homes that are part of the site.

# REVIEW QUESTIONS

1. What role did the "people" play in Washington's inauguration in 1789? What was the purpose of the grand procession, and why were the militia present?

2. What was distinctive about the four regions of the United States in 1790? What were the common values and goals that brought white Americans together?

3. What were the major problems confronting the Washington administration, and how effectively were they resolved? Why was Washington so cautious when confronted with the outbreak of war in Europe?

4. Who were the Federalists and the Republicans, and how did they differ over the meaning of liberty and the power of the national government? What were the major steps in the formation of two distinct parties in the early United States?

5. Why did regional differences tend to pit the North against the South by the late 1790s?

6. How did the XYZ Affair lead to a political crisis in the United States? Why did the Federalists believe that they would benefit from a war against France?

7. Jefferson called his election in 1800 the "revolution of 1800." What do you think he meant? Would you agree with him?

# KEY TERMS

**Alien and Sedition Acts** (p. 213)
**Bill of Rights** (p. 203)
**Deism** (p. 214)
**Federalists** (p. 206)
**Franco-American Accord of 1800** (p. 214)
**Jay's Treaty** (p. 209)
**Judiciary Act of 1789** (p. 203)
**Nullification** (p. 213)
**Pietists** (p. 199)
**Quasi-War** (p. 212)
**Republican** (p. 206)
**States' rights** (p. 213)
**Tariff Act of 1789** (p. 204)
**Treaty of Greenville** (p. 209)
**Treaty of San Lorenzo** (p. 211)
**Whiskey Rebellion** (p. 209)
**XYZ Affair** (p. 212)

# PEARSON myhistorylab™ Connections

Reinforce what you learned in this chapter by studying the many documents, images, maps, review tools, and videos available at **www.myhistorylab.com**.

## Read and Review

✓● Study and Review  Study Plan: Chapter 8

●●●● Read the Document

*George Washington, Farewell Address (1796)*

*The Alien and Sedition Acts (1798)*

*The Jay Treaty (1794)*

*Alexander Hamilton, An Opinion on the Constitutionality of an Act to Establish a Bank (1791)*

*Proclamation of Neutrality (1793)*

*The Treaty of San Lorenzo (1796)*

*George Washington, Proclamation Regarding the Whiskey Rebellion (1794)*

👁● See the Map *Western Land Claims Ceded by the States*

## Research and Explore

●●●● Read the Document
*Personal Journeys Online*

*From Then to Now Online: Advice for an Empire*

*Exploring America: The Partisan Press*

## ((●● Hear the Audio

Hear the audio files for Chapter 8 at
**www.myhistorylab.com**.

## Nullification as a Destructive Force in U.S. Politics

**TRACE** the development of the concept of nullification from an attempt to protect civil liberties to a defense of slavery and a theory that led to secession and the attempt to destroy the Union.

The concept of nullification arose in the early years of the new republic. An undeclared naval war with France was under way and John Adams was president. French warships were seizing American merchant vessels in the Caribbean. Federalists controlled the presidency and the Congress. Hamilton and the High Federalists were clamoring for war with France. Thomas Jefferson and the Democratic Republicans were offering strong support for France and attacking the Adams administration for making war with the very nation that had helped secure American independence during the Revolution. Democratic Republican editors were torching Adams's name in their papers. In response,

the Federalist Congress passed the Alien and Sedition Acts of 1798 that forbade "false, scandalous, and malicious writing" against the president and government officials.

Thomas Jefferson and James Madison were concerned about the violation of civil rights, and especially freedom of the press, contained within the Sedition Act of 1798. Jefferson and Madison secretly produced the Virginia and Kentucky Resolutions in opposition to the Alien and Sedition Acts. They argued the compact theory of government and suggested that states' rights were supreme over the authority of the federal government. Most important, they suggested that states had the authority to declare null and void any federal legislation that the state legislature considered to be unconstitutional. The power of the U.S. Supreme Court to declare federal laws to be unconstitutional had not yet been established; John Marshall was not yet Chief Justice of the U.S. Supreme Court. Jefferson and Madison, under the concept of states' rights, were attempting to assign that power to the states.

## *Protection is afforded to the minority …*

*James Madison*

### Sedition Act of 1798

**Section 1.** Be it enacted by the Senate and House of Representatives of the United States of America, in Congress assembled, That if any persons shall unlawfully combine or conspire together, with intent to oppose any measure or measures of the government of the United States . . . he or they shall be deemed guilty of a high misdemeanor.

SEC. 2. And be it farther enacted, That if any person shall write, print, utter or publish, or shall cause or procure to be written, printed, uttered or published, or shall knowingly and willingly assist or aid in writing, printing, uttering or publishing any false, scandalous and malicious writing or writings against the government of the United States . . . (they) . . . shall be punished by a fine not exceeding two thousand dollars, and by imprisonment not exceeding two years.

### James Madison, Virginia Resolution (1799)

That this Assembly doth explicitly and peremptorily declare, that it views the powers of the federal government, as resulting from the compact, to which the states are parties; as limited by the plain sense and intention of the instrument constituting the compact; as no further valid that they are authorized by the grants enumerated in that compact; and that in case of a deliberate, palpable, and dangerous exercise of other powers, not granted by the said compact, the states who are parties thereto, have the right, and are in duty bound, to interpose for arresting the progress of the evil, and for maintaining within their respective limits, the authorities, rights and liberties appertaining to them.

That the General Assembly doth particularly protest against the palpable and alarming infractions of the Constitution, in the two late cases of the "Alien and Sedition Acts" passed at the last session of Congress; the first of which exercises a power no where delegated to the federal government

. . . the General Assembly doth solemnly appeal to the like dispositions of the other states, in confidence that they will concur with this commonwealth in declaring, as it does hereby declare, that the acts aforesaid, are unconstitutional; and that the necessary and proper measures will be taken by each, for co-operating with this state, in maintaining the Authorities, Rights, and Liberties, referred to the States respectively, or to the people.

## Kentucky Resolution (1799)
## (secretly authored by Thomas Jefferson)

RESOLVED, That this commonwealth considers the federal union, upon the terms and for the purposes specified in the late compact, as conducive to the liberty and happiness of the several states: That it does now unequivocally declare its attachment to the Union, and to that compact, agreeable to its obvious and real intention, and will be among the last to seek its dissolution: That if those who administer the general government be permitted to transgress the limits fixed by that compact, by a total disregard to the special delegations of power therein contained, annihilation of the state governments, and the erection upon their ruins, of a general consolidated government, will be the inevitable consequence: That the principle and construction contended for by sundry of the state legislatures, that the general government is the exclusive judge of the extent of the powers delegated to it, stop nothing short of despotism; since the discretion of those who administer the government, and not the constitution, would be the measure of their powers: That the several states who formed that instrument, being sovereign and independent, have the unquestionable right to judge of its infraction; and that a nullification, by those sovereignties, of all unauthorized acts done under

*Thomas Jefferson*

colour of that instrument, is the rightful remedy: That this commonwealth does upon the most deliberate reconsideration declare, that the said alien and sedition laws, are in their opinion, palpable violations of the said constitution . . .

## South Carolina's Exposition and Protest, 1828 (secretly authored by John C. Calhoun)

But the existence of the right of judging of their powers (the federal government), so clearly established from the sovereignty of States, as clearly implies a veto or control, within its limits, on the action of the General Government, on contested points of authority; and this very control is the remedy which the Constitution has provided to prevent the encroachments of the General Government on the reserved rights of the States; and by which the distribution of power, between the General and State Governments, may be preserved for ever inviolable, on the basis established by the Constitution. It is thus effectual protection is afforded to the minority, against the oppression of the majority. . . .

## President Jackson's Proclamation Regarding Nullification, December 10, 1832

If this doctrine (nullification) had been established at an earlier day, the Union would have been dissolved in its infancy. . . . The discovery of this important feature in our Constitution was reserved to the present day. To the statesmen of South Carolina belongs the invention, and upon the citizens of that State will, unfortunately, fall the evils of reducing it to practice. . . .

I consider, then, the power to annul a law of the United States, assumed by one State, incompatible with the existence of the Union, contradicted expressly by the letter of the Constitution, unauthorized by its spirit, inconsistent with every principle on which It was founded, and destructive of the great object for which it was formed. . . .

## South Carolina Ordinance of Secession, 1860

AN ORDINANCE to dissolve the union between the State of South Carolina and other States united with her under the compact entitled "The Constitution of the United States of America."

We, the people of the State of South Carolina, in convention assembled, do declare and ordain, and it is hereby declared and ordained, That the ordinance adopted by us in convention on the twenty-third day of May, in the year of our Lord one thousand seven hundred and eighty-eight, whereby the Constitution of the United States of America was ratified, and also all acts and parts of acts of the General Assembly of this State ratifying amendments of the said Constitution, are hereby repealed; and that the union now subsisting between South Carolina and other States, under the name of the "United States of America," is hereby dissolved.

*The union . . . is hereby dissolved . . .*

# 9

# The Triumph and Collapse
# of Jeffersonian Republicanism

The British bombardment of Fort McHenry, Baltimore, on September 13–14, 1814, inspired the writing of "The Star-Spangled Banner."

## JEFFERSON'S PRESIDENCY  *(page 224)*

**WHY WAS** the expansion of the
United States so important to Jefferson?

## MADISON AND THE COMING OF WAR  *(page 229)*

**WHAT FACTORS** pushed Madison
into a war with Britain?

## THE WAR OF 1812  *(page 232)*

**WHAT WERE** the consequences
of the War of 1812?

## THE ERA OF GOOD FEELINGS  *(page 235)*

**HOW DID** rising nationalism contribute
to the spirit of the Era of Good Feelings?

## THE BREAKDOWN OF UNITY  *(page 239)*

**WHY DID** slavery become such a divisive issue
in the years preceding the Missouri Compromise?

ONE AMERICAN JOURNEY

*Riversdale, 30 August 1814*

*My dear Sister,*

*Since I started this letter [on Aug. 9] we have been in a state of continual alarm, and now I have time to write only two or three lines to ask you to tell Papa that we are alive, in good health, and I hope safe from danger. I am sure that you have heard the news of the battle of Bladensburg where the English defeated the American troops with Madison 'not at their head, but at their rear.'*

*From there they went to Washington where they burned the Capitol, the President's House, all the public offices, etc. During the battle I saw several cannonballs with my own eyes, and I will write all the details to your husband. At the moment the English ships are at Alexandria which is also in their possession.*

*I don't know how all this will end, but I fear very badly for us. It is probable that it will also bring about a dissolution of the union of the states, and in that case, farewell to the public debt. You know I have predicted this outcome for a long time. Wouldn't it be wise to send your husband here without delay, in order to plan with me the best course to pursue for Papa's interests as well as yours?*

*This letter will go, I think, by a Dutch ship. If I have time with the confusion we are in, I will write again in a few days, perhaps by the same vessel. At present my house is full of people every day and at night my bedroom is full of rifles, pistols, sabers, etc. Many thanks to your husband for the information in his letter of 27 April, and tell him that I invested all his money in the May loan [of the U.S. Treasury]. Please give many greetings to my dear Father and to Charles [her brother]. Embrace your children for me and believe me,*

*Your affectionate sister,*

*Rosalie E. Calvert*

Margaret Law Callcott, ed., *Mistress of Riversdale: The Plantation Letters of Rosalie Stier Calvert, 1795–1821* (Baltimore: Johns Hopkins University Press, 1991), pp. 271–272.

**Read the Document** at **www.myhistorylab.com**

Personal Journeys Online

- George Robert Gleig, *Burning of Washington*, August 23, 1814. A British soldier describes the destruction in Washington.

- Dolley Madison, Letter to her sister, August 23, 1814. Dolley Madison describes the abandonment of the White House.

- Lt. Col. R. E. Parker, Letter to the governor, June 11, 1814. A Virginia soldier relates how the slaves plotted to escape behind British lines.

ROSALIE CALVERT was the youngest of the three children of a wealthy Belgian family that had fled the advancing armies of revolutionary France in 1794. Her father, Henri J. Stier, had planned in advance for his family's departure and brought with him a sizable fortune in gold, U.S. currency, and paintings. The family, unsurprisingly, was strongly Federalist in its political leanings. In 1799, Rosalie married George Calvert, a descendant of the proprietors of the Maryland colony and a kinsman of the Washingtons.

The coming to power of the Jeffersonian Republicans in 1801 triggered bitter memories of the revolutionary turmoil Rosalie had experienced as a young woman in Belgium. In her eyes, Jefferson and his followers were demagogues who catered to the poor and threatened to infect the United States with the political radicalism of the French Revolution. She blamed the War of 1812 on ignorant, ill-conceived Republican policies and feared that the war would unleash massive unrest. Particularly

## CHRONOLOGY

| | |
|---|---|
| **1801** | Thomas Jefferson is inaugurated, the first Republican president. |
| | John Marshall becomes chief justice. |
| **1802** | Congress repeals the Judiciary Act of 1801. |
| **1803** | *Marbury v. Madison* sets the precedent of judicial review by the Supreme Court. |
| | Louisiana Purchase. |
| | Lewis and Clark expedition begins. |
| | Britain and France resume their war after a brief peace. |
| **1804** | Vice President Aaron Burr kills Alexander Hamilton in a duel. |
| | Judges John Pickering and Samuel Chase impeached by Republicans. |
| **1806** | Britain and France issue orders restricting neutral shipping. |
| | Betrayal of the Burr conspiracy. |
| **1807** | *Chesapeake* affair. |
| | Congress passes the Embargo Act. |
| | Congress prohibits the African slave trade. |
| **1808** | James Madison elected president. |
| **1809** | Repeal of the Embargo Act. |
| | Passage of the Nonintercourse Act. |
| **1810–1825** | Revolutions and independence movements in Latin America. |
| **1810** | Macon's Bill No. 2 reopens trade with Britain and France. |
| | United States annexes part of West Florida. |
| | Georgia state law invalidated by the Supreme Court in *Fletcher v. Peck*. |
| **1811** | Battle of Tippecanoe and defeat of the Indian confederation. |
| | Charter of the Bank of the United States expires. |
| **1812** | Congress declares war on Britain. |
| | American loss of Detroit. |
| | Napoleon invades Russia. |

| | |
|---|---|
| **1813** | Perry's victory at Battle of Put-in-Bay. |
| | Battle of the Thames and death of Tecumseh. |
| **1814** | Jackson crushes the Creeks at the Battle of Horseshoe Bend. |
| | British burn Washington, DC, and attack Baltimore. |
| | Macdonough's naval victory on Lake Champlain turns back a British invasion. |
| | Hartford Convention meets. |
| | Treaty of Ghent signed. |
| **1815** | Jackson routs British at the Battle of New Orleans. |
| | Congress of Vienna arranges a peace settlement for Europe after Napoleon's defeat at Waterloo. |
| **1816** | Congress charters the Second Bank of the United States and passes a protective tariff. |
| | James Monroe elected president. |
| **1817** | Rush-Bagot Treaty demilitarizes the Great Lakes. |
| **1818** | Anglo-American Accords on trade and boundaries. |
| | Jackson's border campaign in Spanish East Florida. |
| **1819** | Trans-Continental Treaty between United States and Spain. |
| | Beginning of the Missouri controversy. |
| | Financial panic sends economy into a depression. |
| | *McCulloch v. Maryland* upholds constitutionality of the Bank of the United States. |
| **1820** | Missouri Compromise on slavery in the Louisiana Purchase. |
| | Monroe reelected. |
| **1821** | Greek revolt against the Turks. |
| **1822** | The United States extends diplomatic recognition to the new nations of Latin America. |
| **1823** | Monroe Doctrine proclaims Western Hemisphere closed to further European colonization. |
| **1825** | John Quincy Adams elected president by the House of Representatives. |

alarming was the news that a mob in Baltimore had brutally beaten twelve prominent Federalists for their antiwar stand. Thus the sense of "continual alarm" that runs through her letter in August 1814, at a time when the war had spilled over into her home.

Despite Rosalie's denunciations of the Republicans, Jefferson's party succeeded in promoting the growth and independence of the United States in the first quarter of the nineteenth century. Expansionist policies to the south and west more than doubled the size of the republic and fueled the westward spread of slavery. The war against Britain from 1812 to 1815, if less than a military triumph, nonetheless freed Americans to look inward for economic development.

At the height of Republican success just after the War of 1812, the Federalist Party collapsed, and with it the social and political elitism championed by Rosalie Calvert and her father. Without an organized opposition to enforce party discipline, the Republicans soon followed the Federalists into political oblivion. The nation's expansion produced two crises—a financial panic and a battle over slavery in Missouri—that shattered the facade of Republican unity. By the mid-1820s, a new party system was emerging. ✦

# JEFFERSON'S PRESIDENCY

**WHY WAS** the expansion of the United States so important to Jefferson?

•◖•┤Read the Document
at www.myhistorylab.com
*Margaret Bayard Smith, Reflections Upon Meeting Thomas Jefferson (1801)*

•◖•┤Read the Document
at www.myhistorylab.com
*Thomas Jefferson, First Inaugural Address (1801)*

**WHERE TO LEARN MORE**

★ Monticello, Charlottesville, Virginia
http://www.monticello.org/

Thomas Jefferson believed that a true revolution had occurred in 1800, a peaceful overthrow of the Federalist Party and its hated principles of government consolidation and military force. In his eyes, the defeat of the monarchical Federalists reconfirmed the true political legacy of the Revolution by restoring the Republican majority to its rightful control of the government.

Unlike the Hamiltonian Federalists, whose commercial vision of the United States accepted social and economic inequalities as inevitable, the Jeffersonians wanted a predominantly agrarian republic based on widespread economic equality for white yeomen families to counter any threat posed by the privileged few to the people's liberties. Thus, they favored territorial expansion as a means of adding enough land to maintain self-reliant farmers as the guardians of republican freedoms. They also favored the spread of slavery. As long as racial slavery promoted a sense of unity among free white men, they were confident that a populist democracy could coexist with elite rule.

## REFORM AT HOME

The cornerstone of Republican domestic policy was a return to the frugal, simple federal establishment the Jeffersonians believed to be the original intent of the Constitution. Determined to root out what they viewed as Federalist corruption and patronage, the Republicans began by reforming fiscal policy. Jefferson's secretary of the treasury was Albert Gallatin, a native of Switzerland who emerged in the 1790s as the best financial mind in the Republican Party. He convinced Jefferson that the Bank of the United States was essential for financial stability and blocked efforts to dismantle it. Unlike Hamilton, however, Gallatin thought that a large public debt was a curse, a drag on productive capital, and an unfair burden on future generations. He succeeded in reducing the national debt from $83 million in 1800 to $57 million by 1809.

Gallatin's conservative fiscal policies shrank both the spending and taxes of the national government. The Republicans eliminated all internal taxes, including the despised tax on whiskey. Slashes in the military budget kept government expenditures below the level of 1800. The cuts in military spending, combined with soaring revenues from customs collections, left Gallatin with a surplus in the budget that he could devote to debt repayment.

Jeffersonian reform targeted the political character, as well as the size, of the national government. He moved to break the Federalist stranglehold on federal offices by appointing officials with sound Republican principles. Arch-Federalists, those Jefferson deemed guilty of misusing their offices for openly political reasons, were immediately replaced, and Republicans filled other posts opened up by attrition. By the time Jefferson left the presidency in 1809, Republicans held nearly all the appointive offices.

Jefferson moved most aggressively against the Federalists in the judiciary. Just days before they relinquished power, the Federalists passed the Judiciary Act of 1801, legislation that both enlarged the judiciary and packed it with more Federalists appointed by Adams, the outgoing president.

The Republicans fought back. Now dominant in Congress, they quickly repealed the Judiciary Act of 1801. Frustrated Federalists now turned to John Marshall, a staunch Federalist appointed chief justice of the United States by President Adams in 1801, hoping that he would

The classical design and bucolic setting of Monticello, Jefferson's home outside Charlottesville, Virginia, visually expressed both his aristocratic tastes and his vision of a harmonious agrarian republic.

Jane Braddick Petticolas (1791–1852), "View of the West Front of Monticello and Garden," 1825, watercolor on paper, 13 5/8 × 18 1/18 inches. Edward Owen/Monticello/Thomas Jefferson Foundation, Inc.

rule that Congress had acted unconstitutionally in removing the recently appointed federal judges. Marshall moved carefully to avoid an open confrontation. He was aware that the Republicans contended that Congress and the president had at least a coequal right with the Supreme Court to decide constitutional questions.

The issue came to a head in the case of **Marbury v. Madison** (1803), which centered on Secretary of State James Madison's refusal to deliver a commission to William Marbury, one of Adams's "midnight appointments" (so-called because Adams made them on his next-to-last day in office) as a justice of the peace for the District of Columbia. Marshall held that although Marbury had a legal right to his commission, the Court had no jurisdiction in the case. The Court ruled that the section of the Judiciary Act of 1789 granting it the power to order the delivery of Marbury's commission was unconstitutional because it conferred on the Court a power not specified in the Constitution. Stating that it was "emphatically the province and duty of the judicial department to say what the law is," Marshall created the precedent of judicial review, the power of the Supreme Court to rule on the constitutionality of federal law. This doctrine was of pivotal importance for the future of the Court.

## THE LOUISIANA PURCHASE

In foreign affairs, fortune smiled on Jefferson during his first term. The European war that had almost sucked in the United States in the 1790s subsided. Britain and France agreed on a truce in 1802. The Anglo-French peace allowed Spain and France to reclaim their colonial trade in the Western Hemisphere. The new ruler of France, Napoleon Bonaparte, was also now free to

**Marbury v. Madison**   Supreme Court decision of 1803 that created the precedent of judicial review by ruling as unconstitutional part of the Judiciary Act of 1789.

**Read the Document**
at www.myhistorylab.com
*Marbury v. Madison (1803)*

### QUICK REVIEW

**Judiciary Act of 1801**

♦ Enlarged the judiciary and packed it with Adams's appointees.

♦ Repealed by Republican Congress.

♦ Conflict came to head in case of *Marbury v. Madison* (1803).

 **See the Map**
at www.myhistorylab.com
*The Louisiana Purchase*

Masterful hunters, the Plains Indians encountered by Lewis and Clark depended on the buffalo for their economic survival.

develop his plans for reviving the French empire in America. In a secret treaty with Spain in 1800, Napoleon reacquired for France the Louisiana Territory, a vast, vaguely defined area stretching between the Mississippi River and the Rocky Mountains.

Sketchy, unconfirmed reports of the treaty reached Jefferson in the spring of 1801, and he was immediately alarmed. French control of the Mississippi Valley, combined with the British presence in Canada, threatened to hem in the United States and deprive Jefferson's farmers of their empire of liberty.

Jefferson was prepared to reverse his party's traditional foreign policy to eliminate this threat. He opened exploratory talks with the British on an Anglo-American alliance to drive the French out of Louisiana. He also strengthened U.S. forces in the Mississippi Valley and secured congressional approval for the Lewis and Clark expedition through upper Louisiana. Although best known for its scientific discoveries, this expedition was designed initially as a military mission. Jefferson applied diplomatic and military pressure to induce Napoleon to sell New Orleans and a small slice of coastal territory to its east to the United States. This was his main objective: to possess New Orleans and control the mouth of the Mississippi River, outlet to world markets. To his surprise, Napoleon suddenly decided in early 1803 to sell all of the immense Louisiana Territory to the United States.

Napoleon's failure to reconquer Saint-Domingue (modern-day Haiti) was instrumental in his about-face on plans for a revived French empire in America. He had envisioned this rich sugar island as the jewel of his new empire and intended to use the Louisiana Territory as a granary to supply the island. During the upheavals of the French Revolution, the slaves on the island, led by Touissant L'Ouverture, rebelled in a bloody and successful bid for independence. Napoleon sent a large army to reassert French control, but it succumbed to disease and the islanders' fierce resistance. Without firm French control of Saint-Domingue, Louisiana was of little use to Napoleon. For $15 million (including about $4 million in French debts owed to American citizens), he offered to part with the whole of Louisiana. The cost to the United States was about 3.5 cents per acre.

Jefferson, the strict constructionist, now turned pragmatist. Despite the lack of any specific authorization in the Constitution for the acquisition of foreign territory or the incorporation as U.S. citizens of the 50,000 French and Spanish descendants then living in Louisiana, he accepted Napoleon's deal. The Louisiana Purchase doubled the size of the United States and offered seemingly endless space to be settled by yeoman farmers. It also opened up another frontier for slaveholders in the lower Mississippi Valley.

## FLORIDA AND WESTERN SCHEMES

The magnificent prize of Louisiana did not satisfy Republican territorial ambitions. Still to be gained were river outlets on the Gulf Coast essential for the development of plantation agriculture in Alabama and Mississippi. The boundaries of the Louisiana Purchase were so vague that Jefferson felt justified in claiming Spanish-held Texas and the Gulf Coast eastward from New Orleans to Mobile Bay, including the Spanish province of West Florida. Against stiff Spanish

## AMERICAN VIEWS

###  Protest of French Settlers in Louisiana

In the Louisiana Ordinance of 1804, Congress divided the Louisiana Purchase territory into northern and southern parts along a line that later separated the future state of Louisiana (originally designated the Territory of Orleans) from the territory to the north. No rights of self-government were extended to the settlers in Louisiana. Instead, a territorial government was established for which the president appointed both the governor and his advisory council. Congress also prohibited the inhabitants from engaging in the foreign slave trade and restricted the admission of future slaves to the bona-fide property of the actual settlers. A bill limiting the bondage of incoming slaves to one year passed the House but was rejected in the Senate. The following memorial to Congress registers the grievances of the French settlers over their treatment.

- **What** feature of congressional policy did the settlers single out as a major grievance?
- **Why** were the settlers so insistent that slavery was essential to their economic progress?
- **Why** do you think that Congress quickly abandoned its initial effort to restrict the growth of slavery in the Territory of Orleans?

We the subscribers, Planters, Merchants and other inhabitants of Louisiana respectfully approach the Legislature of the United States with a memorial of our rights, [and] a remonstrance against certain laws which contravene them. . . .

Without any agency in the events which have annexed our country to the United States, we yet considered them as fortunate, and thought our liberties secured even before we knew the terms of the cession. Persuaded that a free people would acquire territory only to extend the blessings of freedom, that an enlightened nation would never destroy those principles on which its government was founded, and that their Representatives would disdain to become the instruments of oppression, we calculated with certainty that their first act of sovereignty would be a communication of all the blessings they enjoyed. . . .

We pray leave to examine the law for erecting Louisiana. . . . This act does not "incorporate us into the Union," that it vests us with none of the "Rights," gives us no advances and deprives us of all the "immunities" of American citizens. . . .

A Governor is to be placed over us, whom we have not chosen, whom we do not even know, who may be ignorant of our language, uninformed of our institutions, and who may have no connections with our Country or interest in its welfare. . . .

We know not with what view the territory North of the 33d degree has been severed from us. . . . If this division should operate as to prolong our state of political tutelage, on account of any supposed deficiency of numbers, we cannot but consider it as injurious to our rights, and therefore enumerate it among those points of which we have reason to complain. . . .

There is one subject however extremely interesting to us, in which great care has been taken to prevent any interference even by the Governor and Council, selected by the President himself. The African trade is absolutely prohibited, and severe penalties imposed on a traffic free to all the Atlantic states, who choose to engage in it, and as far as it relates to procuring the subjects of it from other states [the domestic slave trade], permitted even in the territory of the Mississippi.

It is not our intention to enter into arguments that have become familiar to every reasoner on this question. We only ask the right of deciding it for ourselves, and of being placed in this aspect on an equal footing with other states. To the necessity of employing African labourers, which arises from climate, and the species of cultivation [sugar], pursued in warm latitudes, is added reason in this country peculiar to itself. The banks raised to restrain the waters of the Mississippi can only be kept in repair by those whose natural constitution and habits of labour enable them to resist the combined effects of a deleterious moisture, and a degree of heat intolerable to whites; this labour is great, it requires many hands and it is all important to the very existence of our country. . . .

Another subject . . . of great moment to us, is the sudden change of language in all the public offices and administration of justice. The great mass of the inhabitants speak nothing but the French: the late government was always very careful in their selection of officers, to find men who possessed our language and with whom we could personally communicate. . . .

We therefore respectfully pray that so much of the law mentioned above as provides for the temporary government of this country, as divides it into two territories, and prohibits the importation of slaves, be repealed.

*Source:* Pierre Derbigney, Memorial Presented by the Inhabitants of Louisiana to the Congress of the United States, Washington: Samuel H. Smith, 1804, Gilder Lehman Collection of American History, Pierpont Morgan Library, cited in *The Boisterous Sea of Liberty: A Documentary History of America from Discovery through the Civil War,* ed. by David Brion Davis and Steven Mintz (New York: Oxford University Press, 1998), pp. 290–293.

The PRAIRIE DOG sickened at the sting of the HORNET or a Diplomatic Puppet exhibiting his Deceptions!

This Federalist cartoon satirizes Jefferson, in the form of a prairie dog, coughing up the $2 million bribe to Napoleon for the acquisition of West Florida, while a French diplomat stands by dancing and taunting Jefferson.

## QUICK REVIEW

### Jefferson and Florida

- Jefferson failed in attempts to buy West Florida.
- Westerners demanded that the territory be taken by force.
- Aaron Burr involved in failed conspiracy to seize land in Florida.

opposition, he pushed ahead with his plans to acquire West Florida. This provoked the first challenge to his leadership of the party.

Once it was clear that Spain did not want to sell West Florida to the United States, Jefferson accepted Napoleon's offer to act as a middleman in the acquisition. Napoleon's price was $2 million. He soon lost interest in the project, however, and Jefferson lost prestige in 1806, when he pushed an appropriations bill through Congress to pay for Napoleon's services. Former Republican stalwarts in Congress denounced the bill as bribe money and staged a party revolt against the president's devious tactics.

Jefferson's failed bid for West Florida emboldened westerners to demand that Americans seize the territory by force. In 1805 and 1806, Aaron Burr, Jefferson's first vice president, apparently became entangled in an attempt at just such a land grab.

Republicans had been suspicious of Burr since his dalliance with the Federalists in their bid to make him, rather than Jefferson, president in 1800. He further alienated the party when he involved himself with the efforts of a minority of die-hard Federalists known as the Essex Junto. The members of this group feared that incorporation of the vast Louisiana Purchase into the United States would leave New England powerless in national affairs. They concocted a plan for a northern confederacy in which New York would play a key role. Rebuffed by Hamilton, they turned to Burr and backed him in the New York gubernatorial race of 1804. Burr lost, largely because Hamilton denounced him. The enmity between the two men reached a tragic climax in July 1804, when Burr killed Hamilton in a duel at Weehawken, New Jersey. Burr, indicted for murder in the state of New Jersey, was nonetheless able to return to Washington where he both resumed his duties as vice president and hatched a separatist plot for the West.

The Burr conspiracy remains mysterious. Burr was undoubtedly eager to pry land loose from the Spanish and Indians, and he may have been thinking of carving out a separate western confederacy in the lower Mississippi Valley. Whatever he had in mind, he blundered in relying on General James Wilkinson as a co-conspirator. Wilkinson, the military governor of the Louisiana Territory and also a double agent for Spain, betrayed Burr. He was tried for treason in 1807, and Jefferson made extraordinary efforts to secure his conviction. He was saved by the insistence of Chief Justice Marshall that the Constitution defined treason only as the waging of war against the United States or the rendering of aid to its enemies. The law also required the direct testimony of two witnesses to an "overt act" of treason for conviction. Lacking such witnesses, the government failed to prove its case, and Burr was acquitted.

## EMBARGO AND A CRIPPLED PRESIDENCY

Concern about a possible war against Britain in 1807 soon quieted the uproar over Burr's trial. After Britain and France had resumed their war in 1803, the United States became enmeshed in the same quarrels over neutral rights, blockades, ship seizures, and **impressment** of U.S. sailors that had almost dragged the country into war in the 1790s. Britain proclaimed a blockade of the European continent, which was controlled by Napoleon, and confiscated the cargoes of ships attempting to run the blockade. Napoleon retaliated with seizures of ships that submitted to

**impressment**  The coercion of American sailors into the British navy.

British searches and accepted the British-imposed licensing system for trading with Europe. Caught in the middle, but eager to supply both sides, was the U.S. merchant marine, the world's largest carrier of neutral goods.

U.S. merchants and shippers had taken full advantage of the opportunities opened by the European war. Despite French and British restrictions, American merchants traded with anyone they pleased. They dominated commerce, not only between Britain and the United States, but also between the European continent and the French and Spanish colonies in the West Indies. Profits were so great that merchants made money even when only one-third of their ships evaded the blockades.

In June 1807, however, a confrontation known as the **Chesapeake Incident** nearly triggered an Anglo-American war. A British ship, the *Leopard*, ordered a U.S. frigate, the *Chesapeake*, to submit to a search in coastal waters off Norfolk, Virginia. When the commander of the *Chesapeake* refused, the *Leopard* opened fire. Jefferson resisted the popular outcry for revenge. Instead, he barred U.S. ports to British warships and called both for monetary compensation and an end to impressments, not only because the country was woefully unprepared for war but also because he passionately believed that international law should settle disputes between nations.

In a last burst of the idealism that had animated the republicanism of the Revolution, Jefferson resorted to a trade embargo as a substitute for war. The **Embargo Act of 1807,** an expression of Jefferson's policy of "peaceable coercion," prohibited U.S. ships from leaving port to any nation until Britain and France repealed their trading restrictions on neutral shippers.

The premise of the embargo was that Europe was so dependent on American foods and raw materials that it would do America's bidding if faced with a cutoff. This premise was not so much wrong as unrealistic. The embargo did hurt Europe, but the people who first felt the pain were British textile workers and slaves in the colonies, hardly those who wielded the levers of power. Meanwhile, politically influential landlords and manufacturers benefited from short-term shortages by jacking up prices.

The U.S. export trade and its profits dried up with Jefferson's self-imposed blockade. Except for manufacturers, who now had the U.S. market to themselves, nearly all economic groups suffered under the embargo. Especially hard hit were New England shippers and merchants, and they accused the Republicans of near-criminal irresponsibility for forcing a depression on the country. Jefferson responded to these criticisms and to widespread violations of the embargo with a series of enforcement acts that consolidated executive powers far beyond what the Federalists themselves had been able to achieve while in power.

As the embargo tightened and the 1808 presidential election approached, the Federalist Party revived. The Federalist presidential candidate, Charles C. Pinckney, running against Secretary of State James Madison, Jefferson's handpicked successor, polled three times as many votes as he had in 1804. Madison won only because he carried the South and the West, the Republican heartland.

Before Madison took office, the Republicans abandoned Jefferson's embargo, replacing it with the Nonintercourse Act, a measure that prohibited U.S. trade only with Britain and France. At the president's discretion, trade could be reopened with either nation once it lifted its restrictions on U.S. shipping.

**Chesapeake Incident**   Attack in 1807 by the British ship *Leopard* on the American ship *Chesapeake* in American territorial waters.

**Embargo Act of 1807**   Act passed by Congress in 1807 prohibiting American ships from leaving for any foreign port.

<u>QUICK REVIEW</u>

**Growth of American Trade: 1793–1807**

- Britain and France resumed war in 1803.
- American merchants wanted to supply both sides.
- Value of American exports increased fivefold between 1793 and 1807.

## MADISON AND THE COMING OF WAR

Frail-looking and short, Madison struck most contemporaries as an indecisive and weaker version of Jefferson. Yet in intellectual toughness and resourcefulness he was at least Jefferson's equal. He failed because of an inherited foreign policy that was partly of his own making as Jefferson's secretary of state. The Republicans' idealistic stand on neutral rights was ultimately

**WHAT FACTORS** pushed Madison into a war with Britain?

untenable unless backed up by military and political force. Madison concluded as much when he decided on war against Britain in the spring of 1812.

A war against America's old enemy also promised to restore unity to a Republican Party increasingly divided over Madison's peaceful diplomacy. Thus did Madison and his fellow Republicans push for a war they were eager but unprepared to fight.

## THE FAILURE OF ECONOMIC SANCTIONS

As pressure mounted to reopen all trade routes, Congress responded in 1810 by replacing the Nonintercourse Act with Macon's Bill No. 2, named after Congressman Nathaniel Macon. This measure threw open American trade to everyone but stipulated that if either France or England lifted its restrictions, the president would resume trading sanctions against the other. Napoleon now duplicitously promised to withdraw his decrees against U.S. shipping on the condition that if Britain did not follow suit, Madison would force the British to respect U.S. rights. To Madison's chagrin, French seizures of U.S. ships continued. By the time Napoleon's duplicity became clear, he had already succeeded in worsening Anglo-American tensions. In November 1810, Madison reimposed nonintercourse against Britain, putting the two nations on a collision course.

## THE FRONTIER AND INDIAN RESISTANCE

Mounting frustrations in the South and West also pushed Madison toward a war against Britain. Nearly a million Americans lived west of the Appalachian Mountains in 1810, a tripling of the western population in just a decade. Farm prices, including those for the southern staples of cotton and tobacco, plunged when Jefferson's embargo shut off exports, and they stayed low after the embargo was lifted. Blame for the persistent agricultural depression focused on the British and their stranglehold on overseas trade after 1808. Western settlers also accused the British of inciting Indian resistance. However, it was the unceasing demand of Americans for ever more Indian land, not any British incitement, that triggered the **pan-Indian resistance movement** that so frightened western settlers on the eve of the War of 1812.

In the Treaty of Greenville (1795) (see Chapter 8), the U.S. government had promised that any future acquisitions of Indian land would be approved by all native peoples in the region. Nonetheless, government agents continued to play one group against another and divide groups from within by lavishing money and goods on the more accommodationist Christianized Indians. By such means, William Henry Harrison, the governor of the Indiana Territory, procured most of southern Indiana in the Treaty of Vincennes of 1804. Two extraordinary leaders, the Shawnee chief Tecumseh and his brother, the Prophet Tenkswatawa, channeled Indian outrage over this treaty into a movement to unify tribes throughout the West for a stand against the white invaders.

The message of pan-Indianism was unwavering: White encroachments had to be stopped and tribal and clan divisions submerged in a return to native rituals and belief systems. With the assistance of Tecumseh, Tenkswatawa established the Prophet's Town in 1808. At the confluence of the Wabash and Tippecanoe rivers in north-central Indiana, this encampment became headquarters of an intertribal confederation. As he tried to explain to the worried Governor Harrison, his goals were peaceful. He admonished his followers, "[Do] not take up the tomahawk, should it be offered by the British, or by the long knives [Virginians]: do not meddle with any thing that does not belong to you, but mind your own business, and cultivate the ground, that your women and your children have enough to live on."

That ground, of course, was the very reason the Indians could not live in peace and dignity. White settlers wanted it and would do anything to get it. In November 1811, Harrison marched an army to Prophet's Town and provoked the Battle of Tippecanoe. Losses were heavy on both sides, but Harrison regrouped his forces, drove the surviving Indians away, and burned

**pan-Indian resistance movement** Movement calling for the political and cultural unification of Indian tribes in the late eighteenth and early nineteenth centuries.

the abandoned town. Harrison's victory came at a high cost: Tecumseh now joined forces with the British, leaving the frontier more unsettled than ever.

While Harrison's aggressiveness was converting fears of a British-Indian alliance into a self-fulfilling prophecy, expansionist-minded southerners struck at Britain through Spain, now its ally against Napoleon. With the covert support of President Madison, U.S. adventurers staged a bloodless revolt in Spanish West Florida between Louisiana and the Pearl River. This "republic" was quickly recognized by the U.S. government and annexed as part of Louisiana in 1811.

Hatred of Native Americans, expansionist pressures, the lingering agricultural depression, and impatience with the administration's policy of economic coercion all pointed in the same direction: a war against Britain coupled with a U.S. takeover of British Canada and what remained of Spanish Florida. This was the rallying cry of the **War Hawks,** the forty or so prowar congressmen swept into office in 1810. Generally younger men from the South and West, the War Hawks were led by Henry Clay of Kentucky. Along with other outspoken nationalists, such as John C. Calhoun of South Carolina, Clay played a key role in building congressional support for Madison's growing aggressiveness on the British issue.

## DECISION FOR WAR

In July 1811, Madison issued a Proclamation calling Congress into an early session on November 4. When Congress met, Madison tried to lay the groundwork for war. But the Republican-controlled Congress balked at strengthening the military or raising taxes to pay for war. On June 1, he sent a war message to Congress in which he laid out the stark alternative of submission or resistance to British control of U.S. commerce. Madison was now convinced that British commercial restrictions were not just a defensive measure aimed at France but an aggressive attempt to reduce the United States to the permanent status of colonial dependent.

For Madison and most other Republicans, the impending conflict was a second war for independence. Free and open access to world markets was certainly at stake, but so was national pride. The arrogant British policy of impressment was a humiliating affront to U.S. honor and headed the list of grievances in Madison's war message.

A divided Congress declared war on Britain. Support for the war was strongest in regions whose economies had been damaged the most by the British blockade and control of Atlantic commerce. Thus, the South and the West, trapped in an agricultural depression and anxious to eliminate foreign threats at their frontiers, favored war. Conversely, mercantile New England, a region that had, ironically, prospered as a result of British interference with ocean commerce, opposed the war.

The votes that carried the war declaration came from northern Republicans, who saw the impending struggle as a defense of America's experiment in self-government. Nine-tenths of the congressional Republicans voted for war, but not a single Federalist did so. For the Federalists, the real enemy was France, which had actually seized more U.S. ships than had the British. From their strongholds in coastal New England, the Federalists condemned the war as a French-inspired plot and predicted that it would end in financial ruin.

The Federalists' anger increased when they learned that the British had been prepared to yield on one of the most prominent issues. On June 23, the British government revoked for one year its Orders in Council against the United States. This concession, however, did not address impressment or monetary compensation, and news of it reached America too late to avert a war.

The Prophet Tenkswatawa was the spiritual leader of the pan-Indian movement that sought to revitalize native culture and block the spread of white settlement in the Old Northwest.

**WHERE TO LEARN MORE**

Tippecanoe Battlefield Museum, Battle Ground, Indiana http://www.tcha.mus.in.us/battlefield.htm

## QUICK REVIEW

### Treaties and Resistance

- Treaty of Greenville (1795) promised all further acquisitions of Indian land would be approved by all native peoples in the region.
- Treaty of Vincennes (1804) procured most of southern Indiana in violation of Treaty of Greenville.
- Indian tribes throughout West unified for stand against settlers.

**War Hawks** Members of Congress, predominantly from the South and West, who aggressively pushed for a war against Britain after their election in 1810.

# THE WAR OF 1812

**WHAT WERE** the consequences of the War of 1812?

The Republicans led the nation into a war it was unprepared to fight. (See Map 9–1.) Still, the apparent vulnerability of Canada to invasion and the British preoccupation with Napoleon in Europe made it possible to envision a U.S. victory.

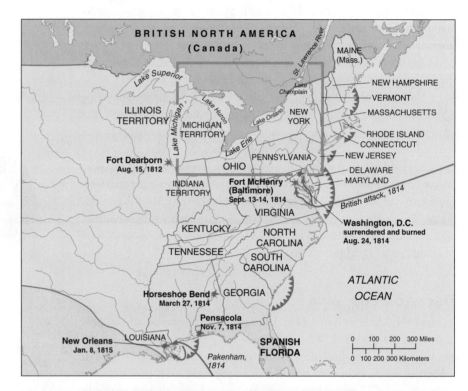

See the **Map**

at www.myhistorylab.com
*The War of 1812*

MAP 9–1   **The War of 1812**   Most of the battles of the War of 1812 were fought along the Canadian-American border, where American armies repeatedly tried to invade Canada. Despite the effectiveness of the British naval blockade, the American navy was successful in denying the British strategic control of the Great Lakes. Andrew Jackson's smashing victory at the Battle of New Orleans convinced Americans that they had won the war.

**Why was** control of the Great Lakes so important to both sides? Why was the Battle of New Orleans so important in shaping the final terms of the peace treaty that ended the war?

## SETBACKS IN CANADA

The **War of 1812** unleashed deep emotions that often divided along religious lines. From their strongholds in the Congregationalist churches in New England, the Federalists preached that all true Christians opposed a war "against the nation from which we are descended, and which for many generations has been the bulwark of the religion we profess." Such antiwar sentiments, however, outraged the Baptists and Methodists, the largest and most popularly rooted denominations. They believed, as resolved by the Georgia Baptist Association in 1813, that the British government was "corrupt, arbitrary, and despotic" and that the war was "just, necessary, and indispensable."

Fiercely loyal to Madison, who had championed religious freedom in Virginia, these Methodists and Baptists harbored old grudges against the established churches of both Britain and New England for suppressing their religious rights. Especially for the Baptists, the war became something of a crusade to secure civil and religious liberties against their traditional enemies.

Madison hoped to channel this Christian anti-British patriotism into the conquest of Canada. Two out of three Canadians were native-born Americans who, it was assumed, would welcome the United States Army with open arms. Only 5,000 British troops were initially stationed in Canada, and Canadian militia were outnumbered nine to one by their U.S. counterparts.

Canada was also the only area where the United States could strike directly against British forces. Although officially a war to defend America's neutrality on the high seas, the War of 1812 was largely a land war. The United States simply did not have enough ships to do more than harass the powerful British navy.

By seizing Canada, Madison also hoped to weaken Britain's navy and undercut its maritime system. Madison had been convinced that withholding U.S. foodstuffs and provisions from the British West Indies would quickly force the British to yield to U.S. economic pressure. But the British had turned to Canada as an alternative source of supplies. Madison hoped to close off that source. And if, as Madison expected, Napoleon denied the British access to the naval stores of the Baltic region in Europe, a U.S. monopoly on Canadian lumber would cripple British naval power. Facing such a threat, the British would have to end the war on U.S. terms.

Madison's strategic vision was clear, but its execution was pathetic. Three offensives against Canada in 1812 were embarrassing failures (see Map 9–1). Republican expectations of victory in Canada had been wishful thinking. Most Canadians fought against, not with, the Americans. Reliance on state militias proved disastrous. Poorly trained and equipped, the militias, when they did show up for battle, could not match the discipline of British soldiers or the fighting skills of their Native American allies. Nor was U.S. generalship on a par with that of the British. Primitive land communications made the movement and coordination of troops a nightmare. New England, the obvious base for operations against the strategically critical St. Lawrence River Valley—the entry point for all British supplies and reinforcements—withheld many of its state forces from national service. Consequently, the invasions were piecemeal, ineffective forays launched from western areas where anti-British and anti-Indian sentiment ran high. All the Republicans had to show for the first year of the war were morale-boosting but otherwise insignificant naval victories. In individual combat between ships, the small U.S. navy acquitted itself superbly. Early in the war, U.S. privateers harassed British merchant vessels, but the easy pickings were soon gone. British naval squadrons were redeployed to protect shipping, and other warships kept up a blockade that stifled U.S. commerce.

Military setbacks and antiwar feeling in much of the Northeast hurt the Republicans in the election of 1812. Madison won only narrowly over DeWitt Clinton, an antiadministration Republican from New York. The now familiar regional pattern in voting repeated itself. Madison

**War of 1812** War fought between the United States and Britain from June 1812 to January 1815 largely over British restrictions on American shipping.

**WHERE TO LEARN MORE**

Fort Meigs Historic Site, Perrysburg, Ohio http://www.fortmeigs.org

**QUICK REVIEW**

**Invasion of Canada**

◆ Madison hoped to conquer Canada.

◆ Three offensives against Canada in 1812 were failures.

◆ By the end of 1812 British controlled half of Old Northwest.

swept the electoral vote of the South and West. He ran poorly in the Northeast and won only because his party held on to Pennsylvania.

## WESTERN VICTORIES AND BRITISH OFFENSIVES

U.S. forces fared better in 1813. In September, the navy won a major engagement on Lake Erie that opened up a supply line in the western theater. Commodore Oliver Hazard Perry attacked the British fleet in the **Battle of Put-in-Bay,** on the southwestern shore of the lake, and forced the surrender of all six British ships. The victory signaled General William Henry Harrison to launch an offensive in the West.

With the loss of Lake Erie, the British were forced to abandon Detroit, a place they had captured in the first year of the war. Harrison caught up with the British garrison and their Indian allies on the banks of the Thames River in southern Ontario. Demonstrating bold leadership and relying on battle-tested western militias, Harrison won a decisive victory. Tecumseh, the most visionary of the Indian warriors, was killed, and the backbone of the Indian resistance was broken. The Old Northwest was again safe for U.S. settlement.

The Battle of the Thames ended British plans for an Indian buffer state. But by 1814, Britain had bigger goals in mind. A coalition of European powers forced Napoleon to abdicate in April 1814, thus freeing Britain to focus on the U.S. war. It now seemed poised to win the war with a clear-cut victory. British strategy in 1814 called for two major offensives—an invasion south from Montreal down Lake Champlain in upstate New York, and an attack on Louisiana aimed at seizing New Orleans with a task force out of Jamaica. The overall objective was nothing less than a reversal of America's post-1783 expansion.

The British attacks could hardly have come at a worse time for the Madison administration. The Treasury was nearly bankrupt. Lacking both a centralized means of directing wartime finances and any significant increase in taxes, the Treasury was forced to rely on makeshift loans. These loans were poorly subscribed, largely because the cash-rich New England banks refused to buy them. Inflation also became a problem when state banks, no longer restrained by the control of a national bank, overissued paper money in the form of bank notes.

As the country's finances tottered toward collapse, political dissent in New England was reaching a climax. In 1814, the British extended their blockade of U.S. commerce northward to include New England. Federalist merchants and shippers, who had earlier profited from their illegal trade with the British, now felt the economic pinch of the war. Cries for resistance against "Mr. Madison's war" culminated in a call issued by the Massachusetts legislature for a convention to consider "a radical reform of the national compact." The convention was scheduled for December in Hartford, Connecticut.

The darkest hour came in August 1814. A British amphibious force occupied and torched Washington, DC, in retaliation for a U.S. raid on York (now Toronto), the capital of Upper Canada. Still, the British actions stiffened U.S. resistance, and the failure of a follow-up attack on Baltimore deprived the British of any strategic gain.

The Chesapeake raids were designed to divert U.S. attention from the major offensive General George Prevost was leading down the shores of Lake Champlain. Prevost commanded the largest and best-equipped army the British had yet assembled, but he was forced to turn back when Commodore Thomas McDonough defeated a British fleet on September 11 at the **Battle of Plattsburgh.**

The tide had turned. When news of the setbacks at Baltimore and Plattsburgh reached England, the Foreign Office scaled back the demands it had been making on U.S. negotiators at peace talks in the city of Ghent, in present-day Belgium. The British were ready for peace, but one of their trump cards had yet to be played—the southern offensive against New Orleans. The outcome of that campaign could still upset whatever was decided at Ghent.

**Battle of Put-in-Bay** American naval victory on Lake Erie in September 1813 in the War of 1812 that denied the British strategic control over the Great Lakes.

### WHERE TO LEARN MORE

★ Perry's Victory and International Peace Memorial, Put-in-Bay, Ohio
http://www.nps.gov/pevi/index.htm

### WHERE TO LEARN MORE

★ Fort McHenry National Monument, Baltimore, Maryland
http://www.nps.gov/fomc/archeology/overview.html

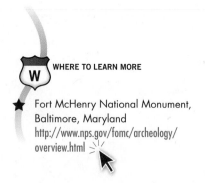

**Battle of Plattsburgh** Victory of Commodore Thomas McDonough over a British fleet in Lake Champlain, September 11, 1814.

## THE TREATY OF GHENT AND THE BATTLE OF NEW ORLEANS

By the fall of 1814, the British were eager to redraw the map of post-Napoleonic Europe, restore profitable relations with America, and reduce their huge war debt. The British negotiators at Ghent agreed to a peace treaty on terms the Americans were delighted to accept. The **Treaty of Ghent,** signed on Christmas Eve, 1814, simply restored relations to their status at the start of the war. No territory changed hands, and nothing was said about impressment or the rights of neutrals. The ink had barely dried on the Treaty of Ghent when the British government sent reinforcements to General Edward Pakenham, the commander of the Louisiana invasion force. By this action, the British indicated that they were not irrevocably committed to the peace settlement, which, though signed, could not be formally ratified until weeks later, when it was sent across the Atlantic. Far from being an anticlimax to a war that was already over, the showdown between British and U.S. forces at the **Battle of New Orleans** in January 1815 had immense strategic significance for the United States.

Among the troops that Jackson led to victory at the Battle of New Orleans were a contingent of African Americans, the free men of color from New Orleans.

The hero of New Orleans, in song and legend, was Andrew Jackson. A planter-politician from Tennessee, Jackson rose to prominence during the war as a ferocious Indian fighter. As a general in the Tennessee militia, Jackson crushed Indian resistance in the Old Southwest at the Battle of Horseshoe Bend in March 1814. The number of Indians who fought and died in this battle was the largest in the history of American-Indian warfare. Jackson then forced the vanquished Creeks to cede two-thirds of their territory to the United States. On the southern frontier as well as the northern, Native Americans emerged as the major losers of the war.

After his Indian conquests, Jackson was promoted to general in the regular army and given command of the defense of the Gulf Coast. In November 1814, he seized Pensacola in Spanish Florida to deny the British its use as a supply depot and then hurried to defend New Orleans. The overconfident British frontally attacked Jackson's lines on January 8, 1815. The result was a massacre. More than 2,000 British soldiers were killed or wounded. U.S. casualties totaled 21.

Strategically, Jackson's smashing victory at New Orleans ended any possibility of a British sphere of influence in Louisiana. Politically, it was a deathblow to Federalism. At the Hartford Convention in December 1814, party moderates had forestalled talk of secession with a series of proposed constitutional amendments designed to limit southern power in national affairs. Set against the revived nationalism that marked the end of the war, the Federalists now seemed to be parochial sulkers who put regional interests above the national good. Worse yet, they struck many Americans as quasi-traitors who had been prepared to desert the country in the face of the enemy. As a significant political force, Federalism was dead.

**Treaty of Ghent**  Treaty signed in December 1814 between the United States and Britain that ended the War of 1812.

•◦◦—Read the Document

at **www.myhistorylab.com**
*The Treaty of Ghent (1814)*

**Battle of New Orleans**  Decisive American War of 1812 victory over British troops in January 1815 that ended any British hopes of gaining control of the lower Mississippi River Valley.

•◦◦—Read the Document

at **www.myhistorylab.com**
*Report and Resolutions of the Hartford Convention (1814)*

# THE ERA OF GOOD FEELINGS

In 1817, on the occasion of a presidential visit by James Monroe, a Boston newspaper proclaimed the **Era of Good Feelings,** an expression that nicely captured the spirit of political harmony and sectional unity that washed over the republic in the immediate postwar years. National pride surged with the humbling of the British at New Orleans, the demise of the Federalists lessened political tensions, and the economy was booming. The Republicans had been vindicated, and for a short time they enjoyed de facto status as the only governing party.

**HOW DID** rising nationalism contribute to the spirit of the Era of Good Feelings?

## ECONOMIC NATIONALISM

The War of 1812 had taught the Republicans to appreciate the old Federalist doctrines on centralized national power. In his annual message of December 1815, Madison outlined a program of economic nationalism that was pushed through Congress by Henry Clay and

**Era of Good Feelings**  The period from 1817 to 1823 in which the disappearance of the Federalists enabled the Republicans to govern in a spirit of seemingly nonpartisan harmony.

John C. Calhoun, the most prominent of the new generation of young, nationalist-minded Republicans.

The first order of business was to create a new national bank. Reliance on state banks for wartime financing had proved a major mistake. Fiscal stability required the monetary coordination and restraint that only a new Bank of the United States could provide. Introduced by Calhoun, the bank bill passed Congress in 1816. Modeled after Hamilton's original bank and also headquartered in Philadelphia, the **Second Bank of the United States** was capitalized at $35 million, making it by far the nation's largest bank. Its size and official status as the depository and dispenser of the government's funds gave the bank tremendous economic power.

After moving to repair the fiscal damage of the war, the Republicans then acted to protect what the war had fostered. Embargoes followed by three years of war had forced U.S. businessmen to manufacture goods they previously had imported. This was especially the case with iron and textile goods long supplied by the British. In 1815 and again in 1816, the British inundated the U.S. market with cheap imports to strangle U.S. industry in its infancy. Responding to this challenge to the nation's economic independence, the Republicans passed the Tariff of 1816, the first protective tariff in U.S. history.

Congress earmarked revenue from the tariff and $1.5 million from the Bank of the United States (a cash payment in return for its charter) for transportation projects. The lack of a road system in the trans-Appalachian region had severely hampered troop movements during the war. Also, as settlers after the war moved onto lands seized from the pro-British Indians, western congressmen demanded improved outlets to eastern markets.

In early 1817, an internal-improvements bill sponsored by Calhoun passed Congress. Though in agreement with the bill's objectives, President Madison was convinced that the Constitution did not permit federal financing of primarily local projects. He vetoed the bill just before he left office.

Congressional passage of Calhoun's internal-improvements bill marked the pinnacle of the Republicans' economic nationalism. Frightened by the sectional disunity of the war years, a new generation of Republicans jettisoned many of the ideological trappings of Jefferson's original agrarian party. Their program was a call for economic, and therefore political, unity. Support for this program was strongest in the mid-Atlantic and western states, the regions that stood to gain the most economically. Opposition centered in the Southeast, notably among die-hard proponents of states' rights in the old tobacco belt of Virginia and North Carolina and in New England, a region not only well served already by banks and a road network but also anxious not to be politically overshadowed by the rising West. This opposition took on an increasingly hard edge in the South as the Supreme Court outlined an ever more nationalist interpretation of the Constitution.

## JUDICIAL NATIONALISM

Under Chief Justice John Marshall, the Supreme Court had long supported the nationalist perspective Republicans began to champion after the war. Two principles defined Marshall's jurisprudence: the primacy of the Supreme Court in all matters of constitutional interpretation and the sanctity of contractual property rights. In *Fletcher v. Peck* (1810), for example, the Court ruled that a Georgia law voiding a land grant made by an earlier legislature—on the grounds that it had involved massive fraud—violated the constitutional provision barring any state from "impairing the obligation of contracts." Marshall held that despite the fraud, the original land grant constituted an unbreakable legal contract.

Out of the political limelight since the Burr trial in 1807, the Court was thrust back into it by two controversial decisions in 1819. The first involved Dartmouth College and the attempt by the New Hampshire legislature to amend its charter in the direction of greater public control over this private institution. In *Dartmouth College v. Woodward,* the Court ruled

---

**Second Bank of the United States**
A national bank chartered by Congress in 1816 with extensive regulatory powers over currency and credit.

**QUICK REVIEW**

**Economic Nationalism**

- Second Bank of the United States established.
- Tariff of 1816 protected American manufacturers.
- Revenue from the tariff earmarked for transportation projects.

*Fletcher v. Peck*   Supreme Court decision of 1810 that overturned a state law by ruling that it violated a legal contract.

*Dartmouth College v. Woodward*
Supreme Court decision of 1819 that prohibited states from interfering with the privileges granted to a private corporation.

that Dartmouth's original royal charter of 1769 was a contract protected by the Constitution. Therefore, the state of New Hampshire could not alter the charter without the prior consent of the college. By sanctifying charters, or acts of incorporation, as contracts, the Court prohibited states from interfering with the rights and privileges they had bestowed on private corporations.

The second important decision in 1819, *McCulloch v. Maryland,* rested on a positive assertion of national power over the states. The case involved the Bank of the United States. In 1818, the Maryland legislature placed a heavy tax on the branch of the Bank of the United States established in Baltimore (and on all other banks in the state established without state legislative authority). James McCulloch, the cashier of the Baltimore branch, refused to pay the tax. This set up a test case that involved two fundamental legal issues: Was the bank itself constitutional? And could a state tax federal property within its borders?

A unanimous Court, in language similar to but even more sweeping than that used by Alexander Hamilton in the 1790s, upheld the constitutional authority of Congress to charter a national bank and thereby regulate the nation's currency and finances. As long as the end was legitimate "within the scope of the Constitution," Congress had full power to use any means not expressly forbidden by the Constitution to achieve that end. As for Maryland's claim of a constitutional right to tax a federal agency, Marshall stressed that "the power to tax involves the power to destroy." Surely, he reasoned, when the people of the United States ratified the Constitution, they did not intend the federal government to be controlled by the states or rendered powerless by state action. Here was the boldest statement to date of the loose, or "implied powers," interpretation of the Constitution.

## Toward a Continental Empire

Marshall's legal nationalism paralleled the diplomatic nationalism of John Quincy Adams, secretary of state from 1817 to 1825. A former Federalist and the son of the second president, Adams broke with the party over its refusal to support an expansionist policy and held several diplomatic posts under the Madison administration. Adams shrewdly exploited Britain's desire for friendly and profitable relations after the War of 1812. The British wanted access to U.S. cotton and foodstuffs in exchange for manufactured goods and investment capital. The United States wanted more trading opportunities in the British Empire and a free hand to deal with Spain's disintegrating empire in the Americas.

The **Rush-Bagot Agreement** of 1817 signaled the new pattern of Anglo-American cooperation. The agreement strictly limited naval armaments on the Great Lakes, thus effectively demilitarizing the border with Canada. The **Anglo-American Accords** of the following year resolved several issues left hanging after the war. The British once again recognized U.S. fishing rights off Labrador and Newfoundland, a concession that was of great importance to New England. The boundary of the Louisiana Territory abutting Canada was set at the 49th parallel, and both nations agreed to the joint occupation of Oregon, the territory in the Pacific Northwest that lay west of the Rocky Mountains.

Having secured the northern flank of the United States, Adams was now free to deal with the South and West. Adams wanted all of Florida and an undisputed American window on the Pacific. The adversary here was Spain. Spain resorted to delaying tactics in trying to hold off the tenacious Adams. Negotiations remained deadlocked until Andrew Jackson gave Adams the leverage he needed.

**McCulloch v. Maryland** Supreme Court decision of 1819 that upheld the constitutional authority of Congress to charter a national bank, and thereby to regulate the nation's currency and finances.

**Rush-Bagot Agreement** Treaty of 1817 between the United States and Britain that effectively demilitarized the Great Lakes by sharply limiting the number of ships each power could station on them.

**Anglo-American Accords** Series of agreements reached in the British-American Conventions of 1818 that fixed the western boundary between the United States and Canada, allowed for joint occupation of Oregon, and restored American fishing rights.

As secretary of state, John Quincy Adams was unrelenting in his pursuit of a continental empire for the United States.

Dagli Orti/Picture Desk, Inc./Kobal Collection

**Trans-Continental Treaty of 1819**
Treaty between the United States and Spain in which Spain ceded Florida to the United States, surrendered all claims to the Pacific Northwest, and agreed to a boundary between the Louisiana Purchase territory and the Spanish Southwest.

•••📖Read the Document
at www.myhistorylab.com
*Exploring America: Continentalism*

In March 1818, Jackson led his troops across the border into Spanish Florida. He destroyed encampments of the Seminole Indians, seized two Spanish forts, and executed two British subjects on the grounds that they were selling arms to the Seminoles for raids on the Alabama-Georgia frontier. Despite later protestations to the contrary, Jackson had probably exceeded his orders. He might well have been censured by the Monroe administration had not Adams supported him, telling Spain that Jackson was defending U.S. interests and warning that he might be unleashed again.

Spain yielded to the U.S. threat in the **Trans-Continental Treaty of 1819.** The United States annexed East Florida, and Spain recognized the prior U.S. seizures of West Florida in 1810 and 1813. Adams secured a U.S. hold on the Pacific Coast by drawing a boundary between the Louisiana Purchase and the Spanish Southwest that ran stepwise up the Sabine, Red, and Arkansas rivers to the Continental Divide and then due west along the 42nd parallel to the Pacific (see Map 9–2). Spain renounced any claim to the Pacific Northwest; the United States

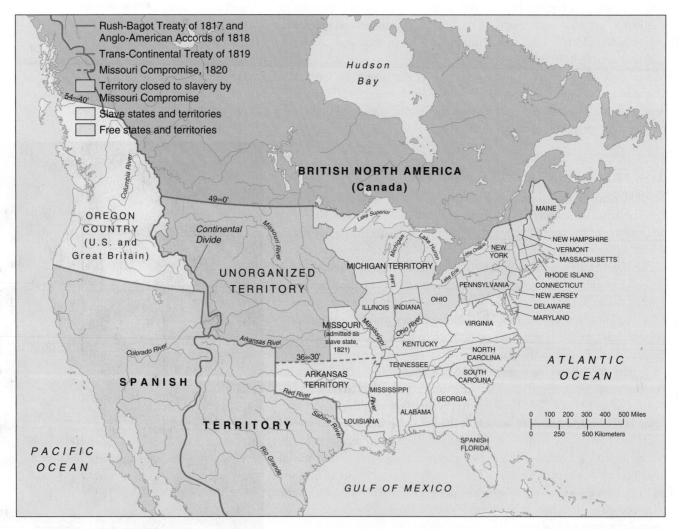

**MAP 9–2   The Missouri Compromise of 1820 and Territorial Treaties with Britain and Spain, 1818–1819**   Treaties with Britain and Spain in 1818 and 1819 clarified and expanded the nation's boundaries. Britain accepted the 49th parallel as the boundary between Canada and the United States and agreed to joint occupation from the Trans-Mississippi West to the Oregon Country. Spain ceded Florida to the United States and agreed to a boundary stretching to the Pacific between the Louisiana Purchase territory and Spanish possessions in the Southwest. Sectional disputes over slavery led to the drawing of the Missouri Compromise line of 1820 that prohibited slavery in the Louisiana Territory north of 36° 30′.

**Considering this** map, where would you predict future conflicts over slavery might occur?

Fittingly placing Monroe next to a globe, this painting depicts one of the cabinet meetings that led to the formulation of the Monroe Doctrine.

in turn renounced its shaky claim to Texas under the Louisiana Purchase and assumed $5 million in Spanish debts to American citizens.

Adams's success in the Spanish negotiations turned on the British refusal to threaten war or assist Spain in the wake of Jackson's high-handed actions in Florida. Spanish possessions were worth little when weighed against the economic advantages of retaining close trading ties with the United States. Moreover, Britain, like the United States, had a vested interest in developing trade with the newly independent Latin American countries. Recognizing this common interest, George Canning, the British foreign minister, proposed in August 1823 that the United States and Britain issue a joint declaration opposing any European attempt to recolonize South America or to assist Spain in regaining its colonies.

President Monroe rejected the British overture, but only at the insistence of Adams. Adams wanted to maintain the maximum freedom of action for future U.S. policy and avoid any impression that America was beholden to Britain. He also wanted to cement relations with the new nations of Latin America that he had refused to recognize formally until 1822. Thus originated the most famous diplomatic statement in early American history, the **Monroe Doctrine.**

In his annual message to Congress in December 1823, Monroe declared that the Americas "are henceforth not to be considered as subjects for future colonization by any European power." In turn, Monroe pledged that the United States would not interfere in the internal affairs of European states. With its continental empire rapidly taking shape and new Latin American republics to be courted, the United States was more than willing to proclaim a special position for itself as the guardian of New World liberties.

**See** the **Map**
at **www.myhistorylab.com**
*The Missouri Compromise
of 1820–1821*

**Monroe Doctrine**   In December 1823, Monroe declared to Congress that the Americas "are henceforth not to be considered as subjects for future colonization by any European power."

# THE BREAKDOWN OF UNITY

For all the intensity with which he pursued his continental vision, John Quincy Adams worried in early 1819 that "the greatest danger of this union was in the overgrown extent of its territory, combining with the slavery question." His words were prophetic. A sectional crisis flared in 1819 over slavery and its expansion when the territory of Missouri sought admission to the Union as

**WHY DID** slavery become such a divisive issue in the years preceding the Missouri Compromise?

a slave state. Simultaneously, a financial panic ended postwar prosperity and crystallized regional discontent over banking and tariff policies. Party unity cracked under these pressures, and each region backed its own presidential candidate in the wide-open election of 1824.

## THE PANIC OF 1819

From 1815 to 1818, Americans enjoyed a wave of postwar prosperity. European markets were starved for U.S. goods after a generation of war and trade restrictions, so farmers and planters expanded production and brought new land into cultivation. The availability of public land in the West on easy terms of credit sparked a speculative frenzy, and land sales soared. State banks and, worse yet, the Bank of the United States fed the speculation by making loans in the form of bank notes far in excess of their hard-currency reserves.

European markets for U.S. cotton and food supplies returned to normal by late 1818. In January 1819, cotton prices sank in England, and the Panic of 1819 was on. Cotton was the most valuable U.S. export, and expected returns from the staple were the basis for an intricate credit network anchored in Britain. The fall in cotton prices triggered a credit contraction that soon engulfed the overextended U.S. economy. Commodity prices fell across the board, and real-estate values collapsed, especially in and around western cities.

A sudden shift in policy by the Bank of the United States virtually guaranteed that the economic downturn would settle into a depression. The Bank stopped all loans, called in all debts, and refused to honor drafts drawn on its branches in the South and West. Hardest hit by these policies were farmers and businessmen in the West, who had mortgaged their economic futures. Bankruptcies mushroomed as creditors forced the liquidation of farms and real estate. For westerners, the Bank of the United States now became "the Monster," a ruthless institution controlled by eastern aristocrats who callously destroyed the hopes of farmers.

Southern resentment over the hard times brought on by low cotton prices focused on the tariff. Planters charged that the Tariff of 1816 unfairly raised their costs and amounted to an unconstitutional tax levied for the sole benefit of northern manufacturers. Unreconstructed Jeffersonians, now known as the Old Republicans, spearheaded a sharp reaction against the South's flirtation with nationalist policies in the postwar period by demanding a return to strict doctrines of states' rights.

## THE MISSOURI COMPROMISE

Until 1819, slavery was not a major divisive issue in U.S. politics. The Northwest Ordinance of 1787, which banned slavery in federal territories north of the Ohio River, and the Southwest Ordinance of 1790, which permitted slavery south of the Ohio, represented a compromise that had allowed slavery in areas where climate and soil conditions favored slave-based agriculture. What was unforeseen in the 1780s, however, was the explosive demand for slave-produced cotton generated by the English textile industry in the early nineteenth century (see Chapter 11). A thriving cotton market was underwriting slavery's expansion across the South, and even Missouri, a portion of the Louisiana Purchase that northerners initially assumed would be inhospitable to slavery, fell under the political control of slaveholders.

The Missouri issue increased long-simmering northern resentment over the spread of slavery and the southern dominance of national affairs under the Virginia presidents. In February 1819, James Tallmadge, a Republican congressman from New York, introduced an amendment in the House mandating a ban on future slave imports and a program of gradual emancipation as preconditions for the admission of Missouri as a state.

Without a two-party system in which each party had to compromise to protect its interests, voting followed sectional lines. The amendment passed in the northern-controlled House, but it was repeatedly blocked in the Senate, which was evenly divided between free and slave states. The debates were heated, and southerners spoke openly of secession if Missouri were denied admission as a slave state.

**QUICK REVIEW**

**Tallmadge Amendment**

- Proposed 1819 amendment banning future slave importations and imposing a program of gradual emancipation as condition of Missouri statehood.
- Passed by the House but rejected by the Senate.
- Voting broke down on regional lines.

The stalemate over Missouri persisted into the next session of Congress. Finally, Speaker of the House Henry Clay engineered a compromise in March 1820. Congress put no restrictions on slavery in Missouri, and the admission of Missouri as a slave state was balanced by the admission of Maine (formerly part of Massachusetts) as a free state. In return for their concession on Missouri, northern congressmen demanded a prohibition on slavery in the remainder of the Louisiana Purchase north of the 36°30' parallel, the southern boundary of Missouri (see Map 9–2). With the **Missouri Compromise,** the Louisiana Purchase was closed to slavery in the future, except for the Arkansas Territory and what would become the Indian Territory of Oklahoma. The compromise almost unraveled when Missouri submitted a constitution the following November that required the state legislature to bar the entry of free black people. Missouri's restrictionist policy obviously denied African American citizens the constitutional right to move from one state to any other state.

The nearly universal acceptance by white Americans of second-class citizenship for free black Americans permitted Clay to dodge the issue. Missouri's constitution was accepted with the proviso that it "shall never be construed" to discriminate against citizens in other states. With these meaningless words, the Missouri Compromise was salvaged. By sacrificing the claims of free black citizens for equal treatment, the Union survived its first great sectional crisis over slavery.

The Missouri crisis made white southerners aware that they were now a political minority within the Union. More rapid population growth in the North had reduced southern representation in the House to just over 40 percent. Of greater concern was the crystallization in Congress of a northern majority array against the expansion of slavery. Southern threats of secession died out in the aftermath of the Missouri Compromise, but it was an open question whether the sectional settlement really solved the intertwined issues of slavery and expansion or merely sidestepped them for a day of final reckoning.

## THE ELECTION OF 1824

The election of 1820 made Monroe, like both his Republican predecessors, a two-term president. The Federalists were too weak to run a candidate, and although Monroe won all but one of the electoral votes, Republican unity was more apparent than real. After Monroe's victory, Republicans split into factions as they began jockeying almost immediately for the election of 1824 (see Map 9–3).

Monroe had no obvious successor, and five candidates competed to replace him. All of them were nominal Republicans, and three were members of his cabinet. Secretary of War John C. Calhoun soon dropped out. He preferred to accept a nomination as vice president, confident that his turn would come in 1828. The other candidates, Secretary of the Treasury William Crawford from Georgia, Secretary of State John Quincy Adams from Massachusetts, Henry Clay from Kentucky, and Andrew Jackson from Tennessee, each had a strong regional following. As the Republican Party fragmented, sectional loyalties were replacing partisan allegiances.

None of the candidates ran on a platform, but Crawford was identified with states' rights, and Clay and Adams with centralized government. Clay in particular was associated with the national bank, protective tariffs, and federally funded internal improvements, a package of federal subsidies he called the **American System.** Jackson took no stand on any of the issues.

**Missouri Compromise** Sectional compromise in Congress in 1820 that admitted Missouri to the Union as a slave state and Maine as a free state and prohibited slavery in the northern Louisiana Purchase territory.

**American System** The program of government subsidies favored by Henry Clay and his followers to promote American economic growth and protect domestic manufacturers from foreign competition.

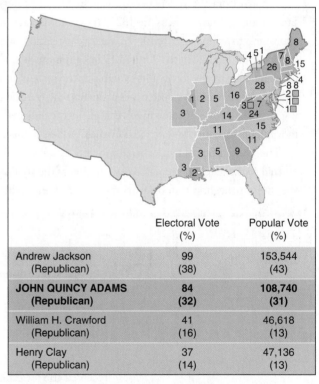

| | Electoral Vote (%) | Popular Vote (%) |
|---|---|---|
| Andrew Jackson (Republican) | 99 (38) | 153,544 (43) |
| **JOHN QUINCY ADAMS (Republican)** | **84 (32)** | **108,740 (31)** |
| William H. Crawford (Republican) | 41 (16) | 46,618 (13) |
| Henry Clay (Republican) | 37 (14) | 47,136 (13) |

**MAP 9–3 The Election of 1824** The regional appeal of each of the four presidential candidates in the election of 1824 prevented any candidate from receiving a majority of the electoral vote. Consequently, and as set forth in the Constitution, the House of Representatives now had to choose the president from the three leading candidates. Its choice was John Quincy Adams.

**What does** this map tell you about the state of the Republican Party in 1824?

## GLOBAL CONNECTIONS

### THE U.S. RESPONSE TO INDEPENDENCE MOVEMENTS

"America . . . proclaimed to mankind the inextinguishable rights of human nature, and the only lawful foundations of government. . . . Wherever the standard of freedom and Independence has been or shall be unfurled, there will her heart, her benedictions and her prayers be. But she goes not abroad, in search of monsters to destroy. . . . She well knows that by once enlisting under other banners than her own, were they even the banners of foreign independence, she would involve herself beyond the power of extrication, in all the wars of interest and intrigue, of individual avarice, envy, and ambition, which assume the colors and usurp the standards of freedom. The fundamental maxims of her policy would insensibly change from liberty to force. . . . She might become the dictatress of the world. She would no longer be the ruler of her spirit. . . . [America's] glory is not dominion, but liberty. Her march is the march of the mind."

Drawn from the Independence Day speech of Secretary of State John Quincy Adams in 1821, these words gave classic expression to an enduring tension in America's relations with the outside world: Should the United States promote liberty and independence by the force of its example or the force of its arms? Adams was responding to political opponents who were demanding that the United States involve itself in the independence movements in Latin America and Greece. Adams refused to do so. The United States had no vital interests at stake in Greece, and aid to the rebels or premature recognition of the government they were struggling to form carried the risk of embroiling the

United States in a conflict with their enemies, the Turks and Russians. Moreover, direct involvement in a European affair would set a dangerous precedent that Europeans could cite to intervene in the Western Hemisphere, where Adams wanted the United States to have a free hand.

As for the Latin American revolutionaries, Adams noted their disregard of the civil rights for which Americans had contended during the Revolution. He had no doubt that the independence movements to the south would eventually succeed, but he believed that the United States could best support them and the cause of liberty by championing and vindicating its own freedom and independence. To intervene abroad in an effort to transform foreign societies was to endanger liberty at home.

At the insistence of President Monroe, Adams extended diplomatic recognition to the new Latin American nations in 1822. In so doing, he insisted that the United States would recognize only governments that promised to adhere to all of their international obligations. Recognition, he stressed, carried no moral approval. This was the recognition policy followed by the U.S. government for ninety years, until President Woodrow Wilson committed it to a policy of liberal interventionism abroad.

- What is your position on the stand taken by Adams against the involvement of the United States in wars of liberty and independence?

Jackson's noncommittal stance turned out to be a great asset. It helped him to project the image of a military hero, fresh from the people, who was unsullied by any connection with Washington politicians, whom the public associated with hard times and sectional controversies. He was the highest vote-getter (43 percent of the popular vote), but none of the four candidates had a majority in the electoral college.

As in 1800, the election was thrown into the House of Representatives. Clay, who had received the fewest electoral votes, was eliminated. Crawford had suffered a debilitating stroke and was no longer a viable candidate. Thus it came down to Adams or Jackson. Anxious to undercut Jackson, his chief rival in the West, Clay used his influence as speaker of the House to line up support for Adams, a fellow advocate of a strong centralized government. Adams won the election, and he immediately named Clay as his secretary of state, the office traditionally viewed as a stepping-stone to the presidency. Jackson and his followers were outraged. They smelled a "corrupt bargain" in which Clay had bargained away the presidency to the highest bidder. Vowing revenge, they began building a new party that would usher in a more democratic era of mass-based politics.

## CONCLUSION

In 1800, the Republicans were an untested party whose rise to power frightened many Federalists into predicting the end of the Union and constitutional government. The Federalists were correct in sensing that their days of power had passed, but they underestimated the ideological flexibility the Republicans would reveal once in office and the imaginative ways in which Jefferson and his successors would wield executive power to expand the size of the original Union. Far from being anarchists and demagogues, the Republicans were shrewd empire builders astute enough to add to their base of political support in the South and West. They also paved the way for the nation to evolve as a democratic republic rather than the more aristocratic republic preferred by the Federalists and Rosalie Calvert and her family.

With no Federalist threat to enforce party discipline, the Republicans lost their organizational strength. Embracing economic nationalism after the war made the party's original focus on states' rights all but meaningless. Ideologically and organizationally adrift, the party split into regional coalitions in the wake of the Missouri controversy and the panic of 1819. But before it dissolved, the party left as its most enduring legacy the foundations of a continental empire.

# WHERE TO LEARN MORE

**Fort McHenry National Monument, Baltimore, Maryland.** This historic site preserves the fort that was the focal point of the British attack on Baltimore and contains a museum with materials on the battle and the writing of "The Star-Spangled Banner." For the military history of the fort and the archaeological work at the site, see http://www.nps.gov/fomc/archeology/overview.html.

**Fort Meigs Historic Site, Perrysburg, Ohio.** Part of the War of 1812 Heritage Trail, this site features a reconstructed War of 1812 fort and museum. Information on visits and activities can be found at http://www.fortmeigs.org.

**Tippecanoe Battlefield Museum, Battle Ground, Indiana.** This museum includes artifacts from the Indian and white settlement of Indiana and visual materials on the Battle of Tippecanoe of 1811. The museum's website at http://www.tcha.mus.in.us/battlefield.htm includes an account of the battle and its aftermath.

**Monticello, Charlottesville, Virginia.** The architecturally unique home of Thomas Jefferson and the headquarters for his plantation serves as a museum that provides insights into Jefferson's varied interests. Information on educational programs and upcoming events at Monticello, as well as the new Jefferson Library in Charlottesville, can be found at http://www.monticello.org/.

**Perry's Victory and International Peace Memorial, Put-in-Bay, Ohio.** At the site of Perry's decisive victory on Lake Erie in 1813 now stands a museum that depicts the role of the Old Northwest in the War of 1812. For a printable travel guide and information on the new visitor center, see http://www.nps.gov/pevi/index.htm.

# REVIEW QUESTIONS

1. What changes did the Republicans bring to the federal government? How did their policies differ from those of their Federalist predecessors?

2. Why were the Republicans so intent on expanding the boundaries of the United States, and why did the Federalists oppose an expansionist program?

3. What factors accounted for the Federalists' inability to regain national power after they lost the election of 1800?

4. What external and internal factors drew the United States into war against Britain? Could the war have been avoided?

5. What accounted for the difficulties of the United States in waging the War of 1812, and why was the war widely viewed as a great U.S. victory? How did the war lead to an increasing pattern of diplomatic cooperation between the United States and Britain?

6. Why was Rosalie Calvert so critical of the Republican Party and U.S. entry into the War of 1812? To what extent would New England Federalists have shared her views?

7. What explains the upsurge of nationalism that underlay the Era of Good Feelings? Why were the Republicans unable to maintain their party unity after 1819?

8. What accounted for the noninvolvement of the United States in the revolutionary movements in Latin America and the long delay in extending formal recognition to the new governments established there?

# KEY TERMS

**American System** (p. 241)
**Anglo-American Accords** (p. 237)
**Battle of New Orleans** (p. 235)
**Battle of Plattsburgh** (p. 234)
**Battle of Put-in-Bay** (p. 234)
*Chesapeake* **Incident** (p. 229)
*Dartmouth College v. Woodward* (p. 236)
**Embargo Act of 1807** (p. 229)
**Era of Good Feelings** (p. 235)
*Fletcher v. Peck* (p. 236)
**Impressment** (p. 228)
*Marbury v. Madison* (p. 225)

*McCulloch v. Maryland* (p. 237)
**Missouri Compromise** (p. 241)
**Monroe Doctrine** (p. 239)
**Pan-Indian resistance movement** (p. 230)
**Rush-Bagot Agreement** (p. 237)
**Second Bank of the United States** (p. 236)
**Trans-Continental Treaty of 1819** (p. 238)
**Treaty of Ghent** (p. 235)
**War Hawks** (p. 231)
**War of 1812** (p. 233)

# myhistorylab Connections

Reinforce what you learned in this chapter by studying the many documents, images, maps, review tools, and videos available at **www.myhistorylab.com**.

## Read and Review

✓●─ **Study** and **Review**   **Study Plan: Chapter 9**

●●●─ **Read** the **Document**

*Constitutionality of the Louisiana Purchase (1803)*

*Marbury v. Madison (1803)*

*Thomas Jefferson, First Inaugural Address (1801)*

*James Madison, First Inaugural Address (1809)*

*Margaret Bayard Smith, Reflections Upon Meeting Jefferson (1801)*

*Pennsylvania Gazette, "Indian hostilities" (1812)*

*The Treaty of Ghent (1814)*

*Dolley Payne Madison to Lucy Payne Todd (1814)*

*Opinion of the Supreme Court for McCulloch v. Maryland (1819)*

*Monroe Doctrine (1823)*

*Report and Resolutions of the Hartford Convention (1814)*

*The Star-Spangled Banner (1814)*

👁─ **See** the **Map**

*The Louisiana Purchase*

*Missouri Compromise of 1820–1821*

*The War of 1812*

## Research and Explore

●●●─ **Read** the **Document**

*Personal Journeys Online*

*From Then to Now Online: The Lewis and Clark Expedition in Their World and Ours*

*Exploring America: Continentalism*

((●─ **Hear** the **Audio**

*Jefferson and Liberty.*
*Star Spangled Banner*

●●─ **Watch** the **Video** *Lewis and Clark: What Were They Trying to Accomplish?*

---

((●─ **Hear** the **Audio** ─

Hear the audio files for Chapter 9 at
**www.myhistorylab.com**.

# 10
# The Jacksonian Era

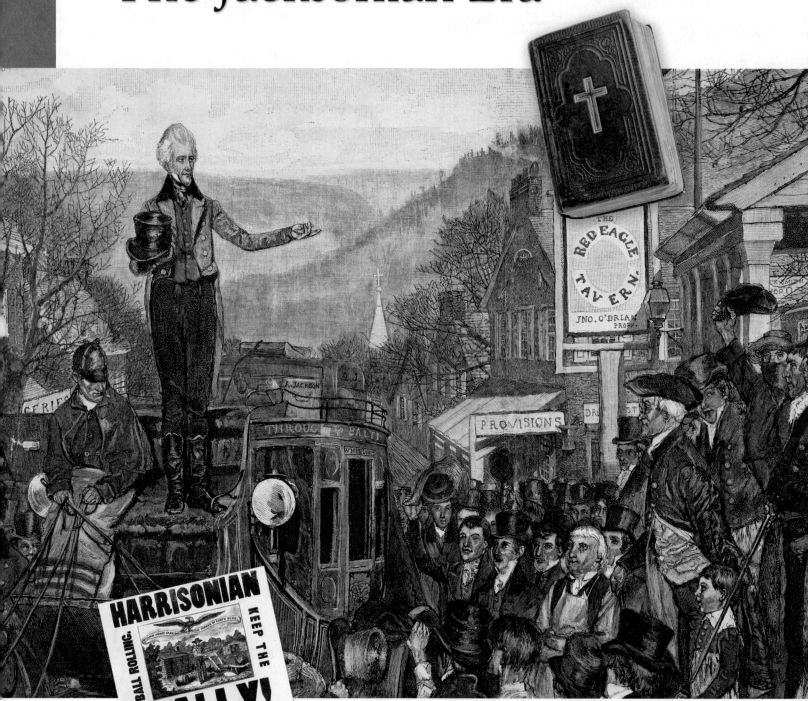

President-elect Andrew Jackson addresses a crowd from a stage coach on his way to Washington in 1829.

((●—[ **Hear** the **Audio**

Hear the audio files for Chapter 10 at **www.myhistorylab.com**.

### THE EGALITARIAN IMPULSE  *(page 249)*

**WHAT FACTORS** contributed to the democratization of American politics and religion in the early nineteenth century?

### JACKSON'S PRESIDENCY  *(page 254)*

**HOW DID** the Jacksonian Democrats capitalize on the new mass politics?

### VAN BUREN AND HARD TIMES  *(page 262)*

**WHAT CHALLENGES** did Van Buren face during his presidency?

### THE RISE OF THE WHIG PARTY  *(page 265)*

**WHAT WAS** the basis of Whig popularity? What did they claim to stand for?

### THE WHIGS IN POWER  *(page 268)*

**WHY WAS** William Henry Harrison's death such a blow to the Whig agenda?

ONE AMERICAN JOURNEY

*Newport, New Hampshire*

*September 1828*

*Wherever a person may chance to be in company, he will hear nothing but politicks discussed. In the ballroom, or at the dinner table, in the Stagecoach & in the tavern; even the social chitchat of the tea table must yield up to the everlasting subject.*

*How many friendships are broken up! With what rancor the political war is carried on between the editorial corps! To what meanness[,] vulgarity & abuse is that champion of liberty, in proper hands, the press prostituted! With what lies and scandal does the columns of almost every political paper abound! I blush for my country when I see such things, & I often tremble with apprehension that our Constitution will not long withstand the current which threatens to overwhelm it. Our government is so based that an honest difference between American citizens must always exist. But the rancorous excitement which now threatens our civil liberties and a dissolution of this Union does not emanate from an honest difference of opinion, but from a determination of an unholy league to trample down an Administration, be it ever so pure, & be its acts ever so just. It must not be. There is a kind Providence that overlooks the destinies of this Nation and will not suffer it to be overthrown by a party of aspiring office seekers & political demagogues.*

*Benjamin B. French*

Donald B. Cole and John J. McDonough, eds., *Witness to the Young Republic: A Yankee's Journal, 1828–1870* (Hanover, NH: University Press of New England, 1989), pp. 15–16.

**Read the Document** at www.myhistorylab.com

Personal Journeys Online

- **Alexis de Tocqueville,** *Travel account,* **1835. A Frenchman gives his impressions of American democracy.**

- **Michael Chevalier,** *Travel,* **1831. A Frenchman describes the spectacle of spectacle politics.**

---

BENJAMIN BROWN FRENCH, a young editor and county clerk in Newport, New Hampshire, penned these words in his journal in September 1828. Like most other Americans, he was amazed, indeed, shocked, by the intense, seemingly all-pervasive partisanship stirred up in the presidential election of 1828 between Andrew Jackson and John Quincy Adams. Whether measured by the vulgar personal attacks launched by a partisan press, the amount of whiskey and beef consumed at political barbecues, or the huge increase in voter turnout, this election marked the entrance of ordinary Americans onto the political stage.

The sense of shock soon wore off for French. The son of a wealthy Federalist lawyer with whom he was always at odds, French broke with his father at the age of 25, when he married without his permission. With no income, job, or family support, he now began to make a business out of law, politics, and journalism.

In so doing he was part of the first generation of professional politicians, young men who compensated for their lack of social connections and family wealth by turning to politics. The partisanship that French found so disturbing in 1828 quickly became the basis of his livelihood. After rejecting his father's politics by joining the Democrats in 1831, he spent most of his subsequent years as a political officeholder in Washington, holding a variety of appointive jobs until his death in 1870.

What made French's career possible was the ongoing democratization of U.S. politics in the early decades of the nineteenth century. The number and potential power of the voters expanded, and professional politicians realized that party success now depended on reaching and organizing this enlarged electorate. Men like French, working for the party, could help them do this. ◆

## CHRONOLOGY

| | |
|---|---|
| **1826** | Disappearance of William Morgan. |
| **1827** | Emergence of the Anti-Masons, the first third party. |
| **1828** | Andrew Jackson elected president. |
| | John C. Calhoun writes *The South Carolina Exposition and Protest*. |
| **1830** | Congress passes the Indian Removal Act. |
| | Greek independence established. |
| | July Revolution in France. |
| | Revolutions break out in Belgium, Poland, and Italian states. |
| **1831** | William Lloyd Garrison starts publication of the *Liberator*. |
| | Nat Turner leads a slave uprising in Virginia. |
| **1832** | Jackson vetoes bill for rechartering the Second Bank of the United States; Bank War begins. |
| | South Carolina nullifies the Tariffs of 1828 and 1832. |
| | Jackson reelected. |
| | Election reform bill passes in Britain. |

| | |
|---|---|
| **1833** | Congress passes the Force Act and the Compromise Tariff. |
| | American Anti-Slavery Society established. |
| **1834** | Whig Party begins to organize. |
| **1836** | Texas War of Independence and establishment of the Republic of Texas. |
| | Congress passes first gag rule on abolitionist petitions. |
| | Van Buren elected president. |
| **1837** | Panic of 1837 sets off a depression. |
| **1840** | Independent Treasury Act passes. |
| | William Henry Harrison elected first Whig president. |
| **1841** | John Tyler succeeds to presidency on death of Harrison. |
| **1842** | United States and Britain sign the Webster-Ashburton Treaty. |
| **1844** | James K. Polk elected president. |
| | Gag rule repealed. |
| **1845** | Texas admitted to the Union. |

# THE EGALITARIAN IMPULSE

Political democracy, defined as the majority rule of white males, was far from complete in early nineteenth-century America. Barriers to political participation, however, came under increasing attack after 1800 and were all but eliminated by the 1820s. As politics opened to mass participation, popular styles of religious leadership and worship emerged in a broad reaction to the formalism and elitism of the dominant Protestant churches. The same egalitarian impulse drove these twin democratic revolutions, and both represented an empowerment of the common man. Popular movements now spoke his language and appealed to his quest for republican equality. (Women would have to wait longer.)

**WHAT FACTORS** contributed to the democratization of American politics and religion in the early nineteenth century?

## THE EXTENSION OF WHITE MALE DEMOCRACY

In 1789, Congress set the pay of representatives and senators at $6 a day plus travel expenses. By 1816, inflation had so eroded this salary that many government clerks earned more than members of Congress. Thus Congress thought itself prudent and justified when it voted itself a hefty raise to $1,500 a year. The public thought otherwise. So sharp was the reaction against the Salary Act of 1816 that 70 percent of the members of Congress were turned out of office at the next election. Chastised congressmen quickly repealed the salary increase.

The uproar over the Salary Act marked a turning point in the transition from the deferential politics of the Federalist-Republican period to the egalitarianism of the coming Jacksonian era. The public would no longer passively accept decisions handed down by local elites or established national figures. Individual states, not the federal government, defined who could vote. Six states, Indiana, Mississippi, Illinois, Alabama, Missouri, and Maine, entered the Union between 1816 and 1821, and none of them required voters to own property. Meanwhile, proponents of suffrage liberalization won major victories in the older states. Constitutional conventions in Connecticut in 1818 and Massachusetts and New York in 1821 eliminated property requirements for voting. By the end of the 1820s, near universal white male suffrage was the norm everywhere except Rhode Island, Virginia, and Louisiana.

**Extending the suffrage and democratic reform.**    Broadening the suffrage was part of a general democratization of political structures and procedures in the state governments. Most significant for national politics, voters acquired the power to choose presidential electors. In 1800, only two states had provided for a statewide popular vote in presidential elections. By 1824, most did so, and by 1832 only South Carolina still clung to the practice of having the state legislature choose the electors.

Several currents swelled the movement for democratic reform. Limiting voting rights to those who owned land property seemed increasingly elitist when economic changes were producing new classes—workers, clerks, and small tradesmen—whose livelihoods were not tied directly to the land. Renters, more than 77 percent of the voters in New York City by 1814, joined homeowners in an expanded electorate. The middling and lower ranks of society demanded the ballot and access to offices to protect themselves from the commercial and manufacturing interests that benefited most from economic change.

Of greatest importance, however, was the incessant demand that all white men be treated equally. The logical extension of the ideology of the American Revolution, with its leveling attacks against kings and aristocrats, this demand for equality made republicanism by the 1820s synonymous with simple majority rule. If any white male was the equal of any other, regardless of wealth or property holdings, then only the will of the majority could be the measure of a republican government.

**The disfranchisement of free blacks and women.**    As political opportunities expanded for white males, they shrank for women and free black people. In the state constitutions of the Revolutionary era, free black males who met the minimum property requirements usually had the same voting rights as white males. By the early 1800s, race and gender began to replace wealth and status as the basis for defining the limits of political participation. In state after state, the same constitutional conventions that embraced universal suffrage for white men deprived black men of the vote or burdened them with special property qualifications. Moreover, none of the ten states that entered the Union from 1821 to 1861 allowed black suffrage.

Advocates of greater democratization explicitly argued that only white males had the intelligence and love of liberty to be entrusted with political rights. Women, they said, were too weak and emotional, black people too lazy and lascivious. In denouncing distinctions drawn on property as artificial and demeaning, the white egalitarians simultaneously erected new distinctions based on race and sex that were supposedly natural and hence immutable. Thus personal liberties were now to be guarded not by propertied gentlemen but by all white men, whose equality ultimately rested on assumptions of their shared natural superiority over women and non-white people.

## THE POPULAR RELIGIOUS REVOLT

In religion as well as politics, ordinary Americans demanded a greater voice in the early nineteenth century. Insurgent religious movements rejected the formalism and traditional Calvinism of the Congregational and Presbyterian churches, the dominant Protestant denominations in Washington's America. In a blaze of fervor known as the **Second Great Awakening** (recalling the Great Awakening of colonial America), evangelical sects led by the Methodists and Baptists radically transformed the religious landscape between 1800 and 1840. A more popularly rooted

**Second Great Awakening**    Series of religious revivals in the first of the nineteenth century characterized by great emotionalism in large public meetings.

## GLOBAL CONNECTIONS

### ❧ AN AGE OF REFORM ❧

"Turn where we may—within, around—the voice of great events is proclaiming to us, 'Reform, that you may preserve.' Now, therefore . . . take counsel . . . of the signs of this most portentous time. . . . The danger is terrible. The time is short. If this Bill should be rejected, I pray to God that none of those who concur in rejecting it may ever remember their votes with unavailing regret, amidst the wreck of laws, the confusion of ranks, the spoliation of property, and the dissolution of social order."

Thomas Babington Macaulay used this argument in the British Parliament to support the Reform Bill of 1832, legislation that extended the vote to Britain's industrial middle classes. Social changes produced by the Industrial Revolution had resulted in massive inequities and corruption in an electoral system that traditionally had consolidated power in the hands of wealthy conservative landowners. Events on the European continent gave greater weight to Macaulay's warning that England must reform or face revolution at home. The July Revolution of 1830 in France had deposed a conservative king and replaced him with one acceptable to the upper middle class. In the same year the Belgians succeeded in establishing their independence, but Austrian troops crushed a nationalist revolution in Italy, and Russian troops did likewise in Poland.

The revolutions of 1830 made it clear that the conservative order imposed on Europe at the Congress of Vienna in 1815 could not withstand the demands for political change unleashed by the American and French Revolutions or the economic change associated with the Industrial Revolution. Revolutionary ideals of legal equality and the right of cultural communities to determine their own fate as independent nations intersected with demands by the new middle and working classes for access to political power. The result was a continuing challenge to the status quo that periodically erupted into uprisings and revolutions. The next great wave of unrest that spilled over Europe after 1830 was the revolutions of 1848.

With the glaring exception of slavery, the United States by the 1830s was already a reformed society by the standards of Europe and the rest of the world. Liberal notions of individualism and self-improvement were wedded to mass democratic politics and a vibrant nationalism. But as long as slavery remained, America's national purpose would be tainted and tragically flawed.

- What lessons in establishing a republican government did the United States offer Europe in the nineteenth century?

---

Christianity moved outward and downward as it spread across frontier areas and converted marginalized and common folk. By 1850, one in three Americans was a regular churchgoer, a dramatic increase since 1800.

The Baptists and Methodists, both spinning off numerous splinter groups, grew spectacularly and were the largest religious denominations by the 1820s. The key to their success was their ability to give religious expression to the popular impulse behind democratic reform. Especially in the backcountry of the South and West, where the first revivals occurred, itinerant preachers reshaped religion to fit the needs and values of ordinary Americans.

The evangelical religion of the traveling preachers was democratic in its populist rejection of traditional religious canons and its encouragement of organizational forms that gave a voice to popular culture. Salvation was no longer simply bestowed by an implacable God, as taught by the Calvinist doctrine of individual predestination (see Chapter 1). Ordinary people could now actively choose salvation, and this possibility was exhilarating.

**Evangelicalism and minority rights.**    Evangelicalism was a religion of the common people, and it appealed especially to women and African Americans. The revivals converted about twice as many women as men. Excluded from most areas of public life, women found strength and comfort in the evangelical message of Christian love and equality. As the wife of a Connecticut minister explained, church membership offered women a welcome release from "being treated like beasts of burden [and] drudges of domineering masters." In the first flush of

**Read the Document**

at www.myhistorylab.com
*Charles Finney, What a Revival of Religion Is (1835)*

**Interpreting the Past**
*The Second Great Awakening and Religious Diversity in America*
(pp. 334–335)

The Second Great Awakening originated on the frontier. Preachers were adept at arousing emotional fervor, and women in particular responded to the evangelical message of spiritual equality open to all who would accept Christ into their lives.

Collection of the New-York Historical Society, Negative #26275.

evangelical excitement, female itinerant preachers spread the gospel up and down the East Coast. By thus defying social convention, these women offered a model of independent action. Other women organized their own institutions within denominations still formally controlled by men. Women activists founded and largely directed hundreds of church-affiliated charitable societies and missionary associations.

Evangelicalism also empowered black Americans. African American Christianity experienced its first sustained growth in the generation after the Revolutionary War. As a result of their uncompromising commitment to convert slaves, the Baptists and Methodists led the way. Many of the early Baptist and Methodist preachers directly challenged slavery. In converting to Methodism, one slave stated that "from the sermon I heard, I felt that God had made all men free and equal, and that I ought not be a slave." Perceiving in it the promise of liberty and deliverance, the slaves received the evangelical gospel in loud, joyous, and highly emotional revivals. They made it part of their own culture, fusing Christianity with folk beliefs from their African heritage.

**The limits of equality.**    But for all its liberating appeal to women and African Americans, evangelicalism was eventually limited by race and gender in much the same way as the democratic reform movement. Denied positions of authority in white-dominated churches and resentful of white opposition to integrated worship, free black northerners founded their own independent churches.

As increasing numbers of planters embraced evangelicalism after the 1820s, southern evangelicals first muted their attacks on slavery and then developed a full-blown religious defense of it based on the biblical sanctioning of human bondage. They similarly cited the Old Testament patriarchs to defend the unquestioned authority of fathers over their households, the masters of slaves, women, and children.

Whether in religion or politics, white men retained the power in Jacksonian America. Still, the Second Great Awakening removed a major intellectual barrier to political democracy. Traditional Protestant theology, whether Calvinist, Anglican, or Lutheran, viewed the mass of humanity as sinners predestined to damnation and hence was loath to accept the idea that those same sinners, by majority vote, should make crucial political decisions. In rejecting this theology, ordinary Americans made a fundamental intellectual breakthrough. "Salvation open to all" powerfully reinforced the legitimacy of "one man, one vote."

## THE RISE OF THE JACKSONIANS

The Jacksonian Democrats were the first party to mold and organize the democratizing impulse in popular culture. At the core of the Jacksonian appeal was the same rejection of established authority that marked the secular and religious populists. Much like the revivalists and the democratic reformers, the Jacksonians fashioned communications techniques that tapped into the hopes and fears of ordinary Americans. In so doing, they built the first mass-based party in U.S. history.

In Andrew Jackson the new **Democratic Party** that formed between 1824 and 1828 had the perfect candidate for the increasingly democratic temperament of the 1820s. Lacking any formal education, family connections, or inherited wealth to ease his way, Jackson relied on his own wits and raw courage to carve out a career as a frontier lawyer and planter in Tennessee. He won fame as the military savior of the republic with his victory at the Battle of New Orleans. Conqueror of the British, the Spanish, and the Indians, all of whom had blocked frontier expansion, he achieved incredible popularity in his native South.

Jackson lost the election of 1824, but his defeat turned out to be a blessing in disguise. The wheeling and dealing in Congress that gave the presidency to John Quincy Adams enveloped his administration in a cloud of suspicion from the start. It also enhanced Jackson's appeal as the honest tribune of the people whose rightful claim to the presidency had been spurned by intriguing politicians in Washington by the "corrupt bargain" between Adams and Clay (see page 242).

When Adams delivered his first annual message to Congress in 1825, he presented a bold vision of an activist federal government promoting economic growth, social advancement, and scientific progress. Such a vision might have received a fair hearing in 1815, when postwar nationalism was in full stride. By 1825, postwar nationalism had dissolved into sectional bickering and burning resentments against banks, tariffs, and the political establishment, which were blamed for the hard times after the Panic of 1819.

**Democratic Party** Political Party formed in the 1820s under the leadership of Andrew Jackson; favored states' rights and a limited role for the federal government.

### QUICK REVIEW

**Andrew Jackson**

- Self-made man from the southern backcountry.
- Frontier lawyer and planter in Tennessee.
- Hero of the Battle of New Orleans.

To the opponents of the Jacksonians, elections had become a degrading spectacle in which conniving Democratic politicians, such as the one shown below handing a voting ticket to the stereotypical Irishman in the light coat, were corrupting the republic's political culture.

*First State Election in Detroit, Michigan*, 1837, c. 1837. Thomas Mickell Burnham. Gift of Mrs. Samuel T. Carson. Photograph ©1991 The Detroit Institute of Arts/ The Bridgeman Art Library, NY.

This bust portrait of Jackson in uniform, issued as print during the 1832 presidential race, invokes his military image and especially his victory at New Orleans in 1815.

((•—Hear the **Audio**
at **www.myhistorylab.com**
*Van Buren*

**Albany Regency**   The tightly disciplined state political machine built by Martin Van Buren in New York.

**HOW DID** the Jacksonian Democrats capitalize on the new mass politics?

•••—Read the **Document**
at **www.myhistorylab.com**
*Andrew Jackson, First Annual Message to Congress (1829)*

Little of Adams's program passed Congress, and his nationalist vision drove his opponents into the Jackson camp. Southern planters jumped onto the Jackson bandwagon out of fear that Adams might use federal power against slavery; westerners joined because Adams revived their suspicions of the East. The most important addition came from New York, where Martin Van Buren had built the **Albany Regency,** a tightly disciplined state political machine.

Van Buren belonged to a new breed of professional politicians. In battling against the system of family-centered wealth and prestige on which politics had previously been based, Van Buren redefined parties as something good in and of themselves. Indeed, he and his followers argued that parties were indispensable instruments for the successful expression of the popular will against the dominance of elites.

State leaders such as Van Buren organized the first national campaign that relied extensively on new techniques of mass mobilization. In rallying support for Jackson against Adams in 1828, these state leaders put together chains of party-subsidized newspapers and coordinated a frantic schedule of meetings and rallies. Grassroots Jackson committees reached out to voters by knocking on their doors, pressing party literature into their hands, dispensing mass-produced medals and buttons with a likeness of Jackson, and lavishly entertaining all who would give them a hearing. Politics became a folk spectacle as torchlight parades awakened sleepy towns and political barbecues doled out whiskey and food to farmers from the surrounding countryside.

The election of 1828 centered on personalities, not issues. This in itself was a victory for Jackson's campaign managers, who proved far more skillful in the new presidential game of image making than did their Adams counterparts, now known as the National Republicans. Jackson carried every state south and west of Pennsylvania in 1828 and polled 56 percent of the popular vote. Voter turnout shot up to 55 percent from the apathetic 25 percent of 1824. Adams ran well only in New England and in commercialized areas producing goods for outside markets. Aside from the South, where he was virtually untouchable, Jackson's appeal was strongest among ordinary Americans who valued their local independence and felt threatened by outside centers of power beyond their control. He rolled up heavy majorities from Scots-Irish farmers in the Baptist–Methodist evangelical belt of the backcountry and from unskilled workers with an Irish Catholic background. To these voters, Jackson was a double hero, for he had defeated their hated British enemy and promised to do the same to the Yankee capitalists of the Northeast and all the elitist politicians.

# JACKSON'S PRESIDENCY

Once in office, Jackson proved to be the most forceful and energetic president since Jefferson. Like a military chieftain tolerating no interference from his subordinates, Jackson dominated his presidency with the sheer force of his personality.

The Jacksonians had no particular program in 1828. Apart from removing Indians to areas west of the Mississippi River, Jackson's first term was notable primarily for its political infighting. Two political struggles that came to a head in 1832–1833, the Bank War and the nullification crisis, stamped the Jacksonians with a lasting party identity.

## JACKSON'S APPEAL

Although they were led by wealthy planters and entrepreneurs—hardly average Americans—the Jacksonians skillfully depicted themselves as the champions of the common man against aristocratic interests that had enriched themselves through special privileges granted by the government. Jackson proclaimed his task as one of restoring the federal government to the ideal of Jeffersonian republicanism, in which farmers and artisans could pursue their individual liberty free of any government intervention that favored the rich and powerful.

Jackson began his assault on special privilege by proclaiming a reform of the appointment process for federal officeholders. Accusing his predecessors, especially Adams, of having created a social elite of self-serving bureaucrats, he vowed to make government service more responsive to the popular will. He insisted that federal jobs required no special expertise or training and proposed to rotate honest, hard-working citizens in and out of the civil service.

Jackson's reform of the federal bureaucracy had more style than substance. He removed only about one-fifth of the officeholders he inherited, and most of his appointees came from the same relatively high-status groups as the Adams people. But by providing a democratic rationale for government service, he opened the way for future presidents to move more aggressively against incumbents. Thus emerged the **spoils system,** in which the victorious party gave government jobs to its supporters and removed the appointees of the defeated party.

When Jackson railed against economic privilege, he most often had in mind Henry Clay's American System (see Chapter 9). Clay's program called for a protective tariff, a national bank, and federal subsidies for internal improvements; his goal was to bind Americans together in an integrated national market. To the Democrats, Clay's system represented government favoritism at its worst, a set of costly benefits at the public's expense for special-interest groups that corrupted politicians in their quest for economic power. In 1830, Jackson struck a blow for the Democratic conception of the limited federal role in economic development. He vetoed the Maysville Road Bill, which would have provided federal money for a road to be built entirely within Kentucky, Clay's home state. The bill was unconstitutional, he claimed, because it benefited only the citizens of Kentucky and not the U.S. people as a whole.

On the issue of internal improvements, as with bureaucratic reform, the Democrats placed party needs ahead of ideology. Jackson's Maysville veto did not rule out congressional appropriations for projects deemed beneficial to the general public. This pragmatic loophole gave Democrats all the room they needed to pass more internal-improvement projects during Jackson's presidency than during all of the previous administrations together. Having built a mass party, the Democrats soon discovered that they had to funnel federal funds to their constituents back home.

The Democrats also responded to the demand for Indian removal that came out of their strongholds in the South and West. By driving Native Americans from these regions, Jackson more than lived up to his billing as the friend of the common (white) man.

Even at a Washington ball in his home in 1824, Adams, shown on the left, had to share the spotlight with his arch rival Jackson, the striking figure in the middle of the painting.

**WHERE TO LEARN MORE**

★ The Hermitage, Hermitage, Tennessee
http://www.thehermitage.com/

**spoils system**  The awarding of government jobs to party loyalists.

## INDIAN REMOVAL

Some 125,000 Indians lived east of the Mississippi when Jackson became president. The largest concentration was in the South, where five Indian nations, the Cherokees, Creeks, Choctaws, Chickasaws, and Seminoles, controlled millions of acres of land in what soon would become the great cotton frontiers of southwestern Georgia and central Alabama and Mississippi. That, of

**Interpreting the Past**
*Jacksonian Democracy and American Politics* (pp. 274–275)

SE-QUO-YAH

Sequoyah, a Cherokee scholar, developed a written table of syllables for the Cherokee language that enabled his people to publish a tribal newspaper in both Cherokee and English.

## QUICK REVIEW

### Georgia and the Cherokees

◆ Georgia stole land of Creek Indians in 1825.

◆ Georgia moved against Cherokees in 1828, stripping them of all legal rights.

◆ Stage was set for Indian Removal Act.

**Indian Removal Act**   President Andrew Jackson's measure that allowed state officials to override federal protection of Native Americans.

**Trail of Tears**   The forced march in 1838 of the Cherokee Indians from their homelands in Georgia to the Indian Territory in the West.

**Black Hawk's War**   Short 1832 war in which federal troops and Illinois militia units defeated the Sauk and Fox Indians led by Black Hawk.

course, was the problem: Native Americans held land that white farmers coveted for their own economic gain.

Pressure from the states to remove the Indians had been building since the end of the War of 1812. It was most intense in Georgia. In early 1825, Georgia authorities finalized a fraudulent treaty that ceded most of the Creek Indians' land to the state. In 1828, Georgia moved against the Cherokees, the best-organized and most advanced (by white standards) of the Indian nations. By now a prosperous society of small farmers with their own newspaper and schools for their children, the Cherokees wanted to avoid the fate of their Creek neighbors. In 1827, they adopted a constitution declaring themselves an independent nation with complete sovereignty over their land. The Georgia legislature reacted by placing the Cherokees directly under state law, annulling Cherokee laws and even the right of the Cherokees to make laws, and legally defining the Cherokees as tenants on land belonging to the state of Georgia. By also prohibiting Indian testimony in cases against white people, the legislature stripped the Cherokees of any legal rights. Alabama and Mississippi followed Georgia's lead in denying Indians legal rights.

Thus the stage was set for what Jackson always considered the most important measure of the early days of his administration, the **Indian Removal Act.** Jackson had long considered the federal policy of negotiating with the Indians as sovereign entities a farce. But it was awkward politically for the president to declare that he had no intention of enforcing treaty obligations of the U.S. government. The way out of this dilemma was to remove Native Americans from the center of the dispute. In his first annual message, Jackson sided with state officials in the South and advised the Indians "to emigrate beyond the Mississippi or submit to the laws of those States."

Congress acted on Jackson's recommendation in the Indian Removal Act of 1830. The act appropriated $500,000 for the negotiation of new treaties under which the southern Indians would surrender their territory and be removed to land in the trans-Mississippi area (primarily present-day Oklahoma). Although force was not authorized and Jackson stressed that removal should be voluntary, no federal protection was provided for Indians harassed into leaving by land-hungry settlers.Ultimately, Jackson did deploy the U.S. Army, but only to round up and push out Indians who refused to comply with the new removal treaties.

And so most of the Indians left the eastern United States, the Choctaws in 1830, the Creeks and Chickasaws in 1832, and the Cherokees in 1838 (see Map 10–1). The government was ill prepared to supervise the removal. The private groups that won the federal contracts for transporting and provisioning the Indians were the ones that had entered the lowest bids; they were a shady lot, interested only in a quick profit. Thousands of Indians, perhaps as many as one-fourth of those who started the trek, died on the way to Oklahoma, the victims of cold, hunger, disease, and the general callousness of the white people they met along the way. It was indeed, as recalled in the collective memory of the Cherokees, a **Trail of Tears.**

Tribes that resisted removal were attacked by white armies. Federal troops joined local militias in 1832 in suppressing the Sauk and Fox Indians of Illinois and Wisconsin in what was called **Black Hawk's War.** More a frantic attempt by the Indians to reach safety on the west bank of the Mississippi than an actual war, this affair ended in the slaughter of 500 Indian men, women, and children by white troops and their Sioux allies. The Seminoles, many of whose leaders were runaway slaves adopted into the tribe, fought the army to a standstill in the swamps of Florida in what became the longest Indian war in U.S. history.

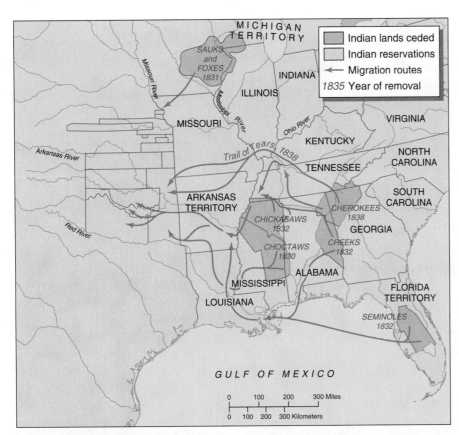

MAP 10–1   **Indian Removals**  The fixed policy of the Jackson administration and pressure from the states forced Native Americans in the 1830s to migrate from their eastern homelands to a special Indian reserve west of the Mississippi River.

> **Which states** were at the center of Indian Removal? What explains the intense pressure for removal in those states?

Jackson forged ahead with his removal policy despite the opposition of eastern reformers and Protestant missionaries. Aligned with conservatives concerned by Jackson's cavalier disregard of federal treaty obligations, they came within three votes of defeating the removal bill in the House of Representatives. Jackson ignored their protests (see American Views: Native Americans Speak Out) as well as the legal rulings of the Supreme Court. In *Cherokee Nation v. Georgia* (1831) and *Worcester v. Georgia* (1832), the Court ruled that Georgia had violated the U.S. Constitution in extending its jurisdiction over the Cherokees. Aware that southerners and westerners were on his side, Jackson ignored the Supreme Court rulings and pushed Indian removal to its tragic conclusion.

## THE NULLIFICATION CRISIS

Jackson's stand on Indian removal confirmed the impression of many of his followers that when state and national power conflicted, he could be trusted to side with the states. But when states' rights forces in South Carolina precipitated the **nullification crisis** by directly challenging Jackson in the early 1830s over tariff policy, Jackson revealed himself to be an ardent nationalist on the issue of majority rule in the Union.

After the first protective tariff in 1816, rates increased further in 1824 and then jumped to 50 percent in 1828 in what was denounced as the "Tariff of Abominations," a measure contrived by northern Democrats to win additional northern support for Jackson in the upcoming presidential campaign. The outcry was loudest in South Carolina, an old cotton state losing population to the West in the 1820s as cotton prices remained low after the Panic of 1819. For all of

**WHERE TO LEARN MORE**

Cherokee Trail of Tears Commemorative Park, Hopkinsville, Kentucky
http://www.trailoftears.org

**See** the **Map**
at **www.myhistorylab.com**
*Native American Removal*

**Read** the **Document**
at **www.myhistorylab.com**
*Black Hawk, Autobiography of Ma-ka-tai-me-she-kia-kiak, or Black Hawk (1833)*

**nullification crisis**   Sectional crisis in the early 1830s in which a states' rights party in South Carolina attempted to nullify federal law.

**Read** the **Document**
at **www.myhistorylab.com**
*Proclamation Regarding Nullification (1832)*

For the Cherokees, the Trail of Tears stretched 1,200 miles from the homeland in the East to what became the Indian Territory in Oklahoma.

**WHERE TO LEARN MORE**

★ Rice Museum, Georgetown, South Carolina
http://www.ricemuseum.org

**QUICK REVIEW**

**Fear of Rebellion and Northern Intentions**

- African Americans were majority of South Carolina's population.
- Rebellions convinced planters that anti-slavery movement was feeding slave unrest.
- Southerners feared that protective tariffs were a prelude to emancipation.

**Interpreting the Past**

*Nullification as a Destructive Force in U.S. Politics* (pp. 218–219)

the economic arguments against high tariffs, the tariff issue was a stalking-horse for the more fundamental issue of setting limits on national power so that the federal government could never move against slavery.

South Carolina was the only state where African Americans made up the majority of the population. Slaves were heavily concentrated in the marshes and tidal flats south of Charleston, the low-country district of huge rice plantations. Ever fearful that growing anti-slavery agitation in the North and in England was feeding slave unrest, state leaders such as James Hamilton, Jr. warned that the time had come to "stand manfully at the Safety Valve of Nullification."

With the low-country planters in charge, the antitariff forces in South Carolina controlled state politics by 1832. They called themselves the nullifiers, a name derived from the constitutional theory developed by John C. Calhoun. Calhoun argued that a state, acting through a popularly elected convention, had the sovereign power to declare an act of the national government null and inoperative. On the basis of this theory, a South Carolina convention in November 1832 nullified the tariffs of 1828 and 1832 (a compromise tariff that did not reduce rates to a low enough level to satisfy the nullifiers). The convention decreed that customs duties were not to be collected in South Carolina after February 1, 1833.

Jackson considered nullification a dangerous and nonsensical perversion of the Constitution, and he vowed to crush any attempt to block the enforcement of federal laws. In January 1833, Jackson, asked for and received from Congress the Force Bill giving him full authorization to put down nullification by military force. Meanwhile, a compromise tariff in 1833 provided for the lowering of tariff duties to 20 percent over a 10-year period. Up against this combination of the carrot and the stick, the nullifiers backed down, but not before they scornfully nullified the Force Bill.

Jackson's stand established the principle of national supremacy grounded in the will of the majority. Despite his victory, however, states' rights doctrines remained popular both in the South and among many northern Democrats. South Carolina had been isolated in its stand on nullification, but many southerners, and especially slaveholders, agreed that the powers of the national government had to be strictly limited. By dramatically affirming his right to use force against a state in defense of the Union, Jackson drove many planters out of the Democratic Party. In the shock waves set off by the nullification crisis, a new anti-Jackson coalition began to form in the South.

## THE BANK WAR

What amounted to a war against the Bank of the United States became the centerpiece of Jackson's presidency and a defining event for the Democratic Party. The **Bank War** erupted in 1832, when Jackson vetoed draft legislation for the early rechartering of the national bank.

Like most westerners, Jackson distrusted banks. Because gold and silver coins were scarce and the national government did not issue or regulate paper currency, money consisted primarily of notes issued as loans by private and state banks. These bank notes fluctuated in value according to the reputation and creditworthiness of the issuing banks. In the credit-starved West, banks were particularly unreliable. All of this struck many Americans, and especially farmers and workers, as inherently dishonest. They wanted to be paid in "real" money, gold or silver coin, and they viewed bankers as parasites who did nothing but fatten their own pockets by manipulating paper money. The largest and most powerful bank was the Bank of the United States, and citizens who were wiped out or forced to retrench drastically by the Panic of 1819 never forgave the Bank for saving itself at the expense of its debtors. Still, under the astute leadership of a new president, Nicholas Biddle of Philadelphia, the Bank performed well in the 1820s. Prosperous times had returned, and the Bank underwrote the economic expansion with its healthy credit reserves, stable bank notes, and policing of the state banks through its policy of returning their notes for redemption in specie. By 1832, the Bank was as popular as it ever would be.

Searching for an issue to use against Jackson in the presidential campaign of 1832, Clay forced Jackson's hand on the Bank. Clay convinced Biddle to apply to Congress for a new charter, even though the current charter would not expire until 1836. Confident of congressional approval, Clay reasoned that he had Jackson trapped. If Jackson went along with the new charter, Clay could take credit for the measure. If he vetoed it, Clay could attack Jackson as the enemy of a sound banking system.

Clay's clever strategy backfired. Jackson turned on him and the Bank with a vengeance. Jackson and his advisers realized that the Bank was vulnerable as a symbol of privileged monopoly, a monstrous institution that deprived common Americans of their right to compete equally for economic advantage. Moreover, many of these advisers were also state bankers and local developers, who backed Jackson precisely because they wanted to be free of federal restraints on their business activities. On July 10, 1832, Jackson vetoed the rechartering bill for the Bank in a message that appealed both to state bankers and to foes of all banks. He took a ringing "stand against all new grants of monopolies and exclusive privileges, against any prostitution of our Government to the advancement of the few at the expense of the many."

The business community and eastern elites lashed out at Jackson's veto as the demagogic ravings of an economic fool. In rejecting Jackson's claims that the Bank had fostered speculative and corrupt financial practices, the pro-Bank forces had the better of the economic argument. But Jackson won the political battle, and he went to the people in the election of 1832 as their champion against the banking aristocracy. Although his support was no stronger than it had been in 1828, he easily defeated Clay, the candidate of the short-lived National Republican Party.

●●●■ Read the Document
at **www.myhistorylab.com**
*The Force Bill (1833)*

**Bank War**  Successful effort by President Andrew Jackson to block the rechartering of the Second Bank of the United States.

●●●■ Read the Document
at **www.myhistorylab.com**
*From Then to Now Online: Banks and the Government*

●●●■ Read the Document
at **www.myhistorylab.com**
*Andrew Jackson, Veto of the Bank Bill (1832)*

# AMERICAN VIEWS

## ❧ Native Americans Speak Out ❧

### Memorial and Protests of the Cherokee Nation, 1836

Of the major tribes in the Southeast, the Cherokees fought longest and hardest against the Jacksonian policy of Indian removal. Led by their principal chief, John Ross, the son of a Scot and a mixed-blood Cherokee woman, they submitted the following protest to Congress against the fraudulent 1835 Treaty of New Echota forced on them by the state of Georgia. Although clearly opposed by an overwhelming majority of the Cherokees, this treaty provided the legal basis for the forced removal of the Cherokee people from Georgia to the Indian Territory.

- **On what** legal grounds did the Cherokees base their protest? What pledges had been made to them by the U.S. government?
- **What** did the Cherokees mean when they said they had been "taught to think and feel as the American citizen"? If the Cherokees had become "civilized" by white standards, why did most whites still insist on their removal?
- **Why** would President Jackson have allowed white intruders to remain on land reserved by treaties for the Cherokees?
- **Do** you feel that the Cherokees were justified in believing that they had been betrayed by the U.S. government?

The undersigned representatives of the Cherokee nation, east of the river Mississippi, impelled by duty, would respectfully submit . . . the following statement of facts: It will be seen, from the numerous treaties between the Cherokee nation and the United States, that from the earliest existence of this government, the United States, in Congress assembled, received the Cherokees and their nation into favor and protection; and that the chiefs and warriors, for themselves and all parts of the Cherokee nation, acknowledged themselves and the said Cherokee nation to be under the protection of the United States of America, and of no other sovereign whatsoever: they also stipulated, that the said Cherokee nation will not hold any treaty with any foreign power, individual State, or with individuals of any State: that for, and in consideration of, valuable concessions made by the Cherokee nation, the United States solemnly guaranteed to said nation all their lands not ceded, and pledged the faith of the government, that "all white people who have intruded, or may hereafter intrude, on the lands reserved for the Cherokees, shall be removed by the United States, and proceeded against, according to the provisions of the act, passed 30th March, 1802," entitled "An act to regulate trade and intercourse with the Indian tribes, and to preserve peace on the frontiers." It would be useless to recapitulate the numerous provisions for the security and protection of the rights of the Cherokees, to be found in the various treaties between their nation and the United States. The Cherokees were happy and prosperous under a scrupulous observance of treaty stipulations by the government of the United States, and from the fostering hand extended over them, they made rapid advances in civilization, morals, and in the arts and sciences. Little did they anticipate, that when taught to think and feel as the American citizen, and to have with him a common interest, they were to be despoiled by their guardian, to become strangers and wanderers in the land of their fathers, forced to return to the savage life, and to seek a new home in the wilds of the far west, and that without their consent. An instrument purporting to be a treaty with the Cherokee people, has recently been made public by the President of the United States, that will have such an operation, if carried into effect. This instrument, the delegation aver before the civilized world, and in the presence of Almighty God, is fraudulent, false upon its face, made by unauthorized individuals, without the sanction, and against the wishes, of the great body of the Cherokee people. Upwards of fifteen thousand of those people have protested against it, solemnly declaring they will never acquiesce.

*Source:* U.S. Congress, *Executive Documents* (1836).

## The Militant Consciousness of William Apess

Although virtually erased in the historical record, the Native Americans of New England had not vanished by the nineteenth century. They persisted, both as individuals and as a culture. Numbering no more than a few thousand, most lived impoverished on reservations where they were denied the local self-governance extended to whites. The young left early, searching for whatever paying jobs they could find. One of these marginalized, transient Indians, the Pequot William Apess, produced a remarkable collection of autobiographical and protest writings that he began publishing in pamphlet form in 1829. The following excerpts reveal the anger, passion, and eloquence he brought to his indictment of white injustices to his people in Massachusetts.

- **Why** does Apess link the plight of Indians in Massachusetts with that of Indians in Georgia?
- **How** does he use the military contributions of Indians on the patriot side in the American Revolution to stake a claim for himself and his people to the liberties of republicanism?
- **In what** way does his condemnation of the dispossession of Indian lands by whites change or complicate the traditional approach to American history as an unfolding story of freedom and opportunity?

Perhaps you have heard of the oppression of the Cherokees and lamented over them much, and thought the Georgians were hard and cruel creatures; but did you ever hear of the poor, oppressed and degraded Marshpee Indians in Massachusetts and lament over them? . . . And we do not know why the people of this Commonwealth want to cruelize us any longer, for we are sure that our fathers *fought, bled, and died for the liberties of* their now weeping and suffering children. . . . *Oh, white man! white man!* The blood of our fathers, spilt in the Revolutionary War, cries from the ground of our native soil, to break the chains of oppression, and let our children *go free!"* . . .

No doubt there are many good people in the United States who would not trample upon the rights of the poor, but there are many others who are willing to roll in their coaches upon the tears and blood of the poor and unoffending natives—those who are ready at all times to speculate on the Indians and defraud them out of their rightful possessions. Let the poor Indian attempt to resist the encroachments of his white neighbors, what a hue and cry is instantly raised against him. It has been considered as a trifling thing for the whites to make war on the Indians for the purpose of driving them from their country and taking possession thereof. This was, in their estimation, all right, as it helped to extend the territory and enriched some individuals. But let the thing be changed. Suppose an overwhelming army should march into the United States for the purpose of subduing it and enslaving the citizens; how quick would they fly to arms, gather in multitudes around the tree of liberty, and contend for their rights with the last drop of their blood. And should the enemy succeed, would they not eventually rise and endeavor to regain their liberty? And who would blame them for it?

*Source:* Barry O'Connell, ed., *On Our Own Ground: The Complete Writings of William Apess, a Pequot* (University of Massachusetts Press, 1992).

**Jackson and the Bank of the United States**

- Jackson and most westerners distrusted banks.
- Jackson vetoed rechartering the Bank of the United States.
- Struggle over future of Bank ended with victory for Jackson at expense of Democrat's image.

After Congress failed to override his veto, Jackson then set out to destroy the Bank. He claimed that the people had given him a mandate to do so by reelecting him in 1832. In Roger B. Taney he finally found a secretary of the treasury (his first two choices refused) who agreed to sign the order removing federal deposits from the Bank in 1833. Drained of its lifeblood, the deposits, the Bank was reduced by 1836 to seeking a charter as a private corporation in the state of Pennsylvania. In the meantime, the government's moneys were deposited in "pet banks," state banks controlled by loyal Democrats.

Jackson won the Bank War, but he left the impression that the Democrats had played fast and loose with the nation's credit system. The economy overheated in his second term. High commodity prices and abundant credit, both at home and abroad, propelled a buying frenzy of western lands. Prices soared, and inevitably the speculative bubble had to burst. When it did, the Democrats would be open to the charge of squandering the people's money by shifting deposits to reckless state bankers who were part of a corrupt new alliance between the government and private economic interests. Jackson was out of office when the Panic of 1837 hit; Van Buren, his successor, paid the political price for Jackson's economic policies.

# VAN BUREN AND HARD TIMES

**WHAT CHALLENGES** did Van Buren face during his presidency?

Like John Adams and James Madison, Martin Van Buren followed a forceful president who commanded a strong popular following. Fairly or not, he would come out, as they did, second-best compared to his predecessor.

Facing a sharp economic downturn, Van Buren appeared indecisive and unwilling to advance a bold program. When the rise of a radical **abolitionist movement** in the North revived

Broken families and demoralized workers were among the litany of evils blamed on the Panic of 1837.

sectional tensions over slavery, he awkwardly straddled the divisive issue. In the end, he undermined himself by failing to offer a compelling vision of his presidency.

## THE PANIC OF 1837

Van Buren was barely settled into the White House when the nation was rocked by a financial panic. For over a decade, the economy had benefited from a favorable business cycle. A banking crisis in 1837 painfully reintroduced economic reality.

Even as it expanded, the U.S. economy had remained vulnerable to disruptions in the supply of foreign capital and the sale of agricultural exports that underpinned prosperity. The key foreign nation was Britain, a major source of credit and demand for exports. In late 1836, the Bank of England tightened its credit policies. Concerned about the large outflow of specie to the United States, it raised interest rates and reduced the credit lines of British merchants heavily involved in U.S. trade. Consequently, the British demand for cotton fell and with it the price of cotton (see Figure 10–1). Because cotton, as the leading export, was the main security for most loans issued by U.S. banks and mercantile firms, its drop in value set off a chain reaction of contracting credit and falling prices. When panic-stricken investors rushed to the banks to redeem their notes in specie, the hard-pressed banks suspended specie payments.

**abolitionist movement**  A radical antislavery crusade committed to the immediate end of slavery that emerged in the three decades before the Civil War.

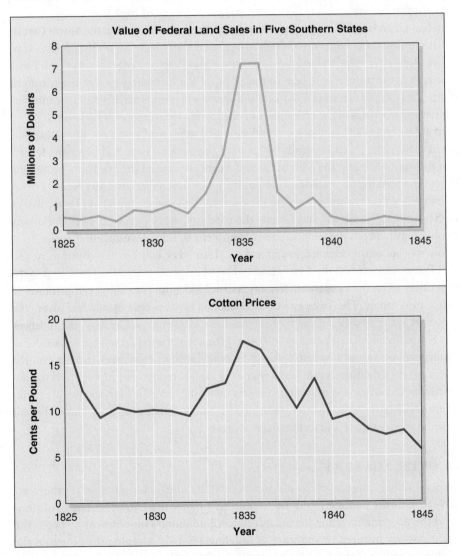

FIGURE 10–1    **Cotton Prices and the Value of Federal Land Sales in Five Southern States, 1825–1845.**

**WHERE TO LEARN MORE**

★ Martin Van Buren National Historic
Site, Kinderhook, New York
http://www.nps.gov/mava/index.htm

**Whig Party**    Political party, formed in
the mid-1830s in opposition to the
Jacksonian Democrats, that favored a
strong role for the national government
for promoting economic growth.

**Specie Circular**    Proclamation issued
by President Andrew Jackson in 1836
stipulating that only gold or silver could
be used as payment for public land.

**Independent Treasury System**    Fiscal
arrangement first instituted by President
Martin Van Buren in which the federal
government kept its money in regional
vaults and transacted its business in
hard money.

What began as a bank panic soon dragged down the entire economy. As unemployment
mounted and workers mobilized mass protest meetings in eastern cities, conservatives feared the
worst. "Workmen thrown out of employ by the hundred daily," nervously noted a wealthy merchant in New York City in May 1837. He half expected that "we shall have a revolution here."

After a brief recovery in 1838, another round of credit contraction drove the economy into
a depression that did not bottom out until 1843. In the manufacturing and commercial centers
of the Northeast, unemployment reached an unheard-of 20 percent. The persistence of depressed
agricultural prices meant that farmers and planters who had incurred debts in the 1830s faced
the constant threat of losing their land or their slaves. Many fled west to avoid their creditors.

## THE INDEPENDENT TREASURY

Although the Democrats bore no direct responsibility for the economic downturn, they could
not avoid being blamed for it. Their political opponents, now coalescing as the **Whig Party,**
claimed that Jackson's destruction of the Bank of the United States had undermined business
confidence. In their view, Jackson had then compounded his error by trying to force a hard-money
policy on the state banks that had received federal deposits. The "pet banks" were required to replace small-denomination bank notes with coins or hard money. This measure, it was hoped,
would protect the farmers and workers from being paid in depreciated bank notes.

Jackson had taken his boldest step against paper money when he issued the **Specie Circular**
of 1836, which stipulated that large tracts of public land could be bought only with specie. Aimed
at breaking the speculative spiral in land purchases, the Specie Circular contributed to the Panic
of 1837 by requiring the transfer of specie to the West for land transactions just when eastern
banks were strapped for specie reserves. Bankers and speculators denounced Jackson for interfering with the natural workings of the economy and blundering into a monetary disaster.

Conservative charges of Democratic irresponsibility were overblown, but the Democrats
were caught in a dilemma. By dramatically politicizing the banking issue and removing federal
moneys from the national bank, the Democrats had in effect assumed the burden of protecting
the people from the banking and business community. Once they shifted treasury receipts to selected state banks, they had to try to regulate these banks. Otherwise they would be accused of
creating a series of little "monsters" and feeding the paper speculation they so decried. But any
regulatory policy contradicted the Democratic commitment to limit governmental power.

The only way out of the dilemma was to make a clean break between the government and
banking. Van Buren reestablished the Democrats' tarnished image as the party of limited government when he came out for the **Independent Treasury System.** Under this plan, the government would
dispense with banks entirely. The Treasury would conduct its business only in gold and silver coin
and would store its specie in regional vaults or subtreasuries. First proposed in 1837, the Independent Treasury System finally passed Congress in 1840 on the heels of a second wave of bank failures.

The Independent Treasury System made more political than economic sense. It restored
the ideological purity of the Democrats as the friends of honest money, but it prolonged the depression. Specie locked up in government vaults was unavailable for loans in the private banking system that could have expanded the credit needed to revive the economy. The end result
was to reduce the money supply and further depress prices.

## UPROAR OVER SLAVERY

In 1831, William Lloyd Garrison of Boston inaugurated a radical new phase in northern attacks on slavery with the publication of his abolitionist paper the *Liberator*. The abolitionists embraced the doctrine of immediatism, an immediate moral commitment to begin the
work of emancipation. Inspired by the wave of religious revivals sweeping the North in the
late 1820s, they seized on slavery as the greatest sin of all. (For more on the abolitionists,
see Chapter 12.)

The abolitionists touched off a political uproar when they launched a propaganda offensive in 1835. Taking advantage of technological improvements in the printing industry, they produced over a million pieces of antislavery literature, much of which was sent to the South through the U.S. mail. Alarmed white southerners vilified the abolitionists as fanatics intent on enticing the slaves to revolt. Abolitionist tracts were burned, and, with the open approval of Jackson, southern postmasters violated federal law by censoring the mail to keep out antislavery materials.

Unable to receive an open hearing in the South, the abolitionists now focused on Congress. Beginning in 1836 and continuing through Van Buren's presidency, hundreds of thousands of antislavery petitions, some with thousands of signatures, flooded into Congress. Most called for the abolition of slavery in the District of Columbia. Southern congressmen responded by demanding that free speech be repressed in the name of southern white security. Repression took the form of the **gag rule,** a procedural device whereby antislavery petitions were automatically tabled with no discussion.

The gag rule first passed in 1836 and was renewed in a series of raucous debates through 1844. Only the votes of some three-fourths of the northern Democrats enabled the southern minority to have its way. With Van Buren's reluctant support, the gag rule became a Democratic Party measure, and it identified the Democrats as a prosouthern party in the minds of many northerners. Ironically, while Van Buren was attacked in the North as a lackey of the slave interests, he was damned in the South, if only because he was a nonslaveholder from the North, as being unsafe on the slavery issue. In short, tensions over slavery and the economy doomed Van Buren to be cast as a vacillating president fully trusted by neither section.

**gag rule** A procedural device whereby antislavery petitions were automatically tabled in Congress with no discussion.

# THE RISE OF THE WHIG PARTY

The early opponents of the Democrats were known as the National Republicans, a label that captured the nationalist vision of former Jeffersonian Republicans who adhered to the economic program of Henry Clay and John Quincy Adams. The Bank War and Jackson's reaction to nullification shook loose pro-Bank Democrats and many southern states' righters from the original Jacksonian coalition, and these groups joined the opposition to Jackson. By 1834, the anti-Jacksonians started to call themselves Whigs, a name associated with eighteenth-century American and British opponents of monarchical tyranny. The name stuck because of the party's constant depiction of Jackson as King Andrew, a tyrant who ran roughshod over congressional prerogatives and constitutional liberties.

By 1840, the Whigs had mastered the techniques of political organization and mobilization pioneered by the Democrats in the late 1820s. They ran William Henry Harrison, their own version of a military hero, and swept to victory. The **second party system** of intense national competition between Whigs and Democrats was now in place (see the Overview table, The Second Party System). It would dominate politics until the rise of the antislavery Republican Party in the 1850s.

WHAT WAS the basis of Whig popularity? What did they claim to stand for?

**William Henry Harrison of Ohio**
- Untainted by association with Bank of the United States, Masonic Order, or slaveholding.
- Hero of War of 1812.
- Selected John Tyler of Virginia as his running mate.

**second party system** The national two-party competition between Democrats and Whigs from the 1830s through the early 1850s.

## THE PARTY TAKING SHAPE

The Whig Party was born in the congressional reaction to Jackson's Bank veto and his subsequent attacks on the national bank. What upset the congressional opposition, apart from the specific content of Jackson's policies, was how he enforced his will. Jackson wielded his executive power like a bludgeon. Whereas all earlier presidents together had used the veto only ten times, Jackson did so a dozen times. He openly defied the Supreme Court and Congress, and unlike his predecessors, he took each case directly to the people.

Local and state Whig coalitions sent an anti-Jackson majority to the House of Representatives in 1835. The most powerful of these coalitions was in New York, where a third party, the **Anti-Masons,** joined the Whigs. The party had originated in western New York in the late 1820s as a grassroots response to the sudden disappearance and presumed murder of William

**Anti-Masons** Third party formed in 1827 in opposition to the presumed power and influence of the Masonic order.

Whig political rally in 1840.

Morgan, an itinerant artisan who threatened to expose the secrets of the Order of Freemasons. An all-male order steeped in ritual and ceremony, the Masons united urban and small-town elites into a tightly knit brotherhood through personal contacts and mutual aid. When efforts to investigate Morgan's disappearance ran into a legal dead end, rumors spread that the exclusivist Masons constituted a vast conspiracy that conferred special privileges and legal protection on its members.

Western New York, an area of religious fervor and rapid economic change after the opening of the Erie Canal in 1825, provided fertile ground for the growth of the new party. With close ties to rural landlords and town creditors, the Masons were vulnerable to the charge of economic favoritism. In addition, evangelicals accused the Masons of desecrating the Christian faith with their secret rituals. The Anti-Masons were thus the first party to combine demands for equal opportunity with calls for the moral reform of a sinful society. They were also the first party to select their presidential ticket in a national nominating convention, a precedent immediately followed by the Whigs and Democrats.

Although it spread into New England and the neighboring mid-Atlantic states, the Anti-Mason Party was unable to sustain itself. Recognizing that the opponents of the Anti-Masons were usually the entrenched local interests of the Democratic Party, shrewd politicians, led by Thurlow Weed and William Seward of New York, took up the movement and absorbed most of it into the anti-Jackson coalition. They did so by calling for equal opportunity and for such evangelical reforms as a ban on the sale of alcohol. The Whigs thus broadened their popular base and added an egalitarian message to their appeal.

By 1836, the Whigs were strong enough to mount a serious challenge for the presidency. However, they still lacked an effective national organization that could unite their regional coalitions behind one candidate. Instead, they ran four sectional candidates. Van Buren won an electoral majority by holding on to the populous mid-Atlantic states and improving on Jackson's showing in New England. Still, the Whigs were encouraged by the results. Compared to Jackson, Van Buren did poorly in what had been the overwhelmingly Democratic South, which was now open to further Whig inroads.

OVERVIEW  **The Second Party System**

## OVERVIEW  The Second Party System

|  | Democrats | Whigs |
|---|---|---|
| Ideology | Favor limited role of federal government in economic affairs and matters of individual conscience; support territorial expansion | Favor government support for economic development and controls over individual morality; opposed to expansion |
| Voter support | Mainly subsistence farmers, unskilled workers, and Catholic immigrants | Mainly manufacturers, commercial farmers, skilled workers, and northern evangelicals |
| Regional strength | South and West | New England and Upper Midwest |

## WHIG PERSUASION

Whereas the Democrats attributed the threat to those liberties to privileged monopolies of government-granted power, the Whigs found it in the expansive powers of the presidency as wielded by Jackson and in the party organization that put Jackson and Van Buren into office. In 1836, the Whigs called for the election of "a president of the nation, not a president of party." Underlying this call was the persistent Whig belief that parties undermined individual liberties and the public good by fostering and rewarding the selfish interests of the party faithful. Although the Whigs dropped much of this ideology when they matured as a party, they never lost their fear of the presidency as an office of unchecked, demagogic power.

Most Whigs viewed governmental power as a positive force to promote economic development. They favored the spread of banking and paper money, chartering corporations, passing protective tariffs to support U.S. manufacturers, and opening up new markets for farmers through government-subsidized transportation projects. Such policies, they held, would widen economic opportunities for Americans and provide incentives for material self-improvement.

Whether as economic promoters or evangelical reformers, Whigs believed in promoting social progress and harmony through an interventionist government. Whig ideology blended economic, social, and spiritual reform into a unified message of uplift. An activist government would provide economic opportunities and moral guidance for a harmonious, progressive society of freely competing individuals whose behavior would be shaped by the evangelical norms of thrift, sobriety, and self-discipline. Much of the Whigs' reform impulse was directed against non-English and Catholic immigrants, those Americans who the Whigs believed most needed to be taught the virtues of self-control and disciplined work habits. Not coincidentally, these groups, the Scots-Irish in the backcountry, the Reformed Dutch, and Irish and German Catholics, were the most loyal Democrats. They resented the Whigs' aggressive moralism and legislative attempts to interfere with their drinking habits and Sunday amusements. These Democrats were typically subsistence farmers on the periphery of market change and unskilled workers forced by industrial change to abandon their hopes of ever opening their own shops. They equated an activist government with special privileges for the economically and culturally powerful and identified with the Democrats' desire to keep the government out of the economy and individual religious practices.

## THE ELECTION OF 1840

One of the signs of the Whigs' maturing as a party was their decision in 1840 to place victory above principle. Because of the lingering economic depression, Democratic rule had been discredited for many voters. Henry Clay, who promised that his American System would revive

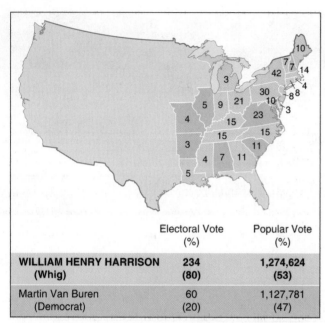

| | Electoral Vote (%) | Popular Vote (%) |
|---|---|---|
| **WILLIAM HENRY HARRISON (Whig)** | **234 (80)** | **1,274,624 (53)** |
| Martin Van Buren (Democrat) | 60 (20) | 1,127,781 (47) |

MAP 10–2 **The Election of 1840** Building upon their strength in the commercializing North, the Whigs attracted enough rural voters in the South and West to win the election of 1840.

**Which Democratic** strongholds proved vulnerable to the Whigs in 1840? Why?

the economy with government aid, appeared the most likely Whig candidate for president against Van Buren in 1840. Yet Whig power brokers dumped Clay, who represented the party's ideological heart, for a popular military hero, William Henry Harrison of Ohio.

Unlike Clay, Harrison was untainted by any association with the Bank of the United States, the Masonic Order, or slaveholding. As the victor at the Battle of Tippecanoe and a military hero in the War of 1812, he enabled Whig image-makers to cast him, like Jackson, as the honest, patriotic soldier worthy of the people's trust. In a decision that came back to haunt them, the Whigs geographically balanced their ticket by selecting John Tyler, a planter from Virginia, as Harrison's running mate. Tyler was an advocate of states' rights and a former Democrat who had broken with Jackson over the Force Bill.

Much to the disgust of Benjamin French, who accused the Whigs of running a campaign based on "fraud & humbug," the Whigs beat the Democrats at their own game of mass politics in 1840. They reversed the roles and symbolism of the Jackson-Adams election of 1828 and seized the high ground as the party of the people. In a further adaptation of earlier Democratic initiatives, the Whigs put together a frolicking campaign of slogans, parades, and pageantry.

The Whigs gained control of both Congress and the presidency in 1840. Harrison won 53 percent of the popular vote, and for the first time the Whigs carried the South (see Map 10–2). With the arrival of politics as mass spectacle, the turnout surged to an unprecedented 78 percent of eligible voters, a whopping increase over the average of 55 percent in the three preceding presidential elections (see Figure 10–2). The Whigs claimed most of the new voters and were now fully competitive with the Democrats in all parts of the nation. As the new majority party, they finally had the opportunity, or so they thought, to implement their economic program.

# THE WHIGS IN POWER

**WHY WAS** William Henry Harrison's death such a blow to the Whig agenda?

Although the Whigs had been noncommittal on their plans during the campaign of 1840, it was common knowledge that Clay would move quickly on Whig economic policies by marshaling his forces in Congress and trying to dominate a pliant Harrison. But Harrison died from pneumonia in April 1841, barely a month after his inauguration, ruining Clay's plans.

## HARRISON AND TYLER

Harrison had pledged to follow the dictates of party leaders in Congress and defer to the judgment of his cabinet. Bowing to Clay's demands, he agreed to call Congress into special session to act on Whig Party measures. Precisely because he was the type of president the Whigs needed and wanted, his death was a real blow to Whig hopes of establishing the credibility of their party as an effective agent for positive change.

Just how serious that blow was soon became apparent when Tyler became president, the first vice president to succeed on the death of a president. Tyler subscribed to a states' rights agrarian philosophy that put him at odds with the urban and commercial elements of the Whig Party even in his home state of Virginia. Clay's economic nationalism struck him

**QUICK REVIEW**

**The Election of 1844**

- Henry Clay (Whig) versus James K. Polk (Democrat).
- Annexation of Texas and Oregon key issues.
- Polk's expansionist program united Democrats.
- Tyler used Polk's victory as mandate for annexation of Texas.

as a program of rank corruption that surrendered the constitutional rights of the South to power-hungry politicians and manufacturers in the North. Clay forged ahead with the party agenda, the repeal of the Independent Treasury System and its replacement by a new national bank, a protective tariff, and the distribution of the proceeds of the government's public land sales to the states as funds for internal improvements.

Tyler used the negative power of presidential vetoes to stymie the Whig program. He twice vetoed bills to reestablish a national bank. The second veto led to the resignation of the cabinet he had inherited from Harrison, save for Secretary of State Daniel Webster, who was in the midst of negotiations with the British. Enraged congressional Whigs then expelled Tyler from the party. Clay's legislative wizardry got him nowhere. In the end, Clay had no national bank, no funds for internal improvements, and only a slightly higher tariff. Although Clay's leadership of the Whigs was strengthened, Tyler had deprived that leadership of meaning by denying the Whigs the legislative fruits of their victory in 1840.

## THE TEXAS ISSUE

Constrained by his states' rights view to a largely negative role in domestic policy, Tyler was a much more forceful president in foreign policy, an area in which the Constitution gives the chief executive considerable latitude. In 1842, Tyler's secretary of state, Daniel Webster, wrapped up his negotiations with the British over a long-standing boundary dispute. Webster now resigned from the cabinet to join his fellow Whigs, allowing Tyler to follow a pro-southern policy of expansion that he hoped would gain him the Democratic nomination for the presidency in 1844. His goal was the annexation of Texas.

Texas had been a slaveholding republic since 1836, when rebellious Americans, joined by some *tejanos* (Texans of Mexican descent), declared their independence from Mexico. Jackson extended diplomatic recognition before leaving office, but he refused the new nation's request to be annexed to the United States out of fear of provoking a war with Mexico, which did not recognize Texan independence, and damaging Van Buren's chances in the election of 1836.

For the sake of sectional harmony, party leaders sidestepped the Texas issue after 1836. Tyler renewed the issue in 1843 to curry favor among southern and western Democrats. He replaced Webster as secretary of state with a proannexationist Virginian, Abel P. Upshur, and secretly opened negotiations with the Texans. After Upshur's death in an accidental explosion on the battleship *Princeton,* John C. Calhoun, his successor, completed the negotiations and dramatically politicized the slavery issue. In the spring of 1844, Calhoun and Tyler submitted to the Senate a secretly drawn up treaty annexing Texas to the United States. Calhoun also made public his correspondence with Richard Pakenham, the British minister in Washington. In his letter, Calhoun accused the British of seeking to force emancipation on Texas in return for economic aid and a British-brokered Mexican recognition of Texan independence. These British efforts, warned Calhoun, were just the opening wedge in a master plan to block U.S. expansion and destroy slavery in the South. After pointedly defending slavery as a benign institution, Calhoun concluded that the security and preservation of the Union demanded the annexation of Texas. The Pakenham letter hit the Senate like a bombshell, convincing antislavery Northerners that the annexation of Texas was a slaveholders' conspiracy to extend slavery and swell the political power of the South. In June 1844, the Senate rejected Calhoun's treaty of annexation by a two-to-one margin. Still, the issue was hardly dead. Thanks to Tyler and Calhoun, Texas dominated the election of 1844.

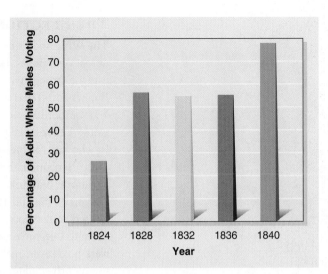

**FIGURE 10–2** **Voter Turnout in Presidential Elections, 1824–1840** The creation of mass-based political parties dramatically increased voter turnout in presidential elections. Voting surged in 1828 with the emergence of the Jacksonian Democratic Party and again in 1840 when the Whig party learned to appeal to the mass electorate.

*Data Source:* Richard P. McCormick, "New Perspectives on Jacksonian Politics," in *The Nature of Jacksonian America,* ed. Douglas T. Miller (1972), p. 103.

## THE ELECTION OF 1844

The Whig and Democratic National Conventions met in the spring of 1844 in the midst of the uproar over Texas. Both Clay, who had the Whig nomination locked up, and Van Buren, who was the strong favorite for the Democratic one, came out against immediate annexation. Van Buren's anti-Texas stand cost him his party's nomination. In a carefully devised strategy, western and southern Democrats united to deny him the necessary two-thirds vote of convention delegates. A deadlocked convention turned to James K. Polk of Tennessee, a confirmed expansionist who had the blessing of Jackson, the party's patriarch.

To counter the charge that they were a prosouthern party, the Democrats ran in 1844 on a platform that linked Oregon to Texas as a territorial objective. Some 6,000 Americans were in Oregon by the mid-1840s, and demands mounted, especially from northern Democrats, that the United States abandon its 1818 agreement of joint occupation with the British and lay exclusive claim to Oregon as far north as the 54°4' parallel, the border with Russian-owned Alaska. These were bold, even reckless, demands, because the actual area of U.S. settlement in Oregon was south of the Columbia River, itself well south of even the 49th parallel.

The Democratic ticket in 1844 highlighted the Texas issue and linked Jackson's name to it.

Polk's expansionist program united the Democrats and enabled them to campaign with much more enthusiasm than in 1840. Acquiring Texas and Oregon not only held out the hope of cheap, abundant land to debt-burdened farmers in the North and planters in the South but also played on the anti-British sentiments of many voters. In contrast, the Whig campaign was out of focus. Clay sensed that his opposition to the immediate annexation of Texas was hurting him in the South, and he started to hedge by saying that he would accept Texas if the conditions were right. This wavering, however, failed to stem the defection of proslavery southern Whigs to the Democrats and cut into his support among antislavery Whigs in the North. Clay lost to Polk by less than 2 percent of the popular vote.

Tyler claimed Polk's victory as a mandate for the immediate annexation of Texas. He knew that it would still be impossible to gain the two-thirds majority in the Senate necessary for the approval of a treaty. Thus, he resorted to the constitutionally unprecedented expedient of a joint resolution in Congress inviting Texas to join the Union. By the narrow margin of 27 to 25, the Senate concurred with the House in favor of annexation. Tyler signed the joint resolution on March 1, 1845.

# CONCLUSION

The Jacksonian era ushered in a revolution in U.S. political life. Responding to a surge of democratization that was in full swing by the 1820s, politicians learned how to appeal to a mass electorate and to build disciplined parties that channeled popular desires into distinctive party positions. In the two decades after 1824, voter participation in national elections tripled, and Democrats and Whigs competed on nearly equal terms in every region.

Although the origins of a national political culture can be traced back to the Federalists and the Jeffersonian Republicans, politics did not fully enter the mainstream of U.S. life until the rise of the second party system of Democrats and Whigs. The election of 1824 revived interest in presidential politics, and Jackson's forceful style of leadership highlighted the presidency as the focal point of U.S. politics. Professional politicians soon mastered the art of tailoring issues and images to reach the widest popular audience. Voters in favor of government aid for economic development and a social order based on Protestant moral controls turned to the Whigs. Conversely, those who saw an activist government as a threat to their economic and cultural equality turned to the Democrats.

The national issues around which the Democrats and Whigs organized and battled down to 1844 were primarily economic. As long as this was the case, party competition tended to diffuse sectional tensions and strengthen a national political culture. Slavery, in the form of the Texas question, replaced the economy as the decisive issue in the election of 1844. With this shift, party appeals began to focus on the place of slavery in U.S. society, creating an escalating politics of sectionalism that saw such loyal party workers as Benjamin French switch their allegiance to a new sectional party. Within a decade, the slavery issue would rip apart the second party system.

# WHERE TO LEARN MORE

**Rice Museum, Georgetown, South Carolina.** Rice planters were the leaders of the nullification movement, and the interpretive materials here on the history of rice cultivation help one understand how slave labor was employed to produce their great wealth. Maps to the museum and news of special events can be found at http://www.ricemuseum.org.

**The Hermitage, Hermitage, Tennessee.** This site, the plantation home of Andrew Jackson, includes a museum with artifacts of Jackson's life. Its website, http://www.thehermitage.com, lists events and programs and examines the archaeological projects undertaken at the Hermitage.

**Martin Van Buren National Historic Site, Kinderhook, New York.** The site preserves Lindenwald, Van Buren's home after he left the presidency, and includes a library with materials on Van Buren and his political era. Its recently expanded website, http://www.nps.gov/mava/index.htm, discusses the history of Lindenwald and includes a virtual tour of its art collection.

**Cherokee Trail of Tears Commemorative Park, Hopkinsville, Kentucky.** Used as an encampment by the Cherokees in 1838 and 1839, this historic park is a documented site of part of the actual trail followed by the Cherokees during their forced removal. http://www.trailoftears.org.

**Trail of Tears National Historic Trail.** For access and information on the land and water routes followed by the Cherokees as they were forced out of the East, see http://www.nps.gov/trte/index.htm.

# REVIEW QUESTIONS

1. Explain the democratic movements of the early nineteenth century. What role did race and gender play in these movements? What evidence is there for the existence of similar democratic sentiments in Europe?

2. What distinguished Jackson's presidency from those of his predecessors? How did he redefine the role of the president?

3. How was the Bank War central to the development of the Democratic and Whig parties? Why did the political debates of the 1830s focus on financial issues?

4. In terms of ideology and voter appeal, how did the Democrats and Whigs differ? How did each party represent a distinctive response to economic and social change?

5. How would you describe the changes in U.S. politics between 1824 and 1840? What accounted for these changes?

6. How did the annexation of Texas emerge as a political issue in the early 1840s? Why were the Democrats more in favor of territorial expansion than the Whigs?

7. What do you think accounted for the sense of shock, even outrage, with which Benjamin Brown French reacted to the partisanship of the election of 1828?

# KEY TERMS

**Abolitionist movement** (p. 263)
**Albany Regency** (p. 254)
**Anti-Masons** (p. 265)
**Bank War** (p. 259)
**Black Hawk's War** (p. 256)
**Democratic Party** (p. 253)
**Gag rule** (p. 265)
**Independent Treasury System** (p. 264)
**Indian Removal Act** (p. 256)
**Nullification crisis** (p. 257)
**Second Great Awakening** (p. 250)
**Second party system** (p. 265)
**Specie Circular** (p. 264)
**Spoils system** (p. 255)
**Trail of Tears** (p. 256)
**Whig Party** (p. 264)

# PEARSON
# myhistorylab Connections

Reinforce what you learned in this chapter by studying the many documents,
images, maps, review tools, and videos available at **www.myhistorylab.com**.

## Read and Review

✓●—Study and Review    **Study Plan: Chapter 10**

●ᐧ●—Read the **Document**

*Andrew Jackson, First Annual Message to
Congress (1829)*

*Andrew Jackson, Veto of the Bank Bill (1832)*

*Charles Finney, "What a Revival of Religion Is" (1835)*

*Memorial of the Cherokee Nation (1830)*

*Proclamation Regarding Nullification (1832)*

*The Force Bill (1833)*

*Black Hawk, Autobiography of Ma-ka-tai-me-she-kia-kiak,
or Black Hawk (1833)*

*South Carolina's Ordinance of Nullification (1832)*

◉—See the **Map**

*Native American Land Cessions to 1829*

*Native American Removal*

*The Slave, Free Black, and White Population of the
United States in 1830*

## Research and Explore

●ᐧ●—Read the **Document**

*Personal Journeys Online*

*From Then to Now Online: Banks and the Government*

((•●—Hear the **Audio** *Van Buren*

((•●—Hear the **Audio**

Hear the audio files for Chapter 10 at
**www.myhistorylab.com**.

## Jacksonian Democracy and American Politics

**TO WHAT** degree was the election of 1824 a turning point in American political history? Considering the role of the common man, changes in party operations and campaign tactics, and the growing influence of political patronage, how did the events initiated in that election change American politics between 1824 and 1840?

Historians have referred to the years of Jackson's presidency as the Age of the Common Man and the Rise of Democracy. Perhaps this does carry a little too much elaboration with it, but the time of Andrew Jackson was a period of great ferment and change. The Second Great Awakening was stirring the religious and reform values of American citizens. The rise of the second two-party system was creating both conflict and confrontation in the American politics. The issues of national tariffs and slavery were beginning to divide the states, and the slow movement toward civil war was becoming clearly apparent. John Adams, Andrew Jackson, and Henry Clay and the election of 1824 comprise a turning point in U.S. politics. With a field of four candidates, the election for president was thrown to the U.S. House of Representatives, where Henry Clay was the Speaker of the House and had heavy influence upon the vote of the members of that chamber. After Adams was elected over Jackson, who had the largest share of popular votes, Adams appointed Clay as secretary of state then seen as a stepping stone to the presidency. Jackson's supporters immediately screamed "corrupt bargain" and the campaign of 1828 was under way before Adams was even inaugurated. Jackson's people coalesced into the Democratic Party. Adams's followers became the National Republicans, later evolving into the Whigs.

## *Mr. Clay came at six ...*

*Henry Clay*

**9TH.** . . . Mr. Clay came at six, and spent the evening with me in a long conversation explanatory of the past and prospective of the future. He said that the time was drawing near when the choice must be made in the House of Representatives of a President from the three candidates presented by the electoral colleges; that he had been much urged and solicited with regard to the part in that transaction that he should take, and had not been five minutes landed at his lodgings before he had been applied to by a friend of Mr. Crawford's, in a manner so gross that it had disgusted him; that some of my friends also, disclaiming, indeed, to have any authority from me, had repeatedly applied to him, directly or indirectly, urging considerations personal to himself as motives to his cause. He had thought it best to reserve for sometime his determination to himself: first, to give a decent time for his own funeral solemnities as a candidate; and, secondly, to prepare and predispose all his friends to a state of neutrality between the three candidates who would be before the House, so that they might be free ultimately to take that course which might be most conducive to the public interest. The time had now come at which he might be explicit in his communication with me, and he had for that purpose asked this confidential interview. He wished me, as far as I might think proper, to satisfy him with regard to some principles of great public importance, but without any personal considerations for himself. In the question to come before the House between General Jackson, Mr. Crawford, and myself, he had no hesitation in saying that his preference would be for me.

*Source:* Charles Francis Adams, ed. Memoirs of John Quincy Adams, 12 Volumes (Philadelphia: J. B. Lippincott & Co., 1875).

## Presidential Candidates and Political Parties, 1788–1840

**IN THE** slightly more than fifty years covered in this list, some parties flourished and some died. Some parties rose up to replace earlier parties and some changed into a new political alliance with a different name and evolved political goals.

| | |
|---|---|
| 1788 | George Washington – No Party Designation |
| | John Adams – No Party Designation |
| 1792 | George Washington – No Party Designation |
| | John Adams – No Party Designation |
| | George Clinton – No Party Designation |
| 1796 | John Adams – Federalist |
| | Thomas Jefferson – Democratic-Republican |
| | Thomas Pinckney – Federalist |
| | Aaron Burr – Democratic-Republican |
| 1800 | Thomas Jefferson – Democratic-Republican |
| | Aaron Burr – Democratic-Republican |
| | John Adams – Federalist |
| | Charles C. Pinckney – Federalist |
| 1804 | Thomas Jefferson – Democratic-Republican |
| | Charles C. Pinckney – Federalist |
| 1808 | James Madison – Democratic-Republican |
| | Charles C. Pinckney – Federalist |
| | George Clinton – Democratic-Republican |
| 1812 | James Madison – Democratic-Republican |
| | De Witt Clinton – Federalist |
| 1816 | James Monroe – Democratic-Republican |
| | Rufus King – Federalist |

| | |
|---|---|
| 1820 | James Monroe – Democratic-Republican |
| | John Q. Adams – Independent Republican |
| 1824 | John Q. Adams – Democratic-Republican |
| | Andrew Jackson – Democratic-Republican |
| | William H. Crawford – Democratic-Republican |
| | Henry Clay – Democratic-Republican |
| 1828 | Andrew Jackson – Democratic |
| | John Q. Adams – National Republican |
| 1832 | Andrew Jackson – Democratic |
| | Henry Clay – National Republican |
| | William Wirt – Anti-Masonic |
| | John Floyd – National Republican |
| 1836 | Martin Van Buren – Democratic |
| | William H. Harrison – Whig |
| | Hugh L. White – Whig |
| | Daniel Webster – Whig |
| | W. P. Mangum – Whig |
| 1840 | William H. Harrison – Whig |
| | Martin Van Buren – Democratic |

# *. . . to the victors belong the spoils*

**SENATOR WILLIAM** Marcy gave the name "spoils system" to the practice of awarding political office to the supporters of your own party once you had won control of either state or federal government. His famous statement on the floor of the U.S. Senate: "When they are contending for victory, they avow the intention of enjoying it. If they are defeated, they expect to retire from office. If they are successful, they claim as matter of right the advantages of success. They see nothing wrong in the rule that to the victors belong the spoils of the enemy." This principle had been used heavily in the states of New York and Pennsylvania where Marcy engaged brutally in applying the practice. It was not until Jackson's election in 1828 that the spoils system was introduced at the federal level. Previous presidents had been circumspect in removing federal office servers from their jobs. Washington had removed only 9 in two terms, Adams had removed 9 in one term. After the Federalists were defeated in 1800 and the Democratic-Republicans took office, Jefferson refused to utilize the spoils system and removed only 39 federal office holders in two terms. Madison then dropped only 5 in two terms, Monroe removed only 9 in two terms and John Q. Adams fired only 2 in one administration. This changed in 1829 when Jackson removed a total of 734 federal office holders in a single year of his first administration. The age of the spoils system had arrived. The Democrats clearly used the spoils system to their advantage. How did the other political parties respond to this concept?

*William Learned Marcy (1786–1857), American political leader.*

# 11

# Slavery and the Old South

"Slavery and the Old South, 1800–1860." A slave auction in Virginia, 1861. English engraving.

These shackles were found at a Plantation Slave Quarter site on Wadmalaw Island, S.C. approximately 25 miles from Charleston. They are blacksmith made.

Hear the audio files for Chapter 11 at **www.myhistorylab.com**.

### THE LOWER SOUTH  (*page 279*)

**HOW DID** the increasing demand for cotton shape the development of slavery in the Lower South?

### THE UPPER SOUTH  (*page 282*)

**WHAT CAUSED** the decline of slavery after 1800 in the Upper South?

### SLAVE LIFE AND CULTURE  (*page 285*)

**WHAT WAS** life like for African American slaves in the first half of the nineteenth century?

### FREE SOCIETY  (*page 292*)

**HOW WAS** free society in the South structured?

### THE PROSLAVERY ARGUMENT (*page 297*)

**HOW DID** the southern defense of slavery change between the early nineteenth century and the 1850s?

ONE AMERICAN JOURNEY

*Had Mrs Wheeler condemned me to the severest corporal punish, or exposed me to be sold in the public slave market in Wilmington [New Carolina] I should probably have resigned myself with apparent composure to her cruel behests. But when she sought to force me into a compulsory union with a man whom I could only hate and despise it seemed that rebellion would be a virtue, that duty to myself and my God actually required it, and that whatever accidents or misfortunes might attend my flight nothing could be worse than what threatened my stay.*

*Marriage like many other blessings I considered to be especially designed for the free, and something that all the victims of slavery should avoid as tending essentially to perpetuate that system. Hence to all overtures of that kind from whatever quarter they might come I had invariably turned a deaf ear. I had spurned domestic ties not because my heart was hard, but because it was my unalterable resolution never to entail slavery on any human being. And now when I had voluntarily renounced the society of those I might have learned to love should I be compelled to accept one, whose person, and speech, and manner could not fail to be ever regarded by me with loathing and disgust. Then to be driven in to the fields beneath the eye and lash of the brutal overseer, and those miserable huts, with their promiscuous crowds of dirty, obscene and degraded objects, for my home I could not, I would not bear it.*

*Hannah Crafts*

Henry Louis Gates, Jr., ed., *The Bondwoman's Narrative* (New York: Warner Books, 2002), pp. 206–207.

**Read the Document** at **www.myhistorylab.com**

**Personal Journeys Online**

- **Marie Perkins, Letter, 1852. A slave writes her husband informing him of the sale of their son.**

- **Lucy Skipwith, Letter, 1855. A slave writes her master in Virginia from his plantation in Alabama.**

- **Stephen Pembroke, Speech by a slave, 1854. A former slave describes his life under slavery.**

HANNAH CRAFTS was the name an African American woman adopted after she escaped from slavery in the late 1850s. This passage is from *The Bondwoman's Narrative*, a recently discovered manuscript that stands as the only known novel written by a female black slave. Although the precise identity of Crafts remains uncertain, the evidence strongly suggests that she was a house slave of John Hill Wheeler of North Carolina who fled north in the spring of 1857, married a Methodist clergyman, and merged into the black middle class of southern New Jersey. The novel contains searingly candid observations on the brutalized living conditions that field slaves were forced to endure.

Only the system of slavery that Crafts described with revulsion makes it possible to speak of the antebellum South as a single region despite its geographical and cultural diversity. It was black slavery that created a bond among white southerners and cast them in a common mold.

Not only did slavery make the South distinctive, it was also the source of the region's immense agricultural wealth, the foundation on which planters built their fortunes, the basis for white upward mobility, and the means by which white people controlled a large black minority. Precisely because slavery was so deeply embedded in southern life and customs, white leadership reacted to the mounting attacks on slavery after 1830 with an ever more defiant defense of the institution. That defense, in turn, reinforced a growing sense of sectionalism among white southerners, the belief that their values divided them from their fellow citizens in the Union.

Economically and intellectually, the Old South developed in stages. The South of 1860 was geographically much larger and

## CHRONOLOGY

| | | | |
|---|---|---|---|
| **1790s** | Large-scale conversions of slaves to Christianity begin. | **1831–1832** | Virginia legislature debates and rejects gradual emancipation. |
| **1793** | Eli Whitney patents the cotton gin. | **1832** | Thomas R. Dew publishes the first full-scale defense of slavery. |
| **1800** | Gabriel Prosser leads a rebellion in Richmond, Virginia. | **1837–1845** | Slavery issue divides Presbyterians, Methodists, and Baptists into separate sectional churches. |
| **1807** | Britain abolishes the slave trade. | | |
| **1808** | Congress prohibits the African slave trade. | **1845** | Florida and Texas, the last two slave states, are admitted to the Union. |
| **1811** | Slaves rebel in Louisiana. | | |
| **1816–1819** | First cotton boom in the South. | **1848** | France outlaws slavery. |
| **1822** | Denmark Vesey's Conspiracy fails in Charleston, South Carolina. | **1850s** | Cotton production doubles. |
| | | **1857** | Hinton R. Helper publishes *The Impending Crisis of the South*. |
| **1823** | Spain outlaws slavery. | | |
| **1831** | Nat Turner leads a rebellion in Southampton County, Virginia. | | |

more diverse than it had been in 1800. It was also more uniformly committed to a single cash crop, cotton. Cotton became king, as contemporaries put it, and it provided the economic basis for southern sectionalism. During the reign of King Cotton, however, regional differences emerged between the Lower South, where the linkage between cotton and slavery was strong, and the Upper South, where slavery was relatively less important and the economy was more diversified. In both regions the control mechanisms of slavery were very tight, and Hannah Crafts was exceptional in her successful flight to freedom. ✦

# THE LOWER SOUTH

South and west of South Carolina stretched some of the best cotton land in the world. A long growing season, adequate rainfall, navigable rivers, and untapped fertility gave the Lower South incomparable natural advantages for growing cotton. Ambitious white southerners exploited these advantages by extending slavery to the newer cotton lands that opened up in the Lower South after 1800 (see Map 11–1). Cotton production and slavery thus went hand in hand.

**HOW DID** the increasing demand for cotton shape the development of slavery in the Lower South?

## COTTON AND SLAVES

Before 1800, slavery was associated with the cash crops of tobacco, rice, and sea island (or long-staple) cotton. Tobacco, the mainstay of the colonial Chesapeake economy, severely depleted the soil. Its production stagnated after the Revolutionary War, when it lost its formerly protected markets in Britain. Rice and long-staple cotton, named for its long, silky fibers, were profitable but geographically limited to the humid sea islands and tidal flats off the coast of South Carolina and Georgia. Like sugar cane, introduced into Louisiana in the 1790s, they required a huge capital investment in special machinery, dikes, and labor. Upland, or short-staple, cotton faced none of these constraints, once the cotton gin removed the technical barrier to its commercial production (see Chapter 12). It could be planted far inland, and small farmers could grow it profitably because it required no additional costs for machinery or drainage systems.

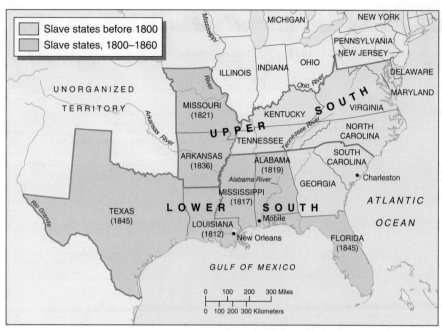

**MAP 11–1    The Spread of Slavery: New Slave States Entering the Union, 1800–1850**
Seven slave states entered the Union after 1800 as cotton production shifted westward.

**Why was** cotton production especially suited to slave labor?

**WHERE TO LEARN MORE**

★ Cottonlandia Museum,
Greenwood, Mississippi
http://www.cottonlandia.org/

**gang system**    The organization and
supervision of slave field hands into
working teams on southern plantations.

Read the Document

at www.myhistorylab.com
*From Then to Now Online:
Overcoming the Economic Legacy
of Slavery*

As a result, after the 1790s, the production of short-staple cotton boomed. Moreover, like the South's other cash crops, upland cotton was well suited for slave labor because it required fairly continuous tending throughout the year. The long work year maximized the return on capital invested in slave labor.

The linkage of cotton and slaves was at the heart of the plantation system that spread westward after the War of 1812. From its original base in South Carolina and Georgia, the cotton kingdom moved into the Old Southwest and then into Texas and Arkansas. As wasteful agricultural practices exhausted new lands, planters moved to the next cotton frontier farther west. Cotton output exploded from 73,000 bales (a bale weighed close to 500 pounds) in 1800 to more than 2 million bales by midcentury, thanks to the fertility of virgin land and to technological changes, such as improved seed varieties and steam-powered cotton gins (see Figure 11–1). Slave labor accounted for more than 90 percent of cotton production.

Plantations, large productive units specializing in a cash crop and employing at least 20 slaves, were the leading economic institution in the Lower South. Planters were the most prestigious social group, and, although less than 5 percent of white families were in the planter class, they controlled more than 40 percent of the slaves, cotton output, and total agricultural wealth. Most had inherited or married into their wealth, but they could stay at the top of the South's class structure only by continuing to profit from slave labor.

Plantations were generally more efficient producers of cotton than small farms. A variety of factors contributed to this efficiency. Most important, the ownership of 20 or more slaves enabled planters to use gangs to do both routine and specialized agricultural work. This **gang system,** a crude version of the division of labor that was being introduced in northern factories, permitted a regimented work pace. Teams of field hands, made up of women as well as men, had to work at a steady pace or else feel the lash.

The plantation districts of the Lower South stifled the growth of towns and economic enterprise. Planters, as well as ordinary farmers, strove to be self-sufficient. The most significant economic exchange, exporting cotton, took place in international markets and was handled by specialized commission merchants in Charleston, Mobile, and New Orleans. The Lower South had amassed great wealth, but most outsiders saw no signs of progress there.

## THE PROFITS OF SLAVERY

Slavery was profitable on an individual basis. Most modern studies indicate that the average rate of return on capital invested in a slave was about 10 percent a year, a rate that at least equaled that of alternative investments in the South or the North. Not surprisingly, the newer regions of the cotton kingdom in the Lower South, with the most productive land and the greatest commitment to plantation agriculture, consistently led the nation in per capita income.

The profitability of slavery ultimately rested on the enormous demand for cotton outside the South. Demand was so strong that prices held steady at around 10 cents a pound in the 1850s, even as southern production of cotton doubled. Textile mills in Britain were always the largest market, but demand in continental Europe and the United States grew even faster after 1840.

**The slave trade.** Southern law defined slaves as chattel, the personal property of their owners, and their market value increased along with the profitability of slavery. Prices for a male field hand rose from $250 in 1815 to $900 by 1860. Prices at any given time varied according to the age, sex, and skills of the slave, as well as overall market conditions, but the steady rise in prices meant that slave owners could sell their human chattel and realize a profit over and above what they had already earned from the slaves' labor. This was especially the case with slave mothers; the children they bore increased the capital assets of their owners. Slave women of childbearing age were therefore valued nearly as much as male field hands.

The domestic slave trade brought buyers and sellers of slaves together. Slaves flowed from the older areas of the Upper South to the newer plantation districts in the Lower South. This trade was extensive: More than 800,000 slaves were moved between regions in the South from 1790 to 1860. The sheer size of the internal slave trade indicates just how profit-driven slave owners were. Few of them hesitated to break up slave families for sale when market conditions were right. About half of all slave sales separated family members. Slave children born in the Upper South after 1820 stood a one-in-three chance of being sold during their lifetime. Most of the profits from slave labor and sales went into buying more land and slaves. As long as slaves employed in growing cash staples returned 10 percent a year, slave owners had little economic incentive to shift their capital resources into manufacturing or urban development. The predictable result was that industrialization and urbanization fell far behind the levels in the free states.

Nowhere was the indifference of planters to economic diversification more evident than in the Lower South, which had the smallest urban population and the fewest factories. Planters here were not opposed to economic innovations that promised greater profits, but they feared social changes that might undermine the stability of slavery. Urbanization and industrialization both entailed such risks. Most planters suspected that the urban environment weakened slavery.

**Urban slavery.** Urban slaves were artisans, semiskilled laborers, and domestics, and, unlike their rural counterparts, they usually lived apart from their owners. They had much more freedom than field hands to move around, interact with white people and other black people, and experiment with various social roles. Many of them, especially if they had a marketable skill, such as carpentry or tailoring, could hire out their labor and retain some of their wages for themselves after reimbursing their owners. In short, the direct authority of the slave owner was less clear-cut in the town than in the country.

Urban slavery declined from 1820 to 1860 as slaves decreased from 22 percent to 10 percent of the urban population. This decline reflected both doubts about the stability of slavery in an urban setting and the large profits that slave labor earned for slave owners in the rural cotton economy.

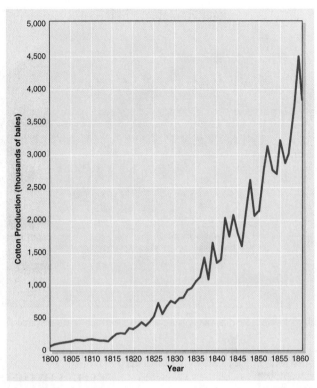

**FIGURE 11–1  U.S. Cotton Production, 1800–1860** Cotton production spiraled upward after 1800, and the South became the world's leading supplier.
*Data Source:* U.S. Bureau of the Census, *Historical Statistics of the United States* (1960).

**QUICK REVIEW**

**Economy of Slavery**

◆ Prices for average male field hand: $250 in 1815, $900 in 1860.

◆ Female slaves of childbearing age valued almost as highly as male field hands.

◆ Large and profitable regional market in slaves.

**QUICK REVIEW**

**Urban Slavery**

◆ 1820–1860: slaves decreased from 22 percent to 10 percent of urban population.

◆ Planters had a general ambivalence toward industrialization.

◆ Many planters saw factory work as a threat to slave discipline.

# CASH!

**All persons that have SLAVES to dispose of, will do well by giving me a call, as I will give the**

## HIGHEST PRICE FOR

# Men, Women, & CHILDREN.

**Any person that wishes to sell, will call at Hill's tavern, or at Shannon Hill for me, and any information they want will be promptly attended to.**

*Thomas Griggs.*

**Charlestown, May 7, 1835.**

PRINTED AT THE FREE PRESS OFFICE, CHARLESTOWN.

Like most slave traders, Thomas Griggs of Charleston offered cash for all slaves he purchased.

**Industrial slavery.**    The ambivalence of planters toward urban slavery also characterized their attitudes toward industrial slavery and, indeed, to industrialization itself. If based on free labor, industrialization risked promoting an antislavery class consciousness among manufacturing laborers that would challenge the property rights of slave owners. But the use of slaves as factory operatives threatened slave discipline because an efficient level of production required special incentives. A Virginian noted of slaves that he had hired out for industrial work, "They were worked hard, and had too much liberty, and were acquiring bad habits. They earned money by overwork, and spent it for whisky, and got a habit of roaming about and *taking care of themselves;* because, when they were not at work in the furnace, nobody looked out for them."

No more than 5 percent of the slaves in the Lower South ever worked in manufacturing, and most of these were in rural enterprises serving local markets too small to interest northern manufacturers. Ever concerned to preserve slavery, planters would not risk slave discipline or the profits of cotton agriculture by embracing the unpredictable changes that industrialization was sure to bring.

# THE UPPER SOUTH

**WHAT CAUSED** the decline of slavery after 1800 in the Upper South?

Climate and geography distinguished the Upper South from the Lower South. The eight slave states of the Upper South lay north of the best growing zones for cotton. The northernmost of these states—Delaware, Maryland, Kentucky, and Missouri—bordered on free states and were known as the Border South. The four states south of them—Virginia, North Carolina, Tennessee, and Arkansas—constituted a middle zone. Slavery was entrenched in all these states, but it was less dominant than in the cotton South.

The key difference between the Upper and Lower South was the suitability of the Lower South for growing cotton with gangs of slave laborers. Except for prime cotton districts in middle Tennessee, eastern Arkansas, and parts of North Carolina, the Upper South lacked the fertile soil and long growing season necessary for the commercial production of cotton, rice, or sugar (see Map 11–2). Consequently, the demand for slaves was weaker than in the Lower South. Percentages of slave ownership and of slaves in the overall population were roughly half those in the cotton South. While the Lower South was undergoing a cotton boom after the War of 1812, the Upper South was mired in a long economic slump, from which it did not emerge until the 1850s. The improved economy of the Upper South in the late antebellum period increasingly relied on free labor, a development that many cotton planters feared would diminish southern unity in defense of slavery.

## A PERIOD OF ECONOMIC ADJUSTMENT

To inhabitants and visitors alike, vast stretches of the Upper South presented a dreary spectacle of exhausted fields and depopulation in the 1820s and 1830s. The soil was most depleted where tobacco had been cultivated extensively. Even where the land was still fertile, farmers could not compete against the fresher lands of the Old Southwest. Land values fell as farmers dumped their property and headed west.

Agricultural reform emerged in the 1830s as one proposed solution to this economic crisis. Its leading advocate was Edmund Ruffin, a Virginia planter who tirelessly promoted the use of marl (calcium-rich seashell deposits) to neutralize the overly acidic and worn-out soils of the Upper South. He also called for deeper plowing, systematic rotation of crops, and upgrading the breeding stock for animal husbandry.

Ruffin's efforts, and those of the agricultural societies and fairs spawned by the reform movement, met with some success, especially in the 1840s, when the prices of all cash staples fell. Still, only a minority of farmers ever embraced reform. These were generally the well-educated planters who read the agricultural press and could afford to change their farming practices.

Although soil exhaustion and wasteful farming persisted, agriculture in the Upper South had revived by the 1850s. A rebound in the tobacco market accounted for part of this revival, but the growing profitability of general farming was responsible for most of it.

Particularly in the Border South, the trend was toward agricultural diversification. Farmers and planters lessened their dependence on slave labor or on a single cash crop and practiced a thrifty, efficient agriculture geared to producing grain and livestock for urban markets. Western Maryland and the Shenandoah Valley and northern sections of Virginia grew wheat, and in the former tobacco districts of the Virginia and North Carolina Tidewater, wheat, corn, and garden vegetables became major cash crops.

Expanding urban markets and a network of internal improvements facilitated the transition to general farming. Both these developments were outgrowths of the movement for industrial diversification launched in the 1820s in response to the heavy outflow of population from the Upper South.

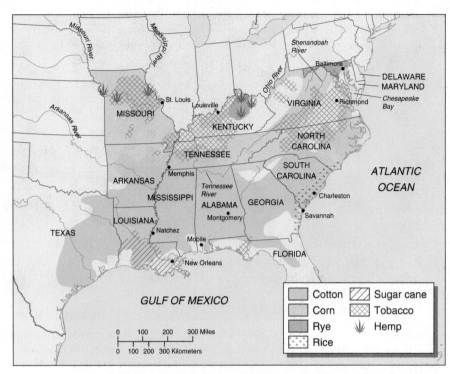

MAP 11–2 **Cotton and Other Crops in the South, 1860** Most of the Upper South was outside the Cotton Belt, where the demand for slave labor was greatest.

**Why was** the increasing dominance of cotton cultivation in the Lower South accompanied by a growing concentration of slaves in that region? What agricultural trends help explain the relative decline of slavery in the Upper South?

**Growing urbanization.** Although not far advanced by northern standards, urbanization and industrialization in the Upper South were considerably greater than in the Lower South. The region had twice the percentage of urban residents of the cotton South, and it contained the leading manufacturing cities in the slave states, St. Louis, Baltimore, and Louisville. Canals and railroads linked cities and countryside in a denser transportation grid than in the Lower South.

With an economy more balanced among agriculture, manufacturing, and trade than a generation earlier, the Upper South at midcentury was gradually becoming less tied to plantation agriculture and slave labor. The rural majority increasingly prospered by growing foodstuffs for city-dwellers and factory workers. The labor market for railroad construction and manufacturing work attracted northern immigrants, helping to compensate for the loss of the native-born population through migration to other states.

The economic adjustment in the Upper South converted the labor surplus of the 1820s into a labor scarcity by the 1850s. "It is a fact," noted Edmund Ruffin in 1859, "that labor is greatly deficient in all Virginia, and especially in the rich western counties, which, for want of labor, scarcely yet yield in the proportion of one tenth of their capacity." Ruffin's commitment to agricultural reform was exceeded only by his devotion to slavery. He now feared that free labor was about to replace scarce and expensive slave labor in Virginia and much of the Upper South.

## THE DECLINE OF SLAVERY

Slave owners tended to exaggerate all threats to slavery, and Ruffin was no exception. But slavery was clearly growing weaker in the Upper South by the 1850s (see Figure 11–2). The decline

**QUICK REVIEW**

**Economic Trends in the Upper South**

- Increased agricultural diversity.
- Expanding urban markets.
- Growing urbanization.
- Decreased reliance on plantation agriculture and slave labor.

The internal slave trade was the primary means by which the slaves of the Upper South were brought into the plantation markets of the Old Southwest. This illustration shows professional slave traders driving a chained group of slaves, known as a coffle, to prospective buyers in the Lower South.

Collection of The New-York Historical Society.

●•●─┤**Read** the **Document**

at **www.myhistorylab.com**
*A Slave Tells of His Sale at Auction
(1848)*

**FIGURE 11–2  The Changing Regional Pattern of Slavery in the South, 1800–1860**  As the nineteenth century progressed, slavery increasingly became identified with the cotton-growing Lower South.

was most evident along the northern tier of the Upper South, where the proportion of slaves to the overall population fell steadily after 1830.

Elsewhere in the Upper South, slavery was holding its own by the 1850s. Tobacco and cotton planters in North Carolina and Tennessee continued to rely heavily on slave labor, but most small farmers were indifferent, if not opposed, to the institution. Only in Arkansas, whose alluvial lands along the Mississippi River offered a new frontier for plantation agriculture, was slavery growing rapidly.

The region's role as a slave exporter to the Lower South hastened the decline of slavery in the Upper South. In every decade after 1820, the internal slave trade drained off about 10 percent of the slaves in the Upper South, virtually the entire natural increase. Selling slaves to the Lower South reinforced the Upper South's economic stake in slavery at a time when the institution was otherwise barely profitable there. The sale of surplus slaves was a windfall for planters whose slaves had become an economic burden. This same windfall gave planters the capital to embark on agricultural reform and shift out of tobacco production. Investment capital in the Upper South was not flowing into slave property but into economic diversification that expanded urban manufacturing. Both of these structural changes increasingly put slavery at a competitive disadvantage against free labor.

The wheat, corn, oats, and fodder crops that replaced tobacco in much of the Upper South did not require continuous attention. Unlike tobacco, wheat needed intensive labor only at planting and harvest. Thus, as planters abandoned tobacco, they kept fewer slaves and relied on cheap seasonal workers to meet peak labor demand.

The cheapness and flexibility of free labor made it better suited than slave labor for general farming. Urban manufacturers likewise wanted workers who could be hired and fired at a moment's notice. Despite the successful use of slaves in tobacco manufacturing and at the

On June 8, 1857, the slaves on the Stirrup Branch plantation in Bishopville, South Carolina, had their picture taken in the rear of their owner's house. The occasion was the seventy-fifth birthday of Captain James Rembert.

large Tredegar Iron Works in Richmond, immigrant workers displaced slaves in most of the factories in the Border South. By 1860, slaves made up just 1 percent of the population in St. Louis and Baltimore, the South's major industrial cities.

Slavery was in economic retreat across the Upper South after 1830. There were still plantation districts with large concentrations of slaves, and slave owners retained enough political power to defeat all challenges to their property interests. Nevertheless, the gradual turn to free labor was unmistakable.

# SLAVE LIFE AND CULTURE

Nearly 4 million slaves lived in the South by 1860, a more than fivefold increase since the ratification of the Constitution. This population gain was overwhelmingly due to an excess of births over deaths. The British-led effort to suppress the foreign slave trade was successful in closing off fresh supplies from Africa after 1807.

**WHAT WAS** life like for African American slaves in the first half of the nineteenth century?

Almost all southern slaves were thus native-born by the mid-nineteenth century. They were not Africans but African Americans, and they shared the common fate of bondage. By resisting an enslavement they could not prevent, they shaped a culture of their own that eased their pain and raised their hopes of someday being free. They retained their dignity in the face of continual humiliation and relied on their family life and religious beliefs as sources of strength under nearly intolerable circumstances.

## WORK ROUTINES AND LIVING CONDITIONS

Being treated as a piece of property to be worked for profit and bought and sold when financially advantageous to one's owners, this was the legal and economic reality that all slaves confronted. Each southern state had its own **slave codes,** laws defining the status of slaves and the rights of masters; the codes gave slave owners near-absolute power over their human property.

Slaves could not own property, make contracts, possess guns or alcohol, legally marry (except in Louisiana), leave plantations without the owner's written permission, or testify against their masters or any other white person in a court of law. Many states also prohibited

**slave codes** A series of laws passed mainly in the southern colonies in the late seventeenth and early eighteenth centuries to defend the status of slaves and codify the denial of basic civil rights to them.

⬤•⬤┤**Read** the **Document**

at **www.myhistorylab.com**
*Georgia Slave Codes (1848)*

## GLOBAL CONNECTIONS

### COTTON IS KING

"*But if there were no other reason why we should never have war, would any sane nation make war on cotton? Without firing a gun, without drawing a sword, should they make war on us we could bring the whole world to our feet. . . . What would happen if no cotton was furnished for three years? . . . England would topple headlong and carry the whole civilized world with her, save the South. No, you dare not make war on cotton. No power on earth dares to make war upon it. Cotton is king.*"

With these words delivered in a debate in the U.S. Senate on March 4, 1858, Senator James Henry Hammond of South Carolina popularized the phrase "Cotton is King," one that had first appeared in 1855 as the title of a work by the Cincinnati merchant David Christy decrying the world's dependence on southern-supplied cotton. Hammond would be proved wrong in his proclamation of the South's cotton-based invincibility, as Confederate diplomats discovered to their dismay during the Civil War, but by the 1850s the South's chief staple did indeed appear to be omnipotent.

As Hammond was speaking, the production, marketing, and consumption of cotton had spun a global web that constituted a veritable cotton empire of staggering proportions. Worldwide, perhaps as many 20 million workers were employed in the manufacturing of cotton and cotton cloth. No other manufacturing activity then rivaled cotton. Entire towns and regions stretching from the textile centers of New England to the mill districts of England, France, and Germany on to the suburbs of Moscow in Russia were critically dependent on a reliable and abundant source of cheap cotton. That source was overwhelmingly the American slave South. By the late 1850s cotton planters and their slaves provided England with 77 percent of its raw cotton, France 90 percent, Germany 60 percent, and Russia up to 92 percent. England's economy in particular, whether measured by its manufacturing, financial, or export sectors, seemed hostage to the South's continuing ability and willingness to keep it supplied with the product essential for its prosperity. No wonder Hammond was confident to the point of cockiness.

Hammond's speech politicized the growing faith of planters in the indispensability of their cotton to the global economy and pushed many of them to view secession from the Union as not only desirable but feasible. What Hammond and these planters overlooked was that cotton had become so important to the global economy that any major disruption in southern cotton would quickly compel foreign purchasers to develop alternative sources of cotton that were more directly under their political control. The cutting off of southern cotton during the Civil War resulted in a new global configuration of cotton production that permanently displaced King Cotton from its throne.

- What do you think were the main contours of the new global web of cotton production that emerged during and after the American Civil War, and what do you suspect was the likely impact on the rural populations of India, Egypt, and parts of Brazil?

teaching a slave to read or write. The murder of a slave by a master was illegal, but in practice, the law and community standards looked the other way if a disobedient slave was killed while being disciplined.

The slave codes penalized any challenge to a master's authority or any infraction of plantation rules. Whippings were the most commonly authorized punishment. Striking a master, committing arson, or conspiring to rebel were punishable by death. Most masters recognized that it made good business sense to feed, clothe, and house their slaves well enough to ensure productive labor and to encourage a family life that would enable the slave population to reproduce itself. Thus planters' self-interest probably improved the living standards for slaves in the first half of the nineteenth century, and the slave population grew at a rate only slightly below that of white southerners.

**Diet and housing.**     Planters rarely provided their slaves with more than the bare necessities. The slaves lived mainly on rations of cornmeal and salt pork, supplemented with vegetables they grew on the small garden plots that many planters permitted and with occasional catches of game

QUICK REVIEW

### Health and Welfare

- Planters provided the bare necessities.
- Slave diets were insufficient in vitamins and nutrients.
- Clothing and shelter were rudimentary.
- Life expectancy at birth for slaves was roughly half that of whites.

and fish. This diet provided ample calories but was often insufficient in vitamins and nutrients. Infant mortality was twice as high among slaves as among white southerners in 1850; so was mortality among slave children up to age 14. According to one study, the life expectancy for slaves at birth was 21 to 22 years, roughly half the white life expectancy.

Planters furnished slaves with two sets of coarse clothing, one for summer and one for winter. Their housing, typically a 15-by-15-foot one-room cabin for five or six occupants, provided little more than basic shelter against the elements. Large planters placed these cabins in a row, an arrangement that projected precision and undifferentiated order. Slaves expressed their individuality by furnishing their cabins with handmade beds and benches and by pushing for the right to put in gardens.

**Working conditions.**    The diet and housing of most slaves may have been no worse than that of the poorest whites in both the North and the South, but their workload was undoubtedly heavier. Just over half of the slave population at midcentury was concentrated on plantation units with 20 or more slaves, and most of these slaves worked as field hands in gang labor. Overseers freely admitted that they relied on whippings to make slaves in the gangs keep at their work.

Most plantation slaves toiled at hard physical labor from sunup to sundown. The work was more intense and sustained than that of white farmers or white factory hands. The fear of the whip on a bare back set the pace.

Some 15 to 20 percent of plantation slaves were house servants or skilled artisans who had lighter and less regimented workloads than field hands. Some planters used the prospect of transfer to these relatively privileged positions as an incentive to field hands to work harder. Extra rations, time off on weekends, passes to visit a spouse on a nearby plantation, and the right to have a garden plot were among the other incentives planters used to keep labor productivity high. However, what a planter viewed as privileges, benevolently bestowed, slaves quickly came to see as customary rights. Despite the power of the whip, if planters failed to respect these "rights," slave morale would decline, and the work routine would be interrupted.

Nearly three-fourths of the slaves worked on plantations and medium-sized farms. Most of the remainder, those in units with fewer than 10 slaves, worked on small farms in close contact with the master's family. Their workloads were more varied and sometimes less taxing than those of plantation hands, but these slaves were also more directly exposed to the whims of their owners and less likely to live in complete family units. Slave couples on small holdings were more likely to live on separate farms. Owners with only a few slaves were also more vulnerable than planters to market downturns that could force them to sell slaves and further divide families.

Of all slaves, 10 percent were not attached to the land, laboring instead at jobs that most white workers shunned. Every southern industry, but most particularly extractive industries such as mining and lumbering, relied heavily on slaves. Racial tensions often flared in southern industry, and when the races worked together, skilled white laborers typically insisted on being placed in supervisory positions.

Digging coal as miners or shoveling it as stokers for boilers on steamboats, laying down iron for the railroads or shaping hot slabs of it in a foundry, industrial slaves worked at least as hard as field hands. Compared to plantation slaves, however, they had more independence off the job and greater opportunities to earn money of their own. Because many of them had to house and feed themselves, they could also enjoy more time free from direct white scrutiny. By undertaking extra factory work, known as "overwork," industrial slaves could earn $50 or more a month, money they could use to buy goods for their families or, in rare cases, to purchase their freedom.

Especially on large plantations, slave nursemaids cared for the young children in the white planter's family.

From the Collection of the Louisiana State Museum.

Read the **Document**

at **www.myhistorylab.com**
*Memoirs of a Monticello Slave (1847)*

## FAMILIES AND RELIGION

The core institution of slave life was the family. Except in Louisiana, southern law did not recognize slave marriages, but masters permitted, even encouraged, marital unions in order to raise the morale of their labor force and increase its value by having it produce marketable children. Slaves embraced their families as a source of loving warmth and strength in a system that treated them as commodities.

Despite all the obstacles arrayed against them, many slave marriages produced enduring commitments and a supportive moral code for family members. Most slave unions remained intact until the death or, frequently, the sale of one spouse. Close to one-third of slave marriages were broken up by sales or forced removals.

Both parents were present in about two-thirds of slave families, the same ratio as in contemporary peasant families in Western Europe. Although the father's role as protector of and provider for his wife and children had no standing under slavery, most slave fathers struggled to help feed their families by hunting and fishing, and they risked beating and death to defend their wives against sexual abuse by the overseer or master. Besides their field labors, slave mothers had all the burdens of pregnancy, child care, laundry, and cooking.

No anguish under slavery was more heartrending than that of a mother whose child was sold away from her. "Oh, my heart was too full!" recalled Charity Bowery on being told that her boy Richard had been sold. "[My mistress] had sent me away on an errand, because she didn't want to be troubled with our cries. I hadn't any chance to see my poor boy. I shall never see my poor boy. I shall never see him again in this world. My heart felt as if it was under a great load."

Charity Bowery's experience was hardly unique. Slave parents had to suppress the rage they felt at their powerlessness to protect their children from the cruelties of slavery. Most parents could only teach their children the skills of survival in a world in which white people had a legal monopoly on violence. The most valuable of these skills was the art of hiding one's true feelings from white people and telling them what they wanted to hear.

Extensive kinship ties provided a support network for the vulnerable slave family. Thickest on the older and larger plantations, these networks included both blood relatives and other significant people. Children were taught to address elders as "Aunt" and "Uncle" and fellow slaves as "sister" and "brother." If separated from a parent, a child could turn to relatives or the larger slave community for care and assistance.

Slaves followed West African customs by prohibiting marriage between cousins and by often naming their children after departed grandparents. They also drew on an African heritage kept alive through folklore and oral histories to create a religion that fit their needs. The ancestors of nineteenth-century slaves brought no common religion with them when they were taken to the New World. However, beliefs common to a variety of African religions survived. Once slaves began to embrace Christianity in the late eighteenth century, they blended these beliefs into an African Christianity. In keeping with African traditions, the religion of the slaves fused the natural and spiritual worlds, accepted the power of ghosts over the living, and relied on an expressive form of worship in which the participants shouted and swayed in rhythm with the beat of drums and other instruments.

By most estimates, no more than 30 percent of slaves ever converted to Christianity. Those who did found in Christianity a message of deliverance rooted in the liberation of Moses's people from bondage in Egypt. The Jesus of the New Testament spoke to them as a compassionate God who had shared their burden of suffering, so that all peoples could hope to find the Promised Land of love and justice. By blending biblical imagery into their spirituals, the slaves expressed their yearning for freedom: "Didn't my Lord deliver Daniel/Then why not every man?"

The initial exposure of slaves to Christianity usually came from evangelical revivalists, and slaves always favored the Baptists and Methodists over other denominations. The evangelical message of universal spiritual equality confirmed the slaves' sense of personal worth. Less formal in both their doctrines and organization than the Presbyterians and Episcopalians, the evangelical sects

**QUICK REVIEW**

**Slave Families**

◆ Both parents present in two-thirds of slave families.

◆ Most slave fathers did extra work and risked punishment to support and defend their families.

◆ Parents concentrated on teaching children survival skills.

**Read the Document**

at **www.myhistorylab.com**
*Charles C. Jones, The Religious Instruction of the Negroes in the United States (1842)*

allowed the slaves more leeway to choose their own preachers and engage in their physical call-and-response pattern of worship.

Most planters were pragmatic about encouraging Christianity among their slaves. They wished to control religion, as they did other aspects of slaves' lives. Thus, while many planters allowed black preachers at religious services on their plantations, they usually insisted that white observers be present. Worried that abolitionist propaganda might attract the slaves to Christianity as a religion of secular liberation, some planters in the late antebellum period tried to convert their slaves to their own version of Christianity. They invited white ministers to their plantations to preach a gospel of passivity and obedience, centered on Paul's call for servants to "obey in all things your Masters."

Although most slaves viewed the religion of their owners as hypocritical and the sermons of white ministers as propaganda, they feigned acceptance of the religious wishes of their masters. As much as they could, the slaves hid their genuine religious life from white people. Many slaves experienced religion as a spiritual rebirth that gave them the inner strength to endure their bondage. As one recalled, "I was born a slave and lived through some hard times. If it had not been for my God, I don't know what I would have done."

## RESISTANCE

Open resistance to slavery was futile. The persistently disobedient slave would be sold "down river" to a harsher master or, in extreme cases, killed. Although the odds of succeeding were infinitesimal, desperate slaves did plot rebellion in the nineteenth century. The first major uprising, **Gabriel Prosser's Rebellion** in 1800, involved about 50 armed slaves around Richmond, though perhaps as many as 1,000 slaves knew about Prosser's plans. The rebels' failure to seize a key road to Richmond and a slave informer's warning to white authorities doomed the rebellion before it got under way. State authorities executed Prosser and 25 of his followers.

A decade later, in what seems to have been a spontaneous bid for freedom, several hundred slaves in the river parishes (counties) above New Orleans marched on the city. Poorly armed, they were no match for the U.S. Army troops and militiamen who stopped them. More than 60 slaves died, and the heads of the leading rebels were posted on poles along the Mississippi River to warn others of the fate that awaited rebellious slaves.

The most carefully planned slave revolt (at least in the minds of whites who resorted to torture to gain "confessions"), **Denmark Vesey's Conspiracy,** like Prosser's, failed before it got started. Vesey, a literate carpenter and lay preacher in Charleston who had purchased his freedom, allegedly planned the revolt in the summer of 1822. The plot collapsed when two domestic servants betrayed it. White authorities responded swiftly and savagely. They hanged 35 conspirators, including Vesey, and banished 37 others from the state. After destroying the African Methodist Episcopal church where Vesey had preached and the purported conspirators had met, they tried to seal off the city from subversive outsiders by passing the Negro Seamen's Act, which mandated the imprisonment of black sailors while their ships were berthed in Charleston.

One slave revolt, **Nat Turner's Rebellion,** in Southampton County, Virginia, did erupt before it could be suppressed. Turner was a literate field hand driven by prophetic visions of black vengeance against white oppressors. Convinced by what he called "signs in heaven" that he should "arise and prepare myself and slay my enemies with their own weapons," he led a small band of followers on a murderous rampage in late August 1831. The first white man to be killed was Joseph Travis, Turner's owner. In the next two days, the rebels killed 60 other white people. An enraged posse, aided by slaves, captured or killed most of Turner's party. Turner hid for two months before being apprehended. He and more than 30 other slaves were executed, and panicky white people killed more than 100 others.

Slaves well understood that the odds against a successful rebellion were insurmountable. They could see who had all the guns. White people were also more numerous. Surveillance by

**QUICK REVIEW**

**Fear of Rebellion and Northern Intentions**

- African Americans were the majority of South Carolina's population.
- Rebellions convinced planters that the antislavery movement was feeding slave unrest.
- Southerners feared that protective tariffs were a prelude to emancipation.

**See** the **Map**

at **www.myhistorylab.com**
*Slave Conspiracies and Uprisings, 1800–1831*

**Gabriel Prosser's Rebellion**  Slave revolt that failed when Gabriel Prosser, a slave preacher and blacksmith, organized a thousand slaves for an attack on Richmond, Virginia, in 1800.

**Denmark Vesey's Conspiracy**  The most carefully devised slave revolt in which rebels planned to seize control of Charleston in 1822 and escape to freedom in Haiti, a free black republic, but they were betrayed by other slaves, and seventy-five conspirators were executed.

**Nat Turner's Rebellion**  Uprising of slaves led by Nat Turner in Southampton County, Virginia, in the summer of 1831 that resulted in the death of 55 white people.

**Read** the **Document**

at **www.myhistorylab.com**
*Nat Turner, Confession (1831)*

This contemporary woodcut of Nat Turner's Rebellion depicts the fervency of both the actions of the slaves and the response of the whites.

Watch the Video

at **www.myhistorylab.com**
*Underground Railroad*

**Underground Railroad** Support system set up by antislavery groups in the Upper South and the North to assist fugitive slaves in escaping the South.

mounted white patrols, part of the police apparatus of slavery, limited organized rebellion by slaves to small, local affairs that were quickly suppressed.

Nor could many slaves escape to freedom. Few runaways made it to Canada or to a free state. White people could stop black people and demand to see papers documenting their freedom or right to travel without a master. The **Underground Railroad,** a secret network of stations and safe houses organized by Quakers and other black and white antislavery activists, provided some assistance. However, fellow slaves or free black people, especially in the cities of the Border South, provided the only help most runaways could count on. Out of more than 3 million slaves in the 1850s, only about 1,000 a year permanently escaped. (See American Views: A Letter from an Escaped Slave to His Former Master.)

After fleeing from slavery in Maryland in 1849, Harriet "Moses" Tubman, standing on the left, risked reenslavement by returning to the South on several occasions to assist in the escapes of other slaves. She is photographed here with some of those she helped free.

## AMERICAN VIEWS

### � A Letter from an Escaped Slave to His Former Master ✑

In 1859, Jackson Whitney was one of 6,000 fugitive slaves living in Canada, a sanctuary of freedom beyond the reach of the Fugitive Slave Act of 1850. Like most fugitives, he was male, and he had been forced to leave his family behind in Kentucky. His letter, as well as other direct testimony by African Americans about their experiences and feelings while enslaved, gives us information about slavery that only the slaves could provide.

- **How** would you characterize the tone of Whitney's letter? How did he express his joy at being a free man?
- **How** did Whitney feel that Riley, his former owner, had betrayed him?
- **What** did Whitney mean by the phrase "a slave talking to 'massa' "? How did he indicate that he had been hiding his true feelings as a slave?
- **How** did Whitney contrast his religious beliefs and those of Riley? How did he expect Riley to be punished?
- **What** pained Whitney about his freedom in Canada, and what did he ask of Riley?

March 18, 1859

Mr. Wm. Riley, Springfield, Ky.,

Sir:

I take this opportunity to dictate a few lines to you, supposing you might be curious to know my whereabouts. I am happy to inform you that I am in Canada, in good health, and have been here several days. Perhaps, by this time, you have concluded that robbing a woman of her husband, and children of their father does not pay, at least in your case; and I thought, while lying in jail by your direction, that if you had no remorse or conscience that would make you feel for a poor, broken-hearted man, and his worse-than-murdered wife and child, . . . and could not by any entreaty or permission be induced to do as you promised you would, which was to let me go with my family for $800, but contended for $1,000, when you had promised to take the same you gave for me (which was $660.) at the time you bought me, and let me go with my dear wife and children! but instead would render me miserable, and lie to me, and to your neighbors . . . and when you was at Louisville trying to sell me! then I thought it was time for me to make my feet feel for Canada, and let your conscience feel in your pocket.

Now you cannot say but that I did all that was honorable and right while I was with you, although I was a slave. I pretended all the time that I thought you, or some one else had a better right to me than I had to myself, which you know is rather hard thinking.

You know, too, that you proved a traitor to me in the time of need, and when in the most bitter distress that the human soul is capable of experiencing; and could you have carried out your purposes there would have been no relief. But I rejoice to say that an unseen, kind spirit appeared for the oppressed, and bade me take up my bed and walk, the result of which is that I am victorious and you are defeated. I am comfortably situated in Canada, working for George Harris [another fugitive slave from Kentucky who had bought a farm in Canada] . . .

There is only one thing to prevent me being entirely happy here, and that is the want of my dear wife and children, and you to see us enjoying ourselves together here. I wish you could realize the contrast between Freedom and slavery; but it is not likely that we shall ever meet again on this earth.

But if you want to go to the next world and meet a God of love, mercy, and justice, in peace; who says, "Inasmuch as you did it to the least of them my little ones, you did it unto me," making the professions that you do, pretending to be a follower of Christ, and tormenting me and my little ones as you have done, [you] had better repair the breaches you have made among us in this world, by sending my wife and children to me; thus preparing to meet your God in peace; for, if God don't punish you for inflicting such distress on the poorest of His poor, then there is no use of having any God, or talking about one . . .

I hope you will consider candidly, and see if the case does not justify every word I have said, and ten times as much. You must not consider that it is a slave talking to 'massa' now, but one as free as yourself.

I subscribe myself one of the abused of America, but one of the justified and honored of Canada.

Jackson Whitney

*Source:* John W. Blassingame, ed., *Slave Testimony: Two Centuries of Letters, Speeches, Interviews, and Autobiographies* (Louisiana State University Press, 1977).

**WHERE TO LEARN MORE**

Aboard the Underground Railroad
http://www.nps.gov/history/
nr/travel/underground

Running away was common, but most runaways fled no farther than to nearby swamps and woods. Most voluntarily returned or were tracked down by bloodhounds within a week. Aside from those who were protesting a special grievance or trying to avoid punishment, slaves who ran away usually did so to visit a spouse or loved one. Occasionally, runaways could bargain for lenient treatment in return for faithful service in the future. Most were severely punished. Such temporary flights from the master's control siphoned off some of the anger that might otherwise have erupted in violent, self-destructive attacks on slave owners. All planters had heard about the field hand who took an ax to an overseer, the cook who poisoned her master's family, or the house servant who killed a sleeping master or mistress.

Slaves resisted complete domination by their masters in less overt ways. They mocked white people in folktales like those about Br'er Rabbit, for example, in which weak but wily animals cunningly outsmart their stronger enemies. Slave owners routinely complained of slaves malingering at work, abusing farm animals, losing tools, stealing food, and committing arson. These subversive acts of protest never challenged the system of slavery itself, but they did help slaves to maintain a sense of dignity and self-respect.

HOW WAS free society in the South structured?

# FREE SOCIETY

The abolitionists and the antislavery Republican party of the 1850s portrayed the social order of the slave South as little more than haughty planters lording it over shiftless poor white people. The reality was considerably more complex. Planters, who set the social tone for the South as a whole, did act superior, but they were a tiny minority and had to contend with an ambitious middle class of small slaveholders and a majority of nonslaveholding farmers. Some landless white people on the margins of rural society fit the stereotype of "poor whites," but they were easily outnumbered by self-reliant farmers who worked their own land. Southern cities, though small by northern standards, provided jobs for a growing class of free workers who increasingly clashed with planters over the use of slave labor. These same cities, notably in the Upper South, were also home to the nation's largest concentration of free black people.

((•—[Hear the Audio

at www.myhistorylab.com
*Remembering Slavery*

## THE SLAVEHOLDING MINORITY

**Large planters.**   Only in the rice districts of the South Carolina low country and in the rich sugar- and cotton-growing areas of the Mississippi Delta were large planters more than a small minority of the slaveholding class, let alone the general white population. Families of the planter class, those who held a minimum of 20 slaves, constituted only around 3 percent of all southern families in 1860. Fewer than one out of five planter families, less than 1 percent of all families, owned more than 50 slaves. Far from conspicuously exhibiting their wealth, most planters lived in drab log cabins, not grand, white-columned houses. Most planters wanted to acquire wealth, not display it. They were restlessly eager to move on and abandon their homes when the allure of profits from a new cotton frontier promised to relieve them of the debts they had incurred to purchase their slaves.

**Planters' wives.**   Most planters expected their wives to help supervise the slaves and run the plantation. Besides raising her children, the plantation mistress managed the household staff, oversaw the cooking and cleaning, gardened, dispensed medicine and clothing to the slaves, and often assisted in their religious instruction. When guests or relatives came for an extended visit, the wife had to make all the special arrangements that such occasions entailed. When the master was called off on a business or political trip, she kept the plantation accounts. In many respects, she worked harder than her husband.

**QUICK REVIEW**

**Plantation Mistresses**

- Mistresses ran the household staff.
- Mistresses were responsible for arrangements for visitors.
- Planter's wives found the management of slaves a burden.

| **OVERVIEW** Structure of Free Society in the South, c. 1860 | | |
| --- | --- | --- |
| **Group** | **Size** | **Characteristics** |
| Large planters | Less than 1 percent of white families | Owned 50 or more slaves and plantations in excess of 1,000 acres; the wealthiest class in United States |
| Planters | About 3 percent of white families | Owned 20 to 49 slaves and plantations in excess of 100 acres; controlled bulk of southern wealth and provided most of the political leaders |
| Small slaveholders | About 20 percent of white families | Owned fewer than 20 slaves and most often fewer than five; primarily farmers, though some were part of a small middle class in towns and cities |
| Nonslaveholding whites | About 75 percent of white families | Mostly yeomen farmers who owned their own land and stressed production for family use; one in five owned neither slaves nor land and squatted on the least desirable land where they planted some corn and grazed some livestock; in cities they worked as artisans or, more typically, day laborers |
| Free blacks | About 3 percent of all free families | Concentrated in the Upper South; hemmed in by legal and social restrictions; mostly tenants or farm laborers; about one-third lived in cities and generally were limited to lowest paying jobs |

Planters' wives often complained in their journals and letters of their isolation from other white women and the physical and mental toil of managing slaves. The women with whom they had the closest daily contact were often their female domestic slaves. As Hannah Crafts noted, they treated some of these slaves with an intimacy that abolitionist propaganda refused to acknowledge. Whatever their misgivings about slavery, plantation mistresses enjoyed a wealth and status unknown to most southern women and only rarely questioned the institution of slavery. Their deepest anger stemmed from their humiliation by husbands who kept slave mistresses or sexually abused slave women. Bound by their duties as wives not to express this anger publicly, and unwilling to renounce the institution that both victimized and benefited them, white women tended to vent their frustrations on black women whose alleged promiscuity they blamed for the sexual transgressions of white males.

**Small slaveholders.**    Despite the tensions and sexual jealousies it aroused, owning slaves was the surest means of social and economic advancement for most white families. Most slave owners, however, never attained planter status. Nine out of 10 slave owners in 1860 owned fewer than 20 slaves, and fully half of them had fewer than five. Many white people also rented a few slaves on a seasonal basis.

Generally younger than the planters, small slaveholders were a diverse lot. About 10 percent were women, and another 20 percent or so were merchants, businessmen, artisans, and urban professionals. Most were farmers trying to acquire enough land and slaves to become planters. To keep costs down, they often began by purchasing children, the cheapest slaves available, or a young slave family, so that they could add to their slaveholdings as the slave mother bore more children.

Small slaveholders had scant economic security. A deadly outbreak of disease among their slaves or a single bad crop could destroy their credit and force them to sell their slaves to clear their debts. Owners of fewer than ten slaves stood a fifty-fifty chance within a decade of dropping out of the slaveholding class. Nor could small holders hope to compete directly with the planters. In any given area suitable for plantations, they were gradually pushed out as planters bought up land to raise livestock or more crops. In general, only slave owners who had established themselves in business or the professions had the capital reserves to rise into the planter elite.

## THE WHITE MAJORITY

Three-fourths of southern white families owned no slaves in 1860. Although most numerous in the Upper South, nonslaveholders predominated wherever the soil and climate were not suitable for plantation agriculture. Most were yeoman farmers who worked their own land with family labor.

These farmers were quick to move when times were bad and their land was used up, but once settled in an area, they formed intensely localized societies in which fathers and husbands held sway over their families. The community extended 5 to 10 miles around the nearest country store or county courthouse. Networks of kin and friends provided labor services when needed, fellowship in evangelical churches, and staple goods that an individual farm could not produce. Social travel and international markets, so central to the lives of planters, had little relevance in the farmers' community-centered existence. The yeomanry aimed to be self-sufficient and limited their market involvement to the sale of livestock and an occasional cotton crop that could bring in needed cash.

Yeoman farmers jealously guarded their independence, and in their tight little worlds of face-to-face relationships, they demanded that planters treat them as social equals. Ever fearful of being reduced to dependence, they avoided debt and sought to limit government authority. Rather than risk financial ruin by buying slaves on credit to grow cotton, they grew food crops and depended on their sons and, when needed, their wives and daughters to work the fields.

Nonslaveholding farmers from the mountains and planters on the bottomlands rarely mixed, and their societies developed in isolation from each other. In areas where there were both small farms and scattered plantations, the interests of the yeomen and the planters were often complementary. Planters provided local markets for the surplus grain and livestock of nonslaveholders and, for a small fee, access to gristmills and gins for grinding corn and cleaning cotton. They lent small sums to poorer neighbors in emergencies or to pay taxes. The yeomen staffed the slave patrols and became overseers on the plantations. Both groups sought to protect property rights from outside interference and to maintain a system of racial control in which white liberties rested on black degradation.

When yeomen and planters clashed, it was usually over economic issues. Large slaveholders needing better credit and marketing facilities gravitated toward the Whig Party, which called for banks and internal improvements. Nonslaveholding farmers, especially in the Lower South, tended to be Democrats who opposed banks and state-funded economic projects. They viewed bankers as grasping outsiders who wanted to rob them of their economic independence, and they suspected that state involvement in the economy led only to higher taxes and increased public debt. These partisan battles, however, rarely involved a debate about the merits of slavery. As long as planters deferred to the egalitarian sensibilities of the yeomen by courting them at election time and promising to safeguard their liberties, the planters were able to maintain broad support for slavery across class lines.

Around 15 percent of rural white families owned neither land nor slaves. These were the so-called poor whites, stigmatized by both abolitionists and planters as lazy and shiftless. The abolitionists considered them a kind of underclass who proved that slavery so degraded the dignity of labor that it led people to shun work and lapse into wretched poverty. To the planters, they were a constant nuisance and a threat to slave discipline. Planters habitually complained that poor whites demoralized their slaves by showing that a person could survive without steady labor.

Some landless white people did live down to their negative stereotype. Still, the "poor white trash" label with which they were stigmatized is misleading. Most were resourceful and enterprising enough to supply themselves with all the material comforts they wanted. Not having to do steady work for survival, they hunted, fished, and took orders from no one. Although poor by most standards, they were also defiantly self-reliant.

Nonslaveholders were a growing majority in southern cities, especially among the working classes. These urban workers shared no agricultural interests or ties with the planters. Nor were most of them, especially in the unskilled ranks, southern-born. Northerners and immigrants dominated the urban work force. Free workers, especially Irish and German immigrants, increasingly replaced slaves in urban labor markets. These white workers bitterly resented competition from black slaves, and their demands to exclude slaves from the urban workplace reinforced planters' belief that cities bred abolitionism.

# FREE BLACK PEOPLE

A small minority of southern black people, 6 percent of the total in 1860, were "free persons of color." They constituted 3 percent of the free population in the South (see Figure 11–3). These free black people occupied a precarious and vulnerable position between degraded

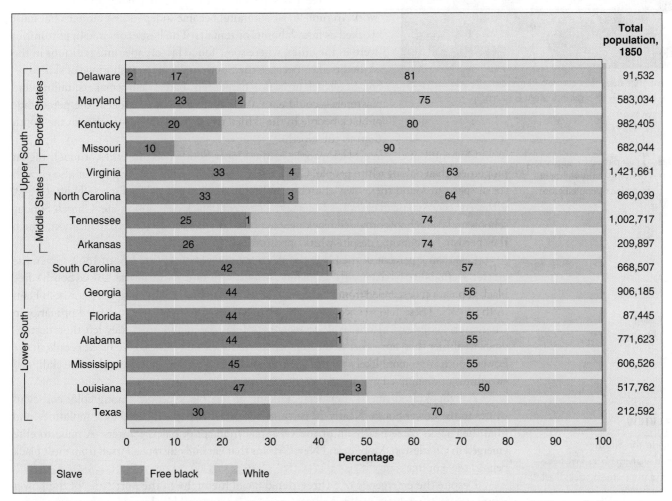

FIGURE 11–3 **Slave, Free Black, and White Population in Southern States, 1850** Except for Texas, slaves by 1850 comprised over 40 percent of the population in every state of the Lower South. The small population of free black people was concentrated in the Upper South.

Barbering was one of the skilled trades open to black men during the antebellum years. Several wealthy African Americans began their careers as barbers.

The Granger Collection, New York.

**black codes** Laws passed by states and municipalities denying many rights of citizenship to free black people before the Civil War.

enslavement and meaningful freedom. White intimidation and special legal provisions known as **black codes** (found throughout the North as well) denied them nearly all the rights of citizenship. Because of the legal presumption in the South that all black people were slaves, they had to carry freedom papers, official certificates of their freedom. They were shut out of the political process and could not testify against white people in court. Many occupations, especially those involved in the communication of ideas, such as the printing trades, were closed to them.

Every slave state forbade the entry of free black people, and every municipality had rules and regulations that forced them to live as an inferior caste. Any sign of upward mobility or intimation of equal standing was ruthlessly suppressed. More than four-fifths of the southern free black population lived in the Upper South. Most were the offspring of slaves freed by private manumissions between 1780 and 1800, when slavery temporarily loosened in the Chesapeake region in the wake of the Revolutionary War. Manumissions dropped sharply after 1810, the result of heightened white anxieties after Prosser's Rebellion and the rising demand for slaves in the Lower South.

As in the North, legal barriers and white prejudice generally confined free black people to the poorest paying and most menial work. In rural areas, a handful became independent farmers, but most worked as farm laborers or tenants. The best economic opportunities were in the cities, where some found factory jobs and positions in the skilled trades. Because the South had a general shortage of skilled labor, free black artisans—carpenters, barbers, shoemakers, tailors, and plasterers—could earn a respectable income. Indeed, the percentage of black people in the skilled trades was generally higher in the South than in the North.

One-third of the free black people in the Upper South lived in cities, a much higher proportion than among white people. Cities offered black people not only jobs but also enough social space to found their own churches and mutual-aid associations. Especially after 1840, urban African American churches became the center of black community life. Church Sunday schools and day schools provided black people practically their only access to education, which they persisted in pursuing despite white opposition.

Less than 2 percent of the black people in the Lower South were free in 1860. Given the greater profitability of slavery there, manumissions were rare. Most of the Lower South's free black population descended from black emigrants who had fled the revolutionary unrest in Haiti in the 1790s. These refugees were artisans, shopkeepers, and farmers who settled primarily in Charleston and New Orleans. Able to secure a solid economic footing, they left their descendants wealthier than any other free black people in the United States. Free black people in the Lower South were more likely than those in the Upper South to have a marketable skill, and two-thirds of them lived in cities.

A light skin enhanced the social standing of free black people among color-conscious whites in the Lower South. Nearly 70 percent of free black people in 1860 were mulattoes, and from their ranks came nearly all of the very small number of black planters. A mulatto elite emerged in Charleston, Mobile, and New Orleans that carefully distanced itself from most black people, slave or free.

Despite the emergence of a three-tiered racial hierarchy in the port cities of the Lower South, white officialdom insisted on maintaining a white and black racial dichotomy. As the racial defense of slavery intensified in the 1850s, more calls were made for laws to banish or enslave free black people. Arkansas passed such a law in 1859, and similar bills were proposed in Florida, Tennessee, Mississippi, and Missouri. Even Maryland held a referendum in 1859 on whether to reenslave its free black population, among the largest in the South. Only the opposition of nonslaveholders heavily dependent on cheap free black labor defeated the referendum.

# THE PROSLAVERY ARGUMENT

In the early nineteenth century, white southerners made no particular effort to defend slavery, because the institution was not under heavy outside attack. If pressed, most white people would have called slavery a necessary evil, an unfortunate legacy from earlier generations that was needed to maintain racial peace.

The 1830s marked a turning point. After the twin shocks of Nat Turner's Rebellion and the onset of the abolitionist crusade (for more on this crusade, see Chapter 12), white mobs emerged to stifle any open criticism of slavery in the Lower South. White southerners also began to develop a defense of slavery. By the 1850s, politicians, intellectuals, and evangelical ministers were arguing that slavery was a positive good.

**HOW DID** the southern defense of slavery change between the early nineteenth century and the 1850s?

•◀—Read the Document
at **www.myhistorylab.com**
*Thomas R. Dew's Defense of Slavery (1832)*

## RELIGIOUS ARGUMENTS

Evangelical Protestantism dominated southern religious expression by the 1830s, and its ministers took the lead in combating abolitionist charges that slavery was a moral and religious abomination. Except for a radical minority of antislavery evangelicals in the Upper South, southern churches had always supported slavery. This support grew more pronounced and articulate once the abolitionists stepped up their attacks on slavery in the mid-1830s.

Southern evangelicals accepted the Bible as God's literal word, and through selective reading they found abundant evidence to proclaim slavery fully in accord with His moral dictates. Southern evangelicals also turned to the Bible to support their argument that patriarchal authority, the unquestioned power of the father, was the basis of all Christian communities. Part of that authority extended over slaves, and slavery thus became a matter of family governance, a domestic institution in which Christian masters of slaves, unlike capitalist masters of free "wage slaves" in the North, accepted responsibility for caring for their workers in sickness and old age. Far from being a moral curse, therefore, slavery was part of God's plan to Christianize an inferior race and teach its people how to produce raw materials that benefited the world's masses.

The growing commitment of southern evangelicals to slavery as a positive good clashed with the antislavery position and the generally more liberal theology of northern evangelicals. In 1837, the Presbyterians split along sectional lines in part because of differences over slavery. In 1844, as a direct result of the slavery issue, the Methodist Episcopal Church, the nation's largest, divided into northern and southern churches. The Baptists did the same a year later. These religious schisms foreshadowed the sectionalized political divisions of the 1850s; they also severed one of the main emotional bonds between whites in the North and the South. The religious defense of slavery was central to the slaveholding ethic of

As this printed label from the 1850s for a box of cigars reveals, antebellum manufacturers of consumer goods produced by slave labor had every incentive to present an idealized picture of slave life in the South.

paternalism that developed after 1830. By the 1850s, planters commonly described slaves as members of an extended family who were treated better than free workers in the North.

The crusade to sanctify slavery won few converts outside the South. Most northern churches did not endorse abolitionism but did have moral qualms about slavery. In a particularly stinging rebuke to southern church leaders in the 1850s, black abolitionists succeeded in having slaveholders barred from international religious conventions.

## RACIAL ARGUMENTS

More common than the biblical defense of slavery was the racial argument that black people were unfit for freedom. Drawing in part on the scientific wisdom of the day, the racial defense alleged that black people were naturally lazy and inherently inferior to white people. If freed, so went the argument, they would turn to crime and sexually assault white women. Only the controls of slavery enabled the races to coexist in the South.

The racial argument resonated powerfully among white people because nearly all of them, including those otherwise opposed to slavery, dreaded emancipation. The attitude of a Tennessee farmer, as recorded by a northern traveler in the 1850s, was typical: "He said he'd always wished there hadn't been any niggers here . . . , but he wouldn't like to have them free." Unable to conceive of living in a society with many free black people, most white people could see no middle ground between slavery and the presumed social chaos of emancipation.

The existence of *black* slavery also had egalitarian implications for the nonslaveholding majority of whites. Slavery supposedly spared white southerners from the menial, degrading labor that white northerners had to perform. Moreover, because slaves lacked political rights, champions of slavery argued that black bondage buttressed the political liberties of all white males by removing from politics the leveling demands of the poor and propertyless for a redistribution of wealth.

Despite its apparent success in forging white solidarity, the racial argument could be turned on its head and used to weaken slavery. Most white northerners were about as racist as their southern counterparts, but they were increasingly willing to end slavery on the grounds that the stronger white race should help black people improve themselves as free persons. In short, nothing in the internal logic of racist doctrines required enslaving black people. The same logic also encouraged some white southerners to challenge the economic prerogatives of slaveholders. Why, for example, should any white people, as members of the master race, be forced into economic competition against skilled slave artisans? Why should not all non-agricultural jobs be legally reserved for white people? Doctrines of black inferiority could not prevent white unity from cracking when the economic interests of nonslaveholders clashed with those of planters.

---

# CONCLUSION

The proslavery argument depicted a nearly ideal society blessed by class and racial harmony. In reality, social conditions in the slave South were contradictory and conflict-ridden. Slaves were not content in their bondage. Hannah Crafts spoke for nearly all of them when she described slavery as a coarse, brutalizing institution that demeaned all it touched. They dreamed of freedom and sustained that dream through their own forms of Christianity and the support of family and kin. Relations between masters and their slaves were antagonistic, not affectionate, and wherever the system of control slackened, slaves resisted their owners. Nor did all white southerners, who confronted increasing economic inequality after 1830, accept racial slavery as in their best interests. It divided as well as united them.

During the 1850s, the size of the slaveholding class fell from 31 percent of southern white families to 25 percent. Slave owners were a shrinking minority, and slavery was in decline throughout the Upper South. In the Border South, free labor was replacing slavery as the dominant means of organizing economic production. In these states, slavery was a vulnerable institution. Planters were not fooled by the public rhetoric of white unity. They knew that slavery was increasingly confined to the Lower South, and that elsewhere in the South white support for it was gradually eroding. Planters feared the double-edged challenge to their privileged position posed by outside interference with slavery and internal white disloyalty. By the 1850s, many of them were concluding that the only way to resolve their dilemma was to make the South a separate nation.

# WHERE TO LEARN MORE

**Aboard the Underground Railroad.** For a National Register of Historic Places Travel Itinerary that provides maps and descriptions and photographs of sixty historic places associated with the Underground Railroad, go to http://www.nps.gov/history/nr/travel/underground/.

**The Anacostia Museum Center for African American History.** This museum of the Smithsonian Institution explores American history and cultures from an African American perspective. Go to http://anacostia.si.edu for information on its exhibits and a calendar of events.

**Appalachian Museum of Berea College, Berea, Kentucky.** This museum is an excellent source for understanding the lifestyle and material culture of the nonslaveholding farmers in the Appalachian highlands. For an overview of its exhibits, see http://www.berea.edu/appalachiancenter/artifactsexhibits.asp.

**Cottonlandia Museum, Greenwood, Mississippi.** The library and museum depict the history of cotton in the Mississippi Delta. Special collections include some Native American artifacts. Information on its displays can be found at http://www.cottonlandia.org/.

# REVIEW QUESTIONS

1. What factors accounted for the tremendous expansion of cotton production in the South? How was this expansion linked to slavery and westward movement?

2. What differentiated the Upper South from the Lower South? What role did slavery play in each region after 1815?

3. How would you characterize the life of a plantation slave? What insights does Hannah Crafts's opening account provide into the special vulnerability of slave women? Why were religion and family such key features of the world that slaves built for themselves? What evidence is there of resistance and rebellion among the slaves?

4. How did most nonslaveholding white southerners live? What values did they prize most highly? Why did most nonslaveholders accept slavery or at least not attack it directly?

5. What was the position of free black southerners in southern society? How were their freedoms restricted?

6. How did white southerners attempt to defend slavery and reconcile it with Christianity?

7. How was the development of the Old South linked to the international cotton market?

# KEY TERMS

Black codes (p. 296)
Denmark Vesey's Conspiracy (p. 289)
Gabriel Prosser's Rebellion (p. 289)
Gang system (p. 280)
Nat Turner's Rebellion (p. 289)
Slave codes (p. 285)
Underground Railroad (p. 290)

# PEARSON myhistorylab Connections

Reinforce what you learned in this chapter by studying the many documents, images, maps, review tools, and videos available at **www.myhistorylab.com**.

## Read and Review

✓●— **Study** and **Review** Study Plan: Chapter 11

•◦•—**Read** the **Document**

*Memoirs of a Monticello Slave (1847)*

*Nat Turner, Confession (1831)*

*A Slave Tells of His Sale at Auction (1848)*

*Georgia Slave Codes (1848)*

*Charles C. Jones, The Religious Instruction of the Negroes in the United States (1842)*

*Senator Sees Slavery as a "Positive Good" (1837)*

*Thomas R. Dew's Defense of Slavery (1832)*

👁—**See** the **Map**

*Slavery in the South*

*Agriculture, Industry, and Slavery in the Old South, 1850*

*Slave Conspiracies and Uprisings, 1800–1831*

*The Underground Railroad*

## Research and Explore

•◦•—**Read** the **Document**

*Personal Journeys Online*

*From Then to Now Online: Overcoming the Economic Legacy of Slavery*

((•●—**Hear** the **Audio**

*Go Down Moses; sung by Bill McAdoo*

*Pick a Bale of Cotton*

*Remembering Slavery*

((•●—**Watch** the **Video** *Underground Railroad*

---

((•●—**Hear** the **Audio**

Hear the audio files for Chapter 11 at
**www.myhistorylab.com**.

# 12

# The Market Revolution and Social Reform

An abolitionist freeing a slave from his shackles: colored woodcut, c. 1840, from an American antislavery almanac.
Top image: Map of proposed route of Erie Canal, 1811 Negative Number 420757, © Collection of the New-York Historical Society, New York City.

((●─ **Hear** the **Audio**

Hear the audio files for Chapter 12 at **www.myhistorylab.com**.

## INDUSTRIAL CHANGE AND URBANIZATION  *(page 305)*

**HOW DID** industrialization contribute to growing inequality and the creation of new social classes?

## REFORM AND MORAL ORDER  *(page 317)*

**WHAT ROLE** did women play in the reform movements that followed the War of 1812?

## INSTITUTIONS AND SOCIAL IMPROVEMENT  *(page 321)*

**HOW DID** Enlightenment ideas shape the reform of institutions for the poor, criminals, and the mentally ill?

## ABOLITIONISM AND WOMEN'S RIGHTS  *(page 325)*

**WHAT WAS** the relationship between abolitionism and the women's rights movement?

ONE AMERICAN JOURNEY

*East Boylston, Mass. 10th mo. 2d, 1837*

*Dear Friend: . . .*

*The investigation of the rights of the slave has led me to a better understanding of my own. I have found the Anti-Slavery cause to be the high school of morals in our land—the school in which human rights are more fully investigated, and better understood and taught, than in any other. Here a great fundamental principle is uplifted and illuminated, and from this central light, rays innumerable stream all around. Human beings have rights, because they are moral beings: the rights of all men grow out of their moral nature; and as all men have the same moral nature, they have essentially the same rights. These rights may be wrested from the slave, but they cannot be alienated: his title to himself is as perfect now, as is that of Lyman Beecher [a prominent minister]: it is stamped on his moral being, and is, like it, imperishable. Now if rights are founded on the nature of our moral being, then the mere circumstance of sex does not give to man higher rights and responsibilities, than to woman. . . . My doctrine then is, that whatever it is morally right for man to do, it is morally right for woman to do. Our duties originate, not from difference of sex, but from the diversity of our relations in life, the various gifts and talents committed to our care, and the different eras in which we live.*

    Angelina Emily Grimké

Angelina E. Grimke, *Letters to Catherine Beecher, in reply to an Essay of Slavery and Abolition,* Addressed to A. E. Grimke, rev. ed., Boston: Isaac Knapp, 1838, pp. 114–21.

**◆•◆—Read the Document** at **www.myhistorylab.com**

Personal Journeys Online

- **Margaret Fuller, Excerpt from *Women in the Nineteenth Century*, 1845. Arguments for women's rights.**
- **Lydia Maria Child, Letter, 1839. Issue of women's rights in the antislavery movement.**

**BORN IN 1805** to a wealthy slaveholding family in Charleston, Angelina was the daughter of a prominent jurist. Despite all the social and economic benefits that membership in the planter class conferred upon her, she passionately rejected slavery when she became a young adult. As was also true for her sister Sarah, this rejection was part of a religious conversion to Quakerism. Angelina left her home in Charleston in 1829 and joined her sister in Philadelphia. The sisters joined the abolitionist movement in 1835, and within two years had become the crusade's most celebrated (and notorious) platform lecturers.

Although Angelina, in her commitment to radical reform, was hardly typical of antebellum U.S. women, let alone women of the planter class, her journey from a privileged life in Charleston to one of social activism in the North speaks to the radicalizing potential of the reform impulse that swept over the nation after the War of 1812. This reform impulse was strongest in the North, where

traditional social and economic relations were undergoing wrenching changes as a market revolution accelerated the spread of cities, factories, and commercialized farms. New middle and working classes evolved in response to such changes, which were the most pronounced in the Northeast. The North was also the area where the emotional fires of evangelical revivals burned the hottest.

The religious message of the Second Great Awakening, which began in the early 1800s, provided a framework for responding to the changes that accompanied the market revolution. Evangelicalism taught that in both the spiritual and secular realms, individuals were accountable for their own actions. Through Christian activism, individuals could strive toward moral perfectibility and cleanse society of its evils.

The first wave of reform after the War of 1812 focused on individual behavior, targeting drinking, gambling, sexual misconduct, and Sabbath-breaking. By the 1830s, a second phase

## CHRONOLOGY

| | |
|---|---|
| **1790** | Samuel Slater opens the first permanent cotton mill in Rhode Island. |
| **1793** | Eli Whitney patents the first cotton gin. |
| **1807** | Robert Fulton's steamboat, the *Clermont*, makes its pioneering voyage up the Hudson River. |
| **1814** | The Boston Associates opens its Waltham mill, the first textile factory to mechanize all phases of production. |
| **1817** | Construction of the Erie Canal begins. |
| | American Colonization Society is founded. |
| **1819–1823** | Economic depression. |
| **1820s** | The new nations of Latin America commit themselves to policies of gradual emancipation. |
| **1824** | In *Gibbons v. Ogden*, the Supreme Court strikes down a state monopoly over steamboat navigation. |
| **1825** | Erie Canal is completed. |
| | Opening of the Stockton and Darlington Railroad in England. |
| **1826** | American Temperance Society launches its crusade. |
| **1828** | The Baltimore and Ohio, the most important of the early railroads, is chartered. |
| **1829** | David Walker publishes *Appeal to the Colored Citizens of the World*. |
| **1830** | Joseph Smith founds the Church of Jesus Christ of Latter-Day Saints. |
| **1830–1831** | Evangelical revivals are held in northern cities. |
| **1831** | William Lloyd Garrison begins publishing the *Liberator*. |
| **1833** | Slaves in the British Empire are emancipated. |

| | |
|---|---|
| | American Anti-Slavery Society is organized. |
| **1834** | New York Female Reform Society is founded. |
| | Female workers at the Lowell Mills stage their first strike. |
| **1836** | Congress passes gag rule. |
| **1837** | Horace Mann begins campaign for school reform in Massachusetts. |
| | Antiabolitionist mob kills Elijah P. Lovejoy. |
| | In *Charles River Bridge v. Warren Bridge*, the Supreme Court encourages economic competition by ruling that presumed rights of monopolistic privileges could not be used to block new economic enterprises. |
| **1839–1843** | Economic depression. |
| **1840** | Abolitionists split into Garrisonian and anti-Garrisonian societies. |
| | Political abolitionists launch the Liberty Party. |
| **1841** | Brook Farm is established. |
| | Dorothea Dix begins her work to improve conditions for the mentally ill. |
| **1842** | Massachusetts Supreme Court in *Commonwealth v. Hunt* strengthens the legal right of workers to organize trade unions. |
| **1845** | Potato famine in Ireland sets off a mass migration of Irish to the United States. |
| **1846–1848** | Mormons migrate to the West. |
| **1847** | John Humphrey Noyes establishes the Oneida Community. |
| **1848** | Seneca Falls Convention outlines a program for women's rights. |

of reform turned to institutional solutions for crime, poverty, and social delinquency, largely untouched by voluntary moral suasion. The third phase of the reform cycle rejected the social beliefs and practices that prescribed fixed and subordinate positions to certain Americans based on race and also on sex. This radical phase culminated in abolitionism and the campaign for women's rights, movements that came together in Angelina Grimké's journey out of her native South. ✦

# INDUSTRIAL CHANGE AND URBANIZATION

In 1820, 80 percent of the free labor force worked in agriculture, and manufacturing played a minor role in overall economic activity. Over the next three decades, however, the United States joined England as a world leader in industrialization.

The most direct cause of this rapid and sustained surge in manufacturing was increased consumption within the United States of the goods the country was producing. The

**HOW DID** industrialization contribute to growing inequality and the creation of new social classes?

## Table 12-1

**Impact of the Transportation Revolution on Traveling Time**

| Route | 1800 | 1830 | 1860 |
|---|---|---|---|
| New York to Philadelphia | 2 days | 1 day | Less than 1 day |
| New York to Charleston | More than 1 week | 5 days | 2 days |
| New York to Chicago | 6 weeks | 3 weeks | 2 days |
| New York to New Orleans | 4 weeks | 2 weeks | 6 days |

**transportation revolution** Dramatic improvements in transportation that stimulated economic growth after 1815 by expanding the range of travel and reducing the time and cost of moving goods and people.

**transportation revolution** dramatically reduced transportation costs and shipping times, opened up new markets for farmers and manufacturers alike, and provided an incentive for expanding production (see Table 12–1). As agricultural and manufactured goods were exchanged more efficiently, a growing home market continually stimulated the development of U.S. manufacturing.

## THE TRANSPORTATION REVOLUTION

Aside from some 4,000 miles of toll roads in the Northeast, the nation had nothing approaching a system of transportation in 1815. The cost of moving goods by land transportation was prohibitively high. It cost just as much to haul heavy goods by horsedrawn wagons 30 miles into the interior as to ship them 3,000 miles across the Atlantic Ocean. Water transportation was much cheaper, but it was limited to the coast or navigable rivers. Thus, only farmers located near a city or a river could grow surplus crops for sale in an outside market. Western farm surpluses followed the southerly flow of the Ohio and Mississippi river systems to market outlets in New Orleans.

**Steamboats and canals.** Steamboats provided the first transportation breakthrough. By the 1820s, steamboats had reduced the cost and the time of upriver shipments by 90 percent. As steamboats spread to western waters, more and more farmers could reap the economic benefits of exporting corn, pork, and other foodstuffs.

Western trade did not start to flow eastward until the completion of the Erie Canal in 1825, the first and most successful of the artificial waterways designed to link eastern seaboard cities with western markets (see Map 12–1). Funded by the New York legislature, the Erie Canal stretched 364 miles from Albany to Buffalo, a small port on Lake Erie. An immediate success, the Erie Canal reduced the cost of sending freight from Buffalo to New York City by more than 90 percent, and by the 1840s, it was pulling in more western trade than was being sent to New Orleans on the Mississippi River.

Anxious to match the Erie's success, other states launched plans for competing canals to the West. More than 3,000 miles of canal were in place by 1840, but no other canal could overcome the tremendous advantage of the Erie's head start in fixing trading patterns along its route.

**Railroads.** Railroads were the last and ultimately the most important of the transportation improvements that spurred economic development in Jacksonian America. Moving at 15 to 20 miles per hour, four times as fast as a canal boat and twice the speed of a stagecoach, the railroads of the 1830s were a radically new technology that overturned traditional notions of time and space.

In 1825, the same year the Erie Canal was completed, the world's first general-purpose railroad opened in England. The construction of the first American railroads began in the late 1820s, and they all pushed outward from seaboard cities eager to connect to the western market. By 1840, the railroads had become the most dynamic booster of interregional trade. Whereas the canal network stopped expanding after 1840, the railroads tripled their mileage in the 1840s. By

**WHERE TO LEARN MORE**

Erie Canal Museum, Syracuse, New York
http://www.eriecanalmuseum.org

**Hear the Audio**
at www.myhistorylab.com
*The Erie Canal*

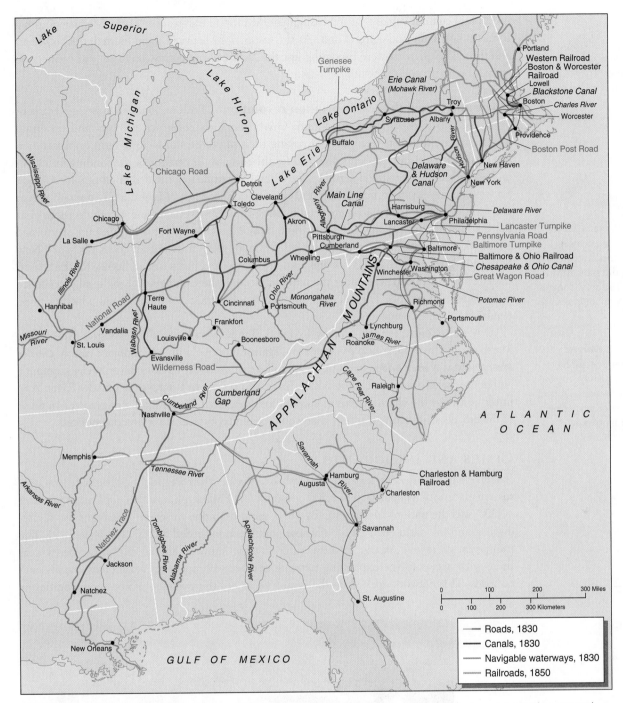

MAP 12–1 **The Transportation Revolution** By 1830, a network of roads, canals, and navigable rivers was spurring economic growth in the first phase of the transportation revolution. By 1850, railroads, the key development in the second phase of the transportation revolution, were opening up additional areas to commercial activity.

**Which cities** probably benefited the most from the new transportation infrastructure and why?

1849, trunk lines built westward from Atlantic Coast cities had reached the Great Lakes and the Ohio Valley and were about to enter the Mississippi Valley.

The rail network in place by midcentury was already altering the North-South sectional balance. The bulk of western trade no longer went downriver to New Orleans but was shipped east by rail. Moving in the opposite direction, to the West, were northern-born settlers, manufactured

**Gibbons v. Ogden** Supreme Court decision of 1824 involving coastal commerce that overturned a steamboat monopoly granted by the state of New York on the grounds that only Congress had the authority to regulate interstate commerce.

**Charles River Bridge v. Warren Bridge** Supreme Court decision of 1837 that promised economic competition by ruling that the broader rights of the community took precedence over any presumed right of monopoly granted in a corporate charter.

goods, and cultural values that increasingly unified the free states east of the Mississippi into a common economic and cultural unit. As the distinctions between them blurred, the Northeast and the Old Northwest were becoming just the North. Significantly, no direct rail connection linked the North and the South.

**Government and the transportation revolution.** Both national and state government promoted the transportation revolution. Given the high construction costs and uncertain profits, private investors were leery of risking their scarce capital in long-term transportation projects. State legislatures stepped in and furnished some 70 percent of the funding for canals and about half of all railroad capital. The federal government provided engineers for railroad surveys, lowered tariffs on iron used in rail construction, and granted subsidies to the railroads in the form of public land. Most important, however, were two Supreme Court decisions that helped open up the economy to competition. In **Gibbons v. Ogden** (1824), the Court overturned a New York law that had given Aaron Ogden a monopoly on steamboat service between New York and New Jersey. Thomas Gibbons, Ogden's competitor, had a federal license for the coastal trade. The right to compete under the national license, the Court ruled, took legal precedence over Ogden's monopoly. The decision affirmed the supremacy of the national government to regulate interstate commerce.

A new Court presided over by Roger B. Taney, who became chief justice when John Marshall died in 1835, struck a bolder blow against monopoly in the landmark case of **Charles River Bridge v. Warren Bridge** in 1837. Taney ruled that the older Charles River Bridge Company had not received a monopoly from Massachusetts to collect tolls across the Charles River. Any uncertainties in the charter rights of corporations, reasoned Taney, should be resolved in favor of the broader community interests that would be served by free and open competition.

## CITIES AND IMMIGRANTS

Barely one in twenty Americans in the 1790s lived in an urban area (defined by the federal census as a place with a population of 2,500 or more), and Philadelphia, with a population just over 40,000, was the nation's largest city. By 1850, more than one in seven Americans was a city-dweller, and the nation had 10 cities whose population exceeded 50,000 (see Map 12–2). The transportation revolution triggered this surge in urban growth. The cities that prospered were those with access to the expanding network of cheap transport on steamboats, canals, and railroads. This network opened up the rural interior for the purchase of farm commodities by

Canal boats below a lock at the Junction of the Erie with the Northern (Champlain) Canal. Aquatint by John Hill.

MAP 12–2 **The Growth of Cities, 1820–1860** In 1820, most cities were clustered along the Atlantic seaboard. By 1860, new transportation outlets—canals and railroads—had fostered the rapid growth of cities in the interior, especially at trading locations with access to navigable rivers or to the Great Lakes. Much of this growth occurred in the 1850s.

*Data Source: Statistical Abstract of the United States.*

**Which region** saw the least urban growth? Why?

city merchants and the sale of finished goods by urban importers and manufacturers. A huge influx of immigrants after the mid-1840s and simultaneous advances in steam engines provided the cheap labor and sources of power that increasingly made cities focal points of manufacturing production.

**The port cities.** America's largest cities in the early nineteenth century were its Atlantic ports: New York, Philadelphia, Baltimore, and Boston. All these cities grew as a result of transportation improvements, but only New York experienced phenomenal growth. By 1810, New York had become the largest U.S. city, and by the 1850s its population exceeded 800,000.

New York's harbor gave oceangoing ships direct, protected access to Manhattan Island, and from there, the Hudson River provided a navigable highway flowing 150 miles north to Albany, deep in the state's agricultural interior. No other port was so ideally situated for trade. And no other had the advantage of access to the Erie Canal. New Yorkers plowed the profits of this commerce into local real estate, which soared in value fiftyfold between 1823 and 1836, and into financial institutions such as the New York Stock Exchange, founded in 1817. The city's banks brought together the capital that made New York the country's chief financial center.

As they grew, the Atlantic ports pioneered new forms of city transportation. Omnibuses, horsedrawn coaches carrying up to 20 passengers, and steam ferries were in common use by the 1820s. At mid-century, horsedrawn street railway lines moved at speeds of about 6 miles an hour, overcoming some of the limitations of the "walking cities" of the early nineteenth century. Accompanying this growth were the first slums, the most notorious of which was the Five Points district of New York City.

**Inland cities.** The fastest growing cities were in the interior. Pittsburgh, at the head of the Ohio River, was the first western city to develop a manufacturing sector to complement its exchange function. With access to the extensive coalfields of western Pennsylvania, Pittsburgh had a cheap fuel that provided the high heat needed to manufacture iron and glass. Cincinnati, downstream on the Ohio, was the West's first meatpacking center. St. Louis, just below the merger of the Missouri and Mississippi rivers, prospered by servicing American trade with the trans-Mississippi West.

By the 1840s, the Great Lake ports of Cleveland, Detroit, Milwaukee, and Chicago were the dynamic centers of western urbanization. Their combined population increased twenty-five-fold between 1830 and 1850. The Great Lakes served as an extension of the Erie Canal, and cities on

New York City's busy harbor was the entry to the largest metropolitan center that emerged in the nineteenth-century United States.

the lakes where incoming and outgoing goods had to be unloaded for transshipment benefited enormously. They attracted settlers and soon evolved into regional economic centers. They also aggressively promoted themselves into major rail hubs and thus reaped the economic advantages of being at the junctions of both water and rail transport.

**New industrial cities.**   The only other cities growing as fast as the Great Lakes ports were the new industrial towns. The densest cluster of these was in rural New England along the fall line of rivers, where the rapidly falling water provided cheap power to drive the industrial machinery of factories and machine shops. Each town was tied to a transportation network that brought in raw cotton for the textile mills from the mercantile centers of Boston and Providence and shipped out the finished goods.

Lowell, Massachusetts, was America's first large-scale planned manufacturing city. Founded in 1822 by Boston businessmen, Lowell was built around the falls of the Merrimack River. Within a decade, rural fields had been transformed into a city of 18,000 people. Lowell's success became a model for others to follow, and by 1840, New England led the North in both urbanization and industrialization.

**Immigration.**   Swelling the size of nearly all the cities was a surge of immigrants after the 1830s. The number of immigrants from 1840 to 1860, 4.2 million, represented a tenfold increase over the number that had come in the two preceding decades. Most of these immigrants were Irish and German (see Figure 12–1).

In the 1840s, economic and political upheavals in Europe spurred mass migration, mostly to the United States. Catholic peasants in Ireland, dominated by their Protestant English landlords, eked out a subsistence as tenants on tiny plots of land. A potato blight wiped out the crop in 1845 and 1846, and in the next five years about 1 million Irish died of malnutrition and disease. Another 1.5 million fled, many to the United States.

The Irish had no money to buy land or move west unless they joined construction gangs for canals and railroads. Without marketable skills, they had to take the worst and lowest paying jobs. Packed into dark cellars, unventilated attics, and rank tenements, the Irish suffered from very high mortality rates. Still, cash wages and access to food made the U.S. city preferable to the prospect of starvation in Ireland.

**WHERE TO LEARN MORE**

★ Lowell National Historical Park
http://www.nps.gov/lowe/index.htm

•••—⌐Read the **Document**

at **www.myhistorylab.com**
*The Harbinger, Female Workers of Lowell (1836)*

•••—⌐Read the **Document**

at **www.myhistorylab.com**
*From Then to Now Online:
Immigration: An Ambivalent Welcome*

Lowell was the nation's leading textile center and the second-largest city in Massachusetts by 1850. The building with the cupola and the structure with dormers and chimneys were part of the mill complex. The two detached buildings were boardinghouses for the young women who worked in the mills.

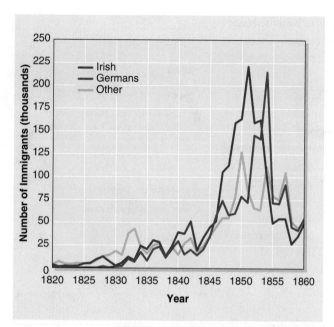

**FIGURE 12–1 Immigration to the United States, 1820–1860**
The potato famine in Ireland and economic and political unrest on the continent led to a surge in immigration in the 1840s. The pace slackened in the mid-1850s, when economic conditions in Europe improved.

*Data Source:* U.S. Bureau of the Census, *Historical Statistics of the United States, Colonial Times to 1957* (1960), p. 57.

**QUICK REVIEW**

**Immigration at Midcentury**

◆ Surge of immigrants fueled growth of cities after the 1830s.

◆ Economic and political upheaval spurred mass migration from Europe.

◆ Famine drove 1.5 million Irish to America.

**putting-out system** System of manufacturing in which merchants furnished households with raw materials for processing by family members.

**WHERE TO LEARN MORE**

★ Slater Hill Historic Site, Pawtucket, Rhode Island
http://www.slatermill.org/museum/about

German immigrants were second in number only to the Irish by the 1850s. They came to America to escape poor harvests and political turmoil. Far more Germans than Irish had owned property as farmers, artisans, and shopkeepers and had the capital to purchase land in the West and the skills to join the ranks of small businessmen in the cities. They were also more likely than the Irish to have entered the country through Baltimore or New Orleans, southern ports engaged in the tobacco and cotton trade with continental Europe. From there they fanned out into the Mississippi and Ohio valleys. With their diversified skills, they found ample economic opportunities in the fast-growing cities of the West and a setting in which to build tightly knit communities with German-speaking shops, churches, schools, and benevolent societies. About four in five of all the immigrants arriving after 1840 settled in the New England and mid-Atlantic states. Their sheer numbers transformed the size and ethnic composition of the working class, especially in the cities of the Northeast. And their cheap labor provided the final ingredient in the expansion of industrialization that began after the War of 1812.

## THE INDUSTRIAL REVOLUTION

The Northeast led America's industrial revolution. In 1815, this region had the largest cities, the most developed capital markets, the readiest access to the technological skills of artisans, and the greatest supply of available labor. The first large-scale factories, the textile mills, were erected in New England in the 1820s. For the next 30 years, the United States had the most rapidly developing industrial economy in the world.

The household and the small workshop were the sites of manufacturing in Jefferson's America. Wider markets for household manufactures began to develop in the late eighteenth century with the coming of the **putting-out system.** Local merchants furnished ("put out") raw materials to rural households and paid at a piece rate for the labor that converted the raw materials into manufactured products. The supplying merchant then marketed and sold these goods.

In the cities and larger towns, most manufacturing was done by artisans, skilled craftsmen known as mechanics. Working in their own shops and with their own tools, they produced small batches of finished goods. Each artisan had a specific skill that set him above common laborers—shoemaking, furniture making, silver smithing. These skills came from hands-on experience and craft traditions that were handed down from one generation to the next.

Master craftsmen taught the "mysteries of the craft" to the journeymen and apprentices who lived with them and worked in their shops. Journeymen had learned the skills of their craft but lacked the capital to open their own shops. Apprentices were adolescent boys legally sent by their fathers to live with and obey a master craftsman in return for being taught a trade.

The factory system of production that would undercut both household and artisanal manufacturing after 1815 could produce goods far more quickly and cheaply per worker than could artisans or rural households. Factories subdivided the specialized skills of the artisan into a series of semiskilled tasks, a process foreshadowed by the putting-out system. Factories also put workers under systematic controls. And in the final stage of industrialization, they boosted workers' productivity through the use of power-driven machinery.

Britain pioneered the technological advances that drove early industrialization. The secrets of this technology, especially the designs for the machines that mechanized textile production, were closely guarded by the British government. Despite attempts to prohibit the emigration of artisans who knew how the machinery worked, some British mechanics made it to the United States. Samuel Slater was one of them, and he took over the operation of a fledgling mill in Providence,

Rhode Island. With his knowledge of how to build the water-powered spinning machinery, he converted the mill into the nation's first permanent cotton factory in 1790.

The first real spurt of factory building came with the closing off of British imports during the embargo and the War of 1812. Hundreds of new cotton and woolen mills were established from 1808 to 1815. But the great test of U.S. manufacturing came after 1815, when peace with Britain brought a flood of cheap British manufactured goods. If factories were to continue to grow, U.S. manufacturers had to reach more consumers in their home market and overcome the British advantage of lower labor costs.

**Sources of labor.**   Industrial labor was more expensive in America than in England, where the high cost of land forced the rural poor into the cities to find work. In contrast, land was cheap and plentiful in the United States, and Americans preferred the independence of farm work to the dependence of factory labor. Consequently, the first mill workers were predominantly children. The owners set up the father on a plot of company-owned land, provided piecework for the mother, and put the children to work in the mills.

Although this so-called **Rhode Island system** of family employment sufficed for small mills, it was inadequate for the larger, more mechanized factories that were built in New England after the War of 1812. The owners of these mills recruited unmarried adolescent daughters of farmers from across New England as their laborers in the **Waltham system.** Although factory wages were low, they were more than these young women could earn doing piecework in the home or as domestics. The wages also brought a liberating degree of financial independence. "When they felt the jingle of silver in their pockets," recalled Harriet Hanson Robinson of her fellow workers at Lowell in the 1830s, "there for the first time, their heads became erect and they walked as if on air."

**Rhode Island system**   During the industrialization of the early nineteenth century, the recruitment of entire families for employment in a factory.

**Waltham system**   During the industrialization of the early nineteenth century, the recruitment of unmarried young women for employment in factories.

To overcome parental fears that their daughters might be exposed to morally corrupting conditions in the mills and mill towns, New England manufacturers set up paternalistic moral controls. Single female workers had to live in company-owned boardinghouses that imposed curfews, screened visitors, and mandated church attendance. The mill women worked six days a week from dawn to dusk for low wages. There were limits to what the women would endure, and in 1834 and 1836 the female hands at Lowell "turned out" to protest wage reductions in demonstrations that were the largest strikes in American history up to that time.

After the economic downturn of the late 1830s, conditions in the mills grew worse. By the mid-1840s, however, the Irish, desperate for work, sent their children into the mills at an earlier age than Yankee families. These workers did not leave after two or three years of building up a small dowry for marriage, as many New Englanders did. By the early 1850s, more than half the textile operatives were Irish women.

In the mid-Atlantic region, where the farm population was more prosperous than in New England and fewer young women were available for factory work, immigrants were an important source of manufacturing workers as early as the 1820s. They played an especially crucial role in urban manufacturing. The port cities lacked usable waterpower, but by drawing on a growing pool of cheap, immigrant labor, manufacturers could expand production while driving down the cost.

Except in New England textile factories and the smaller factories and shops in the seaboard cities, native-born males were the

At midcentury most industrial work was still done by hand. Shown here are two foundry workers holding floor rammers used for packing sand against molds.

**American system of manufacturing**
A technique of production pioneered in the United States in the first half of the nineteenth century that relied on precision manufacturing with the use of interchangeable parts.

largest group of early manufacturing workers. They came from poor rural families that lacked enough land to pass on to male heirs. As late as 1840, women, including those working at home, made up about half of the manufacturing work force and one-quarter of the factory hands. Few of these workers brought any specific skills to their jobs, and thus they had little bargaining power. Economic necessity forced them to accept low wages and harsh working conditions. The sheer increase in their numbers, as opposed to any productivity gains from technological innovations, accounted by 1850 for two-thirds of the gains in manufacturing output.

**Technological gains.**    After 1815, U.S. manufacturers began to close the technological gap with Britain by drawing on the versatile skills of U.S. mechanics. Mechanics experimented with new designs, improved old ones, and patented inventions that found industrial applications outside their own crafts.

The most famous early American invention was the cotton gin. Eli Whitney, a Massachusetts Yankee, built the prototype of the gin in 1793 while working as a tutor on a Georgia plantation. By cheaply and quickly removing the seeds from cotton fibers, the cotton gin spurred the cultivation of cotton across the South.

Whitney also pushed the idea of basing production on interchangeable parts. After receiving a federal contract to manufacture muskets, he designed new milling machines and turret lathes that transformed the technology of machine tool production. The new techniques were first applied in 1815 to the manufacture of wooden clocks and by the 1840s to sewing machines, farm machinery, and watch parts. The **American system of manufacturing,** low-cost, standardized mass production, built around interchangeable parts stamped out by machines, was America's unique contribution to the industrial revolution.

As the pace of technological innovation accelerated after 1840, so did the growth of manufacturing. Indeed, the 1840s registered the highest rate of expansion in the manufacturing sector of the economy in the nineteenth century. The adoption of the stationary steam engine in urban manufacturing fueled much of this expansion. High-pressure steam engines enabled power-driven industry to locate in the port cities of the Northeast and the booming cities on the Great Lakes. With limited access to waterpower, early manufacturing in the West was confined to the processing of farm goods. By turning to steam power and new machine tools, western manufacturers after 1840 enlarged their region's industrial base and created a new industry, the mass production of agricultural implements. The West was the center of the farm-machinery industry, and the region produced 20 percent of the nation's manufacturing output by the 1850s.

A greater control over natural resources, as well as new technologies, drove industrial growth. To provide their mills with a steady, reliable source of water, one that would not be affected by the whims of nature, the Boston Associates constructed a series of dams and canals that

Shown here working at power looms under the supervision of a male overseer, young single women constituted the bulk of the labor force in the first textile factories of New England.

extended to the headwaters of the Merrimack River in northern New Hampshire. Inevitably, the ecology of the region changed. The level of the lakes was altered, the flow of rivers interrupted, the upward migration of spawning fish blocked, and the foraging terrain of wild game flooded. Farmers protested when their fields and pastures were submerged, but lawyers for the Boston Associates successfully argued that water, like other natural resources, should be treated as a commodity that could contribute to economic progress. Increasingly, the law treated nature as an economic resource to be engineered and bought and sold.

## GROWING INEQUALITY AND NEW CLASSES

In the first half of the nineteenth century, the economy grew three times faster than in the eighteenth century, and per capita income doubled. Living standards for most Americans improved. There was a price to be paid, however, for the benefits of economic growth. Half of the adult white males were propertyless at midcentury. Wealth had become more concentrated, and extremes of wealth and poverty eroded the Jeffersonian ideal of a republic of independent proprietors who valued liberty because they were economically free.

The gap between the rich and the poor widened considerably in the early phases of industrialization (see Figure 12–2). In 1800, the richest 10 percent of Americans owned 40 to 50 percent of the national wealth. By the 1850s, their share was about 70 percent. The most glaring discrepancies in wealth appeared in the large cities. In all cities by the 1840s, the top 10 percent of the population owned 80 percent of urban wealth.

**The new middle class.** The faster pace of economic growth that enabled the urban rich to increase their wealth also created opportunities for a rapidly expanding new middle class. This class grew as the number of nonmanual jobs increased. Most of these jobs were in northern cities and bustling market towns, where the need was greatest for office and store clerks, managerial personnel, sales agents, and independent retailers. The result by midcentury was a new middle class superimposed on the older one of independent farmers, artisans, shopkeepers, and professionals. The separation of work and home constituted the first step in an evolving sense of class consciousness. As the market revolution advanced, the workplace increasingly became a specialized location of production or selling. Middle-class fathers now left for work in the morning, while mothers governed households that were primarily residential units and places of material comfort, where growing quantities of consumer goods were on display. Having servants became a status symbol. Shunned as degrading by most native-born white women, these low-paying jobs were filled by African American and young immigrant (especially Irish) women. Work had not left the middle-class home; instead, it was disguised as the "domestic duties" of middle-class wives who supervised the servants.

Besides turning to etiquette books for advice on proper manners in public and in the home, the middle class also tried to shape its behavior by the tenets of evangelical religion. Revivals swept northern cities in the late 1820s. Preachers like Charles G. Finney stressed that both economic and moral success depended on the virtues of sobriety, self-restraint, and hard work. Aggressiveness and ambition at work were not necessarily sinful so long as businessmen reformed their own moral lives and helped others do the same. This message was immensely reassuring to employers and entrepreneurs, for it confirmed and sanctified their own pursuit of economic self-interest. It also provided them with a religious inspiration for

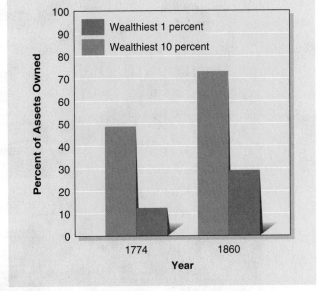

**FIGURE 12–2 Growth in Wealth Inequality, 1774–1860** The two benchmark years for the gathering of data on the nationwide distribution of wealth are 1774 and 1860. Specialized studies on regions and subregions indicate that wealth inequality increased most sharply from the 1820s to 1850, the period that coincides with early industrialization.

*Data Source:* Jeffrey G. Williamson and Peter H. Lindert, *American Inequality: A Macroeconomic History* (1980), p. 38.

**temperance** Reform movement originating in the 1820s that sought to eliminate the consumption of alcohol.

## QUICK REVIEW

### Class Consciousness

♦ Separation of home and work first step in evolving class consciousness.

♦ Home a place of material comfort for rising middle class.

♦ Having servants a sign of status.

♦ Middle class shaped by evangelical religion.

**⬥⬥⬥ Read the Document**

at **www.myhistorylab.com**
*Catharine Esther Beecher, American Woman's Home (1869)*

**cult of domesticity** The belief that women, by virtue of their sex, should stay home as the moral guardians of family life.

attempting to exert moral control over their communities and employees. **Temperance,** the prohibition of alcoholic beverages, was the greatest of the evangelically inspired reforms, and abstinence from alcohol became the most telling evidence of middle-class respectability.

**Women and the cult of domesticity.** In a reversal of traditional Calvinist doctrine, the evangelical ministers of the northern middle class enshrined women as the moral superiors of men. Though considered weak and passive, women were also held to be uniquely pure and pious. Women, who easily outnumbered men at Sunday services and weeknight prayer meetings, were now responsible for converting their homes into loving, prayerful centers of domesticity, and the primary task of motherhood became the Christian nurturing of souls entrusted to a mother's care.

This sanctified notion of motherhood reflected and reinforced shifting patterns of family life. Families became smaller as the birthrate fell by 25 percent in the first half of the nineteenth century. The decline was greatest in the urban middle class after 1820. Middle-class couples consciously limited the size of their families, and women stopped having children at an earlier age. As a result, parents devoted more care and financial resources to child rearing.

Beginning in the 1820s, ministers and female writers elevated the family role of middle-class women into a **cult of domesticity.** This idealized conception of womanhood insisted that the biological differences of God's natural order determined separate social roles for men and women. Characterized as strong, aggressive, and ambitious, men naturally belonged in the competitive world of business and politics. Women's providential task was to preserve religion and morality in the home and family.

**The working classes.** The economic changes that produced a new middle class also fundamentally transformed the working class. In the preindustrial United States, the working

This pen-and-watercolor drawing of a middle-class family in 1832 illustrates how the home, as it lost its productive functions, became idealized as a center of domestic refinement and material comfort.

"Family Group," Joseph H. Davis, American, 1811–1865, Graphite pencil and watercolor on paper, Sheet: 24.8 × 41 cm (9 3/4 × 16 1/8 in.), Museum of Fine Arts, Boston, Gift of Maxim Karolik for the proposed M. and M. Karolik Collection of American Watercolors, © 2003 Museum of Fine Arts, Boston.

class was predominantly native-born and of artisan origins. By midcentury, most urban workers were immigrants or the children of immigrants and had never been artisans in a skilled craft.

Job skills, sex, race, and ethnicity all divided workers after 1840. Master craftsmen were the most highly skilled and best-paid workers. As industrialization proceeded, the unity of the old artisan class splintered. Ambitious master craftsmen with access to capital rose into the ranks of small businessmen and manufacturers. They expanded output and drove down the cost of production by contracting out work at piece wages and hiring the cheapest workers they could find. The result was to transform the apprentice system into a system of exploited child labor.

By the 1830s, journeymen were becoming permanent wage earners with little prospect of opening their own shops. To protect their liberties from what they considered a new aristocracy of manufacturers, they organized workingmen's parties in the 1830s, centered in the eastern cities. At the top of these parties' lists of reforms were free public education, the abolition of imprisonment for debt, and a 10-hour workday.

**Early trade unions.**    Journeymen also turned to trade union activity in the 1820s and 1830s to gain better wages, shorter hours, and enhanced job security. Benefiting from a strong demand for their skills, workers in the building trades organized the first unions. They were soon followed by shoemakers, printers, and weavers, workers in trades where pressure on urban journeymen was the most intense. Locals from various trades formed the National Trades Union, the first national union, in 1834. The new labor movement launched more than 150 strikes in the mid-1830s.

Although the Panic of 1837 decimated union membership, the early labor movement did achieve two notable victories. First, by the late 1830s, it had forced employers to accept the 10-hour day as the standard for most skilled workers. Second, in a landmark decision handed down in 1842, the Massachusetts Supreme Court ruled in *Commonwealth v. Hunt* that a trade union was not necessarily subject to laws against criminal conspiracies and that a strike could be used to force employers to hire only union members.

The unions defended artisanal rights and virtues, and they ignored workers whose jobs had never had craft status. As massive immigration merged with industrialization after 1840, this basic division between workers widened. On one side was the male, Protestant, and native-born class of skilled artisans. On the other side was the working-class majority of factory laborers and unskilled workers, predominantly immigrants and women who worked for a wage as domestics or factory hands.

Increasingly fearing these workers as a threat to their job security and Protestant values, in the 1840s U.S.-born artisans joined **nativist** organizations that sought to curb mass immigration from Europe and limit the political rights of Catholic immigrants. Whereas immigrants viewed temperance as business-class meddling in their lives, nativist workers tended to embrace the evangelical, middle-class ideology of temperance and self-help. One of the few issues that brought immigrants and nativists together was the nearly universal demand of white workers that black workers be confined to the most menial jobs.

Gender also divided workers. Working-class men shared the dominant ideology of female dependence. They measured their own status as husbands by their ability to support their wives and daughters. Beginning in the 1830s, male workers argued that their wages would be higher if women were barred from the labor force. With these views, male workers helped lock wage-earning women into the lowest paying and most exploited jobs.

**nativist**   Favoring the interests and culture of native-born inhabitants over those of immigrants.

### QUICK REVIEW

**Unions**

- In the late 1830s and early 1840s unions won important victories.
- Unions concentrated on artisanal rights and virtues.
- American-born artisans increasingly saw immigrants as a threat to job security.

# REFORM AND MORAL ORDER

The rapidity and extent of the social and economic changes that accompanied the market revolution were disorienting, even frightening, to many Americans, particularly religious leaders and wealthy businessmen in the East. They saw signs of moral wickedness and disorder all around them in the more fluid, materialistic society that was emerging. Alarmed by

**WHAT ROLE** did women play in the reform movements that followed the War of 1812?

**benevolent empire** Network of reform associations affiliated with Protestant churches in the early nineteenth century dedicated to the restoration of moral order.

what they perceived as a breakdown in moral authority, they sought to impose moral discipline on Americans.

These eastern elites, with the indispensable support of their wives and daughters, created a network of voluntary church-affiliated reform organizations known collectively as the **benevolent empire.** Revivals in the 1820s and 1830s broadened the base of reform to include the newly evangelicalized middle class in northern cities and towns.

## THE BENEVOLENT EMPIRE

Evangelical businessmen in the seaboard cities backed the call to restore moral order. Worried by the increasing number of urban poor, wealthy merchants contributed vital financial support for a network of reform associations. The reform societies built on the Second Great Awakening's techniques of organization and communication. The Protestant reformers sent out speakers on regular schedules along prescribed routes. They developed organizations that maintained a constant pressure for reform. National and local boards of directors supervised the work of salaried managers, who inspired volunteers to combat sin among the unconverted. When steam presses and stereotype plates halved the cost of printing and dramatically increased its speed, the American Bible Society was the first organization to exploit this revolution in the print media. Between 1790 and 1830, the number of religious newspapers grew from 14 to more than 600. By then, religious presses were churning out more than 1 million Bibles and 6 million tracts a year.

A host of local societies targeted individual vices. Their purpose, as summed up by a Massachusetts group, the Andover South Parish Society for the Reformation of Morals, was "to discountenance [discourage] immorality, particularly Sabbath-breaking, intemperance, and profanity, and to promote industry, order, piety, and good morals." These goals linked social and moral discipline, appealing both to churchgoers concerned about godlessness and profit-oriented businessmen eager to curb their workers' unruly behavior.

**Sabbatarian movement** Reform organization founded in 1828 by Congregationalist and Presbyterian ministers that lobbied for an end to the delivery of mail on Sundays and other Sabbath violations.

The boldest expression of the drive to enhance Protestant Christian power was the **Sabbatarian movement.** In 1828, evangelicals led by Lyman Beecher formed the General Union for Promoting the Observance of the Christian Sabbath. Their immediate goal was the repeal of a law passed by Congress in 1810 directing post offices to deliver mail on Sunday. Their broader mission was to enforce local statutes that shut down business and leisure activities on Sundays.

In 1829, insisting on the separation of church and state, the Democratic Congress upheld the postal law of 1810. The Sabbatarians had outraged canal operators, hotelkeepers, tavern owners, and other businesses threatened with the loss of their Sunday trade. Businessmen, workingmen, southern evangelicals, and religious conservatives all felt that the Sabbath purists had gone too far in a movement now seen as a threat to civil liberties and the rights of private property.

The General Union disbanded in 1832, but it left an important legacy for future reform movements. On the one hand, it developed techniques that converted the reform impulse into direct political action. In raising funds, training speakers, holding rallies, disseminating literature, lobbying for local Sunday regulations, and coordinating a petition to Congress, the Sabbatarians created an organizational model for other reformers to follow in mobilizing public opinion and influencing politicians. On the other hand, the failure of the Sabbatarians revealed that a new approach was needed that encouraged individuals to reform themselves without coercive controls. It soon emerged in the temperance movement.

## QUICK REVIEW

**The Birth of Reform**

- Anxieties over social and economic change fueled reform efforts.
- Reform societies built on techniques and ideas of the Second Great Awakening.
- Local societies targeted individual vices.
- Reformers linked social and moral discipline to reform.

 Watch the Video

at **www.myhistorylab.com**
*Drinking and the Temperance Movement in Nineteenth-Century America*

## THE TEMPERANCE MOVEMENT

Temperance, the drive against the consumption of alcohol, had the greatest impact on the most people of any reform movement. Its success rested on what Lyman Beecher called "a new moral power." Dismayed by popular resistance to the coercive moralism of the first wave of Protestant reform, evangelicals concluded that reform had to rest on persuasion, and it had to begin with the voluntary decision of individuals to free themselves from sin.

## OVERVIEW Changes Promoting Growth in the Transformed Economy

| Sector | 1815 | 1850 |
|---|---|---|
| Travel and transportation | By foot and horsedrawn wagon | Cheaper and faster with canals, steamboats, and railroads opening up new markets |
| Population | Overwhelmingly native-born, rural, and concentrated east of Appalachian Mountains | Four times larger as a result of natural increase and surge of immigration after 1840; settlement of West and growth of cities |
| Wage labor | Native-born, primarily women and children in manufacturing | Expanding as rural poor and immigrants enter manufacturing workforce |
| Power | Water-driven mills | Steam-driven engines |
| Farming | Subsistence-oriented; surplus sold in localized markets | Commercialized agriculture spreading in response to improvements in transportation |
| Manufacturing | Small-scale production in household units and artisan shops | Large-scale production in eastern cities and factories |

In 1826, evangelicals founded the **American Temperance Society.** Their goal was to bring about a radical change in U.S. attitudes toward alcohol and its role in social life. Taverns easily outnumbered churches as gathering places. Alcohol was used to pay common laborers and itinerant preachers on the early Methodist circuit. Masters and journeymen shared a drink as a customary way of taking a break from work, and no wedding, funeral, or meeting of friends was complete without alcohol.

For the temperance crusade to succeed, the reformers had to finance a massive propaganda campaign and link it to an organization that could mobilize and energize thousands of people. They built such a mass movement by merging temperance into the network of churches and lay volunteers that the benevolent empire had developed and by adopting the techniques of revivals to win converts.

Evangelical reformers denounced intemperance as the greatest sin of the land. Alcohol represented all that was wrong in America, crime, poverty, insanity, broken families, boisterous politicking, Sabbath-breaking. This message thundered from the pulpit and the public lectern. Thanks to the generous financial subsidies of wealthy benefactors, it was also broadcast in millions of tracts printed on the latest high-speed presses. Like revivals, temperance rallies combined emotionally charged sermons with large, tearful prayer meetings to evoke guilt among sinners, who would then seek release by taking the pledge of abstinence.

Within a decade, the American Temperance Society had more than 5,000 local chapters and statewide affiliates, most in the Northeast.

**American Temperance Society**
National organization established in 1826 by evangelical Protestants that campaigned for total abstinence from alcohol and was successful in sharply lowering per capita consumption of alcohol.

Temperance cartoon.

A million members had pledged abstinence by 1833. Women constituted one-third to more than one-half of the members in local temperance societies. Lacking legal protections against abusive husbands who drank away the family resources, women had a compelling reason to join the crusade. As the moral protectors of the family, they pressured their husbands to take the teetotaler's pledge and stick by it, raised sons to shun alcohol, and banished liquor from their homes. By the 1840s, temperance and middle-class domesticity had become synonymous.

The first wave of temperance converts came from the upper and middle classes. Businessmen welcomed temperance as a model of self-discipline in their efforts to regiment factory work. Young, upwardly mobile professionals and petty entrepreneurs learned in temperance how to be thrifty, self-controlled, respectable, and creditworthy. Temperance made its first significant inroads among the working classes during the economic depression of 1839–1843. Joining together in what they called Washington Temperance Societies, small businessmen and artisans, many of them reformed drunkards, carried temperance into working-class districts. The Washingtonians insisted that workers could survive the depression only if they stopped drinking and adopted the temperance ethic of frugality and self-help. Their wives organized auxiliary societies and pledged to enforce sobriety and economic restraint at home. In a telling measure of the temperance movement's success, per capita alcohol consumption fell from an all-time high of 7.1 gallons per year in 1830 to less than 2 gallons per year by 1845.

## WOMEN'S ROLE IN REFORM

The first phase of women's reform activities represented an extension of the domestic ideal promoted in the cult of domesticity. Assumptions about women's unique moral qualities permitted, and even encouraged, them to assume the role of "social mother" by organizing on behalf of the orphaned and the widowed. Founded in 1797, the Society for the Relief of Poor Widows with Small Children in New York typified these early approaches to reform. The women in the society came from socially prominent families. Motivated by religious charity and social duty, they visited poor women and children, dispensed funds, and set up work programs. However, they limited their benevolence to the "deserving poor," socially weak but morally strong people who had suffered personal misfortune, and screened out all who were thought to be unworthy.

A second phase in the reform efforts by women developed in the 1830s. Unlike their benevolent counterparts, the reformers now began to challenge male prerogatives and move beyond moral suasion. The crusade against prostitution exemplified the new militancy. Women seized leadership of the movement in 1834 with the founding of the New York Female Moral Reform Society. In the pages of their journal, *Advocate for Moral Reform,* members identified male greed and licentiousness as the causes for the fallen state of women. Identified, too, were the male patrons of the city's brothels. The society blamed businessmen for the low wages that forced some women to resort to prostitution and denounced lustful men for engaging in "a regular crusade against [our] sex."

In 1839, this attack on the sexual double standard became a national movement with the establishment of the **American Female Moral Reform Society.** With 555 affiliates throughout the evangelical heartland of the North, female activists mounted a lobbying campaign that, unlike earlier efforts, bypassed prominent men and reached out to a mass audience. By the 1840s, such unprecedented political involvement enabled women to secure the first state laws criminalizing seduction and adultery.

Other women's groups developed a more radical critique of U.S. society and its male leadership. The Boston Seamen's Aid Society, founded in 1833 by Sarah Josepha Hale, a widow with five children, soon rejected the benevolent tradition of distinguishing between "respectable" and "unworthy" poor. Hale discovered that her efforts to guide poor women toward self-sufficiency flew in the face of the low wages and substandard housing that trapped her clients in poverty.

---

●•▶ Read the Document

at **www.myhistorylab.com**

*Lyman Beecher, "Six Sermons on Intemperance" (1828)*

---

**American Female Moral Reform Society** Organization founded in 1839 by female reformers that established homes of refuge for prostitutes and petitioned for state laws that would criminalize adultery and the seduction of women.

Hale attacked male employers for exploiting the poor. "Combinations of selfish men are formed to beat down the price of female labor," she wrote in her 1836 annual report, "and then they call the diminished rate the market price."

## BACKLASH AGAINST BENEVOLENCE

Some of the benevolent empire's harshest critics came out of the populist revivals of the early 1800s. They considered the Protestant reformers' program a conspiracy of orthodox Calvinists from old-line denominations to impose social and moral control on behalf of a religious and economic elite.

These criticisms revealed a profound mistrust of the emerging market society. In contrast to the evangelical reformers, drawn from the well-educated business and middle classes who were benefiting from economic change, most evangelical members of the grassroots sects and followers of the itinerant preachers were unschooled, poor, and hurt by market fluctuations that they could not control. Socially uprooted and economically stranded, they found a sense of community in their local churches and resisted control by wealthier, better-educated outsiders. Above all, they clung to beliefs that shored up the threatened authority of the father over his household.

With the elevation of women to the status of moral guardians of the family and agents of benevolent reform outside the household, middle-class evangelicalism in the Northeast was becoming feminized. This new social role for women was especially threatening, indeed, galling, for men who were the casualties of the more competitive economy. Raised on farms where the father had been the unquestioned lawgiver and provider, these men attacked feminized evangelicalism for undermining their paternal authority. They found in Scripture an affirmation of patriarchal power for any man, no matter how poor or economically dependent.

The **Church of Jesus Christ of Latter-day Saints** (also known as the **Mormon Church**) represented the most enduring religious backlash of economically struggling men against the aggressive efforts of reforming middle-class evangelicals. Joseph Smith, who established the church in upstate New York in 1830, came from a New England farm family uprooted and impoverished by market speculations gone sour. He and his followers were alienated not only from the new market economy but also from what they saw as the religious and social anarchy around them. Based on Smith's divine revelations as set forth in the Book of Mormon (1830), their new faith offered converts both a sanctuary as a biblical people and a release from social and religious uncertainties.

Mormonism provided a defense of communal beliefs centered on male authority. It assigned complete spiritual and secular authority to men. Only through subordination and obedience to their husbands could women hope to gain salvation. To be a Mormon was to join a large extended family that was part of a shared enterprise. Men bonded their labor in a communal economy to benefit all the faithful. Driven by a strong sense of social obligation, the Mormons forged the most successful alternative vision in antebellum America to the individualistic Protestant republic of the benevolent reformers. (For the Mormons' role in the westward movement, see Chapter 13.)

**Church of Jesus Christ of Latter-day Saints (Mormon Church)**   Church founded in 1830 by Joseph Smith and based on the revelations in a sacred book he called the Book of Mormon.

**Interpreting the Past**
*The Second Great Awakening and Religious Diversity in America* (pp. 334–335)

# INSTITUTIONS AND SOCIAL IMPROVEMENT

Although evangelical Protestantism was its mainspring, antebellum reform also had its roots in the European Enlightenment. Like the evangelicals inspired by religious optimism, reformers drawing on Enlightenment doctrines of progress had unbounded faith in social improvement. They saw in the United States an unlimited potential to fashion a model republic of virtuous, intelligent citizens.

**HOW DID**
Enlightenment ideas shape the reform of institutions for the poor, criminals, and the mentally ill?

## SCHOOL REFORM

Before the 1820s, schooling in America was an informal, haphazard affair that nonetheless met the basic needs for reading, writing, and arithmetic skills of an overwhelmingly rural population. Private tutors and academies for the wealthy, a few charitable schools for the urban poor, and rural one-room schoolhouses open for a few months each year constituted formal education at the primary level.

The first political demands for free tax-supported schools originated with the **Workingmen's Movement** in eastern cities in the 1820s. In pushing for "equal republican education," workers sought to guarantee that all citizens, no matter how poor, could achieve meaningful liberty and equality. Their proposals, however, met stiff resistance from wealthier property holders, who refused to pay taxes to support the education of working-class children.

The breakthrough in public education came in New England, where the disruptive forces of industrialization and urbanization were felt the earliest. Increased economic inequality, growing numbers of impoverished Irish Catholic immigrants, and the emergence of a mass democracy based on nearly universal white male suffrage convinced reformers of the need for state-supported schools.

In 1837, the Massachusetts legislature established the nation's first state board of education. The head of the board for the next twelve years was Horace Mann, a former Whig politician and temperance advocate who now tirelessly championed educational reform. Mann demanded that the state government assume centralized control over Massachusetts schools.

Democrats in the Massachusetts legislature denounced Mann's program as "a system of centralization and of monopoly of power in a few hands, contrary in every respect, to the true spirit of our democratic institutions." The laboring poor, who depended for economic survival on the wages their children could earn, resisted compulsory-attendance laws and a longer school year. Farmers fought to maintain local control over schooling and to block the higher taxes needed for a more comprehensive and professionalized system. The Catholic Church protested the thinly veiled attempts of the reformers to indoctrinate all students in the moral strictures of middle-class Protestantism. Catholics began, at great expense, to build their own parochial schools.

Mann and his allies nonetheless prevailed in most of the industrializing states, with strong support from the professional and business constituencies of the Whig Party. Manufacturers hoped that the schools would turn out a more obedient and punctual labor force, and the more skilled and prosperous workers saw in public education a key to upward mobility for their children. Most important for its political success, school reform appealed to the growing northern middle class. Schools would instill the moral and economic discipline that the middle class deemed essential for a progressive and ordered society.

Out of the northern middle class also came the young female teachers who increasingly staffed elementary schools. Presumed by their nature to be more nurturing than men, women now had an entry into teaching, the first profession open to them. Besides, women could also be paid far less than men; school boards assumed that they would accept low wages while waiting to be married.

Just over 50 percent of the white children between 5 and 19 years of age in the United States were enrolled in school in 1850, the highest percentage in the world at the time. Working-class parents pulled their children out of school at an earlier age than higher-income middle-class parents. Planters continued to rely on private tutors or academies, and southern farmers saw little need for public education. The slave states, especially in the Lower South, lagged behind the rest of the nation in public education.

## PRISONS, WORKHOUSES, AND ASYLUMS

Up to this time, Americans had depended on voluntary efforts to cope with crime, poverty, and social deviance. Convinced that these efforts were inadequate, reformers turned to public authorities to establish a host of new institutions to deal with social problems.

The reformers held that people's environments shaped their character for good or evil. The Boston Children's Friend Society was devoted to the young, "whose plastic natures may be molded

---

**Workingmen's Movement**
Associations of urban workers who began campaigning in the 1820s for free public education and a ten-hour workday.

**Watch the Video**
at **www.myhistorylab.com**
*Who was Horace Mann and why are so many schools named after him?*

**Read the Document**
at **www.myhistorylab.com**
*Horace Mann on Education and National Welfare*

into images of perfect beauty, or . . . perfect repulsiveness." Samuel Gridley Howe, a prison reformer, proclaimed: "Thousands of convicts are made so in consequence of a faulty organization of society. . . ." In the properly ordered environment of new institutions, discipline and moral character would be instilled in criminals and other deviants who lacked the self-control to resist the society's corrupting vices and temptations.

Reformers had particularly high expectations for the penitentiary systems pioneered in Pennsylvania and New York in the 1820s. Unlike earlier prisons, the penitentiaries were huge, imposing structures that isolated the prisoners from each other and the outside world. No longer were criminals to be brutally punished or thrown together under inhumane conditions that perpetuated a cycle of moral depravity. Cut off from all corrupting influences, forced to learn that hard work teaches moral discipline, and uplifted by religious literature, criminals would be guided toward becoming law-abiding, productive citizens.

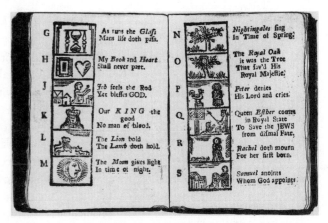

Moral lessons, such as this one for boys at play, filled the pages of the McGuffey's readers.

Library of Congress

**Workhouses.**    The same philosophy of reform provided the rationale for asylums to house the poor and the insane. The number of transient poor and the size of urban slums increased as commercial capitalism uprooted farmers from the land and undercut the security of craft trades. Believing that the poor, much like criminals, had only themselves to blame, public officials and their evangelical allies prescribed a therapeutic regimen of discipline and physical labor to cure the poor of their moral defects. The structured setting for the regimen was the workhouse.

The custodians of the workhouses banished drinking, gambling, and idleness. Their prime responsibility was to supervise the inmates in a tightly scheduled daily routine built around manual labor. Once purged of their laziness and filled with self-esteem as the result of work discipline, the poor would be released to become useful members of society.

**Asylums for the mentally ill.**    Public insane asylums offered a similar order for the mentally ill. Reformers believed that too many choices in a highly mobile, materialistic, and competitive society drove some people insane. Following the lead of New York and Massachusetts in the 1830s, 28 states had established mental hospitals by 1860. These facilities set rigid rules and work assignments to teach patients how to order their lives.

In the early 1840s Dorothea Dix, a Massachusetts schoolteacher, discovered that the insane in her home state were dumped into jails and almshouses, where they suffered filthy, inhumane treatment. Horrified, Dix lobbied state legislatures across the nation for the next twenty years to improve treatment for the mentally ill.

While the reformers did provide social deviants with cleaner, safer living conditions, their penitentiaries and asylums succeeded more in classifying and segregating inmates than in reforming them. Submission to routine turned out not to be the best builder of character. Penitentiaries, reformatories, and workhouses failed to eliminate or noticeably check poverty, crime, and vice. Refusing to question their basic premise that repressive institutions could promote individual responsibility, reformers abandoned their environmental explanations for deviance. By midcentury, they were defining deviants and dependents as permanent misfits with ingrained character defects. The asylums remained; but, stripped of their earlier optimism, they became little more than holding pens for the outcasts of society.

In the concern etched in her face, this photograph captures the compassion that Dorothea Dix brought to her crusade for mental health reform.

## UTOPIAN ALTERNATIVES

Unlike the reformers, who aimed to improve the existing order by guiding individuals to greater self-discipline, the utopians sought perfection by withdrawing from society and its confining institutions. A radically new social order, not an improved old one, was their goal.

Though following different religious and secular philosophies of communitarian living, all the utopians wanted to fashion a more rational and personally satisfying alternative to the competitive materialism of antebellum America. Nearly all the communities sought to transform the organization and rewards of work, thus challenging the prevailing dogmas about private property.

The most successful utopian communities were religious sects whose reordering of both sexual and economic relations departed sharply from middle-class norms. The **Shakers,** at their height in the 1830s, attracted some 6,000 followers. Organized around doctrines of celibate **communism,** Shaker communities held all property in common. The sexes worked and lived apart from each other. Dancing during religious worship brought men and women together and provided an emotional release from enforced sexual denial. In worldly as well as spiritual terms, women enjoyed an equality in Shaker life that the outside world denied them. For this reason, twice as many women as men joined the Shakers.

John Humphrey Noyes, a graduate of Dartmouth who studied for the ministry at Yale, established the **Oneida Community** in upstate New York in 1847. He attracted over 200 followers with his perfectionist vision of plural marriage, community nurseries, group discipline, and common ownership of property. Charged with adultery, Noyes fled to Canada in 1879, but the Oneida Community, reorganized in 1881 as a joint-stock company in the United States and committed thereafter to conventional sexual mores, survived into the twentieth century.

Secular utopians aspired to perfect social relations through rationally designed planned communities. Bitter critics of the social evils of industrialization, they tried to construct models for a social order free from poverty, unemployment, and inequality. They envisioned cooperative communities that balanced agricultural and industrial pursuits in a mixed economy that recycled earnings to the laborers who actually produced the wealth.

Despite their high expectations, nearly all the planned communities ran into financial difficulties and soon collapsed. The pattern was set by the first of the controversial socialist experiments, **New Harmony** in Indiana, the brainchild of the wealthy Scottish industrialist and philanthropist Robert Owen. A proponent of utopian **socialism,** Owen promised to create a new order where "the degrading and pernicious practices in which we are now well trained, of buying cheap and selling dear, will be rendered unnecessary" and "union and co-operation will supersede individual interest." But within two years of its founding in 1825, New Harmony fell victim to inadequate financing and internal bickering.

About the only secular cooperative that gained lasting fame was **Brook Farm** in West Roxbury, Massachusetts (today part of Boston). Established in 1841, Brook Farm was a showcase for the transcendentalist philosophy of Ralph Waldo Emerson. A former Unitarian minister in Boston, Emerson taught that intuition and emotion could grasp a truer ("transcendent") reality than could the senses alone. Although disbanded after six years as an economic failure, Brook Farm inspired intellectuals such as Nathaniel Hawthorne, who briefly lived there. In turn, his writings and those of other writers influenced by **transcendentalism** flowed into the great renaissance of American literature in the mid-nineteenth century, an outpouring of work that grappled with Emersonian themes of individualism and the reshaping of the American character.

**A distinctly national literature.**   In an 1837 address at Harvard titled "The American Scholar," Emerson called for a distinctly national literature devoted to the democratic possibilities of American life. Writers soon responded to Emerson's call.

Walt Whitman, whose *Leaves of Grass* (1855) foreshadowed modern poetry in its use of free verse, shared Emerson's faith in the possibilities of individual fulfillment, and his poems celebrated the democratic variety of the American people. Henry David Thoreau, Emerson's friend

---

**Shakers**   The followers of Mother Ann Lee, who preached a religion of strict celibacy and communal living.

**communism**   A social structure based on the common ownership of property.

**Oneida Community**   Utopian community established in upstate New York in 1848 by John Humphrey Noyes and his followers.

**New Harmony**   Short-lived utopian community established in Indiana in 1825, based on the socialist ideas of Robert Owen, a wealthy Scottish manufacturer.

**socialism**   A social order based on government ownership of industry and worker control over corporations as a way to prevent worker exploitation.

**Brook Farm**   A utopian community and experimental farm established in 1841 near Boston.

**transcendentalism**   A philosophical and literary movement centered on an idealistic belief in the divinity of individuals and nature.

**W WHERE TO LEARN MORE**

Historic New Harmony, New Harmony, Indiana
http://www.usi.edu/hnh/index2.asp

•••• Read the Document

at **www.myhistorylab.com**
*Nathaniel Hawthorne, A Letter from Brook Farm (1841)*

and neighbor, embodied the transcendentalist fascination with nature and self-discovery by living in relative isolation for 16 months at Walden Pond, near Concord, Massachusetts. His *Walden; or, Life in the Woods* (1854) became an American classic. Nathaniel Hawthorne and Herman Melville, the greatest novelists of the American renaissance, focused on the existence of evil and the human need for community.

Much of the appeal of the utopian communities flowed from the same concern about the splintering and selfishness of antebellum society that animated Hawthorne and Melville. The works of these novelists have endured, but the utopian experiments quickly collapsed. Promising economic security and social harmony to buttress a threatened sense of community, the utopians failed to lure all but a few Americans from the acquisitiveness and competitive demands of the larger society.

# ABOLITIONISM AND WOMEN'S RIGHTS

Abolitionism emerged from the same religious impulse that energized reform throughout the North. Like other reformers, the abolitionists came predominantly from evangelical, middle-class families, particularly those of New England stock. What distinguished the abolitionists was their insistence that slavery was *the* great national sin, an evil that mocked American ideals of liberty and Christian morality.

## REJECTING COLONIZATION

In the early nineteenth century, when slavery was expanding westward, almost all white Americans regardless of class or region were convinced that emancipation would lead either to a race war or the debasement of their superior status through racial interbreeding. This paralyzing fear of general emancipation, rooted in pervasive racism, long shielded slavery from sustained attack.

In 1817, antislavery reformers from the North and the South founded the **American Colonization Society.** Slaveholding politicians from the Upper South, notably Henry Clay, James Madison, and President James Monroe, were the leading organizers of the society. Gradual emancipation accompanied by the removal of black people from America to Africa was the only solution these white reformers could imagine for ridding the nation of slavery and avoiding a racial bloodbath. Their goal was to make America all free *and* all white.

The American Colonization Society had no real chance of success. No form of emancipation, no matter how gradual, could appeal to slaveowners who could profit from the labor of their slaves. Moreover, the society could never afford to purchase the freedom of any significant number of slaves.

Free African Americans bitterly attacked the colonizers' central assumption that free black people were unfit to live as citizens in America. They were native-born and considered themselves Americans with every right to enjoy the blessings of republican liberty. Organizing through their own churches in northern cities, free African Americans founded some fifty abolitionist societies, offered refuge to fugitive slaves, and launched the first African American newspaper in 1827, *Freedom's Journal.* David Walker, a free black man who had moved from North Carolina to Massachusetts, published his *Appeal to the Colored Citizens of the World* in 1829. In a searing indictment of white greed and hypocrisy, he rejected colonization and insisted that "America is more our country, than it is the whites', we have enriched it with our *blood and tears*." He warned white America that "wo, wo, will be to you if we have to obtain our freedom by fighting."

As if in response to this call for revolutionary resistance by the enslaved, Nat Turner's Rebellion exploded in the summer of 1831 (see Chapter 11). Both alarmed and inspired by the increased tempo of black militancy, a small group of antislavery white people abandoned all illusions about colonization and embarked on a radically new approach for eradicating slavery.

WHAT WAS the relationship between abolitionism and the women's rights movement?

●●●–Read the **Document**
at **www.myhistorylab.com**
*National Convention of Colored People, Report on Abolition (1847)*

**American Colonization Society**   Organization, founded in 1817 by antislavery reformers, that called for gradual emancipation and the removal of freed blacks to Africa.

## OVERVIEW Types of Antislavery Reform

| Type | Definition | Example |
|---|---|---|
| Gradualist | Accepts notions of black inferiority and attempts to end slavery gradually by purchasing the freedom of slaves and colonizing them in Africa | American Colonization Society |
| Immediatist | Calls for immediate steps to end slavery and denounces slavery and racial prejudice as moral sins | Abolitionists |
| Political antislavery | Recognizes slavery in states where it exists but insists on keeping slavery out of the territories | Free-Soilers |

((•──┤**Hear** the **Audio**

at **www.myhistorylab.com**
*The Liberator*

**American Anti-Slavery Society**  The first national organization of abolitionists, founded in 1833.

## ABOLITIONISM

William Lloyd Garrison, a Massachusetts printer and the leading figure in early abolitionism, became coeditor of an antislavery newspaper in Baltimore in 1829. Before the year was out, Garrison was arrested and convicted of criminal libel for his editorials against a Massachusetts merchant engaged in the domestic slave trade, and he spent seven weeks in jail before a New York City philanthropist paid his $100 fine. Recognizing that his lack of freedom in jail paled against that of the slave, Garrison emerged with an unquenchable hatred of slavery. Returning to Boston, he launched his antislavery newspaper, the *Liberator,* in 1831. A year later, he was instrumental in founding the New England Anti-Slavery Society.

As militant as the free African Americans who comprised the bulk of the early subscribers to the *Liberator,* Garrison thundered, "If we would not see our land deluged in blood, we must instantly burst asunder the shackles of the slaves." He committed abolitionism to the twin goals of immediatism, an immediate moral commitment to end slavery, and racial equality. Only by striving toward these goals, he insisted, could white America ever hope to end slavery without massive violence.

The abolitionists' demand for the legal equality of black people was as unsettling to public opinion as their call for immediate, uncompensated emancipation. Denied the vote outside New England, segregated in all public facilities, prohibited from moving into several western states, and excluded from most jobs save menial labor, free black people everywhere were walled off as an inferior caste.

Garrison, harsh and uncompromising in denouncing slavery and advocating black rights, instilled the antislavery movement with moral urgency. But without the organizational and financial resources of a national society, the message of the early Garrisonians rarely extended beyond free black communities in the North. The success of British abolitionists in 1833, when gradual, compensated emancipation was enacted for Britain's West Indian colonies, inspired white and black abolitionists to gather at Philadelphia in December 1833 and form the **American Anti-Slavery Society.**

The abolitionists spread their message through revivals, rallies, paid lecturers, children's games and toys, and the printed word. Drawing on the experience of reformers in Bible and tract societies, the abolitionists harnessed steam power to the cause of moral suasion. They distributed millions of antislavery tracts, and by the late 1830s, abolitionist sayings appeared on posters, emblems, song sheets, and even candy wrappers.

Women were essential in all of these activities. From the very beginning of the movement, they established their own antislavery societies as auxiliaries to the national organizations run and dominated by men. Initially, their role was limited to raising funds, circulating petitions, and visiting homes to gain converts. Often operating out of local churches, women were grass-roots organizers of a massive petition campaign launched in the mid-1830s. Women signed more than half of the antislavery memorials sent to Congress.

The abolitionists focused their energies on mass propaganda because they saw their role as social agitators who had to break through white apathy and change public opinion. By 1840 they had succeeded in enlisting nearly 200,000 northerners in 2,000 local affiliates of the American Anti-Slavery Society. Most whites, however, remained unmoved, and some violently opposed the abolitionists.

Antiabolitionist mobs in the North went on a rampage in the mid-1830s (see Figure 12–3). They disrupted antislavery meetings, beat and stoned speakers, destroyed printing presses, burned the homes of the wealthy benefactors of the movement, and vandalized free black neighborhoods in a wave of terror that drove many black people from several northern cities. Local elites, especially those with profitable ties to the slave economy of the South, often incited the mobs, whose fury expressed the anxiety of semiskilled and common laborers that they might lose their jobs if freed slaves moved north.

In the South, the hostility to abolitionism took the form of burning and censoring antislavery literature, offering rewards for the capture of leading abolitionists to stand trial for allegedly inciting slave revolts, and tightening up slave codes and the surveillance of free black people. Meanwhile, Democrats in Congress yielded to slaveholding interests in 1836 by passing a gag rule that automatically tabled antislavery petitions with no debate.

The hostility and violence abolitionism provoked convinced Garrison and some of his followers that U.S. institutions and values were fundamentally flawed. In 1838, Garrison helped found the New England Non-Resistant Society, dedicated to the belief that a complete moral regeneration, based on renouncing force in all human relationships, was necessary if the United States were ever to live up to its Christian and republican ideals. The Garrisonian nonresistants rejected all coercive authority, whether expressed in capital punishment, human bondage, clerical support of slavery, male dominance in the patriarchal family, the racial oppression of back people, or the police power of government. The logic of their stand as Christian **anarchists** drove them to denounce all formal political activities and even the legitimacy of the Union, based as it was on a pact with slaveholders.

Garrison's opponents within the abolitionist movement accused him of alienating the public by identifying the antislavery cause with radical attacks on traditional authority. His support for the growing demand of antislavery women to be treated as equals in the movement brought the factional bickering to a head and split the American Anti-Slavery Society. In turn, the opposition of most male abolitionists to the public activities of their female counterparts provoked a militant faction of these women into founding their own movement to achieve equality in U.S. society.

**FIGURE 12–3   Mob Violence and the Abolitionists**   Civil disturbances resulting in attacks on individuals or property increased sharply in the 1830s. The abolitionist campaign to flood the country with antislavery literature triggered much of this surge. Nearly half of the mob activity in the 1830s was directed against abolitionists.

*Data Source:* Leonard L. Richards, *"Gentlemen of Property and Standing." Anti-Abolitionist Mobs in Jacksonian America* (1970).

**anarchists**   A person who believes that all government interferes with individual liberty and should be abolished by whatever means.

## THE WOMEN'S RIGHTS MOVEMENT

Feminism grew out of abolitionism because of the parallels many women drew between the exploited lives of the slaves and their own subordinate status in northern society. "In striving to cut [the slave's] irons off, we found most surely that we were manacled *ourselves*," argued Abby Kelley, a Quaker abolitionist.

In 1837, Angelina and Sarah Grimké, the South Carolina–born abolitionists, attracted large crowds of men and women to their antislavery lectures in New England. By publicly lecturing to a "promiscuous" (mixed) audience of men and women, they defied restrictions on women's proper role and enraged the Congregational clergy of Massachusetts. Harshly criticized

**Read** the **Document**

at www.myhistorylab.com
*Exploring America: Angelina Grimké*

# AMERICAN VIEWS

## Appeal of a Female Abolitionist

*Lydia Maria Child's Appeal, published in Boston in 1833, was a landmark in abolitionist literature for both the thoroughness of its attack on slavery and its refutation of racist ideology and discrimination. This condemnation of racial prejudice was the most radical feature of abolitionist ideology. It directly challenged the deeply held beliefs and assumptions of nearly all white Americans, in the North as well as the South. Racism and slavery, as Child shows in this excerpt from her Appeal, fed off one another in the national curse of slavery.*

- **How** does Child argue that northern white people must bear some of the responsibility for perpetuating slavery?
- **What** arguments does Child make against racial discrimination in northern society?
- **What** did Child mean when she wrote that "the Americans are peculiarly responsible for the example they give"? Do you agree with her?
- **How** does Child deal with the charge that the abolitionists threatened the preservation of the Union?

While we bestow our earnest disapprobation on the system of slavery, let us not flatter ourselves that we are in reality any better than our brethren of the South. Thanks to our soil and climate, and the early exhortions of the Quakers, the form of slavery does not exist among us; but the very spirit of the hateful and mischievous thing is here in all its strength. . . . Our prejudice against colored people is even more inveterate than it is at the South. The planter is often attached to his negroes, and lavishes caresses and kind words upon them, as he would on a favorite hound: but our cold-hearted, ignoble prejudice admits of no exception, no intermission.

The Southerners have long continued habit, apparent interest and dreaded danger, to palliate the wrong they do; but we stand without excuse. . . . If the free States wished to cherish the system of slavery forever, they could not take a more direct course than they now do. Those who are kind and liberal on all other subjects, unite with the selfish and the proud in their unrelenting efforts to keep the colored population in the lowest state of degradation; and the influence they unconsciously exert over children early infuses into their innocent minds the same strong feelings of contempt. . . .

The state of public feeling not only makes it difficult for the Africans to obtain information, but it prevents them from making profitable use of what knowledge they have. A colored man, however intelligent, is not allowed to pursue any business more lucrative than that of a barber, a shoeblack, or waiter. These, and all other employments, are truly respectable, whenever the duties connected with them are faithfully performed; but it is unjust that a man should, on account of his complexion, be prevented from performing more elevated uses in society. Every citizen ought to have a fair chance to try his fortune in any line of business, which he thinks he has ability to transact. Why should not colored men be employed in the manufactories of various kinds? If their ignorance is an objection, let them be enlightened, as speedily as possible. If their moral character is not sufficiently pure, remove the pressure of public scorn, and thus supply them with motives for being respectable. All this can be done. It merely requires an earnest wish to overcome a prejudice, which . . . is in fact opposed to the spirit of our religion, and contrary to the instinctive good feelings of our nature. . . . When the majority heartily desire a change, it is effected, be the difficulties what they may. The Americans are peculiarly responsible for the example they give; for in no other country does the unchecked voice of the people constitute the whole of government. . . .

The strongest and best reason that can be given for our supineness on the subject of slavery, is the fear of dissolving the Union. The Constitution of the United States demands our highest reverence. . . . But we must not forget that the Constitution provides for any change that may be required for the general good. The great machine is constructed with a safety valve, by which any rapidly increasing evil may be expelled whenever the people desire it.

If the Southern politicians are determined to make a Siamese question of this also, if they insist that the Union shall not exist without slavery, it can only be said that they join two things, which have no affinity with each other, and which cannot permanently exist together. They chain the living and vigorous to the diseased and dying; and the former will assuredly perish in the infected neighborhood.

The universal introduction of free labor is the surest way to consolidate the Union, and enable us to live together in harmony and peace. If a history is ever written entitled "The Decay and Dissolution of the North American Republic," its author will distinctly trace our downfall to the existence of slavery among us.

*Source:* Lydia Maria Child, *An Appeal in Favor of That Class of Americans Called Africans* (originally published 1833), ed. Carolyn L. Karcher (University of Massachusetts Press, 1996).

for their unwomanly behavior, the Grimkés publicly responded with an indictment of the male patriarchy and the shocking assertion that "men and women are *created equal!* They are both moral and accountable beings and whatever is right for man to do is right for woman."

Now more sensitive than ever to the injustice of their assigned role as men's submissive followers, antislavery women demanded an equal voice in the abolitionist movement. Despite strong opposition from many of his fellow male abolitionists, Garrison helped Abby Kelley win a seat on the business committee of the American Anti-Slavery Society at its convention in 1840. The anti-Garrisonians walked out of the convention and formed a separate organization, the American and Foreign Anti-Slavery Society.

What was rapidly becoming known as the "woman question" also disrupted the 1840 World Anti-Slavery Convention in London. The refusal of the convention to seat the U.S. female delegates was the final indignity that transformed the discontent of women into a self-conscious movement for women's equality. Two of the excluded delegates, Lucretia Mott and Elizabeth Cady Stanton, vowed to build an organization to "speak out for *oppressed* women."

Their work went slowly. Early feminists were dependent on the abolitionists for most of their followers, and they were unable to do more than hold local meetings and sponsor occasional speaking tours. In 1848, Stanton and Mott were finally able to call the first national convention ever devoted to women's rights at Seneca Falls, in upstate New York. The **Seneca Falls Convention** issued the **Declaration of Sentiments,** a call for full female equality. Modeled directly on the Declaration of Independence, it identified male patriarchy as the source of women's oppression and demanded the vote for women as a sacred and inalienable right of republican citizenship. This call for suffrage raised the prospect of women's self-determination as independent citizens. The Seneca Falls agenda defined the goals of the women's movement for the rest of the century. The feminists' few successes before the Civil War came in economic rights. By 1860, 14 states had granted women greater control over their property and wages.

Despite such successes, the feminist movement did not attract broad support. Most women found in the doctrine of separate spheres a reassuring feminine identity that they could express either at home or in benevolent and reform societies. Within the reform movement as a whole, women's rights were always a minor concern. Abolitionists focused on emancipation.

## POLITICAL ANTISLAVERY

Most of the abolitionists who had broken with Garrison in 1840 believed that emancipation could best be achieved by moving abolitionism into the mainstream of U.S. politics. Political abolitionism had its roots in the petition campaign of the late 1830s. Congressional efforts to suppress the discussion of slavery backfired when John Quincy Adams, the former president who had become a Massachusetts congressman, resorted to an unending series of parliamentary ploys to get around the gag rule (see Chapter 10). Adams became a champion of the constitutional right to petition Congress for redress of grievances. White northerners who had shown no interest in abolitionism as a moral crusade for black people now began to take a stand against slavery when the issue involved the civil liberties of whites and the dominant political power of the South. The hundreds of thousands, they signed abolitionist petitions in 1837 and 1838 to protest the gag rule and the admission of Texas as a slave state.

In 1840, anti-Garrisonian abolitionists tried to turn this new antislavery constituency into an independent political party, the **Liberty Party.** The Liberty Party opposed any expansion of slavery in the territories, condemned racial discrimination in the North as well as slavery in the South, and won the support of most black abolitionists. "To it," recalled Samuel Ward of New York, "I devoted my political activities; with it I lived my political life." In 1843, a national African American convention in Buffalo endorsed the Liberty Party.

This political activism was part of a concerted effort by African Americans to assert leadership in an antislavery movement that rarely treated them as equals. Frederick Douglass was

**Seneca Falls Convention**   The first convention for women's equality in legal rights, held in upstate New York in 1848.

**Declaration of Sentiments**   The resolutions passed at the Seneca Falls Convention of 1848 calling for full female equality, including the right to vote.

**Liberty Party**   The first antislavery political party, formed in 1840.

## GLOBAL CONNECTIONS

### THE INTERNATIONAL DIMENSIONS OF ABOLITION

"The trumpet has sounded through all the colonial dependencies of our country, which proclaims 'liberty to the captives.' O! what heart is there so cold, so seared, so dead, as to feel no thrill of exulting emotion at the thought, that on the morning of this day, eight hundred thousand fellow-men and fellow-subjects, who, during the past night, slept bondmen, awoke freemen! [British emancipation will be] but the first day of a Jubilee year,—of a period of successive triumphs . . . of continuous and rapidly progressive prosperity, to the cause of freedom. [Once America joins Britain in the work of emancipation] the world will be shamed into imitation:—and in no long period, there will not be found on earth a remnant of it."

On August 1, 1834, the day that the British Emancipation Act of 1833 took effect, the Reverend Ralph Wardlaw of Glasgow, Scotland, spoke these words of millennial joy and hope for the future. It was a day of exultation for reformers on both sides of the Atlantic. The spark of freedom was first struck in Britain by the creation in 1787 of the Quaker-inspired Society for the Abolition of the Slave Trade. It exploded into a revolutionary conflagration when the slaves in Saint-Domingue rose up in rebellion in 1791 and unleashed the greatest slave revolt in the Western Hemisphere. By 1808, reformers in Britain and the United States had prohibited the African slave trade. When the Spanish Empire in Latin America began to break up after 1810, the independence movements in Spain's former colonies committed themselves to emancipation. In a startling reversal from the situation in 1800, only Brazil and Cuba remained as major slave areas in Latin America by the 1820s. Then, as the result of a massive grassroots campaign that inundated Parliament with 5,000 petitions and half a million signers, Britain passed the Emancipation Act of 1833, which emancipated the slaves in its colonies as of August 1, 1834.

British emancipation buoyed the abolitionist cause in the United States and was a major factor in emboldening the abolitionists to organize a national society in 1833. It also convinced them, as the Reverend Wardlaw had argued, that Protestant Christianity was poised to take the lead in an epic struggle for human betterment. That was the vision that inspired the abolitionists as they set out to redeem America's revolutionary heritage by cleansing the nation of slavery.

- How does placing the American antislavery movement in a transatlantic context broaden our understanding of the antislavery cause and its place in the intellectual history of the nineteenth century?

their most dynamic spokesman. Increasingly dissatisfied with Garrison's Christian pacifism and his stand against political action, Douglass broke with Garrison in 1847 and founded a black abolitionist newspaper, the *North Star*. The break became irreparable in 1851 when Douglass publicly denied the Garrisonian position that the Constitution was a proslavery document. If properly interpreted, Douglass insisted, "the Constitution is a *glorious liberty document*," and he called for a political war against slavery.

Led by Joshua R. Giddings, a small but vocal bloc of antislavery politicians began to popularize the frightening concept of "the Slave Power," a vast conspiracy of planters and their northern lackeys that controlled the federal government and was plotting to spread slavery and subvert any free institutions that opposed it. As proof, they cited the gag rule, which had shut off debate on slavery, and the campaign of the Tyler administration to annex slaveholding Texas.

The specter of the Slave Power made white liberties, and not black bondage, central to northern concerns about slavery. This shift redefined the evil of slavery to appeal to the self-interest of white northerners who had rejected the moral appeals of the Garrisonians. White people who had earlier been apathetic now began to view slavery as a threat to their rights of free speech and self-improvement.

The image of the Slave Power predisposed many northerners to see the expansionist program of the incoming Polk administration as part of a southern plot to secure more territory for slaveholders at the expense of northern farmers. Northern fears that free labor would be shut out of the new territories won in the Mexican War provided the rallying cry for the Free-Soil Party of 1848, which foreshadowed the more powerful Republican Party of the late 1850s.

## CONCLUSION

With surprising speed after 1815, transportation improvements, technological innovations, and expanding markets drove the economy toward industrialization. Wealth inequality increased, old classes were reshaped, and new ones formed. These changes were most evident in the Northeast, where capital, labor, and growing urban markets spurred the acceleration of manufacturing. The reform impulse that both reflected and shaped these changes was also strongest in the Northeast. The new evangelical Protestantism promised that human perfectibility was possible if individuals strove to free themselves from sin. Influenced by this promise, the northern middle class embraced reform causes that sought to improve human character. Temperance changed U.S. drinking habits and established sobriety as the cultural standard for respectable male behavior. Middle-class reform also emphasized institutional solutions for what were now defined as the social problems of ignorance, crime, and poverty.

The most radical of the reform movements focused on women's equality and the elimination of slavery. The women's rights movement emerged out of women's involvement in reform, especially in abolitionism. Feminism and abolitionism triggered a backlash from the more conservative majority, a response that strengthened the resolve of reformers such as Angelina Grimké. This backlash prevented women from gaining legal and political equality, the major demand of the feminists, and convinced most abolitionists that they had to switch from moral agitation to political persuasion. The political abolitionists soon found that the most effective approach in widening the antislavery appeal was their charge that a Slave Power conspiracy threatened the freedoms of white northerners.

Shown here are seven leaders of the founding generation of American feminists. Clockwise from the top: Lucretia Mott, Elizabeth Cady Stanton, Mary A. Livermore, Lydia Maria Child, Susan B. Anthony, and Grace Greenwood. In the center is Anna E. Dickinson.

# WHERE TO LEARN MORE

**Lowell National Historical Park.** The park is a wonderful resource for visualizing the early stages of America's industrial revolution. *For hours and a schedule of events, see http://www. nps*.gov/lowe/index.htm.

**Slater Hill Historic Site, Pawtucket, Rhode Island.** The Sylvanus Brown House of 1758, the Slaren Mill of 1793, and the Wilkinson Mill of 1810 are on the site. An extensive library and holdings provide insight into the social and economic world of the early industrial revolution. Information on hours, collections, and exhibits can be found at http://www.slatermill.org/museum/about.

**Erie Canal Museum, Syracuse, New York.** The museum houses extensive collections on the building and maintenance of the Erie Canal, and its photo holdings visually record much of the history of the canal. In addition to information on exhibits, tours, *and school programs, its website, http://www.eriecanalmuseum.* org, includes pictures of a replica of an Erie Canal line boat.

**Historic New Harmony, New Harmony, Indiana.** The tours and museum holdings at this preserved site offer a glimpse into the communal living that Robert Owen tried to promote in his utopian plan. For a brief history of New Harmony and links to special events and programs at the site, go to http://www.usi.edu/ hnh/index2.asp.

**Women's Rights Historical Park, Seneca Falls, New York.** The park provides an interpretive overview of the first women's rights convention and includes among its historical sites the restored home of Elizabeth Cady Stanton. Go to http://www. nps.gov/wori/index.htm for links to the museum's summer calendar of events and information on programs.

# REVIEW QUESTIONS

1. Why were improvements in transportation so essential to the growth of the economy after 1815? What were the nature and scope of these improvements?

2. What is an industrial revolution? How can we explain the surge in manufacturing in the United States from 1815 to 1850?

3. What was the religious impulse behind the first wave of reform? What innovations in reaching a mass audience did the benevolent reformers pioneer?

4. What drew women into reform? Why did many of them feel a special affinity for abolitionism?

5. Why was abolitionism the most radical reform of all? How was it linked to an international movement calling for the end of slavery?

6. Why do you think so few southern women of the plantation class followed Angelina Grimké on her journey from social privilege to social activism?

# KEY TERMS

**American Anti-Slavery Society** (p. 326)
**American Colonization Society** (p. 325)
**American Female Moral Reform Society** (p. 320)
**American system of manufacturing** (p. 314)
**American Temperance Society** (p. 319)
**Anarchists** (p. 327)
**Benevolent empire** (p. 318)
**Brook Farm** (p. 324)
***Charles River Bridge v. Warren Bridge*** (p. 308)
**Church of Jesus Christ of Latter-Day Saints (Mormon Church)** (p. 321)
**Communism** (p. 324)
**Cult of domesticity** (p. 316)

**Declaration of Sentiments** (p. 329)
***Gibbons v. Ogden*** (p. 308)
**Liberty Party** (p. 329)
**Nativist** (p. 317)
**New Harmony** (p. 324)
**Oneida Community** (p. 324)
**Putting-out system** (p. 312)
**Rhode Island system** (p. 313)
**Sabbatarian movement** (p. 318)
**Seneca Falls Convention** (p. 329)
**Shakers** (p. 324)
**Socialism** (p. 324)
**Temperance** (p. 316)
**Transcendentalism** (p. 324)
**Transportation revolution** (p. 306)
**Waltham system** (p. 313)
**Workingmen's Movement** (p. 322)

# PEARSON
# myhistorylab Connections

Reinforce what you learned in this chapter by studying the many documents,
images, maps, review tools, and videos available at **www.myhistorylab.com**.

## Read and Review

✓● Study and Review    Study Plan: Chapter 12

●●● Read the Document

*Horace Mann on Education and National Welfare*

*National Convention of Colored People, Report on Abolition (1847)*

*The Harbinger, Female Workers of Lowell (1836)*

*Catharine Esther Beecher, American Woman's Home (1869)*

*Nathaniel Hawthorne, A Letter from Brook Farm (1841)*

*John Humphrey Noyes and Bible Communism (1845 and 1849)*

*Lyman Beecher, "Six Sermons on Intemperance" (1828)*

👁 See the Map

*Expanding America and Internal Improvements*

*Utopian Communities before the Civil War*

## Research and Explore

●●● Read the Document

*Personal Journeys Online*

*From Then to Now Online: Immigration: An Ambivalent Welcome*

*Exploring America: Angelina Grimké*

((●● Hear the Audio

*If There is No Struggle, There is No Progress; excerpt from speech by Frederick Douglass; read by Ossie Davis*

*The Erie Canal*

*The Liberator*

*What if I am a Woman; speech by Maria W. Stewart; read by Ruby Dee*

📡 Watch the Video

*Drinking and the Temperance Movement in Nineteenth-Century America*

*The Women's Rights Movement in Nineteenth-Century America*

*Who Was Horace Mann and Why Are So Many Schools Named after Him?*

((●● Hear the Audio

Hear the audio files for Chapter 12 at
**www.myhistorylab.com**.

## The Second Great Awakening and Religious Diversity in America

The Second Great Awakening (1800–1830s) led to the creation of many new religious affiliations within the American religious community and an increased diversity within American religious life. What were the similarities and differences among some of these new denominations? How did this growing diversity impact American society?

One of the reasons that separation of church and state has worked so well in the United States is the wide diversity of religious affiliations within the American population. From the beginning of English colonial efforts to the time of the American Revolution this happy scenario was not necessarily present. In the northern colonies the Congregationalist Church was the established state religion among Puritan settlers. In the middle and southern colonies the Anglican Church or Church of England was the established church.

Religious diversity was slow in growing in the early years of the American colonies and nation. The First Great Awakening of the 1730s and 1740s strengthened the Presbyterian, Baptist, and Methodist churches in their quest to win over the followers of the Congregationalist and Anglican churches and create diversity in the camp of American religions. The Second Great Awakening of the 1800s through the 1830s created even greater diversity.

## *They are ancient men, men of another age . . .*

*Charles Grandison Finney was the quintessential revival preacher of the Second Great Awakening. Finney emphasized revivals and evangelism; he empowered women in the church, preached against slavery, and believed in salvation by faith rather than good works. He is credited with bringing hundreds of thousands of individuals to the Christian faith.*

### Charles Grandison Finney, Lectures on the Revival of Religion, 1835

I would say nothing to undervalue, or lead you to undervalue a thorough education for ministers. But I do not call that a thorough education, which they get in our colleges and seminaries. It does not fit them for their work. . . . Those fathers who have the training of our young ministers are good men, but they are ancient men, men of another age and different stamp from what is needed in these days of excitement, when the church and world are rising to new thought and action. Those dear fathers will not, I suppose, see this; and will perhaps think hard of me for saying it; but it is the cause of Christ.

### From Autobiography of Peter Cartwright, The Backwoods Preacher

*The revival or "camp meeting" was the signal event of the Second Great Awakening. The Cane Ridge experience became an annual event in Kentucky and was copied all over the nation in large and small camp meetings to revive the faith of Christians or to convert new believers.*

Somewhere between 1800 and 1801, in the upper part of Kentucky, at a memorable place called "Cane Ridge," there was appointed a sacramental meeting by some of the Presbyterian ministers, at which meeting, seemingly unexpected by ministers or people, the mighty power of God was displayed in a very extraordinary manner; many were moved to tears, and bitter and loud crying for mercy. The meeting was protracted for weeks. Ministers of almost all denominations flocked in from far and near. The meeting was kept up by night and day. Thousands heard of the mighty work, and came on foot, on horseback, in carriages and wagons. It was supposed that there were in attendance at times during the meeting from twelve to twenty-five thousand people. Hundreds fell prostrate under the mighty power of

*Shaker Dance, Joseph Becker, Frank Leslie's Illustrated Newspaper, 1873*

God, as men slain in battle. Stands were erected in the woods from which preachers of different Churches proclaimed repentance toward God and faith in our Lord Jesus Christ, and it was supposed, by eye and ear witnesses, that between one and two thousand souls were happily and powerfully converted to God during the meeting.

## Simple Gifts

*"Simple Gifts" is a Shaker quick dance or dancing song used in worship services such as the one illustrated above. The hymn was written by Elder Joseph Brackett, Jr. in 1848.*

'Tis the gift to be simple, 'tis the gift to be free,
'Tis the gift to come down where we ought to be,
And when we find ourselves in the place just right,
'Twill be in the valley of love and delight.
When true simplicity is gain'd,
To bow and to bend we shan't be asham'd,
To turn, turn will be our delight,
Till by turning, turning we come round right.

## Joseph Smith, The Beginnings of Mormonism (1823)

While I was thus in the act of calling upon God, I discovered a light appearing in my room, which continued to increase until the room was lighter than at noonday, when immediately a personage appeared at my bedside, standing in the air, for his feet did not touch the floor. . . .

He called me by name, and said unto me that he was a messenger sent from the presence of God to me, and that his name was Moroni; that God had a work for me to do; and that my name should be had for good and evil among all nations, kindreds, and tongues, or that it should be both good and evil spoken of among all people. . . .

. . . I returned to my father in the field, and rehearsed the whole matter to him. He replied to me that it was of God, and told me to go and do as commanded by the messenger. I left the field, and went to the place where the messenger had told me the plates were deposited; and owing to the distinctness of the vision which I had had concerning it, I knew the place the instant that I arrived there. . . .

At length the time arrived for obtaining the plates, the Urim and Thummim, and the breastplate. . . . the same heavenly messenger delivered them up to me with this charge: that I should be responsible for them; that if I should let them go carelessly, or through any neglect of mine, I should be cut off; but that if I would use all my endeavors to preserve them, until he, the messenger, should call for them, they should be protected.

. . . For no sooner was it known that I had them, than the most strenuous exertions were used to get them from me. . . . The persecution became more bitter and severe than before, and multitudes were on the alert continually to get them from me if possible. But by the wisdom of God, they remained safe in my hands. When, according to arrangements, the messenger called for them, I delivered them up to him; and he has them in his charge until this day. . . .

On the 5th day of April, 1829, Oliver Cowdery came to my house, until which time I had never seen him. He stated to me that . . . the family related to him the circumstances of my having received the plates, and accordingly he had come to make inquiries of me.

Two days after the arrival of Mr. Cowdery (being the 7th of April) I commenced to translate the Book of Mormon, and he began to write for me.

*Thousands heard of the mighty work . . .*

# 13
# The Way West

In his painting. *The Oregon Trail,* 1869, Albert Bierstadt (1830–1902) captures a wagon train progressing through the dramatic landscape of mountain cliffs and an expansive sky. Oil on canvas, 31 × 49" (78.74 × 124.46 cm).
Butler Institute of American Art, Youngstown, OH, USA/Gift of Joseph G. Butler III 1946/Bridgeman Art Library.

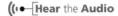 Hear the **Audio**

Hear the audio files for Chapter 13 at **www.myhistorylab.com**.

### THE AGRICULTURAL FRONTIER  *(page 339)*

**HOW DID** economic and demographic pressures in the East spur western migration?

### THE FRONTIER OF THE PLAINS INDIANS  *(page 344)*

**WHAT STRATEGIES** did the Sioux use to maintain their power on the Great Plains?

### THE MEXICAN BORDERLANDS  *(page 348)*

**WHAT FORCES** contributed to the Americanization of Texas?

### POLITICS, EXPANSION, AND WAR  *(page 355)*

**WHY WAS** James K. Polk so eager to provoke a war with Mexico?

ONE AMERICAN JOURNEY

*On an occasion when I had interrogated a Sioux chief, on the upper Missouri, about their Government, their punishments and tortures of prisoners, for which I had freely condemned them for the cruelty of the practice, he took occasion, when I had got through, to ask me some questions relative to modes in the civilized world, which, with his comments upon them, were nearly as follows: and struck me, as I think they must every one, with great force.*

*He . . . told me he had often heard that white people hung their criminals by the neck, and choked them to death like dogs, and those their own people; to which I answered, "yes." He then told me he had learned that they shut each other up in prisons, where they keep them a great part of their lives because they can't pay money! I replied in the affirmative to this, which occasioned great surprise and excessive laughter, even among the women. . . . He said . . . that he had been along the Frontier, and a good deal amongst the white people, and he had seen them whip their little children, a thing that is very cruel, he had heard also, from several white medicine-men, that the Great Spirit of the white people was the child of a white woman, and that he was at the last put to death by the white people! This seemed to be a thing that he had not been able to comprehend, and he concluded by saying, "the Indians' Great Spirit got no mother—the Indians no kill him, he never die." He put me a chapter of other questions as to the trespasses of the white people on their lands, their continual corruption of the morals of their women, and digging open the Indians' graves to get their bones, &c. To all of which I was compelled to reply in the affirmative, and quite glad to close my note-book, and quietly to escape from the throng that had collected around me, and saying (though to myself and silently), that these and an hundred other vices belong to the civilized world, and are practiced upon (but certainly, in no instance, reciprocated by) the "cruel and relentless savage."*

*George Catlin*

George Catlin, *Letters and Notes on the Manners, Customs, and Condition of the North American Indians,* Vol. II, pp. 756–57, 1841.

•◦—[ Read the Document at **www.myhistorylab.com**

Personal Journeys Online

- **Edward Harris, Journal excerpt, 1843. Account by a naturalist of the smallpox epidemic of 1837 on the Upper Missouri.**

- **Pierre Jean de Smet, S. J., Letter from a Catholic priest, 1841. Impressions of the character and intelligence of Indians in the Rocky Mountains.**

GEORGE CATLIN, one of the great illustrators of the American Indians, recorded these words in the 1830s when he traveled over the trans-Mississippi West painting and sketching, in his words, "the looks and customs of the vanishing races of native man in America." Unlike most whites of his generation, he approached Indian cultures with respect, and he realized that native peoples had a valid critique of the culture and values of white America.

From his first contact with the tribes along the upper Missouri River in the early 1830s, Catlin sensed that he was witness to a way of life that was about to vanish. He worked at a feverish pace to create a pictorial record of what he saw in a collection of art he called "Catlin's Indian Gallery." The proceeds from exhibiting his work in Europe enabled him to live quite comfortably in the 1840s, but he suffered a severe setback in 1852 when a financial speculation went sour. A failure as an entrepreneur, he nonetheless succeeded brilliantly as an artist in depicting the Native American peoples of the trans-Mississippi West just as they were about to be engulfed by a surging tide of white settlement.

## CHRONOLOGY

| | |
|---|---|
| **1803–1806** | Lewis and Clark travel up the Missouri River in search of a water route to the Pacific. |
| **1816** | Settlers surge into the trans-Appalachian region. |
| **1821** | Mexico gains its independence from Spain. |
| | Santa Fe Trail opens. |
| | Stephen F. Austin establishes the first American colony in Texas. |
| **1824** | Rocky Mountain Fur Company begins the rendezvous system. |
| **1830** | Congress creates the Indian Territory. |
| **1834** | Protestant missions are established in Oregon. |
| | Santa Anna seizes power in Mexico. |
| **1836** | Texas wins its independence from Mexico. |
| **1837** | Smallpox epidemic hits the Plains Indians. |
| **1842** | First large parties of migrants set out on the Oregon Trail. |
| **1845** | United States annexes Texas. |
| | Democrats embrace Manifest Destiny. |
| | The Great Irish Famine begins. |
| **1846** | Mexican War breaks out. |
| | United States and Britain reach an agreement in Oregon. |
| **1847** | Mormons begin settlement of Utah. |
| **1848** | Oregon Territory is organized. |
| | Treaty of Guadalupe Hidalgo ends the Mexican War. |
| | Revolutions sweep across Europe. |
| **1851** | Fort Laramie Treaty with the Plains Indians is signed. |

Some 300,000 Americans traveled the Oregon Trail in the 1840s and 1850s in a trek that eventually made the United States a nation that spanned the continent. These overlanders, as they came to be known, were part of a restless tide of white migration that eventually saw more than 50,000 Americans a year migrate west of the Appalachians after the War of 1812.

The West became a meeting ground of people from diverse cultures as Anglo-Americans came into contact and conflict with the Indians of the Plains and the Mexicans of the Southwest. Convinced of the superiority of their political and cultural values, Anglo-Americans asserted a God-given right to spread across the continent and impose their notions of liberty and democracy on peoples whose land they coveted. In the process, they forever changed much in the Native American culture that Catlin had so respectfully painted. ✦

# THE AGRICULTURAL FRONTIER

The U.S. population ballooned from 5.3 million in 1800 to more than 23 million by 1850. As the population expanded, it shifted westward. Fewer than one in ten Americans lived west of the Appalachians in 1800; by 1850, about half did (see Map 13–1).

**HOW DID** economic and demographic pressures in the East spur western migration?

The tremendous amount of land available for settlement accounted for both phenomena. Through purchase and conquest, the land area of the United States more than tripled in the first half of the nineteenth century. Here was space where Americans could raise the large families of a rural society in which, on average, six to eight children survived to adolescence.

Declining soil fertility and rising population pressure in the rural East propelled these migrations. A common desire for greater economic opportunity, however, resulted in two distinct western societies by the 1840s. North of the Ohio River, in the Old Northwest, free labor and family farms defined the social order. South of the Ohio was the Old Southwest, a society dominated by slave labor and the plantation.

## THE CROWDED EAST

By the early nineteenth century, land was scarce in the East, especially in New England. After generations of population growth and subdivisions of landholdings to male heirs, most New England communities no longer had enough arable land to satisfy all the young men who

MAP 13–1  **The Westward Shift of the United States Population, 1790–1850**  With a speed that was unimaginable in 1790, the United States quickly became a continental nation that stretched from the Atlantic to the Pacific by 1850. Particularly dramatic was the population growth in what became the Midwest.

**What regions** west of the Appalachian Mountains were most densely populated in 1850? What explains the demographic pattern shown in the 1850 map?

340

wanted their own farms. Even such recently opened areas as Vermont felt the pressure of rural overpopulation.

Land was more productive and expensive farther south, in the mid-Atlantic states. Keyed to the major export crop of wheat, agriculture was more commercialized than in New England, and economic inequality was thus higher. Successful farmers became wealthy by specializing in wheat and hiring the rural poor to work their fields. One-third to one-half of the young men in the commercialized agricultural districts of New Jersey and Pennsylvania were landless by the end of the eighteenth century. These men and their families, many of whom were recently arrived Scots-Irish and German immigrants, led the western migration from Pennsylvania. The pressure to move west was greatest in the slave states along the eastern seaboard. Although population density here was just two-thirds of that in New England, landholdings were more concentrated and the soil more exhausted than in the Northeast. Tenants who wanted their own land and small farmers tired of competing against slave labor were forced west across the mountains. They were joined by the sons of planters. Despite marriages arranged to keep land within the wealthy families, there was no longer enough good land left to carve out plantations for all the younger sons.

By the early 1800s, the young and the poor in the rural East had every incentive to head west, where fertile land was abundant, accessible, and, at $2 to $3 per acre, far cheaper than in the East. Land was the basis of wealth and social standing, and its ownership separated the independent from the dependent, the rooted from the rootless.

The western settler, observed a traveler on the Missouri frontier in the 1820s, wanted "to be a freeholder, to have plenty of rich land, and to be able to settle his children around him." Government policy under the Jeffersonian Republicans and Jacksonian Democrats attempted to promote these goals. Central to the land policy of the federal government after 1800 was the conviction that political liberties rested on the broadest possible base of land ownership. Thus, public policy and private aspirations merged in the belief that access to land was the key to preserving U.S. freedom.

When Jefferson took office in 1801, the minimum price for public land was $2 per acre, and a block of 320 acres had to be purchased at one time. By the 1830s, the price was down to $1.25 per acre, and the minimum purchase was only 80 acres. Congress also protected squatters, who had settled on public land before it was surveyed, from being outbid by speculators at land sales. The Preemption Act of 1841 guaranteed the right to purchase up to 160 acres at the minimum price of $1.25 when the public auction was held.

## THE OLD NORTHWEST

The number of Americans who settled in the heartland of the Old Northwest, Ohio, Indiana, and Illinois, rose tenfold from 1810 to 1840. The end of the War of 1812 and the abandonment by the British of their former Indian allies opened the region to a flood of migrants.

Travelers passing through the Ohio Valley just after the war were astonished by the number of Americans trekking west. Wagonloads of migrants bounced along turnpikes to disembark on the Ohio River at Pittsburgh and Wheeling, where they bought flatboats to carry them down to the interior river valleys. Moving north across the Ohio were families from the hill country of Virginia and Kentucky. These two streams of migrants, one predominantly northern and the other southern, met in the lower Midwest and viewed each other as strangers.

**A mosaic of settlements.** The Old Northwest was less a melting pot in which regional cultures merged than a mosaic of settlements in which the different values and folkways of regional cultures from throughout the East took root and expanded. Belts of migration generally ran along a line from east to west as settlers sought out soil types and ecological conditions similar to those they had left behind. Thus, the same North-South cultural differences that existed along the Atlantic seaboard in 1800 were to be found half a century later in the Mississippi Valley.

A transplanted Yankee culture from New England and upstate New York spread over the upper Midwest, northern Ohio, Indiana, and Illinois, as well as Michigan and Wisconsin. These westerners were Whiggish in their politics, tended to be antislavery, and valued a communal sense of responsibility that regulated moral behavior and promoted self-improvement. The highland southerners who settled the lower Midwest, southern Ohio, Indiana, and Illinois, as well as Kentucky, were Democrats: They fiercely distrusted any centralized authority, political or moral, and considered Yankees intolerant do-gooders. Holding the balance of cultural and political power were the migrants from Pennsylvania and New Jersey, who were accustomed to ethnic diversity and the politics of competing economic groups. They settled principally in central Ohio, Indiana, and Illinois. By emphasizing economic growth and downplaying the cultural politics that pitted Yankees against southerners, they built a consensus around community development.

It took about ten years of backbreaking labor to create an 80-acre farm in heavily wooded sections. The work of women was essential for the success of the farm and the production of any salable surplus. Wives and daughters helped to tend the field crops, milked cows, and churned butter, and they produced the homespun cloth that, along with their dairy goods, found a market in the first country stores on the frontier.

Because outside labor was scarce and expensive, communities pooled their efforts for such tasks as raising a cabin. Groups of settlers also acted as cooperative units at public land auctions. Local associations known as **claims clubs** enforced the extralegal right of squatters to enter noncompetitive bids on land they had settled and improved. Members of the clubs physically intimidated speculators and refused to step aside until local settlers had acquired the land they wanted. The high cost of hauling goods to outside markets kept the early frontier economy barely above self-sufficiency. This initial economy, however, soon gave way to a more commercially oriented agriculture when steamboats, canals, and railroads opened up vast new markets (see Chapter 12).

The first large market was in the South, down the corridor of the Ohio and Mississippi rivers, and its major staples were corn and hogs. By the 1830s, the Erie Canal and its feeder waterways in the upper Midwest began to reorient much of the western farm trade to the Northeast. Wheat, because of its ready marketability for milling into flour, became the major cash crop for the northern market.

**claims clubs** Groups of local settlers on the nineteenth-century frontier who banded together to prevent the price of their land claims from being bid up by outsiders at public land auctions.

Although southern cotton was the raw material that fueled New England textile factories in the first stages of industrialization, the commercialization of agriculture in the West also contributed to the growth of eastern manufacturing. Western farms supplied eastern manufacturers with inexpensive raw materials for processing into finished goods. By flooding national markets with corn and wheat, western produce not only supplied eastern workers with cheap food but also forced noncompetitive eastern farmers either to move west or to work in factories in eastern cities. In turn, the West itself became an ever-growing market for eastern factory goods. For example, nearly half of the nation's iron production in the 1830s was fashioned into farm implements.

In the 1820s, the Old Northwest was just emerging from semisubsistence and depended on the southern trade. Thirty years later it had become part of a larger Midwest whose economy was

Cyrus McCormick pioneered the development of horse-drawn mechanical reapers. Shown here demonstrating his reaper to potential customers, McCormick helped revolutionize American agriculture with labor-saving machinery that made possible far larger harvests of grain crops.

increasingly integrated with that of the Northeast. Settlers continued to pour into the region, and three additional states, Michigan (1837), Iowa (1846), and Wisconsin (1848), joined the Union.

The combination of favorable farm prices and steadily decreasing transportation costs generated a rise in disposable income that was spent on outside goods or invested in internal economic development. A network of canals and railroads was laid down, and manufacturing cities grew from towns favorably situated by water or rail transport. There was still room for subsistence farming, but the West north of the Ohio was now economically specialized and socially diverse.

## THE OLD SOUTHWEST

"The *Alabama Feaver* rages here with great violence and has carried off vast numbers of our Citizens," wrote a North Carolina planter in 1817 about the westward migration from his state. About as many people migrated from the old slave states in the East to the Old Southwest as those states gained by natural increase in the 1820s and 1830s. By 1850, more than 600,000 white settlers from Maryland, Virginia, and the Carolinas lived in slave states to the south and west, and many of them had brought their slaves with them. Indeed, from 1790 to 1860, more than 800,000 slaves were moved or sold from the South Atlantic region into the Old Southwest.

Soaring cotton prices after the War of 1812 and the smashing of Indian confederations during the war, which opened new lands to white settlement, propelled the first surge of migration into the Old Southwest (see Map 13–1). Before cotton prices plunged in the Panic of 1819, planters flooded into western Tennessee and the Black Belt, a crescent-shaped band of rich, black loamy soil arcing westward from Georgia through central Alabama and Mississippi. Migration surged anew in the 1830s when cotton prices were again high and the Chickasaws and Choctaws had been forced out of the incredibly fertile Delta country between the Yazoo and Mississippi rivers (see Chapter 10). The 1840s brought Texas fever to replace the Alabama fever of the 1810s, and a steady movement to the Southwest rounded out the contours of the cotton South. In less than thirty years, six new slave states—Mississippi (1817), Alabama (1819), Missouri (1821), Arkansas (1836), Florida (1845), and Texas (1845)—joined the Union (see the Overview table, Westward Expansion and the Growth of the Union, 1815–1850).

The southwestern frontier attracted both slaveholding planters and small independent farmers. The planters, though a minority, had the capital or the credit to acquire the best lands and the slave labor to make those lands productive. The slaveholders were responding both to the need for fresh land and to the extraordinary demand for short-staple cotton.

The most typical settlers on the southern frontier were the small independent yeomen farmers who generally owned no slaves. Usually settling in the valleys, on the ridges, and in the hill country, they often soon sold out to neighboring planters and headed west again.

The yeomanry moved onto the frontier in two waves. The first consisted of stockmen-hunters, a restless, transient group that spread from the pine barrens in the Carolina backcountry to the coastal plain of eastern Texas. These pioneers prized unfettered independence and measured their wealth in the livestock left to roam and fatten on the sweet grasses of uncleared forests. They were quick to move on when farmers, the second wave, started to clear the land for crops.

The yeoman farmers practiced a diversified agriculture aimed at feeding their families. Corn and pork were the mainstays of their diet, and both could readily be produced as long as there was room for the open-range herding of swine and for patches of corn. The more ambitious farmers, usually those who owned one or two slaves, grew some cotton, but most preferred to avoid the economic risks of cotton production. The yeoman's chief source of labor was his immediate family, and to expand that labor force to produce cotton meant going into debt to purchase slaves. The debt could easily cost the yeoman his farm if the price of cotton fell.

Measured by per capita income, and as a direct result of the profits from slave-produced cotton on virgin soils, the Old Southwest was a wealthier society than the Old Northwest in

## OVERVIEW    Westward Expansion and the Growth of the Union, 1815–1850

| New Free States | New Slave States | Territories (1850) |
| --- | --- | --- |
| Indiana, 1816 | Mississippi, 1817 | Minnesota |
| Illinois, 1818 | Alabama, 1819 | Oregon |
| Maine, 1820 | Missouri, 1821 | New Mexico |
| Michigan, 1837 | Arkansas, 1836 | Utah |
| Iowa, 1846 | Florida, 1845 | |
| Wisconsin, 1848 | Texas, 1845 | |

1850. In the short term, the settlement of the Old Southwest was also more significant for national economic development. Cotton accounted for more than half the value of all U.S. exports after the mid-1830s. More than any other commodity, cotton paid for U.S. imports and underpinned national credit. But southern prosperity was not accompanied by the same economic development and social change as in the Old Northwest. Compared to the slave West in 1860, the free-labor West was twice as urbanized, and far more of its workforce was engaged in nonagricultural pursuits.

The Southwest Ordinance, enacted by Congress in 1790, opened all territories south of the Ohio River to slavery. Slaves, land, and cotton were the keys to wealth on the southern frontier, and agricultural profits were continually plowed back into more land and slaves to produce more cotton. In contrast, prosperous farmers in the Old Northwest had no slaves to work additional acres. Hence, they were much more likely to invest their earnings in promotional schemes designed to attract settlers whose presence would raise land values and increase business for local merchants and entrepreneurs. As early as the 1840s, rural communities in the Old Northwest were supporting bustling towns that offered jobs in trade and manufacturing on a scale far surpassing anything in the slave West. By the 1850s, the Midwest was almost as urbanized as the Northeast had been in 1830, and nearly half its labor force no longer worked on farms.

The Old Southwest remained overwhelmingly agricultural. Once the land was settled, the children of the first generation of slaveholders and yeomen moved west to the next frontier rather than compete for the good land that was left. Relatively few newcomers took their place. By the 1850s, Kentucky, Tennessee, Alabama, and Mississippi, the core states of the Old Southwest, were all losing more migrants than they were gaining.

**WHAT STRATEGIES** did the Sioux use to maintain their power on the Great Plains?

## THE FRONTIER OF THE PLAINS INDIANS

Few white Americans had ventured west of the Mississippi by 1840. Moreover, Americans had no legal claim to much of the trans-Mississippi West, or merely the paper title of the Louisiana Purchase, to which none of the native inhabitants had acquiesced. Beyond Texas and the boundary line drawn by the Trans-Continental Treaty of 1819 lay the northern possessions of Mexico. Horse-mounted Indian tribes dominated by the Sioux were a formidable power throughout the central Plains.

Before the 1840s, only fur trappers and traders, who worked with and not against the powerful Sioux, had pushed across the Great Plains and into the Rockies. The 1840s brought a sudden change, a large migration westward that radically altered the ecology of the Great Plains. Farm families trapped in an agricultural depression and enticed by Oregon's bounty turned the trails blazed by the fur traders into ruts on the **Oregon Trail,** the route that led to the first large settlement of Americans on the Pacific Coast.

## TRIBAL LANDS

At least 350,000 Native Americans lived in the plains and mountains of the trans-Mississippi West in 1840. They were loosely organized into tribal groups, each with its own territory and way of life. Most inhabited the Great Plains region, which lay north and west of the Indian Territory reserved for eastern tribes in the present state of Oklahoma. The point where the prairies of the Midwest gave way to the higher, drier plains marked a rough division between predominantly agricultural tribes to the east and nomadic, hunting tribes to the west.

In the 1830s, the U.S. government set aside a broad stretch of country between the Platte River to the north and the Red River to the south (most of what is now Oklahoma and eastern Kansas) exclusively for tribes resettled from the East under the Indian Removal Act of 1830 and for village-living groups native to the area. Many government officials envisioned this territory as a permanent sanctuary that would separate Indians from white people and allow them to live in peace on allotments of land granted as compensation for the territory they had ceded to the federal government. However, even as Congress was debating the idea of a permanent Indian reserve, the pressure on native peoples in the Mississippi Valley both from raiding parties of Plains Indians and the incessant demands of white farmers and speculators for land was rendering a stable Indian-white boundary meaningless.

On the eve of Indian removal in the East, the Sauks, Foxes, Potawatomis, and other Indian peoples inhabited Iowa. The defeat of the Sauks and Foxes in what white Americans called Black Hawk's War in 1832 opened Iowa to white settlement and forced tribes to cede land (see Chapter 10). In 1838, Congress created the Territory of Iowa, which encompassed all the land between the Mississippi and Missouri rivers north of the state of Missouri. The remaining Indians were now on the verge of being pushed completely out of the region. Throughout the upper Mississippi Valley in the 1830s, other groups suffered a similar fate, and the number of displaced Indians swelled.

The first to be displaced were farming peoples whose villages straddled the woodlands to the east and the open plains to the west. These border tribes were caught in a vise between the loss of their land to advancing white people and the seizure of their horses and agricultural provisions by Indian raiders such as the Sioux from the plains. The Pawnees were among the hardest hit.

By the 1830s, the Pawnees were primarily an agricultural people who embarked on seasonal hunts for game in the Platte River Valley. In 1833, they signed a treaty with the U.S. government in which they agreed to withdraw north of the Platte in return for subsidies and military protection from the hostile Indians on the plains. Once the Pawnees moved north of the Platte, Sioux attacked them and seized control of the prime hunting grounds. When the Pawnees in desperation filtered back south of the Platte, in violation of the treaty of 1833, they encountered constant harassment from white settlers. In vain the Pawnee leaders cited the provisions of the treaty that promised them protection from the Sioux. Forced back north of the Platte by the U.S. government, the Pawnees were eventually driven out of their homeland by the Sioux.

**Oregon Trail**   Overland trail of more than two thousand miles that carried American settlers from the Midwest to new settlements in Oregon, California, and Utah.

Shown here is a Lakota shirt, c. 1850, that was specially woven for Sioux warriors who had distinguished themselves in battle. The blue and yellow dyes symbolize sky and earth, and the strands of human hair represent acts of bravery performed in defense of the Lakota people.

Shirt, about 1860s, unknown Sioux artist. Deer skin, hair, quills, feathers, paint, Denver Art Museum Collection, Native Arts Acquisitions Funds, 1947. 235 © Photo by the Denver Art Museum. All Rights Reserved.

### QUICK REVIEW

#### The Pawnees

- By 1830s, the Pawnees were primarily an agricultural people.
- Agreed in 1833 treaty to move north.
- Attacked by Sioux in the north and white settlers in the south.

**W**  **WHERE TO LEARN MORE**

★ Indian Museum of North America, Crazy Horse, South Dakota
http://www.crazyhorsememorial
.org/monument/

**Read the Document**

at www.myhistorylab.com
*Exploring America:*
*America and the Horse*

### QUICK REVIEW

#### Sources of Sioux Power

- Horses.
- Guns.
- Political skill.
- Relative insusceptibility to European diseases.

The Sioux were the dominant power on the northern and central Great Plains, more than able to hold their own against white Americans in the first half of the nineteenth century. In the eighteenth century, the western Sioux had separated from their woodland kin (known as the Santee Sioux), left their homeland along the headwaters of the Mississippi River, and pushed onto the Minnesota prairies. Armed with guns they had acquired from the French, the western Sioux dominated the prairies east of the Missouri River by 1800.

The Sioux learned to use the horse from the Plains Indians. Introduced to the New World by the Spanish, horses had revolutionized the lives of native peoples on the Great Plains. As they acquired more horses through trading and raids, the Plains Indians evolved a distinctly new nomadic culture. The Sioux were the most successful of all the tribes in melding two facets of white culture, the gun and the horse, into an Indian culture of warrior-hunters.

As the demand for buffalo hides from American and European traders increased in the early 1800s, the Sioux extended their buffalo hunts. In a loose alliance with the Cheyennes and Arapahos, Sioux war parties pushed aside or subjugated weaker tribes to the south and west of the Missouri River basin. Reduced to a dependent status, these tribes were forced to rely on the Sioux for meat and trading goods.

Epidemic diseases brought to the plains by white traders helped Sioux expansion. Because they lived in small wandering bands, the Sioux were less susceptible to these epidemics than the more sedentary village peoples. The Sioux were also one of the first tribes to be vaccinated against smallpox by doctors sent up the Missouri River by the Bureau of Indian Affairs in the early 1830s. Smallpox reached the plains in the 1780s, and a major epidemic in 1837 probably halved the region's Indian population. Particularly hard hit were tribes attempting to resist the Sioux advance. Sioux losses were relatively light and, unlike the other tribes, their population grew.

By 1850, the Sioux had increased in power and numbers since they first encountered American officials during the Lewis and Clark Expedition in 1804 and 1805. Americans could vilify the Sioux, but they could not force them into dependence in the first half of the nineteenth century. The Sioux continued to extend their influence, and they were shrewd enough to align themselves with the Americans whenever their interests dictated conciliation.

## THE FUR TRADERS

The western fur trade originated in the rivalry between British and U.S. companies for profitable furs, especially beaver pelts. Until the early 1820s, the Hudson's Bay Company, a well-capitalized

The annual rendezvous in Wyoming of fur trappers and traders was a multinational affair in which Anglo Americans, French Canadians, Mexican Americans, and Native Americans gathered to trade, drink, and swap stories.

The Denver Public Library, Western History Department.

British concern, dominated the trans-Mississippi fur trade. A breakthrough for U.S. interests came in 1824 when two St. Louis businessmen, William Henry Ashley and Andrew Henry of the Rocky Mountain Fur Company, developed the rendezvous system, which eliminated the need for permanent and costly posts deep in Indian territory. In keeping with Indian traditions of periodic intertribal meetings, the rendezvous system brought together trappers, Indians, and traders in a grand annual fair at a designated site in the high mountain country of Wyoming. White trappers and Indians exchanged the animal skins they had gathered in the seasonal hunt for guns, traps, tobacco, whiskey, textiles, and other trading goods with agents of the fur companies in St. Louis.

Living conditions in the wilderness were primitive, even brutal. Mortality rates among trappers ran as high as 80 percent a year. Death could result from an accidental gunshot wound, an encounter with a grizzly, or an arrow from an Indian whose hunting grounds a trapper had transgressed.

For all its dangers, the life of a trapper appealed to unattached young men. They were fleeing the confinements, as well as the comforts, of white civilization and were as free as they could be. When on a hunt with the Indians, they were part of a spectacle unknown to other white Americans, one that was already passing into history.

Such spectacles were increasingly rare after 1840, the year of the last mountain men's rendezvous on the Green River in Wyoming. The most exploitative phase of the fur trade in the 1830s had ravaged the fur-bearing animals and accelerated the spread of smallpox among the tribes. Whiskey, the most profitable item among the white man's trading goods, had corrupted countless Indians and undermined the vitality of tribal cultures.

The mountain men were about to pass into legend, but before they did, they explored every trail and path from the front (or eastern) range of the Rockies to the Pacific. The main trading corridor of the fur trade, up the lower Missouri to the North Platte and across the plains to the South Pass, a wide plateau crossing the Continental Divide, and into the Wyoming basin, became the main overland route to the West in the 1840s. The mountain men had removed the mystery of western geography, and in so doing they hastened the end of the frontier conditions that had made their unique way of life possible.

## THE OREGON TRAIL

Before the 1830s, few Americans had heard of Oregon, and practically none lived there. Under an agreement reached in 1818, the Oregon Country was still jointly administered by the United States and Great Britain. Furs, whether beaver pelts or the skins of the Pacific sea otter, had attracted a few U.S. trappers and merchants, but the British-controlled Hudson's Bay Company dominated the region. Protestant missionaries established the first permanent white settlements in the 1830s. Reports of Oregon's fertility that the missionaries sent east sparked the first popular interest in the region, especially among midwestern farmers stuck in the agricultural depression that followed the Panic of 1837.

The first large party of overlanders on the Oregon Trail left Independence, Missouri, for the Willamette Valley in 1842. Independence and St. Joseph in Missouri and, by the 1850s, Council Bluffs in Iowa were the jumping-off points for the Oregon Trail. (See Map 13–2.) Most overlanders were young farm families from the Midwest, who had moved

●●●◗**Read** the **Document**

at **www.myhistorylab.com**
*Elizabeth Dixon Smith Geer, Oregon Trail Journal (1847, 1848)*

**WHERE TO LEARN MORE**

★ Scotts Bluff National Monument, Gering, Nebraska
http://www.nps.gov/scbl/index.htm

**MAP 13–2  Western Overland Trails**  The great overland trails to the West began at the Missouri River. The Oregon Trail crossed South Pass in Wyoming and then branched off to Oregon, California, or Utah. The Santa Fe Trail carried American goods and traders to the Mexican Southwest.

**What role** did geography play in determining overland trails?

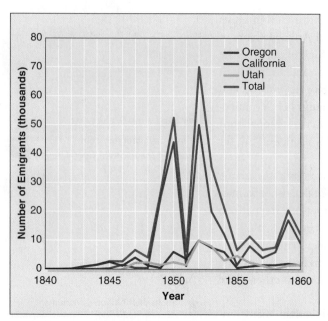

**FIGURE 13–1    Overland Emigration to the West, 1840–1860**
Immigration to the trans-Mississippi West steadily increased in the 1840s as farm families moved to Oregon or Utah. After the discovery of gold in California in 1849, California attracted the bulk of the emigrants, many of whom were single men hopeful of striking it rich.

*Data Source:* John D. Unruh, Jr., *The Plains Across: The Overland Emigrants and the Trans-Mississippi West, 1840–60* (1982), pp. 84–85.

●●●—**Read the Document**

at **www.myhistorylab.com**
*The Treaty of Fort Laramie (1851)*

**QUICK REVIEW**

**The Oregon Trail**

♦ First large party of overlanders left Missouri in 1842.

♦ Most overlanders were young farm families.

♦ In the 1840s, five thousand of the ninety thousand people who attempted the trip died.

at least once before in their restless search for the perfect farm that would keep them out of debt. (See Figure 13–1.)

The journey was long and dangerous. In the 1840s, some 5,000 of the 90,000 men, women, and children who set out on the Oregon Trail died along the way. But although the overlanders were terrified of encountering Indians, who they assumed would be hostile, few died from Indian attacks. As long as the wagon trains were just passing through, the Plains Indians left the white people alone. At first they watched with bemused curiosity, and then, as the white migrants kept coming, they traded game for clothing and ammunition. Indians killed only 115 migrants in the 1840s, and trigger-happy white migrants provoked most of the clashes. Disease, especially cholera, was the great killer. Second to disease were accidents, especially drownings that resulted when drivers tried to force overloaded wagons across swollen rivers.

Cooperation between families was the key to a successful overland crossing. The men in a party often drew up a formal, written constitution at the start of a trip spelling out the assignments and work responsibilities of each wagon. Before the trail was well marked, former mountain men hired on as captains to lead wagon trains. Timing was crucial. A wagon train had to leave late enough in the spring to get good grass in Nebraska for the oxen and mules. Too early a departure, and the wagon train risked getting bogged down in spring mud; too late, and it risked being trapped in the snows of the Pacific coastal ranges.

Before "Oregon fever" had run its course, the flow of white settlers across the continent radically changed the economy and ecology of the Great Plains. Pressure mounted on plants and animals, reducing the land's ability to support all the tribes accustomed to living off it. Intertribal warfare intensified as the supply of buffalo and other game dwindled. Far from being separated from white people by a permanent line of division, the Plains Indians now stood astride the main path of white migration to the Pacific.

In response, officials in the Bureau of Indian Affairs organized a great gathering of the tribes in 1851. At this conference they pushed through the Fort Laramie Treaty, the first U.S. government attempt to draw boundaries within which to contain the Plains Indians. In exchange for accepting limitations on their movements and for the loss of game, the tribes were to receive annual compensation of $50,000 a year for fifty years (later reduced by the U.S. Senate to ten years).

Most of the Indians at the Fort Laramie conference were Sioux and their allies. The Sioux viewed the treaty as confirming their dominance on the Great Plains. When U.S. negotiators tried to restrict Sioux hunting to north of the Platte, the Sioux demanded and received treaty rights to lands south of the Platte as well.

The Fort Laramie Treaty represented a standoff between the Sioux and the U.S. government, the two great powers on the Plains. If neither yielded its claim to the region, war between them would be inevitable.

**WHAT FORCES**
contributed to the Americanization of Texas?

# THE MEXICAN BORDERLANDS

By the mid-1840s, parties of emigrant Americans were beginning to branch off the main Oregon Trail on their way to Utah and California, which were then part of Mexico's northern borderlands (see Map 13–2). Mostly a semiarid and thinly populated land of high plateaus, dry basins, and desert bisected north to south by mountain ranges, the borderlands had been part of the Spanish Empire in North America. Mexico inherited this territory when it won independence from Spain in 1821. Mexico's hold on the region was always weak. It lost Texas in 1837, and, in the next decade, the U.S. penetration of Utah and California set the stage for the U.S. seizure of most of the rest in the Mexican War.

## THE PEOPLES OF THE SOUTHWEST

Diverse peoples lived in the Southwest. Imperial Spain had divided them into four main groupings: Indians, full-blooded Native Americans who retained their own languages and customs; *mestizos*, people of racially mixed ancestry, usually Spanish and Indian; *criollos*, U.S.-born whites of Spanish ancestry; and Spaniards. By far the smallest group was the Spaniards. Compared to the English, few Spaniards emigrated to the New World, and most who did were men. Consequently, Spanish males married or lived with native women, creating a large class of *mestizos*. Despite their small numbers, the Spanish, along with the *criollos*, monopolized economic and political power. This wealthy elite controlled the labor of the *mestizos* in the predominantly ranching economy of the borderlands.

The largest single group in the borderlands were the Indians, about half the population in the 1820s. Most had not come under direct Spanish or Mexican control. Those who had were part of the mission system. This instrument of Spanish imperial policy forced Indians to live in a fixed area, convert to Catholicism, and work as agricultural laborers.

Spanish missions, most of them established by the Franciscan order, aimed both to Christianize and "civilize" the Indians, making them loyal imperial subjects. Mission Indians were forced to abandon their native economies and culture and settle in agricultural communities under the tight supervision of the friars (see Chapter 1). Spanish soldiers and royal officials, who lived in military garrisons known as *presidios*, accompanied the friars.

The largest concentration of Indians, some 300,000 when the Spanish friars arrived in the 1760s, was in California. Most of these, the Paiutes, Chumashes, Pomos, Shastas, and a host of smaller tribes, occupied their own distinct ecological zones where they gathered and processed what the rivers, forests, and grasslands provided. Fish and game were abundant, and wild plants and nuts, especially acorns, provided grain and flour.

The major farming Indians east of California were the Pueblo peoples of Arizona and New Mexico. Named after the adobe or stone communal dwellings in which they lived atop mesas or on terraces carved into cliffs, the Pueblo Indians were a peaceful people closely bound to small, tightly knit communities. (*Pueblo* is Spanish for "village.") Indeed, some of their dwellings, such as those of the Hopis in Arizona or the Acomas in New Mexico, have been continuously occupied for more than 500 years. Corn and beans were the staples of their irrigation-based agriculture. Formally a part of the Spanish mission system, they had incorporated the Catholic God and Catholic rituals into their own polytheistic religion, which stressed the harmony of all living things with the forces of nature. They continued to worship in their underground sanctuaries known as *kivas*.

Once the Pueblos made their peace with the Spaniards after their great revolt in 1680 (see Chapter 3), their major enemies were the nomadic tribes that lived by hunting and raiding. These tribes outnumbered the Pueblos four to one and controlled most of the Southwest until the 1850s. The horse, which many of the tribes acquired during Spain's temporary retreat from the region during the late seventeenth century in the wake of the Pueblo Revolt, was the basis of their way of life. As the horse frontier spread, the peoples of the southern Plains gained enormous mobility and the means of ranging far and wide for the economic resources that sustained their transformation into societies of mounted warriors.

West of the pueblos around Taos was the land of the Navajos, who herded sheep, raised some crops, and raided other tribes from their

This painting by Alfred James Miller depicts the busy interior of Fort Laramie in 1837.

Alfred Jacob Miller, "The Interior of Fort Laramie," 1858–60. The Walters Art Museum, Baltimore.

The paintings by George Catlin are among the best visual sources for understanding the material culture of the Plains Indians. Shown here in a c. 1837 painting are the circular lodges of a Mandan village.

Smithsonian American Art Museum, Washington, DC/Art Resource, NY

**WHERE TO LEARN MORE**

★ Indian Pueblo Cultural Center, Albuquerque, New Mexico
http://www.indianpueblo.org/

**QUICK REVIEW**

**Peoples of the Southwest**

◆ Indians.

◆ Spanish.

◆ Mestizos: those of racially mixed ancestry.

◆ Criollos: American-born whites of Spanish ancestry.

*Tejano*   A person of Spanish or Mexican descent born in Texas.

*empresarios*   Agents who received a land grant from the Spanish or Mexican government in return for organizing settlements.

mountain fastnesses. Spilling over onto Navajo lands, the Southern Utes ranged up and down the canyon lands of Utah. The Gila Apaches were the dominant tribe south of Albuquerque and westward into Arizona. To the east in the Pecos River Valley roamed bands of Mescalero and Jicarillo Apaches. On the broad plains rolling northward from the Texas panhandle and southward into northern Mexico were war parties of Comanches and Kiowas.

The Comanches, a branch of the mountain Shoshonis who moved to the plains when horses became available, were the most feared of the nomadic peoples. Utterly fearless, confident, and masterful horsemen, they gained a reputation of mythic proportions for their prowess as mounted warriors. For food and clothing, they relied on the immense buffalo herds of the southern plains. For guns, horses, and other trading goods, they lived off their predatory raids. When the Santa Fe Trail opened in the early 1820s, their shrewdness as traders gave them a new source of firearms that strengthened their raiding prowess.

The three focal points of white settlement in the northern borderlands of Mexico, Texas, New Mexico, and Alta California (as distinguished from Lower, or Baja, California), were never linked by an effective network of communications or transportation. Each of these settlements was an isolated offshoot of Hispanic culture with a semiautonomous economy based on ranching and a mostly illegal trade with French, British, and U.S. merchants that brought in a trickle of needed goods.

Neither Spain, which tried to seal off its northern outposts from economic contact with foreigners, nor Mexico, which opened up the borderlands to outsiders, had integrated this vast region into a unified economic or political whole. Indeed, Mexico's most pressing problem in the 1820s was protecting its northern states from the Comanches. To serve as a buffer against the Comanches, the Mexican government in 1821 invited Americans into Texas, opening the way to the eventual U.S. takeover of the territory.

## THE AMERICANIZATION OF TEXAS

The Mexicans faced the same problems governing Texas that the Spanish had. Mexico City was about a thousand miles from San Antonio, the center of Hispanic settlement in Texas, and communications were slow and cumbersome. The ranching elite of *Tejanos* (Spanish-speaking Mexicans born in Texas) had closer economic ties to American Louisiana than they did to Coahuila, the Mexican state to which Texas was formally attached. The low agricultural productivity, combined with the low birthrate among mission Indians, outbreaks of disease, and the generally hostile frontier environment, sharply restricted population growth. Only some 5,000 Mexicans lived in Texas in the 1820s.

Sparsely populated and economically struggling, Mexican Texas shared a border with the United States along the Sabine River in Louisiana and the Red River in the Arkansas Territory (see Map 13–2). The threat that the nearby Americans posed to Mexico's security was obvious to Mexican officials. However, attempts to promote Mexican immigration into Texas failed. Reasoning that the Americans were going to come in any event and anxious to build up the population of Texas against Indian attacks, the Mexican government encouraged Americans to settle in Texas by offering huge grants of land in return for promises to accept Mexican citizenship, convert to Catholicism, and obey the authorities in Mexico City.

The first American *empresario,* the recipient of a large grant in return for a promise to bring in settlers, was Stephen F. Austin. After having the grant confirmed by the new Mexican government in 1821, Stephen Austin founded the first American colony in Texas. The Austin grant encompassed 18,000 square miles. Other grants were smaller but still lavish. The *empresarios* stood to grow wealthy by leasing out land, selling parcels to settlers, and organizing the rest into large-scale farms that produced cotton with slave labor in the bottomlands of the Sabine, Colorado, and Brazos rivers. As early as 1830, eastern and south-central Texas was becoming an extension of the plantation economy of the Gulf coastal plain. More than 25,000 white settlers, with around 1,000 slaves, had poured into the region (see American Views, A Mexican View of the Texans in 1828).

More Americans moved into Texas with slaves than the Mexicans had anticipated. Many settlers simply ignored Mexican laws, especially the Emancipation Proclamation of 1829, which forbade slavery in the Republic of Mexico. In 1830, the Mexican government attempted to assert its authority. It levied the first taxes on the Americans, prohibited the further importation of slaves, and closed the international border to additional immigration. Still, another 10,000 Americans spilled across the border in the early 1830s, and they continued to bring in slaves.

Unlike the *empresarios*, many of whom became Catholic and married into elite *Tejano* families, these newcomers lived apart from Mexicans and rejected Mexican citizenship. Cultural tensions escalated. Believing that they belonged to a superior race of liberty-loving white Anglo-Saxons, most of these new arrivals sneered at the Mexicans as a mongrelized race of black people, Indians, and Spaniards and resented having to submit to their rule. A clash became inevitable in 1835 when General Santa Anna, elected president of Mexico in 1833, overturned the liberal Mexican constitution of 1824. He established himself as a dictator in 1834, and his centralist rule ended any hope of the Americans *empresarios* and their *Tejano* allies that Texas might become an autonomous state within a federated Mexico. Skirmishing between Mexican troops and rebellious Texans began in the fall of 1835.

At first, the Anglo-*Tejano* leadership sought to overthrow Santa Anna, restore the constitution of 1824, and win separate statehood for Texas within a liberal Mexican republic. Santa Anna, however, refused to compromise. When he raised a large army to crush the uprising, he radicalized the rebellion and pushed its leaders to declare complete independence on March 2, 1836. Four days later, a Mexican army of 4,000 annihilated the 187 defenders of the **Alamo,** an abandoned mission in San Antonio. A few weeks later at Goliad, another 300 Texans were killed after they had agreed to surrender (see Map 13–3).

"Remember the Alamo!" and "Remember Goliad!" were powerful rallying cries for the beleaguered Texans. Volunteers from the U.S. South rushed to the aid of the main Texan army, commanded by Sam Houston. Houston's victory in April 1836 at the Battle of San Jacinto established the independence of Texas. Captured while trying to flee, Santa Anna signed a treaty in May 1836, recognizing Texas as an independent republic with a boundary on the south and west at the Rio Grande. However, the Nueces River to the north of the Rio Grande had been the administrative border of Texas under Mexican rule. The Mexican Congress rejected the treaty, and the boundary remained in dispute.

Soon forgotten during the ensuing eight years of Texas independence was the support that many *Tejanos* had given to the successful revolt against Mexican rule. In part because Mexico refused to recognize the Texas Republic, Anglos feared *Tejanos* as a subversive element. Pressure mounted on them to leave, especially after Santa Anna launched a major counterattack in 1842, capturing San Antonio. Those who stayed lost much of their land and economic power as Anglos used their knowledge of U.S. law or just plain chicanery to reduce the *Tejanos* to second-class citizens.

**Alamo**   Franciscan mission at San Antonio, Texas, that was the site in 1836 of a siege and massacre of Texans by Mexican troops.

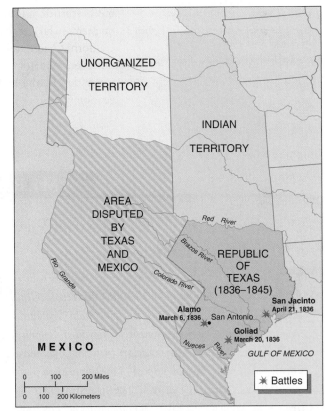

MAP 13–3   **Texas and Mexico after the Texas Revolt**   The Battle of San Jacinto was the decisive American victory that gained the independence of Texas, but the border dispute between Texas and Mexico would not be resolved until the Mexican War a decade later.

**Why might** the Mexican government have thought it so important to establish the border of Texas at the Nueces River? What potential dangers might the government have seen in an expanded Texas?

More difficult to subordinate were the Comanches. While president of Texas, Houston tried to fix a permanent boundary between the Comanches and white settlers, but Texas pride and ongoing white encroachments on Indian land undercut his efforts. By the early 1840s, Texans and Comanches were in a state of nearly permanent war. Only the force of the federal army after the Civil War ended the Comanches' long reign over the high, dry plains of northern and western Texas.

## The Push into California and the Southwest

**California.**    Mexican rule in California was always weak. The Sonoran Desert and the resistance of the Yuman Indians in southeastern California cut off Mexico from any direct land contact with Alta California. Only irregular communications were maintained over a long sea route. For **Californios,** Californians of Spanish descent, Mexico was literally *la otra banda,* "the other shore." In trying to strengthen its hold on this remote and thinly populated region, the Mexican government relied on a program of economic development. As in Texas, however, Mexican policy had unintended consequences.

The centerpiece of the Mexican program was the secularization of the missions, opening up the landholdings of the Catholic Church to private ownership and releasing the mission Indians from paternalistic bondage. Small allotments of land were set aside for the Indians, but most returned to their homelands. Those who remained became a source of cheap labor for the *rancheros* who carved up the mission lands into huge cattle ranches. Thus, by the 1830s, California had entered what is called the *rancho* era. The main beneficiaries of this process, however, were not the Mexican authorities who had initiated it but the American traders who responded to the economic opportunities presented by the privatization of the California economy.

*Californios*    Persons of Spanish descent living in California.

**QUICK REVIEW**

**Mexican Rule in California**

◆ Mexican rule in California weak.

◆ Government initiated program of economic development to help strengthen its control over region.

◆ Centerpiece of program: secularization of missions.

## AMERICAN VIEWS

### Mexican Views of the U.S. Expansion

#### A Mexican View of the Texans, 1828

By the late 1820s, Mexico was reassessing its policy of encouraging American immigration to Texas. Concerned over the large numbers and uncertain loyalties of the American settlers, the government appointed a commission in 1827 ostensibly to survey the boundary between Louisiana and the province of Texas. The real purpose of the commission was to recommend policy changes that would strengthen Mexico's hold on Texas. The following excerpt is from a journal kept by José María Sánchez, the draftsman of the boundary commission.

- **Why** was the Mexican government so ineffective in maintaining control over Texas?
- **What** was the appeal of Texas for Americans? How did most of them enter Texas and take up land?

- **Why** did Sánchez have such a low opinion of the Americans in the Austin colony? What did he think of Stephen Austin?
- **Why** did the Mexicans fear that they would lose Texas?

The Americans from the north have taken possession of practically all the eastern part of Texas, in most cases without the permission of the authorities. They immigrate constantly, finding no one to prevent them, and take possession of the *sitio* [location] that best suits them without either asking leave or going through any formality other than that of building their homes. Thus the majority of inhabitants in the Department are North Americans, the Mexican population being reduced to only Bejar, Nacogdoches, and La Bahía del Espíritu Santo, wretched settlements that between them do not number three thousand inhabitants, and the new village of Guadalupe Victoria that has scarcely more than seventy settlers. The government of the state, with its seat at Saltillo, that should watch over the preservation of its most precious and interesting department, taking measures to prevent its being stolen by foreign hands, is the one that knows the least not only about actual conditions, but even about its territory. . . . Repeated and urgent appeals have been made to the Supreme Government of the Federation regarding the imminent danger in which this interesting Department is of becoming the prize of the ambitious North Americans, but never has it taken any measures that may be called conclusive. . . .

[Sánchez goes on to describe the village of Austin and the American colony founded by Stephen Austin.]

Its population is nearly two hundred persons, of which only ten are Mexicans, for the balance are all Americans from the North with an occasional European. Two wretched little stores supply the inhabitants of the colony: one sells only whiskey, rum, sugar, and coffee; the other, rice, flour, lard, and cheap cloth. . . . The Americans from the North, at least the great part of those I have seen, eat only salted meat, bread made by themselves out of corn meal, coffee, and home-made cheese. To these the greater part of those who live in the village add strong liquor, for they are in general, in my opinion, lazy people of vicious character. Some of them cultivate their small farms by planting corn; but this task they usually entrust to their negro slaves, whom they treat with considerable harshness. Beyond the village in an immense stretch of land formed by rolling hills are scattered the families brought by Stephen Austin, which today number more than two thousand persons. The diplomatic policy of this empresario, evident in all his actions, has, as one may say, lulled the authorities into a sense of security, while he works diligently for his own ends. In my judgment, the spark that will start the conflagration that will deprive us of Texas, will start from this colony. All because the government does not take vigorous measures to prevent it. Perhaps it does not realize the value of what it is about to lose.

*Source:* José María Sánchez, excerpted from "A Trip to Texas in 1828," trans. Carlos E. Castaneda from *Southwestern Historical Quarterly,* vol. 29 Copyright 1926. Reprinted courtesy of Texas State Historical Association, Austin, Texas. All rights reserved.

## A Mexican Rebel in 1859

*The U.S. victory in the Mexican War intensified cultural conflict along the now expanded Hispanic frontier. The Anglos (as Mexicans called white Americans) quickly assumed positions of political and economic dominance. They broke treaties designed to protect the property rights and land titles of Mexican Americans and under the cover of legality bullied peoples of Mexican descent. The resulting anger and resentment flared up in a brief revolt in 1859 in the lower Rio Grande valley led by Juan Cortina, a ranch owner who had fought for Mexico in the Mexican War. The following is from one of the proclamations issued by Cortina.*

- **What** was Cortina's opinion of the Anglos?
- **What** reasons did he cite for the uprising?
- **How** did he attempt to rally support for his cause?

Mexicans! When the State of Texas [became] an integrant part of the Union, flocks of vampires, in the guise of men, came and scattered themselves in the settlements, without any capital except the corrupt heart and the most perverse intentions. Some, brimful of laws, pledged to us their protection against the attacks of the rest; others assembled in shadowy councils, attempted and excited the robbery and burning of our relatives on the other side of the river Bravo; while others, to the abusing of our unlimited confidence, when we entrusted them with our titles [to land], which secured the future of our families, refused to return them under false and frivolous pretexts. . . . Many of you have been robbed of your property, incarcerated, chased, murdered, and hunted like wild beasts, because your labor was fruitful, and because your industry excited the vile avarice which led them.

Mexicans! Is there no remedy for you? . . . Mexicans! My part is taken; the voice of revelation whispers to me that to me is entrusted the work of breaking the chains of your slavery, and that the Lord will enable me, with powerful arm, to fight against our enemies, in compliance with the requirements of that Sovereign Majesty [God], who, from this day forward, will hold us under His protection. On my part, I am ready to offer myself as a sacrifice for your happiness; and counting upon the means necessary for the discharge of my ministry, you may count upon my cooperation, should no cowardly attempt put an end to my days.

*Source:* House Executive Documents, No. 52, 36th Congress, 1st session, 1860, pp. 80–82.

New England merchants had been trading in California since the 1780s. What first attracted them were the seal fisheries off the California coast, a source of otter pelts highly prized in the China trade. After the seals had been all but exterminated by the 1820s, Yankee merchants shipped out hides and tallow to New England for processing into shoes and candles. Ships from New England and New York sailed around Cape Horn to California ports, where they unloaded trading goods. Servicing this trade in California was a resident colony of American agents, some 300 strong by the mid-1840s.

Whereas Yankees dominated the American colonies in coastal California, it was mostly midwestern farm families who filtered into the inner valleys of California from the Oregon Trail in the 1830s and 1840s (see Map 13–2). Nearly a thousand Americans lived in the Sacramento River Valley by 1846.

California belonged to Mexico in name only by the early 1840s. The program of economic development had strengthened California's ties to the outside world at the expense of Mexico. American merchants and California *rancheros* ran the economy, and both groups had joined separatist movements against Mexican rule. Unlike the *Californios*, who were ambivalent about their future political allegiance, the Americans wanted to be part of the United States and assumed that California would shortly be annexed. With the outbreak of the Mexican War in 1846, their wish became reality.

**New Mexico.**   Except for Utah, the American push into the interior of the Mexican Southwest followed the California pattern of trade preceding settlement. When Mexico liberalized the formerly restrictive trading policies of Spain, American merchants opened up the 900-mile-long **Santa Fe Trail** from Independence, Missouri, to Santa Fe, New Mexico. Starved for mercantile goods, the New Mexicans were a small but highly profitable market. They paid for their American imports with gold, silver, and furs.

Bent's Old Fort, an impregnable adobe structure built on the Arkansas River at the point where the Santa Fe Trail turned to the southwest, was the fulcrum for the growing economic influence of Americans over New Mexican affairs. Completed in 1832, the fort enabled the Bent brothers from Missouri to control a flourishing and almost monopolistic trade with Indians, trappers, caravans on the Santa Fe Trail, and the large landowners and merchants of New Mexico. This trade pulled New Mexico into the cultural and economic orbit of the United States and undermined what little sovereign power Mexico held in the region.

Although only a few hundred Americans were permanent residents of New Mexico in the 1840s, they had married into the Spanish-speaking landholding elite and were themselves beginning to receive large grants of land. Ties of blood and common economic interests linked this small group of American businessmen with the local elite. American merchants and New Mexican landlords were further united by their growing disdain for the instability of Mexican rule, Santa Anna's dictatorship, and sporadic attempts by Mexico to levy heavy taxes on the Santa Fe trade. Another bond was their concern over the aggressive efforts of the Texans to seize eastern New Mexico. After thwarting an 1841 Texan attempt to occupy Santa Fe, the leaders of New Mexico increasingly looked to the United States to protect their local autonomy. They quickly decided to cooperate with the U.S. army of invasion when the Mexican War got under way.

**Utah.**   At the extreme northern and inner reaches of the Mexican borderlands lay Utah. Aside from trade with the Utes, Spain and Mexico had largely ignored this remote region. Its isolation and lack of white settlers, however, were precisely what made Utah so appealing to the Mormons, the Church of Jesus Christ of Latter-day Saints. For the Mormons in the 1840s, Utah became the promised land in which to build a new Zion.

Founded by Joseph Smith in upstate New York in the 1820s, Mormonism grew rapidly within a communitarian framework that stressed hard work and economic cooperation under the leadership of patriarchal leaders (see Chapter 12). The economic success of close-knit Mormon

**WHERE TO LEARN MORE**

Fort Union National Monument, Watrous, New Mexico
http://www.nps.gov/foun/index.htm

**Santa Fe Trail**   The 900-mile trail opened by American merchants for trading purposes following Mexico's liberalization of the formerly restrictive trading policies of Spain.

communities, combined with the righteous zeal of their members, aroused the fears and hostility of non-Mormons. Harassed out of New York, Ohio, and Missouri, the Mormons thought they had found a permanent home by the late 1830s in Nauvoo, Illinois. But the murder of Joseph Smith and his brother by a mob in 1844 convinced the beleaguered Mormons that they had to leave the settled East for a refuge in the West. In 1846 a group of Mormons migrated to the Great Basin in Utah. Under the leadership of Brigham Young, they established a new community in 1847 at the Great Salt Lake on the western slopes of the Wasatch Mountains. An annual influx of about 2,000 converts enabled the initial settlement to grow rapidly.

The Mormons succeeded by concentrating their farms along the fertile and relatively well-watered Wasatch Front. They dispensed land and organized an irrigation system that coordinated water rights with the amount of land under production. To their dismay, however, they learned in 1848 that they had not left the United States after all. The Union acquired Utah, along with the rest of the northern borderlands of Mexico, as a result of the Mexican War.

# POLITICS, EXPANSION, AND WAR

The Democrats viewed their victory in the election of 1844 (see Chapter 10) as a popular mandate for expansion. James K. Polk, the new Democratic president, fully shared this expansionist vision. The greatest prize in his eyes was California. When he was stymied in his efforts to purchase California and New Mexico, he tried to force concessions from the Mexican government by ordering American troops to the mouth of the Rio Grande, far within the territory claimed by Mexico. When the virtually inevitable clash of arms occurred in late April 1846, war broke out between the United States and Mexico.

**WHY WAS** James K. Polk so eager to provoke a war with Mexico?

Victory resulted in the **Mexican Cession of 1848,** which added a half-million square miles to the United States. Polk's administration also finalized the acquisition of Texas and reached a compromise with the British on the Oregon Territory that recognized U.S. sovereignty in the Pacific Northwest up to the 49th parallel. The United States was now a nation that spanned a continent.

**Mexican Cession of 1848**   The addition of half a million square miles to the United States as a result of victory in the 1846 war between the United States and Mexico.

## MANIFEST DESTINY

With a phrase that soon entered the nation's vocabulary, John L. O'Sullivan, editor and Democratic politician, proclaimed in 1845 America's "manifest destiny to overspread and to possess the whole of the continent which Providence has given us for the development of the great experiment of Liberty and federated self-government entrusted to us." Central to **Manifest Destiny** was the assumption that white Americans were a special people, a view that dated back to the Puritans' belief that God had appointed them to establish a New Israel cleansed of the corruption of the Old World.

**Manifest Destiny**   Doctrine, first expressed in 1845, that the expansion of white Americans across the continent was inevitable and ordained by God.

What distinguished the special U.S. mission as enunciated by Manifest Destiny was its explicitly racial component. Between 1815 and 1850, the term Anglo-Saxon, originally loosely applied to English-speaking peoples, acquired racial overtones. Caucasian Anglo-Saxon Americans, as the descendants of ancient Germanic tribes that had purportedly brought the seeds of free institutions to England, were now said to be the foremost race in the world. The superior racial pedigree they claimed for themselves gave white Americans the natural right to expand westward, a chosen people carrying the blessings of democracy and progress. Only they, it was argued, had the energy, industriousness, and innate love of liberty to establish a successful free government.

●●●─[Read the **Document**

at **www.myhistorylab.com**
*From Then to Now Online:
Manifest Destiny and American
Foreign Policy*

Manifest Destiny was closely associated with the Democratic Party. For Democrats, expansionism would counterbalance the debilitating effects of industrialization and urbanization. As good Jeffersonians, they stressed the need for more land to realize the ideal of a democratic republic rooted in the virtues and rough equality of independent farmers. For their working-class

## GLOBAL CONNECTIONS

### THE NINETEENTH-CENTURY FRONTIER

"*If I was to till you of our own township how it is growing as if it were by m[a]gic and also our market town Castlemaine you would not feel much interest in them. But realy they astonish me. As to our digging there is little new but likely I will send you a newspaper which will give you all the information of these Things. . . . Our great railroad is now all the talk but is not begun yet. . . . There is a great many goldmining compenys starting up about this place I believe five or six some of them so large as 2000 shares. It is causing work to get more plenty for those who is willing to work for wages and if our great railway was started I think there need not be many idle. But I think that wages will never be high again as there is still a goodly number waiting in hops of the same perhaps more Than will work when they get the chance.*"

In this letter, with words and details that we might expect from an American prospecting for gold in California, John McCance, an Irish emigrant to Australia, wrote back home describing the conditions he faced in the goldfields in the province of Victoria. Settling a frontier, and displacing and subjugating native peoples in the process, was not a unique American experience in the nineteenth century. It was part of a worldwide process replicated by migrants, especially of European origin, in such areas as Latin America, Canada, South Africa, Australia, and New Zealand. Population growth on a global scale, combined with improved and cheap forms of international travel, fed a stream of migrants into the frontier regions of the Southern Hemisphere and the North American West. In a radical environmental adaptation that made possible a tremendous increase in global supplies of food, vast, open expanses of grasslands, increasingly accessible by railroads, were transformed for the commercial production of grain and livestock. As newcomers poured in, indigenous foraging and pastoral peoples were wiped out, displaced, herded onto reservations, or forced to fundamentally change their ways of living, the victims of disease and superior military force and technology. The advance of global frontiers and the growing dominance of European-based societies went hand-in-hand in the nineteenth century.

- How would you define a frontier?
- To what extent would you argue that the U.S. frontier experience has been unique?

Irish constituency, the Democrats touted the broad expanses of the West as the surest means to escape the misery of wage slavery.

Manifest Destiny captured the popular imagination when the country was still mired in depression after the Panic of 1837. The way out of the depression, according to many Democrats, was to revive the export trade to soak up the agricultural surplus.

In this late-1872 evocation of the spirit of Manifest Destiny, Indians retreat westward as white settlers, guided by a diaphanously clad America, spread the benefits of American civilization.

### THE MEXICAN WAR

Once in office, Polk proved far more conciliatory with the British than with the Mexicans. Polk was willing to compromise on Oregon because he dreaded the possibility of a two-front war against both the Mexicans and the British. Mexico had severed diplomatic ties with the United States over the annexation of Texas (see Chapter 10), and a war could break out at any time.

In the spring of 1846, after Polk had abrogated the agreement on the joint occupation of Oregon, the British offered a compromise that they had earlier rejected. They agreed to a boundary at the 49th parallel if they were allowed to retain Vancouver Island in Puget Sound. Polk sent the offer to the Senate, which quickly approved it in June 1846.

Unlike Oregon, where he backed off from extravagant territorial claims, Polk refused to budge on the U.S. claim (inherited from the Texans when the

United States annexed Texas in 1845) that the Rio Grande was the border between Texas and Mexico. The Mexicans insisted that the Nueces River, 100 miles north of the Rio Grande, was the border, as it had been when Texas was part of Mexico.

Citing rumors of a Mexican invasion, Polk sent 3,500 troops under General Zachary Taylor to the Nueces River in the summer of 1845. Polk also stepped up his efforts to acquire California. He instructed Thomas Larkin, the U.S. consul in Monterey, California, to inform the *Californios* and Americans that the United States would support them if they revolted against Mexican rule. Polk also secretly ordered the U.S. Pacific naval squadron to seize California ports if war broke out with Mexico. Polk's final effort at peaceful expansion was the Slidell mission in November 1845. He sent John L. Slidell to Mexico City to offer $30 million to purchase California and New Mexico and to secure the Rio Grande boundary.

When Polk learned that the Mexican government had refused to receive Slidell, he set out to draw Mexico into a war that would result in the U.S. acquisition of California. In early 1846, he ordered General Taylor to advance to the Rio Grande, deep in the disputed border region. Taylor blockaded the mouth of the Rio Grande and built a fort on the northern bank across from the Mexican town of Matamoros. The Mexicans attacked and were repulsed on April 24.

Even before the news reached Washington, Polk had decided on war. Informed of the clash between Mexican and American troops in early May (it took ten days for the news to reach Washington), he sent a redrafted war message to Congress on May 9 asserting that Mexico "has invaded our territory, and shed American blood on American soil." Congress declared war on May 13, 1846.

The war was a stunning military success for the United States (see Map 13–4), in large measure because a decade of Comanche raids had so pillaged and demoralized settlements across northern Mexico that the local inhabitants were in no condition to resist any invader. The Mexicans fought bravely, but they lacked the leadership, modern artillery, and naval capacity to check the U.S. advances. By the end of 1846, Polk had gained his objectives in the Mexican borderlands. An army sent west under Colonel Stephen W. Kearny occupied New Mexico. The

THE MEXICAN RULERS,
*migrating from Matamoras with their Treasures.*

This anti-Catholic lithograph sarcastically depicts the "rulers" of Mexico as lecherous Catholic clerics who were quick to desert the Mexican town of Matamor as when U.S. troops arrived in May 1846. The priest and monk ride out of Matamoras accompanied by young women, bottles of wine, and other booty.

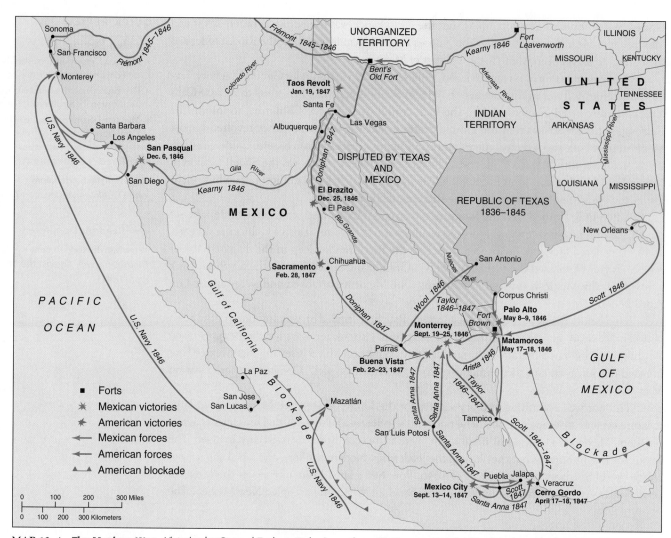

**MAP 13–4    The Mexican War**  Victories by General Zachary Taylor in northern Mexico secured the Rio Grande as the boundary between Texas and Mexico. Colonel Stephen Kearny's expedition won control of New Mexico, and reinforcements from Kearny ensured the success of American troops landed by the Pacific Squadron in gaining Alta California for the United States. The success of General Winfield Scott's amphibious invasion at Vera Cruz and his occupation of Mexico City brought the war to an end.

**Why did** the United States feel the need to employ naval blockades to the east and west of Mexico?

See the **Map**

at **www.myhistorylab.com**
*Mexican-American War,
1846–1848*

Watch the **Video**

at **www.myhistorylab.com**
*The Annexation of Texas*

conquest was relatively bloodless, because most of the local elite cooperated with the U.S. forces. Sporadic resistance was largely confined to poorer Mexicans and the Pueblo Indians, who feared that their land would be confiscated.

Kearny's army then moved to Tucson and eventually linked up in southern California with pro-American rebels and U.S. forces sent ashore by the Pacific squadron. As in New Mexico, the stiffest resistance came from ordinary Mexicans and the Spanish-speaking Indians.

Despite the loss of its northern provinces, Mexico refused to concede defeat. After Taylor had established a secure defensive line in northeastern Mexico with a victory at Monterrey in September 1846 and repulsed a Mexican counterattack at Buena Vista in February 1847, Polk directed General Winfield Scott to invade central Mexico. Following an amphibious assault on Vera Cruz in March 1847, Scott captured Mexico City in September.

After a frustrating delay while Mexico reorganized its government, peace talks finally got under way and concluded in the Treaty of Guadalupe Hidalgo, signed on February 2, 1848. Mexico surrendered its claim to Texas north of the Rio Grande and ceded Alta California and

New Mexico (including present-day Arizona, Utah, and Nevada). The United States paid $15 million, assumed over $3 million in claims of American citizens against Mexico, and agreed to grant U.S. citizenship to Mexican residents in its new territories.

Polk had gained his strategic goals, but the cost was 13,000 American lives (most from diseases such as measles and dysentery), 50,000 Mexican lives, and the poisoning of Mexican-American relations for generations. The war also, as will be seen in Chapter 14, heightened sectional tensions over slavery and weakened the political structure that was vital to preserving the Union.

# CONCLUSION

Americans were an expansionist people. Their surge across the continent between 1815 and 1850 was fully in keeping with their restless desire for personal independence on a plot of land. Population pressure on overworked farms in the East impelled much of this westward migration, but by the 1840s, expansion had seemingly acquired a momentum all its own, one that increasingly rejected the claims of other peoples to the land. Far from being a process of peaceful, evolutionary, and democratic change, expansion involved the spread of slavery, violent confrontations, and the uprooting and displacement of native peoples. As Catlin sensed in the 1830s, the coming of white settlement quickly had a devastating impact on the native peoples he visited and befriended. By 1850, the earlier notion of reserving the trans-Mississippi West as a permanent Indian country had been abandoned. The Sioux and Comanches were still feared by white settlers, but their final subjugation was not far off. The derogatory stereotypes of Mexican Americans that were a staple of both popular thought and expansionist ideology showed clearly that U.S. control after the Mexican War would relegate Spanish-speaking people to second-class status. However misleading and false much of it was, the rhetoric of Manifest Destiny did highlight a central truth. Broad, popular support existed for expanding across the continent. As the Mexican War made clear, the United States was now unquestionably the dominant power in North America. The only serious threat to its dominance in the near future would come from inside, not outside, its domain.

**QUICK REVIEW**

**War with Mexico**

- Polk sought a war that would give the United States control of California.
- Mexico fought bravely but could not match American military.
- Treaty of Guadalupe Hidalgo (1848): Mexico gave up claim to Texas north of Rio Grande, Alta California, and New Mexico.

# WHERE TO LEARN MORE

**Indian Pueblo Cultural Center, Albuquerque, New Mexico.** This center provides an excellent orientation to the culture, crafts, and community life of the Pueblo and southwestern Indians. It also includes much material on archaeological findings. Visit http://www.indianpueblo.org for a calendar of events and an introduction to the history of the nineteen pueblos.

**Indian Museum of North America, Crazy Horse, South Dakota.** This is one of the best sources for learning about the culture of the Teton Sioux and other American and Canadian tribes on the Great Plains. Holdings include outstanding examples of Indian art and artifacts. For information on exhibits, educational and cultural programs, and special collections of Native American art, go to http://www.crazyhorsememorial.org/monument/.

**Scotts Bluff National Monument, Gering, Nebraska.** Scotts Bluff was a prominent landmark on the Oregon Trail, and the museum exhibits here have interpretive material on the trail and the western phase of expansion. Go to http://www.nps.gov/scbl/index.htm to print a park travel guide and to access a website devoted to the frontier photographer and artist William Henry Jackson.

**Conner Prairie, Noblesville, Indiana.** The museum and historic area re-create a sense of life on the Indiana frontier during the period of the Old Northwest. See http://www.connerprairie.org.

**Fort Union National Monument, Watrous, New Mexico.** Fort Union was a nineteenth-century military post, and the holdings and exhibits in the museum relate to frontier military life and the Santa Fe Trail. For a printable travel guide and a history of the park that includes bibliographical aids, go to http://www.nps.gov/foun/index.htm.

# REVIEW QUESTIONS

1. What accounted for the westward movement of Americans? How did the presence or absence of slavery affect developmental patterns in the new settlements?

2. How was the West of the Plains Indians transformed after 1830 as peoples migrated both within the region and into it from various directions? Why were the Sioux so powerful? How did they interact with other Native Americans and the U.S. government?

3. Who lived in the Mexican borderlands of the Southwest? Why was it so difficult for the Mexican government to maintain effective control of the region? What role did trade play in the American penetration of the Southwest?

4. What did Americans mean by Manifest Destiny? Why was territorial expansion so identified with the Democratic Party?

5. Who was responsible for the outbreak of the Mexican War? Were Mexicans the victims of American aggression? Why did the British make no effort to intervene?

6. How valid was the Sioux chief's indictment of the pretensions of white civilization as related to George Catlin?

# KEY TERMS

**Alamo** (p. 351)
*Californios* (p. 352)
**Claims clubs** (p. 342)
*Empresarios* (p. 350)
**Manifest Destiny** (p. 355)

**Mexican Cession of 1848** (p. 355)
**Oregon Trail** (p. 345)
**Santa Fe Trail** (p. 354)
*Tejano* (p. 350)

# PEARSON myhistorylab™ Connections

Reinforce what you learned in this chapter by studying the many documents, images, maps, review tools, and videos available at **www.myhistorylab.com**.

## Read and Review

✓●─ **Study** and **Review** Study Plan: Chapter 13

●●●─ **Read** the **Document**

Chief Seattle, Oration (1854)

Polk's 1st Inaugural Address (1845)

Elizabeth Dixon Smith Geer, Oregon Trail Journal (1847, 1848)

John O'Sullivan, Annexation (1845)

Lydia Allen Rudd, Diary of Westward Journey (1852)

The Treaty of Fort Laramie (1851)

Thomas Corwin, Against the Mexican War (1847)

William Barret Travis, Letter from the Alamo (1836)

### History Bookshelf

James Fenimore Cooper, The Pioneers (1823)

Francis Parkman, The Oregon Trail: Sketches of Prairie and Rocky-Mountain Life (1847)

👁─ **See** the **Map**

Mexican-American War, 1846–1848

Native American Land Cessions, 1840

## Research and Explore

●●●─ **Read** the **Document**

Personal Journeys Online

From Then to Now Online: Manifest Destiny and American Foreign Policy

Exploring America: America and the Horse

📻─ **Watch** the **Video** The Annexation of Texas

───── ((●●─ **Hear** the **Audio** ─────

Hear the audio files for Chapter 13 at
**www.myhistorylab.com**.

# 14

# The Politics of Sectionalism

The slave Eliza is attacked by vicious dogs while crossing a frozen river with her baby in this 1881 poster advertising a production of *Uncle Tom's Cabin*.

((•—Hear the **Audio**

Hear the audio files for Chapter 14 at **www.myhistorylab.com**.

### SLAVERY IN THE TERRITORIES  *(page 366)*

**WHY WAS** the issue of slavery in the territories so contentious?

### POLITICAL REALIGNMENT  *(page 372)*

**WHAT FACTORS** contributed to the Republicans' rise to political prominence?

### THE ROAD TO DISUNION  *(page 381)*

**WHY WERE** southerners so alarmed by the election of Abraham Lincoln in 1860?

ONE AMERICAN JOURNEY

*December 16, 1852*

*My Dear Madam,*

*So you want to know what sort of woman I am! Well, if this is any object, you shall have statistics free of charge. To begin, then, I am a little bit of a woman, somewhat more than forty, about as thin and dry as a pinch of snuff, never very much to look at in my best days and looking like a used up article now.*

*I was married when I was twenty-five years old to a man rich in Greek and Hebrew and Latin and Arabic, and alas, rich in nothing else. . . . But then I was abundantly furnished with wealth of another sort. I had two little curly headed twin daughters to begin with and my stock in this line has gradually increased, till I have been the mother of seven children, the most beautiful and the most loved of whom lies buried near my Cincinnati residence. It was at his dying bed and at his grave that I learned what a poor slave mother may feel when her child is torn away from her. In those depths of sorrow which seemed to me immeasurable, it was my only prayer to God that such anguish might not be suffered in vain. There were circumstances about his death of such peculiar bitterness, of what seemed almost cruel suffering that I felt that I could never be consoled for it unless this crushing of my own heart might enable me to work out some great good to others.*

*I allude to this here because I have often felt that much that is in that book had its root in the awful scenes and bitter sorrow of that summer. It has left now, I trust, no trace on my mind except a deep compassion for the sorrowful, especially for mothers who are separated from their children. . . .*

*This horror, this nightmare abomination! Can it be in my country! It lies like lead on my heart, it shadows my life with sorrow; the more so that I feel, as for my own brothers, for the South, and am pained by every horror I am obliged to write, as one who is forced by some awful oath to disclose in court some family disgrace. . . .*

*Yours affectionately,*

*H. B. Stowe*

Harriet Beecher Stowe to Eliza Cabot Follen, December 16, 1852; from Jeanne Boydston, Mary Kelley, and Anne Margolis, *The Limits of Sisterhood* (Chapel Hill: University of North Carolina Press, 1988), pp. 178–180.

**Read the Document** at **www.myhistorylab.com**

Personal Journeys Online

- **Carl Schurz, *Reminiscences*, 1908.** Account of his participation in Germany's failed Revolution of 1848 and his subsequent journey to freedom in the United States.

- **Frederick Douglass, three excerpts: "What of the Night?" May 5, 1848; "A Letter to American Slaves," September 5, 1850; "Letter to James Redpath, June 29, 1860."** These excerpts chart the famous black abolitionist's journey from a belief in moral suasion and political action as the best strategy to liberate the nation's slaves to an embrace of direct action and violence as the only remedy for emancipation.

**HARRIET BEECHER STOWE,** in her letter to the poet and fellow abolitionist Eliza Cabot Follen in the year that *Uncle Tom's Cabin* became an international best seller, revealed how being a wife and a mother had influenced her perception of slavery and inspired her writing. When she was barely out of her teens, her family left their New England home for the raw frontier town of Cincinnati in 1832. Stowe's father, Lyman Beecher, already a famous Protestant evangelical preacher, moved there to save the West from Roman Catholicism. Stowe wrote a geography textbook, married a young scholar from her father's seminary,

## CHRONOLOGY

| | |
|---|---|
| **1846** | Wilmot Proviso is submitted to Congress but is defeated. |
| **1848** | Gold is discovered in California. |
| | Whig Party candidate Zachary Taylor defeats Democrat Lewis Cass and Free-Soiler Martin Van Buren for the presidency. |
| | Revolutions in Europe; publication of Karl Marx and Friedrich Engels's *Communist Manifesto*. |
| **1850** | California applies for statehood. |
| | President Taylor dies; Vice President Millard Fillmore succeeds him. |
| | Compromise of 1850 is passed. |
| **1851** | Harriet Beecher Stowe publishes *Uncle Tom's Cabin*. |
| **1852** | Democrat Franklin Pierce is elected president in a landslide over Whig candidate Winfield Scott. |
| | Whig Party disintegrates. |
| **1853** | National Black Convention convened in Rochester, New York, to demand repeal of the Fugitive Slave Act. |
| | Crimean War erupts between Russia and Turkey over Russian demand to protect Christian shrines in Palestine; soon engulfs Britain and France; eventually leads to the unification of Germany and Italy. |
| **1854** | Ostend Manifesto is issued. |
| | Kansas-Nebraska Act repeals the Missouri Compromise. |
| | Know-Nothing and Republican parties are formed. |
| **1855** | Civil war erupts in "Bleeding Kansas." |
| | William Walker attempts a takeover of Nicaragua. |
| **1856** | "Sack of Lawrence" occurs in Kansas; John Brown makes a retaliatory raid at Pottawatomie Creek. |

| | |
|---|---|
| | Democratic congressman Preston Brooks of South Carolina canes Massachusetts senator Charles Sumner in the U.S. Senate. |
| | Democrat James Buchanan is elected president over Republican John C. Frémont and American (Know-Nothing) candidate Millard Fillmore. |
| **1857** | Supreme Court issues *Dred Scott* decision. |
| | Kansas territorial legislature passes the proslavery Lecompton Constitution. |
| | Panic of 1857 begins. |
| **1858** | Senatorial candidates Abraham Lincoln and Stephen A. Douglas hold series of debates in Illinois. |
| **1859** | John Brown's Raid fails at Harpers Ferry, Virginia. |
| **1860** | Constitutional Union Party forms. |
| | Democratic Party divides into northern and southern factions. |
| | Republican candidate Abraham Lincoln is elected president over southern Democratic candidate John C. Breckinridge, northern Democratic candidate Stephen A. Douglas, and Constitutional Unionist candidate John Bell. |
| | South Carolina secedes from the Union. |
| **1861** | The rest of the Lower South secedes from the Union. |
| | Crittenden Plan and Tyler's Washington peace conference fail. |
| | Jefferson Davis assumes presidency of the Confederate States of America. |
| | Lincoln is inaugurated. |
| | Fort Sumter is bombarded; Civil War begins. |
| | Several Upper South states secede. |
| | Tsar Alexander II of Russia frees the serfs. |

and settled into motherhood. The growing antislavery crusade prompted her to write a few articles on the subject. Not until the death of her beloved son, Charley, in a cholera epidemic in 1849, however, did she make the connection between her own tragedy and the national tragedy of human bondage.

Slavery was an abstract concept to most white northerners at the time. Stowe personalized it in a way that made them see it as an institution that did not just oppress black people but also destroyed families and debased well-meaning Christian masters. The deep piety expressed in the letter permeated the book and changed people's moral perceptions about slavery.

As slavery took on a personal and tragic meaning for Stowe, so it would move from being just another political issue to a moral crusade. Stowe's personal journey transformed it into a political passion; for the millions who read her book, the political became personal. Yet the anguish she expressed in her writing and the outrage it generated among her readers was hardly prefigured when a relatively obscure congressman from Pennsylvania stepped forward in 1846 with a modest proposal that not only placed slavery front and center as a national political issue, a position that only strengthened over the next fifteen years, but would shake the Union to its very core. ◆

Slavery was not, of course, a new political issue. But after 1846, the clashes between northern and southern congressmen over issues relating to slavery became more frequent and more difficult to resolve. In the coming years, several developments, including white southerners' growing consciousness of themselves as a minority, the mixture of political issues with religious questions, and the rise of the Republican Party, would aggravate sectional antagonism. The flash point was the issue of slavery in the territories acquired from Mexico.

# SLAVERY IN THE TERRITORIES

**WHY WAS** the issue of slavery in the territories so contentious?

Whatever its boundaries over the years, the West symbolized the hopes and dreams of white Americans. It was the region of fresh starts, of possibilities. To exclude slavery from the western territories was to exclude white southerners from pursuing their vision of the American dream. Northern politicians disagreed. They argued that exclusion preserved equality, the equality of all white men and women to live and work without competition from slave labor or rule by despotic slaveholders. The issue of slavery in the territories became an issue of freedom for both sides. From the late 1840s until 1861, northern and southern leaders attempted to fashion a solution to the problem of slavery in the territories. Four proposals dominated the debate:

- Outright exclusion
- Extension of the Missouri Compromise line to the Pacific
- Popular sovereignty, allowing the residents of a territory to decide the issue
- Protection of the property of slaveholders (meaning their right to own slaves) even if few lived in the territory

The first major debate on these proposals occurred during the early days of the Mexican War and culminated in the Compromise of 1850.

## THE WILMOT PROVISO

In August 1846, David Wilmot, a Pennsylvania Democrat, offered an amendment to an appropriations bill for the Mexican War. The language of the **Wilmot Proviso** stipulated that "as an express and fundamental condition to the acquisition of any territory from the Republic of Mexico . . . neither slavery nor involuntary servitude shall ever exist in any part of said territory."

Wilmot explained that he wanted only to preserve the territories for "the sons of toil, of my own race and own color." By thus linking the exclusion of slavery in the territories to freedom for white people, he hoped to generate support across the North, regardless of party, and even in some areas of the Upper South. Linking freedom for white people to the exclusion of slaves infuriated southerners. It implied that the mere proximity of slavery was degrading and that white southerners were therefore a degraded people, unfit to join other Americans in the territories.

Northern lawmakers, a majority in the House of Representatives (because the northern states had a larger population than the southern states), passed more than 50 versions of the proviso between 1846 and 1850. In the Senate, however, where each state had equal representation, the proviso was consistently rejected and never became law.

The proviso debate sowed distrust and suspicion between northerners and southerners. Congress had divided along sectional lines before, but seldom had the divisions become so personal.

Religious differences also sharpened the sectional conflict over the proviso. The leading evangelical Protestant denominations—Methodists, Baptists, and Presbyterians—split along sectional lines by the mid-1840s. Growing numbers of northern evangelicals advocated political action. Southern evangelicals recoiled from such mixing of church and state, charging northerners with abandoning the basic tenets of evangelical Christianity: the importance of individual salvation above all, and the Bible as the unerring word of God. The leaders of the Democratic and Whig parties, disturbed that the issue of slavery in the territories could so

**Wilmot Proviso** The amendment offered by Pennsylvania Democrat David Wilmot in 1846 which stipulated that "as an express and fundamental condition to the acquisition of any territory from the Republic of Mexico . . . neither slavery nor involuntary servitude shall ever exist in any part of said territory."

## THE REVOLUTIONS OF 1848

Nᴇw Yorkers greeted the "Magnificent Magyar," Hungarian patriot Louis Kossuth, as a conquering hero in December 1851. Supporters rushed the stage from which he was to deliver a speech, and one female admirer tore off a section of his coat as a prized souvenir. To New Yorkers, Kossuth embodied the democratic ideals of their nation founded on the principles of liberty and equality.

Fueled by rapid industrial and urban transformation, democratic sentiment spread over the European continent among the new working and middle classes in the 1840s. France showed the way. When the government of King Louis-Philippe failed to respond to demands for economic and political reforms, these groups banded together to overthrow the monarchy in February 1848. But the resulting government and new constitution under Charles Louis Napoleon Bonaparte, the nephew of the famous ruler, offered only superficial change, as reformers squandered their advantage with internal bickering between radicals and moderates.

When students at the University of Bonn heard the news of Louis-Philippe's downfall, they rushed into the town square to demand civil and religious liberties and the formation of a German national state. "We were dominated by a vague feeling," one student recalled, "as if a great outbreak of elemental forces had begun, as if an earthquake was impending of which we had felt the first shock." But the authoritarian rulers of the nine German states, while they allowed the formation of an all-German parliament and the drafting of a republican constitution, ignored both and the revolution failed.

A similar scenario played out in the Austrian Empire, a conglomeration of eleven different ethnic peoples, including Kossuth's Hungary. The ruling Hapsburg monarchy initially accepted some of the reformers' demands but then ruthlessly suppressed uprisings in Prague, Vienna, and Buda (Hungary). The Austrians also reestablished their control over portions of Italy, successfully overcoming a movement for Italian unity and reform.

These setbacks troubled Americans. Their initial enthusiasm for the revolutionary movements of 1848 was rooted in the belief that mankind naturally prefers liberty and equality and that the American experiment was exportable to other peoples. President James K. Polk hailed developments in Europe in 1848: "The great principles of popular sovereignty which were proclaimed in 1776 by the immortal author of our Declaration of Independence, seem now to be in the course of rapid development throughout the world."

The failure of these revolutionary movements made the American experiment that much more precious, and it also highlighted some contradictions in American democratic life. Frederick Douglass wondered how Americans could lionize a Hungarian freedom fighter, but hunt down Americans with the same aspirations. Events of the 1850s would sorely test that experiment.

- How did Americans come to view their own ideals in the aftermath of the revolutions of 1848 in Europe?

---

monopolize Congress and poison sectional relations, sought to defuse the issue as the presidential election of 1848 approached.

## THE ELECTION OF 1848

Both Democrats and Whigs wanted to avoid identification with either side of the Wilmot Proviso controversy, and they selected their 1848 presidential candidates accordingly. The Democrats nominated Michigan senator Lewis Cass, a party stalwart, whose public career stretched back to the War of 1812. Cass understood the destructive potential of the slavery issue. In 1847, he suggested that territorial residents, not Congress, should decide slavery's fate. This solution, **popular sovereignty,** had a do-it-yourself charm: Keep the politicians out of it, and let the people decide. Cass was deliberately ambiguous, however, on when the people should decide. The timing was important. If residents could decide only when applying for statehood, slavery would be legal up to that point. The ambiguity aroused more fears than it allayed.

**popular sovereignty**  A solution to the slavery crisis suggested by Michigan senator Lewis Cass by which territorial residents, not Congress, would decide slavery's fate.

The Whigs were silent on the slavery issue. Reverting to their winning 1840 formula of nominating a war hero, they selected General Zachary Taylor of Mexican War fame. Taylor belonged to no party and had never voted. If one had to guess his views, his background provided some clues. He owned a hundred-slave plantation in Louisiana, and his now-deceased daughter had been married to Jefferson Davis, Mississippi's staunch proslavery senator.

Taylor's background disturbed many antislavery northern Whigs. These Conscience Whigs, along with remnants of the old Liberty Party and a scattering of northern Democrats, bolted their parties and formed the Free-Soil Party. The name reflected the party's vow to keep the territories free. Its slogan, "Free soil, free speech, free labor, free men," was a catalog of white liberties that the South had allegedly threatened over the previous decade. The Free-Soilers' appeal centered on their opposition to slave labor in the territories. Free labor, they believed, could not compete with bonded labor. The party nominated former president Martin Van Buren.

Chalking up one out of seven northern votes, Van Buren ran strongly enough in 11 of the 15 northern states to deny the winning candidate in those states a majority of the votes cast. But he could not overcome Taylor's strength in the South. Taylor was elected, giving the nation its first president from the Lower South.

## THE GOLD RUSH

Events in distant California, recently acquired from Mexico, would leave Taylor little time to savor his victory. By the time he took office in March 1849, a gold rush was under way there.

Through 1849 and 1850, more than 100,000 hopefuls flooded into California. Though the trek to California took months, whether overland or by the sea route, and travelers battled disease, weather, and each other, the lure of gold, easy to get at with just simple tools, was a powerful motivator.

Huge fortunes accrued, not only from the gold, but from supplying the miners. Young Levi Strauss experimented with trousers made out of canvas that miners particularly favored; two brothers, Henry Wells and William Fargo, offered banking, transportation, and mail services for the newcomers. The rush also attracted migrants from around the world. California soon became a polyglot empire of Chinese, Chileans, Mexicans, Irish, Germans, and Turks. Blacks, mostly slaves brought by southern masters, also roamed the gold fields.

By 1853 gold-mining operations had undergone structural and technological changes that made many miners superfluous. The new hydraulic extraction techniques severely damaged the pristine rivers of central California. Almost overnight, San Francisco was transformed from a modest port to a cosmopolitan metropolis. The image of California, and of the West in general, as wild or golden, dates from this era. But the romance of California and the wealth it generated loomed more troubling back east as the territory filled up with people in 1849. For the western dream would soon become ensnared in the conflict over slavery.

## THE COMPROMISE OF 1850

When the California territory's new residents began asking for statehood and drafted a state constitution, the document contained no provision for slavery. The constitution reflected antiblack rather than antislavery sentiment. Keeping California white would shield residents against social and economic interaction with black people. If Congress accepted the residents' request for statehood, California would enter the Union as a free state. The Union at the time consisted of 15 free states and 15 slave states. The admission of California would tip the balance. New Mexico appeared poised to follow

The California Gold Rush attracted a multinational population. Here, Chinese miners relax at their camp. The placid scene masks the occasionally violent confrontations between different racial and ethnic groups drawn to the gold fields.

suit and enter the Union as the seventeenth free state. Southerners saw their political power slipping away. Northern leaders saw an opportunity to stop the extension of slavery and reduce southern influence in the federal government.

When Congress confronted the issue of California statehood in December 1849, partisans on both sides began marshaling forces for what promised to be a long and bitter struggle. Because nine Free-Soil candidates had won seats in the House of Representatives, neither Whigs nor Democrats held a majority there.

No one, at first, knew where Taylor stood. He supported, it turned out, a version of popular sovereignty and favored allowing California and the other territories acquired from Mexico to decide the slavery issue for themselves. Under normal circumstances, the residents of a new territory organized a territorial government under the direction of Congress. When the territory's population approached 30,000 or so, residents could draft a constitution and petition Congress for statehood. California already easily exceeded the population threshold. Taylor proposed bypassing the territorial stage, and congressional involvement in it, and having California and New Mexico admitted as states directly. The result would be to bring both into the Union as free states.

Southerners resisted Taylor's plan, and Congress deadlocked on the territorial issue. Henry Clay then stepped forward with his last great compromise. To break the impasse, Clay urged that Congress should take five steps:

- Admit California as a free state, as its residents clearly preferred.
- Allow the residents of the New Mexico and Utah territories to decide the slavery issue for themselves.
- End the slave trade in the District of Columbia.
- Pass a new fugitive slave law to enforce the constitutional provision stating that a person "held to Service or Labor in one state . . . escaping into another . . . shall be delivered upon Claim of the party to whom such Service or Labor may be due."
- Set the boundary between Texas and New Mexico and pay Texas $10 million for the territory given up to New Mexico. (Texas, incidentally, would use this payment to retire its state debt and fund a public school system.)

Clay's proposal provoked a historic Senate debate that began in February 1850, featuring America's three most prominent statesmen, Clay, John C. Calhoun, and Daniel Webster, together for the last time. Calhoun argued that the compromise did not resolve the slavery issue to the South's satisfaction, and he proposed to give southerners in Congress the right to veto legislation as a way to safeguard their minority rights. Webster stood up to support the compromise, at deep political peril to himself. His Massachusetts constituents detested the fugitive slave provision, which gave southern slaveholders the right to "invade" northern states to reclaim escaped slaves. After tumultuous deliberation that lasted into the summer of 1850, the Senate rejected the compromise.

President Taylor, who had vowed to veto any compromise, died unexpectedly of a stomach ailment after overindulging in cherries and milk in the hot sun at a July 4 celebration in Washington. Vice President Millard Fillmore, a pro-Clay New Yorker, assumed the presidency after Taylor's death. Fillmore let it be known that he favored Clay's package and would sign it if passed.

Although the Senate had rejected the compromise, Illinois senator Stephen A. Douglas kept it alive. Like Webster, Douglas feared for the Union if the compromise failed. Realizing that it would never pass as a package, he proposed to break it up into its components and hold a separate vote on each. With a handful of senators voting for all parts, and with different sectional blocs supporting one provision or another, Douglas engineered a majority for the compromise, and Fillmore signed it.

The **Compromise of 1850** (see Map 14–1) was not a compromise in the sense of each opposing side consenting to certain terms desired by the other. The North gained California but would have done so in any case. Southern leaders looked to the West and saw no slave territories

**•••• Read the Document**
at **www.myhistorylab.com**
*The Compromise of 1850*

**QUICK REVIEW**

**The Compromise of 1850: Key Figures**

- Senator Henry Clay: Kentucky (Whig).
- Senator John C. Calhoun: South Carolina (Democrat).
- Senator Daniel Webster: Massachusetts (Whig).

**Compromise of 1850**   The four-step compromise which admitted California as a free state, allowed the residents of the New Mexico and Utah territories to decide the slavery issue for themselves, ended the slave trade in the District of Columbia, and passed a new fugitive slave law.

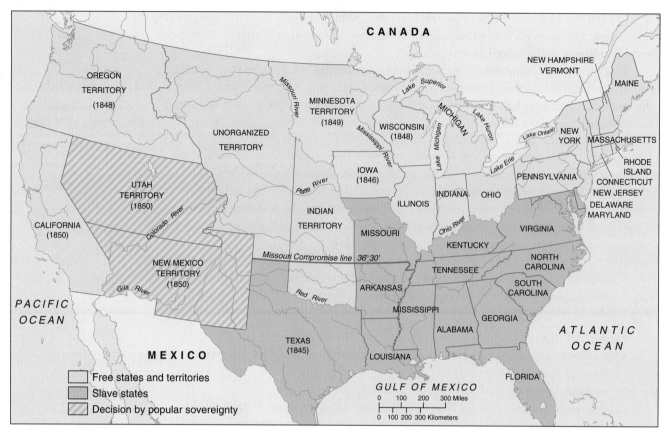

CANADA

MAP 14–1  **The Compromise of 1850**  Given the unlikely prospect that any of the western territories would opt for slavery, the compromise sealed the South's minority status in the Union.

**What were** the results of the Compromise of 1850, and how did the country react to the news of the Compromise?

**Fugitive Slave Act**  Law, part of the Compromise of 1850, that required the authorities in the North to assist southern slave catchers and return runaway slaves to their owners.

**○●○ Read the Document**

**at www.myhistorylab.com**
*The Fugitive Slave Act (1850)*

**W**  **WHERE TO LEARN MORE**

★ The Underground Railroad Freedom Center, Cincinnati, Ohio
http://www.freedomcenter.org/

awaiting statehood. Their future in the Union appeared to be one of numerical and economic decline, and the survival of their institutions seemed doubtful. They gained the **Fugitive Slave Act,** which reinforced their right to seize and return to bondage slaves who had fled to free territory, but it was slight consolation. And the North's hostile reception to the law made southerners doubt its commitment to the compromise.

## RESPONSE TO THE FUGITIVE SLAVE ACT

The Fugitive Slave Act was ready-made for abolitionist propaganda mills and heartrending stories. A few months after Congress passed it, a Kentucky slaveholder visited Madison, Indiana, and snatched a black man from his wife and children, claiming that the man had escaped nineteen years earlier. Black people living in northern communities feared capture, and some fled across the Canadian border. Several northern cities and states vowed resistance, but except for a few publicized cases, northern authorities typically cooperated with southern slave owners to help them retrieve their runaway property. The effect of the act on public opinion, however, was to polarize North and South even further.

The strongest reaction to the act was in the black communities of the urban North. Previously, black abolitionists in the North had focused on freeing slaves in the South. The Fugitive Slave Act brought the danger of slavery much closer to home. No black person was safe under the new law. Mistaken identity, the support of federal courts for slaveholders' claims, and the presence of informants made reenslavement a real possibility. The lives that 400,000 black northerners had constructed, often with great difficulty, appeared suddenly uncertain.

Black northerners formed associations to protect each other and repel, violently if necessary, any attempt to capture and reenslave them. Frederick Douglass, an escaped slave himself, explained the need for such organizations: "We must be prepared . . . see the streets . . . running with blood . . . should this law be put into operation." Some black people left the United States. In October 1850, 200 left Pittsburgh for Ontario, Canada, vowing that "they would die before being taken back into slavery." As many as 20,000 African Americans may have found their way across the border during the 1850s in response to fears over capture and reenslavement.

## UNCLE TOM'S CABIN

Sectional controversy over the Fugitive Slave Act was relatively modest compared to the firestorm ignited by abolitionist writer Harriet Beecher Stowe with the publication of a novel about southern slavery. *Uncle Tom's Cabin,* which first appeared in serial form in 1851, moved many northern white people from the sidelines of the sectional conflict to more active participation.

*Uncle Tom's Cabin* created a sensation in the United States and abroad. The book sold 10,000 copies in its first week and 300,000 within a year. By the time of the Civil War, it had sold an unprecedented 3 million copies in the United States and tens of thousands more in Europe. Stowe's book gave slavery a face; it changed people's moral perceptions about the institution in an era of deep Protestant piety; it was a Sermon on the Mount for a generation of northerners seeking witness for their Christianity and a crusade on behalf of their faith. It transformed abolitionism, bringing the movement, whose extreme rhetoric many northerners had previously viewed with disapproval, to the edge of respectability, and moving the nation a bit further on its journey to fulfill its founding ideals.

For southerners, *Uncle Tom's Cabin* was a damnable lie, a political tract disguised as literature. Some southerners retaliated with crude plays and books of their own. In these versions of slavery, no slave families were broken up, no slaves were killed, and all masters were models of Christian behavior. Few northerners, however, read these southern responses. The writers penned them more to convince fellow southerners that slavery was necessary and good than to change opinions in the North.

Black northerners embraced *Uncle Tom's Cabin.* Frederick Douglass's National Black Convention resolved that the book was "a work plainly marked by the finger of God" on behalf of black people. Some black people hoped that the book's popularity would highlight the hypocrisy of white northerners who were quick to perceive evil in the South but were often blind to discrimination against African Americans in the North. Despite reactions to Stowe's book, however, black northerners continued to face voting restrictions, segregation, and official harassment.

## THE ELECTION OF 1852

While the nation was reading and reacting to *Uncle Tom's Cabin,* a presidential election campaign took place. The Compromise of 1850 had divided the Whigs deeply. Northern Whigs perceived it as a capitulation to southern slaveholding interests and refused to support the renomination of President Millard Fillmore. Many southern Whigs, angered by the suspicions and insults of their erstwhile northern colleagues, abandoned the party. Although the Whigs

**CAUTION!!**

**COLORED PEOPLE**

**OF BOSTON, ONE & ALL,**

You are hereby respectfully CAUTIONED and advised, to avoid conversing with the

**Watchmen and Police Officers of Boston,**

For since the recent ORDER OF THE MAYOR & ALDERMEN, they are empowered to act as

**KIDNAPPERS**

AND

**Slave Catchers,**

And they have already been actually employed in KIDNAPPING, CATCHING, AND KEEPING SLAVES. Therefore, if you value your LIBERTY, and the *Welfare of the Fugitives* among you, *Shun* them in every possible manner, as so many *HOUNDS* on the track of the most unfortunate of your race.

**Keep a Sharp Look Out for KIDNAPPERS, and have TOP EYE open.**

*APRIL 24, 1851.*

The Fugitive Slave Act threatened the freedom of escaped slaves living in the North, and even of free black northerners. This notice, typical of warnings posted in northern cities, urged Boston's African American population to take precautions.

**Watch** the **Video**

at **www.myhistorylab.com**
*Harriet Beecher Stowe and the Making of* Uncle Tom's Cabin

An advertisement for *Uncle Tom's Cabin.* The book became a worldwide best-seller illuminating the tragedy of slavery in its corruption of family, human dignity, and Christianity.

nominated Mexican War hero and Virginian Winfield Scott for president, few southern Whigs viewed the nonslaveholding general as a friend of their region.

The Democratic Party entered the campaign more united. Despite reservations, the northern and southern wings of the party both announced their support for the Compromise of 1850. Southern Democrats viewed the party's nominee, Franklin Pierce of New Hampshire, as safe on the slavery issue despite his New England heritage. Pierce satisfied northerners as a nationalist devoted to the idea of Manifest Destiny. He belonged to Young America, a mostly Democratic group that advocated extending American influence into Central and South America and the Caribbean with an aggressive foreign policy. His service in the Mexican War and his good looks and charm won over doubters from both sections.

Given the disarray of the Whigs and the relative unity of the Democrats, the election results were predictable. Pierce won overwhelmingly with 254 electoral votes to Scott's 42. But Pierce's landslide victory could not obscure the deep fissures in the American party system. The Whigs, although they would continue to run local candidates through the rest of the 1850s, were finished as a national party. And the Democrats, despite their electoral success, emerged frayed from the election. In the Lower South, conflicts within the party between supporters and opponents of the Compromise of 1850 had overshadowed the contests between Democrats and Whigs. Southern Democrats had wielded great influence at the party's nominating convention and dominated party policy, clouding its prospects in the North. During the election, much of the party's support in the North had come from the first-time votes of mainly Catholic immigrants. But the growing political influence of Catholics alarmed evangelical Protestants of both parties, thus adding religious bigotry to the divisive issues undermining the structure of the national parties.

# POLITICAL REALIGNMENT

**WHAT FACTORS** contributed to the Republicans' rise to political prominence?

The conflicts over slavery and religion wrecked the Second American Party system. The Whigs disintegrated, though remnants persisted in several states and localities, and the Democrats became more southern and more closely identified with immigrants, especially Roman Catholics. The Republicans, a new party, combined the growing antislavery and antisouthern sentiment in the North with religious nativism. Whether America would dissolve into warring factions over slavery or sectarian strife was anyone's guess in the mid-1850s. Eventually, the issue of slavery overwhelmed ethnic and religious concerns.

Franklin Pierce hoped to duck the slavery issue by focusing on Young America's dreams of empire. But his attempts to forge national sentiment around an aggressive foreign policy failed. And his administration's inept handling of a new territorial controversy in Kansas forced him to confront the slavery debate.

### YOUNG AMERICA'S FOREIGN MISADVENTURES

Pierce's first missteps occurred in pursuit of Young America's foreign ambitions. The administration turned a greedy eye toward Spanish-ruled Cuba, just 90 miles off the coast of Florida. Spanish authorities were harassing American merchants exporting sugar from Cuba and the American naval vessels protecting the merchants' ships. Southerners supported an aggressive

Cuba policy, seeing the island as a possible new slave state. And nationalists saw great virtue in replacing what they perceived as a despotic colonial regime with a democratic government under the guidance of the United States.

In October 1854, three American diplomats met in Ostend, Belgium, to discuss Cuba. It is not clear whether Pierce approved or even knew of their meeting, but the diplomats believed that they had the administration's blessing. One of them, the American minister to Spain, Pierre Soulé of Louisiana, was especially eager for the United States to acquire Cuba. The group composed a document on Cuba called the **Ostend Manifesto** that claimed that the island belonged "naturally to the great family of states of which the Union is the Providential Nursery." The implication was that Spain's control of Cuba was unnatural. The United States would offer to buy Cuba from Spain, but if Spain refused to sell, the authors warned, "by every law, human and Divine, we shall be justified in wresting it from Spain."

The Ostend Manifesto caused an uproar and embarrassed the Pierce administration when it became public. Other nations quickly denounced it as a "buccaneering document" and a "highwayman's plea." It provoked a similar reaction in the United States, raising suspicions in the North that the South was willing to provoke a war with Spain to expand the number of slaveholding states.

While Pierce fumbled in the area of foreign policy, Senator Stephen A. Douglas of Illinois was developing a national project that also promised to draw the country together, the construction of a transcontinental railroad and the settling of the land it traversed. The result was worse conflict and the first outbreak of sustained sectional violence.

## STEPHEN DOUGLAS'S RAILROAD PROPOSAL

Douglas, like many westerners, wanted a transcontinental railroad. He himself had a personal stake in railroad building in that he owned some Chicago real estate and speculated in western lands. But beyond personal gain, Douglas, the supreme nationalist, understood that a transcontinental railroad would enhance the nation's journey toward becoming a continental empire. Not only would it physically link East and West, it would also help spread American democracy.

Douglas had in mind a transcontinental route extending westward from Chicago through the Nebraska Territory. Unfortunately for his plans, Indians already occupied this region, many of them on land the U.S. government had set aside as Indian Territory and barred to white settlement. Removing the "Indian barrier" and establishing white government were "first steps," in the senator's view, toward a "tide of emigration and civilization."

Once again, and not for the last time, the federal government responded by reneging on earlier promises and forcing Indians to move. In 1853, President Pierce sent agents to convince the Indians in the northern part of the Indian Territory to cede land for the railroad.

With the Indian "obstacle" removed, Douglas sought congressional approval to establish a government for the Nebraska Territory. But southern senators defeated his proposal. They objected to it not only because it called for a northern rather than southern route for the transcontinental railroad but also because the new territory lay above the Missouri Compromise line and would enter the Union as yet another free state. Bowing to southern pressure, Douglas rewrote his bill and resubmitted it in January 1854. He predicted that the new bill would "raise a hell of a storm." He was right.

## THE KANSAS-NEBRASKA ACT

Douglas's Kansas-Nebraska Bill split the Nebraska Territory into two territories, Kansas and Nebraska, with the implicit understanding that Kansas would become a slave state and Nebraska a free state. Consistent with Douglas's belief in popular sovereignty, it left the actual decision on slavery to the residents of the territories. But because it allowed southerners to bring slaves into an area formerly closed to slavery, it repealed the Missouri Compromise.

**Kansas-Nebraska Act**    Law passed in 1854 creating the Kansas and Nebraska Territories but leaving the question of slavery open to residents, thereby repealing the Missouri Compromise.

Northerners of all parties were outraged. The Missouri Compromise had endured for thirty-four years as a basis for sectional accord on slavery. Now it was threatened, northern leaders charged, by the South's unquenchable desire to spread slavery and expand its political power. President Pierce, however, backed the bill, ensuring the support of enough northern Democrats to secure it a narrow victory. The **Kansas-Nebraska Act** was law.

## "BLEEDING KANSAS"

Because of its fertile soil, favorable climate, and location adjacent to the slave state of Missouri, Kansas was the most likely of the new territories to support slavery. As a result, both southerners and antislavery northerners began an intensive drive to recruit settlers and establish a majority there.

As proslavery residents of Missouri poured into Kansas, antislavery organizations funded and armed their own migrants. In March 1855, proslavery forces, relying on the ineligible votes of Missouri residents, fraudulently elected a territorial legislature. This legislature promptly passed a series of harsh measures, including a law mandating the death penalty for aiding a fugitive slave and another making it a felony to question slaveholding in Kansas. For good measure, the proslavery majority expelled the few free-staters elected to the assembly. In response, free-staters established their own government in Topeka and vowed to make Kansas white.

**"Bleeding Kansas"**    Violence between pro- and antislavery forces in Kansas Territory after the passage of the Kansas-Nebraska Act in 1854.

A sporadic civil war erupted in Kansas in November 1855 and reached a climax in the spring of 1856. Journalists dubbed the conflict **"Bleeding Kansas."** On May 21, a group of proslavery officials attacked the free-state stronghold of Lawrence, subjecting it to a heavy artillery barrage. No one was killed, but the town suffered substantial damage. Eastern newspapers, exaggerating the incident, called it "the sack of Lawrence." Three days later, antislavery agitator John Brown, originally from Connecticut, went with several sympathizers to Pottawatomie Creek south of Lawrence in search of proslavery settlers. Armed with razor-sharp broadswords, they split the skulls and hacked the bodies of five men.

The memory of the failed revolutions in Europe remained fresh in the minds of Americans concerned about their own fragile democratic institutions. The disintegration of law and order on the Plains brought a foreboding recognition to many Americans. The double outrage of a fraudulent election followed by severe legislation resembled more the despotism of restored regimes in Europe than the extension of American democracy.

👁 See the **Map**

at **www.myhistorylab.com**
*The Compromise of 1850 and the Kansas-Nebraska Act*

Kansans were not the only Americans bleeding over slavery. Five days before the "sack of Lawrence," Massachusetts senator Charles Sumner delivered a longwinded diatribe, "The Crime Against Kansas," full of personal insults against several southerners, especially elderly South Carolina senator Andrew P. Butler. Two days after Sumner's outburst, and a day after the story of the sack of Lawrence appeared in the newspapers, Butler's cousin, South Carolina congressman Preston Brooks, entered the mostly vacant Senate chamber, where Sumner sat working on a speech. Seeking to defend his cousin's honor, Brooks raised his walking cane and beat Sumner over the head. Bloody and unconscious, the senator slumped to the floor. He recovered but did not return to the Senate for over three years. His empty chair offered northerners' mute confirmation of their growing conviction that southerners were despotic. Southerners showered Brooks with new walking canes.

Armed Missourians cross the border into Kansas to vote illegally for a proslavery government in 1855.

# KNOW-NOTHINGS AND REPUBLICANS: RELIGION AND POLITICS

The Sumner incident, along with the Kansas-Nebraska Bill and the civil war in Kansas, further polarized North and South, widening sectional divisions within the political parties. Some northern Democrats distanced themselves from their party and looked for political alternatives; northern Whigs seized on changing public opinion to form new coalitions; and free-soil advocates gained new adherents. From 1854 to 1856, northerners moved into new political parties that altered the national political landscape and sharpened sectional conflict.

Although the slavery issue was mainly responsible for the party realignment in the North, other factors played a role as well. Nearly 3.5 million immigrants entered the United States between 1848 and 1860, the greatest influx in American history in proportion to the total population. Some of these newcomers, especially the Germans, were escaping failed democratic revolutions in Europe. They were predominantly middle-class Protestants who, along with the smaller number of German Catholics and Jews, settled mostly in the cities, where they established shops and other businesses. More than 1 million of the immigrants, however, were poor Irish Roman Catholics, fleeing their homeland to avoid starvation.

The Irish immigrants made their homes in northern cities, which were in the midst of Protestant revivals and reform. They also competed for jobs with native-born Protestant workers. Because the Irish would work for lower wages, the job competition bred animosity and sometimes violence. But it was their Roman Catholic religion that most concerned some urban Protestants, who associated Catholicism with despotism and immorality, the same evils they attributed to southerners. For their part, the Irish made it clear that they had little use for Protestant reform, especially temperance and abolitionism. The clash of cultures would soon further disturb a political environment increasingly in flux over the slavery issue.

New parties emerged from this cauldron of religious, ethnic, and sectional strife. Anti-immigrant, anti-Catholic sentiment gave rise to the **Know-Nothing Party,** which began as a secret organization in July 1854. Its name derived from the reply that members gave when asked about the party: "I know nothing." Although strongest in the North, Know-Nothing chapters blossomed in several southern cities that had experienced some immigration since 1848, among them Richmond, Louisville, New Orleans, and Savannah. The party's members in both North and South were mostly former Whigs. In addition to their biases against Catholics and foreigners, the Know-Nothings shared a fear that the slavery issue could destroy the Union. But because attempts to solve the issue seemed only to increase sectional tensions, the Know-Nothings hoped to ignore it.

Know-Nothing candidates fared surprisingly well in local and congressional elections during the fall of 1854, carrying 63 percent of the statewide vote in Massachusetts and making strong showings in New York and Pennsylvania. In office, Know-Nothings achieved some notable reforms. In Massachusetts, where they pursued an agenda similar to that of the Whigs in earlier years, they secured administrative reforms and supported public health and public education programs.

The Know-Nothings' anti-Catholicism, however, overshadowed their reform agenda. In several states and cities, they passed legislation barring Catholics from public office and unsuccessfully sought to increase the time required for an immigrant to become a citizen from one year to 21 years. The Know-Nothings also fostered anti-Catholic violence, such as the bloody election day riot that erupted in Louisville, Kentucky, in 1855.

One of Thomas Nast's vitriolic comments on the separation between Church (i.e., the Roman Catholic church) and State.

**Read** the **Document**

at **www.myhistorylab.com**
*From Then to Now Online: Religion and Politics*

**Know-Nothing Party**   Anti-immigrant party formed from the wreckage of the Whig Party and some disaffected northern Democrats in 1854.

**Republican Party** Party that emerged in the 1850s in the aftermath of the bitter controversy over the Kansas-Nebraska Act, consisting of former Whigs, some northern Democrats, and many Know-Nothings.

**QUICK REVIEW**

**Republican Values**
- Supporters of reform.
- Opposed to slavery.
- Antisouthern sectional party.

Ethnic and religious bigotry were weak links to hold together a national party. Southern and northern Know-Nothings soon fell to quarreling over slavery despite their vow to avoid it, and the party split. Many northern Know-Nothings soon found a congenial home in the new **Republican Party.** The Republican Party formed in the summer of 1854 from a coalition of anti-slavery Conscience Whigs and Democrats disgusted with the Pierce administration's Kansas policy. Like the Know-Nothings, the Republicans advocated strong state and federal governments to promote economic and social reforms. But the new party did not espouse the Know-Nothings' anti-Catholic and anti-immigrant positions. The overriding bond among Republicans was their opposition to the extension of slavery in the territories.

Reflecting its opposition to slavery, the Republican Party was an antisouthern sectional party. Northern Whig merchants and entrepreneurs who joined the party were impatient with southern obstruction in Congress of federal programs for economic development, such as a transcontinental railroad, harbor and river improvements, and high tariffs to protect American industries (located mostly in the North) from foreign competition. In a bid to keep slavery out of the territories, the Republicans favored limiting homesteads in the West to 160 acres. Not incidentally, populating the territories with northern whites would ensure a western base for the new party.

Heightened sectional animosity laced with religious and ethnic prejudice fueled the emergence of new parties and the weakening of old political affiliations in the early 1850s. Accompanying the political realignment were diverging views on the proper role of government. As the nation prepared for the presidential election of 1856, the Democrats had become a party top-heavy with southerners; the Know-Nothings splintered along sectional lines; some Whigs remained active under the old party name, mainly on the state and local levels in North and South; and the Republican Party was becoming an important political force in the North and, to southerners, the embodiment of evil.

## THE ELECTION OF 1856

The presidential election of 1856 proved to be one of the strangest in American history. The Know-Nothings and the Republicans faced a national electorate for the first time while the Democrats were deeply divided over the Kansas issue.

The upstart Republicans held their convention in Philadelphia in mid-July. The platform condemned the "twin relics of barbarism"—slavery and polygamy. There was no epidemic, current or pending, of men and women seeking multiple partners. But, as everyone understood at the time, the Mormons in Utah Territory espoused, though did not require, polygamy. Memories of Mormon settlements in the Midwest and the turmoil they generated remained fresh in the minds of residents in a region where Republicans hoped to pick up significant support. While antisouthern sentiment varied, few voters were sympathetic to the Mormons.

The Republicans passed over their most likely candidate, the New York senator and former Whig William H. Seward. Instead, they followed a tried-and-true Whig precedent and nominated a military hero, John C. Frémont, a handsome, dark-haired soldier of medium height and medium intelligence. His wife, Jessie Benton, the daughter of Missouri senator Thomas Hart Benton, was his greatest asset. In effect, she ran the campaign and wisely encouraged her husband to remain silent. The Know-Nothings split into "South Americans" and "North Americans." The South Americans nominated Millard Fillmore, although he was not a Know-Nothing. The North Americans eventually and reluctantly embraced Frémont, despite the widespread but mistaken belief that he was a Roman Catholic.

The Democrats, facing a northern revolt and southern opposition to any candidate who did not support the extension of slavery, turned to Pennsylvania's James Buchanan whose greatest virtue was that he had been out of the country the previous four years as ambassador to Great Britain. Southerners accepted him as electable and sensitive to slavery. Northern Democrats hoped for the best.

Democratic Party strategy in the North focused on shoring up its immigrant base by connecting the Republicans to the Know-Nothings and simultaneously appealing to evangelical Protestants by intimating that Frémont had received a Catholic education, had studied for the priesthood, or was himself a Roman Catholic secretly attending Mass and "going through all the crosses and gyrations, eating wafers," take your pick. Democratic papers cried out that Frémont was "*the instrument of vice, and the foe of God and of Freedom.*"

The importance of evangelical imagery in the political campaigns of the major parties was especially evident among the Republicans. A participant in the party convention likened the party platform to "God's revealed Word," and a minister supporting the Republican ticket saw the election "as a decisive struggle . . . between freedom and Slavery, truth and falsehood, justice and oppression, God and the devil."

Away from the pulpit, Republican campaigners sometimes found tough going in the North, indicating how much the slavery extension debate had overtaken sectarian issues. A portion of the northern electorate viewed the Republican Party as a gilded version of the radical antislavery parties of the 1840s, promoting racial equality and emancipation to the detriment of whites.

James Buchanan emerged victorious. The only national party had won a national election. The Democrats did it by holding the lower North as Pennsylvania, New Jersey, Illinois, Indiana, and California voted for Buchanan, and sweeping the Lower South. But "Old Buck's" victory was narrow in these northern states; the Republicans performed remarkably well considering it was the first time they had fielded a presidential candidate. They had achieved a "victorious defeat," making Buchanan the first candidate to win without carrying the North since 1828. Republicans eagerly looked forward to the next presidential contest and the good prospects of prying at least Pennsylvania, Indiana, and Illinois from the Democratic column. For the first time ever, an avowedly antislavery party had carried eleven free states.

The South had not yet lapsed into one-party politics. Millard Fillmore garnered 40 percent of the popular vote in the South, but won only the state of Maryland. He fared poorly in the Lower South. The states that had the greatest stake in the slave economy voted solidly Democratic.

Buchanan, who brought more than a generation of political experience to the presidency, would need every bit and more. He had scarcely settled into office when two major crises confronted him: a Supreme Court decision that challenged the right of Congress to regulate slavery in the territories and renewed conflict over Kansas.

## THE DRED SCOTT CASE

Dred Scott was a slave owned by an army surgeon based in Missouri. In the 1830s and early 1840s, he had traveled with his master to the state of Illinois and the Wisconsin Territory before returning to Missouri. In 1846, Scott sued his master's widow for freedom on the grounds that the laws of Illinois and the Wisconsin Territory barred slavery. After a series of appeals, the case reached the Supreme Court. Chief Justice Roger Taney of Maryland, joined by five other justices of the nine-member Supreme Court (five of whom came from slave states), dismissed Scott's suit two days after Buchanan's inauguration in March 1857.

Taney's opinion contained two bombshells. First, he argued that black people were not citizens of the United States. Because Scott was not a citizen, he could not sue. The framers, according to Taney, respected a long-standing view that slaves were "beings of an inferior order . . . so far inferior that they had no rights which the white man was bound to respect."

Second, Taney held that even if Scott had standing in court, his residence in the Wisconsin Territory did not make him a free man. This was because the Missouri Compromise, which was still in effect in the 1840s, was, in Taney's view, unconstitutional. (The Wisconsin Territory lay above the compromise line.) The compromise, the chief justice explained, deprived citizens

●•●—Read the Document
at **www.myhistorylab.com**
*Opinion of the Supreme Court for* Dred
Scott v. Sanford *(1857)*

Dred Scott and his wife, Harriet, are portrayed here with their children as an average middle-class family, an image that fueled northern opposition to the Supreme Court's 1857 decision that denied Scott's freedom and citizenship.

**Dred Scott decision**  Supreme Court ruling, in a lawsuit brought by Dred Scott, a slave demanding his freedom based on his residence in a free state and a free territory with his master, that slaves could not be U.S. citizens and that Congress had no jurisdiction over slavery in the territories.

**Lecompton Constitution**  Proslavery draft written in 1857 by Kansas territorial delegates elected under questionable circumstances; it was rejected by two governors, supported by President Buchanan, and decisively defeated by Congress.

of their property (slaves) without the due process of law granted by the Fifth Amendment to the U.S. Constitution. In effect, Taney ruled that Congress could not bar slavery from the territories.

The **Dred Scott** decision was especially unsettling to the tens of thousands of free blacks throughout the country, especially in the South. The Court, in stripping their citizenship, made them vulnerable to reenslavement or expulsion. The case also accelerated restrictions on the southern free black population as its legal recourse vanished with the decision. Several cities, including Charleston, experimented with requirements that free blacks purchase and wear badges identifying them as free. For African Americans, the enemy was no longer the slaveholder, but the very government from which they had hoped for redress.

The decision also shocked Republicans. The right of Congress to ban slavery from the territories, which Taney had apparently voided, was one of the party's central tenets. Republicans responded by ignoring the implications of the decision for the territories while promising to abide by it so far as it affected Dred Scott himself. Once in office, Republicans vowed, they would seek a reversal. This position allowed them to attack the decision without appearing to defy the law.

The *Dred Scott* decision boosted Republican fortunes in the North even as it seemed to undercut the party. Fears of a southern Slave Power conspiracy now seemed ever more justified. If Congress could not ban slavery from the territories, Republicans asked, how secure was the right of states to ban slavery within their borders? A small group of slaveholders, they charged, was holding nonslaveholding white people hostage to the institution of slavery.

## THE LECOMPTON CONSTITUTION

Establishing a legitimate government in Kansas was the second major issue to bedevil the Buchanan administration. The president made a good start, sending his friend and fellow Pennsylvanian Robert Walker (then a resident of Mississippi) to Kansas as territorial governor to oversee the election of a constitutional convention in June 1857.

The violence had subsided in Kansas, and prospects had grown for a peaceful settlement. But free-staters, fearing that the slavery forces planned to stuff the ballot box with fraudulent votes, announced a boycott of the June election. As a result, proslavery forces dominated the constitutional convention, which was held in Lecompton. And Walker, although a slaveholder, let it be known that he thought Kansas would never be a slave state. He thus put himself at odds with proslavery residents from the outset.

Walker persuaded the free-staters to vote in October to elect a new territorial legislature. The returns gave the proslavery forces a narrow victory, but Walker discovered irregularities. Walker threw out the fraudulent returns, and the free-staters took control of the territorial legislature for the first time.

Undeterred, the proslavery forces drafted a proslavery constitution at the constitutional convention in Lecompton. Buchanan, who had promised southerners a proslavery government in Kansas, dismissed Walker before he could rule on the Lecompton Constitution, then ignored the recommendation of Walker's successor that he reject it. He submitted the **Lecompton Constitution** to the Senate for approval even though it clearly sidestepped the popular sovereignty requirement of the Kansas-Nebraska Act.

Like the Kansas-Nebraska Act, the Lecompton Constitution outraged many northerners. Northern Democrats facing reelection refused to support a president of their own party, and, though the constitution passed in the Senate, Democratic opposition killed it in the House. Congress would eventually admit Kansas to the Union as a free state in January 1861.

The *Dred Scott* decision and Buchanan's support of the Lecompton Constitution helped the Republicans and hurt northern Democrats in the 1858 congressional elections. The **Panic of 1857,** a severe economic recession that lingered into 1858, also worked to the advantage of the Republicans.

The Democratic administration did nothing as unemployment rose; starvation stalked the streets of northern cities, and homeless women and children begged for food and shelter. Republicans claimed that government intervention, specifically, Republican-sponsored legislation to raise certain tariffs, give western land to homesteaders, and fund transportation projects, if passed by Congress, could have prevented the panic. The Democrats' inaction, they said, reflected the southern Slave Power's insensitivity to northern workers.

Southerners disagreed. The panic had scarcely touched them. Cotton prices were high, and few southern banks failed. Cotton seemed indeed to be king. The financial crisis in the North reinforced the southern belief that northern society was corrupt and greedy. The Republicans' proposed legislative remedies, in their view, would enrich the North and beggar the South.

**Panic of 1857**   Banking crisis that caused a credit crunch in the North; it was less severe in the South, where high cotton prices spurred a quick recovery.

## THE RELIGIOUS REVIVAL OF 1857–1858

In the midst of economic depression and sectional controversy, a religious revival swept across the nation's cities in the winter of 1857–1858. Beginning with lunchtime prayer meetings among businessmen in New York City, the phenomenon spread throughout the country, though concentrating in the larger urban centers of the Northeast. The sectional crisis and the economic downturn had a part in bringing urban middle-class men into churches and meeting halls at the noon hour, but the gatherings emphasized prayer and personal reflection, avoiding political discussion and focusing on individual redemption. Sectional strife had diverted attention from personal salvation, and the financial panic served as a reminder that wealth and possessions could be fleeting, but the soul was everlasting. Ministers and lay leaders of the movement encouraged men to turn away from the reform "isms" of the era—feminism, abolitionism, and socialism among them. Men, they suggested, should not worship secular ideologies, but should make the Bible the foundation of their behavior and thought. And they should reestablish their leadership both in spiritual and family matters.

Religion provided not only solace but also explanations for a time beset by increasing uncertainty. The revival, which peaked in early 1858, did not change society dramatically any more than it pulled the nation out of the economic doldrums. But now with each turn in the political arena many more people, not only the fervent evangelicals, came to understand that these mere events held transcendent meaning.

Some feared that the growing integration of religion and politics could harm the nation's religious life and burden the political process with sharper divisions than were necessary. But by 1858, it became increasingly difficult to distinguish the political from the spiritual. The Illinois senatorial contest between Democrat Stephen A. Douglas and Abraham Lincoln of the Republican Party proved a case in point. Their debates underscored the moral dimensions of political questions and the resulting difficulties of effecting compromises.

## THE LINCOLN-DOUGLAS DEBATES

Douglas faced a forceful opponent in his 1858 reelection campaign. The Republicans had nominated Abraham Lincoln, a 49-year-old lawyer and former Whig congressman. The Kentucky-born Lincoln had risen from modest circumstances to become a prosperous lawyer in the Illinois state capital of Springfield. After one term in Congress from 1847 to 1849, he returned to his law practice but maintained his interest in politics. Strongly opposed to the extension of slavery into the territories, he considered joining the Republican Party after the passage of the Kansas-Nebraska Act. Most Illinois voters opposed the extension of slavery into the territories, although generally not out of concern for the slaves. Illinois residents, like most northerners, wanted to keep the territories free for white people. Few voters would support dissolving the Union over the slavery issue. Douglas, who knew his constituents well, branded Lincoln a dangerous radical for warning, in a biblical paraphrase, that the United States, like "a house divided against itself," could not "endure permanently half slave and half free."

Lincoln could not allow the charge of radicalism to go unanswered. So, in July 1858, he challenged Douglas to a series of debates across the state. Douglas was reluctant to provide exposure for his lesser-known opponent, but he could not reject Lincoln's offer outright, lest voters think he was dodging his challenger. He agreed to debates in seven of the state's nine congressional districts.

The **Lincoln-Douglas debates** were a defining event in American politics. For Douglas, slavery was not a moral issue. What mattered was what white people wanted. If they wanted slavery, fine; if they did not, fine also. Lincoln and many Republicans had a very different view. For them, slavery was a moral issue. As such, it was independent of what the residents of a territory wanted.

Lincoln not only identified the cause of the Republican Party with the forces of liberty and freedom all over the world, but also framed the debate as a contest between good and evil. Evangelical rhetoric had pervaded political discourse for nearly two decades. But coming on the heels of a national religious revival, Lincoln's assertion reinforced the perception that the nation was approaching a crossroads, not only a secular divide, but a battle that could determine the future of mankind for eternity: "As I view the contest, it is not less than a contest for the advancement of the kingdom of Heaven or the kingdom of Satan."

Lincoln tempered his moralism with practical politics. He took care to distance himself from the abolitionists, asserting that he abided by the Constitution and did not seek to interfere in places where slavery existed. Moreover, Lincoln, like most Republicans, hated the institution of slavery, but held ambivalent views about African Americans. These views would change in time, sometimes prodded by events, other times by thought and prayer. About slavery, there was little ambiguity in his position, even if he tried to project a moderate image on the campaign trail. Privately, he hoped for its demise. To Lincoln, slavery was immoral, but inequality was not. The Republican Party was antislavery, but it did not advocate racial equality.

Illinois voters retained a narrow Democratic majority in the state legislature, which reelected Douglas to the U.S. Senate. (State legislatures elected senators until 1913, when the Seventeenth Amendment provided for direct election by the people.) But Douglas alienated southern Democrats with his strong defense of popular sovereignty and lost whatever hope he had of becoming the standard-bearer of a united Democratic Party in 1860. Lincoln lost the senatorial contest but won national respect and recognition.

Despite Lincoln's defeat in Illinois, the Republicans made a strong showing in the 1858 congressional elections across the North. The increased Republican presence and the sharpening sectional divisions among Democrats portended a bitter debate over slavery in the new Congress. Americans, more than ever before, were viewing issues and each other in sectional terms. *Northern* and *southern* took on meanings that expressed a great deal more than geography.

**Read the Document**

at **www.myhistorylab.com**
*The Lincoln-Douglas Debates of 1858*

**Lincoln-Douglas debates**   Series of debates in the 1858 Illinois senatorial campaign during which Douglas and Lincoln staked out their differing opinions on the issue of slavery.

Abraham Lincoln making a point at Coles County (Illinois) Fairgrounds, 1858. His U.S. Senate opponent, Stephen A. Douglas, sitting at Lincoln's right, waits his turn. The Lincoln-Douglas debates captivated Illinois voters, who turned out in great numbers to witness the rhetorical fireworks.

# THE ROAD TO DISUNION

The unsatisfying Compromise of 1850, "Bleeding Kansas" and "Bleeding Sumner," the *Dred Scott* case, and Lecompton convinced many northerners that southerners were conspiring with the federal government to restrict their political and economic liberties. Southerners saw these same events as evidence of a northern conspiracy to reduce the South's political and economic influence. There were no conspiracies, but with so little goodwill on either side, hostility predominated. Slavery, above all, accounted for the growing divide.

**WHY WERE** southerners so alarmed by the election of Abraham Lincoln in 1860?

In 1859 abolitionist John Brown, who had avenged the "sack of Lawrence" in 1856, led a raid against a federal arsenal at Harpers Ferry, Virginia, in the vain hope of sparking a slave revolt. This event brought the frustrations of both sides of the sectional conflict to a head. The presidential election campaign of 1860 began before the uproar over the raid had subsided. In the course of that contest, one of the last nationally unifying institutions, the Democratic Party, broke apart. The election of Abraham Lincoln, an avowedly sectional candidate, triggered a crisis that defied peaceful resolution.

Although the crisis spiraled into a civil war, this outcome did not signal the triumph of sectionalism over nationalism. Ironically, in defending their stands, both sides appealed to time-honored nationalist and democratic sentiments. Southern secessionists believed they were the true keepers of the ideals that had inspired the American Revolution. They were merely re-creating a more perfect Union. It was not they, but the Republicans, who had sundered the old Union by subverting the Constitution's guarantee of liberty. Lincoln similarly appealed to nationalist themes, telling northerners that the United States was "the last best hope on earth."

Northerners and southerners both appealed to nationalism and democracy but applied different meanings to these concepts. The differences underscored how far apart the sections had grown. When southerners and northerners looked at each other, they no longer saw fellow Americans; they saw enemies. The reason was slavery.

Slavery and its corollary, white supremacy, lay at the core of the sectional crisis that prompted secession and the bloody civil war that followed. For many white southerners, the journey from the ideals of the American Revolution led naturally to a Slave Republic: Enslavement of blacks guaranteed the freedom and equality of whites. Many northerners believed that slavery represented a tragic detour from the nation's founding principles, especially as articulated in the Declaration of Independence. Contemporaries understood that these fundamentally different views of slavery led directly to the breakup of the Union.

## NORTH-SOUTH DIFFERENCES

Slavery accounted for or played a role in creating distinctions between North and South that transcended their shared heritage.

**Economic differences.**    Behind the ideological divide that separated North and South lay real and growing social and economic differences (see the Overview table, South and North Compared in 1860). As the North became increasingly urban and industrial, the South remained primarily rural and agricultural. The urban population of the free states increased from 10 to 26 percent between 1820 and 1860. In the South, in the same period, it increased only from 5 to 10 percent. Likewise the proportion of the northern workforce in agriculture declined from 68 percent to 40 percent between 1800 and 1860, whereas in the South it increased from 82 percent to 84 percent. Northern farmers made up for the decline in farm workers by relying on machinery. In 1860, the free states had twice the value of farm machinery per worker as the slave states.

The demand for farm machinery in the North reflected the growing demand for manufactured products in general. The need of city-dwellers for ready-to-wear shoes and clothing, household iron products, processed foods, homes, workplaces, and public amenities boosted industrial production in the North. In contrast, in the South, the slower rate of urbanization, the lower proportion of immigrants, and the region's labor-intensive agriculture kept industrial development modest. The proportion of U.S. manufacturing capital invested in the South declined from 31 to 16 percent between 1810 and 1860. In 1810, per capita investment in industrial enterprises was 2.5 times greater in the North than in the South; in 1860, it was 3.5 times greater.

These economic developments generated communities of innovation in the North, especially in the rapidly expanding cities, where people traded ideas and technical information and skills. One of the most important innovations of the era was the telegraph, pioneered by Samuel F. B. Morse, who convinced the government to subsidize a line from Washington, DC, to Baltimore, Maryland, in 1843 and then electrified his patrons with instantaneous reports from the political party conventions of 1844. As information became a valuable currency for a new age, such improvements in communications and transportation tended to reinforce the economic dominance of the Northeast.

**Social and religious differences.**   More subtle distinctions between North and South became evident as well by midcentury. The South had a high illiteracy rate, nearly three times greater than the North, eight times greater if black southerners are included. Northerners supported far more public schools and libraries than southerners. In the South, education was barred by law to slaves and limited for most white people. Many white leaders viewed education more as a privilege for the well-to-do than a right for every citizen.

Evangelical Protestantism attracted increasing numbers in both North and South, but its character differed in the two regions. In the North, evangelical Protestants viewed social reform as a prerequisite for the Second Coming of Christ. As a result, they were in the forefront of most reform movements. Southern evangelicals generally defended slavery.

**The effects of slavery.**   Slavery permeated southern society. Investment in land and slaves limited investment in manufacturing and railroads. The availability of a large slave labor force reduced the need for farm machinery and limited the demand for manufactured products. Slaves were relatively immobile. They did not migrate to cities in massive numbers as did northern farmers. Nor could they quickly fill the labor demands of an expanding urban economy. Agriculture usually took precedence.

Slavery also divided northern from southern churches. And it accounted for the contrast between the inward, otherworldly emphasis of southern theology and the reformist theology of northern evangelicals. Southerners associated black slavery with white freedom; northerners associated it with white degradation.

Slavery contributed to the South's martial tradition and its lukewarm attitude toward public education. Fully 95 percent of the nation's black population lived in the South in 1860, and 90 percent of these were slaves. As a result, the South was often a region on edge. Fearful of revolt, especially in the 1850s, when rumors of slave discontent ran rampant, white people felt compelled to maintain patrols and militias in constant readiness. The South was also determined to keep slaves as ignorant as possible. Educated slaves would be susceptible to abolitionist propaganda and more inclined to revolt.

The South's defense of slavery and the North's attack on it fostered an array of stereotypes that exaggerated the real differences between the sections. Like all stereotypes, these reduced individuals to dehumanized categories. They encouraged the people of each section to view those of the other less as fellow Americans than as aliens in their midst.

Ironically, although slavery increasingly defined the character of the South in the 1850s, a growing majority of white southerners did not own slaves. Slavery nonetheless implicated non-slaveholders in ways that ensured their support for it. By satisfying the demand for labor on large plantations, it relieved many rural white southerners from serving as farmhands and enabled them to work their own land. Slaveholders also recruited nonslaveholders to suppress slave violence or rebellion. It was nonslaveholders, for example, who often manned patrols and militia companies. Some nonslaveholders hoped to purchase slaves someday. Many dreamed of migrating westward to the next cotton frontier where they might find greater opportunity to own land and slaves. Finally, regardless of a white man's social or economic status, he shared an important feature with the largest slaveholder: As long as racial slavery existed, the color of his skin made him a member of a privileged class that could never be enslaved.

While white southerners were more united on slavery than on other issues, their defense of slavery presented them with a major dilemma. By the 1850s, most Western nations had condemned and abolished the institution. And because northerners controlled the flow of information through the popular newspapers and the national network of communications, credit, and commerce, southerners were likely to find themselves increasingly isolated. A minority in their own country and a lonely voice for a despised institution that was for them a significant source of wealth, southerners were understandably jittery.

## JOHN BROWN'S RAID

Shortly after he completed his mayhem at Pottawatomie Creek, John Brown left Kansas and approached several New England abolitionists for funds to continue his private war in the territory. But when Brown returned to Kansas in late 1857, he discovered that peace had settled over that troubled territory. Residents now cared more about making money than about making war. Leaving Kansas for the last time, he went east with a new plan. He proposed to attack and capture the federal arsenal at Harpers Ferry, Virginia, a small town near the Maryland border. The assault, Brown imagined, would spark a slave uprising that would eventually spread to the rest of the state. With funds from his New England friends, he equipped a few dozen men and hired an English army officer to train them.

Brown and his "army" moved to a Maryland farmhouse in the summer of 1859 to train and complete planning for the raid. On the night of October 16, 1859, he and 22 followers captured the federal arsenal at Harpers Ferry and waited for the slaves to rally to his banner. Meanwhile, the townspeople alerted outside authorities. The Virginia militia and a detachment of United States Marines under the command of Colonel Robert E. Lee arrived and put a quick end to **John Brown's Raid.** They wounded Brown and killed or captured most of his force.

Brown had launched the operation without provisions and at a site from which escape was impossible. Although the primary goal of the attack had been to inspire a slave insurrection, no one had bothered to inform the local slaves. And despite the secret nature of the expedition, Brown had left behind a mountain of documents at the Maryland farmhouse. Was he crazy? As the *Boston Post* editorialized after the raid, "John Brown may be a lunatic, [but if so] then one-fourth of the people of Massachusetts are madmen."

Although the *Post* may have exaggerated, the editorial reflected an article of faith among many abolitionists that, given the signal, slaves would immediately throw off their chains, slaughter their masters, and join a rebellion. But even those slaves in the area who knew of the raid understood the odds against Brown and had the good sense not to join him.

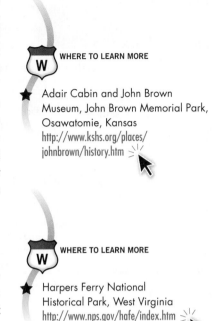

**W** WHERE TO LEARN MORE

★ Adair Cabin and John Brown Museum, John Brown Memorial Park, Osawatomie, Kansas
http://www.kshs.org/places/johnbrown/history.htm

**W** WHERE TO LEARN MORE

★ Harpers Ferry National Historical Park, West Virginia
http://www.nps.gov/hafe/index.htm

**John Brown's Raid** New England abolitionist John Brown's ill-fated attempt to free Virginia's slaves with a raid on the federal arsenal at Harpers Ferry, Virginia, in 1859.

John Brown on trial for treason and murder at Charlestown, Virginia. The image of the wounded and prostrate Brown eloquently defending his actions before his accusers touched many northerners who otherwise condemned his action. Even a few southerners, including Virginia's governor Henry A. Wise, admired his courage.

## OVERVIEW South and North Compared in 1860

| | South | North |
|---|---|---|
| Population | Biracial; 35 percent African American | Overwhelmingly white; less than 2 percent African American |
| Economy | Growing, though relatively undiversified; 84 percent of workforce in agriculture | Developing through industrialization and urbanization; 40 percent of workforce in agriculture |
| Labor | Heavily dependent on slave labor, especially in Lower South | Free wage labor |
| Factories | 15 percent of national total | 85 percent of national total; concentrated in the Northeast |
| Railroads | Approximately 10,000 miles of track; primarily shorter lines, with fewer links to trunk lines | Approximately 20,000 miles of track; more effectively linked in trunk lines connecting east and west |
| Literacy | 17 percent illiteracy rate for free population | 6 percent illiteracy rate |

**Read the Document**

at www.myhistorylab.com
*John Brown, Address before Sentencing (1859)*

**Hear the Audio**

at www.myhistorylab.com
*John Brown: An Address by Frederick Douglass*

The raid, though foolish and unsuccessful, played on southerners' worst fears of slave rebellion, adding a new dimension: Here was an attack engineered not from within the South but from the North. Some southern white people may have dismissed the ability or even the desire of slaves to mount revolts on their own, but they less easily dismissed the potential impact of outside white agitators. The state of Virginia tried Brown on the charge of treason to the state. The trial was swift but fair. The jury sentenced Brown to hang.

The outpouring of northern grief over Brown's death convinced white southerners that the threat to their security was not over. The discovery of Brown's correspondence at his Maryland farmhouse further fueled southern rancor, and southerners increasingly ceased to believe northern disclaimers about the raid. John Brown's Raid significantly changed southern public opinion. However much they defended slavery, most southerners were for the Union. The northern reaction to John Brown's trial and death, however, troubled them. The *Richmond Whig*, a newspaper that reflected moderate Upper South opinion, observed in early 1860 "recent events have wrought almost a complete revolution in the sentiments, the thoughts, the hopes, of the oldest and steadiest conservatives in all the southern states. . . . There are thousands upon . . . thousands of men in our midst who, a month ago, scoffed at the idea of a dissolution of the Union as a madman's dream, but who now hold the opinion that its days are numbered, its glory perished."

It was one thing to condemn slavery in the territories but another to attack it violently where it was long established. Southerners now saw in the Republican Party the embodiment of John Brown's ideals and actions. So, in their view, the election of a Republican president would be a death sentence for the South.

### THE ELECTION OF 1860

An atmosphere of mutual sectional distrust and animosity characterized the campaign for the presidential election of 1860. In April, the Democratic Party, the sole surviving national political organization, held its convention in Charleston, South Carolina. Northern Democrats arrived in Charleston united behind Stephen A. Douglas. Although they constituted a majority of the delegates, they could not muster the two-thirds majority necessary to nominate their candidate. Other issues, however, were decided on a simple majority vote, permitting northern Democrats to defeat a platform proposal for a federal slave code in the territories.

Southern extremists who favored secession hoped to disrupt the convention and divide the party. They reasoned that the Republicans would then win the presidency, providing the South with the justification to secede. The platform vote gave them the opportunity they were seeking. Accompanied by spectators' cheers, delegates from five Lower South states, South Carolina, Florida, Mississippi, Louisiana, and Texas, walked out. The Arkansas and Georgia delegations joined them the following day.

Still without a nominee, the Democrats agreed to reconvene in Baltimore in June. This time, the Upper South delegations marched out when Douglas Democrats, in a commanding majority, refused to seat the Lower South delegations that had walked out in Charleston. The remaining delegates nominated Douglas for president. The bolters, who included almost all the southern delegates plus a few northerners loyal to President Buchanan, met in another hall and nominated John C. Breckinridge of Kentucky.

The disintegration of the national Democratic Party alarmed those southerners who understood that it would ensure the election of a Republican president in November. The *Memphis Appeal* warned that "the odium of the Black-Republican party has been that it is *Sectional.*" Should southerners now allow a group of "restless and reckless or misguided men to destroy the national Democratic party?" the *Appeal* asked. Its emphatic answer was "No!"

The *Appeal* reflected the sentiment of many former Whigs, mainly from the Upper South, who would not support Breckinridge and could not support Douglas. Together with Whig allies in the North who had not defected to the Republican Party, they met in Baltimore in May 1860 to form the **Constitutional Union Party** and nominated John Bell of Tennessee for president.

Sensing victory, the Republicans convened in Chicago. If they could hold the states won by Frémont in 1856, add Minnesota (a new Republican-leaning state), and win Pennsylvania and one of three other Lower North states, Illinois, Indiana, or New Jersey, their candidate would win. These calculations dictated a platform and a candidate who could appeal to the four Lower North swing states, where antislavery sentiment was not so strong.

In selecting an appropriate presidential nominee, the Republicans faced a dilemma. Senator William H. Seward came to Chicago as the leading candidate. But his immoderate condemnation of southerners and slavery worried moderate northern voters—precisely the voters the party needed for victory.

Reservations about Seward benefited Abraham Lincoln. Lincoln's lieutenants at the convention stressed their candidate's moderation and morality, distancing him from both the abolitionists and Seward. Moreover, Chicago was Lincoln's home turf, and he had many friends working for him at the convention. When Seward faltered, Lincoln rose and won the Republican nomination.

The presidential campaign of 1860 actually comprised two campaigns. In the South, the contest was between Breckinridge and Bell; in the North, it was Lincoln against Douglas. Breckinridge and Bell had scattered support in the North, as did Douglas in the South, but in the main this was a sectional election. Lincoln did not even appear on the ballot in most southern states.

Lincoln became the nation's sixteenth president, with 40 percent of the popular vote (see Map 14–2). Douglas, though second after Lincoln in the popular balloting, won the undivided electoral vote of only one state, Missouri.

Lincoln took most northern states by significant margins and won all the region's electoral votes except three in New Jersey. This gave him a substantial majority of 180 electoral votes. Breckinridge won eleven southern states but received a majority of the popular

**Constitutional Union Party**   National party formed in 1860, mainly by former Whigs, that emphasized allegiance to the Union and strict enforcement of all national legislation.

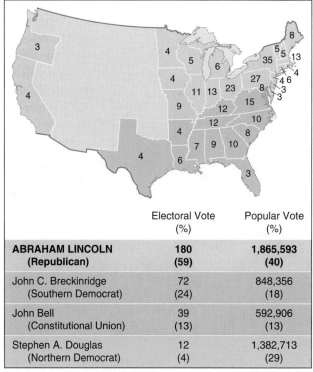

| | Electoral Vote (%) | Popular Vote (%) |
|---|---|---|
| **ABRAHAM LINCOLN** (Republican) | **180** **(59)** | **1,865,593** **(40)** |
| John C. Breckinridge (Southern Democrat) | 72 (24) | 848,356 (18) |
| John Bell (Constitutional Union) | 39 (13) | 592,906 (13) |
| Stephen A. Douglas (Northern Democrat) | 12 (4) | 1,382,713 (29) |

**MAP 14–2   The Election of 1860**   The election returns from 1860 vividly illustrate the geography of sectionalism.

**Based on** the geographic sectionalism shown in this map, what issues were important to voters in the election of 1860?

vote in just four. In the South as a whole, his opponents, Bell and Douglas, together reaped 55 percent of the popular vote, confirming Republicans' skepticism about southern determination to secede.

## SECESSION AND SLAVERY

The events following Lincoln's election demonstrated how wildly mistaken were those who dismissed southern threats of secession. Four days after Lincoln's victory, the South Carolina legislature called on the state's citizens to elect delegates to a convention to consider secession. Meeting on December 20, the delegates voted unanimously to leave the Union. By February 1, six other states had all held similar conventions and decided to leave the Union. Representatives from the seven seceding states met to form a separate country, the **Confederate States of America.** On February 18, Jefferson Davis was sworn in as its president.

The swiftness of secession in the Lower South obscured the divisions in most southern states over the issue. Secessionists barely secured a majority in the Georgia and Louisiana conventions. In Mississippi, Florida, and Alabama, the secessionist majority was more comfortable, but pro-Union candidates polled a significant minority of votes. With Lincoln headed for the White House, the greatest support for secession came from large landowners in counties in which slaves comprised a majority of the population. Support for secession was weakest among small, nonslaveholding farmers.

The secessionists mounted an effective propaganda campaign, deftly using the press to persuade voters to elect their delegates to the state conventions. Framing the issue as a personal challenge to every southern citizen, they argued that it would be cowardly to remain in the Union, a submission to despotism and enslavement. Most of all, secessionists focused on the threat to the institution of slavery as the primary cause for leaving the Union. (See American Views, The Cause of the Civil War.)

The delegates who voted to take Texas out of the Union, for example, charged that a Lincoln administration would result in "the abolition of negro slavery" and "the recognition of political equality between the white and negro races." South Carolina delegates justified secession by alleging that northerners "have encouraged and assisted thousands of our slaves to leave their homes; and those who remain, have been incited by emissaries, books and pictures to servile insurrection." Leaders in Georgia and Mississippi issued similar declarations. Just in case there was any doubt as to what the Confederate States of America stood for, Vice President Alexander Stephens proclaimed the "cornerstone" of the new government "rests upon the great truth that the negro is not equal to the white man; that slavery, subordination to the superior race, is his natural and moral condition." Slavery thus defined the South, and any attempt to lure the errant slave states back into the Union required unprecedented negotiating skills and a willingness to compromise. Neither the outgoing nor incoming administrations would possess these attributes.

## PRESIDENTIAL INACTION

Because Lincoln would not take office until March 4, 1861, the Buchanan administration had to cope with the secession crisis during the critical months of December and January. The president's failure to work out a solution with Congress as secession fever swept the Lower South undermined Unionist forces in the seceding states.

When Buchanan lost the support of northern Democrats over the Lecompton Constitution, he turned to the South for support and filled his cabinet with southerners. Now, facing the secession crisis, he proposed holding a constitutional convention to amend the Constitution in ways that would satisfy the South's demands on slavery. This outright surrender to southern demands, however, had no chance of passing in Congress. Buchanan's

---

**Confederate States of America** Nation proclaimed in Montgomery, Alabama, in February 1861, after the seven states of the Lower South seceded from the United States.

---

**QUICK REVIEW**

**Buchanan and Secession**

- Buchanan had to deal with secession crisis in the months between Lincoln's election and inauguration.
- Buchanan failed to work with Congress to find a solution.
- Buchanan hoped waiting would bring the South to its senses.

administration quickly fell apart. As the Lower South states left the Union, their representatives and senators left Washington, and with them went Buchanan's closest advisers and key cabinet officials.

Buchanan, a lame duck, bereft of friends and advisers, did little more than condemn secession. He was reluctant to take action that would limit the options of the incoming administration or, worse, tip the balance in the Upper South toward secession. He hoped that waiting might bring an isolated Lower South to its senses and give efforts to mediate the sectional rift a chance to succeed.

## PEACE PROPOSALS

Previous sectional conflicts, dating from the Missouri Compromise of 1820, had brought forth the ingenuity and goodwill of political leaders to effect compromise and draw the Union back from the brink of disintegration. Both ingenuity and goodwill were scarce commodities in the gray secession winter of 1860–1861. The two conflicting sides had little trust in each other, and the word "compromise" was viewed as more a synonym for capitulation than salvation.

Kentucky senator John J. Crittenden chaired a Senate committee that proposed a package of constitutional amendments in December 1860 designed to solve the sectional crisis. The central feature of the Crittenden Plan was the extension of the Missouri Compromise line through the territories all the way to California. The plan was of marginal interest to the South, because it was unlikely to result in any new slave states. And Republicans opposed it because it contradicted one of their basic principles, the exclusion of slavery from the territories.

Meanwhile, ex-president John Tyler emerged from retirement to lead an effort by the Border States, the Upper South and the Lower North, to forge a peace. Delegates from these states met in February 1861, but their plan differed little from Crittenden's, and it, too, got nowhere in Congress.

## LINCOLN'S VIEWS ON SECESSION

President-elect Lincoln monitored the secession of the Lower South states and the attempts to reach a compromise from his home in Springfield. Although he said nothing publicly, he made it known that he did not favor compromises like those proposed by Crittenden and Tyler.

Lincoln counted on Unionist sentiment to keep the Upper South from seceding. Like Buchanan, he felt that the longer the Lower South states remained isolated, the more likely they would be to return to the fold. For a while, events seemed to bear him out.

One by one, Upper South states registered their support for the Union. North Carolinians went to the polls in February and turned down the call for a secession convention. Also in February, Virginians elected Unionists to their convention by a five-to-one margin. In Missouri, not one secessionist won election to the state convention. In Kentucky, the legislature adjourned without taking action on a convention or a statewide referendum on secession. And the Maryland legislature, already out of session, showed no inclination to reconvene.

A closer look, however, reveals that there were limits to the Upper South's Unionism. Most voters in the region went to the polls assuming that Congress would eventually reach a compromise based on the Crittenden proposals, Tyler's peace conference, or some other remedy. Leaders in the Upper South saw themselves as peacemakers. As one Virginian explained, "Without submission to the North or desertion of the South, Virginia has that moral position within the Union which will give her power to arbitrate between the sections." But what if arbitration failed? Or what if the Lower South states precipitated a crisis that forced the Upper South to choose sides? It was unlikely that the Upper South would abide the use of federal force against its southern neighbors.

Lincoln believed that the slavery issue had to come to a crisis before the nation could solve it. Although he said in public that he would never interfere with slavery in the slave states, the deep moral revulsion he felt toward the institution left him more ambivalent in private. As he confided to a colleague in 1860, "The tug has to come, and better now, than any time hereafter."

## FORT SUMTER: THE TUG COMES

In his inaugural address on March 4, 1861, Abraham Lincoln denounced secession and vowed to uphold federal law but tempered his firmness with a conciliatory conclusion. Addressing southerners specifically, he assured them, "We are not enemies but friends. . . . Though passion may have strained, it must not break our bonds of affection. The mystic chords of memory, stretching from every battlefield, and patriot grave, to every living heart and hearthstone, all over this broad land, will yet swell the chorus of the Union, when again touched, as surely they will be, by the better angels of our nature."

Southerners wanted concessions, not conciliation, however. The new president said nothing about slavery in the territories, nothing about the constitutional amendments proposed by Crittenden and Tyler, and nothing about the release of federal property in the South to the Confederacy. Even some northerners hoping for an olive branch were disappointed. But Lincoln was hoping for time—time to get the Lower South states quarreling with one another, time to allow Union sentiment to build in the Upper South, and time to convince northerners that the Union needed preserving. He did not get that time.

One day after Lincoln's inauguration, Major Robert Anderson, the commander of **Fort Sumter** in Charleston harbor, informed the administration that he had only four to six weeks' worth of provisions left. Anderson assumed that Lincoln would order him to evacuate the fort. The commanding General of the Army, Winfield Scott, advised the president accordingly, as did many members of his cabinet. Lincoln stalled.

The issue was simple, though the alternatives were difficult: Do not provision Fort Sumter and the garrison would fall to the Confederate government; provision the fort and risk a military confrontation as the Confederate authorities would perceive such action as an act of war. Lincoln had vowed in his inaugural address to uphold the Constitution and "to protect and defend" the country's interests; yet, he had also promised that he would not make any aggressive movements against the South.

News of Anderson's plight changed the mood in the North. The Slave Power, some said, was holding him and his men hostage. Frustration grew over Lincoln's silence and inaction. The Confederacy's bold resolve seemed to contrast sharply with the federal government's confusion and inertia.

In early April, Lincoln ordered an expedition to provision Fort Sumter. Hoping to avoid a confrontation, the president did not send the troops that Anderson had requested. Instead, he ordered unarmed ships to proceed to the fort, deliver the provisions, and leave. Only if the Confederates fired on them were they to force their way into the fort with the help of armed reinforcements. Lincoln notified South Carolina authorities that he intended to do nothing more than "feed the hungry."

At Charleston, Confederate general P. G. T. Beauregard had standing orders to turn back any relief expedition. But President Davis wanted to take Sumter before the provisions arrived to avoid fighting Anderson and the reinforcements at the same time. He also realized that the outbreak of fighting could compel the Upper South to join the Confederacy. But his impatience to force the issue placed the Confederacy in the position of firing, unprovoked, on the American flag and at Major Anderson, who had become a hero to the North.

W **WHERE TO LEARN MORE**

★ Fort Sumter National Monument,
Charleston, South Carolina
http://www.nps.gov/fosu/index.htm

**Fort Sumter** Begun in the late 1820s to protect Charleston, South Carolina, it became the center of national attention in April 1861 when President Lincoln attempted to provision federal troops at the fort, triggering a hostile response from on-shore Confederate forces, opening the Civil War.

**Watch the Video**

at **www.myhistorylab.com**
*What Caused the Civil War?*

## QUICK REVIEW

**From Inauguration to War**

♦ Lincoln struck conciliatory tone in inaugural address.

♦ South wanted concessions, not conciliation.

♦ Crisis over Fort Sumter sparks the war.

## The Cause of the Civil War

The matter of causation has become controversial only in subsequent generations. Writers have cited economic differences between the sections, clashing interpretations of the Constitution, the tariff, and states' rights as factors in addition to slavery that brought about the Civil War. This is not surprising. People do not want to ascribe the death of 350,000 young southern men to the cause of human bondage, especially if one can identify an ancestor or two among the fallen. Contemporaries, however, had no need to dissemble about their actions or their society. The following excerpts from prominent southern politicians, a noted physician-writer, and a leading clergyman reflected the broad consensus in the South that secession and the war that would follow centered on the issue of slavery and the consequences of its abolition.

### Speech of Henry L. Benning before the Virginia Convention, February 18, 1861

What was the reason that induced Georgia to take the step of secession? This reason may be summed up in one single proposition. It was a conviction, a deep conviction on the part of Georgia, that a separation from the North was the only thing that could prevent the abolition of her slavery.

*Source: Addresses delivered before the Virginia state convention by Hon. Fulton Anderson, commissioner from Mississippi, Hon. Henry L. Benning, commissioner from Georgia, and Hon. John S. Preston, commissioner from South Carolina, February 1861. (Richmond: W. M. Elliott, printer, 1861).*

### Speech of Alexander Stephens, Vice President of the Confederate States of America, Savannah, Georgia, March 21, 1861

The new constitution [of the C.S.A.] has put at rest, forever, all the agitating questions relating to our peculiar institution African slavery as it exists amongst us the proper status of the negro in our form of civilization. . . .

Our new government is founded upon . . . its foundations are laid, its cornerstone rests, upon the great truth that the negro is not equal to the white man; that slavery and subordination to the superior race is his natural and normal condition. This, our new government, is the first, in the history of the world, based upon this great physical, philosophical, and moral truth.

*Source: Henry Cleveland, Alexander H. Stephens, in Public and Private: With Letters and Speeches, Before, During, and Since the War (Philadelphia: National Publishing Company, 1866): 717–728.*

### Sermon of Rev. Benjamin M. Palmer, Thanksgiving Day, November 29, 1860, New Orleans, LA

[W]hat, at this juncture, is [our] providential trust? I answer that it is to conserve and to perpetuate the institution of domestic slavery as now existing. . . . Need I pause to show how this system is interwoven with our entire social fabric . . . and sanctioned in the Scriptures of God . . . ? Must I pause to show how it has fashioned our modes of life, and determined all our habits of thought and feeling, and moulded the very type of our civilization? How then can the hand of violence be laid upon it without involving our existence?

*Source: Thanksgiving Sermon, Delivered at the First Presbyterian Church, New Orleans, on Thursday, November 29, 1860 (New York: G. F. Hesbit & Co., Printers, 1860).*

### William H. Holcombe, MD, "The Alternative: A Separate Nationality, or the Africanization of the South," February 1861.

Opposition to slavery, to its existence, its extension and its perpetuation, is the sole cohesive element of the triumphant faction. . . . The question is at length plainly presented: submission or secession. The only alternative left us is this: *a separate nationality or the Africanization of the South.* He has not analyzed this subject aright nor probed it to the bottom, who supposes that the real quarrel between the North and the South is about the Territories, or the decision of the Supreme Court, or even the constitution itself. . . . The division is broader and deeper and more incurable than this. The antagonism is fundamental and ineradicable. The true secret of it lies in the total reversion of public opinion which has occurred in both sections of the country in the last quarter of a century on the subject of slavery.

*Source: Southern Literary Messenger, February 1861: 81–88.*

- **How** do these excerpts reflect the merger of religion and politics?
- **What** connections do these leaders make between slavery and white supremacy?
- **Given** the views expressed in these excerpts, what could the Lincoln administration have done to restore the Union short of war?

## OVERVIEW    The Emerging Sectional Crisis

| Event | Year | Effect |
| --- | --- | --- |
| Wilmot Proviso | 1846 | Congressman David Wilmot's proposal to ban slavery from territories acquired from Mexico touched off a bitter sectional dispute in Congress. |
| Compromise of 1850 | 1850 | Law admitted California as a free state, granted the population of Utah and New Mexico Territories the right to decide on slavery, and established a new and stronger Fugitive Slave Act, all of which "solved" the territorial issue raised by the Wilmot Proviso but satisfied neither North nor South and planted the seeds of future conflict. |
| Election of 1852 | 1852 | Results confirmed demise of the Whig Party, initiating a period of political realignment. |
| Kansas-Nebraska Act | 1854 | Law created the Kansas and Nebraska Territories and repealed the Missouri Compromise of 1820 by leaving the question of slavery to the territories' residents. Its passage enraged many northerners, prompting some to form the new Republican Party. |
| "Bleeding Kansas" | 1855–1856 | Sometimes violent conflict between pro- and antislavery forces in Kansas further polarized the sectional debate. |
| Election of 1856 | 1856 | Presidency was won by Democrat James Buchanan of Pennsylvania, but a surprisingly strong showing by the recently formed Republican Party in the North set the stage for the 1860 election. |
| *Dred Scott* Case | 1857 | The Supreme Court ruling that slaves were not citizens and that Congress had no authority to ban slavery from the territories boosted Republican prospects in the North. |
| Lecompton Constitution | 1857 | Proslavery document, framed by a fraudulently elected constitutional convention in Kansas and supported by President Buchanan, further convinced northerners that the South was subverting their rights. |
| John Brown's Raid | 1859 | Unsuccessful attempt to free the South's slaves, this attack on a federal arsenal in Harpers Ferry, Virginia, increased sectional tension. |
| Election of 1860 | 1860 | Republican Abraham Lincoln won a four-way race for the presidency. The last major national party, the Democrats, disintegrated. Lower South states seceded. |
| Fort Sumter | 1861 | Confederate forces attacked the fort in April 1861, Lincoln called for troops, and several Upper South states seceded. The Civil War was underway. |

Black smoke billows from Fort Sumter in the Charleston harbor during the first engagement of the Civil War.

On April 10, Davis ordered Beauregard to demand the immediate evacuation of Fort Sumter. Anderson refused but wondered what the hurry was, considering that his provisions would run out in a few days. The remark gave Beauregard pause and prompted additional negotiations. Anderson did not yield, and as unarmed Federal supply vessels appeared before dawn on April 12, 1861, the first Confederate shell whistled down on the fort. After more than a day of shelling, during which more than 5,000 artillery rounds struck Fort Sumter, Anderson surrendered. Remarkably, neither side suffered any casualties, a deceptive beginning to an exceptionally bloody war.

When the verdict of Fort Sumter reached President Lincoln, he called on the southern states still in the Union to send troops to put down the rebellion. Refusing to make war on South Carolina, the Upper South states of Virginia, North Carolina, Tennessee, and Arkansas seceded, and the Confederacy expanded to eleven states.

# CONCLUSION

When David Wilmot submitted his amendment to ban slavery from the territories gained from Mexico, he could not have foreseen that the debate he unleashed would end in civil war just fifteen years later. Northerners and southerners had lived together in one nation for nearly eighty years. During that time, they had reached accommodations on slavery at the Constitutional Convention of 1787, in the Compromises of 1820 and 1850, and on numerous lesser occasions. But by the 1850s the slavery issue had become weighted with so much moral and political freight that it defied easy resolution. Throughout the Western world, attitudes toward slavery were changing. Northern evangelical Protestants in the 1840s and 1850s branded slavery a sin and slaveholders sinners. The overwhelming popularity of *Uncle Tom's Cabin* both tapped and fed this sentiment. America could no longer continue its journey as a nation half slave and half free.

The political conflict over slavery coalesced around northern efforts to curtail southern expansion and power and southern attempts to maintain power and influence in the federal government by planting the institution in the western territories. This conflict eventually helped undo the Compromise of 1850 and turned Stephen A. Douglas's railroad bill into a battle royal over Kansas. Unable to resolve sectional differences over slavery, the Whigs disintegrated, and the Democrats divided into northern and southern factions. The Republican Party was formed from the political debris. Ethnic and religious conflicts further disturbed the political landscape and contributed to party realignment.

Northerners and southerners eventually interpreted any incident or piece of legislation as an attempt by one side to gain moral and political advantage at the other's expense. Northerners viewed the *Dred Scott* decision, the Lecompton Constitution, and the southern reaction to John Brown's Raid as evidence of a Slave Power conspiracy to deny white northerners their constitutional rights. Southerners interpreted the northern reaction to these same events as evidence of a conspiracy to rob them of security and equality within the Union.

Ironically, as Americans in both sections talked of freedom and self-determination, the black men and women in their midst had little of either. Their American journey generated scant recognition. Lincoln went to war to preserve the Union; Davis, to defend a new nation. Slavery was the spark that ignited the conflict, but white America seemed more comfortable embracing abstract ideals than real people. Northerners and southerners would confront this irony during the bloodiest war in American history, but they would not resolve it.

# WHERE TO LEARN MORE

**The Underground Railroad Freedom Center, Cincinnati, Ohio.** The Center provides information on the northern response to the Fugitive Slave Act. See its website at http://www.freedomcenter.org/.

**Adair Cabin and John Brown Museum, John Brown Memorial Park, Osawatomie, Kansas.** Maintained by the Kansas Historical Society, the cabin (which once belonged to John Brown's sister) and the museum are located on the site of the Battle of Osawatomie, one of the critical events of "Bleeding Kansas." Its website is http://www.kshs.org/places/johnbrown/history.htm.

**Harpers Ferry National Historical Park, West Virginia.** Exhibits interpret John Brown's Raid and re-create some of the atmosphere and structures of the 1850s village and the federal arsenal. Its website is http://www.nps.gov/hafe/index.htm.

**Fort Sumter National Monument, Charleston, South Carolina.** This historic site interprets the bombardment of the fort and the events that immediately preceded the Civil War. Go to http://www.nps.gov/fosu/index.htm.

# REVIEW QUESTIONS

1. How do you account for the great success of Harriet Beecher Stowe's *Uncle Tom's Cabin?*

2. How did the failure of democratic revolutions in Europe affect Americans' perspectives on their own system of government?

3. Discuss the role of evangelical religion in sharpening the sectional conflict between North and South.

4. Between the time he was elected president in November and his inauguration in March, what options did Abraham Lincoln have for resolving the sectional crisis?

5. Northerners and southerners appealed to the same American ideals in support of their respective positions. Could they both have been correct?

# KEY TERMS

**"Bleeding Kansas"** (p. 374)
**Compromise of 1850** (p. 369)
**Confederate States of America** (p. 386)
**Constitutional Union Party** (p. 385)
***Dred Scott* decision** (p. 378)
**Fort Sumter** (p. 388)
**Fugitive Slave Act** (p. 370)
**John Brown's Raid** (p. 383)
**Kansas-Nebraska Act** (p. 374)

**Know-Nothing Party** (p. 375)
**Lecompton Constitution** (p. 378)
**Lincoln-Douglas debates** (p. 380)
**Ostend Manifesto** (p. 373)
**Panic of 1857** (p. 379)
**Popular sovereignty** (p. 367)
**Republican Party** (p. 376)
**Wilmot Proviso** (p. 366)

# myhistorylab Connections

Reinforce what you learned in this chapter by studying the many documents, images, maps, review tools, and videos available at **www.myhistorylab.com**.

## Read and Review

✓●─ Study and Review **Study Plan: Chapter 14**

●●●●─ Read the **Document**

*Edward Gould Buffum, Six Months in the Gold Mines (1850)*

*George Fitzhugh, The Blessings of Slavery (1857)*

*Harriet Beecher Stowe,* Uncle Tom's Cabin *(1852)*

*A Catechism for Slaves (1854)*

*An African American Novel Critiques Racism in the North (1859)*

*Benjamin Drew, from Narratives of Fugitive Slaves in Canada (1855)*

*John Brown's Address before Sentencing (1859)*

*John C. Calhoun, Proposal to Preserve the Union (1850)*

*Opinion of the Supreme Court for* Dred Scott v. Sanford *(1857)*

*The Compromise of 1850*

*The Fugitive Slave Act (1850)*

*The Lincoln-Douglas Debates of 1858*

👁─ See the **Map**

*Slave Population Patterns, 1790 and 1860*

*The Compromise of 1850 and the Kansas-Nebraska Act*

*United States Territorial Expansion in the 1850s*

## Research and Explore

●●●●─ Read the **Document**

*Personal Journeys Online*

*From Then to Now Online: Religion and Politics*

((●●─ Hear the **Audio** *John Brown: An Address by Frederick Douglass*

📷─ Watch the **Video**

*Harriet Beecher Stowe and the Making of* Uncle Tom's Cabin

*What Caused the Civil War?*

─ ((●●─ **Hear** the **Audio** ─

Hear the audio files for Chapter 14 at
**www.myhistorylab.com**.

# 15
# Battle Cries and Freedom Songs: The Civil War

Uniformed black soldiers of the Guard, 107th U.S. Colored Infantry stand with their rifies in front of a rundown guard house

((•—Hear the **Audio**
Hear the audio files for Chapter 15 at **www.myhistorylab.com**.

## MOBILIZATION, NORTH AND SOUTH  *(page 397)*

**WHAT WERE** the North's key advantages at the outset of the war?

## THE EARLY WAR, 1861–1862  *(page 402)*

**HOW DID** the two sides' objectives dictate their strategies in the early years of the war?

## TURNING POINTS, 1862–1863  *(page 407)*

**WHAT CONVINCED** Lincoln to issue the Emancipation Proclamation?

## WAR TRANSFORMS THE NORTH  *(page 417)*

**WHAT IMPACT** did the war have on the North's economy?

## THE CONFEDERACY DISINTEGRATES  *(page 420)*

**HOW DID** the war affect civilian life in the South?

## THE UNION PREVAILS, 1864–1865  *(page 423)*

**WHAT WAS** Grant's strategy for ending the war?

ONE AMERICAN JOURNEY

*July 14, 1861*

*Camp Clark, Washington, DC*

*My very dear Sarah:*

*The indications are very strong that we shall move in a few days, perhaps tomorrow. And lest I should not be able to write you again I feel impelled to write a few lines that may fall under your eye when I am no more. Our movement may be one of a few days' duration and be full of pleasure. And it may be one of severe conflict and death to me. "Not my will but thine O God be done." If it is necessary that I should fall on the battle-field for my Country I am ready. I have no misgivings about, or lack of confidence in the cause in which I am engaged, and my courage does not halt or falter. I know how American Civilization now leans upon the triumph of the government and how great a debt we owe to those who went before us through the blood and suffering of the Revolution. And I am willing, perfectly willing, to lay down all my joys in this life, to help maintain this government, and to pay that debt. But my dear wife, when I know that with my own joys I lay down nearly all of yours, . . . is it weak or dishonorable that while the banner of my purpose floats calmly and proudly in the breeze, underneath, my unbounded love for you my darling wife children should struggle in fierce though useless contest with my love of country? . . .*

*Sarah, my love for you is deathless, it seems to bind me with mighty cables that nothing but omnipotence can break; and yet my love of Country comes over me like a strong wind and bears me irresistibly with all those chains to the battle-field.*

*The memories of the blissful moments I have enjoyed with you come crowding over me, and I feel most deeply grateful to God and you, that I have enjoyed them for so long. And how hard it is for me to give them up and burn to ashes the hopes and future years, when, God willing, we might still have lived and loved together, and see our boys grown up to honorable manhood around us. . . . If I do not [return], my dear Sarah, never forget how much I loved you, nor that when my last breath escapes me on the battle-field, it will whisper your name.*

*Forgive my many faults, and the many pains I have caused you. How thoughtless, how foolish I have sometimes been! . . .*

*But, O Sarah, if the dead can come back to this earth and flit unseen around those they love, I shall be with you, in the gladdest days and the darkest nights . . . always, always, and if there be a soft breeze upon your cheek, it shall be my breath[;] as the cool air fans your throbbing temple, it shall be my spirit passing by. Sarah do not mourn me dead; think I am gone and wait for thee, for we shall meet again. . . .*

*Sullivan*

••▶ Read the Document at **www.myhistorylab.com**

Personal Journeys Online

- Sam R. Watkins, Co. "Aytch": *A Confederate Memoir of the Civil War*, 1882. A Confederate soldier recounts the horrors of war he witnessed in a southern hospital and on the battlefield.

- Ambrose Bierce, "What I Saw of Shiloh," *Civil War Stories*, 1909. Account of a Union soldier's experiences at the Battle of Shiloh.

## CHRONOLOGY

| | | |
|---|---|---|
| **1861 January** | Benito Juarez becomes president of Mexico, dedicated to restoring national unity. | |
| **March** | Tsar Alexander II emancipates Russia's serfs. | |
| | Kingdom of Italy proclaimed. | |
| **April** | Confederates fire on Fort Sumter; Civil War begins. | |
| **July** | First Battle of Bull Run. | |
| **1862 February** | Forts Henry and Donelson fall to Union forces. | |
| **March** | Peninsula Campaign begins. | |
| | Battle of Glorieta Pass, New Mexico. | |
| **April** | Battle of Shiloh. | |
| | New Orleans falls to Federal forces. | |
| **May** | Union captures Corinth, Mississippi. | |
| **July** | Seven Days' Battles end. | |
| | Congress passes the Confiscation Act. | |
| **August** | Second Battle of Bull Run. | |
| **September** | Battle of Antietam. | |
| **December** | Battle of Fredericksburg. | |
| **1863 January** | Emancipation Proclamation takes effect. | |
| **May** | Battle of Chancellorsville; Stonewall Jackson is mortally wounded. | |
| **June** | French forces capture Mexico City. | |
| **July** | Battle of Gettysburg. | |

| | |
|---|---|
| | Vicksburg falls to Union forces. |
| | New York Draft Riot occurs. |
| | Black troops of the 54th Massachusetts Volunteer Infantry Regiment assault Fort Wagner outside Charleston. |
| **September** | Battle of Chickamauga. |
| **November** | Battle of Chattanooga. |
| **1864 May** | Battle of the Wilderness. |
| **June** | Battle of Cold Harbor. |
| | Ferdinand Maximilian Joseph, archduke of Austria, crowned emperor of Mexico with support of French troops. |
| **September** | Sherman captures Atlanta. |
| **November** | President Lincoln is reelected. |
| | Sherman begins his march to the sea. |
| **1865 January** | Congress passes Thirteenth Amendment to the Constitution, outlawing slavery (ratified December 1865). |
| **February** | Charleston surrenders. |
| **March** | Confederate Congress authorizes enlistment of black soldiers. |
| **April** | Federal troops enter Richmond. |
| | Lee surrenders to Grant at Appomattox Court House. |
| | Lincoln is assassinated. |

SULLIVAN BALLOU'S letter to his wife on the eve of the First Battle of Bull Run typified the sentiments of the civilian armies raised by both North and South: a clear purpose of the importance of their mission, a sense of foreboding, an appeal and acknowledgment of the guiding hand of God, and, most of all, words of love for family.

Sullivan Ballou took the ultimate journey for his beliefs and his love. The Civil War preserved the Union, abolished slavery, and killed at least 620,000 soldiers, more than in all the other wars the country fought from the Revolution to the Korean conflict combined. To come to terms with this is to try to reconcile the war's great accomplishments with its awful consequences. ✦

# MOBILIZATION, NORTH AND SOUTH

Neither side was prepared for a major war. The Confederacy lacked a national army. Each southern state had a militia, but by the 1850s, these companies had become more social clubs than fighting units. Aside from privately owned ships and some captured Federal vessels, the Confederacy also lacked a navy. The Union had a regular army of only 16,000 men, most of whom were stationed west of the Mississippi River. Their major responsibility had been to intervene between white settlers and Indians.

**WHAT WERE** the North's key advantages at the outset of the war?

Watch the Video
at **www.myhistorylab.com**
*What Caused the Civil War?*

Read the Document
at **www.myhistorylab.com**
*A Nation Divided: The Civil War*

Each government augmented these meager military reserves with thousands of new recruits and developed a bureaucracy to mount a war effort. At the same time, the administrations of Presidents Lincoln and Davis secured the loyalty of their civilian populations and devised military strategies for a war of indeterminate duration. How North and South went about these tasks reflected both the different objectives of the two sides and the distinctive personalities of their leaders, Abraham Lincoln and Jefferson Davis.

## WAR FEVER

The day after Major Robert Anderson surrendered Fort Sumter, President Lincoln moved to enlarge his small, scattered army by mobilizing state militias for 90 days. Four states—Virginia, Arkansas, North Carolina, and Tennessee—refused the call and seceded from the Union. About one-third of the officer corps of the regular army, including some of the highest ranking officers, resigned their commissions to join the Confederacy. Still, Lincoln seemed likely to meet his target of 75,000 troops.

Lincoln's modest 90-day call-up reflected the general belief, North and South, that the war would end quickly. Not everyone thought the war would be brief. William T. Sherman, who had recently headed a Louisiana military academy and would become one of the Union's few great commanders, wrote in April 1861, "I think it is to be a long war, very long, much longer than any politician thinks."

Northerners closed ranks behind the president after the Confederacy's attack on Fort Sumter. Stephen A. Douglas, a leading Democrat, called on the Republican Lincoln to offer his and his party's support. "There can be no neutrals in this war," Douglas said, "only patriots, or traitors." Residents of New York City, where sympathy for the South had probably been greater than anywhere else in the North, now sponsored huge public demonstrations in support of the war effort.

Southerners were equally eager to support their new nation. Enlistment rallies, wild send-offs at train stations, and auctions and balls to raise money for the troops were staged throughout the Confederacy. As in the North, war fever fired hatred of the enemy.

Appeals to God were commonplace on both sides. The feeling that a holy war was unfolding energized recruits. A Union soldier expressed his feelings in a letter home at the beginning of the war: "I believe our cause to be the cause of liberty and light . . . the cause of God, and holy and justifiable in His sight, and for this reason, I fear not to die in it if need be." Equally convinced of the righteousness of his cause, a Confederate soldier wrote: "Our Cause is Just and God is Just and we shall finally be successful whether I live to see the time or not." As war fever gripped North and South, volunteers on both sides rushed to join, quickly filling the quotas of both armies.

By early spring of 1862, however, the Confederate government was compelled to order the first general draft in American history. It required three years of service for men between 18 and 35 (a range later expanded from 17 to 50). In 1864, the Confederate Congress added a compulsory reenlistment provision. At that point, the only way a recruit could get out of the army was to die or desert.

The Confederate draft law allowed several occupational exemptions. Among them was an infamous provision that allowed one white man on any plantation with more than 20 slaves to be excused from service. The reason for the exemption was to ensure the security and productivity of large plantations, not to protect the privileged, but it led some southerners to conclude that the struggle had become "a rich man's war but a poor man's fight."

The initial flush of enthusiasm faded in the North as well. Responding to a call for additional troops, some northern states initiated a draft during the summer of 1862. In March 1863, Congress passed the Enrollment Act, a draft law that, like the Confederate draft, allowed for occupational exemptions. A provision that allowed a draftee to hire a substitute aroused resentment among working-class northerners. Anger at the draft, as well as poor working conditions, sparked several riots during 1863. But the North was less dependent on conscription than was the South. Only 8 percent of the Union's soldiers were drafted, compared to 20 percent for the Confederacy.

## THE NORTH'S ADVANTAGE IN RESOURCES

The resources of the North, including its population, industrial and agricultural capacity, and transportation network, greatly exceeded those of the South (see Figure 15–1). The 2.1 million men who fought for the Union represented roughly half the men of military age in the North. The 900,000 men who fought for the

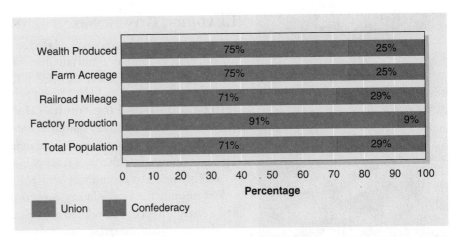

**FIGURE 15–1   A Comparison of the Union and Confederate Control of Key Resources at the Outset of the Civil War**

Confederacy, by contrast, represented fully 90 percent of its eligible population. Irish and German immigrants continued to flow into the North during the war, although at a slower rate than before, and thousands of them enlisted, often as substitutes for native-born northerners. Nearly 200,000 African Americans, most of them ex-slaves from the South, took up arms for the Union. Not until the last month of the war did the Confederacy consider arming slaves.

At the beginning of the war, the North controlled 90 percent of the nation's industrial capacity. The North had dozens of facilities for producing war matériel; the South had only one munitions plant, the Tredegar Iron Works in Richmond. Northern farms, more mechanized than their southern counterparts, produced record harvests of meat, grain, and vegetables. Southern farms were also productive, but the South lacked the North's capacity to transport and distribute food efficiently. The railroad system in the North was more than twice the size of the South's.

Thanks to the North's abundance of resources, no soldier in any previous American army had ever been outfitted as well as the blue-uniformed Union trooper. The official color of the Confederate uniform was gray, although a dusty brown shade was more common. Most southern soldiers, however, did not wear distinguishable uniforms, especially toward the end of the war. They also often lacked proper shoes or any footwear at all. Still, the South never lost a battle because of insufficient supplies or inadequate weaponry. New foundries opened, and manufacturing enterprises in Augusta, Georgia; Selma, Alabama; and elsewhere joined the Tredegar Iron Works in keeping the Confederate armies equipped.

Unstable finances proved more of a handicap for the Confederacy than its relatively low industrial capacity. The Confederate economy, and its treasury, depended heavily on cotton exports. But a Union naval blockade and the ability of textile manufacturers in Europe to find new sources of supply restricted this crucial source of revenue. The imposition of taxes would have improved the Confederacy's finances, but southerners resisted taxation. The government sold interest-bearing bonds to raise money, but as Confederate fortunes declined, so did bond sales. With few other options, the Confederacy financed more than 60 percent of the $1.5 billion it spent on the war with printing-press money. Inflation spiraled out of control, demoralizing civilians.

The Union had more abundant financial resources than the Confederacy, and the federal government was more successful than the Confederate government at developing innovative ways to meet the great cost of the war. Like the Confederacy, the Federal government issued paper money, bills derisively known as "greenbacks," that was not backed by gold or silver. But the Federal government also offset its expenses with the country's first income tax, which citizens could pay in greenbacks, a move that bolstered the value and credibility of the paper currency. These financial measures eliminated the need for wage and price controls and rationing and warded off ruinous inflation in the North.

**QUICK REVIEW**

**Northern Advantages**

- Twice the number of soldiers.
- North controlled 90 percent of nation's industrial capacity.
- Naval superiority.

**Read the Document**

at **www.myhistorylab.com**
*Jefferson Davis, Address to the Provisional Congress (1861)*

Jefferson Davis, Confederate president, was born in Kentucky. After attending West Point and serving for seven years in the military, Davis became a gentleman planter. He returned to military service during the Mexican War, became a senator in 1847, and served as secretary of war under President Franklin Pierce, then returned to the Senate in 1857.

## LEADERS, GOVERNMENTS, AND STRATEGIES

Leadership ability, like resources, played an important role in the war. It was up to the leaders of the two sides to determine and administer civilian and military policy, to define war objectives, and to inspire a willingness to sacrifice in both citizens and soldiers.

**Jefferson Davis and the South.**   The Confederate president, Jefferson Davis, had to build a government from scratch during a war. Abraham Lincoln at least had the benefit of an established governmental structure, a standing army, healthy financial resources, and established diplomatic relations with the nations of Europe.

Although Davis's military and political background qualified him for the prodigious task of running the Confederacy, aspects of his character compromised his effectiveness. He had a sharp intellect but related awkwardly to people. Colleagues found him aloof. He was inclined to equate compromise with weakness and interpreted any opposition as a personal attack.

**Abraham Lincoln and the North.**   Northerners, like southerners, needed a convincing reason to endure the prolonged sacrifice of the Civil War. For them, the struggle was a distant one, fought mostly on southern soil. Lincoln and other northern leaders secured support by convincing their compatriots of the importance of preserving the Union. The president viewed the conflict in global terms, its results affecting the hopes for democratic government around the world. He concluded that the war "presents to the whole family of man, the question, whether a constitutional republic . . . can or cannot maintain its territorial integrity, against its own domestic foes."

**Lincoln's fight for the border states.**   The secession of Virginia, Arkansas, North Carolina, and Tennessee left four border slave states, Maryland, Delaware, Kentucky, and Missouri, hanging in the balance. Were Maryland and Delaware to secede, the federal capital at Washington, DC, would be surrounded by Confederate territory. The loss of Kentucky and Missouri would threaten the borders of Iowa, Illinois, Indiana, and Ohio and remove the Deep South from the threat of imminent invasion. Kentucky's manpower, livestock, and waterways were important to both sides.

Lincoln adopted a "soft" strategy to secure the border states, stressing the restoration of the Union as the sole objective of Federal military operations and assuring border residents that his government would not interfere with slavery. Union commanders barred fugitive slaves from their camps during the first year of the war, promising "to keep the war a lily-white crusade," as one officer put it. But early reports from the four states were troubling. The four governors displayed polite indifference or overt hostility to the federal government.

Maryland's strategic location north of Washington, DC, rendered its loyalty to the Union vital. Although a majority of its citizens opposed secession, a mob attack on Union troops passing through Baltimore in April 1861 indicated strong prosouthern sentiment. Lincoln dispatched Federal troops to monitor the fall elections in the state, placed its legislature under military surveillance, and arrested officials who opposed the Union cause, including the mayor of Baltimore. This show of force guaranteed the pro-Union candidate for governor an overwhelming victory and saved Maryland for the Union. Delaware, although nominally a slave state, remained staunchly for the Union.

Missourians settled their indecision by combat. The fighting culminated with a Union victory in March 1862 at the Battle of Pea Ridge, Arkansas. The Union victory was notable for two reasons. First, the Confederate force included 3,500 mounted Indians led by Colonel Stand Watie, a Cherokee, who achieved one of the rare Rebel victories during the two-day battle. The Cherokees joined the Confederate cause in the hopes of securing a better deal than they had received from Washington. The decisive Union victory at Pea Ridge also secured Missouri and northern Arkansas for federal forces, further diminishing Confederate influence in the Upper South.

Kentucky never seceded but attempted to remain neutral at the outset of the war. The legislature was pro-Union, the governor prosouthern. Both sides actively recruited soldiers in the state. In September 1861, when Confederate forces invaded Kentucky and Union forces moved to expel them, the state became one of the war's battlegrounds.

Although Virginia went with the Confederacy, some counties in the western part of the state opposed secession and, as early as the summer of 1861, took steps to establish a pro-Union state. In June 1863, West Virginia became the nation's thirty-fifth state.

**Strategies and tactics.**   To a great extent, the political objectives of each side determined its military strategy. Southerners wanted independence and protection of their institutions; northerners fought to preserve the Union. The North's goal required conquest. Federal forces had to invade the South, destroy its armies, and rout its government, a difficult assignment considering the vast geographic extent of the Confederacy. The Confederacy, for its part, did not need to conquer the North. Fighting a defensive battle in its own territory, the South had only to hang on until growing northern opposition to the war or some decisive northern military mistake convinced the Union to stop fighting.

But the South's strategy had two weaknesses. First, it demanded more patience than the South had shown in impulsively attacking Fort Sumter. Second, the South might not have sufficient resources to draw out the war long enough to swing northern public opinion behind peace. The question was: What would break first, northern support for the war or southern ability to wage it?

## THE SOUTHERN LANDSCAPE

The southern landscape played a significant strategic role in the Civil War. The South covered 800,000 square miles, about the size of Spain, Italy, France, Germany, and Poland combined. The region was mostly rural with a 3,500-mile coastline, impenetrable forests and swamps, numerous rivers, a mountain chain, and irregular terrain except on the coast. Union and Confederate officers who had attended West Point learned open field combat with two armies arrayed against each other in close formation, firing weapons with limited range and accuracy. The introduction of rifled muskets and light artillery increased the accuracy, range, and deadliness of weaponry. Attacking entrenched soldiers or troops with commanding geographical positions rarely proved successful and usually resulted in high casualties for the attacking army.

The dense forests of the South also hampered traditional battle tactics. Bullets and artillery shells often ignited the underbrush, creating an inferno that trapped troops. The dense smoke caused by fire and weapons restricted visibility. Some soldiers became victims of friendly fire as a result.

Then there was the cloying heat and humidity of the South. Most of the major

The southern landscape played a major role in the Civil War. The undulating terrain and the obstacles presented by rivers, streams, woods, and cultivated fields are all on display here as Union troops under General Ambrose Burnside take the bridge (today named after the General) over Antietam Creek in September 1862. Rebel forces held the higher ground, however, and pushed the Federals back later in the day.

engagements occurred in the late spring, summer, and fall. Wool uniforms exhausted troops, and unsanitary conditions, compounded by the absence of frost until the late fall, heightened the casualties from disease. The moisture and excessive heat also generated sustained and often violent thunderstorms.

Downpours turned roads into mud and gentle streams into raging rivers. The condition of southern roads, never very good even in fine weather, played a role in delaying deployment of troops, the coordination of attacks, and the pursuit of a defeated foe.

The South's uneven terrain also hampered traditional battle tactics. At Antietam, for example, the numerous depressions, or valleys, between hills meant that soldiers disappeared from view every so often. In hilly terrain the artillery echoed off hills, making it difficult for troops to determine the direction of firing.

These environmental idiosyncrasies of the South should have given Confederate troops a significant advantage. They fought on their home turf and they maneuvered among friendly residents. The Confederates, however, like most of their Union counterparts, had rarely ventured beyond their neighborhoods growing up and often found themselves in unfamiliar terrain. Thus, for the most part, the respective commanders adapted to the geography on the fly. The Union's superiority in railroads, steamships, and telegraphy, especially during the last eighteen months of the war, enabled commanders to transcend environmental barriers and the South's immense territory to move troops and information quickly.

## THE EARLY WAR, 1861–1862

**HOW DID** the two sides' objectives dictate their strategies in the early years of the war?

The North's offensive strategy dictated the course of the war for the first two years. In the West, the federal army's objectives were to hold Missouri, Kentucky, and Tennessee, to control the Mississippi River, and eventually to detach the area west of the Appalachians from the rest of the Confederacy. In the East, Union forces sought to capture Richmond, the Confederate capital. The U.S. Navy imposed a blockade along the Confederate coast and pushed into inland waterways to capture southern ports.

The Confederates defended strategic locations throughout their territory or abandoned them when prudence required. Occasionally, taking advantage of surprise or terrain, southern forces ventured out to engage Union armies. Between engagements, each side sniped at, bushwhacked, and trapped the other.

By the end of 1862, the result remained in the balance. Although Union forces had attained some success in the West, the southern armies there remained intact. In the East, where resourceful Confederate leaders several times stopped superior Union forces, the southerners clearly had the best of it.

### FIRST BULL RUN

By July 1861, when the border states appeared more secure for the Union, President Lincoln shifted his attention southward and ordered General Irvin McDowell to move his forces into Virginia to take Richmond (see Map 15–1). Confronting McDowell 20 miles southwest of Washington at Manassas was a Confederate army under General P. G. T. Beauregard. The two armies clashed on July 21 at the First Battle of Bull Run (known to the Confederacy as the First Battle of Manassas). The Union troops seemed at first on the verge of winning. But Beauregard's forces, along with General Joseph E. Johnston's reinforcements, repulsed the assault, scattering not only the Union army but also hundreds of picnickers who had come out from Washington to watch the fight.

Bull Run dispelled some illusions and reinforced others. It boosted southerners' confidence and seemed to confirm their boast that one Confederate could whip ten Yankees, even

**QUICK REVIEW**

**The First Battle of Bull Run**

◆ July 21, 1861: Beauregard (Confederacy) and McDowell (Union) meet at Manassas.

◆ Confederate troops repulse a strong Union attack.

◆ Destroyed belief in North that the war would be over quickly.

## GLOBAL CONNECTIONS

### ∼ THE CIVIL WAR IN EUROPE ∼

The American Civil War was not, of course, a global conflict. The growing power of the United States during the first half of the nineteenth century, however, ensured that the war would generate considerable interest in Europe. The elite of both Great Britain and France could barely conceal their delight at the possible breakup of a rival nation and one whose government stood as a living rebuke to exclusive religious and political institutions.

The staunchest supporter of the Union cause was Russia. That the most despotic regime on the continent supported the most democratic nation was strictly a matter of geopolitics. The Russians viewed a united America as an effective rival to their perennial enemies, France and England. When the Russian Atlantic and Pacific fleets called on New York and San Francisco, respectively, in 1863, many observers interpreted the maneuver as a signal of support for the federal navy and a warning against British or French intervention. In truth, the tsar wished to remove his fleet from Russia's ice-bound harbors for the winter in case tensions with Great Britain escalated into war.

The British and French positions were of vital interest to the Confederacy. Early in the conflict, both countries recognized the Confederate States of America as a belligerent, which enabled the Davis administration to obtain loans and munitions. When a U.S. naval ship intercepted a British vessel carrying two Confederate envoys and detained them, British authorities threatened retaliation and sent two troop vessels to Canada to support their claim. The Lincoln administration wisely apologized and released the captives. The crisis passed.

The Confederacy was never able to gain recognition from Britain and France as an independent nation. The European powers feared American reprisal and the military situation of the Confederacy deteriorated after the losses at Gettysburg and Vicksburg in July 1863. Also, Europe had experienced a number of short grain crops and now relied increasingly on shipments from the North.

The French would not intrude into the American conflict without the British, though they managed to make trouble elsewhere, invading Mexico in 1862 over the alleged nonpayment of a debt and installing Maximilian of Austria as Emperor. They were confident that the Americans, engaged in a civil war, would not interfere. When the Civil War ended in April 1865, the Lincoln administration massed troops at the Mexican border as a warning, and the French withdrew. Mexican nationalists overthrew Maximilian and established a republic in 1867.

Though the British aristocracy favored the Confederacy, the middle and working classes championed the Union cause, especially once emancipation became a war aim. Even the textile workers who suffered from the cessation of the cotton trade supported the Union cause. A statue of Abraham Lincoln adorns a square in the center of Manchester, England. The inscription on the pedestal reads in part, "This statue commemorates the support that the working people of Manchester gave in their fight for the abolition of slavery during the American Civil War."

- What factor was most important in deterring Great Britain and France from recognizing the independence of the Confederate States of America?

---

though the opposing armies were of relatively equal strength when the fighting began. The Union rout planted the suspicion in northern minds that perhaps the Confederates were invincible and destroyed the widespread belief in the North that the war would be over quickly.

◉ See the **Map**

at **www.myhistorylab.com**
*The Civil War Part I: 1861–1862*

## THE WAR IN THE WEST

Federal forces may have retreated in Virginia, but they advanced in the west. Two Confederate forts on the Tennessee-Kentucky border, Fort Henry on the Tennessee River and Fort Donelson on the Cumberland River, guarded the strategic waterways that linked Tennessee

**MAP 15–1   From First Bull Run to Antietam: The War in the East, 1861–1862**   The early stages of the war demonstrated the strategies of the Confederacy and the Union. Federal troops stormed into Virginia hoping to capture Richmond and bring a quick end to the war. Through a combination of poor generalship and Confederate tenacity, they failed Confederate troops hoped to defend their territory, prolong the war, and eventually win their independence as northern patience evaporated. They proved successful initially, but, with the abandonment of the defensive strategy and the invasion of Maryland in the fall of 1862, the Confederates suffered a political and morale setback at Antietam.

**Why did** the South abandon its defensive strategy in the fall of 1862?

●●●⌐Read the Document
at **www.myhistorylab.com**
*Clara Barton, Memoirs about Medical Life at the Battlefield (1862)*

and Kentucky to the Mississippi Valley. The forts also defended Nashville, the Tennessee state capital (see Map 15–2). In February 1862, Union general Ulysses S. Grant coordinated a land and river campaign against the forts, with Flag Officer Andrew H. Foote commanding a force of ironclad Union gunboats.

Grant appreciated the strategic importance of river systems in the conquest of the western Confederacy. His combined river and land campaign caught the southerners unprepared and outflanked. By February 16, both forts had fallen. The Union victory drove a wedge into southern territory and closed the Confederacy's quickest path to the west from Virginia and the Carolinas. The Confederacy's only safe link across the Appalachians was now through Georgia. The Confederacy never recovered its strategic advantage in the West after the loss of Forts Henry and Donelson.

Grant next moved his main army south to Pittsburg Landing on the Tennessee River, to prepare for an assault on the key Mississippi River port and rail center of Vicksburg. After blunting a surprise Confederate attack at Shiloh Church near Pittsburg Landing, Grant pushed the southerners back to Corinth, Mississippi.

Federal forces complemented their victories at Shiloh and Corinth with another important success at New Orleans. Admiral David G. Farragut, who remained a Unionist even though born in Tennessee, blasted the Confederate river defenses protecting New Orleans and sailed a federal fleet to the city in April 1862. With the fall of Memphis to Union forces in June, Vicksburg remained the only major river town still in Confederate hands. The western losses exposed a major problem in the Confederates' defensive strategy: Their military resources were stretched too thin to defend their vast territory.

## THE REAL WAR

The fierce fighting at Shiloh wrought unprecedented carnage. More American soldiers were lost at Shiloh than in all of the nation's wars combined up to that time. Each side suffered more than 10,000 casualties. By the time the smoke had cleared, the soldiers' initial enthusiasm and bravado were replaced by the sober realization that death or capture was a likely outcome, and that heroism, courage, and piety did not guarantee survival. "Too shocking, too horrible," a Confederate survivor of Shiloh wrote. "God grant that I may never be the partaker in such scenes again . . . when released from this I shall ever be an advocate of peace."

All wars are bloody, none more so in American history than the Civil War. Old military tactics combined with modern weapons accounted for some of the gore, and primitive medical practice added to the toll. Death and physical wounds were not the only results of battle. The experience of combat and the scenes of human and natural destruction had a profound psychological impact on the soldiers.

Some soldiers coped with the gore by writing about it, thus distancing themselves from the awful reality. At the brutal battle of Spotsylvania in May 1864, only an earthen parapet separated the two armies firing at close range. A Union soldier wrote, "The dead and wounded were torn to pieces. . . . The mud was half-way to our knees, and by our constant movement the dead were almost buried at our feet." Many men were "nothing but a lump of meat or clot of gore."

Other soldiers were consumed by the death and suffering. The war changed them forever. Union soldier and future U.S. Supreme Court Justice Oliver Wendell Holmes, Jr. wrote to his parents, "Before you get this you will know how immense the butcher's bill has been. [T]hese nearly two weeks have contained all of the fatigue & horror that war can furnish. . . . I am not the same man." The same feeling gripped a young man on the other side, Marion Hill Fitzpatrick of Georgia. "I have changed much in my feelings," he wrote to his parents. "The bombs and balls excite me but little and a battlefield strewed with dead and wounded is an every day consequence."

Yet, after the war many writers presented the conflict as a tableau of flying flags, heroic combatants, noble causes, and triumphal parades. Walt Whitman, who served as a nurse during the conflict, worried that "the real war will never get into the history books." Soldiers understood that once the war was over, memory would sanitize the conflict. The "real war" lives on in their letters and diaries. Daniel Bond of the 1st Minnesota began a diary: "Believing war to be a concentration of all that is wicked; and the most cruel invention of the worst enemy of the human race. And believing that were the real truth with regard to its extreme cruelty known, much would be done at least to soften its horrors . . . I have written this Journal with a view to telling some truths that will not be recorded in its histories." (See American Views: The Costs of War.)

The war became more brutal after Shiloh. Civilian populations became fair game, and when Confederate marksmen used severely wounded Union combatants for target practice as they lay below them at Fredericksburg that winter, it was clear that the war was entering a new, more brutal phase. Total war? As far back as the Peloponnesian War, officers had targeted civilians. But the Civil War was the first industrialized war and the impact on combat was devastating. The length of the war contributed to its brutality. The North became more desperate to end the struggle, and the South to prolong it in order to exhaust the patience of northerners. Both

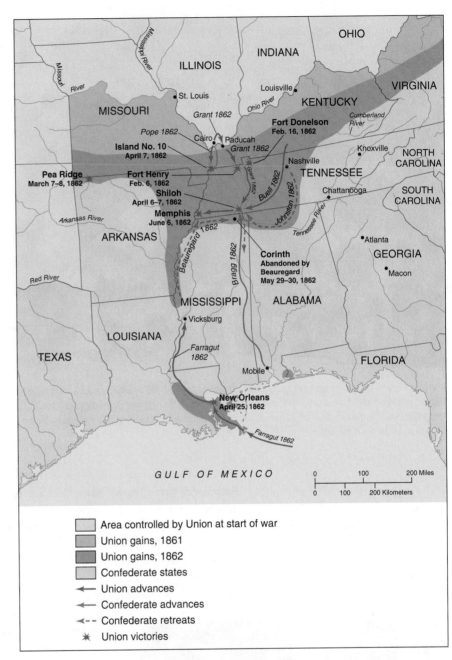

**MAP 15–2   The War in the West, 1861–1862**   Because of the early Union emphasis on capturing Richmond, the war in the West seemed less important to northerners. But from a strategic standpoint, the victories at Forts Henry and Donelson, which drove a wedge into southern territory and closed the Confederacy's quickest path to the West from Virginia and the Carolinas, and the capture of New Orleans and its Mississippi River port were crucial and set the stage for greater federal success in the West in 1863.

**Based on** this map, what was the Union's overall strategy in these campaigns?

**Read** the **Document**
at www.myhistorylab.com
*From Then to Now Online:*
*The Soldiers' War*

A surgeon prepares to amputate the leg of a wounded Union soldier after the Battle of Gettysburg. Such primitive field hospitals functioned without the rudiments of sanitation and contributed to the staggering casualties on each side. Amputations were the most common surgical procedures performed during the war. Cutting off a limb was usually the first option to prevent a fatal infection.

objectives were prescriptions for tragedy. The journey to war had been easy. The journey out of it would be very hard.

## THE WAR IN THE EAST

With Grant and Farragut squeezing the Confederacy in the West, Lincoln ordered a new offensive against Richmond in the East that he believed would end the war. Following the defeat at Bull Run, he had shaken up the Union high command and appointed General George B. McClellan to lead what was now called the Army of the Potomac. McClellan was well liked by his soldiers, who referred to him affectionately as "Little Mac." McClellan returned their affection, perhaps too much. A superb organizer, he would prove overly cautious on the field of battle.

In March 1862, at the outset of the Peninsula Campaign, McClellan moved his 112,000-man army out of Washington and maneuvered his forces by boat down the Potomac River and Chesapeake Bay to the peninsula between the York and James rivers southeast of the Confederate capital (see Map 15–1). Union forces took Yorktown, Williamsburg, and Norfolk. Confederate general Joseph E. Johnston withdrew his forces up the peninsula toward Richmond, preparing for what most felt would be the decisive battle of the war. McClellan, moving ponderously up the peninsula, clashed with Johnston's army inconclusively at Seven Pines in late May 1862. Johnston was badly wounded in the clash, and President Davis replaced him with General Robert E. Lee, who renamed the forces under his command the Army of Northern Virginia.

Lee's reserved and aristocratic bearing masked a gambler's disposition. A fellow officer noted, "his name might be Audacity. He will take more chances, and take them quicker than any other general in this country." Under his daring leadership, the Confederacy's defensive strategy underwent an important shift.

Lee seized the initiative on June 25, 1862, attacking McClellan's right flank. Although inconclusive, the attack pushed the nervous McClellan into a defensive position. For a week, the armies sparred in a series of fierce engagements known collectively as the Seven Days' Battles. More than 30,000 men were killed or wounded on both sides, the deadliest week of the war so far. Although McClellan prevailed in these contests, the carnage so shocked him that he withdrew to Harrison's Landing on the James River. An exasperated Lincoln replaced McClellan with John Pope. Although Lee had saved Richmond, his troops had suffered frightfully. He had lost one-fourth of his 80,000-man army, but he remained convinced of the wisdom of his offensive-defensive strategy.

Lee went to work to vindicate these tactics. A series of inconclusive skirmishes brought Union and Confederate armies together once more near Manassas Junction. The Second Battle of Bull Run was as much a disaster for the Union as the first had been. Lee's generalship

Civil War generals Ulysses S. Grant (left) and Robert E. Lee (right).

befuddled Pope and again saved Richmond. Lee and the Army of Northern Virginia were developing a reputation for invincibility.

# TURNING POINTS, 1862–1863

**WHAT CONVINCED** Lincoln to issue the Emancipation Proclamation?

The impressive Confederate victories in the East masked the delicate condition of southern fortunes. Lee's offensive-defensive strategy seemed to be working, but it raised the possibility that the Confederacy could exhaust its men and resources before it sealed its independence.

The waning summer months of 1862 brought other concerns to the Davis administration in Richmond. The Union navy was choking the South's commercial link with Europe. Davis looked to the nations of Europe for diplomatic recognition as well as for trade.

Having stymied the Union war machine, Lee contemplated a bold move, a thrust into northern territory to bring the conflict to the North and stoke northerners' rising hostility to the war. President Lincoln also harbored a bold plan. Gradually, during the spring and summer of 1862, the president had concluded that emancipation of the Confederacy's slaves was essential for preserving the Union. But Lincoln was reluctant to take this step before the Union's fortunes on the battlefield improved. As the fall of 1862 approached, the Union and Confederate governments both prepared for the most significant conflicts of the war to date.

## THE NAVAL WAR

The Union's naval strategy was to blockade the southern coast and capture its key seaports and river towns. The intention was to prevent arms, clothing, and food from reaching the Confederacy and keep cotton and tobacco from leaving. Destroying the South's ability to carry on trade would prevent the Confederacy from raising money to purchase the goods it needed to wage war. This vital trade brought the Confederacy into contact with European nations, a connection its leaders hoped to reinforce on the diplomatic front.

Neither side had much of a navy at the outset of the war. With more than 3,000 miles of Confederate coastline to cover, the Union blockade was weak at first. As time passed and the number of ships in the Union navy grew, the blockade tightened.

Understandably, the Confederate naval strategy was to break the blockade and defend the South's vital rivers and seaports. The Confederacy built several warships to serve as blockade runners and as privateers to attack Union merchant ships, and they briefly disrupted federal operations before Union vessels regained the advantage. The Confederacy was heavily dependent on the flow of trade and restriction of its flow hurt the southern cause.

## ANTIETAM

The alarming arithmetic of the offensive-defensive strategy convinced Lee that the South could not sustain a prolonged conflict. He knew that his army must keep up the pressure on the Union forces and, if possible, destroy them quickly. Union success in the Mississippi Valley threatened to cut the Confederacy in two and deprive it of the resources of a vast chunk of territory. Within a year, the Confederacy might cease to exist west of the Appalachians. He desperately needed a dramatic victory.

In September 1862, Lee crossed the Potomac into Maryland (see Map 15–1). He was on his way to cut the Pennsylvania Railroad at Harrisburg. Lee established camp at Frederick, scattering his army at various sites, convinced that McClellan and the Army of the Potomac would not attack him.

Luck intervened for the North. At an abandoned Confederate encampment, a Union corporal found three wrapped cigars on the ground, evidently tossed away by a careless Confederate officer. To the corporal's amazement, the wrapping was a copy of Lee's orders for the disposition

**Turning Point: Antietam**

- Kept Lee from directly threatening the North.
- Prompted Britain and France to abandon plans to recognize the Confederacy.
- Provided Lincoln with the opportunity to announce the Emancipation Proclamation.

**Confiscation Act** Second confiscation law passed by Congress, ordering the seizure of land from disloyal southerners and the emancipation of their slaves.

**Emancipation Proclamation** Decree announced by President Abraham Lincoln in September 1862 and formally issued on January 1, 1863, freeing slaves in all Confederate states still in rebellion.

of his army. But even with this information, "Little Mac" moved so cautiously that Lee had time to retreat to defensive positions at Sharpsburg, Maryland, along Antietam Creek. There Lee's army of 39,000 men came to blows with McClellan's army of 75,000.

The Battle of Antietam saw the bloodiest single day of fighting in American history. About 2,100 Union soldiers and 2,700 Confederates died, and another 18,500, equally divided, were wounded. Although the armies had fought to a tactical draw, the battle was a strategic defeat for the Confederacy. In the battle's aftermath, Lee's troops limped back across the Potomac into Virginia and McClellan did not pursue them.

Antietam marked a major turning point in the war. It kept Lee from directly threatening northern industry and financial institutions. It prompted Britain and France to abandon plans to grant recognition to the Confederacy as an independent nation. And it provided Lincoln with the victory he needed to announce the abolition of slavery.

## EMANCIPATION

President Lincoln despised slavery, but he had always maintained that preserving the Union was his primary war goal. "If I could save the Union without freeing any slave I would do it," he wrote to the newspaper editor Horace Greeley in August 1862, "and if I could save it by freeing all the slaves I would do it; and if I could save it by freeing some and leaving others alone, I would also do that." But from the war's outset, the possibility of emancipation as a war objective was considered in the Republican Congress, in the Union army, and among citizens throughout the northern states. As a result, pressure grew within the Union army to declare emancipation as a way of depriving the South and the Confederate army of their labor force.

Lincoln had said in his inaugural address that he had "no purpose, directly or indirectly, to interfere with the institution of slavery in the states where it exists." By March 1862, however, his moral repugnance for slavery, and the military arguments for abolition, led him to propose a resolution, which Congress adopted, supporting the compensated emancipation of slaves. The measure died, however, when Congress failed to appropriate funds for it and slaveholders in the border states expressed no interest in the plan.

Pressure from some northern civilians and Union soldiers and from Congress for some form of emancipation mounted in the spring of 1862. In response, the Republican Congress prohibited slavery in the territories and abolished slavery in the District of Columbia. The act emancipating the district's slaves called for compensating slave owners and colonizing the freed slaves in black republics, such as Haiti and Liberia. Then, in July 1862, Congress passed the **Confiscation Act,** which ordered the seizure of land from disloyal southerners and the emancipation of their slaves.

Although support for emancipation had grown both in the army and among civilians, Lincoln still faced political considerations that dictated against it. Emancipation was still not favored by a majority in the North, especially not in the border states. The thousands of Irish Catholic immigrants who entered the Union army and who had competed with black workers for jobs in northern cities during the 1850s were especially opposed to emancipation, fearing a loss of economic security. But other considerations favored emancipation. Freeing the slaves would appeal to the strong antislavery sentiment in Britain and gain support for the Union cause abroad. And it would weaken the Confederacy's ability to wage war by removing a crucial source of labor.

**The Emancipation Proclamation.** By mid-1862, the president had resolved to act on his moral convictions and proclaim emancipation. Taking the advice of Secretary of State Seward, however, he decided to wait for a battlefield victory so that the measure would not appear an act of desperation. Antietam gave the president his opening, narrow though it was, and on September 22, 1862, he announced his intention to issue the **Emancipation Proclamation,** to take

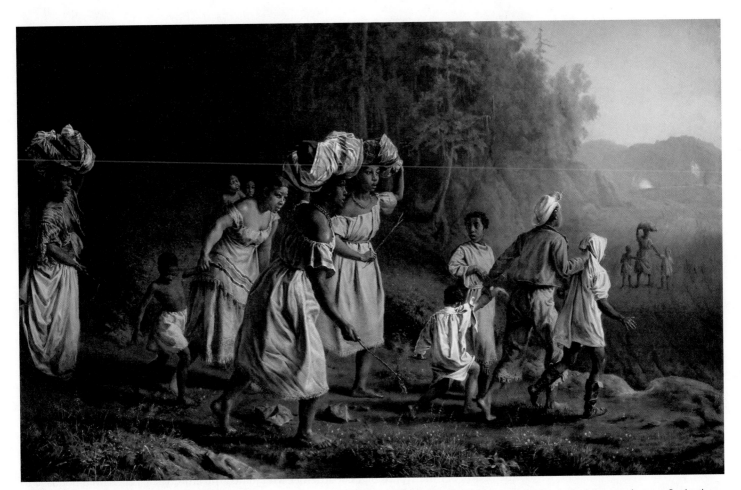

Even before the Emancipation Proclamation, slaves throughout the South "stole" their freedom. After the Proclamation, the trickle of black slaves abandoning their masters became a flood as they sought freedom behind Union lines.

Theodore Kaufman (1814–1896), *On to Liberty,* 1867, Oil on canvas, 36" × 56" (91.4 × 142.2 cm). The Metropolitan Museum of Art. Gift of Erving and Joyce Wolf, 1982 (1982.443.3). Photograph © The Metropolitan Museum of Art/Art Resource, NY

effect January 1, 1863, in all states still in rebellion. The proclamation exempted slaves in the border states loyal to the Union and in areas under Federal occupation. By raising the stakes of the war, President Lincoln hoped to shorten it. And, by leaving slaves in the border states untouched, he maintained their loyalty, or at least their neutrality.

Southerners reacted to the Emancipation Proclamation with outrage. Some viewed it as an invitation to race war and conjured up fears of freed slaves slaying white women and children while their men were at the battlefront. Jefferson Davis, taking a positive view, thought that the proclamation would invigorate the southern war effort.

Northerners generally approved of the Emancipation Proclamation. Although abolitionists comprised a minority of the northern population, most civilians and soldiers recognized the military advantages of emancipation.

The Emancipation Proclamation represented far more than its qualified words and phrases expressed. "A mighty act," Massachusetts governor John Andrew called it. Lincoln had freed the slaves. He and the Union war effort were now tied to the cause of freedom. What had begun as a war to save the Union was now a holy war of deliverance. Freedom and Union entwined in the public consciousness of the North. As Lincoln noted in his December 1862 message to Congress,

**Read the Document**

at **www.myhistorylab.com**
*The Emancipation Proclamation (1863)*

"[I]n giving freedom to the slave, we assure freedom to the free." Emancipation also unified the Republican Party and strengthened the president's hand in conducting the war. America had moved further along in the journey toward fulfilling its founding ideals.

**"Stealing" freedom.**   As word of the Emancipation Proclamation raced through the slave grapevine, slaves rejoiced. But the proclamation only continued a process that had begun when the first Union armies invaded the South. In the months before freedom came, many slaves had run away to Union camps, dug Union trenches, and scouted for Federal troops.

Southern masters fought to deter their slaves by severely punishing the families of black men who fled to the Union lines. They used the courts and slave catchers to reclaim runaways. Some Confederate masters protected their investments by removing slaves to Texas or to areas far from federal forces. And a few slaveowners whipped, sold, and even killed their slaves to prevent them from joining the Union troops.

But in the end, slaveholders could not stem the tide of slaves fleeing toward the Union lines and freedom. The 1862 Confiscation Act included slaves with other Confederate property as "contraband" of war and subject to confiscation. As they helped the Union cause, contrabands also sought to help fellow slaves "steal" their freedom. When Union forces occupied part of the Georgia coast in April 1862, for example, March Haynes, a slave who had worked as a river pilot in Savannah, began smuggling slaves to the Union lines. Federal general Quincy Adams Gilmore provided a fast boat for Haynes's missions. In return, Haynes supplied Gilmore with "exact and valuable information" on the strength and location of Confederate defenses.

The Emancipation Proclamation accelerated the slaves' flight from bondage. After 1863, ex-slaves served in increasing numbers in the Union army.

**Black troops in the Union army.**   More than 80 percent of the roughly 180,000 black soldiers and 20,000 black sailors who fought for the Union were slaves and free black men from the South. For the typical black southerner who joined the army, the passage from bondage to freedom came quickly. Making his escape from his master, he perhaps "stole" his family as well. He typically experienced his first days of freedom behind Union lines, where he may have learned to read and write. Finally, he put on the federal uniform, experiencing, as one black southern volunteer commented, "the biggest thing that ever happened in my life."

President Lincoln strongly advocated enlisting former slaves. In March 1863, he wrote, with exaggerated enthusiasm, that "the bare sight of 50,000 armed and drilled black soldiers on the banks of the Mississippi would end the rebellion at once." On the contrary, the appearance of black Union troops infuriated the Confederates.

The Confederate government formally labeled white officers leading black troops as instigators of slave rebellion and punished them accordingly, presumably by hanging. Black soldiers, when captured, were returned to slavery. The Lincoln administration retaliated by suspending prisoner exchanges, which resulted in horrible conditions in Confederate and Union prisons. Roughly 56,000 prisoners died in captivity, a toll that would have been much lower had Confederate authorities treated black prisoners of war the same as whites.

But for black volunteers, the promise of freedom and redemption outweighed the dangers

⊙ See the **Map**
at **www.myhistorylab.com**
*Effects of the Emancipation Proclamation*

**QUICK REVIEW**

"Stealing" Freedom

- Emancipation Proclamation accelerated process of slaves running away to Union camps.
- "Contrabands" helped fellow slaves to "steal" their freedom.
- Ex-slaves served in increasing numbers in Union army.

◆▶ Read the **Document**
at **www.myhistorylab.com**
*Susie King Taylor, Reminiscences of an Army Laundress (1902)*

Black Union troops—former slaves—repelling Confederates at New Bern, NC, February 1864. African Americans, both free and slave, fought valiantly and often fiercely for their freedom; the alternative was sometimes execution on the spot or reenslavement.

of combat. Black abolitionists campaigned tirelessly for the enlistment of free black men and fugitive slaves in the Union army. Frederick Douglass, whose son Lewis distinguished himself in the all-black 54th Massachusetts Volunteer Infantry Regiment, explained in early 1863, "Once let the black man get upon his person the brass letters, 'U.S.,' let him get an eagle on his buttons and a musket on his shoulder and bullets in his pockets, and there is no power on earth which can deny that he has earned the right to citizenship in the United States."

Although black soldiers were eager to engage the enemy and fought as ably as their white comrades, they received lower pay and performed the most menial duties in camp. Abolitionists and black leaders pressured President Lincoln for more equitable treatment of African American recruits.

Despite discrimination, black soldiers fought valiantly at Port Hudson, Louisiana; near Charleston; and, late in the war, at the siege of Petersburg, Virginia. The most celebrated black encounter with Confederate troops occurred in July 1863, during a futile assault by the 54th Massachusetts Regiment on Fort Wagner outside Charleston. The northern press, previously lukewarm toward black troops, heaped praise on the effort. "Through the cannon smoke of that dark night," intoned a writer in the *Atlantic Monthly*, "the manhood of the colored race shines before many eyes that would not see."

If only President Lincoln could find such gallantry among his generals! George McClellan had failed to follow his advantage at Antietam in September 1862, allowing Lee's army to escape to Virginia and remain a formidable fighting force. And despite Union successes in the West, the Confederate forces massed there remained largely intact.

## FROM FREDERICKSBURG TO GETTYSBURG

In late 1862, after Antietam, the president replaced McClellan with General Ambrose E. Burnside. Burnside was shy and insecure. Claiming incompetence, he had twice refused the command. His judgment proved better than Lincoln's.

**Fredericksburg.**   Moving swiftly against Lee's dispersed army in northern Virginia, Burnside reached the Rappahannock River opposite Fredericksburg in November 1862 (see Map 15–3). But the pontoon bridges to ford his 120,000 soldiers across the river arrived three weeks late, giving Lee an opportunity to gather his 78,000 men. On December 13, the Union forces launched a poorly coordinated and foolish frontal assault that the Confederates repelled, inflicting heavy federal casualties. Burnside, having performed to his own expectations, was relieved of command, and Major General Joseph Hooker was installed in his place.

**Chancellorsville.**   The hard-drinking Hooker lacked Burnside's humility but not his incompetence. Resuming the offensive in the spring of 1863, Hooker hoped to outflank Lee. But the Confederate commander surprised Hooker by sending Stonewall Jackson to outflank the Union right. Between May 1 and May 4, Lee's army delivered a series of crushing attacks on Hooker's forces at Chancellorsville. Outnumbered two to one, Lee had pulled off another stunning victory, but at a high cost. Lee lost some 13,000 men, fewer than Hooker's 17,000, but more than the Confederacy could afford.

Lee also lost Stonewall Jackson at Chancellorsville. Nervous Confederate sentries mistakenly shot and wounded him as he returned from a reconnoitering mission, and he died a few days later. Lee recognized the tragedy of Jackson's loss for himself and his country. "Any victory," the Confederate commander wrote, "would be dear at such a price. I know not how to replace him."

Still, Lee appeared invincible. Chancellorsville thrust Lincoln into a bout of despair. "My God!" he exclaimed in agony, "What will the country say! What will the country say!" Meanwhile, Lee, to take advantage of the Confederacy's momentum and the Union's gloom, planned another bold move. On June 3, 1863, the 75,000-man Army of Northern Virginia broke camp and headed north once again.

**QUICK REVIEW**

### Blacks in the Union Army

- 80 percent of black Union soldiers were slaves or free blacks from the South.
- President Lincoln strongly advocated enlisting former slaves.
- Black Union troops infuriated the Confederates.
- Danger and discrimination did not stop blacks from fighting for the Union.

**W**  **WHERE TO LEARN MORE**

★ Gettysburg National Military Park, Gettysburg, Pennsylvania
http://www.nps.gov/gett/index.htm

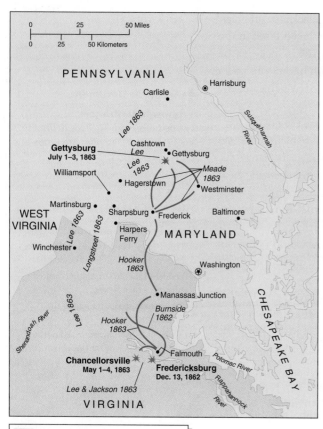

Area controlled by Union
Area controlled by Confederacy
← Union advances
← Confederate advances
◄-- Confederate retreats
✳ Union victories
✳ Confederate victories

**MAP 15–3    From Fredericksburg to Gettysburg: The War in the East, December 1862–July 1863**    By all logic, the increasingly outgunned and outfinanced Confederacy should have been showing signs of faltering by 1863. But bungling by Union generals at Fredericksburg and Chancellorsville sustained southern fortunes and encouraged Robert E. Lee to attempt another invasion of the North.

**How was** Robert E. Lee able to press on, outgunned and outfinanced, into 1863 and beyond?

👁 See the Map
at **www.myhistorylab.com**
*The Civil War Part II: 1863–1865*

**Gettysburg.**    President Lincoln sent the Union Army of the Potomac after Lee. But General Hooker dallied, requested more troops, and allowed the Confederates to march from Maryland into Pennsylvania. An infuriated Lincoln replaced Hooker with George Gordon Meade.

Lee's Army of Northern Virginia occupied a wide swath of Pennsylvania territory from Chambersburg to Wrightsville along the Susquehanna River, across from the state capital at Harrisburg. When Lee learned of Meade's movements, he ordered his troops to consolidate in a defensive position at Cashtown, 45 miles from Harrisburg. That the greatest battle of the war erupted at nearby Gettysburg was pure chance. A Confederate brigade left Cashtown to confiscate much-needed shoes from a factory in Gettysburg. Meeting federal cavalry resistance near the town, the brigade withdrew. On July 1, 1863, a larger Confederate force advanced toward Gettysburg to disperse the cavalry and seize the shoes. What the Confederates did not realize was that the entire Army of the Potomac was coming up behind the cavalry (see Map 15–4).

During the first day of battle, July 1, the Confederates appeared to gain the upper hand, forcing Union troops back from the town to a new position on Cemetery Hill. On the second day, the entire Union army was in place, but the Confederates took several key locations along Cemetery Ridge before federal forces pushed them back to the previous day's positions. Although the opposing sides had suffered heavy casualties, both armies were intact; and, if anything, Lee had the advantage. On July 3, the third day of the battle, Lee made a fateful error. Believing that the center of Meade's line was weak, he ordered an all-out assault against it.

The next morning, a bright, hot summer day, the Confederates launched an assault on Culp's Hill, only to fall back by noon. The key battle of the day occurred at three in the afternoon at Cemetery Ridge, preceded by a fierce artillery duel. When the Union guns suddenly went silent, the Confederates, thinking they had knocked them out, began a charge led by General George Pickett. As the Confederate infantry marched out with battle colors flying, the Union artillery opened up again and tore apart the charging southerners. The Confederates retreated down the gentle slope strewn with their fallen comrades, the hopes of a southern victory dashed.

After Pickett's charge, Lee rode among his troops and urged them to brace for a final Union assault. The attack never came. Meade allowed Lee to withdraw into Maryland and cross the Potomac to Virginia. Gettysburg was the bloodiest battle of the war. The Union suffered 23,000 casualties; the Confederacy, 28,000. The battle's outcome boosted morale in the North and drained Lee's army of men and material.

The Union victory at Gettysburg lifted the veil of gloom in the North. People exhaled collectively when Union troops foiled the Confederate invasion. President Lincoln, in his address dedicating the cemetery at Gettysburg in November of that year, used the evangelical metaphor of rebirth to comment on the importance of the sacrifice on that battlefield. On this consecrated ground, he declared, from the "honored dead," will come "a new birth of freedom."

While the battle changed the mood in the North, it did not mark the beginning of the end of the Confederacy. But coupled with the loss of Vicksburg on July 4 (see below), it dealt a serious blow to Rebel fortunes. Many Confederate troops considered the Gettysburg campaign a draw or a temporary setback at worst; but there was no doubting the implications of the Vicksburg surrender on the nation's birthday.

## AMERICAN VIEWS

### ∽ The Costs of War ∾

The main character in southern writer Ellen Glasgow's novel The Battle-Ground (1902) exclaims after his first battle, "I didn't know it was like this. Why, they're no better than mangled rabbits—I didn't know it was like this." Civilians fought the Civil War and nothing in their lives prepared them for the carnage they encountered. The lasting impression from diaries and letters of those who fought is less of grand causes than of horror—of disease, death, and dying. Here is a small sample.

- **If** the scenes of war were so horrible, why did these writers feel compelled to describe the grisly details?
- **Given** these horrors of war, why did the writers continue to serve?
- **The** Civil War proved the final journey for 620,000 men from both sides. The war solved the issues of secession and slavery. Was the sacrifice worth it?

Private Sam Watkins of the Army of Tennessee encountering a comrade after a battle: I overtook another man walking along. I did not know to what regiment he belonged, but I remember of first noticing his left arm was entirely gone. His face was as white as a sheet. The breast and sleeve of his coat had been torn away, and I could see the frazzled end of his shirt sleeve, which appeared to be sucked into the wound. I looked at it pretty close and I said "Great God!" for I could see his heart throb, and the respiration of his lungs. I was filled with wonder and horror at the sight. He was walking along, when all at once he dropped down and died without a struggle or a groan.

*Source:* Reprinted with the permission of Scribner, a Division of Simon & Schuster, Inc., from "CO. AYTCH" by Sam R. Watkins. (NY: Simon & Schuster, Inc., 1997).

Robert Goldthwaite Carter of the 22nd Massachusetts describes his walk across the Gettysburg battlefield the night after the battle ended:

In every direction, among the bodies was the debris of battle—haversacks, canteens, hats, caps, sombreros, blankets of every shade and hue, bayonets, cartridge boxes. . . . Corpses strewed the ground at every step. Arms, legs, heads, and parts of dismembered bodies were scattered all about, and sticking among the rocks, and against the trunks of trees, hair, brains, entrails and

shreds of human flesh still hung, a disgusting, sickening, heart-rending spectacle to our young minds.

*Source:* Robert Goldthwaite Carter, *Four Brothers in Blue: A Story of the Great Civil War from Bull Run to Appomattox* (Norman, OK: University of Oklahoma Press, 1999; original edition, 1913), p. 324.

Kate Cumming, a Scottish immigrant to Mobile, Alabama, became a Confederate nurse ministering to the wounded and ill in all manner of temporary facilities. Here she describes the operating "room" in one of the makeshift hospitals:

I was compelled to pass the place, and the sight I there beheld made me shudder and sick at heart. A stream of blood ran from the table into a tub in which was the arm. It had been taken off at the socket, and the hand . . . was hanging over the edge of the tub, a lifeless thing. I often wish I could become as callous as many seem to be, for there is no end to these horrors. . . . The passage to the kitchen leads directly past the amputating room below stairs, and many a time I have seen the blood running in streams from it.

*Source:* Richard Barksdale Harwell, ed., *Kate: The Journal of a Confederate Nurse* (Baton Rouge: Louisiana State University Press, 1987), p. 25.

Ambrose Bierce fought for the 9th Indiana Volunteers. Like Walt Whitman, the sanitizing of the war after the fact infuriated him. The stories he wrote after the war based on his battle experiences stressed the physical and psychological impact of the war on the civilian soldiers. Here he describes "What I Saw at Shiloh."

. . . the bodies, half buried in ashes; some in the unlovely looseness of attitude denoting sudden death by the bullet, but by far the greater number in postures of agony that told of the tormenting flame. Their clothing was half burnt away – their hair and beard entirely; the rain had come too late to save their nails. Some were swollen to double girth; others shriveled to manikins. According to degree of exposure, their faces were bloated and black or yellow and shrunken. The contraction of muscles which had given them claws for hands had cursed each countenance with a hideous grin.

*Source:* Reprinted with the permission of Scribner, a Division of Simon & Schuster, Inc., from "CO. AYTCH" by Sam R. Watkins. (NY: Simon & Schuster, Inc., 1997).

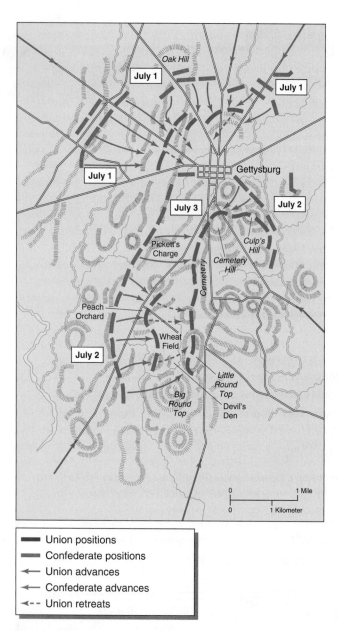

**MAP 15–4 The Battle of Gettysburg, July 1–3, 1863** In a war that lasted four years, it is difficult to point to the decisive battle. But clearly, the outcome during those July days at Gettysburg set the tone for the rest of the war. The result was unclear until the final day of battle, and even then it might have gone either way. Winning by a whisker was enough to propel Union armies to a string of victories over the next year and to throw Confederate forces back on their defenses among an increasingly despairing population. Gettysburg marked the last major southern invasion of the North.

**Why was** the Battle of Gettysburg so crucial?

**Read the Document**

at **www.myhistorylab.com**
*Abraham Lincoln, The Gettysburg Address (1863)*

## VICKSBURG, CHATTANOOGA, AND THE WEST

As Union forces thwarted Confederate dreams in Pennsylvania, other federal troops bore down on strategic Rebel strongholds in the western theater of the war. Union military success in the West would seriously compromise the South's ability to move goods and men across rail lines and over waterways and leave vulnerable the ultimate western prize, the Confederate bread basket, Georgia.

**Vicksburg.** On July 4, one day after Pickett's charge at Gettysburg, the city of Vicksburg, the last major Confederate stronghold on the Mississippi, surrendered to Ulysses S. Grant. Grant had demonstrated an ability to use his forces creatively, swiftly, and with a minimum loss of life in his campaigns in the western Confederacy, but Vicksburg presented him with several strategic obstacles (see Map 15–5). In 1862, the formidable defenses on the city's western edge, which overlooked and controlled the Mississippi, had thwarted a Union naval assault, and the labyrinth of swamps, creeks, and woods protecting the city from the north had foiled General Sherman. The only feasible approaches appeared to be from the south and east.

By March 1863, Grant had devised a brilliant plan to take Vicksburg that called for rapid maneuvering and expert coordination that worked with rather than against the area's geography. Grant had his 20,000 Union troops ferried across the Mississippi from the Louisiana side at a point south of Vicksburg. Then he marched them quickly into the interior of Mississippi. They moved northeastward, captured the Mississippi state capital at Jackson, and turned west toward Vicksburg. On May 22, 1863, Grant settled down in front of the city, less than 600 yards from Confederate positions. Grant's tight siege and the Union navy's bombardment from the river cut the city off completely. As food stores dwindled, residents were forced to eat mules and rats to survive. Their situation hopeless, General John Pemberton and his 30,000-man garrison surrendered on July 4.

**Chattanooga.** As Grant was besieging Vicksburg in June 1863, Union general William S. Rosecrans, commanding the Army of the Cumberland, advanced against Confederate general Braxton Bragg, whose Army of Tennessee held Chattanooga, a "doorway" on the railroad that linked Richmond to the lower South. The capture of the city would complete the uncoupling of the West from the eastern Confederacy.

Bragg lacked confidence in his men and consistently overestimated the force and cunning of his enemy. At Rosecrans's approach, he abandoned Chattanooga and took up positions above nearby Chickamauga Creek. When the two armies clashed at Chickamauga on September 19, Bragg pushed Rosecrans back to Chattanooga. Bragg seized the railroad leading into Chattanooga and bottled up Rosecrans there, much as Grant had confined Pemberton at Vicksburg. Both sides had suffered heavily. Suddenly, the Union's careful strategy for the conquest of the western Confederacy seemed in jeopardy.

The Confederate position on the heights overlooking Chattanooga appeared impregnable. But the Confederate camp was plagued by dissension, with some officers openly questioning Bragg's ability. President Davis considered replacing him but had no one else available with Bragg's experience. Instead, Davis ordered General James Longstreet (along with one-third

**MAP 15–5 Vicksburg and Chattanooga: The War in the West, 1863** Devising a brilliant strategy, Union general Ulysses S. Grant took the last major Mississippi River stronghold from Confederate hands on July 4, 1863, dealing a significant economic and morale blow to the South. Coupled with the defeat at Gettysburg a day earlier, the fall of Vicksburg portended a bitter finale to hopes for southern independence. Grant completed his domination of the West by joining forces with several Union generals to capture Chattanooga and push Confederate forces into Georgia, setting the stage for the capture of that key southern state in 1864.

**What key** military decisions enabled Grant to force the surrender of Vicksburg?

Timothy H. O'Sullivan's photograph of dead Union soldiers at the southern end of the Gettysburg battlefield, July 2, 1863. O'Sullivan titled the work "The Harvest of Death." Note the bodies bloodied and blackened by the July heat. Such photographs brought home the carnage of the war in vivid detail to northern civilians.

of Bragg's army) on a futile expedition against Union forces at Knoxville, Tennessee. Converging on Chattanooga with reinforcements, Union generals Grant, Sherman, and Hooker took advantage of the divided Confederate army to break the siege and force Bragg's army to retreat into Georgia. The Union now dominated most of the West and faced an open road to the East.

**The war in the trans-Mississippi West.** The Confederacy's reverses at Vicksburg and Chattanooga mirrored its misfortunes farther west of the Mississippi River. Although a relatively minor theater of war, the territory west of the Mississippi provided supplies and strategic advantages for the Confederate West. Success in the trans-Mississippi West could divert Federal troops and relieve the pressure on other parts of the Confederacy while allowing food and munitions to reach desperate southern armies.

Native American tribes in the trans-Mississippi West, such as the Navajos, Dakotas, and Lakotas, spent a good deal of the Civil War battling Federal troops for territory and resources, quite apart from the sectional conflict. The Civil War drew federal troops from the frontier, affording Indians an opportunity to press their concerns about tardy and incomplete delivery of food and supplies and the loss of lands granted to them by treaty. The Eastern Sioux in Minnesota confronted both starvation and the migration of whites onto their lands during the fall of 1862. With the white man's war raging in the East, the Sioux struck in the fall of 1862 to call attention to their plight. About 200 Eastern Sioux rampaged across southern Minnesota, striking at white settlements and killing between 350 and 800 men, women, and children. The Minnesota militia quelled the uprising. More than three hundred Sioux were tried and condemned to death, though President Lincoln pardoned all but thirty-eight. Federal authorities removed the remainder of the Eastern Sioux to a desolate area in the Dakota Territory and extinguished all of their remaining land rights in Minnesota.

Texas, however, was the focus of the trans-Mississippi campaign. The state was critical to Confederate fortunes, both as a source of supply for the East and as a base for the conquest of the Far West. Texas was far from secure. It suffered from internal dissent and violence on its borders. Not all Texans supported secession. On the state's western border, Comanches raided homesteaders at will until late 1864. In the east and along the southern frontier in the lower Rio Grande Valley, Union gunboats and troops disrupted Confederate supply lines. By 1864, with the Union in control of the Mississippi, and Federal troops along the Mexican border, Texas had lost its strategic importance.

# WAR TRANSFORMS THE NORTH

The Union successes in 1863 had a profound impact on both sides. For the North, hopes of victory and reunion increased. The federal government expanded its bureaucracy to wage war efficiently, and a Republican-dominated Congress passed legislation that broadened federal power and furthered the war effort. Boosted by federal economic legislation and wartime demand, the northern economy boomed. Women entered the workforce in growing numbers. But labor unrest and class and racial tensions suggested that prosperity had a price.

**WHAT IMPACT** did the war have on the North's economy?

## WARTIME LEGISLATION AND POLITICS

Before the Civil War, the federal government rarely affected citizens' lives directly. But raising troops, protecting territory, and mobilizing the economy for war required a strong and active central government. With the departure of the South from the Union, Republicans dominated all branches of the federal administration. This left them in a position to test the constitutional limits of federal authority.

**Suppressing dissent.** President Lincoln began almost immediately to use executive authority to suppress opposition to the war effort in the North. In one of his most controversial actions, he issued a temporary suspension of the writ of habeas corpus, the constitutional protection against illegal imprisonment. Suspending it allowed the government to arrest suspected Confederate agents and hold them indefinitely, a procedure sanctioned by the Constitution "when in cases of rebellion or invasion the public safety may require it." The suspension became permanent in September 1862 and was used primarily in the border states to detain those suspected of trading with the enemy, defrauding the War Department, or evading the draft.

Executive sanctions fell particularly hard on the Democratic Party. Although many Democrats opposed secession and supported the Union, they challenged the president on the conduct of the war, on emancipation, and on his coolness toward peace initiatives. A few had ties with Confederate agents. Republicans called these dissenters **"Copperheads,"** after the poisonous snake.

Despite the suspension of habeas corpus, Lincoln compiled a fairly good record for upholding basic American civil liberties. Although the authorities shut down a handful of newspapers temporarily, the administration made no attempt to control the news or subvert the electoral process. Two major elections were held during the war. In the first, the off-year election in 1862, Republicans retained control of Congress but lost several seats to Democrats. In the presidential election of 1864, Lincoln won reelection in a hard-fought contest.

While fellow Republicans sometimes chastised the president for violating civil liberties, mismanaging military command assignments, or moving too slowly on emancipation, they rarely threatened to disrupt the party. But there was dissent in the Republican Party, and it had an effect on national policy. **Radical Republicans** hounded Lincoln from early in his administration, establishing the Joint Committee on the Conduct of the War to examine and monitor military policy. Some of them accused Democratic generals, including McClellan, of deliberately subverting the war effort with their poor performance. They also pressed Lincoln for quicker action on emancipation, though they supported the president on most crucial matters.

**Creating a national economy.** Lincoln likewise supported his party on an array of initiatives in Congress. Republicans used the federal government to enhance individual opportunities, especially in the West. The **Homestead Act,** passed in May 1862, granted 160 acres free to any settler in the territories who agreed to improve the land (by cultivating it and erecting a house) within five years of the grant. The act was also a boon for railroad companies.

Other legislation to boost the nation's economy and the fortunes of individual manufacturers and farmers included the **Land Grant College Act** of 1862, a protective tariff that same year, and the National Banking Act of 1863. The Land Grant Act awarded the proceeds from the sale

**Copperheads** A term Republicans applied to northern war dissenters and those suspected of aiding the Confederate cause during the Civil War.

**Radical Republicans** A shifting group of Republican congressmen, usually a substantial minority, who favored the abolition of slavery from the beginning of the Civil War and later advocated harsh treatment of the defeated South.

**Homestead Act** Law passed by Congress in May 1862 providing homesteads with 160 acres of free land in exchange for improving the land within five years of the grant.

**Land Grant College Act** Law passed by Congress in July 1862 awarding proceeds from the sale of public lands to the states for the establishment of agricultural and mechanical colleges.

**Read the Document**

at **www.myhistorylab.com**
*The Homestead Act of 1862*

of public lands to the states for the establishment of colleges offering instruction in "agriculture and mechanical arts." The tariff legislation protected northern industry from foreign competition while raising revenue for the Union. The National Banking Act of 1863 replaced the bank notes of individual states, which were often backed by flimsy reserves and subject to wild fluctuations in value, with a uniform national currency.

Through such initiatives, the Republican-dominated Congress forged a national economy that connected citizens to the fortunes of the national government. Construction began on a transcontinental railroad that, together with the Homestead Act, would help settle the West and bind the nation together in fact. A high protective tariff not only generated revenue for the government, it bolstered northern manufacturing. Through the sale of securities to the general public to help fund the war, hundreds of thousands of citizens now had a stake in the government's survival and success. A federal income tax bound Americans even closer to the government in Washington. A national currency fueled a national economy. Businesses, aided by government-subsidized efficiencies in transportation and communication, became national rather than regional enterprises. Farmers benefited from the Land Grant College Act that offered the latest labor-saving efficiencies for a scientific agriculture. The Constitution of the United States did not explicitly sanction any of these measures. Operating under the broad mandate of the "war powers" allowed the Congress to support the government and protect the citizenry in times of insurrection. The results were a more powerful nation and a more centralized government.

**Read the Document**

at **www.myhistorylab.com**
*"If It Were Not for My Trust in Christ I Do Not Know How I Could Have Endured It":
Testimony from Victims of New York's Draft Riots (1863)*

These measures helped sustain the Union war effort and enjoyed widespread support. The expansion of government into other areas, however, aroused opposition in some quarters, none more than the draft laws.

**Conscription and the draft riots.**    Congress passed the first national conscription law in 1863. Almost immediately, evasion, obstruction, and weak enforcement threatened to undermine it. As military authorities began arresting draft dodgers and deserters, secret societies formed to harbor draftees and instruct them on evasion.

Conflicts between citizens and federal officials over the draft sometimes erupted in violence. The worst draft riot occurred in New York City in July 1863. Competition with blacks for jobs, the use of blacks as strikebreakers, and the feeling that were it not for the Emancipation Proclamation, the war would be over made the Irish population of the city adamant about avoiding fighting and

The lynching of a black New Yorker during the Draft Riot in July 1863. The violence against black people during the riot reflected decades of racial tension, especially between Irish immigrants and black residents, over jobs and housing.

dying for a cause they reviled. The fact that more affluent New Yorkers could buy their way out of the draft by hiring a substitute for $300 made this also a class issue for the mostly working-class and poor Irish residents of the city.

The racial and class issues were apparent in the **New York Draft Riot.** After a mostly Irish mob had destroyed the draft office at the federal marshal's headquarters, it launched an indiscriminate attack on the city's black population and institutions, including burning the Colored Orphan Asylum to the ground and hanging two black New Yorkers who wandered into their path. The rioters also sacked the mayor's house, tore up railroad tracks, looted the Brooks Brothers clothing store, and destroyed commercial and residential property on fashionable Fifth Avenue, crying "Down with the rich!" City officials and the police stood by, unable or unwilling to stem the riot. Army units fresh from Gettysburg, along with militia and naval units, quelled the riot.

## THE NORTHERN ECONOMY

After an initial downturn during the uncertain months preceding the war, the northern economy picked up quickly. High tariffs and massive federal spending soon made up for the loss of southern markets and the closing of the Mississippi River. Profits skyrocketed for some businesses. New industries boomed, and new inventions increased manufacturing efficiency, as in the sewing machine industry, which was first commercialized in the 1850s. Technological advances there greatly increased the output of the North's garment factories. Production of petroleum, used as a lubricant, increased from 84,000 gallons to 128 million gallons during the war.

Despite the loss of manpower to the demands of industry and the military, the productivity of northern agriculture grew during the war.

**Trade unions and strikebreakers.** Working people should have benefited from wartime prosperity. With men off to war and immigration down, labor was in short supply. Although wages increased, prices rose more. Declining real wages led to exploitation, especially of women in garment factories. The trade union movement, which suffered a serious setback in the depression of 1857, revived. Local unions of shoemakers, carpenters, and miners emerged in 1862 across the North, and so did a few national organizations. By 1865, more than 200,000 northern workers belonged to labor unions.

Employers struck back at union organizing by hiring strikebreakers, usually African Americans, who were available because until the war's midpoint, they were unwelcome for military service. Labor conflicts between striking white workers and black strikebreakers sparked riots in New York City and Cincinnati. The racial antagonism accounted in part for workers' opposition to Lincoln's Emancipation Proclamation and for the continued strength of the Democratic Party in northern cities.

**Profiteers and corruption.** The promise of enormous profits bred greed and corruption as well as exploitation. Illicit trade between North and South was inevitable and profiteers not only defied the government to trade with the enemy but also sometimes swindled the government outright. Some merchants reaped high profits supplying the army with shoddy goods at inflated prices.

Deep social and ethical problems were emerging in northern society and would become more pronounced in the decades after the Civil War. For the time being, the benefits of economic development for the Union cause outweighed its negative consequences. The thriving northern economy fed, clothed, and armed the Union's soldiers and kept most civilians employed and well fed. Prosperity and the demands of a wartime economy also provided northern women with unprecedented opportunities.

## NORTHERN WOMEN AND THE WAR

More than 100,000 northern women took jobs in factories, sewing rooms, classrooms, hospitals, and arsenals during the Civil War. Stepping in for their absent husbands, fathers, and sons, they often performed tasks previously reserved for men but at lower pay. The expanding bureaucracy

**New York Draft Riot** A mostly Irish-immigrant protest against conscription in New York City in July 1863 that escalated into class and racial warfare that had to be quelled by federal troops.

**QUICK REVIEW**

**The Draft Riots**

- 1863: Congress passed national conscription law.
- New York, July 1863: Mostly Irish mob burns federal marshal's headquarters.
- Racial and class antagonisms fueled riot.

**QUICK REVIEW**

**The Northern Economy**

- Tariffs and federal spending made up for loss of southern markets.
- Profits skyrocketed in some businesses.
- New industries emerged and new technologies increased efficiency.
- Wages failed to keep up with rising prices.

in Washington also offered opportunities for many women. The United States Treasury alone employed 447 women in the war years. And unlike private industry, the federal government paid women and men equally for the same work.

The new economic opportunities the war created for women left northern society more open to a broader view of women's roles. One indication of this change was the admission of women to eight previously all-male state universities after the war. Like the class and racial tensions that surfaced in northern cities, the shifting role of women during the Civil War hinted at the promises and problems of postwar life. The changing scale and nature of the American economy, the expanded role of government, and the shift in class, racial, and gender relations are all trends that signaled what historians call the "modernization" of American society. Many of these trends began before the war, but the war highlighted and accelerated them.

# THE CONFEDERACY DISINTEGRATES

**HOW DID** the war affect civilian life in the South?

Even under the best of conditions, the newly formed political and economic institutions of the Confederacy would have had difficulty maintaining control over the country's class and racial tensions. But as battlefield losses mounted, the Confederacy disintegrated.

After 1863, defeat infected Confederate politics, ruined the southern economy, and eventually invaded the hearts and minds of the southern people. Disillusionment against the Confederate government did not erode support for Lee and his army. The South pinned its waning hopes on its defensive military strategy. If it could prolong the conflict a little longer, perhaps a war-weary North would replace Lincoln and the Republicans in the 1864 elections with a Democratic president and Congress inclined to make peace.

**WHERE TO LEARN MORE**

★ Museum of the Confederacy, Richmond, Virginia
http://www.moc.org/site/PageServer

## SOUTHERN POLITICS

As the war turned against the Confederacy, southerners increasingly turned against each other. Some joined peace societies, which emerged as early as 1861. North Carolinians opposed to the war formed the Order of the Heroes of America, whose members not only demonstrated for peace but also took control of the Piedmont and mountain sections of the state. Other southerners preferred quieter dissent. They refused to join the army, pay taxes, or obey laws prohibiting trade with the enemy.

States' rights proved an obstacle to the Davis administration's efforts to exert central authority. The governors of Georgia and North Carolina gave the Richmond government particular difficulty, hoarding munitions, soldiers, supplies, food, and money. Even cooperative governors refused to allow state agents to collect taxes for the Confederacy.

Several parts of the South began clamoring for peace during the fateful summer of 1863. By November 1864, the Confederacy was suffering as much from internal disaffection as from the attacks of Union armies. Confederate authorities could not suppress civilian unrest in Virginia, North Carolina, and Tennessee, and Union spies operated openly in Mobile, Wilmington, and Richmond.

Davis and other Confederate leaders might have averted some of these political problems had they succeeded in building a strong sense of Confederate nationalism among soldiers and civilians. They tried several strategies to do so. For example, Davis tried to identify the Confederacy's fight for independence with the American Revolution of 1776. But egalitarian revolutionary ideals quickly lost their appeal in the face of poverty, starvation, and defeat. Davis also tried to cast the Confederacy as a bastion of freedom standing up to Lincoln's despotic abuse of executive authority, but he, too, eventually invoked authority similar to

Lincoln's. Confederate religious leaders sought to distinguish their new nation from the North by referring to southerners as God's "chosen people." But when Confederate military fortunes declined, religious leaders drew back from such visions of collective favor and stressed the need for individual salvation.

## SOUTHERN FAITH

In a devout society convinced it was fighting a holy war, some southerners sought to attribute their mounting losses to a moral failing. Some identified slavery as the culprit. But most Confederates held steadfast to the notion that God was on their side and that battlefield losses represented His temporary displeasure, not abandonment. They asked, as it is written in Judges 6:13, "If the Lord be with us, why then is all this befallen us?" They answered by drawing comfort from the Old Testament account of Job's suffering: "Though he slay me, yet will I trust him."

For black southerners, the Bible held other confirmations. The war was indeed becoming the fulfillment of a biblical prophecy. They turned to the Book of Daniel for its explicit explanation:

> For the king of the north shall return, and shall set forth a multitude greater than the former, and shall certainly come after certain years with a great army and with much riches.
>
> And in those times there shall many stand up against the king of the south: also the robbers of thy people shall exalt themselves to establish the vision; but they shall fall.

## THE SOUTHERN ECONOMY

By 1863, the Confederacy was having a difficult time feeding itself. Destruction of farms by both sides and growing Union control of waterways and rail lines restricted the distribution of food. Speculators held certain commodities off the market to drive up prices, making shortages of food, cloth, and medicines worse. Bread riots erupted in Mobile, Atlanta, and Richmond.

Southern soldiers had marched off to war in neat uniforms with shiny buttons, many leaving behind self-sustaining families. But in August 1863, diarist Mary Chesnut, wife of a Confederate official in Richmond, watched 10,000 men marching near Richmond and commented, "Such rags and tags as we saw now. Most garments and arms were . . . taken from the enemy." The soldiers' families were threadbare as well. In the devastated areas near battle sites, civilians survived by selling fragments of dead soldiers' clothing stripped off their bodies and by collecting spent bullets and selling them for scrap.

The predations of both Union and Confederate soldiers further threatened civilians in the South. The women and children left alone on farms and plantations were vulnerable to stragglers and deserters from both armies who sometimes robbed, burned houses, raped, and murdered. Southerners also feared that slaves on isolated plantations would rise up against their masters. Most slaves, however, were more intent on escape than revenge.

As Confederate casualties mounted, more and more southern women and children, like their northern counterparts, faced the pain of grief. Funeral processions became commonplace in the cities and black

Wartime food shortages, skyrocketing inflation, and rumors of hoarding and price-gouging drove women in several southern cities to protest violently. Demonstrations like the 1863 food riot shown here reflected a larger rending of southern society as Confederate losses and casualties mounted on the battlefield. Some southern women placed survival and providing for their families ahead of boosting morale and silently supporting a war effort that had taken their men away. Their defection hurt the Confederate cause.

the color of fashion. With little food, worthless money, and a husband, son, or father gone forever, the future looked bleak.

## SOUTHERN WOMEN AND THE WAR

In the early days of the Civil War, southern white women continued to live their lives according to antebellum conventions. Magazine articles urged them to preserve themselves as models of purity for men debased by the violence of war.

Women flooded newspapers and periodicals with patriotic verses and songs. A major theme of these works, illustrated by the following example from the *Richmond Record* in September 1863, was the need to suppress grief and fear for the good of the men at the front:

> The maid who binds her warrior's sash
> And smiling, all her pain dissembles,
> The mother who conceals her grief
> [had] shed as sacred blood as e'er
> Was poured upon the plain of battle.

A Virginia woman confided to her diary, "We must learn the lesson which so many have to endure, to struggle against our feelings."

By the time of the Civil War, such emotional concealment had become second nature to planters' wives. They had long had to endure their anguish over their husbands' nocturnal visits to the slave quarters. They were used to the condescension of men who assumed them to be intellectually inferior. And they accepted in bitter, self-sacrificing silence the contradiction between the myth of the pampered leisure they were presumed to enjoy and the hard demands their lives actually entailed. But some southern women chafed at their supporting role and, as Confederate manpower and matériel needs became acute, took on new productive responsibilities. Initially, they did so within the domestic context: Women formed clubs to sew flags and uniforms. To raise money for the war effort, they held benefits and auctions and collected jewelry and other valuables.

Soon, however, the needs of the Confederacy drew women outside the home to fill positions vacated by men. They managed plantations. They worked in the fields alongside slaves. They worked in factories to make uniforms and munitions. They worked in government offices as clerks and secretaries. They taught school. A few, like Belle Boyd and Rose O'Neal Greenhow, spied for the Confederacy. And many, like their northern counterparts, served as nurses. Eventually, battlefield reverses and economic collapse undermined all these roles, leaving women and men alike struggling simply to survive.

As the war dragged on and the southern economy and social order deteriorated, even the patriots suffered from resentment and doubt. By 1864, many women were helping their deserting husbands or relatives elude Confederate authorities.

By 1864, many southern white women had tired of the war. What had begun as a sacred cause had disintegrated into a nightmare of fear and deprivation. Uprooted from their homes, some women wandered through the war-ravaged South, exposed to violence, disease, and hunger and seeking shelter where they could find it. Those women fortunate enough to

**QUICK REVIEW**

**Confederate Women**

◆ As war dragged on, southern women took more active role at home and in the workplace.

◆ Some served as spies and nurses.

◆ Near the end of the war, many women helped their husbands desert.

White family "refugeeing." In advance of Union armies, tens of thousands of southern families fled to safer locales, a bitter exodus that fulfilled the Federals' vow to bring the war to the South's civilian population.

remain in their homes turned to work, others to protest, and many to religion. Some devoutly religious women concluded that it was God, not the Yankees, who had brought destruction on the South for its failure to live up to its responsibilities to women and children. Others blamed their men. Women greeted defeated troops retreating from Vicksburg with shouts of "We are disappointed in you!" However, despite hardship and privation, support for the Confederacy persisted among some women, stoked by fierce hatred of the enemy.

# THE UNION PREVAILS, 1864–1865

**WHAT WAS** Grant's strategy for ending the war?

Despite the Union's dominant military position after Vicksburg and Gettysburg and the Confederacy's mounting homefront problems, three obstacles to Union victory remained. Federal troops under General William T. Sherman controlled Chattanooga and the gateway to Georgia, but the Confederate Army of Tennessee, now commanded by Joseph E. Johnston, was still intact, blocking Sherman's path to Atlanta. Robert E. Lee's formidable Army of Northern Virginia still protected Richmond. And the Confederacy still controlled the rich Shenandoah Valley, which fed Lee's armies and supplied his cavalry with horses. In March 1864, President Lincoln brought General Ulysses S. Grant to Washington and appointed him commander of all Union armies. Grant set about devising a strategy to overcome these obstacles.

## GRANT'S PLAN TO END THE WAR

Grant brought two innovations to the final campaign. First, he coordinated the Union war effort. Before, the Union's armies in Virginia and the West had operated independently, giving Confederate leaders the opportunity to direct troops and supplies to whichever arena most needed them. Now Grant proposed to deprive them of that option. The Union's armies in Virginia and the Lower South would attack at the same time, keeping steady pressure on all fronts. Second, Grant changed the tempo of the war. Before, long periods of rest had intervened between battles. Grant, with the advantage of superior numbers, proposed nonstop warfare.

Although Grant's strategy ultimately worked, several problems and miscalculations undermined its effectiveness. With Sherman advancing in Georgia, Grant's major focus was Lee's army in Virginia. But Grant underestimated Lee. The Confederate general thwarted him for almost a year and inflicted horrendous casualties on his army. Confederate forces under Jubal Early drove Union forces from the Shenandoah Valley in June 1864, depriving Grant of troops and allowing the Confederates to maintain their supply lines. And the incompetence of General Benjamin Butler, charged with advancing up the James River to Richmond in May 1864 to relieve Lee's pressure on Grant, further eroded Grant's plan. Finally, Grant had to contend with disaffection in his officer corps. Many of his officers felt enduring loyalty to General George McClellan, whom Lincoln had dismissed in 1862, and considered Grant a mediocrity who had triumphed in the West only because his opposition there had been third-rate.

Lee's only hope was to make Grant's campaign so costly and time-consuming that the northern general would abandon it before the southerners ran out of supplies and troops. But despite problems and setbacks, Grant kept relentless pressure on Lee. Tied down in Virginia, the Confederate general was unable to send troops to help slow Sherman's advance in Georgia.

**From the Wilderness to Cold Harbor.**    Grant and General George Meade began their campaign against Lee in May 1864, crossing the Rapidan River near Fredericksburg, Virginia, and marching toward an area known as the Wilderness (see Map 15–6). Lee attacked the Army of the Potomac, which outnumbered his forces 118,000 to 60,000, in the thickets of the Wilderness on May 5 and 6 before it could reach open ground. The densely wooded terrain reduced the Union army's advantage in numbers and artillery. Much of the fighting involved fierce hand-to-hand combat. Exchanges of gunfire at close range set the dry underbrush ablaze.

**QUICK REVIEW**

**Grant's Strategy**

- Better coordination of Union effort and the application of steady pressure.
- The waging of nonstop warfare.
- Grant's plan worked in the long run, but at a high cost.

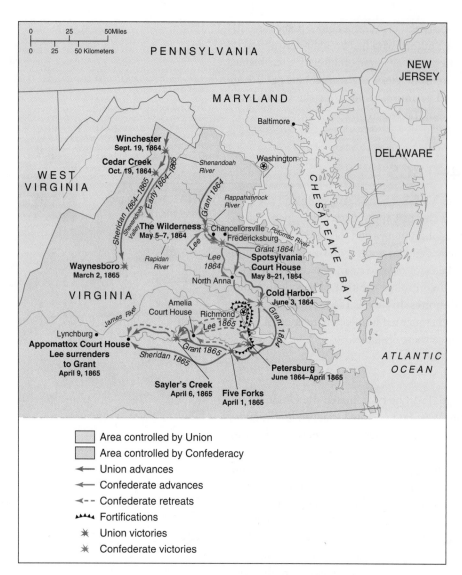

MAP 15–6  **Grant and Lee in Virginia, 1864–1865**  The engagements in Virginia from May 1864 to April 1865 between the two great generals proved decisive in ending the Civil War. Although Lee fared well enough in the Wilderness, Spotsylvania, and Cold Harbor campaigns, the sheer might and relentlessness of Grant and his army wore down the Confederate forces. When Petersburg fell after a prolonged siege on April 2, 1865, Richmond, Appomattox, and dreams of southern independence soon fell as well.

**What happened** at Cold Harbor? What did this battle reveal about the Union's population advantage over the Confederacy?

Wounded soldiers, trapped in the fires, begged their comrades to shoot them before they burned to death. The toll was frightful, 18,000 casualties on the Union side, 10,000 for the Confederates. Other Union commanders would have pulled back and rested after such an encounter. But Grant, relentless in the pursuit of the enemy, startled Lee's army by pushing on, and Lee's offensive in the Battle of the Wilderness was his last. From then on, his army was on the defensive against Grant's relentless pursuit.

Marching and fighting, his casualties always higher than Lee's, Grant continued southward. Attacking the entrenched Confederate army at Spotsylvania, his army suffered another 18,000 casualties to the Confederates' 11,000. Undeterred, Grant moved on toward Cold Harbor, where Lee's troops again awaited him in entrenched positions. Flinging his army against withering Confederate fire on June 3, he lost 7,000 men in eight minutes.

In less than a month of fighting, the Army of the Potomac had lost 55,000 men. The slaughter undermined Grant's support in northern public opinion and led peace advocates to renew their quest for a ceasefire. With antiwar sentiment growing in the North as the presidential elections approached in November, Lee's defensive strategy seemed to be working.

Grant decided to change his tactics. Abandoning his march on Richmond from the north, he shifted his army south of the James River to approach the Confederate capital from the rear. Wasting no time, he crossed his army over the James and, on June 17, 1864, surprised the Confederates with an attack on Petersburg, a critical rail junction 23 miles south of Richmond. It was a brilliant maneuver, but the hesitant actions of Union corps commanders gave Lee time to reinforce the town's defenders. Both armies dug in for a lengthy siege.

**Atlanta.**  While Grant engaged Lee in Virginia, Union forces under William T. Sherman in Georgia engaged in a deadly dance with the Army of Tennessee under the command of Joseph E. Johnston as they began the campaign to take Atlanta. Hoping to lure Sherman into a frontal assault, Johnston settled his forces early in May at Dalton, an important railroad junction in Georgia 25 miles south of Chattanooga and 75 miles north of Atlanta. The wily Union general declined to attack and instead made a wide swing around the Confederates, prompting Johnston to abandon Dalton, rush south, and dig in again at Resaca to prevent Sherman from cutting the railroad. Again Sherman swung around without an assault, and again Johnston rushed south to cut him off, this time at Cassville.

This waltz continued for two months, until Johnston had retreated to a strong defensive position on Kennesaw Mountain, barely 20 miles north of Atlanta. At this point, early in July, Sherman decided to attack, with predictably disastrous consequences. The Union suffered 3,000 casualties, the Confederates only 600. Sherman would not make such a mistake again. He resumed his maneuvering and by mid-July had forced Johnston into defensive positions on Peachtree Creek just north of Atlanta. President Davis feared that Johnston would let Sherman take Atlanta without a fight and "dance" with the Union general until the sea stopped them both. Davis dismissed Johnston and installed John Bell Hood of Texas in his place. This was a grave error. Hood, in the opinion of those who fought for him, had a "lion's heart" but a "wooden head."

In late July, Hood began a series of attacks on Sherman, beginning at Peachtree Creek on July 20, and was thrown back each time with heavy losses. Sherman launched a series of flanking maneuvers around the city in late August that left Hood in danger of being surrounded. The Confederate general had no choice but to abandon Atlanta and save his army. On the night of September 1, Hood evacuated the city, burning everything of military value.

The loss of Atlanta was a severe blow to the Confederacy. Several of the South's major railroads converged at the city, and its industries helped arm and clothe the armies. Atlanta's fall also left Georgia's rich farmland at the mercy of Sherman's army. Most significant, the fall of Atlanta revived the morale of the war-weary North and helped ensure Lincoln's reelection in November. The last hope of the Confederacy, that a peace candidate would replace Lincoln and end the war, had faded.

## THE ELECTION OF 1864 AND SHERMAN'S MARCH

Before Sherman's victory at Atlanta, northern dismay over Grant's enormous losses and his failure to take Richmond raised the prospect of a Democratic election victory. Nominating George B. McClellan, the former commander of the Union's armies, as their presidential candidate, the Democrats appealed to voters as the party of peace. They also appealed to the anti-emancipation sentiment that was strong in some parts of the North.

The fall of Atlanta and the suddenly improved military fortunes of the Union undermined Democratic prospects. Another Union victory three weeks before the elections gave Lincoln a further boost and diminished McClellan's chances. Since September, Union forces under General Philip H. Sheridan had been on the offensive in the Shenandoah Valley (see Map 15–6). In a decisive battle on October 19, they overwhelmed the valley's Confederate defenders. Lee had now been deprived of a vital source of supply.

**The Republican victory.**   In the voting on November 8, Lincoln captured 55 percent of the popular vote, losing only New Jersey, Delaware, and Kentucky. Republicans likewise swept the congressional elections, retaining control of both the Senate and the House of Representatives.

The Republican victory reinforced the Union commitment to emancipation. A proposed constitutional amendment outlawing slavery everywhere in the United States, not just those areas still in rebellion, passed Congress and was ratified as the **Thirteenth Amendment** to the U.S. Constitution in 1865. All the earlier amendments related to government powers and functions; this was the first to outlaw a domestic institution previously protected by the Constitution and state law.

**Sherman's march to the sea.**   After Sherman took Atlanta, he proposed to break Confederate resistance once and for all by marching his army to the sea and destroying everything in its path. Sherman's March got underway on November 15. His force of

**Thirteenth Amendment**
Constitutional amendment ratified in 1865 that freed all slaves throughout the United States.

General Ulysses S. Grant had the pews from a local church moved to a grove of trees where he and his officers planned the following day's assault on Confederate troops at Cold Harbor, Virginia. Grant appears at the left of the photograph, leaning over a bench and studying a map.

60,000 men, encountering little resistance, entered Savannah on December 22, 1864. Just a few weeks earlier, Union forces in Tennessee had routed Hood's army at the Battle of Franklin and then crushed it entirely at the Battle of Nashville. Hood's defeat removed any threat to Sherman's rear.

Sherman resumed his march in February 1865, heading for South Carolina, the heart of the Confederacy and the state where the Civil War had begun. South Carolinians sent taunting messages promising stiff resistance, but these served only to further provoke Sherman's troops. They pushed aside the small force that assembled to oppose them, wreaked greater destruction in South Carolina than they had in Georgia, and burned the state capitol at Columbia. Sherman sent the colonel of a black regiment to receive the surrender of Charleston and ordered black troops to be the first to take possession of the city. The soldiers marched in singing "John Brown's Body," to the cheers of the city's black population.

Sherman ended his march in Goldsboro, North Carolina, in March 1865 after repelling a surprise Confederate attack at Bentonville led by the restored Joseph E. Johnston and the remnants of the Army of Tennessee. Behind the Union army lay a barren swath 425 miles long from Savannah to Goldsboro.

**Lincoln's second inaugural.**    When Abraham Lincoln took the oath of office for a second time on March 4, 1865, the result of the war was a foregone conclusion even if the precise date of its end was not. In a brief but inspirational address, the president provided the spiritual blueprint for reconciliation, though it disappointed some in the crowd who hoped for a declaration of victory, a promise of retribution against the rebel traitors, or at least an acknowledgment that God was clearly on the side of the Union. Instead, Lincoln declared that God had cursed both sides and had visited a destructive war on the nation because of the sin of slavery, a sin, he stressed, that was national, not regional.

> Nor was the president prepared to proclaim victory, despite its inevitability. In fact, the war could continue for some indeterminate time: "Fondly do we hope—fervently do we pray—that this mighty scourge of war may speedily pass away. Yet, if God wills that it continue, until all the wealth piled by the bond-man's two hundred and fifty years of unrequited toil shall be sunk, and until every drop of blood drawn with the lash, shall be paid by another drawn with the sword, as was said three thousand years ago, so still it must be said 'the judgments of the Lord, are true and righteous altogether.'"

> And once the bloody conflict ends, Lincoln intoned, let reconciliation rather than retribution inform the national policy: "With malice toward none; with charity for all; with firmness in the right, as God gives us to see the right, let us strive on to finish the work we are in; to bind up the nation's wounds; to care for him who shall have borne the battle, and for his widow, and his orphan—to do all which may achieve and cherish a just, and a lasting peace, among ourselves, and with all nations." In the meantime, the bitter struggle would continue.

**Arming the Confederacy's slaves.**    In March 1865, in a move reflecting their desperation, Confederate leaders revived a proposal that they had previously rejected: to arm and free slaves. President Davis hoped this action would gain the Confederacy not only a military benefit but also diplomatic recognition from countries that had balked because of slavery.

> On March 13, 1865, a reluctant Confederate Congress passed a bill to enlist black soldiers, but without offering them freedom. Ten days later, President Davis and the War Office issued a general order that promised immediate freedom to slaves who enlisted. The war ended before the order could have any effect. The irony was that in the summer of 1864, a majority of northerners probably would have accepted reunion without emancipation had the Confederacy abandoned its fight.

## THE ROAD TO APPOMATTOX AND THE DEATH OF LINCOLN

With Sherman's triumph in Georgia and the Carolinas and Sheridan's rout of the Confederates in the Shenandoah Valley, Lee's army remained the last obstacle to Union victory. On April 1, Sheridan's cavalry seized a vital railroad junction on Lee's right flank, forcing Lee to abandon Petersburg and the defense of Richmond. Lee tried a daring run westward toward Lynchburg, hoping to secure much-needed supplies and to join Johnston's Army of Tennessee in North Carolina to continue the fight.

> President Davis fled Richmond with his cabinet and headed toward North Carolina. Union troops occupied the Confederate capital on April 3, and two days later, President Lincoln

●●●—Read the Document

at **www.myhistorylab.com**
*Abraham Lincoln, Second Inaugural Address (1865)*

Generals Robert E. Lee and Ulysses S. Grant surrounded by officers in the McLean House at Appomattox Court House, Virginia.

walked through its streets to the cheers of his army and an emotional reception from thousands of black people. "I know I am free," shouted one black spectator, "for I have seen Father Abraham and felt him."

**The surrender at Appomattox.**   Grant's army of 60,000 outran Lee's diminishing force of 35,000 and cut off his escape at Appomattox Court House, Virginia, on April 7. Convinced that further resistance was futile, the Confederate commander met Grant on April 9, 1865, in the McLean house at Appomattox to sign the documents of surrender. The Union general offered generous terms, allowing Lee's men to go home unmolested and to take with them horses or mules "to put in a crop."

Though some southerners entertained fleetingly the idea of launching a guerrilla campaign against Union forces, most were sick of the war. One Confederate leader, traveling through the stricken South in April 1865, reported that soldiers and civilians alike considered any continuation of the conflict "madness." Joseph E. Johnston surrendered to Sherman near Durham, North Carolina, on April 26. On May 10, Union cavalry captured President Davis in southern Georgia. On May 26, Texas general Kirby Smith surrendered his trans-Mississippi army, and the Civil War came to an end.

**The death of Lincoln.**   Washington greeted the Confederate surrender at Appomattox with predictable and raucous rejoicing, torchlight parades, cannon salutes, and crowds spontaneously bellowing "The Star-Spangled Banner." On April 11, President Lincoln addressed a large crowd from the White House balcony and spoke briefly of his plans to reconstruct the South with the help of persons loyal to the Union, including recently freed slaves. At least one listener found the speech disappointing. A sometime actor and full-time Confederate patriot, John Wilkes Booth, muttered to a friend in the throng, "That means nigger citizenship. Now, by God, I'll put him through. That is the last speech he will ever make."

On the evening of April 14, Good Friday, the president went to Ford's Theatre in Washington to view a comedy, *Our American Cousin*. During the performance, Booth shot the president, wounding him mortally, then jumped from Lincoln's box to the stage shouting "*Sic semper tyrannis*" ("Thus ever to tyrants") and fled the theater. Union troops tracked him down to a barn in northern Virginia and killed him. Investigators arrested eight accomplices who

**WHERE TO LEARN MORE**

★ Appomattox Court House,
Appomattox, Virginia
http://www.nps.gov/apco/index.htm

## OVERVIEW   Major Battles of the Civil War, 1861–1865

| Battle or Campaign | Date | Outcome and Consequences |
| --- | --- | --- |
| First Bull Run | July 21, 1861 | Confederate victory, destroyed the widespread belief in the North that the war would end quickly, fueled Confederate sense of superiority |
| Forts Henry and Donelson | February 6–16, 1862 | Union victory, gave the North control of strategic river systems in the western Confederacy and closed an important link between the eastern and western Confederacy |
| Shiloh Church | April 6–7, 1862 | Union victory, high casualties transformed attitudes about the war on both sides |
| Seven Days' Battles | June 25–July 1, 1862 | Standoff, halted McClellan's advance on Richmond in the Peninsula Campaign |
| Second Bull Run | August 29–30, 1862 | Confederate victory, reinforced Robert E. Lee's reputation for invincibility |
| Antietam | September 17, 1862 | Standoff halted Lee's advance into the North, eliminated Confederacy's chance for diplomatic recognition, encouraged Lincoln to issue the Emancipation Proclamation |
| Fredericksburg | December 13, 1862 | Confederate victory, revived morale of Lee's army |
| Chancellorsville | May 2–6, 1863 | Confederate victory, Stonewall Jackson killed, encouraged Lee to again invade North |
| Gettysburg | July 1–3, 1863 | Union victory, halted Confederate advance in the North, major psychological blow to Confederacy |
| Vicksburg | November 1862–July 1863 | Union victory; closed the key Confederate port on the Mississippi, also dealt a severe blow to Confederate cause |
| Chattanooga | August–November 1863 | Union victory, solidified Union dominance in the West |
| Wilderness and Cold Harbor | May and June 1864 | Two Confederate victories, inflicted huge losses on Grant's army; turned public opinion against Grant but failed to force him to withdraw |
| Atlanta | May–September 1864 | Union victory; Confederacy lost key rail depot and industrial center |
| Sherman's March | November 1864–March 1865 | Nearly unopposed, Sherman's army cut a path of destruction through Georgia and South Carolina, breaking southern morale |
| Battles of Franklin and Nashville | November and December 1864 | Union victories in Tennessee; effectively destroyed Army of Tennessee |
| Siege of Petersburg | June 1864–April 1865 | Long stalemate ended in Union victory; led to fall of Richmond and surrender of Lee's army at Appomattox Court House |

had conspired with Booth to murder other high officials in addition to Lincoln. Four of the accomplices were hanged.

Southerners reacted to Lincoln's assassination with surprisingly mixed emotions. Many saw some slight hope of relief for the South's otherwise bleak prospects. But General Johnston and others like him were aware of Lincoln's moderating influence on the radical elements in the Republican Party that were pressing for harsh terms against the South. The president's death, Johnston wrote, was "the greatest possible calamity to the South."

**Watch** the **Video**

at **www.myhistorylab.com**
*The Meaning of the Civil War
for Americans*

# CONCLUSION

Just before the war, William Sherman had warned a friend from Virginia, "You people of the South don't know what you are doing. This country will be drenched in blood. . . . [W]ar is a terrible thing." He was right. More than 365,000 Union soldiers died during the war, 110,000 in battle, and more than 256,000 Confederate soldiers, 94,000 in battle. Total casualties on both sides, including wounded, were more than 1 million.

The southern armies suffered disproportionately higher casualties than the northern armies. One in four Confederate soldiers died or endured debilitating wounds, compared to one in ten federal soldiers. Compounding the suffering of the individuals behind these gruesome statistics was the incalculable suffering, in terms of grief, fatherless children, women who never married, families never made whole, of the people close to them.

The war devastated the South. The region lost one-fourth of its white male population between the ages of 20 and 40. It also lost two-fifths of its livestock and half its farm machinery. Union armies destroyed many of the South's railroads and shattered its industry. Between 1860 and 1870, the wealth of the South declined by 60 percent, and its share of the nation's total wealth dropped from more than 30 percent to 12 percent. The wealth of the North, in contrast, increased by half in the same period.

The Union victory solved the constitutional question about the right of secession and sealed the fate of slavery. The issue that dominated the prewar sectional debate had vanished. Now, when politicians intoned Independence Day orations or campaign speeches about the ideals of democracy and freedom, the glaring reality of human bondage would no longer mock their rhetoric.

The Civil War stimulated societal changes that grew more significant over time. It did not make the Union an industrial nation, but it taught the effectiveness of centralized management, new financial techniques, and the coordination of production, marketing, and distribution. Entrepreneurs would apply these lessons to create the expanding corporations of the postwar American economy. Likewise, the war did not revolutionize gender relations in American society, but by opening new opportunities to women in fields such as nursing and teaching, it helped lay the foundation for the woman's suffrage movement of the 1870s and 1880s.

For many Americans, especially black and white southerners, the war was the most important event in their lives, but it was not responsible for every postwar change in American society, and it left many features of American life intact. The experience of pulling together in a massive war effort, for example, did not soften class antagonisms. Capitalism, not labor, triumphed during the war. And it was industrialists and entrepreneurs, not working people, who most benefited from the war's bonanza.

For black southerners, emancipation was the war's most significant achievement. The war to end slavery changed some American racial attitudes, especially in the North. When Lincoln broadened the war's objectives to include the abolition of slavery, he connected the success of the Union to freedom for the slave. At the outset of the Civil War, only a small minority of northerners considered themselves abolitionists. After the Emancipation Proclamation, every northern soldier became a liberator. The courage of black troops and the efforts of African American leaders to link the causes of reunion and freedom were influential in bringing about this shift.

Most white southerners did not experience a similar enlightenment. Some were relieved by the end of slavery, but most greeted it with fear, anger, and regret.

If the Civil War resolved the sectional dispute of the 1850s by ending slavery and denying the right of the southern states to secede, it created two new equally troubling problems: how to reunite South and North and how to deal with the legacy of slavery. At his last cabinet meeting on April 14, Lincoln seemed inclined to be conciliatory, cautioning against reprisals on Confederate leaders and noting the courage of General Lee and his officers.

America's greatest crisis had closed. In its wake, former slaves tested their new freedom, and the nation groped for reconciliation. The struggle to preserve the Union and abolish slavery had renewed and vindicated the nation's ideals. It was time to savor the hard-fought victories before plunging into the uncertainties of Reconstruction.

# WHERE TO LEARN MORE

**Museum of the Confederacy, Richmond, Virginia.** This museum has rotating exhibits on various aspects of the Confederate effort during the Civil War, both on the home front and on the battlefield. The Confederate White House, which is open to the public, is next door to the museum. Visit its website at http://www.moc.org/site/PageServer.

**Gettysburg National Military Park, Gettysburg, Pennsylvania.** An excellent and balanced interpretation awaits the visitor at this national park. See its website, http://www.nps.gov/gett/index.htm.

**National Museum of the History of Medicine, Washington, DC.** For those interested in the grisly details of Civil War medicine, the museum's permanent exhibit is "To Bind Up the Nation's Wounds: Medicine During the Civil War." The museum also has a long-running exhibit, "Abraham Lincoln: The Final Casualty of the War," which includes the bullet that ended his life. http://nmhm.washingtondc.museum

**Appomattox Court House, Appomattox, Virginia.** What historian Bruce Catton termed "a stillness at Appomattox" can be felt at the McLean house in this south-central Virginia town. The house is much as it was when General Robert E. Lee surrendered his forces to General Ulysses S. Grant on April 9, 1865. An almost reverential solitude covers the house and the well-maintained grounds today. Its website is at http://www.nps.gov/apco/index.htm.

# REVIEW QUESTIONS

1. How did the Union and the Confederacy compare in terms of resources, leadership, and military strategies in the period 1861–1863? What impact did these factors have on the course of the war?

2. What was the significance of the battles of Antietam and Gettysburg? In what ways were they turning points in the Civil War?

3. Given that the federal government was fighting a civil war, why did not European powers, other than France, take advantage of that distraction and meddle in Latin American affairs?

4. What effects did the Emancipation Proclamation have on the Union and Confederate causes?

5. Compare and contrast the roles played by women in the North and in the South during the Civil War, and explain how their actions and activities aided or hindered the war effort of their respective nations.

6. Sullivan Ballou made the ultimate sacrifice for his cause. Why did he fight?

# KEY TERMS*

**Confiscation Act** (p. 408)
**Copperheads** (p. 417)
**Emancipation Proclamation** (p. 408)
**Homestead Act** (p. 417)
**Land Grant College Act** (p. 417)

**New York Draft Riot** (p. 419)
**Radical Republicans** (p. 417)
**Thirteenth Amendment** (p. 425)
*See the Overview table, on p. 429 for important battles of the Civil War.

# PEARSON myhistorylab™ Connections

Reinforce what you learned in this chapter by studying the many documents, images, maps, review tools, and videos available at **www.myhistorylab.com**.

## Read and Review

✓● Study and Review  **Study Plan: Chapter 15**

●●●● Read the Document

*Clara Barton, Memoirs about Medical Life at the Battlefield (1862)*

*Jefferson Davis, Address to the Provisional Congress (1861)*

*Mary Boykin Chesnut, A Confederate Lady's Diary (1861)*

*Susie King Taylor, Reminiscences of an Army Laundress (1902)*

*The Homestead Act of 1862*

*Abraham Lincoln, Second Inaugural Address (1865)*

*Abraham Lincoln, The Gettysburg Address (1863)*

*"I Hope to Fall with My Face to the Foe": Lewis Douglass Describes the Battle of Fort Wagner (1863)*

*"If It Were Not for My Trust in Christ I Do Not Know How I Could Have Endured It": Testimony from Victims of New York's Draft Riots (1863)*

*J. Horace Lacy, "Lee at Fredericksburg" (1886)*

*The Emancipation Proclamation (1863)*

*William T. Sherman, The March Through Georgia (1875)*

◉● See the Map

*The Civil War Part I: 1861–1862*

*The Civil War Part II: 1863–1865*

*Effects of the Emancipation Proclamation*

## Research and Explore

●●●● Read the Document

*Personal Journeys Online*

*From Then to Now Online: The Soldiers' War*

*A Nation Divided: The Civil War*

((●● Hear the Audio

*When This Cruel War Is Over*

*Battle Hymn of the Republic*

●● Watch the Video

*What Caused the Civil War?*

*The Meaning of the Civil War for Americans*

DAVID GOLDFIELD
University of North Carolina, Charlotte

---

((●● Hear the **Audio**

Hear the audio files for Chapter 15 at
**www.myhistorylab.com**.

# 16

# Reconstruction

An elderly man reads a newspaper with the headline "Presidential Proclamation, Slavery," which refers to the January 1863 Emancipation Proclamation in this painting by Henry Louis Stephens (1824–1882).

434

((•─⃗Hear the **Audio**

Hear the audio files for Chapter 16 at **www.myhistorylab.com**.

## WHITE SOUTHERNERS AND THE GHOSTS OF THE CONFEDERACY, 1865 *(page 438)*

### HOW DID southerners remember the war? How did it shape their response to Reconstruction?

## MORE THAN FREEDOM: AFRICAN AMERICAN ASPIRATIONS IN 1865 *(page 439)*

### WHAT WERE African Americans' hopes for Reconstruction?

## FEDERAL RECONSTRUCTION, 1865–1870 *(page 444)*

### HOW DID Presidential Reconstruction differ from Congressional Reconstruction?

## COUNTER-RECONSTRUCTION, 1870–1874 *(page 452)*

### WHAT ROLE did violence play in Counter-Reconstruction?

## REDEMPTION, 1874–1877 *(page 455)*

### WHY DID the federal government abandon African Americans after 1872?

## MODEST GAINS *(page 459)*

### HOW AND why did Reconstruction end?

ONE AMERICAN JOURNEY

AN APPEAL TO THE AMERICAN PEOPLE (1871)

*When a dark and fearful strife*
*Raged around the nation's life,*
*And the traitor plunged his steel*
*Where your quivering hearts could feel,*
*When your cause did need a friend,*
*We were faithful to the end.*

*With your soldiers, side by side,*
*Helped we turn the battle's tide,*
*Till o'er ocean, stream and shore,*
*Wave the rebel flag no more,*
*And above the rescued sod*
*Praises rose to freedom's God.*

*But to-day the traitor stands*
*With crimson on his hands,*
*Scowling 'neath his brow of hate,*
*On our weak and desolate,*
*With the blood-rust on the knife*
*Aimed at the nation's life.*

*Asking you to weakly yield*
*All we won upon the field,*
*To ignore, on land and flood,*
*All the offerings of our blood,*
*And to write above our slain*
*"They have fought and died in vain."*

*Source:* Maryemma Graham, ed., *Complete Poems of Frances E. W. Harper* (New York: Oxford University Press, 1988), pp. 81–83.

✦✦✦ Read the Document at **www.myhistorylab.com**

Personal Journeys Online

- **N. J. Bell,** *Southern Railroad Man,* **1865.** A railroad conductor recalls the aftermath of the Civil War and its impact on a white family in Wilmington, NC.

- **Adelbert Ames, "Letter from the Republican Governor of Mississippi," 1875.** Letter to his wife expressing frustration at the violence against black voters in his state and his hope for federal intervention.

## CHRONOLOGY

| | |
|---|---|
| **1861** | Tsar Alexander II frees the serfs of Russia. |
| **1863** | Lincoln proposes his Ten Percent Plan. |
| **1864** | Congress proposes the Wade-Davis Bill. |
| **1865** | Sherman issues Field Order No. 15. |
| | Freedmen's Bureau is established. |
| | Andrew Johnson succeeds to the presidency, unveils his Reconstruction plan. |
| | Massachusetts desegregates all public facilities. |
| | Black citizens in several southern cities organize Union Leagues. |
| | Former Confederate states begin to pass black codes. |
| **1866** | Congress passes Southern Homestead Act, Civil Rights Act of 1866. |
| | Ku Klux Klan is founded. |
| | Fourteenth Amendment to the Constitution is passed (ratified in 1868). |
| | President Johnson goes on a speaking tour. |
| **1867** | Congress passes Military Reconstruction Acts, Tenure of Office Act. |
| **1868** | President Johnson is impeached and tried in the Senate for defying the Tenure of Office Act. |
| | Republican Ulysses S. Grant is elected president. |
| **1869** | Fifteenth Amendment passed (ratified 1870). |
| **1870** | Congress passes Enforcement Act. |

| | |
|---|---|
| | Republican regimes topple in North Carolina and Georgia. |
| **1871** | Congress passes Ku Klux Klan Act. |
| **1872** | Freedmen's Bureau closes down. |
| | Liberal Republicans emerge as a separate party. |
| | Ulysses S. Grant is reelected. |
| **1873** | Severe depression begins. |
| | Colfax Massacre occurs. |
| | U.S. Supreme Court's decision in the *Slaughterhouse* cases weakens the intent of the Fourteenth Amendment. |
| | Texas falls to the Democrats in the fall elections. |
| **1874** | White Leaguers attempt a coup against the Republican government of New Orleans. |
| | Democrats win off-year elections across the South amid widespread fraud and violence. |
| **1875** | Congress passes Civil Rights Act of 1875. |
| **1876** | Supreme Court's decision in *United States v. Cruikshank* nullifies Enforcement Act of 1870. |
| | Outcome of the presidential election between Republican Rutherford B. Hayes and Democrat Samuel J. Tilden is contested. |
| **1877** | Compromise of 1877 makes Hayes president and ends Reconstruction. |

FRANCES ELLEN WATKINS HARPER, the author of this poem, pleaded with northerners not to abandon African Americans in their quest for full equality. She appealed both to their sense of fairness—that African Americans had fought side-by-side and laid down their lives for the Union cause—and to their self-interest to not allow their winning the war, and the sacrifices that entailed, to be betrayed by losing the peace.

At the time, 1871, Reconstruction was under full assault in the South by white paramilitary groups associated with the Democratic Party. Though violence against the freedmen and their aspirations had been persistent since the end of the Civil War, the growing political power of blacks in the South after 1867 provoked more organized and violent assaults on blacks and some of their white colleagues. The federal government attempted to quell these disturbances with troops and legislation, but these measures were largely ineffective. While a majority of northern whites had opposed slavery, a majority also opposed racial equality. By 1871, a consensus emerged in the North to allow southern whites a free hand in dealing with their political problems. Harper's appeal, therefore, fell on deaf ears. The nation's journey toward a more just society took a major detour in the decade after the Civil War.

Frances Harper's personal journey was more rewarding. She was born into a free black family in Maryland, a slave state, in 1825. Orphaned at the age of 3 and raised by her aunt and uncle, she attended a noted school for free blacks in Baltimore. By the time she was 25, she had become the first woman professor at a seminary in Ohio which later became Wilberforce University. In 1853, Harper moved to Philadelphia where she worked in the Underground Railroad and became one of the few black women lecturers on abolition. In 1860, she married Fenton Harper, and had a daughter with him. When he died in 1864, she took her daughter and resumed lecturing, becoming one of the first women of color to travel throughout the South in the days after emancipation, helping to educate former slaves.

Although she arrived in the South with considerable hope, Harper left after five frustrating years. Violence against African Americans and their white allies had escalated and threatened to reduce the former slaves to a permanent category of second-class citizenship. Her poem was one of her last attempts to reach a northern public already grown weary of the periodic racial disturbances in the South. Harper spent the rest of her life writing novels and poetry, and working for the causes of temperance and of racial and women's rights.

The position of African Americans in American society was one of the two great issues of the Reconstruction era. The other great issue was how and under what terms to readmit the former Confederate states. Between 1865 and 1867, under President Andrew Johnson's Reconstruction plan, white southerners pretty much had their way with the former slaves and with their own state governments. Congressional action between 1867 and 1870 attempted to balance black rights and home rule, with mixed results. After 1870, white southerners gradually regained control of their states and localities, often through violence and intimidation, denying black southerners their political gains while Republicans in Washington and white northerners lost interest in policing their former enemies.

By the time the last federal troops left the South in 1877, the white southerners had prevailed. The Confederate states had returned to the Union with all of their rights and many of their leaders restored. And the freed slaves remained in mostly subservient positions with few of the rights and privileges enjoyed by other Americans. ✦

# WHITE SOUTHERNERS AND THE GHOSTS OF THE CONFEDERACY, 1865

**HOW DID** southerners remember the war? How did it shape their response to Reconstruction?

•••⊸ Read the Document

at www.myhistorylab.com
*Carl Schurz, Report on the Condition of the South (1865)*

**Lost Cause** The phrase many white southerners applied to their Civil War defeat. They viewed the war as a noble cause but only a temporary setback in the South's ultimate vindication.

The casualties of war in the South continued long after the hostilities ceased. Cities such as Richmond, Atlanta, Savannah, Charleston, and Columbia lay in ruins; farmsteads were stripped of everything but the soil; infrastructure, especially railroads, was damaged or destroyed; factories and machinery were demolished; and at least 5 million bales of cotton, the major cash crop, had gone up in smoke. Add a worthless currency, and the loss was staggering, climbing into hundreds of billions of dollars in today's currency.

Their cause lost and their society destroyed, white southerners lived through the summer and fall of 1865 surrounded by ghosts, the ghosts of lost loved ones, joyful times, bountiful harvests, self-assurance, and slavery. Defeat shook the basic tenets of their religious beliefs. Some praised God for delivering the South from the sin of slavery. But many other white southerners refused to accept their defeat as a divine judgment. Instead, they insisted, God had spared the South for a greater purpose. They came to view the war as the **Lost Cause** and interpreted it, not as a lesson in humility, but as an episode in the South's journey to salvation. White southerners transformed the bloody struggle into a symbol of courage against great odds and piety against sin. Eventually, they believed, redemption would come.

The Lost Cause would not merely exist as a memory, but also as a three-dimensional depiction of southern history, in rituals and celebrations, and as the educational foundation for future generations. The statues of the Confederate common soldier erected typically on the most important site in a town, the courthouse square; the commemorations of Confederate Memorial Day, the birthdays of prominent Confederate leaders, and the reunions of veterans, all marked with flourishing oratory, brass bands, parades, and related spectacles; and the textbooks implanting the white history of the South in young minds and carrying the legacy down through the generations—all of these ensured that the Lost Cause would not only be an interpretation of the past, but also the basic reality of the present and the foundation for the future.

Most white southerners approached the great issues of freedom and reunification with unyielding views. They

This engraving shows southerners decorating the graves of rebel soldiers at Hollywood Memorial Cemetery in Richmond, Virginia, in 1867. Northerners and southerners alike honored their war dead. But in the South, the practice of commemorating fallen soldiers became an important element in maintaining the myth of the Lost Cause that colored white southerners' view of the war.

saw African Americans as adversaries whose attempts at self-improvement were a direct challenge to white people's belief in their own racial superiority. White southerners saw outside assistance to black southerners as another invasion. The Yankees might have destroyed their families, their farms, and their fortunes, but they would not destroy the racial order. The war may have ended slavery, but white southerners were determined to preserve strict racial boundaries.

**WHERE TO LEARN MORE**

★ Beauvoir, Biloxi, Mississippi
http://www.beauvoir.org

# MORE THAN FREEDOM: AFRICAN AMERICAN ASPIRATIONS IN 1865

Black southerners had a quite different perspective on the Civil War and Reconstruction, seeing the former as a great victory for freedom and the latter as a time of great possibility. To black southerners the Civil War was a war of liberation, not a Lost Cause. The response of southern whites to black aspirations still stunned African Americans, who believed, naively perhaps, that what they sought—education, land, access to employment, and equality in law and politics— were basic rights and modest objectives. The former slaves did not initially even dream of social equality; far less did they plot murder and mayhem, as white people feared. They did harbor two potentially contradictory aspirations. The first was to be left alone, free of white supervision. But the former slaves also wanted land, voting and civil rights, and education. To secure these, they needed the intervention and support of the white power structure.

In 1865, African Americans had reason to hope that their dreams of full citizenship might be realized. They enjoyed a reservoir of support for their aspirations among some Republican leaders. The first step Congress took beyond emancipation was to establish the Bureau of Refugees, Freedmen, and Abandoned Lands in March 1865. Congress envisioned the **Freedmen's Bureau,** as it came to be called, as a multipurpose agency to provide social, educational, and economic services, advice, and protection to former slaves and destitute white southerners. The bureau marked the federal government's first foray into social welfare legislation. Congress also authorized the bureau to rent confiscated and abandoned farmland to freedmen in 40-acre plots, with an option to buy. This auspicious beginning belied the great disappointments that lay ahead.

**WHAT WERE** African Americans' hopes for Reconstruction?

((●–[ **Hear** the **Audio**

at **www.myhistorylab.com**
*Free At Last*

**Freedmen's Bureau**   Agency established by Congress in March 1865 to provide social, educational, and economic services, advice, and protection to former slaves and destitute whites; lasted seven years.

## EDUCATION

The greatest success of the Freedmen's Bureau was in education. The bureau coordinated more than fifty northern philanthropic and religious groups, which, in turn, established 3,000 freedmen's schools in the South, serving 150,000 men, women, and children.

Initially, single young women from the Northeast comprised much of the teaching force. By 1871, black teachers outnumbered white teachers in the "colored" schools. The financial troubles of northern missionary societies and white northerners' declining interest in the freedmen's condition opened opportunities for black teachers. Support for them came from black churches, especially the African Methodist Episcopal (AME) Church.

At the end of the Civil War, only about 10 percent of black southerners were literate, compared with more than 70 percent of white southerners. Within a decade, black literacy had risen above 30 percent. Joseph Wilson, a former slave, attributed the rise to "this longing of ours for freedom of the mind as well as the body."

Some black southerners went on to one of the thirteen colleges established by the American Missionary Association and black and white churches. Between 1860 and 1880 more than 1,000 black southerners earned college degrees at institutions still serving students today, such as Howard University in Washington, DC, Fisk University in Nashville, Hampton Institute (now University), Tuskegee Institute, and Biddle Institute (now Johnson C. Smith University) in Charlotte.

●●●–[ **Read** the **Document**

at **www.myhistorylab.com**
*The Freedmen's Bureau Bill (1865)*

[ **Watch** the **Video**

at **www.myhistorylab.com**
*The Schools that the Civil War and Reconstruction Created*

## QUICK REVIEW

**Freedom and Education**

♦ The Freedmen's Bureau established 3,000 freedmen's schools.

♦ 1865–1875: Black literacy rises from 10 to 30 percent.

♦ 1860–1880: 1,000 black southerners earn college degrees.

The Freedmen's Bureau, northern churches, and missionary societies established more than 3,000 schools, attended by some 150,000 men, women, and children in the years after the Civil War. At first, mostly young white women from the Northeast staffed these schools.

**W**    WHERE TO LEARN MORE

★ Penn Center Historic District, St. Helena Island, South Carolina http://www.penncenter.com

•••─ Read the Document

at **www.myhistorylab.com**
*Charlotte Forten, Life on the Sea Islands*

**Field Order No. 15**    Order by General William T. Sherman in January 1865 to set aside abandoned land along the southern Atlantic coast for forty-acre grants to freedmen, rescinded by President Andrew Johnson later that year.

Pursuing freedom of the mind involved challenges beyond those of learning to read and write. Many white southerners condemned efforts at "Negro improvement." They viewed the time spent on education as wasted, forcing the former slaves to catch their lessons in bits and pieces between work, often by candlelight or on Sundays. White southerners also harassed white female teachers, questioning their morals and threatening people who rented rooms to them. After the Freedmen's Bureau folded in 1872 and many of the northern societies that supported freedmen's education collapsed or cut back their involvement, education for black southerners became more haphazard.

## "FORTY ACRES AND A MULE"

Although education was important to the freed slaves in their quest for civic equality, land ownership offered them the promise of economic independence. For generations, black people had worked southern farms and had received nothing for their labor.

An overwhelmingly agricultural people, freedmen looked to farm ownership as a key element in their transition from slavery to freedom. "Gib us our own land and we take care of ourselves," a Charleston freedman asserted to a northern visitor in 1865. "But without land, de ole massas can hire or starve us, as dey please." Even before the war's end, rumors circulated through black communities in the South that the government would provide each black family with 40 acres and a mule. These rumors were fueled by General William T. Sherman's **Field Order No. 15** in January 1865, which set aside a vast swath of abandoned land along the South Atlantic coast from the Charleston area to northern Florida for grants of up to 40 acres. The Freedmen's Bureau likewise raised expectations when it was initially authorized to rent 40-acre plots of confiscated or abandoned land to freedmen.

By June 1865, about 40,000 former slaves had settled on Sherman land along the southeastern coast. In 1866, Congress passed the **Southern Homestead Act,** giving black people preferential access to public lands in five southern states. Two years later, the Republican government of South Carolina initiated a land-redistribution program financed by the sale of state bonds. The state used proceeds from the bond sales to purchase farmland, which it then resold to freedmen, who paid for it with state-funded long-term low-interest loans. By the late 1870s, more than 14,000 African American families had taken advantage of this program.

Land ownership did not ensure financial success. Most black-owned farms were small and on marginal land. The value of these farms in 1880 was roughly half that of white-owned farms. Black farmers also had trouble obtaining credit to purchase or expand their holdings. A lifetime of fieldwork left some freedmen without the managerial skills to operate a farm. The hostility of white neighbors also played a role in thwarting black aspirations.

The vast majority of former slaves, however, especially those in the Lower South, never fulfilled their dreams of land ownership. Rumors to the contrary, the federal government never intended to implement a land-redistribution program in the South. General Sherman viewed his field order as a temporary measure to support freedmen for the remainder of the war. President Andrew Johnson nullified the order in September 1865, returning confiscated land to its former owners. Even Republican supporters of black land ownership questioned the constitutionality of seizing privately owned real estate. Most of the land-redistribution programs that emerged after the war, including government-sponsored programs, required black farmers to have capital. But in the impoverished postwar economy of the South, it was difficult for them to acquire it.

Republican Party rhetoric of the 1850s extolled the virtues and dignity of free labor over the degradation of slave labor. Free labor usually meant working for a wage or under some other contractual arrangement. After the war, many white northerners envisioned former slaves assuming the status of free laborers, not necessarily of independent landowners.

Most of the officials of the Freedmen's Bureau shared these views and therefore saw reviving the southern economy as a higher priority than helping former slaves acquire farms. They wanted both to get the crop in the field and start the South on the road to a free labor system. Thus, they encouraged freedmen to work for their former masters under contract and to postpone their quest for land.

At first, agents of the Freedmen's Bureau supervised labor contracts between former slaves and masters. But after 1867, bureau surveillance declined. Agents assumed that both black laborers and white landowners had become accustomed to the mutual obligations of contracts. The bureau, however, underestimated the power of white landowners to coerce favorable terms or to ignore those they did not like. Contracts implied a mutuality that most planters could not accept in their relations with former slaves.

By the late 1870s, most former slaves in the rural South had been drawn into a subservient position in a new labor system called **sharecropping.** The premise of this system was relatively simple: The landlord furnished the sharecroppers with a house, a plot of land to work, seed, some farm animals, and farm implements and advanced them credit at a store the landlord typically owned. In exchange, the sharecroppers promised the landlord a share of their crop, usually one-half. The croppers kept the proceeds from the sale of the other half to pay off their debts at the store and save or spend as they and their families saw fit. In theory, a sharecropper could save enough to secure economic independence.

But white landlords perceived black independence as both contradictory and subversive. With landlords keeping the accounts at the store, black sharecroppers found that the proceeds from their share of the crop never left them very far ahead. Some found themselves in perpetual debt and worked as virtual slaves. Not all white landlords cheated their tenants, but given the sharecroppers' innocence regarding accounting methods and crop pricing, the temptation to do so was great.

**Southern Homestead Act** Largely unsuccessful law passed in 1866 that gave black people preferential access to public lands in five southern states.

**Read** the **Document**

at **www.myhistorylab.com**
*Clinton B. Fisk, "Plain Counsels for Freedmen" (1865)*

**Read** the **Document**

at **www.myhistorylab.com**
*A Sharecrop Contract (1882)*

**sharecropping** Labor system that evolved during and after Reconstruction whereby landowners furnished laborers with a house, farm animals, and tools and advanced credit in exchange for a share of the laborers' crop.

**WHERE TO LEARN MORE**

★ Levi Jordan Plantation, Brazoria County, Texas
http://www.webarchaeology.com

## MIGRATION TO CITIES

Even before the hope of land ownership faded, African Americans looked for alternatives to secure their personal and economic independence. Before the war, the city had offered slaves and free black people a measure of freedom unknown in the rural South. After the war, African Americans moved to cities to find families, seek work, escape the tedium and supervision of farm life, or simply to test their right to move about.

Between 1860 and 1870, the African American population in every major southern city rose significantly. In Atlanta, for example, black people accounted for one in five residents in 1860 and nearly one in two by 1870.

Once in the city, freedmen had to find a home and a job. They usually settled on the outskirts of town, where building codes did not apply. Rather than developing one large ghetto, as happened in many northern cities, black southerners lived in small concentrations in and around cities. Sometimes armed with a letter of reference from their former masters, black people went door to door to seek employment. Many found work serving white families, as guards, laundresses, or maids, for very low wages. Both skilled and unskilled laborers found work rebuilding war-torn cities like Atlanta.

Most rural black southerners, however, worked as unskilled laborers. In both Atlanta and Nashville, black people comprised more than 75 percent of the unskilled workforce in 1870. Their wages were at or below subsistence level. A black laborer in Richmond admitted to a journalist in 1870 that he had difficulty making ends meet on $1.50 a day. "It's right hard," he reported. "I have to pay $15 a month rent, and only two little rooms." His family survived because his wife took in laundry, while her mother watched the children. Considering the laborer's struggle, the journalist wondered, "Were not your people better off in slavery?" The man replied, "Oh, no sir! We're a heap better off now. . . . We're men now, but when our masters had us we was only change in their pockets."

The black church was the center of African American life in the postwar urban South. Most black churches were founded after the Civil War, but some, such as the First African Baptist Church in Richmond, shown here in an 1874 engraving, traced their origins to before 1861.

## FAITH AND FREEDOM

Religious faith framed and inspired the efforts of African Americans to test their freedom on the farm and in the city. White southerners used religion to transform the Lost Cause from a shattering defeat to a premonition of a greater destiny. Black southerners, in contrast, saw emancipation in biblical terms as the beginning of an exodus from bondage to the Promised Land.

Some black churches in the postwar South had originated during the slavery era, but most split from white-dominated congregations after the war. White churchgoers deplored the expressive style of black worship, and black churchgoers were uncomfortable in congregations that treated them as inferiors. A separate church also reduced white surveillance.

The church became a primary focus of African American life. It gave black people the opportunity to hone skills in self-government and administration that white-dominated society denied them. Within the supportive confines of the congregation, they could assume leadership positions, render important decisions, deal with financial matters, and engage in politics. The church also operated as an educational institution. Local governments, especially in rural areas, rarely constructed public schools for black people; churches often served that function.

## GLOBAL CONNECTIONS

### EMANCIPATION AND FREEDOM IN THE UNITED STATES AND RUSSIA

Tsar Alexander II (1855–1881) freed Russia's serfs in 1861, two years before Abraham Lincoln's Emancipation Proclamation. Although Russian serfs had more rights than American slaves, both were tied to the land and to their landlords/masters. The liberation of the serfs was part of a broader reform plan designed to help modernize Russia.

On becoming tsar in 1855, Alexander II had relaxed the speech, travel, and press restrictions imposed by his predecessors, resulting in an influx of Western ideas into Russia. These ideas helped create widespread public support for the liberation of the serfs. The tsar couched his emancipation proclamation in the ideals of God and country, but its origin lay primarily in Russia's economic aspirations and the tsar's political strategy. While most Americans perceived their liberated slaves as forming an agricultural working class, Alexander made land ownership one of the major attractions of emancipation. The government divided farms equally between the landlords and the former serfs, compensating the owners for the divided property.

In theory at least, Russian serfs seemed in a better position than the southern freedmen to secure economic independence, given the land they received. One Russian official exulted, "The people are erect and transformed; the look, the walk, the speech, everything is changed." But the Russian serfs found their economic situation little improved. The land chosen for redistribution was marginal, and redistribution came with a major catch: The former serfs were required to repay the state on the installment plan. Given the quality of the land, the relatively high interest rates attached to the loans, and the vast numbers of serfs and their families, repayment was unrealistic even in the long term. To ensure that the former serfs would pay up, the tsar allowed local governments to keep the peasants on their land until they fulfilled their financial obligations. In other words, they were as much tied to the land after emancipation as before. And, as a method to improve the quality of agricultural cultivation, the multiplicity of small plots and impoverished peasants was also a failure.

As in the United States, violence marred the transition from bondage to freedom. Rebellions flared in several parts of Russia, but the tsar's armies put these uprisings down quickly. Some of the former serfs managed to escape to towns and cities and become part of the growing laboring class, much as freedmen went to southern cities. In the cities, both former serfs and slaves came closer to the free-labor ideal posited but not supported by their respective governments. In rural areas, reform broke down through a lack of planning and a failure of will.

- After emancipation, did the Russian serf or the American slave have a better opportunity to establish economic independence?

The desire to read the Bible inspired thousands of former slaves to attend the church school. The church also spawned other organizations that served the black community, such as burial societies, Masonic lodges, temperance groups, trade unions, and drama clubs. African Americans took great pride in their churches, which became visible measures of their progress. The church and the congregation were a cohesive force in black communities.

The efforts of former slaves in the classroom, on the farm, in cities, and in the churches reflect the enthusiasm and expectations with which black southerners greeted freedom, raising the hopes of those who came to help them, such as Frances Harper. But the majority of white southerners were unwilling to see those expectations fulfilled. For this reason, African Americans could not secure the fruits of their emancipation without the support and protection of the federal government. The issue of freedom was therefore inextricably linked to the other great issue of the era, the rejoining of the Confederacy to the Union, as expressed in federal Reconstruction policy.

# FEDERAL RECONSTRUCTION, 1865–1870

**HOW DID**
Presidential Reconstruction differ from Congressional Reconstruction?

When the Civil War ended in 1865, no acceptable blueprint existed for reconstituting the Union. President Lincoln believed that a majority of white southerners were Unionists at heart, and that they could and should undertake the task of reconstruction. He favored a conciliatory policy toward the South in order, as he put it in one of his last letters, "to restore the Union, so as to make it . . . a Union of hearts and hands as well as of States." He counted on the loyalists to be fair with respect to the rights of the former slaves.

As early as 1863, Lincoln had proposed to readmit a seceding state if 10 percent of its prewar voters took an oath of loyalty to the Union, and it prohibited slavery in a new state constitution. But this Ten Percent Plan did not require states to grant equal civil and political rights to former slaves, and many Republicans in Congress thought it was not stringent enough. In 1864, a group of them responded with the Wade-Davis Bill, which required a majority of a state's prewar voters to pledge their loyalty to the Union and demanded guarantees of black equality before the law. The bill was passed at the end of a congressional session, but Lincoln kept it from becoming law by refusing to sign it (an action known as a "pocket veto"). Lincoln, of course, died before he could implement a Reconstruction plan.

The controversy over the plans introduced during the war reflected two obstacles to Reconstruction that would continue to plague the ruling Republicans after the war. First, neither the Constitution nor legal precedent offered any guidance on whether the president or Congress should take the lead on Reconstruction policy. Second, there was no agreement on what that policy should be. Proposals requiring various preconditions for readmitting a state, loyalty oaths, new constitutions with certain specific provisions, guarantees of freedmen's rights, all provoked vigorous debate.

President Andrew Johnson, some conservative Republicans, and most Democrats believed that because the Constitution made no mention of secession, the southern states had been in rebellion but had never left the Union, and therefore that there was no need for a formal process to readmit them. Moderate and radical Republicans disagreed, arguing that the defeated states had forfeited their rights. Moderates and radicals parted company, however, on the conditions necessary for readmission to the Union. The radicals wanted to treat the former Confederate states as territories, or "conquered provinces," subject to congressional legislation. Moderates wanted to grant the seceding states more autonomy and limit federal intervention in their affairs while they satisfied the conditions of readmission. Neither group held a majority in Congress, and legislators sometimes changed their positions (see the Overview table, Contrasting Views of Reconstruction).

## PRESIDENTIAL RECONSTRUCTION, 1865–1867

When the Civil War ended in April 1865, Congress was not in session and would not reconvene until December. Thus, the responsibility for developing a Reconstruction policy initially fell on Andrew Johnson, who succeeded to the presidency upon Lincoln's assassination. Most northerners, including many Republicans, approved Johnson's Reconstruction plan when he unveiled it in May 1865. Johnson extended pardons and restored property rights, except in slaves, to southerners who swore an oath of allegiance to the Union and the Constitution. Southerners who had held prominent posts in the Confederacy, however, and those with more than $20,000 in taxable property, had to petition the president directly for a pardon. The plan said nothing about the voting rights or civil rights of former slaves.

Northern Democrats applauded the plan's silence on these issues and its promise of a quick restoration of the southern states to the Union. They expected the southern states to favor their party and expand its political power. Republicans approved the plan because it restored property rights to white southerners, although some wanted it to provide for black suffrage. Republicans also hoped that Johnson's conciliatory terms might attract some white southerners to the Republican Party.

On the two great issues of freedom and reunion, white southerners quickly demonstrated their eagerness to reverse the results of the Civil War. Although most states accepted President Johnson's modest requirements, several objected to one or more of them. Mississippi and Texas refused to ratify the Thirteenth Amendment, which abolished slavery. Alabama accepted only parts of the amendment. South Carolina declined to nullify its secession ordinance. No southern state authorized black voting. When Johnson ordered special congressional elections in the South in the fall of 1865, the all-white electorate returned many prominent Confederate leaders to office.

In late 1865, the newly elected southern state legislatures revised their antebellum slave codes. The updated **black codes** allowed local officials to arrest black people who could not document employment and residence or who were "disorderly" and sentence them to forced labor on farms or road crews. The codes also restricted black people to certain occupations, barred them from jury duty, and forbade them to possess firearms. Apprenticeship laws permitted judges to take black children from parents who could not, in the judges' view, adequately support them. Given the widespread poverty in the South in 1865, the law could apply to almost any freed black family. Northerners looking for contrition in the South found no sign of it. Worse, President Johnson did not seem perturbed about this turn of events.

The Republican-dominated Congress reconvened in December 1865 in a belligerent mood. When the radicals, who comprised nearly half of the Republican Party's strength in Congress, could not unite behind a program, their moderate colleagues took the first step toward a congressional Reconstruction plan. The moderates shared the radicals' desire to protect the former slaves' civil rights. But they would not support land-redistribution schemes or punitive measures against prominent Confederates, and disagreed on extending voting rights to the freedmen. The moderates' first measure, passed in early 1866, extended the life of the Freedmen's Bureau and authorized it to punish state officials who failed to extend equal civil rights to black citizens. But President Johnson vetoed the legislation.

Undeterred, Congress passed the Civil Rights Act of 1866 in direct response to the black codes. The act specified the civil rights to which all U.S. citizens were entitled. In creating a category of national citizenship with rights that superseded state laws, the act changed federal-state relations (and in the process overturned the *Dred Scott* decision). President Johnson vetoed the act, but it became law when Congress mustered a two-thirds majority to override his veto, the first time in American history that Congress passed major legislation over a president's veto.

To keep freedmen's rights safe from presidential vetoes, state legislatures, and federal courts, the Republican-dominated Congress moved to incorporate some of the provisions of the 1866 Civil Rights Act into the Constitution. The **Fourteenth Amendment,** which Congress passed in June 1866, addressed the issues of civil and voting rights. It guaranteed every citizen equality before the law. The two key sections of the amendment prohibited states from violating the civil rights of their citizens, thus outlawing the black codes, and gave states the choice of enfranchising black people or losing representation in Congress. Some radical Republicans expressed

**Watch the Video**
at **www.myhistorylab.com**
*Reconstruction in Texas*

**black codes**   Laws passed by states and municipalities denying many rights of citizenship to free blacks after the Civil War.

**Read the Document**
at **www.myhistorylab.com**
*The Mississippi Black Code (1865)*

**Read the Document**
at **www.myhistorylab.com**
*The Civil Rights Act of 1866*

**Fourteenth Amendment**   Passed by Congress in 1866, guaranteed every citizen equality before the law by prohibiting states from violating the civil rights of their citizens, thus outlawing the black codes.

"Selling a Freeman to Pay His Fine at Monticello, Florida." *This 1867 engraving shows how the black codes of the early Reconstruction era reduced former slaves to virtually their pre–Civil War status. Scenes like this convinced northerners that the white South was unrepentant and prompted congressional Republicans to devise their own Reconstruction plans.*

**Read the Document**

at **www.myhistorylab.com**

*The Fourteenth Amendment (1868)*

disappointment that the amendment, in a reflection of northern ambivalence, failed to give the vote to black people outright.

The amendment also disappointed advocates of woman suffrage, for the first time using the word *male* in the Constitution to define who could vote. Susan B. Anthony, who had campaigned for the abolition of slavery before the war and helped mount a petition drive that collected 400,000 signatures for the Thirteenth Amendment, founded the American Equal Rights Association in 1866 with her colleagues to push for woman suffrage at the state level.

The Fourteenth Amendment had little immediate impact on the South. Although enforcement of black codes diminished, white violence against black people increased. In the 1870s, several decisions by the U.S. Supreme Court weakened the amendment's provisions. Eventually, however, it would play a major role in securing the civil rights of African Americans.

President Johnson encouraged southern white intransigence by openly denouncing the Fourteenth Amendment. In August 1866, at the start of the congressional election campaign, he undertook an unprecedented tour of key northern states to sell his message of sectional

# AMERICAN VIEWS

## ◊ Mississippi's 1865 Black Codes ◊

White southerners, especially landowners and business owners, feared that emancipation would produce a labor crisis; freedmen, they expected, would either refuse to work or strike hard bargains with their former masters. White southerners also recoiled from the prospect of having to treat their former slaves as full social equals. Thus, beginning in late 1865, several southern states, including Mississippi, enacted laws designed to control black labor, mobility, and social status. Northerners responded to the codes as a provocation, a bold move to deny the result of the war and its consequences.

- **How** did the black codes fit into President Andrew Johnson's Reconstruction program?
- **Some** northerners charged that the black codes were a backdoor attempt at reestablishing slavery. Do you agree?
- **If** southern states enacted black codes to stabilize labor relations, how did the provisions below effect that objective?

### From an Act to Confer Civil Rights on Freedmen, and for Other Purposes

**Section 1.** All freedmen, free negroes and mulattoes may sue and be sued, implead and be impleaded, in all the courts of law and equity of this State, and may acquire personal property, and choose in action, by descent or purchase, and may dispose of the same in the same manner and to the same extent that white persons may: Provided, That the provisions of this section shall not be so construed as to allow any freedman, free negro or mulatto to rent or lease any lands or tenements except in incorporated cities or towns, in which places the corporate authorities shall control the same.

**Section 7.** Every civil officer shall, and every person may, arrest and carry back to his or her legal employer any freedman, free negro, or mulatto who shall have quit the service of his or her employer before the expiration of his or her term of service

without good cause; and said officer and person shall be entitled to receive for arresting and carrying back every deserting employee aforesaid the sum of five dollars, and ten cents per mile from the place of arrest to the place of delivery; and the same shall be paid by the employer, and held as a set off for so much against the wages of said deserting employee: Provided, that said arrested party, after being so returned, may appeal to the justice of the peace or member of the board of police of the county, who, on notice to the alleged employer, shall try summarily whether said appellant is legally employed by the alleged employer, and has good cause to quit said employer. Either party shall have the right of appeal to the county court, pending which the alleged deserter shall be remanded to the alleged employer or otherwise disposed of, as shall be right and just; and the decision of the county court shall be final.

### From an Act to Amend the Vagrant Laws of the State

**Section 2.** All freedmen, free negroes and mulattoes in this State, over the age of eighteen years, found on the second Monday in January, 1866, or thereafter, with no lawful employment or business, or found unlawfully assembling themselves together, either in the day or night time, and all white persons assembling themselves with freedmen, Free negroes or mulattoes, or usually associating with freedmen, free negroes or mulattoes, on terms of equality, or living in adultery or fornication with a freed woman, freed negro or mulatto, shall be deemed vagrants, and on conviction thereof shall be fined in a sum not exceeding, in the case of a freedman, free negro or mulatto, fifty dollars, and a white man two hundred dollars, and imprisonment at the discretion of the court, the free negro not exceeding ten days, and the white man not exceeding six months.

*Source:* "Laws in Relation to Freedmen," 39 Congress, 2 Session, Senate Executive Document 6, Freedmen's Affairs, 182–86.

---

reconciliation to the public. Although listeners appreciated Johnson's desire for peace, they questioned his claims of southern white loyalty to the Union. The president's diatribes against the Republican Congress won him followers in those northern states with a reservoir of opposition to black suffrage. But the tone and manner of his campaign offended many as undignified. In the November elections, the Democrats suffered embarrassing defeats in the North as Republicans managed better than two-thirds majorities in both the House and Senate, sufficient to override presidential vetoes. Radical Republicans, joined by moderate colleagues buoyed by the election results and revolted by the president's and the South's intransigence, seized the initiative when Congress reconvened.

## CONGRESSIONAL RECONSTRUCTION, 1867–1870

**Congressional Reconstruction**   Name given to the period 1867–1870 when the Republican-dominated Congress controlled Reconstruction era policy.

**Tenure of Office Act**   Passed by the Republican controlled Congress in 1867 to limit presidential interference with its policies, the act prohibited the president from removing certain officeholders without the Senate's consent. President Andrew Johnson, angered at what he believed an unconstitutional attack on presidential authority, deliberately violated the act by firing Secretary of War Edwin M. Stanton. The House responded by approving articles of impeachment against a president for the first time in American history.

The radicals' first salvo in their attempt to take control of Reconstruction occurred with the passing over President Johnson's veto of the Military Reconstruction Acts. The measures, passed in March 1867, inaugurated a period known as **Congressional Reconstruction** or Radical Reconstruction. With the exception of Tennessee, the only southern state that had ratified the Fourteenth Amendment and been readmitted to the Union, Congress divided the former Confederate states into five military districts, each headed by a general (see Map 16–1). The commanders' first order of business was to conduct voter-registration campaigns to enroll black people and bar white people who had held office before the Civil War and supported the Confederacy. The eligible voters would then elect delegates to a state convention to write a new constitution that guaranteed universal manhood suffrage. Once a majority of eligible voters ratified the new constitution and the Fourteenth Amendment, their state would be eligible for readmission to the Union.

The Reconstruction Acts fulfilled the radicals' three major objectives. First, they secured the freedmen's right to vote. Second, they made it likely that southern states would be run by Republican regimes that would enforce the new constitutions, protect former slaves' rights, and maintain the Republican majority in Congress. Finally, they set standards for readmission that required the South to accept the preeminence of the federal government and the end of slavery.

These measures seemed appropriate in view of the war's outcome and the freedmen's status, but white southerners, especially those barred from participation, perceived the state and local governments constructed upon the new basis as illegitimate. Many southern whites would never acknowledge the right of these governments and their officials to rule over them.

To limit presidential interference with their policies, Republicans passed the **Tenure of Office Act,** prohibiting the president from removing certain officeholders without the Senate's consent. Johnson, angered at what he believed was an unconstitutional attack on presidential authority, deliberately violated the act by firing Secretary of War Edwin M. Stanton, a leading radical, in February 1868. The House responded by approving articles of impeachment against a president for the first time in American history. That set the stage for the next step prescribed by the Constitution: a Senate trial to determine whether the president should be removed from office.

Johnson had indeed violated the Tenure of Office Act, a measure of dubious constitutionality even to some Republicans, but enough Republicans felt that his actions fell short of the "high crimes and misdemeanors" standard set by the Constitution for dismissal from office. Seven Republicans deserted their party, and Johnson was acquitted. The seven Republicans who voted against their party did so not out of respect for Johnson but because they feared that a conviction would damage the office of the presidency and violate the constitutional separation of powers. The outcome weakened the radicals and eased the way for Grant, a moderate Republican, to gain the party's nomination for president in 1868.

The Republicans viewed the 1868 presidential election as a referendum on Congressional Reconstruction. They supported black suffrage in the South but equivocated on allowing African Americans to vote in the North. Black northerners could vote in only eight of the twenty-two northern states, and between 1865 and 1869, white northerners rejected equal

MAP 16–1   **Congressional Reconstruction, 1865–1877**   When Congress wrested control of Reconstruction policy from President Andrew Johnson, it divided the South into the five military districts depicted here. The commanding generals for each district held the authority both to hold elections and to decide who could vote.

**What does** the division of the South into military districts that included more than one state tell us about how northern Republicans saw the former Confederacy?

suffrage referendums in eight of eleven states. Republicans "waved the bloody shirt," reminding voters of Democratic disloyalty, the sacrifices of war, and the peace only Republicans could redeem. Democrats denounced Congressional Reconstruction as federal tyranny and, in openly racist appeals, warned white voters that a Republican victory would mean black rule. Grant won the election, but his margin of victory was uncomfortably narrow. Reflecting growing ambivalence in the North over issues of race and federal authority, New York's Horatio Seymour, the Democratic presidential nominee, probably carried a majority of the nation's white vote. Black voters' overwhelming support for Grant probably provided his margin of victory.

The Republicans retained a strong majority in both houses of Congress and managed to pass another major piece of Reconstruction legislation, the **Fifteenth Amendment,** in February 1869. In response to growing concerns about voter fraud and violence against freedmen, the amendment guaranteed the right of American men to vote, regardless of race. Although the amendment provided a loophole allowing states to restrict the right to vote based on literacy or property qualifications, it was nonetheless a milestone. It made the right to vote perhaps the most distinguishing characteristic of U.S. citizenship.

The Fifteenth Amendment allowed states to keep the franchise a male prerogative, angering many in the woman suffrage movement more than had the Fourteenth Amendment. The resulting controversy severed the ties between the movement and Republican politics. Susan B. Anthony broke with her abolitionist colleagues and opposed the amendment. In an appeal brimming with ethnic and racial animosity, Elizabeth Cady Stanton warned that "if you do not wish the lower orders of Chinese, African, Germans and Irish, with their low ideas of womanhood to make laws for you and your daughters . . . awake to the danger . . . and demand that woman, too, shall be represented in the government!" Such language created a major rift in the nascent women's movement.

## SOUTHERN REPUBLICAN GOVERNMENTS, 1867–1870

Away from Washington, the first order of business for the former Confederacy was to draft state constitutions. The documents embodied progressive principles new to the South. They mandated the election of numerous local and state offices. Self-perpetuating local elites could no longer appoint themselves or cronies to powerful positions. The constitutions committed southern states, many for the first time, to public education. Lawmakers enacted a variety of reforms, including social welfare, penal reform, legislative reapportionment, and universal manhood suffrage.

The Republican regimes that gained control in southern states promoted vigorous state government and the protection of civil and voting rights. Three Republican constituencies supported these governments: native whites, native blacks, and northern transplants. The small native white group was mostly made up of yeomen farmers. Residing mainly in the upland regions

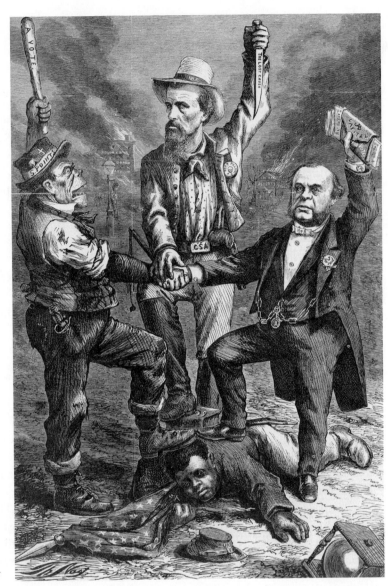

The Democratic Party ran an openly racist presidential campaign in 1868. This pro-Republican drawing by noted cartoonist Thomas Nast includes three Democratic constituencies: former Confederate soldiers (note the "CSA" on the belt buckle); the Irish or immigrant vote (note the almost simian depiction of the Irishman), and the well-dressed Democratic presidential candidate, Horatio Seymour, sporting a "5th Avenue" button and waving a wallet full of bills, a reference to the corrupt Democratic politics in New York City. The three have their feet on an African American soldier. In the background note the "colored orphan asylum" and "southern school" ablaze, and the lynching of black children.

**Fifteenth Amendment** Passed by Congress in 1869, guaranteed the right of American men to vote, regardless of race.

### QUICK REVIEW

**Radical Republican Objectives**

- Secure freedmen's right to vote.
- Make it likely that southern states would have Republican governments.
- Require the South to accept preeminence of the federal government and the end of slavery.

## OVERVIEW  Contrasting Views of Reconstruction: President and Congress

| Politician or Group | Policy on Former Slaves | Policy on Readmission of Former Confederate States |
|---|---|---|
| President Johnson | Opposed to black suffrage | Maintained that rebellious states were already readmitted |
| | Silent on protection of black civil rights | Granted pardons and restoration of property to all who swore allegiance to the United States |
| | Opposed to land redistribution | |
| Radical Republicans | Favored black suffrage | Favored treating rebellious states as territories and establishing military districts[*] |
| | Favored protection of black civil rights | Favored limiting franchise to black people and loyal white people |
| | Favored land redistribution | |
| Moderate Republicans | Favored black suffrage[*] | Favored some restrictions on white suffrage[**] |
| | Favored protection of civil rights | Favored requiring states to meet various requirements before being readmitted[*] |
| | Opposed land redistribution | Split on military rule |

[*]After 1866.
[**]True of most but not all members of the group.

### QUICK REVIEW

**The Tenure of Office Act and Johnson's Impeachment**

- Act prohibited the president from removing certain officeholders without the Senate's consent.
- Johnson deliberately violated the act in February 1868.
- Johnson escaped impeachment by one vote.

**scalawags** Southern whites, mainly small landowning farmers and well-off merchants and planters, who supported the southern Republican Party during Reconstruction.

**carpetbaggers** Northern transplants to the South, many of whom were Union soldiers who stayed in the South after the war.

●●—| Read the Document

at **www.myhistorylab.com**
*From Then to Now Online: African American Voting Rights in the South*

●●—| Read the Document

at **www.myhistorylab.com**
*"Address of the Colored Citizens of Norfolk, Virginia"* (1865)

of the South and long ignored by lowland planters and merchants in state government, they were left devastated by the war. They struggled to keep their land and hoped for an easing of credit and for debt-stay laws to help them escape foreclosure. They wanted public schools for their children and good roads to get their crops to market. Some urban merchants and large planters also called themselves Republicans. They were attracted to the party's emphasis on economic development, especially railroad construction, and would become prominent in Republican leadership after 1867, forming a majority of the party's elected officials. Collectively, opponents called these native white southerners **scalawags.**

Northern transplants, or **carpetbaggers,** as many southern whites called them, constituted a second and smaller group of southern Republicans. Thousands of northerners came south during and after the war. Many were Union soldiers who simply enjoyed the climate and perhaps married a local woman. Most were drawn by economic opportunity. Land was cheap and the price of cotton high. Although most carpetbaggers had supported the Republican Party before they moved south, few became politically active until the cotton economy nosedived in 1866. Financial concerns were not all that motivated carpetbaggers to enter politics; some hoped to aid the freedmen.

Carpetbaggers never comprised more than 2 percent of any state's population. Most white southerners viewed them as an alien presence, instruments of a hated occupying force. Because many of them tended to support extending political and civil rights to black southerners, carpetbaggers were also often at odds with their fellow white Republicans, the scalawags.

African Americans constituted the Republican Party's largest southern constituency. In three states, South Carolina, Mississippi, and Louisiana, they also constituted the majority of eligible voters. They viewed the franchise as the key to civic equality and economic opportunity and demanded an active role in party and government affairs.

Black people began to take part in southern politics even before the end of the Civil War, especially in cities occupied by Union forces. In February 1865, black people in Norfolk, Virginia, gathered to demand a say in the new government that Union supporters were forming in that portion of the state. In April, they created the Colored Monitor Union club, modeled after regular Republican Party organizations in northern cities, called **Union Leagues.** They demanded "the right of universal suffrage" for "all loyal men, without distinction of color." Black people in other southern cities held similar meetings, seeking inclusion in the democratic process to protect their freedom. Despite white threats, black southerners thronged to Union League meetings in 1867, even forging interracial alliances in states such as North Carolina and Alabama. Focusing on political education and recruitment, the leagues successfully mobilized black voters. In 1867, more than 90 percent of eligible black voters across the South turned out for elections. Black women, even though they could not vote, also played a role. During the 1868 presidential campaign, for example, black maids and cooks in the South wore buttons touting the candidacy of the Republican presidential nominee, Ulysses S. Grant.

Black southerners were not content just to vote; they also demanded political office. White Republican leaders in the South often took the black vote for granted. But on several occasions after 1867, black people threatened to run independent candidates, support rival Democrats, or simply stay home unless they were represented among Republican nominees. These demands brought them some success. The number of southern black congressmen in the U.S. House of Representatives increased from two in 1869 to seven in 1873, and more than 600 African Americans, most of them former slaves from plantation counties, were elected to southern state legislatures between 1867 and 1877.

White fears that black officeholders would enact vengeful legislation proved unfounded. African Americans generally did not promote race-specific legislation. Rather, they supported measures such as debt relief and state funding for education that benefited all poor and working-class people. Like all politicians, however, black officials in southern cities sought to enact measures beneficial to their constituents, such as roads and sidewalks.

During the first few years of Congressional Reconstruction, Republican governments walked a tightrope, attempting to lure moderate Democrats and unaffiliated white voters into the party without slighting the black vote. They used the lure of patronage power and the attractive salaries that accompanied public office. In 1868, for example, Louisiana's Republican governor, Henry C. Warmoth, appointed white conservatives to state and local offices, which he divided equally between Confederate veterans and black people, and repealed a constitutional provision disfranchising former Confederate officials.

Republicans also gained support by expanding the role of state government to a degree unprecedented in the South. Southern Republican administrations appealed to hard-pressed upland white constituents by prohibiting foreclosure and passing stay laws that allowed farm owners additional time to repay debts. They undertook building programs that benefited black and white citizens, erecting hospitals, schools, and orphanages. Stepping further into social policy than most northern states at the time, Republican governments in the South expanded women's property rights, enacted legislation against child abuse, and required child support from fathers of

**Union Leagues** Republican Party organizations in northern cities that became an important organizing device among freedmen in southern cities after 1865.

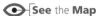
**See** the **Map**

at **www.myhistorylab.com**
*Congressional Reconstruction*

"Time Works Wonders." This Thomas Nast cartoon has Jefferson Davis, former president of the Confederacy, dressed as Iago in William Shakespeare's play *Othello,* declaring with considerable anguish, "For that I suspect the Lusty moor [Othello] hath leap'd into my seat: the thought where of doth like a poisonous mineral gnaw my inwards." Indeed, Hiram Revels occupies Davis's old seat in the U.S. Senate representing the state of Mississippi in 1870.

mulatto children. In South Carolina, the Republican government provided medical care for the poor; in Alabama, it provided free legal aid for needy defendants.

Despite these impressive policies, southern Republicans were unable to hold their diverse constituency together. The excesses of some state governments, high taxes, contests over patronage, and conflicts over the relative roles of white and black party members opened rifts in Republican ranks. Patronage triggered intraparty warfare. Every office secured by a Democrat created a disappointed Republican. Class tensions erupted in the party as economic development policies sometimes superseded relief and social service legislation supported by small farmers. The failure of Alabama Republicans to deliver on promises of debt relief and land redistribution eroded the party's support among up-country white voters. There were differences among black voters too. In the Lower South, divisions that had developed in the prewar era between urban, lighter-skinned free black people and darker, rural slaves persisted into the Reconstruction era. In many southern states, black clergy, because of their independence from white support and their important spiritual and educational role, became leaders. But most preached salvation in the next world rather than equality in this one, conceding more to white people than their rank-and-file constituents.

**WHAT ROLE**
did violence play
in Counter-
Reconstruction?

# COUNTER-RECONSTRUCTION, 1870–1874

Republicans might have survived battles over patronage, policy, expenditures, and taxes. But they could not overcome racism and the violence it generated. Racism killed Republican rule in the South because it deepened divisions within the party, encouraged white violence, and eroded support in the North. Southern Democrats discovered that they could use race baiting and racial violence to create solidarity among white people that overrode their economic and class differences. Unity translated into election victories.

Northerners responded to the persistent violence in the South, not with outrage, but with a growing sense of tedium. They came to accept the arguments of white southerners that it was folly to allow black people to vote and hold office, especially since most northern whites would not extend the franchise to African Americans in their own states.

By 1874, Americans were concerned with an array of domestic problems that overshadowed Reconstruction. A serious economic depression left them more preoccupied with survival than racial justice. Corruption convinced many that politics was part of the nation's problems, not a solution to them. With the rest of the nation thus distracted and weary, white southerners reclaimed control of the South.

## THE USES OF VIOLENCE

Racial violence preceded Republican rule. As African Americans moved about, attempted to vote, haggled over labor contracts, and carried arms as part of the occupying Union forces, they tested the patience of white southerners, to whom any black assertion of equality seemed threatening. African Americans were the face of whites' defeat, of their world turned upside down. If the war was about slavery, then here was the visible proof of the Confederacy's defeat. Many white southerners viewed the term "free black" less as a status than as an oxymoron. The restoration of white supremacy meant the restoration of order and civilization, an objective southern whites would pursue with vengeance.

White paramilitary groups were responsible for much of the violence directed against African Americans. Probably the best-known of these groups was the **Ku Klux Klan.** Founded in Tennessee by six Confederate veterans in 1866, the Klan was initially a social club. Within a year, the Klan had spread throughout the South. In 1867, when black people entered politics in large numbers, the Klan unleashed a wave of terror against them. The Klan directed much of its violence toward subverting the electoral process. One historian has estimated that roughly 10 percent of all black

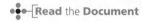

**Read** the **Document**

at **www.myhistorylab.com**
*Hannah Irwin Describes Ku Klux Klan
Ride (Late 1860s)*

**Ku Klux Klan**    Perhaps the most prominent of the vigilante groups that terrorized black people in the South during the Reconstruction era, founded by Confederate veterans in 1866.

delegates to the 1867 state constitutional conventions in the South became victims of political violence during the next decade.

By 1868, white paramilitary organizations permeated the South. Violence was particularly severe in election years in Louisiana, which had a large and active black electorate. The most serious example of political violence in Louisiana, occurred in Colfax in 1873, when a white Democratic mob attempted to wrest control of local government from Republicans. For three weeks, black defenders held the town against the white onslaught. When the white mob finally broke through, they massacred the remaining black defenders, including those who had surrendered and laid down their weapons. It was the bloodiest peacetime massacre in nineteenth-century America.

Racial violence and the combative reaction it provoked both among black people and Republican administrations energized white voters. Democrats regained power in North Carolina, for example, after the state's Republican governor enraged white voters by calling out the militia to counter white violence during the election of 1870. That same year, the Republican regime in Georgia fell as well.

The federal government responded with a variety of legislation. One example was the Fifteenth Amendment. Another was the Enforcement Act of 1870, which authorized the federal government to appoint supervisors in states that failed to protect voting rights. When violence and intimidation persisted, Congress followed with a second, more sweeping measure, the Ku Klux Klan Act of 1871. This law permitted federal authorities, with military assistance, if necessary, to arrest and prosecute members of groups that denied a citizen's civil rights if state authorities failed to do so. The Klan Act was not successful in curbing racial violence, as the Colfax Massacre in 1873 made vividly clear. But with it, Congress, by claiming the right to override state authority to bring individuals to justice, established a new precedent in federal-state relations.

The Klan directed violence at African Americans primarily for engaging in political activity. Here, a black man, John Campbell, vainly begs for mercy in Moore County, North Carolina, in August 1871.

**⬥ Read the Document**

at **www.myhistorylab.com**
*Albion W. Tourgée, Letter on Ku Klux Klan Activities (1870)*

**QUICK REVIEW**

**The Legislative Responses to Political Violence in the South**

◆ 15th Amendment guaranteed the right to vote.

◆ Enforcement Act of 1870 authorized federal supervision of elections in states that failed to support voting rights.

◆ Ku Klux Klan Act of 1871 permitted federal prosecution of members of groups that denied citizen's civil rights if state authorities failed to act.

## NORTHERN INDIFFERENCE

The success of political violence after 1871 reflected both a declining commitment on the part of northern Republicans to support southern Republican administrations and a growing indifference of northerners to the major issues of Reconstruction. That northern base grew increasingly skeptical about Reconstruction policy in general and assistance to the freedmen in particular. Northern Republicans looked around their cities and many saw the local political scene infested with unqualified immigrant voters and corruption. New York City's Democratic boss William M. Tweed and his associates bilked the city of an astounding $100 million. When white southerners charged that unqualified blacks and grasping carpetbaggers corrupted the political process in the South, northerners recognized the argument.

Changing perceptions in the North also indicated a convergence of racial views with white southerners. As a radical Republican congressman from Indiana, George W. Julian, admitted in 1865, white northerners *"hate the negro."* They expressed this hatred in their rejection of black suffrage, racial segregation of their African American population, and periodic violence against black residents, such as during the New York Draft Riots of 1863. Northerners' views were bolstered by prevailing scientific theories of race that "proved" blacks' limited capacities and, therefore, unfitness for either the ballot or skilled occupations.

By the early 1870s, northern public opinion had shifted greatly with respect to black suffrage, in part because of the growing concern about the immigrant vote in northern cities; whereas in the late 1860s cartoons and the press depicted newly enfranchised African Americans nobly, later representations were hostile as this caricature of the South Carolina legislature by Thomas Nast demonstrates.

Northerners also grew increasingly wary of federal power. The emerging scandals of the Grant administration, fueled, it seemed, by government subsidies to railroads and other private businesses, demanded a scaling back of federal power and discretion. When white southerners complained about federal meddling, again, they found resonance in the North.

The excesses and alleged abuses of federal power inspired a reform movement among a group of northern Republicans and some Democrats. In addition, business leaders decried the ability of wealthy lobbyists to influence economic decisions. An influential group of intellectuals and opinion makers lamented the inability of politicians to understand "natural" laws, particularly those related to race. And some Republicans joined the reform movement out of fear that Democrats would capitalize on the turmoil in the South and the political scandals in the North to reap huge electoral victories in 1872.

## LIBERAL REPUBLICANS AND THE ELECTION OF 1872

Liberal Republicans, as the reformers called themselves, put forward an array of suggestions to improve government and save the Republican Party. They advocated civil service reform to reduce reliance on patronage and the abuses that accompanied office seeking. To limit government and reduce artificial economic stimuli, the reformers called for tariff reduction and an end to federal land grants to railroads. For the South, they recommended a general amnesty for white people and a return to "local self-government" by men of "property and enterprise."

When the Liberals failed to convince other Republicans to adopt their program, they broke with the party. Taking advantage of this split, the Democrats forged an alliance with the Liberals. Together, they nominated journalist Horace Greeley to challenge Ulysses S. Grant for the presidency in the election of 1872. Grant won resoundingly, helped by high turnout among black voters in the South, his continued popularity as a war hero, and Greeley's inept campaign.

## ECONOMIC TRANSFORMATION

After 1873, the Republican Party in the South became a liability for the national party, especially as Americans fastened on to economic issues. The major story of the decade would not be equal rights for African Americans, but the changing nature of the American economy. An overextended banking and credit system generated the Panic of 1873 and caused extensive suffering, particularly among working-class Americans. But the depression masked a remarkable economic transformation as the nation moved toward a national industrial economy.

The depression and the economic transformation occupied center stage in the American mentality of the mid-1870s, at least in the North. Most Americans had mentally forsaken Reconstruction long before the Compromise of 1877 made its abandonment a political fact. The sporadic violence against black and white Republicans in the South, and the cries of help from freedmen as their rights and persons were abused by white Democrats, became distant echoes from another era, the era of the Civil War, now commemorated and memorialized, but no longer an active part of the nation's present and future. Of course, for white southerners, the past was not yet past. There was still work to do.

# REDEMPTION, 1874–1877

For southern Democrats, the Republican victory in 1872 underscored the importance of turning out larger numbers of white voters and restricting the black vote. They accomplished these goals over the next four years with a surge in political violence, secure in the knowledge that federal authorities would rarely intervene against them. Preoccupied with corruption and economic crisis and increasingly indifferent, if not hostile, to African American aspirations,

**WHY DID** the federal government abandon African Americans after 1872?

most Americans looked the other way. The elections of 1876 confirmed the triumph of white southerners.

In a religious metaphor that matched their view of the Civil War as a lost crusade, southern Democrats called their victory "Redemption" and depicted themselves as **Redeemers,** holy warriors who had saved the South from the hell of black Republican rule. Generations of American boys and girls would learn this interpretation of the Reconstruction era, and it would affect race relations for nearly a century.

**Redeemers**    Southern Democrats who wrested control of governments in the former Confederacy, often through electoral fraud and violence, from Republicans, beginning in 1870.

## THE DEMOCRATS' VIOLENT RESURGENCE

The violence between 1874 and 1876 differed in several respects from earlier attempts to restore white government by force. Attackers operated more openly and more closely identified themselves with the Democratic Party. Mounted, gray-clad ex-Confederate soldiers flanked Democratic candidates at campaign rallies and "visited" black neighborhoods afterward to discourage black men from voting. With black people intimidated and white people already prepared to vote, election days were typically quiet.

Democrats swept to victory across the South in the 1874 elections. "A perfect reign of terror" redeemed Alabama for the Democrats. The successful appeal to white supremacy inspired a massive white turnout to unseat Republicans in Virginia, Florida (legislature only), and Arkansas. Texas had fallen to the Democrats in 1873. Only South Carolina, Mississippi, and Louisiana, states with large black populations, survived the debacle. But the relentless tide of terror would soon overwhelm them as well.

Democratic leaders in those states announced a "white line" policy, inviting all white men, regardless of party affiliation, to "unite" and redeem the states. They all had the same objective: to eliminate African Americans as a political factor by any means. Black Republicans not only feared for their political future, but also for their lives.

A bold assault occurred in New Orleans in September 1874 when 8,500 White League troops, many of them leading citizens and Confederate veterans, attempted a coup to oust Republican Governor William P. Kellogg and members of his administration. The New Orleans Leaguers overwhelmed the city's racially mixed Metropolitan Police Force under the command of former Confederate general James B. Longstreet. The timely arrival of federal troops, ordered to the scene by President Grant, prevented the takeover. The League was more successful in the Louisiana countryside in the weeks preceding the Democratic victory in November 1874. League troops overthrew or murdered Republican officials in eight parishes.

The Democratic victory in Louisiana encouraged white paramilitarists in Mississippi. Blacks dominated the Warren County government headquartered in Vicksburg. Liners demanded the resignations of all black officials including the sheriff, Peter Crosby, a black Union veteran. Republican Governor Adelbert Ames, a native of Maine, ordered the Liners to disperse and granted Crosby's request to raise a protective militia to respond to future threats.

Peter Crosby's efforts to gather a militia force were too successful. An army of several hundred armed African Americans marched in three columns from the surrounding countryside to Vicksburg. Whites responded to the challenge, firing on the militia and tracking down and terrorizing blacks in the city and county over the next ten days. White Liners (as the Mississippi paramilitarists called themselves) killed at least twenty-nine blacks and wounded countless more. Democrats gained control of the county government.

The Vicksburg incident was a rehearsal for Democratic victories in statewide elections in 1875. Liners focused on the state's majority black counties and vowed to "overawe the negroes and exhibit to them the ocular proof of our power."

The intimidation worked and the Democrats swept to victory in Mississippi. They would not allow Governor Ames to finish his term, threatening him with impeachment. Fearing for his safety, Ames resigned and fled the state. The South's second war of independence was reaching its climax.

July Fourth, 1876. America's one-hundredth birthday. A modest celebration unfolded in Hamburg, South Carolina, a small town in Edgefield County across the Savannah River from Augusta, Georgia. Blacks comprised more than 75 percent of the town's population. They held most of the political offices. An altercation occurred concerning the right of way between the black militia parading in the street and a passing wagon carrying several prominent white residents. When the aggrieved parties met four days later, more than 1,000 armed whites were milling in front of the wooden "armory" where one hundred black militiamen had taken refuge. A shot rang out and shattered a second-floor window and soon a pitched battle was raging. The white attackers fired a cannon that turned most of the building into splinters. As blacks fled, whites tracked them down. The white men also burned homes and shops and robbed residents of the town.

Hamburg was part of a larger pattern of violence and intimidation in the state. In May 1876, South Carolina Democrats drafted *The Plan of the Campaign of 1876*, a manual on how to redeem the state. Some of the recommended strategies included: "Every Democrat must feel honor bound to control the vote of at least one negro, by intimidation, purchase, keeping him away or as each individual may determine how he may best accomplish it. Treat them as to show them, you are the superior race and that their natural position is that of subordination to the white man."

The November election went off in relative calm. In Edgefield County, out of 7,000 potential voters, 9,200 ballots were cast. Similar frauds occurred throughout the state. Still, the result hung in the balance. Both Democrats and Republicans claimed victory and set up rival governments. The following April after a deal brokered in Washington between the parties,

"Declaration of Equality: Justice: 'Five More Wanted.'" An outraged "Justice" in this Thomas Nast cartoon demands the execution of an equal number of white men to balance the six blacks whom whites captured in the aftermath of the Hamburg massacre in July 1876 and then executed. On the pillar to her right are posters with the names of white terrorist groups, the "K.K.K.," the "White League," and the "White Liners," as well as a notice, "Negroes Shot in Cold Blood at Hamburg, S.C." The Hamburg massacre provoked temporary outrage in the North, but little response from the Grant administration. By the fall, widespread violence against blacks in South Carolina generated little comment in the North.

federal troops were withdrawn from South Carolina and a Democratic government installed in Columbia. The victorious Democrats expelled twenty-four Republicans from the state legislature and elected Matthew C. Butler to the U.S. Senate. Butler had led the white attackers at Hamburg.

### THE WEAK FEDERAL RESPONSE

When Governor Daniel H. Chamberlain could no longer contain the violence in South Carolina in 1876, he asked the president for help. Grant acknowledged the gravity of Chamberlain's situation but would offer him only the lame hope that South Carolinians would exercise "better judgment and cooperation" and assist the governor in bringing offenders to justice "without aid from the federal Government."

Congress responded to blacks' deteriorating status in the South with the Civil Rights Act of 1875. The act prohibited discrimination against black people in public accommodations, such as theaters, parks, and trains, and guaranteed freedmen's rights to serve on juries. It had no provision for voting rights, which Congress presumed the Fifteenth Amendment protected. Most judges, however, either interpreted the law narrowly or declared it unconstitutional. In 1883, the U.S. Supreme Court agreed and overturned the act, declaring that only the states, not Congress, could redress "a private wrong, or a crime of the individual."

### THE ELECTION OF 1876 AND THE COMPROMISE OF 1877

Reconstruction officially ended with the presidential election of 1876, in which the Democrat Samuel J. Tilden ran against the Republican Rutherford B. Hayes. When the ballots were counted, it appeared that Tilden, a conservative New Yorker respectable enough for northern voters and Democratic enough for white southerners, had won. But despite a majority in the popular vote, disputed returns in three southern states left him with only 184 of the 185 electoral votes needed to win. The three states—Florida, South Carolina, and Louisiana—were the last in the South still to have Republican administrations.

Both camps maneuvered intensively in the following months to claim the disputed votes. Congress appointed a 15-member commission to settle the issue. Because the Republicans controlled Congress, they held a one-vote majority on the commission.

Southern Democrats wanted Tilden to win, but they wanted control of their states more. They were willing to deal. Hayes intended to remove federal support from the remaining southern Republican governments anyway. It thus cost him nothing to promise to do so in exchange for the contested electoral votes. The so-called **Compromise of 1877** installed Hayes in the White House and gave Democrats control of every state government in the South. Southern Democrats emerged the major winners from the Compromise of 1877. President Hayes and his successors into the next century left the South alone. In practical terms, the Compromise signaled the revocation of civil rights and voting rights for black southerners. The Fourteenth and Fifteenth Amendments would be dead letters in the South until well into the twentieth century. On the two great issues confronting the nation at the end of the Civil War, reunion and freedom, the white South had won. It reentered the Union largely on its own terms with the freedom to pursue a racial agenda consistent with its political, economic, and social interests.

### THE MEMORY OF RECONSTRUCTION

Southern Democrats used the memory of Reconstruction to help maintain themselves in power. Reconstruction joined the Lost Cause as part of the glorious fight to preserve the civilization of the Old South. As white southerners elevated Civil War heroes into saints and battles into holy struggles, they equated Reconstruction with Redemption. White Democrats had rescued the South from a purgatory of black rule and federal oppression. The southern view of

**QUICK REVIEW**

**Civil Rights Act of 1875**

♦ Did not address voting rights.

♦ Prohibited discrimination in public accommodations.

♦ Overturned by the U.S. Supreme Court in 1883.

**Compromise of 1877**   The Congressional settling of the 1876 election which installed Republican Rutherford B. Hayes in the White House and gave Democrats control of all state governments in the South.

Reconstruction permeated textbooks, films, and standard accounts of the period. By the early 1900s, professional historians at the nation's finest institutions concurred in this view, ignoring contrary evidence and rendering the story of African Americans invisible. By that time, therefore, most Americans believed that the policies of Reconstruction had been misguided and had brought great suffering to the white South. The widespread acceptance of this view allowed the South to maintain its system of racial segregation and exclusion without interference from the federal government.

Memorialists did not deny the Redeemers' use of terror and violence. To the contrary; they praised it as necessary. South Carolina senator Benjamin R. Tillman, a participant in the Hamburg massacre, stood in front of his Senate colleagues in 1900 and asserted, "We were sorry we had the necessity forced upon us, but we could not help it, and as white men we are not sorry for it, and we do not propose to apologize for anything we have done in connection with it. We took the government away from them [African Americans] in 1876. We did take it. . . . We of the South have never recognized the right of the negro to govern white men, and we never will." The animosity of southern whites toward Republican governments had much less to do with alleged corruption and incompetence than the mere fact of African Americans casting ballots and making laws.

The national historical consensus grew out of a growing national reconciliation concerning the war, a mutual agreement that both sides had fought courageously and that it was time to move on. Hidden in all the goodwill was the tacit agreement between southern and northern whites that the South was now free to work out its own resolution to race relations. Reconstruction rested on a national consensus of African American inferiority.

# MODEST GAINS

**HOW AND** why did Reconstruction end?

If the overthrow of Reconstruction elicited a resounding indifference from most white Americans, black southerners greeted it with frustration. Their dreams of land ownership faded as a new labor system relegated them to a lowly position in southern agriculture. Redemption reversed their economic and political gains and deprived them of most of the civil rights they had enjoyed under Congressional Reconstruction. Although they continued to vote into the 1890s, they had by 1877 lost most of the voting strength and political offices they held. Rather than becoming part of southern society, they were increasingly set apart from it, valued only for their labor.

Still, the former slaves were better off in 1877 than in 1865. They were free, however limited their freedom. Some owned land; some held jobs in cities. They raised their families in relative peace and experienced the spiritual joys of a full religious life. They socialized freely with relatives and friends, and they moved about. The Reconstruction amendments to the Constitution guaranteed an array of civil and political rights, and eventually these guarantees would form the basis of the civil rights revolution after World War II. But that outcome was long, too long, in the future.

Black southerners experienced some advances in the decade after the Civil War, but these owed little to Reconstruction. Black families functioned as economic and psychological buffers against unemployment and prejudice. Black churches played crucial roles in their communities. Self-help and labor organizations offered mutual friendship and financial assistance. All of these institutions had existed in the slavery era, although on a smaller scale. And some of them, such as black labor groups, schools, and social welfare associations, endured because comparable white institutions excluded black people.

Black people also scored some modest economic successes during the Reconstruction era, mainly from their own pluck. In the Lower South, black per capita income increased 46 percent between 1857 and 1879, compared with a 35 percent decline in white per capita income.

**Watch** the **Video**

at **www.myhistorylab.com**
*The Promise and Failure of Reconstruction*

**Interpreting the Past**
*Realities of Freedom* (pp. 464–465)

**Read** the **Document**

at **www.myhistorylab.com**
*Exploring America:
Did Reconstruction Work for the Freed People?*

**Read** the **Document**

at **www.myhistorylab.com**
*Thirteenth, Fourteenth, and Fifteenth Amendments*

## OVERVIEW Constitutional Amendments and Federal Legislation of the Reconstruction Era

| Amendment or Legislation | Purpose | Significance |
| --- | --- | --- |
| Thirteenth Amendment (passed and ratified in 1865) | Prevented southern states from reestablishing slavery after the war | Final step toward full emancipation of slaves |
| Freedmen's Bureau Act (1865) | Oversight of resettlement, labor for former slaves | Involved the federal government directly in relief, education, and assisting the transition from slavery to freedom; worked fitfully to achieve this objective during its seven-year career |
| Southern Homestead Act (1866) | Provided black people preferential access to public lands in five southern states | Lack of capital and poor quality of federal land thwarted the purpose of the act |
| Civil Rights Act of 1866 | Defined rights of national citizenship | Marked an important change in federal-state relations, tilting balance of power to national government |
| Fourteenth Amendment (passed 1866; ratified 1868) | Prohibited states from violating the rights of their citizens | Strengthened the Civil Rights Act of 1866 and guaranteed all citizens equality before the law |
| Military Reconstruction Acts (1867) | Set new rules for the readmission of former Confederate states into the Union and secured black voting rights | Initiated Congressional Reconstruction |
| Tenure of Office Act (1867) | Required congressional approval for the removal of any official whose appointment had required Senate confirmation | A congressional challenge to the president's right to dismiss cabinet members; led to President Andrew Johnson's impeachment trial |
| Fifteenth Amendment (passed 1869; ratified 1870) | Guaranteed the right of all American male citizens to vote regardless of race | The basis for black voting rights |
| Civil Rights Act of 1875 | Prohibited racial discrimination in jury selection, public transportation, and public accommodations | Rarely enforced; Supreme Court declared it unconstitutional in 1883 |

### QUICK REVIEW

#### Advances

- Black families and institutions played a crucial role in Reconstruction era.
- Fourteenth Amendment guaranteed equality before the law.
- Fifteenth Amendment protected the right to vote.

**Slaughterhouse cases** Group of cases resulting in one sweeping decision by the U.S. Supreme Court in 1873 that contradicted the intent of the Fourteenth Amendment by decreeing that most citizenship rights remained under state, not federal, control.

Sharecropping, oppressive as it was, represented an advance over forced and gang labor. Collectively, black people owned more than $68 million worth of property in 1870, a 240 percent increase over 1860, but the average worth of each piece of property was only $408.

The Fourteenth and Fifteenth Amendments to the Constitution are among the few bright spots in Reconstruction's otherwise dismal legacy. But the benefits of these two landmark amendments did not accrue to African Americans until well into the twentieth century. White southerners effectively nullified the Reconstruction amendments, and the U.S. Supreme Court virtually interpreted them, and other Reconstruction legislation, out of existence.

In the **Slaughterhouse cases** (1873), the Supreme Court contradicted the intent of the Fourteenth Amendment by decreeing that most citizenship rights remained under state, not federal, control. In **United States v. Cruikshank** (1876), the Court overturned the convictions of some of those responsible for the Colfax Massacre, ruling that the Enforcement Act applied only to violations of black rights by states, not individuals. Within the next two decades, the Supreme Court would uphold the legality of racial segregation and black disfranchisement, in effect declaring that the Fourteenth and Fifteenth Amendments did not apply to African Americans.

# CONCLUSION

White southerners robbed black southerners of their gains and sought to reduce them again to servitude and dependence, if not to slavery. But in the process, the majority of white southerners lost as well. Yeoman farmers missed an opportunity to break cleanly from the Old South and establish a more equitable society. Instead, they allowed the old elites to regain power and gradually ignore their needs. They preserved the social benefit of a white skin at the cost of almost everything else. Many lost their farms and sank into tenancy. Few had a voice in state legislatures or the U.S. Congress. A new South, rid of slavery and sectional antagonism, had indeed emerged—redeemed, regenerated, and disenthralled. But the old South lingered on.

The journey toward equality after the Civil War had aborted. Reconstruction had not failed. It was overthrown. In the weeks and months after Appomattox, white southerners launched a war against the freedmen and their allies to return white Democrats to power and African Americans to a position of permanent subordination in southern society. The indifferent and often hostile attitudes of white northerners toward blacks played a role in limiting the federal response and ensuring the success of the white South in prosecuting this war. As with the Civil War, the overthrow of Reconstruction was a national tragedy. By 1877, the "golden moment," an unprecedented opportunity for the nation to live up to its ideals by extending equal rights to all its citizens, black and white alike, had passed.

**United States v. Cruikshank**   Supreme Court ruling of 1876 that overturned the convictions of some of those responsible for the Colfax Massacre, ruling that the Enforcement Act applied only to violations of black rights by states, not individuals.

# WHERE TO LEARN MORE

**Penn Center Historic District, St. Helena Island, South Carolina.**   The Penn School was a sea-island experiment in the education of free black people established by northern missionaries Laura Towne and Ellen Murray in 1862. They operated it until their deaths in the early 1900s. The Penn School became Penn Community Services in 1948, serving as an educational institution, health clinic, and a social service agency. See its website at http://www.penncenter.com.

**_Harper's Magazine_ selected articles and cartoons on Reconstruction.**   This website includes numerous articles and illustrations that appeared in _Harper's_ during the Reconstruction era. This collection is especially good in documenting the violence against African Americans in the South during this era. Go to http://blackhistory.harpweek.com/4Reconstruction/reconlevelone.htm.

**Beauvoir, Biloxi, Mississippi.**   The exhibits at Beauvoir, the home of Jefferson Davis, evoke the importance of the Lost Cause for the white survivors of the Confederacy. Especially interesting is the Jefferson Davis Soldiers Home on the premises and the Confederate Veterans Cemetery. Davis spent his retirement at Beauvoir. Go to http://www.beauvoir.org.

**Levi Jordan Plantation, Brazoria County, Texas.**   This site provides an excellent depiction and interpretation of the lives of sharecroppers and tenants during and immediately after the Reconstruction era. The site is especially valuable for demonstrating the transition from slavery to sharecropping. Go to http://www.webarchaeology.com.

# REVIEW QUESTIONS

1. Both Russia and America hoped to develop a free-labor agricultural class after their respective emancipations. Why didn't these governments follow through on their own objectives?

2. Given the different perspectives on the Civil War's outcome and what the social structure of a postwar South should be, was there any common ground between southern white and southern black on which to forge a Reconstruction policy?

3. Black people did achieve some notable gains during Reconstruction, despite its overall failure. What were those gains?

4. What prompted Frances Harper to write her pleading poem in 1871?

# KEY TERMS

**Black codes** (p. 445)
**Carpetbaggers** (p. 450)
**Compromise of 1877** (p. 458)
**Congressional Reconstruction** (p. 448)
**Field Order No. 15** (p. 440)
**Fifteenth Amendment** (p. 449)
**Fourteenth Amendment** (p. 445)
**Freedmen's Bureau** (p. 439)
**Ku Klux Klan** (p. 452)
**Lost Cause** (p. 438)

**Redeemers** (p. 456)
**Scalawags** (p. 450)
**Sharecropping** (p. 441)
**_Slaughterhouse_ cases** (p. 460)
**Southern Homestead Act** (p. 441)
**Tenure of Office Act** (p. 448)
**Union Leagues** (p. 451)
**_United States v. Cruikshank_** (p. 461)

# PEARSON myhistorylab™ Connections

Reinforce what you learned in this chapter by studying the many documents, images, maps, review tools, and videos available at **www.myhistorylab.com**.

## Read and Review

✓● Study and Review **Study Plan: Chapter 16**

●●●● Read the Document

*A Sharecrop Contract (1882)*

Carl Schurz, *Report on the Condition of the South (1865)*

Clinton B. Fisk, *"Plain Counsels for Freedmen" (1865)*

Albion W. Tourgée, *Letter on Ku Klux Klan Activities (1870)*

*"Address of the Colored Citizens of Norfolk, Virginia" (1865)*

*Address of the Colored State Convention to the People of the State of South Carolina (1865)*

Charlotte Forten, *Life on the Sea Islands*

*Hannah Irwin Describes Ku Klux Klan Ride (Late 1860s)*

*Jourdon Anderson to His Former Master (1865)*

*President Johnson's Veto of the Civil Rights Act 1866*

*The Civil Rights Act of 1866*

*The Fourteenth Amendment (1868)*

*The Freedmen's Bureau Bill (1865)*

*The Mississippi Black Code (1865)*

*Thirteenth, Fourteenth, and Fifteenth Amendments*

👁 See the Map *Congressional Reconstrction*

## Research and Explore

●●●● Read the Document

*Personal Journeys Online*

*From Then to Now Online: African American Voting Rights in the South*

*Exploring America: Did Reconstruction Work for the Freed People?*

((●● Hear the Audio

*Free At Last*

*Remembering Slavery #2*

(●● Watch the Video

*The Promise and Failure of Reconstruction*

*Reconstruction in Texas*

*The Schools that the Civil War and Reconstruction Created*

*Trials of Racial Identity in Nineteenth-Century America*

---

((●● **Hear** the **Audio**

Hear the audio files for Chapter 16 at
**www.myhistorylab.com**.

## Realities of Freedom

**FOLLOWING** emancipation, what economic and social opportunities actually existed for African Americans in the United States? How did these various opportunities available to freedmen improve their life and that of their families after the official end to slavery?

The Freedmen's Bureau established in 1865 by Congress provided freedmen with clothing, temporary shelter, food, and a series of freedmen's schools across the South. Southern response was to fall into the use of terror to deter blacks from becoming economically independent, using the agencies of groups like the Ku Klux Klan. Sharecropping was an insidious economic arrangement that also placed both whites and blacks in a form of economic slavery to large landholders in the South of the post–Civil War era.

Sharecropping, tenant farming, and peonage were new forms of slavery adopted in the South following the Civil War. The story of African Americans after the end of slavery is complex and varied. Some blacks attempted to seek out better places to establish their new lives while others remained in the security of the only home they had known as slaves.

## After slavery we had to get in before night . . .

### An Act to Establish a Bureau for the Relief of Freedmen and Refugees, 1865

**BE IT ENACTED,** That there is hereby established in the War Department, to continue during the present war of rebellion, and for one year thereafter, a bureau of refugees, freedmen, and abandoned lands, to which shall be committed, as hereinafter provided, the supervision and management of all abandoned lands, and the control of all subjects relating to refugees and freedmen from rebel states, or from any district of country within the territory embraced in the operations of the army, under such rules and regulations as may be prescribed by the head of the bureau and approved by the President. The said bureau shall be under the management and control of a commissioner to be appointed by the President, by and with the advice and consent of the Senate . . .

This illustration depicts former slaves outside their sharecropper cabin in Virginia, ca. 1870.

A SPRING SCENE NEAR RICHMOND, VIRGINIA.—[DRAWN BY W. L. SHEPPARD.]

### "When We Worked on Shares, We Couldn't Make Nothing"

After slavery we had to get in before night too. If you didn't, Ku Klux would drive you in. They would come and visit you anyway. . . . When he got you good and scared he would drive on away. They would whip you if they would catch you out in the night time. . . .

I've forgot who it is that told us that we was free. Somebody come and told us we're free now. I done forgot who it was.

After freedom, we worked on shares a while. Then we rented. When we worked on shares, we couldn't make nothing, just overalls and something to eat. Half went to the other man and you would destroy your half if you weren't careful. A man that didn't know how to count would always lose. He might lose anyhow. They didn't give no itemized statement. No, you just had to take their word. They never give you no details. They just say you owe so much. No matter how good account you kept, you had to go by their account and now, Brother, I'm tellin' you the truth about this. It's been that way for a long time. You had to take the white man's work on note, and everything. Anything you wanted, you could git if you were a good hand. You could git anything you wanted as long as you worked. If you didn't make no money, that's all right;

*KKK members, wrapped in sheets like ghosts, threaten a free man in his home.*

they would advance you more. But you better not leave him, you better not try to leave and get caught. They'd keep you in debt. They were sharp. Christmas come, you could take up twenty dollar, in somethin' to eat and much as you wanted in whiskey. You could buy a gallon of whiskey. Anything that kept you a slave because he was always right and you were always wrong if there was difference. If there was an argument, he would get mad and there would be a shooting take place.

### Excerpts from a Sharecropper Contract, 1882

To every one applying to rent land upon shares, the following conditions must be read, and agreed to.

To every 30 or 35 acres, I agree to furnish the team, plow, and farming implements, except cotton planters, and I do not agree to furnish a cart to every cropper. The croppers are to have half of the cotton, corn and fodder (and peas and pumpkins and potatoes if any are planted. . .).

Croppers are to have no part or interest in the cotton seed raised from the crop planted and worked by them. No vine crops of any description, that is, no watermelons, muskmelons, . . . squashes or anything of that kind, except peas and pumpkins, and potatoes, are to be planted in the cotton or corn. All must work under my direction. All plantation work to be done by the croppers. . . .

No cropper to work off the plantation when there is any work to be done on the land he has rented, or when his work is needed by me or other croppers. Trees to be cut down on Orchard, House field & Evanson fences, leaving such as I may designate. . . .

*. . . a bureau of refugees, freedmen, and abandoned lands . . .*

# The Declaration of Independence

When in the course of human events it becomes necessary for one people to dissolve the political bands which have connected them with another and to assume, among the powers of the earth, the separate and equal station to which the laws of nature and of nature's God entitle them, a decent respect to the opinions of mankind requires that they should declare the causes which impel them to the separation.

We hold these truths to be self-evident, that all men are created equal; that they are endowed by their Creator with certain unalienable rights; that among these are life, liberty, and the pursuit of happiness. That, to secure these rights, governments are instituted among men, deriving their just powers from the consent of the governed; that, whenever any form of government becomes destructive of these ends, it is the right of the people to alter or to abolish it, and to institute a new government, laying its foundation on such principles, and organizing its powers in such form, as to them shall seem most likely to effect their safety and happiness. Prudence, indeed, will dictate that governments long established should not be changed for light and transient causes; and, accordingly, all experience hath shown that mankind are more disposed to suffer, while evils are sufferable, than to right themselves by abolishing the forms to which they are accustomed. But when a long train of abuses and usurpations, pursuing invariably the same object, evinces a design to reduce them under absolute despotism, it is their right, it is their duty, to throw off such government and to provide new guards for their future security. Such has been the patient sufferance of these colonies, and such is now the necessity which constrains them to alter their former systems of government. The history of the present King of Great Britain is a history of repeated injuries and usurpations, all having, in direct object, the establishment of an absolute tyranny over these States. To prove this, let facts be submitted to a candid world:

He has refused his assent to laws the most wholesome and necessary for the public good.

He has forbidden his governors to pass laws of immediate and pressing importance, unless suspended in their operation till his assent should be obtained; and, when so suspended, he has utterly neglected to attend to them.

He has refused to pass other laws for the accommodation of large districts of people, unless those people would relinquish the right of representation in the legislature, a right inestimable to them and formidable to tyrants only.

He has called together legislative bodies at places unusual, uncomfortable, and distant from the depository of their public records, for the sole purpose of fatiguing them into compliance with his measures.

He has dissolved representative houses, repeatedly for opposing, with manly firmness, his invasions on the rights of the people.

He has refused, for a long time after such dissolutions, to cause others to be elected; whereby the legislative powers, incapable of annihilation, have returned to the people at large for their exercise; the state remaining, in the meantime, exposed to all the danger of invasion from without and convulsions within.

He has endeavored to prevent the population of these States; for that purpose, obstructing the laws for naturalization of foreigners, refusing to pass others to encourage their migration hither, and raising the conditions of new appropriations of lands.

He has obstructed the administration of justice by refusing his assent to laws for establishing judiciary powers.

He has made judges dependent on his will alone for the tenure of their offices and the amount and payment of their salaries.

He has erected a multitude of new offices and sent hither swarms of officers to harass our people and eat out their substance.

He has kept among us, in time of peace, standing armies, without the consent of our legislatures.

He has affected to render the military independent of, and superior to, the civil power.

He has combined with others to subject us to a jurisdiction foreign to our Constitution and unacknowledged by our laws, giving his assent to their acts of pretended legislation—

For quartering large bodies of armed troops among us;

For protecting them by mock trial, from punishment for any murders which they should commit on the inhabitants of these States;

For cutting off our trade with all parts of the world;

For imposing taxes on us without our consent;

For depriving us, in many cases, of the benefit of trial by jury;

For transporting us beyond seas to be tried for pretended offences;

For abolishing the free system of English laws in a neighboring province, establishing therein an arbitrary government, and enlarging its boundaries, so as to render it at once an example and fit instrument for introducing the same absolute rule into these colonies;

For taking away our charters, abolishing our most valuable laws, and altering, fundamentally, the powers of our governments.

For suspending our own legislatures and declaring themselves invested with power to legislate for us in all cases whatsoever.

He has abdicated government here by declaring us out of his protection and waging war against us.

He has plundered our seas, ravaged our coasts, burnt our towns, and destroyed the lives of our people.

He is, at this time, transporting large armies of foreign mercenaries to complete the works of death, desolation, and tyranny already begun with circumstances of cruelty and perfidy scarcely paralleled in the most barbarous ages, and totally unworthy the head of a civilized nation.

He has constrained our fellow citizens, taken captive on the high seas, to bear arms against their country, to become the executioners of their friends and brethren, or to fall themselves by their hands.

He has excited domestic insurrections amongst us and has endeavored to bring on the inhabitants of our frontiers, the merciless Indian savages, whose known rule of warfare is an undistinguished destruction of all ages, sexes, and conditions.

In every stage of these oppressions, we have petitioned for redress in the most humble terms; our repeated petitions have been answered only by repeated injury. A prince whose character is thus marked by every act which may define a tyrant is unfit to be the ruler of a free people.

Nor have we been wanting in attention to our British brethren. We have warned them, from time to time, of attempts made by their legislature to extend an unwarrantable jurisdiction over us. We have reminded them of the circumstances of our emigration and settlement here. We have appealed to their native justice and magnanimity, and we have conjured them, by the ties of our common kindred, to disavow these usurpations, which would inevitably interrupt our connections and correspondence. They, too, have been deaf to the voice of justice and consanguinity. We must, therefore, acquiesce in the necessity which denounces our separation, and hold them, as we hold the rest of mankind, enemies in war, in peace, friends.

We, therefore, the representatives of the United States of America, in general Congress assembled, appealing to the Supreme Judge of the world for the rectitude of our intentions, do, in the name and by the authority of the good people of these colonies, solemnly publish and declare, that these united colonies are, and of right ought to be, free and independent states: that they are absolved from all allegiance to the British Crown, and that all political connection between them and the state of Great Britain is, and ought to be, totally dissolved; and that, as free and independent states, they have full power to levy war, conclude peace, contract alliances, establish commerce, and to do all other acts and things which independent states may of right do. And, for the support of this declaration, with a firm reliance on the protection of Divine Providence, we mutually pledge to each other our lives, our fortunes, and our sacred honor.

# THE ARTICLES OF CONFEDERATION AND PERPETUAL UNION*

Between the states of New Hampshire, Massachusetts-bay Rhode Island and Providence Plantations, Connecticut, New York, New Jersey, Pennsylvania, Delaware, Maryland, Virginia, North Carolina, South Carolina, and Georgia.

## ARTICLE I

The Stile of this Confederacy shall be "The United States of America."

## ARTICLE II

Each state retains its sovereignty, freedom, and independence, and every power, jurisdiction, and right, which is not by this Confederation expressly delegated to the United States, in Congress assembled.

## ARTICLE III

The said States hereby severally enter into a firm league of friendship with each other, for their common defense, the security of their liberties, and their mutual and general welfare, binding themselves to assist each other, against all force offered to, or attacks made upon them, or any of them, on account of religion, sovereignty, trade, or any other pretense whatever.

## ARTICLE IV

The better to secure and perpetuate mutual friendship and intercourse among the people of the different States in this Union, the free inhabitants of each of these States, paupers, vagabonds, and fugitives from justice excepted, shall be entitled to all privileges and immunities of free citizens in the several States; and the people of each State shall have free ingress and regress to and from any other State, and shall enjoy therein all the privileges of trade and commerce, subject to the same duties, impositions, and restrictions as the inhabitants thereof respectively, provided that such restrictions shall not extend so far as to prevent the removal of property imported into any State, to any other State of which the owner is an inhabitant; provided also that no imposition, duties or restriction shall be laid by any State, on the property of the United States, or either of them.

If any person guilty of, or charged with, treason, felony, or other high misdemeanor in any State, shall flee from justice, and be found in any of the United States, he shall, upon demand of the Governor or executive power of the State from which he fled, be delivered up and removed to the State having jurisdiction of his offense.

Full faith and credit shall be given in each of these States to the records, acts, and judicial proceedings of the courts and magistrates of every other State.

## ARTICLE V

For the most convenient management of the general interests of the United States, delegates shall be annually appointed in such manner as the legislatures of each State shall direct, to meet in Congress on the first Monday in November, in every year, with a power reserved to each State to recall its delegates, or any of them, at any time within the year, and to send others in their stead for the remainder of the year.

No State shall be represented in Congress by less than two, nor by more than seven members; and no person shall be capable of being a delegate for more than three years in any term of six years; nor shall any person, being a delegate, be capable of holding any office under the United States, for which he, or another for his benefit, receives any salary, fees or emolument of any kind.

Each State shall maintain its own delegates in a meeting of the States, and while they act as members of the committee of the States.

In determining questions in the United States in Congress assembled, each State shall have one vote.

Freedom of speech and debate in Congress shall not be impeached or questioned in any court or place out of Congress, and the members of Congress shall be protected in their persons from arrests or imprisonments, during the time of their going to and from, and attendence on Congress, except for treason, felony, or breach of the peace.

## ARTICLE VI

No State, without the consent of the United States in Congress assembled, shall send any embassy to, or receive any embassy from, or enter into any conference, agreement, alliance or treaty with any King, Prince or State; nor shall any person holding any office of profit or trust under the United States, or any of them, accept any present, emolument, office or title of any kind whatever from any King, Prince or foreign State; nor shall the United States in Congress assembled, or any of them, grant any title of nobility.

---

*Agreed to in Congress November 15, 1777; ratified March 1781.

No two or more States shall enter into any treaty, confederation or alliance whatever between them, without the consent of the United States in Congress assembled, specifying accurately the purposes for which the same is to be entered into, and how long it shall continue.

No State shall lay any imposts or duties, which may interfere with any stipulations in treaties, entered into by the United States in Congress assembled, with any King, Prince or State, in pursuance of any treaties already proposed by Congress, to the courts of France and Spain.

No vessel of war shall be kept up in time of peace by any State, except such number only, as shall be deemed necessary by the United States in Congress assembled, for the defense of such State, or its trade; nor shall any body of forces be kept up by any State in time of peace, except such number only, as in the judgement of the United States in Congress assembled, shall be deemed requisite to garrison the forts necessary for the defense of such State; but every State shall always keep up a well-regulated and disciplined militia, sufficiently armed and accoutered, and shall provide and constantly have ready for use, in public stores, a due number of filed pieces and tents, and a proper quantity of arms, ammunition and camp equipage.

No State shall engage in any war without the consent of the United States in Congress assembled, unless such State be actually invaded by enemies, or shall have received certain advice of a resolution being formed by some nation of Indians to invade such State, and the danger is so imminent as not to admit of a delay, till the United States in Congress assembled can be consulted; nor shall any State grant commissions to any ships or vessels of war, nor letters of marque or reprisal, except it be after a declaration of war by the United States in Congress assembled, and then only against the Kingdom or State and the subjects thereof, against which war has been so declared, and under such regulations as shall be established by the United States in Congress assembled, unless such State be infested by pirates, in which case vessels of war may be fitted out for that occasion, and kept so long as the danger shall continue, or until the United States in Congress assembled shall determine otherwise.

## ARTICLE VII

When land forces are raised by any State for the common defense, all officers of or under the rank of colonel, shall be appointed by the legislature of each State respectively, by whom such forces shall be raised, or in such manner as such State shall direct, and all vacancies shall be filled up by the State which first made the appointment.

## ARTICLE VIII

All charges of war, and all other expenses that shall be incurred for the common defense or general welfare, and allowed by the United States in Congress assembled, shall be defrayed out of a common treasury, which shall be supplied by the several States in proportion to the value of all land within each State, granted to or surveyed for any person, as such land and the buildings and improvements thereon shall be estimated according to such mode as the United States in Congress assembled, shall from time to time direct and appoint.

The taxes for paying that proportion shall be laid and levied by the authority and direction of the legislatures of the several States within the time agreed upon by the United States in Congress assembled.

## ARTICLE IX

The United States in Congress assembled, shall have the sole and exclusive right and power of determining on peace and war, except in the cases mentioned in the sixth article; of sending and receiving ambassadors; entering into treaties and alliances, provided that no treaty of commerce shall be made whereby the legislative power of the respective States shall be restrained from imposing such imposts and duties on foreigners, as their own people are subjected to, or from prohibiting the exportation or importation of any species of goods or commodities whatsoever; of establishing rules for deciding in all cases, what captures on land or water shall be legal, and in what manner prizes taken by land or naval forces in the service of the United States shall be divided or appropriated; of granting letters of marque and reprisal in times of peace; appointing courts for the trial of piracies and felonies committed on the high seas and establishing courts for receiving and determining finally appeals in all cases of captures, provided that no member of Congress shall be appointed a judge of any of the said courts.

The United States in Congress assembled shall also be the last resort on appeal in all disputes and differences now subsisting or that hereafter may arise between two or more States concerning boundary, jurisdiction or any other causes whatever; which authority shall always be exercised in the manner following. Whenever the legislative or executive authority or lawful agent of any State in controversy with another shall present a petition to Congress stating the matter in question and praying for a hearing, notice thereof shall be given by order of Congress to the legislative or executive authority of the other State in controversy, and a day assigned for the appearance of the parties by their lawful agents, who shall then be directed to appoint by joint consent, commissioners or judges to constitute a court for hearing and determining the matter in question: but if they cannot agree, Congress shall name three persons out of each of the United States, and from the list of such persons each party shall alternately strike out one, the petitioners beginning, until the number shall be reduced to thirteen; and from that number not less than seven, nor more than nine names as Congress shall direct, shall in the presence of Congress be drawn out by lot, and the persons whose names shall be so drawn or any five of them, shall be commissioners or judges, to hear and finally determine the controversy, so always as a major part of the judges who shall hear the cause shall agree in the determination: and if either party shall neglect to attend at the day appointed, without showing reasons, which Congress shall judge sufficient, or being present shall refuse to strike, the Congress shall proceed to nominate three persons out of each State, and the secretary of Congress shall strike in behalf of such party absent or refusing; and the judgement and sentence of the court to be appointed, in the manner before prescribed, shall be final and conclusive; and if any of the parties shall refuse to submit to the authority of such court, or to appear or defend their claim or cause, the court shall nevertheless proceed to pronounce sentence, or judgement, which shall in like manner be final and decisive, the judgement or sentence and other proceedings being in either case transmitted to Congress, and lodged among the acts of Congress for the security of the parties concerned: provided that every commissioner, before he sits in judgement, shall take an oath to be administered by one of the judges of the supreme or superior court of the State, where the cause shall be tried, "well and truly to hear and determine the matter in question, according to the best of his judgement, without favor, affection or hope of reward:" provided also, that no State shall be deprived of territory for the benefit of the United States.

All controversies concerning the private right of soil claimed under different grants of two or more States, whose jurisdictions as they may respect such lands, and the States which passed such grants are adjusted, the said grants or either of them being at the same time claimed to have originated antecedent to such settlement of jurisdiction, shall on the petition of either party to the Congress of the United States, be finally determined as near as may be in the same manner as is before prescribed for deciding disputes respecting territorial jurisdiction between different States.

The United States in Congress assembled shall also have the sole and exclusive right and power of regulating the alloy and value of coin struck by their own authority, or by that of the respective States; fixing the standards of weights and measures throughout the United States; regulating the trade and managing all affairs with the Indians not members of any of the States; provided that the legislative right of any State within its own limits be not infringed or violated; establishing or regulating post offices from one State to another, throughout all the United States, and exacting such postage on the papers passing through the same as may be requisite to defray the expenses of the said office; appointing all officers of the land forces in the service of the United States, excepting regimental officers; appointing all the officers of the naval forces, and commissioning all officers whatever in the service of the United States; making rules for the government and regulation of the said land and naval forces, and directing their operations.

The United States in Congress assembled shall have authority to appoint a committee, to sit in the recess of Congress, to be denominated "A Committee of the States," and to consist of one delegate from each State; and to appoint such other committees and civil officers as may be necessary for managing the general affairs of the United States under their direction; to appoint one of their members to preside, provided that no person be allowed to serve in the office of president more than one year in any term of three years; to ascertain the necessary sums of money to be raised for the service of the United States, and to appropriate and apply the same for defraying the public expenses; to borrow money, or emit bills on the credit of the United States, transmitting every half year to the respective States an account of the sums of money so borrowed or emitted; to build and equip a navy; to agree upon the number of land forces, and to make requisitions from each State for its quota, in proportion to the number of white inhabitants in such State; which requisition shall be binding, and thereupon the legislature of each State shall appoint the regimental officers, raise the men and cloath, arm and equip them in a soldierlike manner, at the expense of the United States; and the officers and men so cloathed, armed and equipped shall march to the place appointed, and within the time agreed on by the United States in Congress assembled; but if the United States in Congress assembled shall, on consideration of circumstances judge proper that any State should not raise men, or should raise a smaller number of men than the quota thereof, such extra number shall be raised, officered, cloathed, armed and equipped in the same manner as the quota of each State, unless the legislature of such State shall judge that such extra number cannot be safely spared out in the same, in which case they shall raise, officer, cloath, arm and equip as many of such extra number as they judge can be safely spared. And the officers and men so cloathed, armed, and equipped, shall march to the place appointed, and within the time agreed on by the United States in Congress assembled.

The United States in Congress assembled shall never engage in a war, nor grant letters of marque or reprisal in time of peace, nor enter into any treaties or alliances, nor coin money, nor regulate the value thereof, nor ascertain the sums and expenses necessary for the defense and welfare of the United States, or any of them, nor emit bills, nor borrow money on the credit of the United States, nor appropriate money, nor agree upon the number of vessels of war, to be built or purchased, or the number of land or sea forces to be raised, nor appoint a commander in chief of the army or navy, unless nine States assent to the same: nor shall a question on any other point, except for adjourning from day to day be determined, unless by the votes of the majority of the United States in Congress assembled.

The Congress of the United States shall have power to adjourn to any time within the year, and to any place within the United States, so that no period of adjournment be for a longer duration than the space of six months, and shall publish the journal of their proceedings monthly, except such parts thereof relating to treaties, alliances or military operations, as in their judgement require secrecy; and the yeas and nays of the delegates of each State on any question shall be entered on the journal, when it is desired by any delegates of a State, or any of them, at his or their request shall be furnished with a transcript of the said journal, except such parts as are above excepted, to lay before the legislatures of the several States.

### ARTICLE X

The Committee of the States, or any nine of them, shall be authorized to execute, in the recess of Congress, such of the powers of Congress as the United States in Congress assembled, by the consent of the nine States, shall from time to time think expedient to vest them with; provided that no power be delegated to the said Committee, for the exercise of which, by the Articles of Confederation, the voice of nine States in the Congress of the United States assembled is requisite.

### ARTICLE XI

Canada acceding to this confederation, and adjoining in the measures of the United States, shall be admitted into, and entitled to all the advantages of this Union; but no other colony shall be admitted into the same, unless such admission be agreed to by nine States.

### ARTICLE XII

All bills of credit emitted, monies borrowed, and debts contracted by, or under the authority of Congress, before the assembling of the United States, in pursuance of the present confederation, shall be deemed and considered as a charge against the United States, for payment and satisfaction whereof the said United States, and the public faith are hereby solemnly pledged.

### ARTICLE XIII

Every State shall abide by the determination of the United States in Congress assembled, on all questions which by this confederation are submitted to them. And the Articles of this

Confederation shall be inviolably observed by every State, and the Union shall be perpetual; nor shall any alteration at any time hereafter be made in any of them; unless such alteration be agreed to in a Congress of the United States, and be afterwards confirmed by the legislatures of every State.

These articles shall be proposed to the legislatures of all the United States, to be considered, and if approved of by them, they are advised to authorize their delegates to ratify the same in the Congress of the United States; which being done, the same shall become conclusive.

# The Constitution of the United States of America

We the people of the United States, in order to form a more perfect union, establish justice, insure domestic tranquillity, provide for the common defense, promote the general welfare, and secure the blessings of liberty to ourselves and our posterity, do ordain and establish this Constitution for the United States of America.

## Article I

Section 1. All legislative powers herein granted shall be vested in a Congress of the United States, which shall consist of a Senate and House of Representatives.

Section 2. 1. The House of Representatives shall be composed of members chosen every second year by the people of the several States, and the electors in each State shall have the qualifications requisite for electors of the most numerous branch of the State legislature.

2. No person shall be a representative who shall not have attained to the age of twenty-five years, and been seven years a citizen of the United States, and who shall not, when elected, be an inhabitant of that State in which he shall be chosen.

3. Representatives and direct taxes[1] shall be apportioned among the several States which may be included within this Union, according to their respective numbers, which shall be determined by adding to the whole number of free persons, including those bound to service for a term of years, and excluding Indians not taxed, three fifths of all other persons.[2] The actual enumeration shall be made within three years after the first meeting of the Congress of the United States, and within every subsequent term of ten years, in such manner as they shall by law direct. The number of representatives shall not exceed one for every thirty thousand, but each State shall have at least one representative; and until such enumeration shall be made, the State of New Hampshire shall be entitled to choose three, Massachusetts eight, Rhode Island and Providence Plantations one, Connecticut five, New York six, New Jersey four, Pennsylvania eight, Delaware one, Maryland six, Virginia ten, North Carolina five, South Carolina five, and Georgia three.

4. When vacancies happen in the representation from any State, the executive authority thereof shall issue writs of election to fill such vacancies.

5. The House of Representatives shall choose their speaker and other officers; and shall have the sole power of impeachment.

Section 3. 1. The Senate of the United States shall be composed of two senators from each State, chosen by the legislature thereof,[3] for six years; and each senator shall have one vote.

2. Immediately after they shall be assembled in consequence of the first election, they shall be divided as equally as may be into three classes. The seats of the senators of the first class shall be vacated at the expiration of the second year, of the second class at the expiration of the fourth year, and of the third class at the expiration of the sixth year, so that one third may be chosen every second year; and if vacancies happen by resignation, or otherwise, during the recess of the legislature of any State, the executive thereof may make temporary appointments until the next meeting of the legislature, which shall then fill such vacancies.[4]

3. No person shall be a senator who shall not have attained to the age of thirty years, and been nine years a citizen of the United States, and who shall not, when elected, be an inhabitant of that State for which he shall be chosen.

4. The Vice President of the United States shall be President of the Senate, but shall have no vote, unless they be equally divided.

5. The Senate shall choose their other officers, and also a president pro tempore, in the absence of the Vice President, or when he shall exercise the office of the President of the United States.

6. The Senate shall have the sole power to try all impeachments. When sitting for that purpose, they shall be on oath or affirmation. When the President of the United States is tried, the chief justice shall preside: and no person shall be convicted without the concurrence of two thirds of the members present.

7. Judgment in cases of impeachment shall not extend further than to removal from office, and disqualification to hold and enjoy any office of honor, trust or profit under the United States: but the party convicted shall nevertheless be liable and subject to indictment, trial, judgment and punishment, according to law.

Section 4. 1. The times, places, and manner of holding elections for senators and representatives, shall be prescribed in each State by the legislature thereof; but the Congress may at any time by law make or alter such regulations, except as to the places of choosing senators.

2. The Congress shall assemble at least once in every year, and such meeting shall be on the first Monday in December, unless they shall by law appoint a different day.

Section 5. 1. Each House shall be the judge of the elections, returns and qualifications of its own members, and a majority of each shall constitute a quorum to do business; but a smaller number may adjourn from day to day, and may be authorized to compel the attendance of absent members, in such manner, and under such penalties as each House may provide.

---

[1]See the Sixteenth Amendment.
[2]See the Fourteenth Amendment.
[3]See the Seventeenth Amendment.

[4]See the Seventeenth Amendment.

2. Each House may determine the rules of its proceedings, punish its members for disorderly behavior, and, with the concurrence of two thirds, expel a member.

3. Each House shall keep a journal of its proceedings, and from time to time publish the same, excepting such parts as may in their judgment require secrecy; and the yeas and nays of the members of either House on any question shall, at the desire of one fifth of those present, be entered on the journal.

4. Neither House, during the session of Congress, shall, without the consent of the other, adjourn for more than three days, nor to any other place than that in which the two Houses shall be sitting.

SECTION 6. 1. The senators and representatives shall receive a compensation for their services, to be ascertained by law, and paid out of the Treasury of the United States. They shall in all cases, except treason, felony, and breach of the peace, be privileged from arrest during their attendance at the session of their respective Houses, and in going to and returning from the same; and for any speech or debate in either House, they shall not be questioned in any other place.

2. No senator or representative shall, during the time for which he was elected, be appointed to any civil office under the authority of the United States, which shall have been created, or the emoluments whereof shall have been increased, during such time; and no person holding any office under the United States shall be a member of either House during his continuance in office.

SECTION 7. 1. All bills for raising revenue shall originate in the House of Representatives; but the Senate may propose or concur with amendments as on other bills.

2. Every bill which shall have passed the House of Representatives and the Senate, shall, before it become a law, be presented to the President of the United States; If he approves he shall sign it, but if not he shall return it, with his objections, to that House in which it shall have originated, who shall enter the objections at large on their journal, and proceed to reconsider it. If after such reconsideration two thirds of that House shall agree to pass the bill, it shall be sent, together with the objections, to the other House, by which it shall likewise be reconsidered, and if approved by two thirds of that House, it shall become a law. But in all such cases the votes of both Houses shall be determined by yeas and nays, and the names of the persons voting for and against the bill shall be entered on the journal of each House respectively. If any bill shall not be returned by the President within ten days (Sundays excepted) after it shall have been presented to him, the same shall be a law, in like manner as if he had signed it, unless the Congress by their adjournment prevent its return, in which case it shall not be a law.

3. Every order, resolution, or vote to which the concurrence of the Senate and the House of Representatives may be necessary (except on a question of adjournment) shall be presented to the President of the United States; and before the same shall take effect, shall be approved by him, or being disapproved by him, shall be repassed by two thirds of the Senate and House of Representatives, according to the rules and limitations prescribed in the case of a bill.

SECTION 8. 1. The Congress shall have the power.

1. To lay and collect taxes, duties, imposts, and excises, to pay the debts and provide for the common defense and general welfare of the United States; but all duties, imposts, and excises shall be uniform throughout the United States.

2. To borrow money on the credit of the United States;

3. To regulate commerce with foreign nations, and among the several States, and with the Indian tribes;

4. To establish a uniform rule of naturalization, and uniform laws on the subject of bankruptcies throughout the United States;

5. To coin money, regulate the value thereof, and of foreign coin, and fix the standard of weights and measures;

6. To provide for the punishment of counterfeiting the securities and current coin of the United States;

7. To establish post offices and post roads;

8. To promote the progress of science and useful arts, by securing for limited times to authors and inventors the exclusive right to their respective writings and discoveries;

9. To constitute tribunals inferior to the Supreme Court;

10. To define and punish piracies and felonies committed on the high seas, and offenses against the law of nations;

11. To declare war, grant letters of marque and reprisal, and make rules concerning captures on land and water;

12. To raise and support armies, but no appropriation of money to that use shall be for a longer term than two years;

13. To provide and maintain a navy;

14. To make rules for the government and regulation of the land and naval forces;

15. To provide for calling forth the militia to execute the laws of the Union, suppress insurrections and repel invasions;

16. To provide for organizing, arming, and disciplining the militia, and for governing such part of them as may be employed in the service of the United States, reserving to the States respectively, the appointment of the officers, and the authority of training the militia according to the discipline prescribed by Congress;

17. To exercise exclusive legislation in all cases whatsoever, over such district (not exceeding ten miles square) as may, by cession of particular States, and the acceptance of Congress, become the seat of the government of the United States, and to exercise like authority over all places purchased by the consent of the legislature of the State in which the same shall be, for the erection of forts, magazines, arsenals, dockyards, and other needful buildings; and

18. To make all laws which shall be necessary and proper for carrying into execution the foregoing powers, and all other powers vested by this Constitution in the government of the United States, or any department or officer thereof.

SECTION 9. 1. The migration or importation of such persons as any of the States now existing shall think proper to admit, shall not be prohibited by the Congress prior to the year one thousand eight hundred and eight, but a tax or duty may be imposed on such importation, not exceeding ten dollars for each person.

2. The privilege of the writ of habeas corpus shall not be suspended, unless when in cases of rebellion or invasion the public safety may require it.

3. No bill of attainder or ex post facto law shall be passed.

4. No capitation, or other direct, tax shall be laid, unless in proportion to the census or enumeration herein-before directed to be taken.[5]

5. No tax or duty shall be laid on articles exported from any State.

6. No preference shall be given by any regulation of commerce or revenue to the ports of one State over those of another: nor shall vessels bound to, or from, one State be obliged to enter, clear, or pay duties in another.

7. No money shall be drawn from the treasury, but in consequence of appropriations made by law; and a regular statement and account of the receipts and expenditures of all public money shall be published from time to time.

8. No title of nobility shall be granted by the United States: and no person holding any office of profit or trust under them, shall, without the consent of the Congress, accept of any present, emolument, office, or title, of any kind whatever, from any king, prince, or foreign State.

SECTION 10. 1. No State shall enter into any treaty, alliance, or confederation; grant letters of marque and reprisal; coin money; emit bills of credit; make any thing but gold and silver coin a tender in payment of debts; pass any bill of attainder, ex post facto law, or law impairing the obligation of contracts, or grant, any title of nobility.

2. No State shall, without the consent of the Congress, lay any imposts or duties on imports or exports, except what may be absolutely necessary for executing its inspection laws: and the net produce of all duties and imposts laid by any State on imports or exports, shall be for the use of the treasury of the United States; and all such laws shall be subject to the revision and control of the Congress.

3. No State shall, without the consent of the Congress, lay any duty of tonnage, keep troops, or ships of war in time of peace, enter into any agreement or compact with another State, or with a foreign power, or engage in war, unless actually invaded, or in such imminent danger as will not admit of delay.

## ARTICLE II

SECTION 1. 1. The executive power shall be vested in a President of the United States of America. He shall hold his office during the term of four years, and, together with the Vice President, chosen for the same term, be elected, as follows:

2. Each State shall appoint, in such manner as the legislature thereof may direct, a number of electors, equal to the whole number of senators and representatives to which the State may be entitled in the Congress: but no senator or representative, or person holding any office of trust or profit under the United States, shall be appointed an elector.

The electors shall meet in their respective States, and vote by ballot for two persons, of whom one at least shall not be an inhabitant of the same State with themselves. And they shall make a list of all the persons voted for, and of the number of votes for each; which list they shall sign and certify, and transmit sealed to the seat of the government of the United States, directed to the president of the Senate. The president of the Senate shall, in the presence of the Senate and House of Representatives, open all the certificates, and the votes shall then be counted. The person having the greatest number of votes shall be the President, if such number be a majority of the whole number of electors appointed; and if there be more than one who have such majority, and have an equal number of votes, then the House of Representatives shall immediately choose by ballot one of them for President; and if no person have a majority, then from the five highest on the list the said House shall in like manner choose the President. But in choosing the President, the votes shall be taken by States, the representation from each State having one vote; a quorum for this purpose shall consist of a member or members from two thirds of the States, and a majority of all the States shall be necessary to a choice. In every case after the choice of the President, the person having the greatest number of votes of the electors shall be the Vice President. But if there should remain two or more who have equal votes, the Senate shall choose from them by ballot the Vice President.[6]

3. The Congress may determine the time of choosing the electors, and the day on which they shall give their votes; which day shall be the same throughout the United States.

4. No person except a natural born citizen, or a citizen of the United States, at the time of the adoption of this Constitution, shall be eligible to the office of President; neither shall any person be eligible to the office who shall not have attained to the age of thirty-five years, and been fourteen years a resident within the United States.

5. In case of the removal of the President from office, or of his death, resignation, or inability to discharge the powers and duties of the said office, the same shall devolve on the Vice President, and the congress may by law provide for the case of removal, death, resignation or inability, both of the President and Vice President, declaring what officer shall then act as President, and such officer shall act accordingly until the disability be removed, or a President shall be elected.

6. The President shall, at stated times, receive for his services a compensation which shall neither be increased nor diminished during the period for which he shall have been elected, and he shall not receive within that period any other emolument from the United States, or any of them.

7. Before he enter on the execution of his office, he shall take the following oath or affirmation:—"I do solemnly swear (or affirm) that I will faithfully execute the office of President of the United States, and will to the best of my ability, preserve, protect and defend the Constitution of the United States."

SECTION 2. 1. The President shall be commander in chief of the army and navy of the United States, and of the militia of the several States, when called into the actual service of the United States; he may require the opinion in writing, of the principal officer in each of the executive departments, upon any subject relating to the duties of their respective offices, and he shall have power to grant reprieves and pardons for offenses against the United States, except in cases of impeachment.

2. He shall have power, by and with the advice and consent of the Senate, to make treaties, provided two thirds of the senators present concur; and he shall nominate, and by and with the advice and consent of the Senate, shall appoint ambassadors, other public

---

[5]See the Sixteenth Amendment.

[6]Superseded by the Twelfth Amendment.

ministers and consuls, judges of the Supreme Court, and all other officers of the United States, whose appointments are not herein otherwise provided for, and which shall be established by law; but the Congress may by law vest the appointment of such inferior officers, as they think proper, in the President alone, in the courts of laws, or in the heads of departments.

3. The President shall have power to fill up all vacancies that may happen during the recess of the Senate, by granting commissions which shall expire at the end of their next session.

SECTION 3. He shall from time to time give to the Congress information of the state of the Union, and recommend to their consideration such measures as he shall judge necessary and expedient; he may, on extraordinary occasions, convene both Houses, or either of them, and in case of disagreement between them with respect to the time of adjournment, he may adjourn them to such time as he shall think proper; he shall receive ambassadors and other public ministers; he shall take care that the laws be faithfully executed, and shall commission all the officers of the United States.

SECTION 4. The President, Vice President, and all civil officers of the United States, shall be removed from office on impeachment for, and conviction of, treason, bribery, or other high crimes and misdemeanors.

## ARTICLE III

SECTION 1. The judicial power of the United States shall be vested in one Supreme Court, and in such inferior courts as the Congress may from time to time ordain and establish. The judges, both of the Supreme and inferior courts, shall hold their offices during good behavior, and shall, at stated times, receive for their services, a compensation, which shall not be diminished during their continuance in office.

SECTION 2. 1. The judicial power shall extend to all cases, in law and equity, arising under this Constitution, the laws of the United States, and treaties made, or which shall be made, under their authority;—to all cases of admiralty and maritime jurisdiction;—to controversies to which the United States shall be a party;[7]—to controversies between two or more States;—between a State and citizens of another State;—between citizens of different States;—between citizens of the same State claiming lands under grants of different States, and between a State, or the citizens thereof, and foreign States, citizens or subjects.

2. In all cases affecting ambassadors, other public ministers and consuls, and those in which a State shall be party, the Supreme Court shall have original jurisdiction. In all the other cases before mentioned, the Supreme Court shall have appellate jurisdiction, both as to law and fact, with such exceptions, and under such regulations as the Congress shall make.

3. The trial of all crimes, except in cases of impeachment, shall be by jury; and such trial shall be held in the State where the said crimes shall have been committed; but when not committed within any State, the trial shall be such place or places as the congress may by law have directed.

SECTION 3. 1. Treason against the United States shall consist only in levying war against them, or in adhering to their enemies, giving them aid and comfort. No person shall be convicted of treason unless on the testimony of two witnesses to the same overt act, or on confession in open court.

2. The Congress shall have power to declare the punishment of treason, but no attainder of treason shall work corruption of blood, or forfeiture except during the life of the person attained.

## ARTICLE IV

SECTION 1. Full faith and credit shall be given in each State to the public acts, records, and judicial proceedings of every other State. And the Congress may by general laws prescribe the manner in which such acts, records and proceedings shall be proved, and the effect thereof.

SECTION 2. 1. The citizens of each State shall be entitled to all privileges and immunities of citizens in the several States.[8]

2. A person charged in any State with treason, felony, or other crime, who shall flee from justice, and be found in another State, shall on demand of the executive authority of the State from which he fled, be delivered up to be removed to the State having jurisdiction of the crime.

3. No person held to service or labor in one State under the laws thereof, escaping into another, shall, in consequence of any law or regulation therein, be discharged from such service or labor, but shall be delivered up on claim of the party to whom such service or labor may be due.[9]

SECTION 3. 1. New States may be admitted by the Congress into this Union; but no new State shall be formed or erected within the jurisdiction of any other State, nor any State be formed by the junction of two or more States, or parts of States, without the consent of the legislatures of the States concerned as well as of the Congress.

2. The Congress shall have power to dispose of and make all needful rules and regulations respecting the territory or other property belonging to the United States; and nothing in this Constitution shall be so construed as to prejudice any claims of the United States, or of any particular State.

SECTION 4. The United States shall guarantee to every State in this Union a republican form of government, and shall protect each of them against invasion; and on application of the legislature, or of the executive (when the legislature cannot be convened) against domestic violence.

## ARTICLE V

The Congress, whenever two thirds of both Houses shall deem it necessary, shall propose amendments to this Constitution, or, on the application of the legislatures of two thirds of the several States, shall call a convention for proposing amendments, which in either case shall be valid to all intents and purposes, as part of this Constitution, when ratified by the legislatures of three fourths of the several States, or by conventions in three fourths thereof, as the one or the other

---

[7]See the Eleventh Amendment.

[8]See the Fourteenth Amendment, Sec. 1.
[9]See the Thirteenth Amendment.

mode of ratification may be proposed by the Congress; Provided that no amendment which may be made prior to the year one thousand eight hundred and eight shall in any manner affect the first and fourth clauses in the ninth section of the first article; and that no State, without its consent, shall be deprived of its equal suffrage in the Senate.

## ARTICLE VI

1. All debts contracted and engagements entered into, before the adoption of this Constitution, shall be as valid against the United States under this Constitution, as under the Confederation.[10]

2. This Constitution, and the laws of the United States which shall be made in pursuance thereof; and all treaties made, or which shall be made, under the authority of the United States, shall be the supreme law of the land; and the judges in every State shall be bound thereby, any thing in the Constitution or laws of any State to the contrary notwithstanding.

3. The senators and representatives before mentioned, and the members of the several State legislatures, and all executive and judicial officers, both of the United States and of the several States, shall be bound by oath or affirmation to support this Constitution; but no religious test shall ever be required as a qualification to any office or public trust under the United States.

## ARTICLE VII

The ratification of the conventions of nine States shall be sufficient for the establishment of this Constitution between the States so ratifying the same.

Done in Convention by the unanimous consent of the States present the seventeenth day of September in the year of our Lord one thousand seven hundred and eighty-seven, and of the independence of the United States of America the twelfth. In witness whereof we have hereunto subscribed our names.

[Signatories' names omitted]

*Articles in addition to, and amendment of, the Constitution of the United States of America, proposed by Congress, and ratified by the legislatures of the several States, pursuant to the fifth article of the original Constitution.*

## Amendment I

[First ten amendments ratified December 15, 1791]
Congress shall make no law respecting an establishment of religion, or prohibiting the free exercise thereof; or abridging the freedom of speech, or of the press; or the right of the people peaceably to assemble, and to petition the government for a redress of grievances.

## Amendment II

A well regulated militia, being necessary to the security of a free State, the right of the people to keep and bear arms, shall not be infringed.

## Amendment III

No soldier shall, in time of peace be quartered in any house, without the consent of the owner, nor in time of war, but in a manner to be prescribed by law.

---

[10]See the Fourteenth Amendment, Sec. 4.

## Amendment IV

The right of the people to be secure in their persons, houses, papers, and effects, against unreasonable searches and seizures, shall not be violated, and no warrants shall issue, but upon probable cause, supported by oath or affirmation, and particularly describing the place to be searched, and the persons or things to be seized.

## Amendment V

No person shall be held to answer for a capital or otherwise infamous crime, unless on a presentment or indictment of a grand jury, except in cases arising in the land or naval forces, or in the militia, when in actual service in time of war or public danger; nor shall any person be subject for the same offense to be twice put in jeopardy of life or limb; nor shall be compelled in any criminal case to be a witness against himself, nor be deprived of life, liberty, or property, without due process of law; nor shall private property be taken for public use, without just compensation.

## Amendment VI

In all criminal prosecutions, the accused shall enjoy the right to a speedy and public trial, by an impartial jury of the State and district wherein the crime shall have been committed, which district shall have been previously ascertained by law, and to be informed of the nature and cause of the accusation; to be confronted with the witnesses against him; to have compulsory process for obtaining witnesses in his favor, and to have the assistance of counsel for his defense.

## Amendment VII

In suits at common law, where the value in controversy shall exceed twenty dollars, the right of trial by jury shall be preserved, and no fact tried by a jury shall be otherwise reexamined in any court of the United States, than according to the rules of the common law.

## Amendment VIII

Excessive bail shall not be required, nor excessive fines imposed, nor cruel and unusual punishments inflicted.

## Amendment IX

The enumeration in the Constitution of certain rights shall not be construed to deny or disparage others retained by the people.

## Amendment X

The powers not delegated to the United States by the Constitution, nor prohibited by it to the States, are reserved to the States respectively, or to the people.

## Amendment XI [January 8, 1798]

The judicial power of the United States shall not be construed to extend to any suit in law or equity, commended or prosecuted against one of the United States by citizens of another State, or by citizens or subjects of any foreign State.

## Amendment XII [September 25, 1804]

The electors shall meet in their respective States, and vote by ballot for President and Vice President, one of whom, at least, shall not be an inhabitant of the same State with themselves; they shall name in their ballots the person voted for as President, and in distinct ballots, the person voted for as Vice President, and they shall make distinct lists of all persons voted for as President and of all persons voted for as Vice President, and of the number of votes for each, which lists they shall sign and certify, and transmit sealed to the seat of the government of the United States, directed to the President of the Senate;—The President of the Senate shall, in the presence of the Senate and House of Representatives, open all the certificates and the votes shall then be counted;—The person having the greatest number of votes for President, shall be the President, if such number be a majority of the whole number of electors appointed; and if no person have such majority, then from the persons having the highest numbers not exceeding three on the list of those voted for as President, the House of Representatives shall choose immediately, by ballot, the President. But in choosing the President, the votes shall be taken by States, the representation from each State having one vote; a quorum for this purpose shall consist of a member or members from two thirds of the States, and a majority of all the States shall be necessary to a choice. And if the House of Representatives shall not choose a President whenever the right of choice shall devolve upon them, before the fourth day of March next following, then the Vice President shall act as President, as in the case of the death or other constitutional disability of the President. The person having the greatest number of votes as Vice President shall be the Vice President, if such number be a majority of the whole number of electors appointed, and if no person have a majority, then from the two highest numbers on the list, the Senate shall choose the Vice President; a quorum for the purpose shall consist of two thirds of the whole number of Senators, and a majority of the whole number shall be necessary to a choice. But no person constitutionally ineligible to the office of President shall be eligible to that of Vice President of the United States.

### Amendment XIII [December 18, 1865]

SECTION 1. Neither slavery nor involuntary servitude, except as a punishment for crime whereof the party shall have been duly convicted, shall exist within the United States, or any place subject to their jurisdiction.

SECTION 2. Congress shall have power to enforce this article by appropriate legislation.

### Amendment XIV [July 28, 1868]

SECTION 1. All persons born or naturalized in the United States, and subject to the jurisdiction thereof, are citizens of the United States and of the State wherein they reside. No State shall make or enforce any law which shall abridge the privileges or immunities of citizens of the United States; nor shall any State deprive any person of life, liberty, or property, without due process of law; nor deny to any person within its jurisdiction the equal protection of the laws.

SECTION 2. Representatives shall be apportioned among the several States according to their respective numbers, counting the whole number of persons in each State, excluding Indians not taxed. But when the right to vote at any election for the choice of electors for President and Vice President of the United States, representatives in Congress, the executive and judicial officers of a State, or the members of the legislature thereof, is denied to any of the male inhabitants of such State, being twenty-one years of age, and citizens of the United States, or in any way abridged, except for participating in rebellion, or other crime, the basis of representation there shall be reduced in the proportion which the number of such male citizens shall bear to the whole number of male citizens twenty-one years of age in such State.

SECTION 3. No person shall be a senator or representative in Congress, or elector of President and Vice President, or hold any office, civil or military, under the United States, or under any State, who having previously taken an oath, as a member of Congress, or as an officer of the United States, or as a member of any State legislature, or as an executive or judicial officer of any State, to support the Constitution of the United States, shall have engaged in insurrection or rebellion against the same, or given aid or comfort to the enemies thereof. But Congress may by a vote of two thirds of each House, remove such disability.

SECTION 4. The validity of the public debt of the United States, authorized by law, including debts incurred for payment of pensions and bounties for services in suppressing insurrection or rebellion; shall not be questioned. But neither the United States nor any State shall assume or pay any debt or obligation incurred in aid of insurrection or rebellion against the United States, or any claim for the loss or emancipation of any slave; but all such debts, obligations, and claims shall be held illegal and void.

SECTION 5. The Congress shall have the power to enforce, by appropriate legislation, the provisions of this article.

### Amendment XV [March 30, 1870]

SECTION 1. The right of citizens of the United States to vote shall not be denied or abridged by the United States or by any State on account of race, color, or previous condition of servitude.

SECTION 2. The Congress shall have power to enforce this article by appropriate legislation.

### Amendment XVI [February 25, 1913]

The Congress shall have power to lay and collect taxes on incomes, from whatever source derived, without apportionment among the several States, and without regard to any census or enumeration.

### Amendment XVII [May 31, 1913]

The Senate of the United States shall be composed of two senators from each State, elected by the people thereof, for six years; and each senator shall have one vote. The electors in each State shall have the qualifications requisite for electors of the most numerous branch of the State legislature.

When vacancies happen in the representation of any State in the Senate, the executive authority of such State shall issue writs of election to fill such vacancies: Provided, That the legislature of any State may empower the executive thereof to make temporary appointments until the people fill the vacancies by election as the legislature may direct.

This amendment shall not be so construed as to affect the election or term of any senator chosen before it becomes valid as part of the Constitution.

## Amendment XVIII[11] [January 29, 1919]

After one year from the ratification of this article, the manufacture, sale, or transportation of intoxicating liquors within, the importation thereof into, or the exportation thereof from the United States and all territory subject to the jurisdiction thereof for beverage purposes is thereby prohibited.

The Congress and the several States shall have concurrent power to enforce this article by appropriate legislation.

This article shall be inoperative unless it shall have been ratified as an amendment to the Constitution by the legislatures of the several States, as provided in the constitution, within seven years from the date of the submission hereof to the States by Congress.

## Amendment XIX [August 26, 1920]

The right of citizens of the United States to vote shall not be denied or abridged by the United States or by any State on account of sex.

Congress shall have the power to enforce this article by appropriate legislation.

## Amendment XX [January 23, 1933]

SECTION 1. The terms of the President and Vice President shall end at noon on the 20th day of January and the terms of Senators and Representatives at noon on the 3rd day of January, of the years in which such terms would have ended if this article had not been ratified; and the terms of their successors shall then begin.

SECTION 2. The Congress shall assemble at least once in every year, and such meeting shall begin at noon on the 3rd day of January, unless they shall by law appoint a different day.

SECTION 3. If, at the time fixed for the beginning of the term of President, the President-elect shall have died, the Vice President-elect shall become President. If a President shall not have been chosen before the time fixed for the beginning of his term, or if the President-elect shall have failed to qualify, then the Vice President-elect shall act as President until a President shall have qualified; and the Congress may by law provide for the case wherein neither a President-elect nor a Vice President-elect shall have qualified, declaring who shall then act as President, or the manner in which one who is to act shall be selected, and such person shall act accordingly until a President or Vice President shall have qualified.

SECTION 4. The Congress may by law provide for the case of the death of any of the persons from whom, the House of Representatives may choose a President whenever the right of choice shall have devolved upon them, and for the case of the death of any of the persons from whom the Senate may choose a Vice President whenever the right of choice shall have devolved upon them.

SECTION 5. Sections 1 and 2 shall take effect on the 15th day of October following the ratification of this article.

SECTION 6. This article shall be inoperative unless it shall have been ratified as an amendment to the Constitution by the legislatures of

three-fourths of the several States within seven years from the date of its submission.

## Amendment XXI [December 5, 1933]

SECTION 1. The Eighteenth Article of amendment to the Constitution of the United States is hereby repealed.

SECTION 2. The transportation or importation into any State, Territory, or possession of the United States for delivery or use therein of intoxicating liquors in violation of the laws thereof, is hereby prohibited.

SECTION 3. This article shall be inoperative unless it shall have been ratified as an amendment to the Constitution by conventions in the several States, as provided in the Constitution, within seven years from the date of the submission thereof to the States by the Congress.

## Amendment XXII [March 1, 1951]

No person shall be elected to the office of the President more than twice, and no person who has held the office of President, or acted as President, for more than two years of a term to which some other person was elected President shall be elected to the office of the President more than once.

But this article shall not apply to any person holding the office of President when this article was proposed by the Congress, and shall not prevent any person who may be holding the office of President, or acting as President, during the term within which this article becomes operative from holding the office of President or acting as President during the remainder of such term.

This article shall be inoperative unless it shall have been ratified as an amendment to the Constitution by the legislatures of three-fourths of the several States within seven years from the date of its submission to the States by the Congress.

## Amendment XXIII [March 29, 1961]

SECTION 1. The District constituting the seat of Government of the United States shall appoint in such manner as the Congress may direct.

A number of electors of President and Vice President equal to the whole number of Senators and Representatives in Congress to which the District would be entitled if it were a State, but in no event more than the least populous State; they shall be in addition to those appointed by the States, but they shall be considered, for the purposes of the election of President and Vice President, to be electors appointed by a State; and they shall meet in the District and perform such duties as provided by the twelfth article of amendment.

SECTION 2. The Congress shall have power to enforce this article by appropriate legislation.

## Amendment XXIV [January 23, 1964]

SECTION 1. The right of citizens of the United States to vote in any primary or other election for President or Vice President, for electors for President or Vice President, or for Senator or Representative in Congress, shall not be denied or abridged by the United States or any State by reason of failure to pay any poll tax or other tax.

---

[11]Repealed by the Twenty-first Amendment.

SECTION 2. The Congress shall have power to enforce this article by appropriate legislation.

### Amendment XXV [February 10, 1967]

SECTION 1. In case of the removal of the President from office or of his death or resignation, the Vice President shall become President.

SECTION 2. Whenever there is a vacancy in the office of the Vice President, the President shall nominate a Vice President who shall take office upon confirmation by a majority of both Houses of Congress.

SECTION 3. Whenever the President transmits to the President pro tempore of the Senate and the Speaker of the House of Representatives his written declaration that he is unable to discharge the powers and duties of his office, and until he transmits to them a written declaration to the contrary, such powers and duties shall be discharged by the Vice President as Acting President.

SECTION 4. Whenever the Vice President and a majority of either the principal officers of the executive departments or of such other body as Congress may by law provide, transmit to the President pro tempore of the Senate and the Speaker of the House of Representatives their written declaration that the President is unable to discharge the powers and duties of his office, the Vice President shall immediately assume the powers and duties of the office as Acting President.

Thereafter, when the President transmits to the President pro tempore of the Senate and the Speaker of the House of Representatives his written declaration that no inability exists, he shall resume the powers and duties of his office unless the Vice President and a majority of either the principal officers of the executive departments or of such other body as Congress may by law provide, transmit within four days to the President pro tempore of the Senate and the Speaker of the House of Representatives

their written declaration that the President is unable to discharge the powers and duties of his office. Thereupon Congress shall decide the issue, assembling within forty-eight hours for that purpose if not in session. If the Congress, within twenty-one days after receipt of the latter written declaration, or, if Congress is not in session, within twenty-one days after Congress is required to assemble, determines by two-thirds vote of both Houses that the President is unable to discharge the powers and duties of his office, the Vice President shall continue to discharge the same as Acting President; otherwise, the President shall resume the powers and duties of his office.

### Amendment XXVI [June 30, 1971]

SECTION 1. The right of citizens of the United States who are eighteen years of age or older to vote shall not be denied or abridged by the United States or by any State on account of age.

SECTION 2. The Congress shall have power to enforce this article by appropriate legislation.

### Amendment XXVII[12] [May 7, 1992]

No law, varying the compensation for services of the Senators and Representatives, shall take effect until an election of Representatives shall have intervened.

---

[12]James Madison proposed this amendment in 1789 together with the ten amendments that were adopted as the Bill of Rights, but it failed to win ratification at the time. Congress, however, had set no deadline for its ratification, and over the years—particularly in the 1980s and 1990s—many states voted to add it to the Constitution. With the ratification of Michigan in 1992 it passed the threshold of three-fourths of the states required for adoption, but because the process took more than 200 years, its validity remains in doubt.

## Presidential Elections

| Year | Number of States | Candidates | Party | Popular Vote* | Electoral Vote† | Percentage of Popular Vote |
|---|---|---|---|---|---|---|
| 1789 | 11 | GEORGE WASHINGTON | No party designations | | 69 | |
| | | John Adams | | | 34 | |
| | | Other Candidates | | | 35 | |
| 1792 | 15 | GEORGE WASHINGTON | No party designations | | 132 | |
| | | John Adams | | | 77 | |
| | | George Clinton | | | 50 | |
| | | Other Candidates | | | 5 | |
| 1796 | 16 | JOHN ADAMS | Federalist | | 71 | |
| | | Thomas Jefferson | Democratic-Republican | | 68 | |
| | | Thomas Pinckney | Federalist | | 59 | |
| | | Aaron Burr | Democratic-Republican | | 30 | |
| | | Other Candidates | | | 48 | |
| 1800 | 16 | THOMAS JEFFERSON | Democratic-Republican | | 73 | |
| | | Aaron Burr | Democratic-Republican | | 73 | |
| | | John Adams | Federalist | | 65 | |
| | | Charles C. Pinckney | Federalist | | 64 | |
| | | John Jay | Federalist | | 1 | |
| 1804 | 17 | THOMAS JEFFERSON | Democratic-Republican | | 162 | |
| | | Charles C. Pinckney | Federalist | | 14 | |
| 1808 | 17 | JAMES MADISON | Democratic-Republican | | 122 | |
| | | Charles C. Pinckney | Federalist | | 47 | |
| | | George Clinton | Democratic-Republican | | 6 | |
| 1812 | 18 | JAMES MADISON | Democratic-Republican | | 128 | |
| | | DeWitt Clinton | Federalist | | 89 | |
| 1816 | 19 | JAMES MONROE | Democratic-Republican | | 183 | |
| | | Rufus King | Federalist | | 34 | |
| 1820 | 24 | JAMES MONROE | Democratic-Republican | | 231 | |
| | | John Quincy Adams | Independent-Republican | | 1 | |
| 1824 | 24 | JOHN QUINCY ADAMS | Democratic-Republican | 108,740 | 84 | 30.5 |
| | | Andrew Jackson | Democratic-Republican | 153,544 | 99 | 43.1 |
| | | William H. Crawford | Democratic-Republican | 46,618 | 41 | 13.1 |
| | | Henry Clay | Democratic-Republican | 47,136 | 37 | 13.2 |
| 1828 | 24 | ANDREW JACKSON | Democrat | 647,286 | 178 | 56.0 |
| | | John Quincy Adams | National Republican | 508,064 | 83 | 44.0 |
| 1832 | 24 | ANDREW JACKSON | Democrat | 687,502 | 219 | 55.0 |
| | | Henry Clay | National Republican | 530,189 | 49 | 42.4 |
| | | William Wirt | Anti-Masonic | 33,108 | 7 | 2.6 |
| | | John Floyd | | | 11 | |
| 1836 | 26 | MARTIN VAN BUREN | Democrat | 765,483 | 170 | 50.9 |
| | | William H. Harrison | Whig | | 73 | |
| | | Hugh L. White | Whig | | 26 | |
| | | Daniel Webster | Whig | 739,795 | 14 | 49.1 |
| | | W. P. Mangum | Whig | | 11 | |

* Percentage of popular vote given for any election year may not total 100 percent because candidates receiving less than 1 percent of the popular vote have been omitted.
† Prior to the passage of the Twelfth Amendment in 1904, the electoral college voted for two presidential candidates; the runner-up became Vice-President. Data from Historical Statistics of the United States, Colonial Times to 1957 (1961), pp. 682–683, and The World Almanac.

## Presidential Elections (*Continued*)

| Year | Number of States | Candidates | Party | Popular Vote* | Electoral Vote† | Percentage of Popular Vote |
|------|------|------------|-------|------------|------------|------------|
| 1840 | 26 | WILLIAM H. HARRISON | Whig | 1,274,624 | 234 | 53.1 |
|  |  | Martin Van Buren | Democrat | 1,127,781 | 60 | 46.9 |
| 1844 | 26 | JAMES K. POLK | Democrat | 1,338,464 | 170 | 49.6 |
|  |  | Henry Clay | Whig | 1,300,097 | 105 | 48.1 |
|  |  | James G. Birney | Liberty | 62,300 |  | 2.3 |
| 1848 | 30 | ZACHARY TAYLOR | Whig | 1,360,967 | 163 | 47.4 |
|  |  | Lewis Cass | Democrat | 1,222,342 | 127 | 42.5 |
|  |  | Martin Van Buren | Free Soil | 291,263 |  | 10.1 |
| 1852 | 31 | FRANKLIN PIERCE | Democrat | 1,601,117 | 254 | 50.9 |
|  |  | Winfield Scott | Whig | 1,385,453 | 42 | 44.1 |
|  |  | John P. Hale | Free Soil | 155,825 |  | 5.0 |
| 1856 | 31 | JAMES BUCHANAN | Democrat | 1,832,955 | 174 | 45.3 |
|  |  | John C. Frémont | Republican | 1,339,932 | 114 | 33.1 |
|  |  | Millard Fillmore | American ("Know Nothing") | 871,731 | 8 | 21.6 |
| 1860 | 33 | ABRAHAM LINCOLN | Republican | 1,865,593 | 180 | 39.8 |
|  |  | Stephen A. Douglas | Democrat | 1,382,713 | 12 | 29.5 |
|  |  | John C. Breckinridge | Democrat | 848,356 | 72 | 18.1 |
|  |  | John Bell | Constitutional Union | 592,906 | 39 | 12.6 |
| 1864 | 36 | ABRAHAM LINCOLN | Republican | 2,206,938 | 212 | 55.0 |
|  |  | George B. McClellan | Democrat | 1,803,787 | 21 | 45.0 |
| 1868 | 37 | ULYSSES S. GRANT | Republican | 3,013,421 | 214 | 52.7 |
|  |  | Horatio Seymour | Democrat | 2,706,829 | 80 | 47.3 |
| 1872 | 37 | ULYSSES S. GRANT | Republican | 3,596,745 | 286 | 55.6 |
|  |  | Horace Greeley | Democrat | 2,843,446 | * | 43.9 |
| 1876 | 38 | RUTHERFORD B. HAYES | Republican | 4,036,572 | 185 | 48.0 |
|  |  | Samuel J. Tilden | Democrat | 4,284,020 | 184 | 51.0 |
| 1880 | 38 | JAMES A. GARFIELD | Republican | 4,453,295 | 214 | 48.5 |
|  |  | Winfield S. Hancock | Democrat | 4,414,082 | 155 | 48.1 |
|  |  | James B. Weaver | Greenback-Labor | 308,578 |  | 3.4 |
| 1884 | 38 | GROVER CLEVELAND | Democrat | 4,879,507 | 219 | 48.5 |
|  |  | James G. Blaine | Republican | 4,850,293 | 182 | 48.2 |
|  |  | Benjamin F. Butler | Greenback-Labor | 175,370 |  | 1.8 |
|  |  | John P. St. John | Prohibition | 150,369 |  | 1.5 |
| 1888 | 38 | BENJAMIN HARRISON | Republican | 5,447,129 | 233 | 47.9 |
|  |  | Grover Cleveland | Democrat | 5,537,857 | 168 | 48.6 |
|  |  | Clinton B. Fisk | Prohibition | 249,506 |  | 2.2 |
|  |  | Anson J. Streeter | Union Labor | 146,935 |  | 1.3 |
| 1892 | 44 | GROVER CLEVELAND | Democrat | 5,555,426 | 277 | 46.1 |
|  |  | Benjamin Harrison | Republican | 5,182,690 | 145 | 43.0 |
|  |  | James B. Weaver | People's | 1,029,846 | 22 | 8.5 |
|  |  | John Bidwell | Prohibition | 264,133 |  | 2.2 |
| 1896 | 45 | WILLIAM MCKINLEY | Republican | 7,102,246 | 271 | 51.1 |
|  |  | William J. Bryan | Democrat | 6,492,559 | 176 | 47.7 |

*Because of the death of Greeley, Democratic electors scattered their votes.

## Presidential Elections (*Continued*)

| Year | Number of States | Candidates | Party | Popular Vote* | Electoral Vote† | Percent- age of Popular Vote |
|------|------|------|------|------|------|------|
| 1900 | 45 | WILLIAM McKINLEY | Republican | 7,218,491 | 292 | 51.7 |
| | | William J. Bryan | Democrat; Populist | 6,356,734 | 155 | 45.5 |
| | | John C. Woolley | Prohibition | 208,914 | | 1.5 |
| 1904 | 45 | THEODORE ROOSEVELT | Republican | 7,628,461 | 336 | 57.4 |
| | | Alton B. Parker | Democrat | 5,084,223 | 140 | 37.6 |
| | | Eugene V. Debs | Socialist | 402,283 | | 3.0 |
| | | Silas C. Swallow | Prohibition | 258,536 | | 1.9 |
| 1908 | 46 | WILLIAM H. TAFT | Republican | 7,675,320 | 321 | 51.6 |
| | | William J. Bryan | Democrat | 6,412,294 | 162 | 43.1 |
| | | Eugene V. Debs | Socialist | 420,793 | | 2.8 |
| | | Eugene W. Chafin | Prohibition | 253,840 | | 1.7 |
| 1912 | 48 | WOODROW WILSON | Democrat | 6,296,547 | 435 | 41.9 |
| | | Theodore Roosevelt | Progressive | 4,118,571 | 88 | 27.4 |
| | | William H. Taft | Republican | 3,486,720 | 8 | 23.2 |
| | | Eugene V. Debs | Socialist | 900,672 | | 6.0 |
| | | Eugene W. Chafin | Prohibition | 206,275 | | 1.4 |
| 1916 | 48 | WOODROW WILSON | Democrat | 9,127,695 | 277 | 49.4 |
| | | Charles E. Hughes | Republican | 8,533,507 | 254 | 46.2 |
| | | A. L. Benson | Socialist | 585,113 | | 3.2 |
| | | J. Frank Hanly | Prohibition | 220,506 | | 1.2 |
| 1920 | 48 | WARREN G. HARDING | Republican | 16,143,407 | 404 | 60.4 |
| | | James M. Cox | Democrat | 9,130,328 | 127 | 34.2 |
| | | Eugene V. Debs | Socialist | 919,799 | | 3.4 |
| | | P. P. Christensen | Farmer-Labor | 265,411 | | 1.0 |
| 1924 | 48 | CALVIN COOLIDGE | Republican | 15,718,211 | 382 | 54.0 |
| | | John W. Davis | Democrat | 8,385,283 | 136 | 28.8 |
| | | Robert M. La Follette | Progressive | 4,831,289 | 13 | 16.6 |
| 1928 | 48 | HERBERT C. HOOVER | Republican | 21,391,993 | 444 | 58.2 |
| | | Alfred E. Smith | Democrat | 15,016,169 | 87 | 40.9 |
| 1932 | 48 | FRANKLIN D. ROOSEVELT | Democrat | 22,809,638 | 472 | 57.4 |
| | | Herbert C. Hoover | Republican | 15,758,901 | 59 | 39.7 |
| | | Norman Thomas | Socialist | 881,951 | | 2.2 |
| 1936 | 48 | FRANKLIN D. ROOSEVELT | Democrat | 27,752,869 | 523 | 60.8 |
| | | Alfred M. Landon | Republican | 16,674,665 | 8 | 36.5 |
| | | William Lemke | Union | 882,479 | | 1.9 |
| 1940 | 48 | FRANKLIN D. ROOSEVELT | Democrat | 27,307,819 | 449 | 54.8 |
| | | Wendell L. Willkie | Republican | 22,321,018 | 82 | 44.8 |
| 1944 | 48 | FRANKLIN D. ROOSEVELT | Democrat | 25,606,585 | 432 | 53.5 |
| | | Thomas E. Dewey | Republican | 22,014,745 | 99 | 46.0 |
| 1948 | 48 | HARRY S. TRUMAN | Democrat | 24,105,812 | 303 | 49.5 |
| | | Thomas E. Dewey | Republican | 21,970,065 | 189 | 45.1 |
| | | J. Strom Thurmond | States' Rights | 1,169,063 | 39 | 2.4 |
| | | Henry A. Wallace | Progressive | 1,157,172 | | 2.4 |

## Presidential Elections (Continued)

| Year | Number of States | Candidates | Party | Popular Vote* | Electoral Vote† | Percentage of Popular Vote |
|------|------|------------|-------|--------------|---------------|-------------|
| 1952 | 48 | DWIGHT D. EISENHOWER | Republican | 33,936,234 | 442 | 55.1 |
|      |    | Adlai E. Stevenson | Democrat | 27,314,992 | 89 | 44.4 |
| 1956 | 48 | DWIGHT D. EISENHOWER | Republican | 35,590,472 | 457* | 57.6 |
|      |    | Adlai E. Stevenson | Democrat | 26,022,752 | 73 | 42.1 |
| 1960 | 50 | JOHN F. KENNEDY | Democrat | 34,227,096 | 303† | 49.9 |
|      |    | Richard M. Nixon | Republican | 34,108,546 | 219 | 49.6 |
| 1964 | 50 | LYNDON B. JOHNSON | Democrat | 42,676,220 | 486 | 61.3 |
|      |    | Barry M. Goldwater | Republican | 26,860,314 | 52 | 38.5 |
| 1968 | 50 | RICHARD M. NIXON | Republican | 31,785,480 | 301 | 43.4 |
|      |    | Hubert H. Humphrey | Democrat | 31,275,165 | 191 | 42.7 |
|      |    | George C. Wallace | American Independent | 9,906,473 | 46 | 13.5 |
| 1972 | 50 | RICHARD M. NIXON‡ | Republican | 47,165,234 | 520** | 60.6 |
|      |    | George S. McGovern | Democrat | 29,168,110 | 17 | 37.5 |
| 1976 | 50 | JIMMY CARTER | Democrat | 40,828,929 | 297*** | 50.1 |
|      |    | Gerald R. Ford | Republican | 39,148,940 | 240 | 47.9 |
|      |    | Eugene McCarthy | Independent | 739,256 | | |
| 1980 | 50 | RONALD REAGAN | Republican | 43,201,220 | 489 | 50.9 |
|      |    | Jimmy Carter | Democrat | 34,913,332 | 49 | 41.2 |
|      |    | John B. Anderson | Independent | 5,581,379 | | |
| 1984 | 50 | RONALD REAGAN | Republican | 53,428,357 | 525 | 59.0 |
|      |    | Walter F. Mondale | Democrat | 36,930,923 | 13 | 41.0 |
| 1988 | 50 | GEORGE H. W. BUSH | Republican | 48,901,046 | 426**** | 53.4 |
|      |    | Michael Dukakis | Democrat | 41,809,030 | 111 | 45.6 |
| 1992 | 50 | BILL CLINTON | Democrat | 43,728,275 | 370 | 43.2 |
|      |    | George Bush | Republican | 38,167,416 | 168 | 37.7 |
|      |    | H. Ross Perot | United We Stand, America | 19,237,247 | | 19.0 |
| 1996 | 50 | BILL CLINTON | Democrat | 45,590,703 | 379 | 49.0 |
|      |    | Robert Dole | Republican | 37,816,307 | 159 | 41.0 |
|      |    | H. Ross Perot | Reform | 7,866,284 | | 8.0 |
| 2000 | 50 | GEORGE W. BUSH | Republican | 50,459,624 | 271 | 47.9 |
|      |    | Albert Gore, Jr. | Democrat | 51,003,328 | 266 | 49.4 |
|      |    | Ralph Nader | Green | 2,882,985 | | 2.7 |
| 2004 | 50 | GEORGE W. BUSH | Republican | 62,040,610 | 286***** | 50.7 |
|      |    | John F. Kerry | Democrat | 59,028,444 | 251 | 48.3 |
| 2008 | 50 | BARACK OBAMA | Democrat | 69,456,897 | 365 | 52.9 |
|      |    | John McCain | Republican | 59,934,814 | 173 | 45.7 |

*Walter B. Jones received 1 electoral vote.
† Harry F. Byrd received 15 electoral votes.
‡ Resigned August 9, 1974: Vice President Gerald R. Ford became President.
** John Hospers received 1 electoral vote.
*** Ronald Reagan received 1 electoral vote.
**** Lloyd Bentsen received 1 electoral vote.
***** John Edwards received 1 electoral vote.

**Abolitionist movement**  A radical antislavery crusade committed to the immediate end of slavery that emerged in the three decades before the Civil War.

**Acquired immune deficiency syndrome (AIDS)**  A complex of deadly pathologies resulting from infection with the human immunodeficiency virus (HIV).

**Act for Religious Toleration**  The first law in America to call for freedom of worship for all Christians. It was enacted in Maryland in 1649 to quell disputes between Catholics and Protestants, but it failed to bring peace.

**Actual representation**  The practice whereby elected representatives normally reside in their districts and are directly responsive to local interests.

**Affirmative action**  A set of policies to open opportunities in business and education for members of minority groups and women by allowing race and sex to be factors included in decisions to hire, award contracts, or admit students to higher education programs.

**Age of Enlightenment**  Major intellectual movement occurring in Western Europe in the late seventeenth and early eighteenth centuries. Inspired by recent scientific advances, thinkers emphasized the role of human reason in understanding the world and directing its events. Their ideas placed less emphasis on God's role in ordering worldly affairs.

**Alamo**  Franciscan mission at San Antonio, Texas, that was the site in 1836 of a siege and massacre of Texans by Mexican troops.

**Albany Plan of Union**  Plan put forward in 1754 by Massachusetts governor William Shirley, Benjamin Franklin, and other colonial leaders, calling for an intercolonial union to manage defense and Indian affairs. The plan was rejected by participants at the Albany Congress.

**Albany Regency**  Popular name after 1820 for the state political machine in New York headed by Martin Van Buren.

**Alien Friends Act**  Law passed by Congress in 1798 authorizing the president during peacetime to expel aliens suspected of subversive activities; one of the **Alien and Sedition Acts.**

**Alliance for Progress**  Program of economic aid to Latin America during the Kennedy administration.

**Allies**  In World War I, Britain, France, Russia, and other belligerent nations fighting against the **Central Powers** but not including the United States, which insisted upon being merely an associated nation. In World War II, the Allies fighting the **Axis Powers** included the United States as well as the Soviet Union, Great Britain, France, China, and other nations.

**American Anti-Slavery Society**  The first national organization of abolitionists, founded in 1833.

**American Colonization Society**  Organization, founded in 1817 by antislavery reformers, that called for gradual emancipation and the removal of freed blacks to Africa.

**American Federation of Labor (AFL)**  Union formed in 1886 that organized skilled workers along craft lines and emphasized a few workplace issues rather than a broad social program.

**American Female Moral Reform Society**  Organization founded in 1839 by female reformers that established homes of refuge for prostitutes and petitioned for state laws that would criminalize adultery and the seduction of women.

**American Indian Movement (AIM)**  Group of Native American political activists who used confrontations with the federal government to publicize their case for Indian rights.

**Americans with Disabilities Act**  Legislation in 1992 that banned discrimination against physically handicapped persons in employment, transportation, and public accommodations.

**American System**  The program of government subsidies favored by Henry Clay and his followers to promote American economic growth and protect domestic manufacturers from foreign competition.

**American system of manufacturing**  A technique of production pioneered in the United States in the first half of the nineteenth century that relied on precision manufacturing with the use of interchangeable parts.

**American Temperance Society**  National organization established in 1826 by evangelical Protestants that campaigned for total abstinence from alcohol and was successful in sharply lowering per capita consumption of alcohol.

**Anarchist**  A person who believes that all government interferes with individual liberty and should be abolished by whatever means.

**Anglican**  Of or belonging to the Church of England, a Protestant denomination.

**Anglo-American Accords**  Series of agreements reached in the British-American Convention of 1818 that fixed the western boundary between the United States and Canada at the 49th parallel, allowed for the joint occupation of the Oregon Country, and restored to Americans fishing rights off Newfoundland.

**Annapolis Convention**  Conference of state delegates at Annapolis, Maryland, that issued a call in September 1786 for a convention to meet at Philadelphia in May 1787 to consider fundamental changes to the **Articles of Confederation.**

**Antifederalist**  An opponent of the **Constitution** in the debate over its ratification.

**Anti-Masons**  Third party formed in 1827 in opposition to the presumed power and influence of the Masonic order.

*Appeal to the Colored Citizens of the World*  Pamphlet published in 1829 by David, a Boston free black, calling for slaves to rise up in rebellion.

**Articles of Confederation**  Written document setting up the loose confederation of states that comprised the first national government of the United States from 1781 to 1788.

**Atlanta Compromise**  Booker T. Washington's policy accepting segregation and **disfranchisement** for African Americans in exchange for white assistance in education and job training.

**Atlantic Charter**  Statement of common principles and war aims developed by President Franklin Roosevelt and British Prime Minister Winston Churchill at a meeting in August 1941.

**Australian ballot**  Secret voting and the use of official ballots rather than party tickets.

**Axis Powers**  The opponents of the United States and its allies in World War II. The Rome–Berlin Axis was formed between Germany and Italy in 1936 and included Japan after 1940.

**Aztecs**  A warrior people who dominated the Valley of Mexico from about 1100 until their conquest in 1519–21 by Spanish soldiers led by Hernán Cortés.

**Bacon's Rebellion**  Violent conflict in Virginia (1675–1676), beginning with settler attacks on Indians but culminating in a rebellion led by Nathaniel Bacon against Virginia's government.

*Baker v. Carr*  U.S. Supreme Court decision in 1962 that allowed federal courts to review the apportionment of state legislative districts and established the principle that such districts should have roughly equal populations ("one person, one vote").

**Bank War**  The political struggle between President Andrew Jackson and the supporters of the **Second Bank of the United States.**

**Battle of New Orleans**  Decisive American **War of 1812** victory over British troops in January 1815 that ended any British hopes of gaining control of the lower Mississippi River Valley.

**Battle of Plattsburg**  American naval victory on Lake Champlain in September 1814 in the **War of 1812** that thwarted a British invasion from Canada.

**Battle of Put-in-Bay**  American naval victory on Lake Erie in September 1813 in the **War of 1812** that denied the British strategic control over the Great Lakes.

**Battle of the Atlantic**  The long struggle between German submarines and the British and U.S. navies in the North Atlantic from 1940 to 1943.

**Battle of the Little Bighorn**  Battle in which Colonel George A. Custer and the Seventh Cavalry were defeated by the Sioux and Cheyennes under Sitting Bull and Crazy Horse in Montana in 1876.

**Battles of Lexington and Concord**  The first two battles of the American Revolution which resulted in a total of 273 British soldiers dead, wounded, and missing and nearly 100 Americans dead, wounded, and missing.

**Bay of Pigs**  Site in Cuba of an unsuccessful landing by 1,400 anti-Castro Cuban refugees in April 1961.

**Beaver Wars**  Series of bloody conflicts, occurring between 1640s and 1680s, during which the Iroquois fought the French and their Indian allies for control of the fur trade in eastern North America and the Great Lakes region.

**Benevolent empire**  Network of reform associations affiliated with Protestant churches in the early nineteenth century dedicated to the restoration of moral order.

**Berlin blockade**  A three-hundred-day Soviet blockade of land access to United States, British, and French occupation zones in Berlin, 1948–1949.

**Berlin Wall**  Wall erected by East Germany in 1961 and torn down in 1989 that isolated West Berlin from the surrounding areas in Communist-controlled East Berlin and East Germany.

**Bill of Rights**  A written summary of inalienable rights and liberties.

**Black codes**  Laws passed by states and municipalities denying many rights of citizenship to free blacks before the Civil War. Also, during the **Reconstruction era,** laws passed by newly elected southern state legislatures to control black labor, mobility, and employment.

**Black Hawk's War**  Short 1832 war in which federal troops and Illinois militia units defeated the Sauk and Fox Indians led by Black Hawk.

**Black Panthers**  Political and social movement among black Americans, founded in Oakland, California, in 1966 and emphasizing black economic and political power.

**Black Power**  Philosophy emerging after 1965 that real economic and political gains for African-Americans could come only through self-help, **self-determination,** and organizing for direct political influence. Latinos and Native Americans developed their own versions as Brown Power and Red Power, respectively.

**"Bleeding Kansas"**  Violence between pro- and antislavery forces in Kansas Territory after the passage of the **Kansas-Nebraska Act** in 1854.

*Blitzkrieg*  German war tactic in World War II ("lightning war") involving the concentration of air and armored firepower to punch and exploit holes in opposing defensive lines.

**Bolshevik**  Member of the communist movement in Russia that established the Soviet government after the 1917 Russian Revolution; hence, by extension, any radical or disruptive person or movement seeking to transform economic and political relationships.

**Bonus Army**  A group of unemployed veterans who demonstrated in Washington for the payment of service bonuses, only to be dispersed violently by the U.S. Army in 1932.

**Boston Massacre**  After months of increasing friction between townspeople and the British troops stationed in the city, on March 5, 1770, British troops fired on American civilians in Boston.

**Boston Tea Party**  Incident that occurred on December 16, 1773, in which Bostonians, disguised as Indians, destroyed £9,000 worth of tea belonging to the British East India Company in order to prevent payment of the duty on it.

**British Constitution**  The principles, procedures, and precedents that governed the operation of the British government. These could be found in no single written document

**Brook Farm**  A utopian community and experimental farm established in 1841 near Boston.

*Brown v. Board of Education of Topeka*  Supreme Court decision in 1954 that declared that "separate but equal" schools for children of different races violated the **Constitution.**

**Bureau of Reclamation**  Federal agency established in 1902 providing public funds for irrigation projects in arid regions; played a major role in the development of the West by constructing dams, reservoirs, and irrigation systems, especially beginning in the 1930s.

**Cahokia**  Located near modern St. Louis, this was one of the largest urban centers created by Mississippian peoples, containing perhaps 30,000 residents in 1250.

**Californios**  Persons of Spanish descent living in California.

**Camp David Agreement**  Agreement to reduce points of conflict between Israel and Egypt, hammered out in 1977 with the help of U.S. President Jimmy Carter.

**Carpetbaggers**  Pejorative term to describe northern transplants to the South, many of whom were Union soldiers who stayed in the South after the war.

**Central Intelligence Agency (CIA)**  Agency that coordinates the gathering and evaluation of military and economic information on other nations, established in 1947.

**Central Powers**  Germany and its World War I allies Austria, Turkey, and Bulgaria.

**Chain migration**  Process common to many immigrant groups whereby one family member brings over other family members, who in turn bring other relatives and friends and occasionally entire villages.

*Charles River Bridge v. Warren Bridge*  Supreme Court decision of 1837 that promoted economic competition by ruling that the broader rights of the community took precedence over any presumed right of monopoly granted in a corporate charter.

**Cherokee War**  Conflict (1759–1761) on the southern frontier between the Cherokee Indians and colonists from Virginia southward. It caused South Carolina to request the aid of British troops and resulted in the surrender of more Indian land to white colonists.

*Chesapeake* **Incident**  Attack in 1807 by the British ship *Leopard* on the American ship *Chesapeake* in American territorial waters that nearly provoked an Anglo-American war.

**Chisholm Trail**  The route followed by Texas cattle raisers driving their herds north to markets at Kansas railheads.

**Church of Jesus Christ of Latter-day Saints**  See Mormon Church.

**Civil Rights Act of 1866**  Law that defined national citizenship and specified the civil rights to which all national citizens were entitled.

**Civil Rights Act of 1875**  Law that prohibited racial discrimination in jury selection, public transportation, and public accommodations; declared unconstitutional by the U.S. Supreme Court in 1883.

**Civil Rights Act of 1964**  Federal legislation that outlawed discrimination in public accommodations and employment on the basis of race, skin color, sex, religion, or national origin.

**Claims club**  A group of local settlers on the nineteenth-century frontier who banded together to prevent the price of their land claims from being bid up by outsiders at public land auctions.

**Coercive Acts**  Legislation passed by Parliament in 1774; included the Boston Port Act, the Massachusetts Government Act, the Administration of Justice Act, and the **Quartering Act** of 1774.

**Cold War**  The political and economic confrontation between the Soviet Union and the United States that dominated world affairs from 1946 to 1989.

**Collective bargaining**  Representatives of a union negotiating with management on behalf of all members.

**Colored Farmers' Alliance**  An organization of southern black farmers formed in Texas in 1886 in response to the **Southern Farmers' Alliance,** which did not accept black people as members.

**Columbian exchange**  The transatlantic exchange of plants, animals, and diseases that occurred after the first European contact with the Americas.

**Committees of correspondence**  Committees formed in Massachusetts and other colonies in the pre-Revolutionary period to keep Americans informed about British measures that would affect the colonies.

**Committee of Safety**  Any of the extralegal committees that directed the Revolutionary movement and carried on the functions of government at the local level in the period between the breakdown of royal authority and the establishment of regular governments under the new state constitutions. Some Committees of Safety continued to function throughout the Revolutionary War.

**Committee on Public Information (CPI)**  Government agency during World War I that sought to shape public opinion in support of the war effort through newspapers, pamphlets, speeches, films, and other media.

**Communism**  A social structure based on the common ownership of property.

**Compromise of 1850**  The four-step compromise which admitted California as a free state, allowed the residents of the New Mexico and Utah territories to decide the slavery issue for themselves, ended the slave trade in the District of Columbia, and passed a new fugitive slave law to enforce the constitutional provision stating that a slave escaping into a free state shall be delivered back to the owner.

**Compromise of 1877**  The congressional settling of the 1876 election which installed Republican Rutherford B. Hayes in the White House and gave Democrats control of all state governments in the South.

**Conciliatory Proposition**  Plan proposed by Lord North and adopted by the House of Commons in February 1775 whereby Parliament would "forbear" taxation of Americans in colonies whose assemblies imposed taxes considered satisfactory by the British government. The Continental Congress rejected this plan on July 31, 1775.

**Confederate States of America**  Nation proclaimed in Montgomery, Alabama, in February 1861 after the seven states of the Lower South seceded from the United States.

**Confiscation Act of 1862**  Second confiscation law passed by Congress, ordering the seizure of land from disloyal Southerners and the emancipation of their slaves.

**Congressional Reconstruction** Name given to the period 1867–1870 when the Republican-dominated Congress controlled **Reconstruction era** policy. It is sometimes known as Radical Reconstruction, after the radical faction in the **Republican Party.**

**Congress of Industrial Organizations (CIO)** An alliance of industrial unions that spurred the 1930s organizational drive among the mass-production industries.

**Congress of Racial Equality (CORE)** Civil rights group formed in 1942 and committed to nonviolent civil disobedience, such as the 1961 "freedom rides."

**Conservation** The efficient management and use of natural resources, such as forests, grasslands, and rivers, as opposed to **preservation** or uncontrolled exploitation.

**Constitutional Convention** Convention that met in Philadelphia in 1787 and drafted the **Constitution of the United States.**

**Constitutional Union Party** National party formed in 1860, mainly by former **Whigs,** that emphasized allegiance to the Union and strict enforcement of all national legislation.

**Constitution of the United States** The written document providing for a new central government of the United States, drawn up at the **Constitutional Convention** in 1787 and ratified by the states in 1788.

**Containment** The policy of resisting further expansion of the Soviet bloc through diplomacy and, if necessary, military action, developed in 1947–1948.

**Continental Army** The regular or professional army authorized by the Second Continental Congress and commanded by General George Washington during the Revolutionary War. Better training and longer service distinguished its soldiers from the state militiamen.

**Continental Association** Agreement, adopted by the **First Continental Congress** in 1774 in response to the **Coercive Acts,** to cut off trade with Britain until the objectionable measures were repealed. Local committees were established to enforce the provisions of the association.

**Contract theory of government** The belief that government is established by human beings to protect certain rights—such as life, liberty, and property—that are theirs by natural, divinely sanctioned law and that when government protects these rights, people are obligated to obey it. But when government violates its part of the bargain (or contract) between the rulers and the ruled, the people are no longer required to obey it and may establish a new government that will do a better job of protecting them. Elements of this theory date back to the ancient Greeks; John Locke used it in his *Second Treatise on Government* (1682), and Thomas Jefferson gave it memorable expression in the Declaration of Independence, where it provides the rationale for renouncing allegiance to King George III.

**Contract with America** Platform on which many Republican candidates ran for Congress in 1994. Associated with House Speaker Newt Gingrich, it proposed a sweeping reduction in the role and activities of the federal government.

**Copperheads** A term Republicans applied to northern war dissenters and those suspected of aiding the Confederate cause during the Civil War.

**Council of Economic Advisers** Board of three professional economists established in 1946 to advise the president on economic policy.

**Counterculture** Various alternatives to mainstream values and behaviors that became popular in the 1960s, including experimentation with psychedelic drugs, communal living, a return to the land, Asian religions, and experimental art.

**Country (Real Whig) ideology** Strain of thought first appearing in England in the late seventeenth century in response to the growth of governmental power and a national debt. Main ideas stressed the threat to personal liberty posed by a standing army and high taxes and emphasized the need for property holders to retain the right to consent to taxation.

*Coureurs de bois* French for "woods runners," independent fur traders in New France.

**Covenant** A formal agreement or contract.

**Coxey's Army** A protest march of unemployed workers, led by Populist businessman Jacob Coxey, demanding inflation and a public works program during the depression of the 1890s.

**Cult of domesticity** The belief that women, by virtue of their sex, should stay home as the moral guardians of family life.

**Culture areas** Geographical regions inhabited by peoples who share similar basic patterns of subsistence and social organization.

*Dartmouth College v. Woodward* Supreme Court decision of 1819 that prohibited states from interfering with the privileges granted to a private corporation.

**Dawes Act** An 1887 law terminating tribal ownership of land and allotting some parcels of land to individual Indians with the remainder opened for white settlement.

**D-Day** June 6, 1944, the day of the first paratroop drops and amphibious landings on the coast of Normandy, France, in the first stage of **Operation OVERLORD** during World War II.

**Declaration of Independence** The document by which the Second Continental Congress announced and justified its decision (reached July 2, 1776) to renounce the colonies' allegiance to the British government. Drafted mainly by Thomas Jefferson and adopted by Congress on July 4, the declaration's indictment of the king provides a remarkably full catalog of the colonists' grievances, and Jefferson's eloquent and inspiring statement of the **contract theory of government** makes the document one of the world's great state papers.

**Declaration of London** Statement drafted by an international conference in 1909 to clarify international law and specify the rights of neutral nations.

**Declaration of Rights and Grievances** Resolves, adopted by the **Stamp Act Congress** at New York in 1765, asserting that the **Stamp Act** and other taxes imposed on the colonists without their consent, given through their colonial legislatures, were unconstitutional.

**Declaration of Sentiments** The resolutions passed at the **Seneca Falls. Convention** in 1848 calling for full female equality, including the right to vote.

**Declaration of the Causes and Necessity of Taking Up Arms** Document, written mainly by John Dickinson of Pennsylvania and adopted on July 6, 1775, by which the Second Continental Congress justified its armed resistance against British measures.

**Declaratory Act** Law passed in 1766 to accompany repeal of the **Stamp Act** that stated that Parliament had the authority to legislate for the colonies "in all cases whatsoever." Whether "legislate" meant tax was not clear to Americans.

**Deindustrialization** The process of economic change involving the disappearance of outmoded industries and the transfer of factories to new low-wage locations, with devastating effects in the Northeast and Midwest, especially in the 1970s and 1980s.

**Deism** Religious orientation that rejects divine revelation and holds that the workings of nature alone reveal God's design for the universe.

**Democratic Party** Political party formed in the 1820s under the leadership of Andrew Jackson; favored states' rights and a limited role for the federal government, especially in economic affairs.

**Denmark Vesey's Conspiracy** The most carefully devised slave revolt, named after its leader, a free black in Charleston. The rebels planned to seize control of Charleston in 1822 and escape to freedom in Haiti, a free black republic, but they were betrayed by other slaves, and seventy-five conspirators were executed.

**Deregulation** Reduction or removal of government regulations and encouragement of direct competition in many important industries and economic sectors.

*Détente* A lessening of tension, applied to improved American relations with the Soviet Union and China in the mid-1970s.

**Disfranchisement** The use of legal means to bar individuals or groups from voting.

**Dixiecrats** Southern Democrats who broke from the party in 1948 over the issue of civil rights and ran a presidential tickets as the States' Rights Democrats.

**Dollar diplomacy** The U.S. policy of using private investment in other nations to promote American diplomatic goals and business interests.

**Dominion of New England** James II's failed plan of 1686 to combine eight northern colonies into a single large province, to be governed by a royal appointee (Sir Edmund Andros) with an appointed council but no elective assembly. The plan ended with James's ouster from the English throne and rebellion in Massachusetts against Andros's rule.

*Dred Scott* **decision** Supreme Court ruling, in a lawsuit brought by Dred Scott, a slave demanding his freedom based on his residence in a free state and a free territory with his master, that slaves could not be U.S. citizens and that Congress had no jurisdiction over slavery in the territories.

**Eastern Front** The area of military operations in World War II located east of Germany in eastern Europe and the Soviet Union.

**Economic Recovery and Tax Act of 1981 (ERTA)** A major revision of the federal income tax system.

**Eighteenth Amendment** Constitutional revision, ratified in 1919 and repealed in 1933, that prohibited the manufacture or sale of alcohol in the United States.

**Emancipation Proclamation** Decree announced by President Abraham Lincoln in September 1862 and formally issued on January 1, 1863, freeing slaves in all Confederate states still in rebellion.

**Embargo Act of 1807** Act passed by Congress in 1807 prohibiting American ships from leaving for any foreign port.

*Empresario* An agent who received a land grant from the Spanish or Mexican government in return for organizing settlements.

*Encomienda* In the Spanish colonies, the grant to a Spanish settler of a certain number of Indian subjects, who would pay him tribute in goods and labor.

**Enumerated products** Items produced in the colonies and enumerated in acts of Parliament that could be legally shipped from the colony of origin only to specified locations, usually England and other destinations within the British Empire.

**Environmental Protection Agency (EPA)** Federal agency created in 1970 to oversee environmental monitoring and cleanup programs.

**Era of Good Feelings** The period from 1817 to 1823 in which the disappearance of the **Federalists** enabled the **Republicans** to govern in a spirit of seemingly nonpartisan harmony.

**Espionage Act** Law whose vague prohibition against obstructing the nation's war effort was used to crush dissent and criticism during World War I.

**Fair Employment Practices Committee (FEPC)** Federal agency established in 1941 to curb racial discrimination in war production jobs and government employment.

**Farmers' Alliance** A broad mass movement in the rural South and West during the late nineteenth century, encompassing several organizations and demanding economic and political reforms; helped create the **Populist Party.**

**Fascist government** Subscribing to a philosophy of governmental dictatorship that merges the interests of the state, armed forces, and big business; associated with the dictatorship of Italian leader Benito Mussolini between 1922 and 1943 and also often applied to Nazi Germany.

**Federal Deposit Insurance Corporation (FDIC)** Government agency that guarantees bank deposits, thereby protecting both depositors and banks.

**Federal Highway Act of 1956** Measure that provided federal funding to build a nationwide system of interstate and defense highways.

**Federalism** The sharing of powers between the national government and the states.

**Federalist** A supporter of the **Constitution** who favored its ratification.

**Federal Reserve Act** The 1913 law that revised banking and currency by extending limited government regulation through the creation of the Federal Reserve System.

**Federal Trade Commission (FTC)** Government agency established in 1914 to provide regulatory oversight of business activity.

**Field Order No. 15** Order by General William T. Sherman in January 1865 to set aside abandoned land along the southern Atlantic coast for forty-acre grants to freedmen; rescinded by President Andrew Johnson later that year.

**Fifteenth Amendment** Passed by Congress in 1869, guaranteed the right of American men to vote, regardless of race.

**Fireside chats** Speeches broadcast nationally over the radio in which President Franklin Roosevelt explained complex issues and programs in plain language, as though his listeners were gathered around the fireside with him.

**First Continental Congress** Meeting of delegates from most of the colonies held in 1774 in response to the **Coercive Acts.** The Congress endorsed the **Suffolk Resolves,** adopted the **Declaration of Rights and Grievances,** and agreed to establish the **Continental Association** to put economic pressure on Britain to repeal its objectionable measures. The Congress also wrote addresses to the king, the people of Britain, and the American people.

*Fletcher v. Peck* Supreme Court decision of 1810 that overturned a state law by ruling that it violated a legal contract.

**Fort Sumter** Begun in the late 1820s to protect Charleston, South Carolina, it became the center of national attention in April 1861 when President Lincoln attempted to provision federal troops at the fort, triggering a hostile response from on-shore Confederate forces, opening the Civil War.

**Fourierist communities** Short-lived utopian communities in the 1840s based on the ideas of economic cooperation and self-sufficiency popularized by the Frenchman Charles Fourier.

**Fourteenth Amendment** Constitutional amendment passed by Congress in April 1866 incorporating some of the features of the **Civil Rights Act of 1866.** It prohibited states from violating the civil rights of its citizens and offered states the choice of allowing black people to vote or losing representation in Congress.

**Frame of Government** William Penn's 1682 plan for the government of Pennsylvania, which created a relatively weak legislature and strong executive. It also contained a provision for religious freedom.

**Franco-American Accord of 1800** Settlement reached with France that brought an end to the **Quasi-War** and released the United States from its 1778 alliance with France.

**Freedmen's Bureau** Agency established by Congress in March 1865 to provide social, educational, and economic services, advice, and protection to former slaves and destitute whites; lasted seven years.

**Freedom Summer** Voter registration effort in rural Mississippi organized by black and white civil rights workers in 1964.

**Free silver** Philosophy that the government should expand the money supply by purchasing and coining all the silver offered to it.

**Free Speech Movement (FSM)** Student movement at the University of California, Berkeley, formed in 1964 to protest limitations on political activities on campus.

**French and Indian War** The last of the Anglo-French colonial wars (1754–1763) and the first in which fighting began in North America. The war (which merged with the European conflict known as the Seven Years' War) ended with France's defeat and loss of its North American empire.

**Fugitive Slave Act** Law, part of the Compromise of 1850 that required authorities in the North to assist southern slave catchers and return runaway slaves to their owners.

**Fundamental Constitutions of Carolina** A complex plan for organizing the colony of Carolina, drafted in 1669 by Anthony Ashley Cooper and John Locke. Its provisions included a scheme for creating a hierarchy of nobles who would own vast amounts of land and wield political power; below them would be a class of freedmen and slaves. The provisions were never implemented by the Carolina colonists.

**Fundamentalists** Religious conservatives who believe in the literal accuracy and divine inspiration of the Bible; the name derives from an influential series of pamphlets, **The Fundamentals** (1909–1914).

**Gabriel Prosser's Rebellion** Slave revolt that failed when Gabriel Prosser, a slave preacher and blacksmith, organized a thousand slaves for an attack on Richmond, Virginia, in 1800. A thunderstorm upset the timing of the attack, and a slave informer alerted the whites. Prosser and twenty-five of his followers were executed.

**Gag rule** Procedural rule passed in the House of Representatives that prevented discussion of antislavery petitions from 1836 to 1844.

**Gang system** The organization and supervision of slave field hands into working teams on southern plantations.

**Gentlemen's Agreement** A diplomatic agreement in 1907 between Japan and the United States curtailing but not abolishing Japanese immigration.

**GI Bill of Rights** Legislation in June 1944 that eased the return of veterans into American society by providing educational and employment benefits.

*Gibbons v. Ogden* Supreme Court decision of 1824 involving coastal commerce that overturned a steamboat monopoly granted by the state of New York on the grounds that only Congress had the authority to regulate interstate commerce.

**Gilded Age** Term applied to late-nineteenth-century America that refers to the shallow display and worship of wealth characteristic of the period.

*Glasnost* Russian for "openness," applied to Mikhail Gorbachev's encouragement of new ideas and easing of political repression in the Soviet Union.

**Glorious Revolution** Bloodless revolt that occurred in England in 1688 when parliamentary leaders invited William of Orange, a Protestant, to assume the English throne and James II fled to France. James's ouster was prompted by fears that the birth of his son would establish a Catholic dynasty in England.

**Gospel of Wealth** Thesis that hard work and perseverance lead to wealth, implying that poverty is a character flaw.

**Grandfather clause** Rule that required potential voters to demonstrate that their grandfathers had been eligible to vote; used in some southern states after 1890 to limit the black electorate, as most black men's grandfathers had been slaves.

**Grand Settlement of 1701** Separate peace treaties negotiated by Iroquois diplomats at Montreal and Albany that marked the beginning of Iroquois neutrality in conflicts between the French and the British in North America.

**Grange** The National Grange of the Patrons of Husbandry, a national organization of farm owners formed after the Civil War.

**Granger laws** State laws enacted in the Midwest in the 1870s that regulated rates charged by railroads, grain elevator operators, and other middlemen.

**Great Awakening** Tremendous religious revival in colonial America. Sparked by the tour of the English evangelical minister George Whitefield, the Awakening struck first in the Middle Colonies and New England in the 1740s and eventually spread to the southern colonies by the 1760s.

**Great Compromise** Plan proposed by Roger Sherman of Connecticut at the 1787 **Constitutional Convention** for creating a national bicameral legislature in which all states would be equally represented in the Senate and proportionally represented in the House.

**Great Depression** The nation's worst economic crisis, extending throughout the 1930s, producing unprecedented bank failures, unemployment, and industrial and agricultural collapse and prompting an expanded role for the federal government.

**Great League of Peace and Power** Confederation of five Iroquois nations—the Mohawks, Oneidas, Onondagas, Cayugas, and Senecas—formed in the fifteenth century to diminish internal conflict and increase collective strength against their enemies.

**Great Migration** The mass movement of African Americans from the rural South to the urban North, spurred especially by new job opportunities during World War I and the 1920s.

**Great Society** Theme of Lyndon Johnson's administration, focusing on poverty, education, and civil rights.

**Great Uprising** Unsuccessful railroad strike of 1877 to protest wage cuts and the use of federal troops against strikers; the first nationwide work stoppage in American history.

**Greater East Asia Co-Prosperity Sphere** Japanese goal of an East Asian economy controlled by Japan and serving the needs of Japanese industry.

**Greenback Party** A third party of the 1870s and 1880s that garnered temporary support by advocating currency inflation to expand the economy and assist debtors.

**Gulf of Tonkin Resolution** Congressional resolution in August 1964 that authorized the president to take all necessary measures to protect South Vietnam, adopted after reports of North Vietnamese attacks on U.S. navy ships in the Gulf of Tonkin off North Vietnam.

**Halfway Covenant** Plan adopted in 1662 by New England clergy to deal with the problem of declining church membership. It allowed adults who had been baptized because their parents were church members but who had not yet experienced conversion to have their own children baptized. Without the Halfway Covenant, these third-generation children would remain unbaptized until their parents experienced conversion.

**Harlem Renaissance** A new African-American cultural awareness that flourished in literature, art, and music in the 1920s.

**Headright system** A system of land distribution during early colonial era that granted settlers fifty acres for themselves and another fifty for each "head" (or person) they brought to the colony.

**Helsinki Accords** Agreement in 1975 among NATO and Warsaw Pact members that recognized European national boundaries as set after World War II and included guarantees of human rights.

**Holocaust** The systematic murder of millions of European Jews and others deemed undesirable by Nazi Germany.

**Homestead Act** Law passed by Congress in 1862 providing 160 acres of land free to anyone who would live on the plot and farm it for five years.

**Hooverville** Shantytown, sarcastically named after President Hoover, in which unemployed and homeless people lived in makeshift shacks, tents, and boxes. Hoovervilles cropped up in many cities in 1930 and 1931.

**Horatio Alger Stories** A series of best-selling tales about young rags-to-riches heroes first published in 1867 stressing the importance of neat clothes, cleanliness, thrift, and hard work. The books also highlighted the importance of chance in getting ahead and the responsibility of those better off to serve as positive role models.

**Horizontal integration** The merger of competitors in the same industry.

**House Un-American Activities Committee** Congressional committee (1938–1975) that investigated suspected Nazi and Communist sympathizers.

**House of Burgesses** The legislature of colonial Virginia. First organized in 1619, it was the first institution of representative government in the English colonies.

**Hull House** Chicago **settlement house** that became part of a broader neighborhood revitalization and immigrant assistance project led by Jane Addams.

**Immigration and Nationality Act of 1965** Federal legislation that replaced the national quota system for immigration with overall limits of 170,000 immigrants per year from the Eastern Hemisphere and 120,000 per year from the Western Hemisphere.

**Imperialism** The policy and practice of exploiting nations and peoples for the benefit of an imperial power either directly through military occupation and colonial rule or indirectly through economic domination of resources and markets.

**Impressment** The British policy of forcibly enlisting American sailors into the British navy.

**Indentured servant** An individual—usually male but occasionally female—who contracted to serve a master for a period of four to seven years in return for payment of the servant's passage to America. Indentured servitude was the primary labor system in the Chesapeake colonies for most of the seventeenth century.

**Independent Treasury System** Fiscal arrangement first instituted by President Martin Van Buren in which the federal government kept its money in regional vaults ("pet banks") and transacted its business entirely in hard money.

**Indian Removal Act** Legislation passed by Congress in 1830 that provided funds for removing and resettling eastern Indians in the West. It granted the president the authority to use force if necessary.

**Initiative** Procedure by which citizens can introduce a subject for legislation, usually through a petition signed by a specific number of voters.

**Intermediate-Range Nuclear Forces Treaty (INF)** Disarmament agreement between the United States and the Soviet Union under which an entire class of missiles would be removed and destroyed and on-site inspections would be permitted for verification.

**International Monetary Fund (IMF)** International organization established in 1945 to assist nations in maintaining stable currencies.

**Internet** The system of interconnected computers and servers that allows the exchange of e-mail, posting of websites, and other means of instant communication.

**Interstate and Defense Highways** Federal legislation in 1956 committed the federal government to finance more than 40,000 miles of new limited access freeways to criss-cross the United States.

**Interstate Commerce Act** The 1887 law that expanded federal power over business by prohibiting pooling and discriminatory rates by railroads and establishing the first federal regulatory agency, the **Interstate Commerce Commission.**

**Interstate Commerce Commission (ICC)** The first federal regulatory agency, established in 1887 to oversee railroad practices.

**Intolerable Acts** American term for the **Coercive Acts** and the **Quebec Act.**

**Irreconcilables** Group of U.S. senators adamantly opposed to ratification of the **Treaty of Versailles** after World War I.

**Island hopping** In the Pacific Theater during World War II, the strategy in which U.S. forces seized selected Japanese-held islands while bypassing and isolating other islands held by Japan.

**Jacksonian Democrats** See Democratic Party.

**Jay's Treaty** Treaty with Britain negotiated in 1794 in which the United States made major concessions to avert a war over the British seizure of American ships.

**Jazz Age** The 1920s, so called for the popular music of the day as a symbol of the many changes taking place in the mass culture.

**Jim Crow laws**   Segregation laws that became widespread in the South during the 1890s, named for a minstrel show character portrayed satirically by white actors in blackface.

**John Brown's Raid**   New England abolitionist John Brown's ill-fated attempt to free Virginia's slaves with a raid on the federal arsenal at Harpers Ferry, Virginia, in 1859.

**Joint-stock company**   Business enterprise in which a group of stockholders pooled their money to engage in trade or to fund colonizing expeditions. Joint-stock companies participated in the founding of the Virginia, Plymouth, and Massachusetts Bay colonies.

**Judicial review**   A power implied in the **Constitution** that gives federal courts the right to review and determine the constitutionality of acts passed by Congress and state legislatures.

**Judiciary Act of 1789**   Act of Congress that implemented the judiciary clause of the **Constitution** by establishing the Supreme Court and a system of lower federal courts.

**Kansas-Nebraska Act**   Law passed in 1854 creating the Kansas and Nebraska Territories but leaving the question of slavery open to residents, thereby repealing the **Missouri Compromise.**

**Kellogg-Briand Pact**   A 1928 international treaty that denounced aggression and war but lacked provisions for enforcement.

**King George's War**   The third Anglo-French war in North America (1744–1748), part of the European conflict known as the War of the Austrian Succession. During the North American fighting, New Englanders captured the French fortress of Louisbourg, only to have it returned to France after the peace negotiations.

**King Philip's War**   Conflict in New England (1675–1676) between Wampanoags, Narragansetts, and other Indian peoples against English settlers; sparked by English encroachments on native lands.

**King William's War**   The first Anglo-French conflict in North America (1689–1697), the American phase of Europe's War of the League of Augsburg. Ended in negotiated peace that reestablished the balance of power.

**Knights of Labor**   Labor union that included skilled and unskilled workers irrespective of race or gender; founded in 1869, peaked in the 1880s, and declined when its advocacy of the eight-hour workday led to violent strikes in 1886.

**Know-Nothing Party**   Anti-immigrant party formed from the wreckage of the **Whig Party** and some disaffected northern Democrats in 1854.

**Korean War**   War between North Korea and South Korea (1950–1953) in which the People's Republic of China fought on the side of North Korea and the United States and other nations fought on the side of South Korea under teh auspices of the United Nations.

**Ku Klux Klan**   Perhaps the most prominent of the vigilante groups that terrorized black people in the South during **Reconstruction Era,** founded by Confederate veterans in 1866.

**Laissez-faire**   The doctrine that government should not intervene in the economy, especially through regulation.

**Land Grant College Act**   Law passed by Congress in July 1862 awarding proceeds from the sale of public lands to the states for the establishment of agricultural and mechanical (later engineering) colleges. Also known as the Morrill Act, after its sponsor, Congressman Justin Morrill of Vermont.

**Land Ordinance of 1785**   Act passed by Congress under the **Articles of Confederation** that created the grid system of surveys by which all subsequent public land was made available for sale.

**League of Nations**   International organization created by the **Versailles Treaty** after World War I to ensure world stability.

**League of Women Voters**   Group formed in 1920 from the National American Woman Suffrage Association to encourage informed voting and social reforms.

**Lecompton Constitution**   Proslavery draft written in 1857 by Kansas territorial delegates elected under questionable circumstances; it was rejected by two governors, supported by President Buchanan, and decisively defeated by Congress.

**Lend-Lease Act**   Program begun in 1941 through which the United States transferred military equipment to Britain and other World War II allies.

**Liberal Republicans**   Members of a reform movement within the **Republican Party** in 1872 that promoted measures to reduce government influence in the economy and restore control of southern governments to local white elites.

**Liberty Bonds**   Interest-bearing certificates sold by the U.S. government to finance the American World War I effort.

**Liberty Party**   The first antislavery political party, formed in 1840.

**Limited Test Ban Treaty**   Agreement in 1963 between the United States, Britain, and the Soviet Union to halt atmospheric and underwater tests of nuclear weapons.

**Lincoln-Douglas debates**   Series of debates in the 1858 Illinois senatorial campaign during which Democrat Stephen A. Douglas and Republican Abraham Lincoln staked out their differing opinions on the issue of slavery in the territories.

**Lost Cause**   The phrase many white southerners applied to their Civil War defeat. They viewed the war as a noble cause but only a temporary setback in the South's ultimate vindication.

**Lynching**   Execution, usually by a mob, without trial.

**Mahanism**   The ideas advanced by Alfred Thayer Mahan, stressing U.S. naval, economic, and territorial expansion.

**Manhattan Project**   The effort, using the code name Manhattan Engineer District, to develop an atomic bomb under the management of the U.S. Army Corps of Engineers during World War II.

**Manifest Destiny**   Doctrine, first expressed in 1845, that the expansion of white Americans across the continent was inevitable and ordained by God.

*Marbury v. Madison*   Supreme Court decision of 1803 that created the precedent of judicial review by ruling as unconstitutional part of the **Judiciary Act of 1789.**

**Marshall Plan**   The European Recovery Program (1949), which provided U.S. economic assistance to European nations; named for Secretary of State George Marshall.

**Massive retaliation**   Popular name for the military doctrine adopted in the 1950s, whereby the United States promised to respond to any attack on itself or its allies with massive force, including nuclear weapons.

**McCarthyism**   Anticommunist attitudes and actions associated with Senator Joe McCarthy in the early 1950s, including smear tactics and innuendo.

*McCulloch v. Maryland*   Supreme Court decision of 1819 upholding the constitutionality of the Second Bank of the United States and the exercise of federal powers within a state.

**Medicaid**   Supplementary medical insurance for the poor, financed through the federal government; program created in 1965.

**Medicare**   Basic medical insurance for the elderly, financed through the federal government; program created in 1965.

**Mercantilism**   Economic system whereby the government intervenes in the economy for the purpose of increasing national wealth. Mercantilists advocated possession of colonies as places where the mother country could acquire raw materials not available at home.

**Mexican Cession of 1848**   The land ceded to the U.S. by Mexico in the Treaty of Guadalupe Hidalgo.

**Middle Passage**   The voyage between West Africa and the New World slave colonies.

**Minute Men**   Special companies of militia formed in Massachusetts and elsewhere beginning in late 1744. These units were composed of men who were to be ready to assemble with their arms at a minute's notice.

**Missouri Compromise**   Sectional compromise in Congress in 1820 that admitted Missouri to the Union as a slave state and Maine as a free state and prohibited slavery in the **Louisiana Purchase** territory above 36°30′ north latitude.

**Model Cities Program**   Effort to target federal funds to upgrade public services and economic opportunity in specifically defined urban neighborhoods between 1966 and 1974.

**Molly Maguires**   Secret labor organization of mostly Irish miners in the Pennsylvania anthracite coal region in the decade after the Civil War. Named after a woman who led a massive protest against landlords in Ireland in the 1840s, the Maguires carried out selective murders of coal company officials until an infiltrator exposed the group in 1877 and its leaders were arrested, tried, and executed.

**Monroe Doctrine**   Declaration by President James Monroe in 1823 that the Western Hemisphere was to be closed off to further European colonization and that the United States would not interfere in the internal affairs of European nations.

**Mormon Church (Church of Jesus Christ of Latter-day Saints)** Church founded in 1830 by Joseph Smith and based on the revelations in a sacred book he called the Book of Mormon.

**Muckraking** Journalism exposing economic, social, and political evils, so named by Theodore Roosevelt for its "raking the muck" of American society.

**Mugwumps** Elitist and conservative reformers who favored **sound money** and limited government and opposed tariffs and the **spoils system.**

**Multinational corporation** Firm with direct investments, branches, factories, and offices in a number of countries.

**National Aeronautics and Space Administration (NASA)** Federal agency created in 1958 to manage American space flights and exploration.

**National American Woman Suffrage Association** The organization, formed in 1890, that coordinated the ultimately successful campaign to achieve women's right to vote.

**National Association for the Advancement of Colored People (NAACP)** An interracial organization founded in 1910 dedicated to restoring African American political and social rights.

**Nationalists** Group of leaders in the 1780s who spearheaded the drive to replace the **Articles of Confederation** with a stronger central government.

**National Origins Act of 1924** Law sharply restricting immigration on the basis of immigrants' national origins and discriminating against southern and eastern Europeans and Asians.

**National Security Council (NSC)** The formal policymaking body for national defense and foreign relations, created in 1947 and consisting of the president, the secretary of defense, the secretary of state, and others appointed by the president.

**National Security Council Paper 68 (NSC-68)** Policy statement that committed the United States to a military approach to the **Cold War.**

**Nation of Islam** Religious movement among black Americans that emphasizes self-sufficiency, self-help, and separation from white society.

**Nativist/Nativism** Favoring the interests and culture of native-born inhabitants over those of immigrants.

**Nat Turner's Rebellion** Uprising of slaves in Southampton County, Virginia, in the summer of 1831 led by Nat Turner that resulted in the death of fifty-five whites.

**Natural rights** Political philosophy that maintains that individuals have an inherent right, found in nature and preceding any government or written law, to life and liberty.

**Neoliberal** Advocate of or participant in the effort to reshape the **Democratic Party** for the 1990s around a policy emphasizing economic growth and competitiveness in the world economy.

**New Deal** The economic and political policies of the Roosevelt administration in the 1930s.

**New Federalism** President Richard Nixon's policy to shift responsibilities for government programs from the federal level to the states.

**New Freedom** Woodrow Wilson's 1912 program for limited government intervention in the economy to restore competition by curtailing the restrictive influences of trusts and protective tariffs, thereby providing opportunities for individual achievement.

**New Frontier** John F. Kennedy's domestic and foreign policy initiatives, designed to reinvigorate a sense of national purpose and energy.

**New Harmony** Short-lived utopian community established in Indiana in 1825, based on the socialist ideas of Robert Owen, a wealthy Scottish manufacturer.

**New Jersey Plan** Proposal of the New Jersey delegation at the 1787 **Constitutional Convention** for a strengthened national government in which all states would have equal representation in a **unicameral legislature.**

**New Lights** People who experienced conversion during the revivals of the **Great Awakening.**

**New Nationalism** Theodore Roosevelt's 1912 program calling for a strong national government to foster, regulate, and protect business, industry, workers, and consumers.

**New York Draft Riot** A mostly Irish-immigrant protest against conscription in New York City in July 1863 that escalated into class and racial warfare that had to be quelled by federal troops.

**Niagara Movement** African-American group organized in 1905 to promote racial integration, civil and political rights, and equal access to economic opportunity.

**Nineteenth Amendment** Constitutional revision that in 1920 established women citizens' right to vote.

**Nisei** U.S. citizens born of immigrant Japanese parents.

**Nixon Doctrine** In July, 1969, President Nixon described a new American policy toward Asia, in which the United States would honor treaty commitments but would gradually disengage and expect Asian nations to handle military defense on their own.

**Nonimportation movement** A tactical means of putting economic pressure on Britain by refusing to buy its exports to the colonies. Initiated in response to the taxes imposed by the **Sugar** and **Stamp acts,** it was used again against the **Townshend duties** and the **Coercive Acts.** The nonimportation movement popularized resistance to British measures and deepened the commitment of many ordinary people to a larger American community.

**North American Free Trade Agreement (NAFTA)** Agreement reached in 1993 by Canada, Mexico, and the United States to substantially reduce barriers to trade.

**North Atlantic Treaty Organization (NATO)** Military alliance of the United States, Canada, and European nations created in 1949 to protect Europe against possible Soviet aggression.

**Northwest Ordinance of 1787** Legislation passed by Congress under the **Articles of Confederation** that prohibited slavery in the Northwest Territories and provided the model for the incorporation of future territories into the Union as coequal states.

**Nullification** A constitutional doctrine holding that a state has a legal right to declare a national law null and void within its borders.

**Nullification crisis** Sectional crisis in the early 1830s in which a **states' rights** party in South Carolina attempted to nullify federal law.

**Office of Economic Opportunity (OEO)** Federal agency that coordinated many programs of the **War on Poverty** between 1964 and 1975.

**Oligopoly** An industry, such as steel making or automobile manufacturing, that is controlled by a few large companies.

**Olive Branch Petition** Petition, written largely by John Dickinson and adopted by the Second Continental Congress on July 5, 1775, as a last effort of peace that avowed America's loyalty to George III and requested that he protect it from further aggressions. Congress continued military preparations, and the king never responded to the petition.

**Omaha Platform** The 1892 platform of the **Populist Party** repudiating laissez-faire and demanding economic and political reforms to aid distressed farmers and workers.

**Oneida Community** Utopian community established in upstate New York in 1848 by John Humphrey Noyes and his followers.

**Open Door** American policy of seeking equal trade and investment opportunities in foreign nations or regions.

**Open shop** Factory or business employing workers whether or not they are union members; in practice, such a business usually refuses to hire union members and follows antiunion policies.

**Operation Desert Storm** Code name for the successful offensive against Iraq by the United States and its allies in the Persian Gulf War (1991).

**Operation OVERLORD** U.S. and British invasion of France in June 1944 during World War II.

**Oregon Trail** Overland trail of more than 2,000 miles that carried American settlers from the Midwest to new settlements in Oregon, California, and Utah.

**Organization of Petroleum Exporting Countries (OPEC)** Cartel of oil-producing nations in Asia, Africa, and Latin America that gained substantial power over the world economy in the mid- to late 1970s by controlling the production and price of oil.

**Ostend Manifesto** Message sent by U.S. envoys to President Pierce from Ostend, Belgium, in 1854, stating that the United States had a "divine right" to wrest Cuba from Spain.

**Pan American Union** International organization originally established as the Commercial Bureau of American Republics by Secretary of State James Blaine's first Pan-American Conference in 1889 to promote cooperation among nations of the Western Hemisphere through commercial and diplomatic negotiations.

**Panic of 1857** Banking crisis that caused a credit crunch in the North; it was less severe in the South, where high cotton prices spurred a quick recovery.

**Pan-Indian resistance movement** Movement calling for the political and cultural unification of Indian tribes in the late eighteenth and early nineteenth centuries.

**PATRIOT Act** Federal legislation adopted in 2001, in response to the terrorist attacks of September 11, intended to facilitate antiterror actions by federal law enforcement and intelligence agencies.

**Peace of Paris** Treaties signed in 1783 by Great Britain, the United States, France, Spain, and the Netherlands that ended the Revolutionary War. First in a preliminary agreement and then in the final treaty with the United States, Britain recognized the independence of the United States, agreed that the Mississippi River would be its western boundary, and permitted it to fish in some Canadian waters. Prewar debts owed by the inhabitants of one country to those of the other were to remain collectible, and Congress was to urge the states to return property confiscated from Loyalists. British troops were to evacuate United States territory without removing slaves or other property. In a separate agreement, Britain relinquished its claim to East and West Florida to Spain.

**Pendleton Civil Service Act** A law of 1883 that reformed the **spoils system** by prohibiting government workers from making political contributions and creating the Civil Service Commission to oversee their appointment on the basis of merit rather than politics.

**Pentagon Papers** Classified Defense Department documents on the history of the U.S. involvement in Vietnam, prepared in 1968 and leaked to the press in 1971.

**People's Party** See Populist Party.

**Pequot War** Conflict between English settlers (who had Narragansett and Mohegan allies) and Pequot Indians over control of land and trade in eastern Connecticut. The Pequots were nearly destroyed in a set of bloody confrontations, including a deadly English attack on a Mystic River village in May 1637.

*Perestroika* Russian for "restructuring," applied to Mikhail Gorbachev's efforts to make the Soviet economic and political systems more modern, flexible, and innovative.

**Persian Gulf War** War (1991) between Iraq and a U.S.-led coalition that followed Iraq's invasion of Kuwait and resulted in the expulsion of Iraqi forces from that country.

**Pietists** Protestants who stress a religion of the heart and the spirit of Christian living.

**Pilgrims** Settlers of Plymouth Colony, who viewed themselves as spiritual wanderers.

**Platt Amendment** A stipulation the United States had inserted into the Cuban constitution in 1901 restricting Cuban autonomy and authorizing U.S. intervention and naval bases.

*Plessy v. Ferguson* U.S. Supreme Court decision in 1896 affirming the constitutionality of racial segregation by law.

**Pogroms** Government-directed attacks against Jewish citizens, property, and villages in tsarist Russia beginning in the 1880s; a primary reason for Russian Jewish migration to the United States.

**Poll tax** A tax imposed on voters as a requirement for voting. Most southern states imposed poll taxes after 1900 as a way to disfranchise black people; the measures also restricted the white vote.

**Pontiac's War** Indian uprising (1763–1766) led by Pontiac of the Ottawas and Neolin of the Delawares. Fearful of their fate at the hands of the British after the French had been driven out of North America, the Indian nations of the Ohio River Valley and the Great Lakes area united to oust the British from the Ohio-Mississippi Valley. They failed and were forced to make peace in 1766.

**Popular sovereignty** A solution to the slavery crisis suggested by Michigan senator Lewis Cass by which territorial residents, not Congress, would decide slavery's fate.

**Populist Party** A major third party of the 1890s, also known as the **People's Party.** Formed on the basis of the **Southern Farmers' Alliance** and other reform organizations, it mounted electoral challenges against the Democrats in the South and the Republicans in the West.

**Potsdam Declaration** Statement issued by the United States during a meeting of U.S. president Harry Truman, British Prime Minister Winston Churchill, and Soviet premier Joseph Stalin held at Potsdam, near Berlin, in July 1945 to plan the defeat of Japan and the future of Eastern Europe and Germany. In it, the United States declared its intention to democratize the Japanese political system and reintroduce Japan into the international community and gave Japan an opening for surrender.

**Predestination** The belief that God decided at the moment of Creation which humans would achieve salvation.

**Preparedness** Military buildup in preparation for possible U.S. participation in World War I.

**Preservation** Protecting forests, land, and other features of the natural environment from development or destruction, often for aesthetic appreciation.

**Proclamation of 1763** Royal proclamation setting the boundary known as the Proclamation Line.

**Progressive Era** The period of the twentieth century before World War I when many groups sought to reshape the nation's government and society in response to the pressures of industrialization and urbanization.

**Prohibition** A ban on the production, transportation and sale of liquor, achieved temporarily through state laws and the Eighteenth Amendment.

**Prohibition Party** A venerable third party still in existence that has persistently campaigned for the abolition of alcohol but has also introduced many important reform ideas into American politics.

**Proposition 187** California legislation adopted by popular vote in California in 1994, which cuts off state-funded health and education benefits to undocumented or illegal immigrants.

**Proprietary colony** A colony created when the English monarch granted a huge tract of land to an individual or group of individuals, who became "lords proprietor." Many lords proprietor had distinct social visions for their colonies, but these plans were hardly ever implemented. Examples of proprietary colonies are Maryland, Carolina, New York (after it was seized from the Dutch), and Pennsylvania.

**Protestants** Europeans who supported reform of the Catholic Church in the wake of Martin Luther's critique of church practices and doctrines.

**Pueblo Revolt** Rebellion in 1680 of Pueblo Indians in New Mexico against their Spanish overlords, sparked by religious conflict and excessive Spanish demands for tribute.

**Puritans** Individuals who believed that Queen Elizabeth's reforms of the Church of England had not gone far enough in improving the church, particularly in ensuring that church members were among the saved. Puritans led the settlement of Massachusetts Bay Colony.

**Putting-out system** System of manufacturing in which merchants furnished households with raw materials for processing by family members.

**Quakers** Members of the Society of Friends, a radical religious group that arose in the mid-seventeenth century. Quakers rejected formal theology and an educated ministry, focusing instead on the importance of the "Inner Light," or Holy Spirit that dwelt within them. Quakers were important in the founding of Pennsylvania.

**Quartering Acts** Acts of Parliament requiring colonial legislatures to provide supplies and quarters for the troops stationed in America. Americans considered this taxation in disguise and objected. None of these acts passed during the pre-Revolutionary controversy required that soldiers be quartered in an occupied house without the owner's consent.

**Quasi-War** Undeclared naval war of 1797 to 1800 between the United States and France.

**Quebec Act** Law passed by Parliament in 1774 that provided an appointed government for Canada, enlarged the boundaries of Quebec southward to the Ohio River, and confirmed the privileges of the Catholic Church. Alarmed Americans termed this act and the **Coercive Acts** the **Intolerable Acts.**

**Queen Anne's War** American phase (1702–1713) of Europe's War of the Spanish Succession. At its conclusion, England gained Nova Scotia.

**Radical Republicans** A shifting group of Republican congressmen, usually a substantial minority, who favored the abolition of slavery from the beginning of the Civil War and later advocated harsh treatment of the defeated South.

**Reagan Doctrine** The policy assumption that Soviet-influenced governments in Asia, Africa, and Latin America needed to be eliminated if the United States was to win the Cold War.

**Recall** The process of removing an official from office by popular vote, usually after using petitions to call for such a vote.

*Reconquista* The long struggle (ending in 1492) during which Spanish Christians reconquered the Iberian Peninsula from Muslim occupiers, who first invaded in the eighth century.

**Reconstruction Era** The era (1865–1877) when the resolution of two major issues—the status of the former slaves and the terms of the Confederate states' readmission into the Union—dominated political debate.

**Redeemers**  Southern Democrats who wrested control of governments in the former Confederacy, often through electoral fraud and violence, from Republicans beginning in 1870.

**Redemptioners**  Similar to **indentured servants,** except that redemptioners signed labor contracts in America rather than in Europe, as indentured servants did. Shipmasters sold redemptioners into servitude to recoup the cost of their passage if they could not pay the fare upon their arrival.

**Redlining**  Restricting mortgage credit and insurance to properties in neighborhoods defined as being high risk.

**Red Scare**  Post–World War I public hysteria over **Bolshevik** influence in the United States directed against labor activists, radical dissenters, and some ethnic groups.

**Referendum**  Submission of a law, proposed or already in effect, to a direct popular vote for approval or rejection.

**Reformation**  Sixteenth-century movement to reform the Catholic Church that ultimately led to the founding of new Protestant Christian religious groups.

**Regulators**  Vigilante groups active in the 1760s and 1770s in the western parts of North and South Carolina. The South Carolina Regulators attempted to rid the area of outlaws; the North Carolina Regulators sought to protect themselves against excessively high taxes and court costs. In both cases, westerners lacked sufficient representation in the legislature to obtain immediate redress of their grievances. The South Carolina government eventually made concessions; the North Carolina government suppressed its Regulator movement by force.

*Repartimiento*  In the Spanish colonies, the assignment of Indian workers to labor on public works projects.

**Republicanism**  A complex, changing body of ideas, values, and assumptions, closely related to **country ideology,** that influenced American political behavior during the eighteenth and nineteenth centuries. Derived from the political ideas of classical antiquity, Renaissance Europe, and early modern England, republicanism held that self-government by the citizens of a country, or their representatives, provided a more reliable foundation for the good society and individual freedom than rule by kings. The benefits of monarchy depended on the variable abilities of monarchs; the character of republican government depended on the virtue of the people. Republicanism therefore helped give the American Revolution a moral dimension. But the nature of republican virtue and the conditions favorable to it became sources of debate that influenced the writing of the state and federal constitutions as well as the development of political parties.

**Republican Party**  Party that emerged in the 1850s in the aftermath of the bitter controversy over the **Kansas-Nebraska Act,** consisting of former **Whigs,** some northern Democrats, and many **Know-Nothings.**

**Republican Party (Jeffersonian)**  Party headed by Thomas Jefferson that formed in opposition to the financial and diplomatic policies of the **Federalist Party;** favored limiting the powers of the national government and placing the interests of farmers and planters over those of financial and commercial groups; supported the cause of the French Revolution.

*Rescate*  Procedure by which Spanish colonists would pay ransom to free Indians captured by rival natives. The rescued Indians then became workers in Spanish households.

**Reservationists**  Group of U.S. senators favoring approval of the **Treaty of Versailles,** the peace agreement after World War I, after amending it to incorporate their reservations.

**Rhode Island system**  During the industrialization of the early nineteenth century, the recruitment of entire families for employment in a factory.

*Roe v. Wade*  U.S. Supreme Court decision in 1973 that disallowed state laws prohibiting abortion during the first three months (trimester) of pregnancy and established guidelines for abortion in the second and third trimesters.

**Roosevelt Corollary**  President Theodore Roosevelt's policy asserting U.S. authority to intervene in the affairs of Latin American nations; an expansion of the **Monroe Doctrine.**

**Rush-Bagot Agreement**  Treaty of 1817 between the United States and Britain that effectively demilitarized the Great Lakes by sharply limiting the number of ships each power could station on them.

**Sabbatarian movement**  Reform organization founded in 1828 by Congregationalist and Presbyterian ministers that lobbied for an end to the delivery of mail on Sundays and other Sabbath violations.

**"Sack of Lawrence"**  Vandalism and arson committed by a group of proslavery men in Lawrence, the free-state capital of Kansas Territory.

**Sagebrush Rebellion**  Political movement in the western states in the early 1980s that called for easing of regulations on the economic use of federal lands and the transfer of some or all of those lands to state ownership.

**Sand Creek Massacre**  The near annihilation in 1864 of Black Kettle's Cheyenne band by Colorado troops under Colonel John Chivington's orders to "kill and scalp all, big and little."

**Santa Fe Trial**  Overland trial across the southern plains from St. Louis to New Mexico that funneled American traders and goods to Spanish-speaking settlements in the Southwest.

**Scalawags**  Southern whites, mainly small landowning farmers and well-off merchants and planters, who supported the southern **Republican Party** during **Reconstruction** for diverse reasons; a disparaging term.

**Search and destroy**  U.S. military tactic in South Vietnam, using small detachments to locate enemy units and then massive air, artillery, and ground forces to destroy them.

**Second Bank of the United States**  A national bank chartered by Congress in 1816 with extensive regulatory powers over currency and credit.

**Second Continental Congress**  An assemblage of delegates from all the colonies that convened in May 1775 after the outbreak of fighting in Massachusetts between British and American forces. It became the national government that eventually declared independence and conducted the Revolutionary War.

**Second Great Awakening**  Series of religious revivals in the first half of the nineteenth century characterized by great G-9emotionalism in large public meetings.

**Second Party System**  The national two-party competition between Democrats and Whigs from the 1830s through the early 1850s.

**Securities and Exchange Commission (SEC)**  Federal agency with authority to regulate trading practices in stocks and bonds.

**Sedition Act of 1918**  Broad law restricting criticism of America's involvement in World War I or its government, flag, military, taxes, or officials.

**Segregation**  A system of racial control that separated the races, initially by custom but increasingly by law during and after **Reconstruction.**

**Selective Service Act of 1917**  The law establishing the military draft for World War I.

**Selective Service System**  Federal agency that coordinated military conscription before and during the Vietnam War.

**Self-determination**  The right of a people or nation to decide on its own political allegiance or form of government without external influence.

**Seneca Falls Convention**  The first convention for women's equality in legal rights, held in upstate New York in 1848. **See also Declaration of Sentiments.**

**Separatists**  Members of an offshoot branch of Puritanism. Separatists believed that the Church of England was too corrupt to be reformed and hence were convinced that they must "separate" from it to save their souls. Separatists helped found Plymouth Colony.

**Settlement house**  A multipurpose structure in a poor neighborhood that offered social welfare, educational, and homemaking services to the poor or immigrants; usually under private auspices and directed by middle-class women.

**Seventeenth Amendment**  Constitutional change that in 1913 established the direct popular election of U.S. senators.

**Shakers**  The followers of Mother Ann Lee, who preached a religion of strict celibacy and communal living.

**Sharecropping**  Labor system that evolved during and after **Reconstruction** whereby landowners furnished laborers with a house, farm animals, and tools and advanced credit in exchange for a share of the laborers' crop.

**Shays's Rebellion**  An armed movement of debt-ridden farmers in western Massachusetts in the winter of 1786–1787. The rebellion shut down courts and created a crisis atmosphere, strengthening the case of **nationalists** that a stronger central government was needed to maintain civil order in the states.

**Sheppard-Towner Maternity and Infancy Act of 1921**  The first federal social welfare law; funded infant and maternity health care programs in local hospitals.

**Sherman Antitrust Act**  The first federal antitrust measure, passed in 1890; sought to promote economic competition by prohibiting business combinations in restraint of trade or commerce.

**Silicon Valley**  The region of California between San Jose and San Francisco that holds the nation's greatest concentration of electronics firms.

**Sixteenth Amendment**  Constitutional revision that in 1913 authorized a federal income tax.

**Slaughterhouse cases** Group of cases resulting in one sweeping decision by the U.S. Supreme Court in 1873 that contradicted the intent of the **Fourteenth Amendment** by decreeing that most citizenship rights remained under state, not federal, control.

**Slave codes** Sometimes known as "black codes." A series of laws passed mainly in the southern colonies in the late seventeenth and early eighteenth centuries to define the status of slaves and codify the denial of basic civil rights to them. Also, after American independence and before the Civil War, state laws in the South defining slaves as property and specifying the legal powers of masters over slaves.

**Slave Power** A key concept in abolitionist and northern antislavery propaganda that depicted southern slaveholders as the driving force in a political conspiracy to promote slavery at the expense of white liberties.

**Social Darwinism** The application of Charles Darwin's theory of biological evolution to society, holding that the fittest and the wealthiest survive, the weak and the poor perish, and government action is unable to alter this "natural" and beneficial process.

**Social Gospel movement** An effort by leading Protestants to apply religious ethics to industrial conditions and thereby alleviate poverty, slums, and labor exploitation.

**Socialism** A social order based on government ownership of industry and worker control over corporations as a way to prevent worker exploitation.

**Solid South** The one-party (Democratic) political system that dominated the South from the 1890s to the 1950s.

**Songhai Empire** A powerful West African state that flourished between 1450 and 1591, when it fell to a Moroccan invasion.

**Sons of Liberty** Secret organizations in the colonies formed to oppose the **Stamp Act.** From 1765 until independence, they spoke, wrote, and demonstrated against British measures. Their actions often intimidated stamp distributors and British supporters in the colonies.

**Sound money** Misleading slogan that referred to a conservative policy of restricting the money supply and adhering to the gold standard.

**Southeast Asia Treaty Organization (SEATO)** Mutual defense alliance signed in 1954 by the United States, Britain, France, Thailand, Pakistan, the Philippines, Australia, and New Zealand.

**Southern Christian Leadership Conference (SCLC)** Black civil rights organization founded in 1957 by Martin Luther King Jr., and other clergy.

**Southern Farmers' Alliance** The largest of several organizations that formed in the post-Reconstruction South to advance the interests of beleaguered small farmers.

**Southern Homestead Act** Largely unsuccessful law passed in 1866 that gave black people preferential access to public lands in five southern states.

**Southern Manifesto** A document signed by 101 members of Congress from southern states in 1956 that argued that the Supreme Court's decision in *Brown v. Board of Education of Topeka* itself contradicted the **Constitution.**

**Southwest Ordinance of 1790** Legislation passed by Congress that set up a government with no prohibition on slavery in U.S. territory south of the Ohio River.

**Sovereignty** The supreme authority of the state, including both the right to take life and to tax.

**Specie Circular** Proclamation issued by President Andrew Jackson in 1836 stipulating that only gold or silver could be used as payment for public land.

**Spheres of influence** Regions dominated and controlled by an outside power.

**Spoils system** The awarding of government jobs to party loyalists.

**Stamp Act** Law passed by Parliament in 1765 to raise revenue in America by requiring taxed, stamped paper for legal documents, publications, and playing cards. Americans opposed it as "taxation without representation" and prevented its enforcement. Parliament repealed it a year after its enactment.

**Stamp Act Congress** October 1765 meeting of delegates sent by nine colonies, held in New York City, that adopted the **Declaration of Rights and Grievances** and petitioned against the **Stamp Act.**

**States' rights** Favoring the rights of individual states over rights claimed by the national government.

**Stonewall Rebellion** On June 27, 1969, patrons fought back when police raided the gay Stonewall Inn in New York; the name refers to that event and to the increase in militancy by gay Americans that it symbolizes.

**Stono Rebellion** Uprising in 1739 of South Carolina slaves against whites; inspired in part by Spanish officials' promise of freedom for American slaves who escaped to Florida.

**Strategic Arms Limitation Treaty (SALT)** Signed in 1972 by the United States and the Soviet Union to slow the nuclear arms race.

**Strategic Defense Initiative (SDI)** President Reagan's program, announced in 1983, to defend the United States against nuclear missile attack with untested weapons systems and sophisticated technologies; also known as "Star Wars."

**Student Nonviolent Coordinating Committee (SNCC)** Black civil rights organization founded in 1960 and drawing heavily on younger activists and college students.

**Students for a Democratic Society (SDS)** The leading student organization of the New Left of the early and mid-1960s.

**Subtreasury plan** A program promoted by the **Southern Farmers' Alliance** in response to low cotton prices and tight credit. Farmers would store their crop in a warehouse (or "subtreasury") until prices rose, in the meantime borrowing up to 80 percent of the value of the stored crops from the government at a low interest rate.

**Suffolk Resolves** Militant resolves adopted in September 1774 in response to the **Coercive Acts** by representatives from the towns in Suffolk County, Massachusetts, including Boston. They termed the **Coercive Acts** unconstitutional, advised the people to arm, and called for economic sanctions against Britain. The **First Continental Congress** endorsed these resolves.

**Suffrage** The right to vote in a political election.

**Sugar Act** Law passed in 1764 to raise revenue in the American colonies. It lowered the duty from 6 pence to 3 pence per gallon on foreign molasses imported into the colonies and increased the restrictions on colonial commerce.

**Sunbelt** The states of the American South and Southwest.

**Sussex Pledge** Germany's pledge during World War I not to sink merchant ships without warning, on the condition that Britain also observe recognized rules of international law.

**Swann v. Charlotte-Mecklenburg Board of Education** U.S. Supreme Court decision in 1971 that upheld cross-city busing to achieve the racial integration of public schools.

**Sweatshops** Small, poorly ventilated shops or apartments crammed with workers, often family members, who pieced together garments.

**Taft-Hartley Act** Federal legislation of 1947 that substantially limited the tools available to labor unions in labor-management disputes.

**Tammany Hall** New York City's **Democratic Party** organization, dating from well before the Civil War, that evolved into a powerful political machine after 1860, using patronage and bribes to maintain control of the city administration.

**Taos Revolt** Uprising of Pueblo Indians in New Mexico that broke out in January 1847 over the imposition of American rule during the Mexican War; the revolt was crushed within a few weeks.

**Tariff Act of 1789** Apart from a few selected industries, this first tariff passed by Congress was intended primarily to raise revenue and not protect American manufacturers from foreign competition.

**Tariff Act of 1798** Law placing a duty of 5 percent on most imported goods, designed primarily to generate revenue and not to protect American goods from foreign competition.

**Tea Act of 1773** Act of Parliament that permitted the East India Company to sell tea through agents in America without paying the duty customarily collected in Britain, thus reducing the retail price. Americans, who saw the act as an attempt to induce them to pay the Townshend duty still imposed in the colonies, resisted this act through the **Boston Tea Party** and other measures.

**Tejano** A person of Spanish or Mexican descent born in Texas.

**Teller Amendment** A congressional resolution adopted in 1898 renouncing any American intention to annex Cuba.

**Temperance** Reform movement originating in the 1820s that sought to eliminate the consumption of alcohol.

**Temporary Assistance for Needy Families (TANF)** Federal program created in 1996 to replace earlier welfare programs to aid families and children; it involves explicit work requirements for receiving aid and places a time limit on benefits.

**Tenement** Four- to six-story residential dwelling, once common in New York and certain other cities, built on a tiny lot without regard to providing ventilation or light.

**Tennessee Valley Authority (TVA)** Federal regional planning agency established to promote **conservation**, produce electric power, and encourage economic development in seven southern states.

**Tenure of Office Act** Passed by the Republican controlled Congress in 1867 to limit presidential interference with its policies, the act prohibited the president from removing certain officeholders without the Senate's consent. President Andrew Johnson, angered at which he believed as an unconstitutional attack on presidential authority, deliberately violated the act by firing Secretary of War Edwin M. Stanton. The House responded by approving articles of impeachment against a president for the first time in American history.

**Thirteenth Amendment** Constitutional amendment ratified in 1865 that freed all slaves throughout the United States.

**Tories** A derisive term applied to loyalists in America who supported the king and Parliament just before and during the American Revolution. The term derived from late-seventeenth-century English politics when the Tory party supported the duke of York's succession to the throne as James II. Later the Tory party favored the Church of England and the crown over dissenting denominations and Parliament.

**Townshend Duty Act of 1967** Act of Parliament, passed in 1767, imposing duties on colonial tea, lead, paint, paper, and glass. Designed to take advantage of the supposed American distinction between internal and external taxes, the Townshend duties were to help support government in America. The act prompted a successful colonial nonimportation movement.

**Trail of Tears** The forced march in 1838 of the Cherokee Indians from their homelands in Georgia to the Indian Territory in the West; thousands of Cherokees died along the way.

**Transcendentalism** A philosophical and literary movement centered on an idealistic belief in the divinity of individuals and nature.

**Trans-Continental Treaty of 1819** Treaty between the United States and Spain in which Spain ceded Florida to the United States, surrendered all claims to the Pacific Northwest, and agreed to a boundary between the Louisiana Purchase territory and the Spanish Southwest.

**Transportation revolution** Dramatic improvements in transportation that stimulated economic growth after 1815 by expanding the range of travel and reducing the time and cost of moving goods and people.

**Treaty of Fort Laramie** The treaty acknowledging U.S. defeat in the Great Sioux War in 1868 and supposedly guaranteeing the Sioux perpetual land and hunting rights in South Dakota, Wyoming, and Montana.

**Treaty of Ghent** Treaty signed in December 1814 between the United States and Britain that ended the **War of 1812.**

**Treaty of Greenville** Treaty of 1795 in which Native Americans in the Old Northwest were forced to cede most of the present state of Ohio to the United States.

**Treaty of Lancaster** Negotiation in 1744 whereby Iroquois chiefs sold Virginia land speculators the right to trade at the Forks of the Ohio. Although the Iroquois had not intended this to include the right to settle in the Ohio Country, the Virginians assumed that it did. Ohio Valley Indians considered this treaty a great grievance against both the English and the Iroquois.

**Treaty of Paris** The formal end to British hostilities against France and Spain in February 1763.

**Treaty of San Lorenzo** See Pinckney's Treaty.

**Treaty of Tordesillas** Treaty negotiated by the pope in 1494 to resolve the territorial claims of Spain and Portugal. It drew a north–south line approximately 1,100 miles west of the Cape Verde Islands, granting all lands west of the line to Spain and all lands east of the line to Portugal. This limited Portugal's New World empire to Brazil but confirmed its claims in Africa and Asia.

**Treaty of Versailles** The treaty ending World War I and creating the **League of Nations.**

**Troubled Asset Relief Program (TARP)** Federal program in 2008 to purchase or guarantee shaky bank assets to protect the economy from widespread bank failures.

**Truman Doctrine** President Harry Truman's statement in 1947 that the United States should assist other nations that were facing external pressure or internal revolution; an important step in the escalation of the **Cold War.**

**Trusts** In late 19th- and early-20th-century usage, refers to monopolies that eliminated competition and fixed prices and wages in a given industry. Increasing numbers of Americans viewed these entities as threats to the free enterprise system.

**Underground Railroad** Support system set up by antislavery groups in the Upper South and the North to assist fugitive slaves in escaping the South.

**Underwood-Simmons Tariff Act** The 1913 reform law that lowered tariff rates and levied the first regular federal income tax.

**Unicameral legislature** A legislative body composed of a single house.

**Union League** A **Republican Party** organization in northern cities that became an important organizing device among freedmen in southern cities after 1865.

*United States v. Cruikshank* Supreme Court ruling of 1876 that overturned the convictions of some of those responsible for the Colfax Massacre, ruling that the Enforcement Act applied only to violations of black rights by states, not individuals.

*University of California v. Bakke* U.S. Supreme Court case in 1978 that allowed race to be used as one of several factors in college and university admission decisions but made rigid quotas unacceptable.

**Valley Forge** Area of Pennsylvania approximately twenty miles northwest of Philadelphia where General George Washington's continental troops were quartered from December 1777 to June 1778 while British forces occupied Philadelphia during the Revolutionary War. Approximately 2,500 men, about a quarter of those encamped there, died of hardship and disease.

**Vertical integration** The consolidation of numerous production functions, from the extraction of the raw materials to the distribution and marketing of the finished products, under the direction of one firm.

**Viet Cong** Communist rebels in South Vietnam who fought the pro-American government established in South Vietnam in 1954.

**Virginia Plan** Proposal of the Virginia delegation at the 1787 **Constitution Convention** calling for a national legislature in which the states would be represented according to population. The national legislature would have the explicit power to veto or overrule laws passed by state legislatures.

**Virtual representation** The notion, current in eighteenth-century England, that parliamentary members represented the interests of the nation as a whole, not those of the particular district that elected them.

**Volstead Act** The 1920 law defining the liquor forbidden under the Eighteenth Amendment and giving enforcement responsibilities to the Prohibition Bureau of the Department of the Treasury.

**Voting Rights Act** Legislation in 1965 that overturned a variety of practices by which states systematically denied voter registration to minorities.

**Waltham system** During the industrialization of the early nineteenth century, the recruitment of unmarried young women for employment in factories.

**War Hawks** Members of Congress, predominantly from the South and West, who aggressively pushed for a war against Britain after their election in 1810.

**War Industries Board (WIB)** The federal agency that reorganized industry for maximum efficiency and productivity during World War I.

**War of 1812** War fought between the United States and Britain from June 1812 to January 1815 largely over British restrictions on American shipping.

**War on Poverty** Set of programs introduced by Lyndon Johnson between 1963 and 1966 designed to break the cycle of poverty by providing funds for job training, community development, nutrition, and supplementary education.

**Warsaw Pact** Military alliance of the Soviet Union and Communist nations of Eastern Europe from 1955 to 1989.

**Watergate** A complex scandal involving attempts to cover up illegal actions taken by administration officials and leading to the resignation of President Richard Nixon in 1974.

**Webster–Ashburton Treaty** Treaty signed by the United States and Britain in 1842 that settled a boundary dispute between Maine and Canada and provided for closer cooperation in suppressing the African slave trade.

**Welfare capitalism** A paternalistic system of labor relations emphasizing management responsibility for employee well-being. While providing some limited benefits, its function was primarily to forestall the formation of unions or public intervention.

**Whig Party** Political party, formed in the mid-1830s in opposition to the **Jacksonian Democrats,** that favored a strong role for the national government in promoting economic growth.

**Whigs** The name used by advocates of colonial resistance to British measures during the 1760s and 1770s. The Whig party in England unsuccessfully attempted to exclude the Catholic duke of York from succession to the throne as James II; victorious in the **Glorious Revolution,** the Whigs later stood for religious toleration and the supremacy of Parliament over the crown.

**Whiskey Rebellion** Armed uprising in 1794 by farmers in western Pennsylvania who attempted to prevent the collection of the excise tax on whiskey.

**Whitewater**  Arkansas real estate development in which Bill and Hillary Clinton were investors; several fraud convictions resulted from investigations into Whitewater, but evidence was not found that the Clintons were involved in wrongdoing.

**Wide Awakes**  Group of red-shirted, black-caped young men who paraded through city streets in the North extolling the virtues of the **Republican Party** during the 1860 presidential election campaign.

**Wilmot Proviso**  The amendment offered by Pennsylvania Democrat David Wilmot in 1846 which stipulated that "as an express and fundamental condition to the acquisition of any territory from the Republic of Mexico . . . neither slavery nor involuntary servitude shall ever exist in any part of said territory."

**Wobblies**  Popular name for the members of the Industrial Workers of the World (IWW).

**Woman's Christian Temperance Union (WCTU)**  National organization formed after the Civil War dedicated to prohibiting the sale and distribution of alcohol.

**Workingmen's Movement**  Associations of urban workers who began campaigning in the 1820s for free public education and a ten-hour workday.

**World Bank**  Officially the International Bank for Reconstruction and Development, an international organization established in 1845 that assists governments around the world in economic development efforts.

**World Trade Organization**  International organization that sets standards and practices for global trade, and the focus of international protests over world economic policy in the late 1990s.

**World Wide Web**  Since 1991, the Web has expanded the use of the Internet by allowing organizations and companies to create websites that place political and commercial information only a few clicks away from wired consumers.

**Wounded Knee Massacre**  The U.S. Army's brutal winter massacre in 1890 of at least two hundred Sioux men, women, and children as part of the government's assault on the tribe's Ghost Dance religion.

**XYZ Affair**  Diplomatic incident in 1798 in which Americans were outraged by the demand of the French for a bribe as a condition for negotiating with American diplomats.

**Yalta Conference**  Meeting of U.S. president Franklin Roosevelt, British Prime Minister Winston Churchill, and Soviet premier Joseph Stalin held in February 1945 to plan the final stages of World War II and postwar arrangements.

**Yellow-dog contracts**  Employment agreements binding workers not to join a union.

**Yellow press**  A deliberately sensational journalism of scandal and exposure designed to attract an urban mass audience and increase advertising revenues.

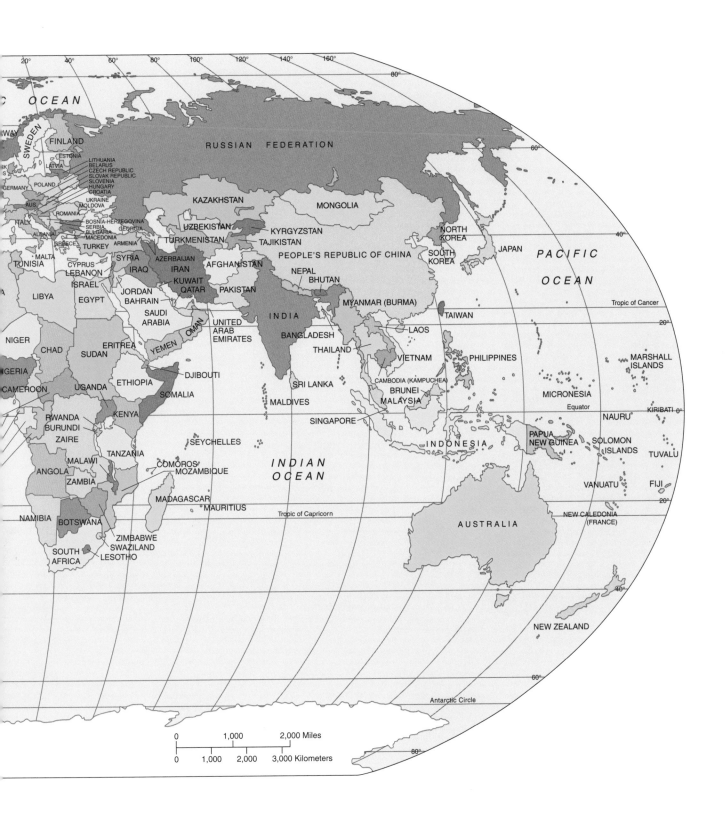

OCEAN

SWEDEN
FINLAND
ESTONIA
LATVIA
LITHUANIA
BELARUS
CZECH REPUBLIC
SLOVAK REPUBLIC
SLOVENIA
HUNGARY
CROATIA
POLAND
AUS
GERMANY
ROMANIA
MOLDOVA
UKRAINE
ITALY
BOSNIA-HERZEGOVINA
SERBIA
BULGARIA
MACEDONIA
ALBANIA
GREECE
GEORGIA
ARMENIA
TURKEY
MALTA
TUNISIA
CYPRUS
LEBANON
ISRAEL
SYRIA
IRAQ
AZERBAIJAN
IRAN
LIBYA
JORDAN
BAHRAIN
EGYPT
KUWAIT
QATAR
SAUDI
ARABIA
OMAN
UNITED
ARAB
EMIRATES
YEMEN

NIGER
CHAD
SUDAN
ERITREA
NGERIA
CAMEROON
UGANDA
ETHIOPIA
DJIBOUTI
SOMALIA
RWANDA
BURUNDI
ZAIRE
KENYA
TANZANIA
MALAWI
ANGOLA
ZAMBIA
COMOROS
MOZAMBIQUE
SEYCHELLES
MADAGASCAR
MAURITIUS
NAMIBIA
BOTSWANA
ZIMBABWE
SWAZILAND
SOUTH
AFRICA
LESOTHO

RUSSIAN FEDERATION

KAZAKHSTAN
MONGOLIA
UZBEKISTAN
KYRGYZSTAN
TURKMENISTAN
TAJIKISTAN
AFGHANISTAN
PEOPLE'S REPUBLIC OF CHINA
NORTH
KOREA
SOUTH
KOREA
JAPAN
NEPAL
BHUTAN
PAKISTAN
INDIA
MYANMAR (BURMA)
TAIWAN
BANGLADESH
LAOS
THAILAND
VIETNAM
PHILIPPINES
SRI LANKA
CAMBODIA (KAMPUCHEA)
MALDIVES
BRUNEI
MALAYSIA
SINGAPORE
INDONESIA
PAPUA
NEW GUINEA

PACIFIC
OCEAN
Tropic of Cancer
MARSHALL
ISLANDS
MICRONESIA
Equator
KIRIBATI
NAURU
SOLOMON
ISLANDS
TUVALU
VANUATU
FIJI
NEW CALEDONIA
(FRANCE)

INDIAN
OCEAN
Tropic of Capricorn

AUSTRALIA

NEW ZEALAND

Antarctic Circle

0        1,000        2,000 Miles

0    1,000    2,000    3,000 Kilometers